INDY 500® RECAPS
THE SHORT CHUTE EDITION

Pat Kennedy

authorHOUSE®

AuthorHouse™
1663 Liberty Drive
Bloomington, IN 47403
www.authorhouse.com
Phone: 1 (800) 839-8640

© 2017 Pat Kennedy. All rights reserved.

No part of this book may be reproduced, stored in a retrieval system, or transmitted by any means without the written permission of the author.

Published by AuthorHouse   03/23/2017

ISBN: 978-1-5246-7272-0 (sc)
ISBN: 978-1-5246-7270-6 (hc)
ISBN: 978-1-5246-7271-3 (e)

Library of Congress Control Number: 2017903615

Print information available on the last page.

Any people depicted in stock imagery provided by Thinkstock are models, and such images are being used for illustrative purposes only.
Certain stock imagery © Thinkstock.

This book is printed on acid-free paper.

Because of the dynamic nature of the Internet, any web addresses or links contained in this book may have changed since publication and may no longer be valid. The views expressed in this work are solely those of the author and do not necessarily reflect the views of the publisher, and the publisher hereby disclaims any responsibility for them.

Dedication

To the courageous drivers who have made the Indianapolis 500 the greatest sporting event in the world over the past 100-plus-years.

PREFACE

This book started as a self-serving exercise to personally organize the major details and interesting facts of each Indianapolis 500 over the 100-plus-year history of the greatest race in the world. For many of us passionate racing fans who have attended a multitude of "500s", there is a tendency for the details of the races to (somewhat) blend together. I hope this book will help to provide clarity in this regard, as well as educate.

During high school, many of us chose to use CliffsNotes to assist in the education process. This book is somewhat patterned after that concept. It falls somewhere between Donald Davidson and Rick Schaffer's Autocourse Official History of the Indianapolis 500—the best and by far the most detailed book on the history of the Indianapolis 500—and a multitude of pictorial books with limited information. I hope it will prove to be an easy read with entertaining and educational information.

ACKNOWLEDGMENTS

This book is dedicated to my dad, William E. Kennedy, Jr.; my great uncle, Big John Berry; and my grandpa, William E. Kennedy, Sr. Their passion for, interest in, and love for the Indianapolis 500 and IndyCar racing was instilled in me at a very young age and continues strong to this day.

I would like to make a special dedication to my mom, Fran Kennedy, who thought her boy could do no wrong! I would also like to dedicate this book to the "Kennedy Clan" for their tremendous support and love, namely: the Shorters—Peggy Kennedy Shorter, Mark Shorter, Mickey Shorter, Kelly Shorter Schneider, Matt Schneider, Logan Schneider, Maddie and Molly Schneider; the Fairchilds—Kathy Kennedy Fairchild, Thom Fairchild, Kyle Fairchild, Kimmie Fairchild Rumer, Justin Rumer, George Rumer and William Rumer; the Bolins—Ann Kennedy Bolin, Paul Bolin, Courtney Bolin, Kevin Bolin, and Brian Bolin; and the Kennedys—Cheryl Kennedy, Maura Kennedy, Bill, Ellen, Kate and Grace Kennedy, Jimmy Kennedy, Patrick Kennedy, and Joey "Kennedy" Gaines. Without this "clan" I could not do what I do!

Special thanks to Angie Brackin, my right hand on this project, whose hard work, understanding, interest, and commitment made this book possible.

Many thanks to Donald Davidson, the savant of the Indianapolis 500, whose tremendous input, fact checking, support, and guidance were very instrumental in elevating the quality of this project.

Thanks to everyone from the Indianapolis Motor Speedway involved in this book, especially Jason Ellison, Mary Ellen Loscar and Mike Roth of the Photo Operation, for their helpful assistance.

Lastly, special thanks to Mark T. Watson, my lifelong best friend, whose artistic talent is responsible for the design of the book cover. Reach him at Spotlight Photography, 317-372-9300.

1911

The partners in the Indianapolis Motor Speedway ownership were: Carl Fisher, James Allison, Arthur Newby and Frank Wheeler.

Drivers had to be able to average 75 mph or better from a flying start over a distance of a quarter mile in order to be included in the starting field. On Friday, four days before the race, time trials were run. Thirty-eight cars were successful. Two others cars were successful on the day before the race.

Qualifiers were lined up by the dates on which the entries were received. There were forty-six entrants total with the first entrant on the pole.

Lewis Strang was on the pole.

Cars were lined up in rows of five. There were forty starters. The pace car and four cars constituted row 1. The ninth row consisted of a single car; all other rows had five cars.

Carl Fisher, the leading partner in the track ownership, drove the Stoddard-Dayton pace car.

A large crowd of approximately 80,000 attended the first "500."

Johnny Aitken led the first lap of the inaugural Indianapolis 500, or the "International 500-Mile Sweepstakes," as it was referred to through 1980.

Prize money was awarded to only the top ten finishers, with $10,000 to the winner (plus accessory prizes, for a total of $14,250), and $500 for tenth place. The total purse was $30,150.

David Bruce-Brown led for most of the first half of the race and at one point opened up a lead of three laps over the second place car. He led a total of eighty-one laps.

Ray Harroun ran a consistently paced race in his six-cylinder Marmon Wasp at approximately 75 mph to minimize tire wear. His testing showed that by reducing his speed from 80 mph to 75 mph he doubled the life of his tires.

Cyrus Patschke relieved Harroun near mid-race and drove for about 35 laps. Patschke would also drive relief for fifth-place finisher Joe Dawson in another Marmon. Ray Harroun led 88 laps total, including laps 182-200, for the victory. All of Harroun's laps led occurred after the 102nd lap. He made four stops and changed three right rear tires.

Harroun drove the only single-seater in the race, with the aid of what is believed to be the first rearview mirror on an automobile. All other cars had riding mechanics. The rearview mirror was the result of Harroun observing a horse-drawn taxi utilizing one back in 1904.

Ralph Mulford, driving a Lozier, ran a charging race, resulting in a greater number of tire changes, fourteen versus four for Harroun. He finished second. David Bruce-Brown finished third in a Fiat.

The race took six hours and forty-two minutes to complete, a 74.6 mph average for Harroun.

There was one fatality in the race, as Art Greiner's (#44) right-rear-wheel came loose and the car overturned on the back stretch on his thirteenth lap, his riding mechanic, Sam Dickson losing his life.

The race was not completed without technological mishaps, as the scoring wire broke on two occasions during the race before being repaired.

Arthur Newby, a partner in the track ownership, was president of the National Motor Vehicle Company and had three cars compete in the race.

Eddie Rickenbacker drove relief for Lee Frayer, who finished thirteenth. Rickenbacker would eventually race in four "500's" with a best finish of 10th in 1914, all before he ever flew a plane.

Harry and Bill Endicott became the first brothers to compete in the "500". Harry finished 16th, while Bill was 26th.

1911 Winner Ray Harroun drove a Marmon Wasp, the only single-seat car in the race.

RACE RESULTS FOR THE 1911 INDIANAPOLIS 500

Finish	Start	Car Num.	Driver	Car Name/ Entrant*	Make/Model	Status	Laps	Led	Winnings
1	28	32	Ray Harroun (R)	Marmon "Wasp"	Marmon/Marmon	74.602	200	88	$14,250
2	29	33	Ralph Mulford (R)	Lozier	Lozier/Lozier	74.285	200	10	$5,200
3	25	28	David Bruce-Brown (R)	Fiat	Fiat/Fiat	72.730	200	81	$3,250
4	11	11	Spencer Wishart (R)	Mercedes	Mercedes/Mercedes	72.648	200	5	$2,350
5	27	31	Joe Dawson (R)	Marmon	Marmon/Marmon	72.365	200	0	$1,500
6	2	2	Ralph DePalma (R)	Simplex	Simplex/Simplex	71.084	200	4	$1,000
7	18	20	Charlie Merz (R)	National	National/National	70.367	200	0	$800
8	12	12	W.H. Turner (R)	Amplex	Amplex/Amplex	68.818	200	0	$700
9	13	15	Fred Belcher (R)	Knox	Knox/Knox	68.626	200	4	$600
10	22	25	Harry Cobe (R)	Jackson	Jackson/Jackson	67.899	200	0	$500
11	10	10	Gil Anderson (R)	Stutz	Stutz/Wisconsin	67.730	200	0	$0
12	32	36	Hughie Hughes (R)	Mercer	Mercer/Mercer	67.630	200	0	$0
13	26	30	Lee Frayer (R)	Firestone-Columbus	Firestone Col./Firestone Col.	Running	N/A	0	$0
14	19	21	Howdy Wilcox (R)	National	National/National	Running	N/A	0	$0
15	33	37	Charlie Bigelow (R)	Mercer	Mercer/Mercer	Running	N/A	0	$0
16	3	3	Harry Endicott (R)	Inter-State	Inter-State/Inter-State	Running	N/A	0	$0
17	36	41	Howard Hall (R)	Velie	Velie/Velie	Running	N/A	0	$0
18	40	46	Billy Knipper (R)	Benz	Benz/Benz	Running	N/A	0	$0
19	39	45	Bob Burman (R)	Benz	Benz/Benz	Running	N/A	0	$0
20	34	38	Ralph Beardsley (R)	Simplex	Simplex/Simplex	Running	N/A	0	$0
21	16	18	Eddie Hearne (R)	Fiat	Fiat/Fiat	Running	N/A	0	$0
22	6	6	Frank Fox (R)	Pope-Hartford	Pope-Hartford/Pope-Hartford	Running	N/A	0	$0
23	24	27	Ernest Delaney (R)	Cutting	Cutting/Cutting	Running	N/A	0	$0
24	23	26	Jack Tower (R)	Jackson	Jackson/Jackson	Running	N/A	0	$0
25	20	23	Mel Marquette (R)	McFarlan	McFarlan/McFarlan	Running	N/A	0	$0
26	37	42	Bill Endicott (R)	Cole	Cole/Cole	Running	N/A	0	$0
27	4	4	Johnny Aitken (R)	National	National/National	Rod	125	8	$0
28	9	9	Will Jones (R)	Case	Case/Wisconsin	Steering	122	0	$0
29	1	1	Lewis Strang (R)	Case	Case/Wisconsin	Steering	108	0	$0
30	7	7	Harry Knight (R)	Westcott	Westcott/Westcott	Accident	90	0	$0
31	8	8	Joe Jagersberger (R)	Case	Case/Wisconsin	Accident	87	0	$0
32	31	35	Herb Lytle (R)	Apperson	Apperson/Apperson	Accident	82	0	$0
33	17	19	Harry Grant (R)	Alco	Alco/Alco	Bearings	51	0	$0
34	15	17	Charles Basle (R)	Buick	Buick/Buick	Mechanical	46	0	$0
35	5	5	Louis Disbrow (R)	Pope-Hartford	Pope-Hartford/Pope-Hartford	Accident	45	0	$0
36	14	16	Arthur Chevrolet (R)	Buick	Buick/Buick	Mechanical	30	0	$0
37	35	39	Caleb Bragg (R)	Fiat	Fiat/Fiat	Mechanical	23	0	$0
38	21	24	Fred Ellis (R)	Jackson	Jackson/Jackson	Fire damage	22	0	$0
39	30	34	Teddy Tetzlaff (R)	Lozier	Lozier/Lozier	Accident	20	0	$0
40	38	44	Art Greiner (R)	Amplex	Amplex/Amplex	Accident	12	0	$0

* - complete car name/entrant data not available for all entries
(R) - Indicated Rookie
(W) - Indicates Past Winner

1912

Riding mechanics became mandatory and would remain so through 1922.

There were twenty-nine entries, and twenty-four cars qualified for the race. Qualifying required greater than a 75 mph average for a full lap. Cars once again started by entry order received. Gil Anderson started on the pole in a Stutz.

This was the first 500 for future track owner Eddie Rickenbacker as a primary driver. He started thirteenth and finished twenty-first.

Teddy Tetzlaff, in a Fiat, led the first two laps, then Ralph DePalma led from lap three to lap 198 in his "Grey Ghost" Mercedes, when a connecting rod broke. He and his riding mechanic, Australian Rupert Jeffkins, unsuccessfully attempted to push the 2500-pound car to the finish.

Joe Dawson and riding mechanic Harry Martin —whose pit manager was fellow driver Johnny Aitken—made up a deficit of over five laps and went on to win in his National in six hours and twenty-one minutes for an average speed of 78.7 mph. Don Herr relieved him for laps 108-144. Teddy Tetzlaff finished second and Hugh Hughes, in a Mercer, finished third. The Mercer was the "smallest" car in the race in relation to piston displacement at only 301 cubic-inches.

As Dawson and the National crew celebrated the victory, DePalma displayed great sportsmanship by approaching and extending a congratulatory handshake to the winner.

The 196 laps led by DePalma are the most by a non-winning driver.

Dawson's car housed a 491 cubic-inch National, which would be the largest on a winning car in history.

The total purse was increased to $50,000, with $20,000 going to the winner.

Joseph Crook Dawson, from Odon, Indiana, was 22 years, 323 days old, and would remain the youngest 500 winner in history until 1952, when Troy Ruttman won at 22 years, 86 days old.

Ralph Mulford finished tenth in 8 hours and 53 minutes in a Knox, after several lengthy stops, including a snack break. Tenth was the last position for which prize money was awarded. Mulford won $1,200. His time was 2 hours and thirty-two minutes longer than the victor.

Bill Endicott finished fifth. He was relieved by his brother Harry. This was the only time a brother relieved a brother in the race.

Ralph DePalma and riding mechanic Rupert Jeffkins push their broken-down Mercedes, eventually finishing in eleventh place.

RACE RESULTS FOR THE 1912 INDIANAPOLIS 500

Finish	Start	Car Num.	Driver	Car Name/Entrant*	Make/Model	Status	Laps	Led	Winnings
1	7	8	Joe Dawson	National	National/National	78.719	200	2	$20,000
2	3	3	Teddy Tetzlaff	Fiat	Fiat/Fiat	76.632	200	2	$10,000
3	17	21	Hughie Hughes	Mercer	Mercer/Mercer	76.307	200	0	$5,000
4	22	28	Charlie Merz	Stutz	Stutz/Wisconsin	76.014	200	0	$3,000
5	15	18	Bill Endicott	Schacht	Schacht/Wisconsin	73.807	200	0	$2,500
6	2	2	Len Zengel (R)	Stutz	Stutz/Wisconsin	73.088	200	0	$2,000
7	11	14	Johnny Jenkins (R)	White	White/White	72.704	200	0	$1,500
8	18	22	Joe Horan (R)	Lozier	Lozier/Lozier	71.491	200	0	$1,400
9	8	9	Howdy Wilcox	National	National/National	69.525	200	0	$1,300
10	16	19	Ralph Mulford	Knox	Knox/Knox	56.285	200	0	$1,200
11	4	4	Ralph DePalma	Mercedes	Mercedes/Mercedes	Piston	198	196	$0
12	12	15	Bob Burman	Cutting	Cutting/Cutting	Accident	156	0	$0
13	10	12	Bert Dingley (R)	Simplex	Simplex/Simplex	Rod	116	0	$0
14	21	25	Joe Matson (R)	Lozier	Lozier/Lozier	Crankshaft	107	0	$0
15	6	7	Spencer Wishart	Mercedes	Mercedes/Mercedes	Water line	82	0	$0
16	1	1	Gil Anderson	Stutz	Stutz/Wisconsin	Accident	79	0	$0
17	14	17	Billy Liesaw (R)	Marquette-Buick	Marquette/Buick	Carb. Fire	72	0	$0
18	24	5	Louis Disbrow	Case	Case/Case	Differ. pin	67	0	$0
19	19	23	Mel Marquette	McFarlan	McFarlan/McFarlan	Accident	63	0	$0
20	5	6	Eddie Hearne	Case	Case/Case	Crankshaft	54	0	$0
21	13	16	Eddie Rickenbacker (R)	Firestone-Columbus	Firestone Col./Firestone Col.	Bearing	44	0	$0
22	23	29	David Bruce-Brown	National	National/National	Valves	24	0	$0
23	9	10	Harry Knight	Lexington	Lexington/Lexington	Engine trouble	7	0	$0
24	20	24	Len Ormsby (R)	Opel	Opel/Opel	Rod	5	0	$0

* - complete car name/entrant data not available for all entries
(R) - Indicated Rookie
(W) - Indicates Past Winner

Pat Kennedy

1913

A new five-story open-sided Japanese style pagoda had been built trackside for officiating and scoring.

From the outset, the Speedway management had intended for the race to be an international event. A few teams accepted the invitation in 1913, including the Peugeot team from France.

The starting order was determined by a blind draw, with twenty-seven starters. A starting field consisting of four cars in each row, instead of five, was implemented for the first time.

Even though the piston displacement had been cut from 600 cubic-inches to 450, the speeds in the qualification trials were higher than the previous year.

Caleb Bragg started on the pole in a Mercer.

Johnny Aitken was pit manager and race strategist for first-year driver Jules Goux in a Peugeot.

On a day with temperatures at 90 degrees Goux led a total of 138 laps, including from lap 136 to the checker. He won by thirteen minutes and eight seconds—a record that still stands as the greatest margin of victory. His speed average was 75.9 mph.

Goux became the first winner to drive the full race without a relief driver, and also became the first foreign-born victor.

Spencer Wishart, in a Mercer, finished second and Charlie Merz finished third in a Stutz, though his car was on fire as he crossed the finish line.

Ten cars received the checkered flag, completing the full 200 laps, while only one other car was still running. Surprisingly, there was only one accident in the race. Seventh-place finisher, Ralph Mulford in a Mercedes, drove the entire 500 miles without a tire change.

After the race Goux was quoted "but for the wine, I would have been unable to drive this race". Goux supposedly refreshed himself with a little champagne during several pit stops.

An estimated crowd of 96,000 attended the race.

Jules Goux with riding mechanic Emil Begin in the winning Peugeot.

RACE RESULTS FOR THE 1913 INDIANAPOLIS 500

Finish	Start	Car Num.	Driver	Car Name/Entrant*	Make/Model	Status	Laps	Led	Winnings
1	7	16	Jules Goux (R)	Peugeot	Peugeot/Peugeot	75.933	200	138	$21,165
2	19	22	Spencer Wishart	Mercer	Mercer/Mercer	73.489	200	0	$10,165
3	16	2	Charlie Merz	Stutz	Stutz/Wisconsin	73.382	200	0	$5,165
4	2	9	Albert Guyot (R)	Sunbeam	Sunbeam/Sunbeam	70.925	200	0	$3,500
5	13	23	Theodore Pilette (R)	Mercedes-Knight	Mercedes/Knight	68.148	200	0	$3,000
6	20	12	Howdy Wilcox	Gray Fox	Pope-Hartford/Pope-Hartford	67.653	200	0	$2,200
7	22	29	Ralph Mulford	Mercedes	Mercedes/Mercedes	66.951	200	0	$1,800
8	23	31	Louis Disbrow	Case	Case/Case	66.793	200	0	$1,600
9	15	35	Willie Haupt (R)	Mason	Duesenberg/Duesenberg	63.481	200	0	$1,500
10	27	25	George Clark (R)	Tulsa	Tulsa/Wisconsin	62.994	200	0	$1,400
11	21	4	Bob Burman	Keeton	Keeton/Wisconsin	Running	N/A	41	$0
12	14	3	Gil Anderson	Stutz	Stutz/Wisconsin	Camshaft	187	18	$0
13	4	5	Bob Evans (R)	Mason	Duesenberg/Duesenberg	Clutch	158	2	$0
14	3	17	Billy Liesaw	Anel	Buick/Buick	Rods	148	0	$0
15	1	19	Caleb Bragg	Mercer	Mercer/Mercer	Pump shaft	128	1	$0
16	11	10	Billy Knipper	Henderson	Knipper/Duesenberg	Clutch	125	0	$0
17	8	27	Teddy Tetzlaff	Isotta-Fraschini	Isotta/Isotta	Broken chain	118	0	$0
18	24	32	Joe Nikrent (R)	Case	Case/Case	Bearings	67	0	$0
19	25	6	Jack Tower	Mason	Duesenberg/Duesenberg	Accident	51	0	$0
20	18	28	Vincenzo Trucco (R)	Isotta-Fraschini	Isotta/Isotta	Loose tank	39	0	$0
21	10	1	Harry Endicott	Nyberg	Nyberg/Nyberg	Drive shaft	23	0	$0
22	26	15	Paolo Zuccarelli (R)	Peugeot	Peugeot/Peugeot	Bearing	18	0	$0
23	12	21	Ralph DePalma	Mercer	Mercer/Mercer	Bearings	15	0	$0
24	6	26	Harry Grant	Isotta-Fraschini	Isotta/Isotta	Broken tank	14	0	$0
25	17	18	Johnny Jenkins	Schacht	Schacht/Schacht	Crankshaft	13	0	$0
26	5	8	Don Herr (R)	Stutz	Stutz/Wisconsin	Clutch shaft	7	0	$0
27	9	33	Bill Endicott	Case	Case/Case	Drive shaft	1	0	$0

* - complete car name/entrant data not available for all entries
(R) - Indicated Rookie
(W) - Indicates Past Winner

1914

Thirty cars competed in the "500."

The starting field was determined by a blind draw that resulted in six lead changes between five drivers in the opening thirteen laps.

Arthur Duray led 77 of the first 115 laps in his Peugeot.

Jean Chassagne, in a Sunbeam, started on the pole and finished twenty-ninth, the second car out.

René Thomas led a total of 102 laps and led from lap 116 to the checker in his first 500, driving a French Delage. Thomas set a new race record of 82.5 mph and won by a margin of more than six minutes. He wore a tie in the race.

The first four finishers were swept by French entries, with second and fourth going to Arthur Duray and Jules Goux in Peugeots and first and third going to Thomas and Albert Guyot in Delages.

Barney Oldfield finished fifth in a Stutz, the top-finishing American team. Billy Carlson finished ninth in a Maxwell with inaugural winner Ray Harroun as team manager. Maxwell had developed a car that ran on kerosene. Ninth-place finisher, Billy Carlson, used only thirty gallons of kerosene to run the full distance. Kerosene was being sold for six cents a gallon, therefore the fuel bill to run the entire 500 miles was only $1.80. Eddie Rickenbacker finished tenth in a Duesenberg.

Joe Dawson was involved in a serious accident on lap forty-five that resulted in his retirement from racing.

An estimated crowd of 110,000 watched the race, as thirteen cars covered the full 500 miles.

A thirteen-year-old boy from Terre Haute, Indiana attended his first Indianapolis 500 in 1914. His name was Anton Hulman, Jr.

René Thomas and riding mechanic Robert Laly in the winning Delage outside the "foreign car" garage.

RACE RESULTS FOR THE 1914 INDIANAPOLIS 500

Finish	Start	Car Num.	Driver	Car Name/Entrant*	Make/Model	Status	Laps	Led	Winnings
1	15	16	Rene Thomas (R)	Delage	Delage/Delage	82.474	200	102	$39,750
2	10	14	Arthur Duray (R)	Peugeot	Peugeot/Peugeot	80.994	200	77	$10,450
3	11	10	Albert Guyot	Delage	Delage/Delage	80.210	200	9	$5,425
4	19	6	Jules Goux (W)	Peugeot	Peugeot/Peugeot	79.491	200	1	$3,500
5	30	3	Barney Oldfield (R)	Stutz	Stutz/Stutz	78.156	200	0	$3,000
6	7	9	Josef Christiaens (R)	Excelsior	Excelsior/Excelsior	77.439	200	9	$2,200
7	26	27	Harry Grant	Sunbeam	Sunbeam/Sunbeam	75.687	200	0	$1,800
8	27	5	Charlie Keene (R)	Beaver Bullet	Keene/Wisconsin	74.822	200	0	$1,600
9	5	25	Billy Carlson (R)	Maxwell	Maxwell/Maxwell	70.972	200	0	$1,500
10	23	42	Eddie Rickenbacker	Duesenberg	Duesenberg/Duesenberg	70.827	200	0	$1,400
11	6	23	Ralph Mulford	Mercedes	Mercedes/Peugeot	69.550	200	0	$0
12	28	43	Willie Haupt	Duesenberg	Duesenberg/Duesenberg	66.660	200	0	$0
13	12	31	Billy Knipper	Keeton	Keeton/Wisconsin	65.790	200	0	$0
14	29	7	Georges Boillot (R)	Peugeot	Peugeot/Peugeot	Frame	148	0	$0
15	18	34	Ernst Friedrich (R)	Bugatti	Bugatti/Bugatti	Pinion	134	0	$0
16	24	1	Louis Disbrow	Burman	Burman/Wisconsin	Rod	128	0	$0
17	25	19	Spencer Wishart	Mercer	Mercer/Mercer	Camshaft	122	0	$0
18	14	2	Earl Cooper (R)	Stutz	Stutz/Stutz	Wheel	118	0	$0
19	9	21	Caleb Bragg	Mercer	Mercer/Mercer	Camshaft	117	1	$0
20	8	15	Art Klein (R)	King	King/Wisconsin	Valve	87	0	$0
21	4	38	Billy Chandler (R)	Braender Bulldog	Mulford/Duesenberg	Rod	69	0	$0
22	3	4	Howdy Wilcox	Gray Fox	Fox/Pope-Hartford	Valve	67	1	$0
23	13	13	George Mason (R)	Mason	Duesenberg/Duesenberg	Piston	66	0	$0
24	22	17	Bob Burman	Burman	Burman/Wisconsin	Rod	47	0	$0
25	17	26	Joe Dawson (W)	Marmon	Marmon/Marmon	Accident	44	0	$0
26	16	24	Gil Anderson	Stutz	Stutz/Stutz	Loose bolts	42	0	$0
27	20	49	Ray Gilhooly (R)	Isotta-Fraschini	Isotta/Isotta	Accident	41	0	$0
28	2	8	Teddy Tetzlaff	Maxwell	Maxwell/Maxwell	Rocker arm	38	0	$0
29	1	12	Jean Chassagne (R)	Sunbeam	Sunbeam/Sunbeam	Accident	20	0	$0
30	21	48	S.F. Brock (R)	Ray	Mercer/Wisconsin	Camshaft	5	0	$0

* - complete car name/entrant data not available for all entries
(R) - Indicated Rookie
(W) - Indicates Past Winner

1915

A rule was adopted that allowed only three cars per make to compete. Several Peugeots and Sunbeams were eliminated because of there already being three of each.

A qualifying procedure of lining the cars up by speed was implemented, with the fastest starting on the pole. Cars were assigned colors as well as numbers. American cars were red and white; Belgian, yellow; English, green; French, blue; German, white and Italian, red. The color scheme by country was dropped after its' inaugural year.

There were only twenty-four starters for the race.

Howdy Wilcox won the pole at 98.9 mph, with Ralph DePalma starting second at 98.6 mph.

The field of cars started four abreast.

The race was postponed from Saturday, May 29 to Monday, May 31 because of rain.

For the fifth and final time Speedway President Carl Fisher drove the pace car to start the race.

Ralph DePalma led for 132 laps total, but with three laps remaining, his connecting rod broke and punched two holes in the crankcase. This time he was able to nurse his cream, red and black Mercedes for the final three laps, the victory avenging the bitter defeat of 1912. His average speed was a record 89.8 mph, more than 7 mph faster than the previous year's record. The new record would stand until 1922.

At one point in the race, Dario Resta led by more than a lap over DePalma. Resta skidded and experienced a blown tire and steering problems later in the race but soldiered his French Peugot to a second-place finish after a fierce duel with DePalma. DePalma's brother John finished 21st in a Delage.

Johnny Aitken came out of retirement and drove relief for Gil Anderson in a Stutz, who finished in third place. Earl Cooper placed fourth.

Attendance was slightly more than half the 110,000 of the previous year. The major reason for the decline in attendance was soft ground from the heavy rains prohibited automobile parking.

Following the 1915 race T.E. "Pop" Myers was made general manager of the track.

1915 Winner Ralph DePalma drove this Mercedes accompanied by riding mechanic Louis Fontaine.

RACE RESULTS FOR THE 1915 INDIANAPOLIS 500

Finish	Start	Car Num.	Driver	Car Name/Entrant*	Make/Model	Status	Laps	Led	Winnings
1	2	2	Ralph DePalma	Mercedes	Mercedes/Mercedes	89.840	200	132	$22,600
2	3	3	Dario Resta (R)	Peugeot	Peugeot/Peugeot	88.911	200	37	$10,900
3	5	5	Gil Anderson	Stutz	Stutz/Stutz	87.602	200	26	$5,600
4	4	4	Earl Cooper	Stutz	Stutz/Stutz	86.624	200	0	$3,700
5	11	15	Eddie O'Donnell (R)	Duesenberg	Duesenberg/Duesenberg	81.473	200	0	$3,000
6	7	8	Bob Burman	Peugeot	Peugeot/Peugeot	80.359	200	0	$2,200
7	1	1	Howdy Wilcox	Stutz	Stutz/Stutz	80.143	200	5	$1,800
8	9	10	Tom Alley (R)	Duesenberg	Duesenberg/Duesenberg	79.972	200	0	$1,600
9	16	19	Billy Carlson	Maxwell	Maxwell/Maxwell	78.962	200	0	$1,500
10	14	7	Noel Van Raalte (R)	Sunbeam	Sunbeam/Sunbeam	75.874	200	0	$1,400
11	24	28	Willie Haupt	Emden	Emden/Emden	70.750	200	0	$0
12	10	14	Harry Grant	Sunbeam	Sunbeam/Sunbeam	Oil Pan	184	0	$0
13	17	21	Tom Orr (R)	Maxwell	Maxwell/Maxwell	Bearing	168	0	$0
14	6	6	Jean Porporato (R)	Sunbeam	Sunbeam/Sunbeam	Piston	164	0	$0
15	15	18	Joe Cooper (R)	Sebring	Duesenberg/Duesenberg	Accident	154	0	$0
16	18	22	Ralph Mulford	Duesenberg	Duesenberg/Duesenberg	Rod	124	0	$0
17	12	12	George Babcock (R)	Peugeot	Peugeot/Peugeot	Cylinder	117	0	$0
18	8	9	Art Klein	Kleinart	Duesenberg/Duesenberg	Disqualified	111	0	$0
19	19	23	Eddie Rickenbacker	Maxwell	Maxwell/Maxwell	Rod	103	0	$0
20	23	27	Louis Chevrolet (R)	Cornelian	Cornelian/Sterling	Valve	76	0	$0
21	13	17	John DePalma (R)	Delage	Delage/Delage	Loose flywheel	41	0	$0
22	20	24	Johnny Mais (R)	Mais	Mais/Mercer	Left track	23	0	$0
23	22	26	George Hill (R)	Bugatti	Bugatti/Bugatti	Pump gear	20	0	$0
24	21	25	C.C. Cox (R)	Cino-Purcell	Cino/Mercer	Timing gears	12	0	$0

* - complete car name/entrant data not available for all entries
(R) - Indicated Rookie
(W) - Indicates Past Winner

1916

The maximum engine displacement was reduced from 450 cubic-inches to 300.

Single-lap qualifications were used and cars were lined up by speed. For the first time, cars were also lined up by day, with first day ahead of second day, second day ahead of third day, etc.

Twenty-one cars started, the lowest number in "500" history. Seven cars were owned by track management under the banner of the Indianapolis Speedway Team Company and the Prest-O-Lite Racing Team.

The race was scheduled for 300 miles, mainly because of wartime efforts of conservation. As a result of the shorter distance, the race was moved from the normal ten a.m. start time to one p.m.

Defending champion Ralph DePalma did not defend his title because he was not successful in getting the Speedway to pay him appearance money.

Johnny Aitken won the pole with a speed of 96.7 mph.

Eddie Rickenbacker started from the front row and led the first nine laps. He was about to gain international recognition as a fighter ace in WWI.

Dario Resta led from lap eighteen to the finish (120 laps) in his Peugeot and collected $12,000 for the win. The Italian born Resta averaged

84.0 mph. Wilbur D'Alene finished second in a Duesenberg and Ralph Mulford finished third in a Peugeot.

A crowd estimated at 83,000 attended the race.

Dario Resta would go on to win the 1916 AAA National Championship.

A second event was run on September 9, 1916. The Harvest Day Classic included races of 25 miles, 50 miles and 100 miles. Each race was won by Johnny Aitken. An estimated crowd of 10,000-12,000 attended.

Dario Resta, with riding mechanic Bob Dahnke in a Peugeot, won the Indianapolis "300."

RACE RESULTS FOR THE 1916 INDIANAPOLIS 500

Finish	Start	Car Num.	Driver	Car Name/Entrant*	Make/Model	Status	Laps	Led	Winnings
1	4	17	Dario Resta	Peugeot	Peugeot/Peugeot	84.001	120	103	$12,000
2	10	1	Wilbur D'Alene (R)	Duesenberg	Duesenberg/Duesenberg	83.237	120	0	$6,000
3	20	10	Ralph Mulford	Peugeot	Peugeot/Peugeot	82.594	120	0	$3,000
4	14	14	Josef Christiaens	Sunbeam	Sunbeam/Sunbeam	79.435	120	0	$2,000
5	5	15	Barney Oldfield	Delage	Delage/Delage	79.185	120	0	$1,700
6	9	4	Pete Henderson (R)	Maxwell	Maxwell/Maxwell	78.284	120	0	$1,400
7	6	29	Howdy Wilcox	Premier	Premier/Premier	76.754	120	0	$1,200
8	17	26	Art Johnson (R)	Crawford	Crawford/Duesenberg	74.411	120	0	$1,000
9	15	24	Billy Chandler	Crawford	Crawford/Duesenberg	74.161	120	0	$900
10	13	9	Ora Haibe (R)	Ostewig	Ostewig/Wisconsin	74.043	120	0	$800
11	19	12	Tom Alley	Ogren	Duesenberg/Duesenberg	73.550	120	0	$0
12	21	8	Louis Chevrolet	Frontenac	Frontenac/Frontenac	Rod	82	0	$0
13	3	28	Gil Anderson	Premier	Premier/Premier	Oil line	75	0	$0
14	18	25	Dave Lewis (R)	Crawford	Crawford/Duesenberg	Fuel tank	71	0	$0
15	1	18	Johnny Aitken	Peugeot	Peugeot/Peugeot	Valve	69	8	$0
16	12	21	Jules DeVigne (R)	Delage	Delage/Delage	Accident	61	0	$0
17	7	27	Tom Rooney (R)	Premier	Premier/Premier	Accident	48	0	$0
18	11	7	Arthur Chevrolet	Frontenac	Frontenac/Frontenac	Magneto	35	0	$0
19	8	19	Charlie Merz	Peugeot	Peugeot/Peugeot	Lubrication	25	0	$0
20	2	5	Eddie Rickenbacker	Maxwell	Maxwell/Maxwell	Steering	9	9	$0
21	16	23	Aldo Franchi (R)	Peusun	Peugeot/Sunbeam	Engine	9	0	$0

* - complete car name/entrant data not available for all entries
(R) - Indicated Rookie
(W) - Indicates Past Winner

No race scheduled—United States in World War I.

No race scheduled—United States in World War I.

1919

The winner from 1914, René Thomas, and his riding mechanic Robert Laly, returned for the first time in five years. Thomas won the pole at a record 104.7 mph and finished eleventh. Crawfordsville, Indiana native Howdy Wilcox started second and was actually the first driver to qualify at over 100 mph (100.01).

Arthur Thurman, an attorney from Washington, DC, became the first driver to lose his life in a "500." Three individuals were fatally injured in the race and two were critically injured.

Thirty-three cars started the race.

Other than the 1911 race, the 1919 field had the largest number of newcomers (19).

Ralph DePalma led 93 of the first 102 laps, but eventually finished sixth in his Packard. Howdy Wilcox, from Crawfordsville, Indiana, led from lap 103-200. Wilcox averaged 88.0 mph to win the race in his Speedway-owned Peugeot.

Howdy Wilcox was the first American to win since 1912. The Peugeot win gave the French automaker it's third win in the last five races.

Wilcox won $20,000 of the $55,275 purse.

Eddie Hearne finished second in a Durant Special, and Jules Goux finished third in a Speedway-owned Peugeot.

Louis Chevrolet's car threw a wheel toward the end of the race. It hit a scoring cable that snapped around and cut the neck of driver Elmer Shannon. Shannon was relieved by his riding mechanic, E.E. Rawlings, who went on to finish thirteenth.

Gaston Chevrolet became the third Chevrolet brother to compete in the "500". He started 16th and finished 10th in his first Indy 500.

Accidents took the lives of drivers Arthur Thurman and Louis LeCocq and riding mechanic Robert Bandini

Howdy Wilcox would become the only driver to compete in each of the first eleven Indianapolis 500's. He finished in the top ten four times plus his 1919 victory. He was killed in a racing accident on the boards at Altoona, Pennsylvania in September of 1923.

Estimated attendance varied from 75,000 to 125,000.

The Speedway adopted the European formula for the 1920 race, cylinder displacement would be reduced from 300 cubic-inches to 183 to slow the cars.

1919 Winner Howdy Wilcox drives his Peugeot with his riding mechanic Maurice Becker. The car was owned by the Indianapolis Speedway Team Company. Leo Banks actually rode in the race with Wilcox.

RACE RESULTS FOR THE 1919 INDIANAPOLIS 500

Finish	Start	Car Num.	Driver	Car Name/Entrant*	Make/Model	Status	Laps	Led	Winnings
1	2	3	Howdy Wilcox	Peugeot	Peugeot/Peugeot	88.050	200	98	$20,000
2	8	14	Eddie Hearne	Durant	Stutz/Stutz	87.087	200	0	$10,000
3	22	6	Jules Goux (W)	Peugeot	Peugeot/Premier	85.935	200	0	$5,000
4	3	32	Albert Guyot	Ballot	Ballot/Ballot	84.443	200	0	$3,500
5	28	26	Tom Alley	Bender	Bender/Bender	82.177	200	0	$3,000
6	4	4	Ralph DePalma (W)	Packard	Packard/Packard	81.042	200	93	$2,200
7	12	7	Louis Chevrolet	Frontenac	Frontenac/Frontenac	81.041	200	9	$1,800
8	10	27	Ira Vail (R)	Hudson	Hudson/Hudson	80.494	200	0	$1,600
9	27	21	Denny Hickey (R)	Stickle	Hoskins/Hudson	80.224	200	0	$1,500
10	16	41	Gaston Chevrolet (R)	Frontenac	Frontenac/Frontenac	79.499	200	0	$1,400
11	1	31	Rene Thomas (W)	Ballot	Ballot/Ballot	78.750	200	0	$0
12	9	8	Earl Cooper	Stutz	Stutz/Stutz	78.600	200	0	$0
13	29	23	Elmer Shannon (R)	Shannon	Shannon/Duesenberg	76.950	200	0	$0
14	26	17	Ora Haibe	Hudson	Hudson/Hudson	65.740	200	0	$0
15	32	37	Andre Boillot (R)	Baby Peugeot	Peugeot/Peugeot	Accident	195	0	$0
16	21	48	Ray Howard (R)	Peugeot	Peugeot/Peugeot	Lubrication	130	0	$0
17	23	22	Wilbur D'Alene	Duesenberg	Duesenberg/Duesenberg	Axle	120	0	$0
18	25	15	Louis LeCocq (R)	Roamer	Duesenberg/Duesenberg	Accident	96	0	$0
19	7	29	Art Klein	Peugeot	Peugeot/Peugeot	Oil line	70	0	$0
20	11	19	Charles Kirkpatrick (R)	Detroit	Mercedes copy/Mercedes copy	Rod	69	0	$0
21	6	33	Paul Bablot (R)	Ballot	Ballot/Ballot	Accident	63	0	$0
22	5	10	Eddie O'Donnell	Duesenberg	Duesenberg/Duesenberg	Piston	60	0	$0
23	24	12	Kurt Hitke (R)	Roamer	Duesenberg/Duesenberg	Bearing	56	0	$0
24	20	1	Cliff Durant (R)	Chevrolet	Stutz/Stutz	Steering	54	0	$0
25	31	9	Tommy Milton (R)	Duesenberg	Duesenberg/Duesenberg	Rod	50	0	$0
26	13	34	Louis Wagner (R)	Ballot	Ballot/Ballot	Wheel	44	0	$0
27	18	18	Arthur Thurman (R)	Thurman	Duesenberg/Duesenberg	Accident	44	0	$0
28	30	43	Omar Toft (R)	Toft/Darco	Miller/Miller	Rod	44	0	$0
29	15	2	Ralph Mulford	Frontenac	Frontenac/Frontenac	Driveshaft	37	0	$0
30	33	36	J.J. McCoy (R)	McCoy	McCoy/N/A	Oil line	36	0	$0
31	14	39	Joe Boyer (R)	Frontenac	Frontenac/Frontenac	Wheel	30	0	$0
32	17	5	W.W. Brown (R)	Richards	Brown/Hudson-Brett	Rod	14	0	$0
33	19	28	Roscoe Sarles (R)	Oldfield	Miller/Miller	Rocker arm	8	0	$0

* - complete car name/entrant data not available for all entries
(R) - Indicated Rookie
(W) - Indicates Past Winner

1920

Four-lap qualification runs were required for the first time. More than one car was permitted to qualify at the same time.

The pole was won by Ralph DePalma at 99.15 mph.

Twenty-three cars started the race.

Former driver Barney Oldfield drove the Marmon pace car.

Joe Boyer led most of the first half of the race.

DePalma led from lap 113 to 186, and was ahead of Gaston Chevrolet by over two laps when his French Ballot slowed and stopped on the north end of the track. He thought he was out of fuel, but instead was experiencing magneto problems. He was able to repair his car and salvaged fifth place. Peter DePaolo, his riding mechanic, was the son of DePalma's sister. DePalma led a total of 79 laps.

Gaston Chevrolet, in a Monroe Special, unlapped himself and went on to victory at an average of 88.6 mph. He went the distance with only two pit stops and no tire changes. This was the first American-built car to win since 1912. The Monroe Special was actually a Frontenac and was designed and built by older brothers Louis and Arthur Chevrolet. The win by Chevrolet represented the last win for a four-cylinder engine until 1934.

René Thomas finished second in a Ballot and Tommy Milton third in a Duesenberg, with rookie Jimmy Murphy posting a fourth place finish also in a Duesenberg.

Roscoe Sarles crashed into the northeast wall on lap 59, and then later, while relieving Bennett Hill, did the same thing in the same turn on lap 115.

Joe Boyer led ninety-three laps, DePalma, seventy-nine laps, and Gaston Chevrolet led the final fourteen laps for the win.

Lap prize money was paid for the first time to the leader of each lap at the rate of $100 per lap.

The crowd was estimated at more than 120,000.

Chevrolet would go on to win the 1920 AAA National Championship.

On Thanksgiving Day of 1920, at twenty-eight years of age, Gaston Chevrolet lost his life in a racing accident at a track in Beverly Hills, California. He was the first 500 winner to lose his life in a racing accident.

1920 Winner Gaston Chevrolet is pictured in his Monroe with riding mechanic John Bresnahan.

RACE RESULTS FOR THE 1920 INDIANAPOLIS 500

Finish	Start	Car Num.	Driver	Car Name/Entrant*	Make/Model	Status	Laps	Led	Winnings
1	6	4	Gaston Chevrolet	Monroe	Frontenac/Frontenac	88.618	200	14	$21,800
2	18	25	Rene Thomas (W)	Ballot	Ballot/Ballot	86.992	200	12	$10,700
3	11	10	Tommy Milton	Duesenberg	Duesenberg/Duesenberg	86.946	200	0	$5,000
4	15	12	Jimmy Murphy (R)	Duesenberg	Duesenberg/Duesenberg	85.101	200	0	$3,500
5	1	2	Ralph DePalma (W)	Ballot	Ballot/Ballot	82.120	200	79	$11,300
6	9	31	Eddie Hearne	Duesenberg	Duesenberg/Duesenberg	81.002	200	0	$2,200
7	4	26	Jean Chassagne	Ballot	Ballot/Ballot	79.941	200	1	$1,900
8	19	28	Joe Thomas (R)	Monroe	Frontenac/Frontenac	78.597	200	0	$1,600
9	23	33	Ralph Mulford	Mulford	Mulford/Duesenberg	68.613	200	0	$1,500
10	17	15	Pete Henderson	Revere	Duesenberg/Duesenberg	67.583	200	0	$1,400
11	14	32	John Boling (R)	Richards	Brett/Brett	Running	199	0	$0
12	2	6	Joe Boyer	Frontenac	Frontenac/Frontenac	Accident	192	93	$9,500
13	10	9	Ray Howard	Peugeot	Peugeot/Peugeot	Camshaft	150	0	$0
14	12	29	Eddie O'Donnell	Duesenberg	Duesenberg/Duesenberg	Oil line	149	0	$0
15	21	16	Jules Goux (W)	Peugeot	Peugeot/Peugeot	Engine	148	0	$0
16	13	34	Willie Haupt	Meteor	Duesenberg/Duesenberg	Running	146	0	$0
17	8	7	Bennett Hill (R)	Frontenac	Frontenac/Frontenac	Accident	115	0	$0
18	3	3	Louis Chevrolet	Monroe	Frontenac/Frontenac	Steering	94	0	$0
19	20	18	Howdy Wilcox (W)	Peugeot	Peugeot/Peugeot	Mechanical	65	0	$0
20	7	5	Roscoe Sarles	Monroe	Frontenac/Frontenac	Accident	58	0	$0
21	5	8	Art Klein	Frontenac	Frontenac/Frontenac	Accident	40	1	$100
22	22	19	Jean Porporato	Gregoire	Gregoire/Gregoire	Ruled off	23	0	$0
23	16	17	Andre Boillot	Peugeot	Peugeot/Peugeot	Engine	16	0	$0

* - complete car name/entrant data not available for all entries
(R) - Indicated Rookie
(W) - Indicates Past Winner

1921

Ralph DePalma won the pole for the second year in a row, driving a Ballot with a speed of 100.75 mph.

On May 27, Frank Wheeler died. He was one of the founding fathers of the Speedway, but no longer a partner at the time of his death.

After five abreast starts in 1911 and 1912, and four abreast starts up through 1920, the rule of three cars per row was implemented and has remained in place ever since.

Twenty-three cars started the race.

Harry C. Stutz drove the pace car bearing his initials—an H.C.S. roadster.

Ralph DePalma led 108 of the first 110 laps before a broken connecting rod eventually ended his race. This brought DePalma's laps led count to 612 total laps. He would remain the all-time lap leader until 1987, when Al Unser, Sr., eclipsed his record.

Once DePalma dropped out, Tommy Milton, driving for the Chevrolet brothers, led the rest of the way. Milton had qualified twentieth of twenty-three starters in his American made Frontenac. Milton averaged 89.6 mph which was just shy of Ralph DePalma's 1915 record of 89.8 mph. He took the checkered flag two laps ahead of Roscoe Sarles in a Duesenberg. Sarles was from Lafayette, Indiana. Percy Ford finished third in Frontenac.

The Chevrolet brothers became the first team to win the "500" in consecutive years.

Ralph DePalma did not finish in the money, as only the top ten finishers earned prize money. He did earn $10,600 in lap prize money and actually earned more than everyone but Milton.

Tommy Milton is believed to have had vision in only one eye.

Estimated attendance was as high as 150,000 fans.

Milton would go on to win the 1921 AAA National Championship.

Tommy Milton in the winning Frontenac. Riding mechanic Harry Frank with glass, Arthur Chevrolet with white shirt and cap, Louis Chevrolet with straw hat and Barnie Oldfield with ever-present cigar, look on.

RACE RESULTS FOR THE 1921 INDIANAPOLIS 500

Finish	Start	Car Num.	Driver	Car Name/ Entrant*	Make/Model	Status	Laps	Led	Winnings
1	20	2	Tommy Milton	Frontenac	Frontenac/Frontenac	89.621	200	90	$26,200
2	2	6	Roscoe Sarles	Duesenberg Straight 8	Duesenberg/Duesenberg	88.608	200	1	$10,100
3	8	23	Percy Ford (R)	Chicago Frontenac	Frontenac/Frontenac	85.025	200	0	$5,000
4	9	5	Eddie Miller (R)	Duesenberg Straight 8	Duesenberg/Duesenberg	84.646	200	0	$3,500
5	13	16	Ora Haibe	Sunbeam	Sunbeam/Sunbeam	84.277	200	0	$3,000
6	14	9	Albert Guyot	Duesenberg Straight 8	Duesenberg/Duesenberg	83.035	200	0	$2,000
7	10	3	Ira Vail	Leach	Leach/Miller	80.152	200	0	$1,800
8	15	21	Bennett Hill	Duesenberg Straight 8	Duesenberg/Duesenberg	79.132	200	0	$1,600
9	21	8	Ralph Mulford	Frontenac	Frontenac/Frontenac	Running	177	0	$1,500
10	17	15	Rene Thomas (W)	Sunbeam	Sunbeam/Sunbeam	Water hose	144	0	$0
11	18	27	Tom Alley	Frontenac	Frontenac/Frontenac	Rod	133	0	$0
12	1	4	Ralph DePalma (W)	Ballot	Ballot/Ballot	Rod	112	108	$10,600
13	4	1	Eddie Hearne	Revere	Duesenberg/Duesenberg	Oil line	111	0	$0
14	19	24	Jimmy Murphy	Duesenberg Straight 8	Duesenberg/Duesenberg	Accident	107	0	$0
15	16	17	Riley Brett (R)	Junior	Brett/Brett	Accident	91	0	$0
16	23	28	C.W. Van Ranst (R)	Frontenac	Frontenac/Frontenac	Water hose	87	0	$0
17	3	7	Joe Boyer	Duesenberg Straight 8	Duesenberg/Duesenberg	Rear axle	74	1	$0
18	6	19	Jean Chassagne	Peugeot	Peugeot/Peugeot	Lost hood	65	0	$0
19	5	22	Jules Ellingboe (R)	Frontenac	Frontenac/Frontenac	Steering	49	0	$0
20	11	14	Andre Boillot	Talbot-Darracq	Sunbeam/Sunbeam	Bearing	41	0	$0
21	7	18	Louis Fontaine (R)	Junior	Brett/Brett	Accident	33	0	$0
22	22	25	Joe Thomas	Duesenberg Straight 8	Duesenberg/Duesenberg	Accident	24	0	$0
23	12	10	Howdy Wilcox (W)	Peugeot	Peugeot/Peugeot	Rod	22	0	$0

* - complete car name/entrant data not available for all entries
(R) - Indicated Rookie
(W) - Indicates Past Winner

1922

There were twenty-seven cars in the race.

Irishman Jimmy Murphy was the owner/driver of a Duesenberg chassis with a straight-eight Miller engine. He won the pole at 100.5 mph and became the first winner to start from the pole. He also became the first driver in history to win in a car entered by himself. Murphy also won the 1921 French Grand Prix at LeMans in this car.

Murphy led 153 of the 200 laps for a two-lap win in his Murphy Special. He averaged 94.5 mph, which broke Ralph DePalma's record from 1915 by 5 mph. Actually, the first five finishers all eclipsed DePalma's record.

Harry Hartz finished second in a Duesenberg after being a riding mechanic for Eddie Hearne in the previous three 500s. Hearne finished in third place in a Ballot.

Duesenberg products also finished second, fourth, fifth, sixth, seventh, eighth, and tenth, thus occupying eight of the first ten places.

The last starting position (27th) was occupied by Jack Curtner. Curtner took over a Fronty Ford that had been crashed by Tommy Mulligan during practice. Curtner was allowed to start in last position without making a qualification run under the condition he would not compete for prize money. Curtner would finish in fourteenth position while completing 165 laps.

The estimated attendance was approximately 135,000.

Jimmy Murphy started his racing career as a riding mechanic and rode with Eddie O'Donnell in the 1919 "500."

Murphy went on to win the 1922 AAA driving title.

A remarkable stretch from 1922 to the mid-1930's was dominated by engines and cars built by Harry Arminius Miller. Miller was a self-taught automotive genius whose cars and engines would win the Indianapolis 500 ten times between 1922 and 1934.

The Speedway announced that the engines for the 1923 "500" could not exceed 122 cubic-inch piston displacement.

Jimmy Murphy with riding mechanic Ernie Olsen takes the checkered flag in his Duesenberg chassis with a Miller engine.

RACE RESULTS FOR THE 1922 INDIANAPOLIS 500

Finish	Start	Car Num.	Driver	Car Name/Entrant*	Make/Model	Status	Laps	Led	Winnings
1	1	35	Jimmy Murphy	Murphy	Duesenberg/Miller	94.484	200	153	$28,075
2	2	12	Harry Hartz (R)	Duesenberg Straight 8	Duesenberg/Duesenberg	93.534	200	42	$10,000
3	23	15	Eddie Hearne	Ballot	Ballot/Ballot	93.042	200	0	$5,000
4	3	17	Ralph DePalma (W)	Duesenberg Straight 8	Duesenberg/Duesenberg	90.613	200	0	$3,500
5	14	31	Ora Haibe	Duesenberg Straight 8	Duesenberg/Duesenberg	90.573	200	0	$3,000
6	7	24	Jerry Wonderlich (R)	Duesenberg Straight 8	Duesenberg/Duesenberg	88.789	200	0	$2,200
7	13	21	I.P. Fetterman (R)	Duesenberg Straight 8	Duesenberg/Duesenberg	87.996	200	0	$1,800
8	9	1	Ira Vail	Disteel Duesenberg	Duesenberg/Duesenberg	86.128	200	0	$1,600
9	12	26	Tom Alley	Monroe	Frontenac/Frontenac	84.295	200	0	$1,500
10	17	10	Joe Thomas	Duesenberg Straight 8	Duesenberg/Duesenberg	82.553	200	0	$1,400
11	16	3	Cliff Durant	Durant	Miller/Miller	77.750	200	0	$0
13	19	22	Douglas Hawkes (R)	Bentley	Bentley/Bentley	74.950	200	0	$0
14	27	18	Jack Curtner (R)	Fronty-Ford	Ford T/Fronty-Ford	Running	165	0	$0
15	18	25	Wilbur D'Alene	Monroe	Frontenac/Frontenac	Running	160	0	$0
16	8	9	Frank Elliott (R)	Leach	Miller/Miller	Rear axle	195	0	$0
17	15	27	L.L. Corum (R)	Monroe	Frontenac/Frontenac	Mechanical	169	0	$0
18	21	19	C. Glenn Howard (R)	Fronty-Ford	Ford T/Fronty-Ford	Mechanical	163	0	$0
19	5	5	Ralph Mulford	Frontenac	Frontenac/Frontenac	Rod	161	0	$0
20	10	7	Pete DePaolo (R)	Frontenac	Frontenac/Frontenac	Accident	110	3	$0
21	25	6	Art Klein	Frontenac	Frontenac/Frontenac	Rod	105	0	$0
22	4	4	Leon Duray (R)	Frontenac	Frontenac/Frontenac	Axle	94	2	$0
23	6	2	Roscoe Sarles	Frontenac	Frontenac/Frontenac	Rod	88	0	$0
24	24	8	Tommy Milton (W)	Leach	Milton/Miller	Fuel tank	44	0	$0
25	22	14	Jules Goux (W)	Ballot	Ballot/Ballot	Axle	25	0	$0
26	20	23	Jules Ellingboe	Duesenberg Straight 8	Duesenberg/Duesenberg	Accident	25	0	$0
27	26	16	Howdy Wilcox (W)	Peugeot	Peugeot/Peugeot	Valve spring	7	0	$0

* - complete car name/entrant data not available for all entries
(R) - Indicated Rookie
(W) - Indicates Past Winner

Indy 500 Recaps The Short Chute Edition

1923

Riding mechanics were no longer mandatory and would not become mandatory again until 1930.

The German Mercedes firm made its' only official attempt at Indy by entering three cars that featured the first superchargers ever used at the Speedway.

Fred Duesenberg drove the Duesenberg Model A pace car.

Tommy Milton, who won the pole at a record of 108.170 mph, broke his own track record by 7 mph. He went on to win in an HCS Special. He averaged 90.9 mph to become the first two-time winner and the second to win from the pole.

The two Harry Stutz entries, called HCS Specials (for his initials), were actually Millers. Miller engines powered 11 of the 24 cars.

This was the most competitive race to date, with twenty-eight lead changes, the prior record being twelve in 1922.

Pinched feet and blistered hands caused Milton to call for relief from Howdy Wilcox for laps 103-151. Milton led thirteen times for 128 laps.

Wilcox, while relieving Milton, led one time for forty-one laps. Wilcox also led in his original car five times for ten laps.

Milton finished three-and-a-half minutes ahead of second place Harry Hartz, followed by Jimmy Murphy and Eddie Hearne, all in Durant-sponsored Millers.

Lora Corum finished a distant fifth-place in a car prepared by Arthur Chevrolet, built almost entirely of Ford Model T parts.

The 1916 winner, Dario Resta, returned to the Indianapolis 500 and qualified in the third position. His race was cut short when the car differential failed on lap 88.

Only three of the starting drivers drove the entire race without a relief driver.

On lap 22, Tom Alley, driving relief for Earl Cooper, crashed through the backstretch fence, killing teenager Bert Schoup. The young man had been watching the race through a knothole.

Attendance was estimated at about 150,000.

On June 11, 1923, Carl Fisher stepped down and named Jim Allison president of the track.

The 24 Hours of LeMans was run for the first time in 1923.

Tommy Milton becomes the first two-time winner in an HCS Miller.

RACE RESULTS FOR THE 1923 INDIANAPOLIS 500

Finish	Start	Car Num.	Driver	Car Name/Entrant*	Make/Model	Status	Laps	Led	Winnings
1	1	1	Tommy Milton (W)	H.C.S.	Miller/Miller	90.954	200	128	$28,700
2	2	7	Harry Hartz	Durant	Miller/Miller	90.063	200	6	$10,100
3	9	5	Jimmy Murphy (W)	Durant	Miller/Miller	88.078	200	11	$7,000
4	14	6	Eddie Hearne	Durant	Miller/Miller	86.646	200	0	$3,500
5	7	23	L.L. Corum	Barber-Warnock Ford	Ford T/Fronty-Ford	82.851	200	0	$3,000
6	16	31	Frank Elliott	Durant	Miller/Miller	82.219	200	0	$2,200
7	10	8	Cliff Durant	Durant	Miller/Miller	82.170	200	4	$2,200
8	20	15	Max Sailer (R)	Mercedes	Mercedes/Mercedes	80.683	200	0	$1,600
9	22	19	Prince de Cystria (R)	Bugatti	Bugatti/Bugatti	77.637	200	0	$1,500
10	24	34	Wade Morton (R)	Duesenberg	Duesenberg/Duesenberg	74.984	200	0	$1,400
11	15	16	Christian Werner (R)	Mercedes	Mercedes/Mercedes	74.650	200	0	$0
12	6	18	Pierre de Viscaya (R)	Bugatti	Bugatti/Bugatti	Rod	166	0	$0
13	21	28	Leon Duray	Durant	Miller/Miller	Rod	136	0	$0
14	3	3	Dario Resta (W)	Packard	Packard/Packard	Differential	87	0	$0
15	11	2	Ralph DePalma (W)	Packard	Packard/Packard	Head gasket	69	0	$0
16	19	26	Harlan Fengler (R)	Durant	Miller/Miller	Fuel tank	69	0	$0
17	8	25	Howdy Wilcox (W)	H.C.S.	Miller/Miller	Clutch	60	51	$2,000
18	13	4	Joe Boyer	Packard	Packard/Packard	Differential	59	0	$0
19	18	35	Bennett Hill	Miller	Miller/Miller	Crankshaft	41	0	$0
20	5	27	Count Louis Zborowski (R)	Bugatti	Bugatti/Bugatti	Rod	41	0	$0
21	12	29	Earl Cooper	Durant	Miller/Miller	Accident	21	0	$0
22	23	22	Raul Riganti (R)	Bugatti	Bugatti/Bugatti	Fuel line	19	0	$0
23	17	14	Christian Lautenschlager (R)	Mercedes	Mercedes/Mercedes	Accident	14	0	$0
24	4	21	Martin de Alzaga (R)	Bugatti	Bugatti/Bugatti	Rod	6	0	$0

* - complete car name/entrant data not available for all entries
(R) - Indicated Rookie
(W) - Indicates Past Winner

1924

Following the lead of Mercedes in 1923, Duesenberg supercharged three of its four cars.

Jimmy Murphy won the pole at 108.0 mph.

Only twenty-two cars started.

Henry Ford, who had attended the first 500 mile race and every one since, served as the Honorary Referee.

For the second consecutive year, a driver was able to lead the race in two different cars. In 1924, it was Joe Boyer, and in 1923, Howdy Wilcox. Boyer led the first lap, but soon experienced supercharger problems in his Duesenberg. On lap 93 Ernie Ansterburg replaced Boyer. On lap 111 Boyer replaced L.L. Corum. On lap 159 Corum replaced Ansterburg in the Boyer car. On lap 176 Thane Houser replaced Corum, and crashed the car on his first lap, finishing in 18th place.

Just past the midpoint of the race, the Duesenberg brothers decided to replace L.L. (Lora Lawrence) "Slim" Corum with Joe Boyer while Corum was running fourth, about two and a half minutes behind the leader. It seemed that Corum was unable to keep pace with Earl Cooper's Studebaker/Miller and Jimmy Murphy's Miller, which dominated the first half of the race.

Boyer led the last 24 laps after Earl Cooper's Studebaker Special had tire trouble, although Cooper was able to finish second. Cooper led for a total of 119 laps. Jimmy Murphy finished third in a Miller.

Because L.L. Corum started the race and Joe Boyer finished, they were declared co-winners. They averaged a record of 98.2 mph. Corum actually completed 110 laps in the winning car before being replaced by Boyer. Corum had started 21st in the twenty-two car field.

The top five finishers all exceeded the previous race record of 94.5 mph.

Of the twenty-two starters, only five cars were eliminated before the finish.

Boyer had the unique distinction of leading the first lap and the last lap—in different cars. Corum gained the unique distinction of being declared a co-winner, while never leading a lap.

Last-place finisher Ernie Ansterburg received $5.25, completing just one lap. This was the smallest amount of prize money ever paid.

Stirling Moss's father, Alfred Moss, drove in the 1924 race and finished sixteenth. Stirling would win sixteen Formula One Grand Prix in his career.

Estimated attendance was 140,000.

In September of 1924, three former winners were fatally injured within two weeks of each other: Joe Boyer at Altoona, Pennsylvania; Dario Resta in England; and Jimmy Murphy at Syracuse, New York.

Lora Corum and Joe Boyer (inset) are declared 1924 co-winners.

RACE RESULTS FOR THE 1924 INDIANAPOLIS 500

Finish	Start	Car Num.	Driver	Car Name/Entrant*	Make/Model	Status	Laps	Led	Winnings
1	21	15	L.L. Corum / Joe Boyer	Duesenberg	Duesenberg/Duesenberg	98.234	200	25	$20,000
2	6	8	Earl Cooper	Studebaker	Miller/Miller	97.788	200	119	$13,700
3	1	2	Jimmy Murphy (W)	Miller	Miller/Miller	97.269	200	56	$7,800
4	2	4	Harry Hartz	Durant	Miller/Miller	96.544	200	0	$3,500
5	5	3	Bennett Hill	Miller	Miller/Miller	96.463	200	0	$3,000
6	13	12	Pete DePaolo	Duesenberg	Duesenberg/Duesenberg	94.297	200	0	$2,200
7	16	14	Fred Comer (R)	Durant	Miller/Miller	93.424	200	0	$1,800
8	15	6	Ira Vail	Vail	Miller/Miller	92.450	200	0	$1,600
9	9	32	Antoine Mourre (R)	Mourre	Miller/Miller	91.764	200	0	$1,500
10	18	19	Bob McDonogh (R)	Miller	Miller/Miller	90.513	200	0	$1,400
11	7	18	Jules Ellingboe	Miller	Miller/Miller	90.570	200	0	$1,049
12	11	7	Jerry Wonderlich	Durant	Miller/Miller	85.480	200	0	$1,049
13	8	16	Cliff Durant	Durant	Miller/Miller	Out of fuel	198	0	$1,038
14	19	26	Bill Hunt (R)	Barber-Warnock Ford	Ford T/Fronty-Ford	Running	190	0	$996
15	17	31	Ora Haibe	Schmidt	Mercedes/Mercedes	Running	181	0	$949
16	20	28	A.E. Moss (R)	Barber-Warnock Ford	Ford T/Fronty-Ford	Running	176	0	$923
17	22	27	Fred Harder (R)	Barber-Warnock Ford	Ford T/Fronty-Ford	Running	175	0	$917
18	4	9	Joe Boyer	Duesenberg	Duesenberg/Duesenberg	Accident	176	0	$973
19	14	1	Eddie Hearne	Durant	Miller/Miller	Fuel tank	150	0	$787
20	12	21	Frank Elliott	Miller	Miller/Miller	Fuel tank	150	0	$787
21	3	5	Tommy Milton (W)	Miller	Miller/Miller	Fuel tank	110	0	$577
22	10	10	Ernie Ansterburg (R)	Duesenberg	Duesenberg/Duesenberg	Accident	1	0	$5

* - complete car name/entrant data not available for all entries
(R) - Indicated Rookie
(W) - Indicates Past Winner

1925

The technology of front-drive cars arrived in May of 1925. Cliff Durant bought a Miller built low slung front-drive machine from the Jimmy Murphy estate after his death. Dave Lewis, Harry Miller's brother-in-law, was assigned to drive the machine.

Leon Duray sat on the pole at a new record of 113.2 mph. Peter DePaolo started second. Earl Cooper was the first driver to eclipse the 110 mph barrier. He eventually started fourth.

Twenty-two cars started the race, with all of them incorporating superchargers.

The race was paced by Captain Eddie Rickenbacker in a Rickenbacker Eight. The Rickenbacker Automobile Company was in receivership two years later. Peter DePaolo's Duesenberg led for 115 laps. His car incorporated a supercharger, rear-wheel-drive and balloon tires. Because his hands were badly blistered, Norm Batten stepped in to relieve him for about thirty-five minutes (22 laps), while his hands received attention.

Steady driving Dave Lewis, who was leading, stopped for relief from Bennett Hill on the 173rd lap, DePaolo had clear sailing to the finish in one of the safest races to date. DePaolo was the first driver to average over 100 mph (101.1 mph), and complete the race in under five hours. For good luck he strapped the shoes of his young son to the front axle.

The first three finishers all eclipsed the 100 mph barrier

Dave Lewis and relief driver Bennett Hill finished second in the first front-wheel-drive car to compete in the 500. They led a total of fifty laps. Phil Shafer, with help from Wade Morton, finished third in a Duesenberg.

Peter DePaolo became the only person to lead the race both as a riding mechanic (with uncle Ralph DePalma) and as a driver.

Estimated attendance was more than 100,000.

DePaolo would go on to win the 1925 AAA National Championship. He would win the championship again in 1927.

The Speedway announced that for the 1926 race, piston displacement would be reduced from 122 cubic-inches to 91 cubic-inches.

The pagoda was burned to the ground the day after the 1925 race to make way for a new pagoda, which was placed further back from the track's edge.

Peter DePaolo in a Duesenberg is the first winner to average more than 100 mph.

RACE RESULTS FOR THE 1925 INDIANAPOLIS 500

Finish	Start	Car Num.	Driver	Car Name/Entrant*	Make/Model	Status	Laps	Led	Winnings
1	2	12	Pete DePaolo	Duesenberg	Duesenberg/Duesenberg	101.127	200	115	$36,150
2	5	1	Dave Lewis	Junior '8' Front Drive	Miller/Miller	100.823	200	50	$15,000
3	22	9	Phil Shafer (R)	Duesenberg	Duesenberg/Duesenberg	100.185	200	13	$8,750
4	3	6	Harry Hartz	Miller	Miller/Miller	98.892	200	3	$4,300
5	11	4	Tommy Milton (W)	Miller	Miller/Miller	97.267	200	0	$3,500
6	1	28	Leon Duray	Miller	Miller/Miller	96.910	200	0	$2,200
7	18	8	Ralph DePalma (W)	Miller	Miller/Miller	96.847	200	0	$1,800
8	9	38	Peter Kreis (R)	Duesenberg	Duesenberg/Duesenberg	96.324	200	0	$2,250
9	14	15	Doc Shattuc (R)	Miller	Miller/Miller	95.742	200	0	$1,500
10	8	22	Pietro Bordino (R)	Fiat	Fiat/Fiat	94.747	200	0	$1,400
11	12	5	Fred Comer	Miller	Miller/Miller	93.670	200	0	$1,096
12	10	27	Frank Elliott	Miller	Miller/Miller	92.230	200	0	$1,037
13	15	24	Earl DeVore (R)	Miller	Miller/Miller	Running	198	0	$981
14	20	14	Bob McDonogh	Miller	Miller/Miller	Truss rod	187	0	$929
15	16	23	Wade Morton	Duesenberg	Duesenberg/Duesenberg	Accident	156	0	$880
16	6	17	Ralph Hepburn (R)	Miller	Miller/Miller	Fuel tank	143	15	$2,334
17	4	2	Earl Cooper	Junior '8'	Miller/Miller	Accident	127	4	$1,191
18	13	3	Bennett Hill	Miller	Miller/Miller	Rear spring	69	0	$750
19	17	29	Herbert Jones (R)	Jones & Whitaker	Miller/Miller	Accident	68	0	$729
20	19	19	Ira Vail	R.J.	Miller/Miller	Rod	61	0	$692
21	21	7	M.C. Jones (R)	Skelly	Ford T/Fronty-Ford	Transmission	32	0	$657
22	7	10	Jules Ellingboe	Miller	Miller/Miller	Steering	24	0	$625

* - complete car name/entrant data not available for all entries
(R) - Indicated Rookie
(W) - Indicates Past Winner

1926

Frank Lockhart, born in Dayton, Ohio, was a very good dirt track racer in California. The original plan was for Lockhart to serve as a relief driver for Bennett Hill, but a few days before qualifications, driver/owner Peter Kreis was hospitalized with pneumonia. The twenty-three year old Lockhart drove Kreis' rear-wheel-drive Miller for his first 500 start.

Earl Cooper, in a front-drive Miller, won the pole at 111.7 mph in the twenty-eight car field. Harry Hartz started second.

There were eighteen Millers in the field.

Louis Chevrolet drove a Chrysler Imperial to pace the start.

Lockhart, who had a lap of 115 mph on one of his two incomplete attempts, qualified on his third attempt and started twentieth in the twenty-eight-car field.

Dave Lewis, who finished second in 1925, led most of the first 60 laps in his front-drive Miller. Frank Lockhart took over for nearly the rest of the race, which was flagged for rain at 160 laps. Lockhart was leading Harry Hartz by two laps when the race was called.

Hartz was in contention for the win in his Miller Special until experiencing problems on his last pit stop.

The race had been stopped by rain on lap seventy-one for more than an hour before it was restarted.

Lockhart was leading at the 380-mile mark when it began to rain again. At 400 miles he was declared the winner as rain fell hard. The rule at the time required that 350 miles be completed in order for the race to be considered official.

This was the first time in history that rain interfered with the race once it was started.

Lockhart's average speed of 95.885 mph for the race was higher than his qualifying speed of 95.782 mph. This also happened in 1924 with the Corum/Boyer Duesenberg.

Attendance was estimated at about 140,000, which was believed to have been the largest in history.

Frank Lockhart wins the 500 in his first try.

RACE RESULTS FOR THE 1926 INDIANAPOLIS 500

Finish	Start	Car Num.	Driver	Car Name/Entrant*	Make/Model	Status	Laps	Led	Winnings
1	20	15	Frank Lockhart (R)	Miller	Miller/Miller	95.904	160	95	$35,600
2	2	3	Harry Hartz	Miller	Miller/Miller	Running	158	6	$13,900
3	14	36	Cliff Woodbury (R)	Boyle	Miller/Miller	Running	158	0	$6,700
4	13	8	Fred Comer	Miller	Miller/Miller	Running	155	0	$4,000
5	27	12	Pete DePaolo (W)	Duesenberg	Duesenberg/Duesenberg	Running	153	0	$3,500
6	8	6	Frank Elliott	Miller	Miller/Miller	Running	152	0	$2,200
7	16	14	Norm Batten (R)	Miller	Miller/Miller	Running	151	0	$1,800
8	15	19	Ralph Hepburn	Miller	Miller/Miller	Running	151	0	$1,600
9	28	18	John Duff (R)	Elcar	Miller/Miller	Running	147	0	$1,500
10	5	4	Phil Shafer	Miller	Miller/Miller	Running	146	16	$3,000
11	12	31	Tony Gulotta (R)	Miller	Miller/Miller	Running	142	0	$615
12	7	16	Bennett Hill	Miller	Miller/Miller	Running	136	0	$607
13	21	33	Thane Houser (R)	Abell	Miller/Miller	Running	102	0	$600
14	17	27	Douglas Hawkes	Eldridge	Eldridge/Anzani	Camshaft	92	0	$593
15	4	1	Dave Lewis	Miller Front Drive	Miller/Miller	Valve	92	43	$4,886
16	1	5	Earl Cooper	Miller Front Drive	Miller/Miller	Transmission	74	0	$579
17	11	9	Cliff Durant	Locomobile Junior 8	Fengler/Locomobile	Fuel leak	61	0	$572
18	18	29	Ben Jones (R)	Duesenberg (Two-Cycle)	Duesenberg/Duesenberg	Accident	54	0	$565
19	23	26	E.A.D. Eldridge (R)	Eldridge	Eldridge/Anzani	Steering	46	0	$558
20	24	23	L.L. Corum (W)	Schmidt	Schmidt/Argyle	Cracked block	45	0	$551
21	22	24	Steve Nemesh (R)	Schmidt	Schmidt/Argyle	Transmission	42	0	$544
22	6	7	Jules Ellingboe	Miller	Miller/Miller	Supercharger	39	0	$538
23	3	10	Leon Duray	Locomobile Junior 8	Fengler/Locomobile	Fuel leak	33	0	$531
24	26	17	Fred Lecklider (R)	Nickel Plate	Miller/Miller	Piston	25	0	$525
25	25	28	Jack McCarver (R)	Hamlin Front Drive	Ford T/Fronty-Ford	Rod	24	0	$519
26	9	34	Bon McDougall (R)	Miller	Miller/Miller	Water leak	19	0	$512
27	10	22	Doc Shattuc	Miller	Miller/Miller	Valve	16	0	$506
28	19	39	Albert Guyot	Guyot	Schmidt/Argyle	Piston	9	0	$500

* - complete car name/entrant data not available for all entries
(R) - Indicated Rookie
(W) - Indicates Past Winner

1927

There were thirty-three starters with twenty-four being Millers. This was the first time since 1919 that there were thirty-three cars starting the race.

Frank Lockhart won the pole in a Miller that he owned at a new record of 120.1 mph. He was the first driver to break the 120 mph barrier. Peter DePaolo started second and George Souders started twenty-second in a Duesenberg owned by Bill White.

Lockhart led the first eighty-one laps. This record for leading the most consecutive laps from the start of the race remained unbroken for the next sixty-three years.

A connecting rod broke on Lockhart's car after he led 110 of the first 119 laps.

George Souders, driving in his first 500, took the lead on lap 150 and led to the finish. He did not use a relief driver, while every car finishing from second to seventeenth used one or more relief drivers. He became the first driver to cover the full 500 miles without either a relief driver or a riding mechanic. Souders was from nearby Lafayette, Indiana.

The margin of victory was the second largest in history (over twelve minutes), as Souders was over eight laps ahead of the second place Earl DeVore when he took the checkered flag. Souders averaged 97.5 mph in his eight-cylinder Duesenberg.

As Souders took the checkered flag, Babe Stapp, who was driving relief for Benny Shoaff, was running second in a Duesenberg three laps behind. Stapp was more than four laps ahead of Earl Devore. On lap 198 Stapp's car slowed and stopped, resulting in Devore overtaking him and finishing second.

The fourth-place finisher was rookie Wilbur Shaw, who received relief from his mechanic Louis Meyer.

On lap twenty-four, Norman Batten stood up in the cockpit as he steered his burning Miller past the fuel-filled pits before jumping out. He was hospitalized but recovered.

Norm Batten steers his flaming Miller before jumping out on lap twenty-four.

RACE RESULTS FOR THE 1927 INDIANAPOLIS 500

Finish	Start	Car Num.	Driver	Car Name/Entrant*	Make/Model	Status	Laps	Led	Winnings
1	22	32	George Souders (R)	Duesenberg	Duesenberg/Duesenberg	97.545	200	51	$30,650
2	15	10	Earl DeVore	Miller	Miller/Miller	93.868	200	0	$12,800
3	27	27	Tony Gulotta	Miller	Miller/Miller	93.139	200	0	$6,000
4	19	29	Wilbur Shaw (R)	Jynx	Miller/Miller	93.110	200	0	$4,000
5	28	21	Dave Evans (R)	Duesenberg	Duesenberg/Duesenberg	90.782	200	0	$3,500
6	7	14	Bob McDonogh	Cooper	Cooper/Miller	90.410	200	0	$5,200
7	18	16	Eddie Hearne	Miller	Miller/Miller	90.064	200	0	$1,800
8	25	6	Tommy Milton (W)	Detroit	Detroit/Miller	85.081	200	0	$1,600
9	14	25	Cliff Bergere (R)	Miller	Miller/Miller	79.929	200	0	$1,500
10	13	5	Frank Elliott	Junior 8	Miller/Miller	78.242	200	0	$1,400
11	33	31	Fred Frame (R)	Miller	Miller/Miller	Running	199	0	$750
12	32	42	Jimmy Hill (R)	Nickel Plate	Miller/Miller	Running	197	0	$600
13	31	24	Benny Shoaff (R)	Perfect Circle Duesenberg	Duesenberg/Duesenberg	Drive gears	198	0	$550
14	26	41	Wade Morton	Thompson Valve	Duesenberg/Duesenberg	Accident	152	0	$500
15	20	44	Al Melcher (R)	Miller	Miller/Miller	Supercharger	144	0	$490
16	23	43	Louis Schneider (R)	Miller	Miller/Miller	Timing gears	137	0	$480
17	12	9	Peter Kreis	Cooper	Cooper/Miller	Front axle	123	0	$470
18	1	2	Frank Lockhart (W)	Perfect Circle Miller	Miller/Miller	Rod	120	110	$11,460
19	6	15	Cliff Woodbury	Boyle Valve	Miller/Miller	Supercharger	108	0	$450
20	17	26	Dutch Baumann (R)	Miller	Miller/Miller	Pinion shaft	90	9	$1,340
21	29	35	Al Cotey (R)	Elcar	Miller/Miller	Universal joint	87	0	$430
22	16	17	Doc Shattuc	Miller	Miller/Miller	Valve	83	0	$420
23	30	23	Fred Lecklider	Elgin Piston Pin	Miller/Miller	Accident	49	0	$410
24	5	19	Ralph Hepburn	Boyle Valve	Miller/Miller	Fuel leak	39	0	$400
25	4	1	Harry Hartz	Erskine Miller	Miller/Miller	Crankshaft	38	0	$390
26	2	3	Pete DePaolo (W)	Perfect Circle Miller	Miller/Miller	Supercharger	31	30	$380
27	3	12	Leon Duray	Miller Front Drive	Miller/Miller	Fuel tank	26	0	$370
28	9	4	Bennett Hill	Cooper	Miller/Miller	Shackle bolt	26	0	$360
29	21	18	Jules Ellingboe	Cooper	Miller/Miller	Accident	25	0	$350
30	10	8	Norm Batten	Miller	Fengler/Miller	Fire	24	0	$340
31	24	38	Babe Stapp (R)	Duesenberg	Duesenberg/Duesenberg	Universal joint	24	0	$330
32	11	22	Jack Petticord (R)	Boyle Valve	Miller/Miller	Supercharger	22	0	$320
33	8	7	Dave Lewis	Miller Front Drive	Miller/Miller	Front axle	21	0	$310

* - complete car name/entrant data not available for all entries
(R) - Indicated Rookie
(W) - Indicates Past Winner

1928

Eddie Rickenbacker and his backers from Detroit purchased the Speedway from Carl Fisher and James Allison in August of 1927.

In April of 1928, Frank Lockhart crashed to his death as a result of a tire failure while trying to break the world land speed record at Daytona Beach. To say that Lockhart's record at the Speedway was impressive is an understatement. In the two races he competed, he led 205 of the 320 laps he was on track.

The field consisted of nineteen Millers, with only one former winner in the race (George Souders).

Joe Dawson became the first former winner to drive the pace car. He drove a Marmon Model 78 to start the race.

Leon Duray was the pole winner with a single-lap record of over 124 mph, which stood as the record for nine years. He also set the four-lap record of 122.4 mph. Duray entered the race as the favorite and led most of the first 150 miles in the twenty-nine car field. His front-drive Miller Special eventually dropped out with overheating problems after 133 laps.

The middle part of the race was primarily led by rookie Jimmy Gleason in his Duesenberg. Tony Gulotta took over from lap 149.

At 180 laps Tony Gulotta was leading Jimmy Gleason by one second with twenty-three-year-old Louis Meyer third.

Gulotta was forced to pit when a fuel line clogged and Gleason pitted and experienced a problem when water was spilled on the magneto. Meyer led the last nineteen laps in his rear-wheel-drive Miller Special, the only laps he led all day. Meyer averaged 99.5 mph in his victory and drove the entire race without relief. Lou Moore finished second in a Miller. George Souders was third, also in a Miller.

Shortly after the Indianapolis 500, George Souders was injured seriously in a race in Detroit. The accident resulted in his left arm having limited use, prompting his retirement from driving.

Louis Meyer would go on to win the 1928 AAA National Championship.

Founding father James Allison passed away on August 4, 1928 after contracting pneumonia.

Norm Batten and 1927 runner-up Earl Devore lost their lives after the 1928 500 when their ship sunk. They were headed for South America for a winter of racing.

Louis Meyer gets his first win in 1928 in a Miller.

RACE RESULTS FOR THE 1928 INDIANAPOLIS 500

Finish	Start	Car Num.	Driver	Car Name/Entrant*	Make/Model	Status	Laps	Led	Winnings
1	13	14	Louis Meyer (R)	Miller	Miller/Miller	99.482	200	19	$28,250
2	8	28	Lou Moore (R)	Miller	Miller/Miller	99.241	200	0	$13,650
3	12	3	George Souders (W)	State Auto Insurance	Miller/Miller	98.034	200	16	$8,400
4	10	15	Ray Keech (R)	Simplex Piston Ring	Miller/Miller	93.320	200	0	$4,300
5	15	22	Norm Batten	Miller	Fengler/Miller	93.228	200	0	$3,200
6	5	7	Babe Stapp	Miller	Miller/Miller	92.638	200	17	$3,900
7	20	43	Billy Arnold (R)	Boyle Valve	Miller/Miller	91.111	200	0	$1,800
8	14	27	Fred Frame	State Auto Insurance	Duesenberg/Duesenberg	90.079	200	0	$1,600
9	9	25	Fred Comer	Boyle Valve	Miller/Miller	88.889	200	0	$1,500
10	4	8	Tony Gulotta	Stutz Blackhawk	Miller/Miller	88.888	200	33	$1,600
11	7	24	Louis Schneider	Armacost Miller	Miller/Miller	87.964	200	0	$652
12	23	12	Dave Evans	Boyle Valve	Miller/Miller	87.401	200	0	$638
13	28	29	Henry Kohlert (R)	Elgin Piston Pin	Miller/Miller	Running	180	0	$625
14	17	23	Deacon Litz (R)	Miller	Miller/Miller	Running	161	0	$610
15	21	39	Jimmy Gleason (R)	Duesenberg	Duesenberg/Duesenberg	Magneto	195	43	$6,196
16	18	5	Cliff Durant	Detroit	Detroit/Miller	Supercharger	175	0	$583
17	11	33	Johnny Seymour (R)	Marmon	Cooper/Miller	Supercharger	170	0	$568
18	24	6	Earl DeVore	Chromolite	Miller/Miller	Accident	161	0	$555
19	1	4	Leon Duray	Miller	Miller/Miller	Overheated	133	59	$6,441
20	16	38	Sam Ross (R)	Aranem	Miller/Miller	Timing gear	132	0	$526
21	27	26	Ira Hall (R)	Duesenberg	Duesenberg/Duesenberg	Accident	115	0	$512
22	19	32	Peter Kreis	Marmon	Cooper/Miller	Rod bearing	73	0	$499
23	2	10	Cliff Woodbury	Boyle Valve	Miller/Miller	Timing gear	55	0	$484
24	6	16	Ralph Hepburn	Miller	Miller/Miller	Timing gear	48	0	$470
25	29	1	Wilbur Shaw	Flying Cloud	Miller/Miller	Timing gear	42	0	$456
26	26	18	Benny Shoaff	Duesenberg	Duesenberg/Duesenberg	Accident	35	0	$442
27	25	41	C.W. Belt (R)	Green	Green/Green	Valve	32	0	$428
28	3	21	Cliff Bergere	Miller	Miller/Miller	Transmission	6	0	$415
29	22	34	Russ Snowberger (R)	Marmon	Cooper/Miller	Supercharger	4	13	$400

* - complete car name/entrant data not available for all entries
(R) - Indicated Rookie
(W) - Indicates Past Winner

1929

The Speedway Golf Course was built with nine holes inside the track and nine holes outside. It was designed by William Diddel.

There were thirty-three starters with fourteen rookies, two former winners, twenty-one Miller cars and twenty-seven cars powered by a Miller.

Cliff Woodbury won the pole at 120.6 mph, but crashed on the third lap and finished thirty-third, becoming the first pole winner to finish last.

Duesenberg driver Bill Spence was fatally injured on his tenth lap when he hit the second turn wall. This was the first race day fatality since 1919.

Deacon Litz led from lap eight to fifty-six, when his Miller was sidelined with mechanical problems.

It appeared Louis Meyer was going to win consecutive races when low oil pressure caused his engine to stall on his final pit stop on lap 157, after he had been in the lead for 65 laps. His pit stop took more than seven minutes.

Philadelphia's Ray Keech took the lead in his Simplex Piston Ring Miller and stayed there to the finish line. He won by over six minutes. He led forty-six laps total. Keech averaged 97.6 mph.

A year earlier, Keech had set the World Land Speed record with a speed of 207.552 mph on the sands of Daytona Beach.

The winning car owner was Maude A. Yagle, the first female car owner to win the Indianapolis 500.

AAA champion Louis Meyer finished second in a Miller when Lou Moore, who was running second in a Miller, broke a connecting rod on his 199th lap. Moore would finish in thirteenth position. Jimmy Gleason finished third in a Duesenberg.

Only twelve cars of the thirty-three starters were running at the finish.

The Hollywood movie "Speedway" was filmed in 1929 starring William Haines and Anita Page.

Ray Keech was fatally injured in a racing accident just sixteen days after his Indianapolis 500 victory on the boards at the same track in Altoona, Pennsylvania, which claimed the lives of former "500" winners Howdy Wilcox and Joe Boyer.

The Monaco Grand Prix was run for the first time in 1929.

Ray Keech wins in 1929 in his Simplex Piston Ring Special—another Miller win.

RACE RESULTS FOR THE 1929 INDIANAPOLIS 500

Finish	Start	Car Num.	Driver	Car Name/Entrant*	Make/Model	Status	Laps	Led	Winnings
1	6	2	Ray Keech	Simplex Piston Ring	Miller/Miller	97.585	200	46	$31,950
2	8	1	Louis Meyer (W)	Miller	Miller/Miller	95.596	200	65	$20,400
3	23	53	Jimmy Gleason	Duesenberg	Duesenberg/Duesenberg	93.699	200	0	$7,250
4	25	43	Carl Marchese (R)	Marchese	Miller/Miller	93.541	200	0	$4,350
5	21	42	Freddie Winnai (R)	Duesenberg	Duesenberg/Duesenberg	88.792	200	0	$3,600
6	28	48	Speed Gardner (R)	Chromolite	Miller/Miller	88.390	200	0	$2,200
7	14	6	Louis Chiron (R)	Delage	Delage/Delage	87.728	200	0	$1,800
8	7	9	Billy Arnold	Boyle Valve	Miller/Miller	83.909	200	0	$1,600
9	32	25	Cliff Bergere	Armacost Miller	Miller/Miller	80.703	200	0	$1,500
10	22	34	Fred Frame	Cooper	Cooper/Miller	Running	193	11	$2,500
11	29	28	Frank Brisko (R)	Burbach	Miller/Miller	Running	180	0	$468
12	18	17	Phil Shafer	Miller	Miller/Miller	Running	150	0	$465
13	13	3	Lou Moore	Majestic Miller	Miller/Miller	Rod	198	22	$2,662
14	26	36	Frank Farmer (R)	Miller	Miller/Miller	Supercharger	140	0	$459
15	24	49	Wesley Crawford (R)	Miller	Fengler/Miller	Carburetor	127	0	$456
16	17	4	Peter Kreis	Detroit	Detroit/Miller	Engine seized	91	0	$453
17	11	23	Tony Gulotta	Packard Cable	Miller/Miller	Supercharger	91	0	$450
18	19	5	Bob McDonogh	Miller Front Drive	Miller/Miller	Oil tank	74	0	$447
19	33	46	Bill Lindau (R)	Pittsburgh Miller	Miller/Miller	Valve	70	0	$444
20	27	31	Herman Schurch (R)	Armacost Miller	Miller/Miller	Tank split	70	0	$441
21	16	38	Johnny Seymour	Cooper	Cooper/Miller	Rear axle	65	0	$438
22	2	21	Leon Duray	Packard Cable	Miller/Miller	Carburetor	65	7	$1,135
23	30	29	Rick Decker (R)	Miller	Miller/Miller	Fuel line	61	0	$432
24	9	26	Deacon Litz	Rusco Durac	Miller/Miller	Rod	56	49	$5,329
25	31	27	Bert Karnatz (R)	Richards Bros.	Miller/Miller	Fuel leak	50	0	$426
26	20	47	Ernie Triplett (R)	Buckeye Duesenberg	Duesenberg/Duesenberg	Rod	48	0	$423
27	10	12	Russ Snowberger	Cooper	Cooper/Miller	Supercharger	45	0	$420
28	4	32	Babe Stapp	Spindler Miller	Duesenberg/Miller	Rear end	40	0	$417
29	15	35	Jules Moriceau (R)	Thompson Products	Amilcar/Amilcar	Accident	30	0	$414
30	5	37	Pete DePaolo (W)	Boyle Valve	Miller/Miller	Steering	25	0	$411
31	3	18	Ralph Hepburn	Packard Cable	Miller/Miller	High gear	14	0	$407
32	12	10	Bill Spence (R)	Duesenberg	Duesenberg/Duesenberg	Accident	9	0	$403
33	1	8	Cliff Woodbury	Boyle Valve	Miller/Miller	Accident	3	0	$400

* - complete car name/entrant data not available for all entries
(R) - Indicated Rookie
(W) - Indicates Past Winner

1930

Supercharging was no longer permitted except for two-cycle engines, and riding mechanics became mandatory again.

Engine sizes, which had been limited to 91 ½ cubic-inches, were allowed up to 336 cubic-inches without superchargers.

New specifications were adopted in an attempt to cut the cost of buying and maintaining a race car, and to encourage the return of American automotive manufacturers.

Initially, Billy Arnold didn't have a ride for the race. Harry Hartz was attempting to make a return from severe injuries that occurred toward the end of the 1927 season. Both Hartz and Arnold practiced in the eight-cylinder front-drive Miller-powered car, with Hartz anticipating using Arnold for possible relief driving during the race. Hartz eventually decided he was not physically up to racing and Arnold became the driver. Arnold had finished seventh in 1928 and eighth in the 1929 500.

Arnold became the third winner to start from the pole position. He also became the first winner in a front-wheel-drive car. His 198 laps led remains the record for most laps led by a winner in a race. Arnold also became the first driver to average more than 100 mph without a relief driver.

The green flag replaced the red flag for starting the race.

There were thirty-eight starters, including nineteen rookies for the eighteenth running of the Indianapolis 500.

AAA champion Louis Meyer led the first two laps, with Arnold leading the remaining 198 to win by seven minutes over rookie Shorty Cantlon. Third place was Louis Schneider in the Bowes Seal Fast car. Arnold averaged 100.4 mph on a day with a temperature of 57 degrees and 20-mile an hour wind. He made one stop for fuel and tires on the 111th lap.

Arnold won $50,350, a record which stood for nearly 20 years.

On lap twenty-nine, Cy Marshall was involved in an accident where his car went over the wall. His riding mechanic, his brother Paul Marshall, was fatally injured and Cy was critically injured. He did not participate in the 500 again for seventeen years. He finished eighth in 1947.

Chet Miller finished in 13th position, completing 160 laps. Miller's near-stock Ford broke a front spring during the race. His innovative crew borrowed one from a nearby passenger car in the infield and the spring was returned after the race without the owner ever knowing.

Attendance was estimated to be the largest ever at 170,000.

Billy Arnold would go on and win the 1930 AAA National Championship.

Billy Arnold and his riding mechanic Spider Matlock won the 1930 race in his Harry Hartz-owned Miller, after leading 198 laps.

RACE RESULTS FOR THE 1930 INDIANAPOLIS 500

Finish	Start	Car Num.	Driver	Car Name/Entrant*	Make/Model	Status	Laps	Led	Winnings
1	1	4	Billy Arnold	Miller-Hartz	Summers/Miller	100.448	200	198	$50,300
2	3	16	Shorty Cantlon (R)	Miller Schofield	Stevens/Miller	98.054	200	0	$13,950
3	4	23	Louis Schneider	Bowes Seal Fast	Stevens/Miller	96.752	200	0	$7,050
4	2	1	Louis Meyer (W)	Sampson	Stevens/Miller	95.253	200	2	$4,450
5	22	6	Bill Cummings (R)	Duesenberg	Stevens/Duesenberg	93.579	200	0	$3,500
6	33	24	Dave Evans	Jones & Maley	Stevens/Miller	92.571	200	0	$2,700
7	8	15	Phil Shafer	Coleman Front Drive	Coleman/Miller	90.921	200	0	$1,800
8	7	22	Russ Snowberger	Russell "8"	Snowberger/Studebaker	89.166	200	0	$1,600
9	9	25	Les Allen (R)	Allen Miller Products	Miller/Miller	85.749	200	0	$1,500
10	17	27	L.L. Corum (W)	Jones Stutz	Stutz/Stutz	85.340	200	0	$1,400
11	16	38	Claude Burton (R)	V8	Oakland/Oakland	Running	196	0	$550
12	30	42	L.P. Cucinotta (R)	Maserati	Maserati/Maserati	Running	185	0	$510
13	15	41	Chet Miller (R)	Fronty Ford	Ford T/Fronty-Ford	Running	160	0	$480
14	38	46	Harry Butcher (R)	Butcher Brothers	Buick/Buick	Running	128	0	$450
15	23	10	Mel Keneally (R)	MAVV	Whippet/Miller	Valve	114	0	$420
16	34	21	Zeke Meyer (R)	Miller	Miller/Miller	Rod	115	0	$385
17	6	17	Ernie Triplett	Guiberson	Whippet/Miller	Piston	125	0	$380
18	13	35	J.C. McDonald (R)	Romthe	Studebaker/Studebaker	Fuel leak	112	0	$375
19	37	28	Roland Free (R)	Slade	Chrysler/Chrysler	Clutch	69	0	$370
20	20	9	Tony Gulotta	MAVV	Whippet/Miller	Valve	79	0	$365
21	11	33	Frank Farmer	Betholine Miller	Miller/Miller	Accident	69	0	$360
22	35	44	Bill Denver (R)	Nardi	Duesenberg/Duesenberg	Rod	41	0	$355
23	26	34	Joe Huff (R)	Gauss Front Drive	Cooper/Miller	Valve	48	0	$350
24	25	3	Wilbur Shaw	Empire State	Smith/Miller	Oil Leak	54	0	$345
25	14	29	Joe Caccia (R)	Alberti	Duesenberg/Duesenberg	Accident	43	0	$340
26	10	36	Cy Marshall (R)	Duesenberg	Duesenberg/Duesenberg	Accident	29	0	$335
27	19	32	Charles Moran, Jr. (R)	DuPont	DuPont/DuPont	Accident	22	0	$330
28	24	7	Jimmy Gleason	Waverly Oil	Miller/Miller	Timing gear	22	0	$325
29	12	14	Lou Moore	Coleman Front Drive	Coleman/Miller	Accident	23	0	$320
30	31	12	Deacon Litz	Duesenberg	Duesenberg/Duesenberg	Accident	22	0	$315
31	32	8	Babe Stapp	Duesenberg	Duesenberg/Duesenberg	Accident	18	0	$310
32	18	39	Johnny Seymour	Gauss Front Drive	Cooper/Miller	Accident	21	0	$305
33	21	5	Pete DePaolo (W)	Duesenberg	Stevens/Duesenberg	Accident	19	0	$300
34	29	45	Marion Trexler (R)	Trexler	Auburn/Lycoming	Accident	19	0	$295
35	27	19	Speed Gardner	Miller Front Drive	Miller/Miller	Bearing	14	0	$290
36	28	26	Baconin Borzachini (R)	Maserati	Maserati/Maserati	Magneto	7	0	$285
37	36	48	Rick Decker	Hoosier Pete	Mercedes/Clemons	Oil tank	8	0	$280
38	5	18	Chet Gardner (R)	Buckeye	Duesenberg/Duesenberg	Skidded out	0	0	$275

* - complete car name/entrant data not available for all entries
(R) - Indicated Rookie
(W) - Indicates Past Winner

1931

A record of seventy entries were received for the 1931 "500." This was twenty-four more than the previous record.

Russ Snowberger won the pole at 112.8 mph.

Billy Arnold was the fastest qualifier at 116.1 mph, but started eighteenth. Arnold had previously won the pole at 113.8 mph, but his run was disallowed because of a technical issue. He had to qualify on a later day.

Joe Caccia and his mechanic, Clarence Grove, were killed in practice when their car climbed the second turn wall.

Forty cars started the race, which was delayed a couple of hours due to morning rain.

Billy Arnold took the lead on the seventh lap and led until lap 162 when, with a five-lap lead, he broke an axle and was in an accident with Luther Johnson. Arnold's Miller went over the wall in flames, seriously injuring both Arnold and his riding mechanic. One of Arnold's wheels cleared the outer wall and crossed Georgetown Road where it fatally injured Wilbur Brink, an eleven-year-old boy, in his front yard.

Tony Gulotta was in second place when Arnold crashed, but he too crashed while unlapping himself. Louis Schneider took the lead in his Stevens chassis and led the final thirty-nine laps to the checker in his self-owned Miller powered rear-drive eight-cylinder Bowes Seal Fast

Special. He averaged 94.6 mph. The speed average was slowed because of drizzling rain for about seventy-five miles early in the race.

Schneider was born in Indianapolis and was a former motorcycle policeman.

Fred Frame finished second in a Duesenberg forty-three seconds behind and Ralph Hepburn was third in a Miller.

Wilbur Shaw, driving relief for Phil Pardee, was uninjured in an accident in turn three that launched his car over the wall. He later drove relief for the other team car.

Dave Evans finished thirteenth, driving a Cummins Diesel and completed the 500 miles without a single pit stop. He finished thirty-eight minutes behind the winner and used a total of thirty-one gallons of crude oil.

Louis Schneider would go on to win the 1931 AAA National Championship.

Former Indianapolis motorcycle policeman Louis Schneider drove his Bowes Seal Fast Special, with riding mechanic "Jigger" Johnson, for the win in 1931.

RACE RESULTS FOR THE 1931 INDIANAPOLIS 500

Finish	Start	Car Num.	Driver	Car Name/Entrant*	Make/Model	Status	Laps	Led	Winnings
1	13	23	Louis Schneider	Bowes Seal Fast	Stevens/Miller	96.629	200	39	$29,500
2	8	34	Fred Frame	Duesenberg	Duesenberg/Duesenberg	96.406	200	0	$12,650
3	10	19	Ralph Hepburn	Harry Miller	Miller/Miller	94.224	200	0	$6,350
4	35	21	Myron Stevens (R)	Jadson	Stevens/Miller	94.142	200	0	$4,000
5	1	4	Russ Snowberger	Russell "8"	Snowberger/Studebaker	49.090	200	0	$3,500
6	20	33	Jimmy Gleason	Duesenberg	Duesenberg/Duesenberg	93.605	200	0	$2,200
7	5	25	Ernie Triplett	Buckeye	Duesenberg/Duesenberg	63.041	200	0	$1,800
8	9	36	H.W. Stubblefield (R)	Jones-Miller	Willys-Knight/Miller	92.434	200	0	$1,950
9	14	28	Cliff Bergere	Elco Royale	Reo/Reo	91.839	200	0	$1,500
10	15	27	Chet Miller	Marr	Hudson/Hudson	89.580	200	0	$1,400
11	30	44	George Howie (R)	G. N. H.	Dodge/Chrysler	87.651	200	0	$500
12	23	12	Phil Shafer	Shafer "8"	Rigling/Buick	86.391	200	0	$470
13	17	8	Dave Evans	Cummins Diesel	Duesenberg/Cummins	86.107	200	0	$450
14	31	72	Al Aspen (R)	William Alberti	Duesenberg/Duesenberg	85.764	200	0	$425
15	37	59	Sam Ross	Miller	Rigling/Miller	85.139	200	0	$400
16	40	69	Joe Huff	Goldberg Brothers	Cooper/Miller	Running	180	0	$375
17	4	5	Deacon Litz	Maley	Duesenberg/Duesenberg	Accident	177	0	$365
18	19	37	Tony Gulotta	Hunt	Rigling/Studebaker	Accident	167	0	$360
19	18	1	Billy Arnold (W)	Miller-Hartz	Summers/Miller	Accident	161	155	$8,905
20	12	57	Luther Johnson (R)	Bill Richards	Studebaker/Studebaker	Accident	156	0	$350
21	36	55	Billy Winn (R)	Hoosier Pete	Rigling/Clemons	Running	138	0	$343
22	27	16	Frank Brisko	Brisko-Atkinson	Stevens/Miller	Steering arm	138	0	$343
23	34	26	Gene Haustein (R)	Fronty-Ford	Ford T/Fronty-Ford	Wheel	117	0	$335
24	16	41	Joe Russo (R)	Russo	Rigling/Duesenberg	Oil	109	0	$330
25	7	17	Speed Gardner	Nutmeg State	Miller/Miller	Frame	107	0	$325
26	38	14	Lou Moore	Boyle Valve	Miller/Miller	Differential	103	0	$320
27	26	2	Shorty Cantlon	Harry Miller	Miller/Miller	Rod	88	0	$315
28	2	3	Bill Cummings	Empire State	Cooper/Miller	Oil line	70	4	$710
29	28	24	Freddie Winnai	Bowes Seal Fast	Stevens/Miller	Accident	60	0	$303
30	11	32	Phil Pardee (R)	Duesenberg	Duesenberg/Duesenberg	Accident	60	0	$303
31	3	31	Paul Bost (R)	Empire State	Rigling/Miller	Crankshaft	35	2	$495
32	22	35	Frank Farmer	Jones-Miller	Willys-Knight/Miller	Rod bearing	32	0	$290
33	32	58	George Wingerter (R)	Wingerter	Duesenberg/Duesenberg	Fuel tank	29	0	$285
34	25	7	Louis Meyer (W)	Sampson	Stevens/Miller	Oil leak	28	0	$330
35	6	39	Babe Stapp	Rigling & Henning	Rigling/Duesenberg	Oil Leak	9	0	$275
36	24	48	John Boling	Grapho Metal	Morton & Brett/M&B	Rod	7	0	$270
37	29	54	Leon Duray	Duray	Stevens:Whippett/Duray	Overheating	6	0	$263
38	33	49	Harry Butcher	Butcher Brothers	Buick/Buick	Accident	6	0	$263
39	39	10	Herman Schurch	Hoosier Pete	Rigling/Clemons	Transmission	5	0	$255
40	21	67	Francis Quinn (R)	Tucker Tappett	Miller/Ford A	Rear axle	3	0	$250

* - complete car name/entrant data not available for all entries
(R) - Indicated Rookie9
(W) - Indicates Past Winner

1932

Lou Moore edged Billy Arnold for the pole position at 117.4 mph.

A record of seventy-two cars were entered.

Forty cars started the race.

Edsel Ford, the only son of Ford founder Henry Ford, drove a Lincoln Model KB to pace the race.

Arnold led from lap two to fifty-eight, when he was involved in an accident trying to avoid a slower car and vaulted the turn-two wall. For the second year in a row, both Arnold and riding mechanic Spider Matlock received serious injuries.

Rookie Bob Carey led the next thirty-six laps before tire problems caused him to drop to twelfth, eventually to climb back to fourth.

Fred Frame led from lap 152 to the finish in his front-drive Hartz-Miller eight. He started in twenty-seventh position and averaged a new race record of 104.1 mph, finally breaking Peter DePaolo's 1925 record, while leading a total of fifty-eight laps. Frame dealt with overheating problems throughout the race resulting in an abnormal six pit stops. He was Billy Arnold's teammate. The win gave car owner/builder Harry Hartz his second "500" win.

The winning car was originally assigned to Cliff Durant but Durant opted out which opened the seat for Frame.

Car owner Harry Hartz was presented with the Wheeler-Schebler trophy. The Wheeler-Schebler trophy was given to the car owner leading at 400 miles. Any car owner achieving this on three occasions would gain permanent possession, which Hartz did by leading with Arnold in 1930 and 1931, and Frame in 1932.

The winning car would compete in the race as late as 1947 and actually practiced in 1948. Ted Horn had finishes of 2nd, 3rd and 4th between 1936 and 1938. Tony Bettenhausen drove this car as a rookie in 1946.

Rookie Howdy Wilcox II finished second in a four-cylinder Miller. He was not related to 1919 winner Howdy Wilcox.

Two men lost their lives in practice. Harry Cox, mechanic for Benny Benefield, was killed in a turn one accident. This was the same car in which Joe Caccia and his mechanic were fatally injured last year. Driver Milton Jones was killed in a turn two accident.

Billy Arnold, recently married, acquiesced to his wife's demands and retired from racing. In the past three races Arnold had a led a remarkable 410 of the 420 laps he had completed.

Fred Frame and riding mechanic Jerry Houck took first in 1932 in the Hartz Miller.

RACE RESULTS FOR THE 1932 INDIANAPOLIS 500

Finish	Start	Car Num.	Driver	Car Name/Entrant*	Make/Model	Status	Laps	Led	Winnings
1	27	34	Fred Frame	Miller-Hartz	Wetteroth/Miller	104.144	200	58	$31,050
2	6	6	Howdy Wilcox II (R)	Lion Head	Stevens/Miller	103.881	200	1	$12,650
3	10	22	Cliff Bergere	Studebaker	Rigling/Studebaker	102.662	200	0	$7,000
4	14	61	Bob Carey (R)	Meyer	Stevens/Miller	101.363	200	36	$6,050
5	4	4	Russ Snowberger	Hupp Comet	Snowberger/Hupmobile	100.791	200	0	$3,500
6	38	37	Zeke Meyer	Studebaker	Rigling/Studebaker	98.476	200	0	$2,500
7	5	35	Ira Hall	Duesenberg	Stevens/Duesenberg	98.207	200	6	$2,600
8	35	65	Freddie Winnai	Foreman Axle Shaft	Duesenberg/Duesenberg	97.437	200	0	$2,200
9	9	2	Billy Winn	Duesenberg	Duesenberg/Duesenberg	97.421	200	0	$2,100
10	15	55	Joe Huff	Highway Truck Parts	Cooper/Cooper	87.586	200	0	$2,000
11	26	33	Phil Shafer	Shafer "8""	Rigling/Buick	Running	197	0	$725
12	40	36	Kelly Petillo (R)	Jones-Miller	Miller/Miller	Running	189	0	$700
13	20	25	Tony Gulotta	Studebaker	Rigling/Studebaker	Running	184	0	$680
14	25	15	H.W. Stubblefield	Gilmore	Adams/Miller	Running	178	0	$660
15	17	18	Peter Kreis	Studebaker	Rigling/Studebaker	Accident	178	0	$635
16	11	46	Luther Johnson	Studebaker	Rigling/Studebaker	Wheel	164	0	$620
17	22	3	Wilbur Shaw	Veedol	Miller/Miller	Rear axle	157	27	$1,915
18	19	24	Deacon Litz	Bowes Seal Fast	Duesenberg/Duesenberg	Rod	152	0	$610
19	12	10	Bill Cummings	Bowes Seal Fast	Stevens/Miller	Crankshaft	151	0	$605
20	32	57	Malcolm Fox (R)	Bill Richards	Studebaker/Studebaker	Spring	132	0	$600
21	29	9	Chet Miller	Hudson	Hudson/Hudson	Engine	125	0	$590
22	31	7	Ernie Triplett	Floating Power	Miller/Miller	Clutch	125	14	$1,290
23	30	1	Louis Schneider (W)	Bowes Seal Fast	Stevens/Miller	Frame	125	0	$590
24	21	41	Joe Russo	Art Rose	Rigling/Duesenberg	Rod	107	0	$580
25	1	8	Lou Moore	Boyle Valve	Miller/Miller	Timing gear	79	1	$575
26	36	14	Juan Gaudino (R)	Golden Seal	Chrysler/Chrysler	Clutch	71	0	$570
27	18	29	Al Miller (R)	Hudson	Hudson/Hudson	Engine	66	0	$565
28	39	42	Doc MacKenzie (R)	Brady	Studebaker/Studebaker	Engine	65	0	$560
29	13	32	Frank Brisko	Brisko-Atkinson	Stevens/Miller	Clutch	61	0	$555
30	34	72	Ray Campbell (R)	Folly Farm	Graham/Graham	Crankshaft	60	0	$550
31	2	5	Billy Arnold (W)	Miller-Hartz	Summers/Miller	Accident	59	57	$3,345
32	3	27	Bryan Saulpaugh (R)	Harry Miller	Miller/Miller	Oil line	55	0	$540
33	7	16	Louis Meyer (W)	Sampson	Stevens/Miller	Crankshaft	50	0	$535
34	23	21	Al Aspen	Brady & Nardi	Duesenberg/Studebaker	Rod	31	0	$530
35	33	49	Johnny Kreiger (R)	Consumers Petroleum Oil	Duesenberg/Duesenberg	Rod	30	0	$525
36	16	48	Wesley Crawford	Boyle Valve	Miller/Duesenberg	Crankshaft	28	0	$520
37	8	17	Paul Bost	Empire State	Cooper/Miller	Crankshaft	18	0	$515
38	24	58	Bob McDonogh	F.W.D.	Miller/Miller	Oil line	7	0	$510
39	28	45	Gus Schrader (R)	Harry Miller	Miller/Miller	Accident	3	0	$505
40	37	26	Al Gordon (R)	Lion Tamer	Miller/Miller	Accident	2	0	$500

* - complete car name/entrant data not available for all entries
(R) - Indicated Rookie
(W) - Indicates Past Winner

1933

Prize money was reduced, the 1932 winner receiving just over $31,000, while the 1933 winner received only $18,000.

Other changes:

On-board fuel tanks restricted to a minimum of fifteen gallons.

No more than six gallons of oil carried on board and none could be added during the race.

Qualifying increased from four laps to ten laps.

There were forty-two starters, the most ever. There were also five former winners—a record.

Five men lost their lives during the month, including three drivers and two riding mechanics. The drivers were Mark Billman, Lester Spangler and Bill Denver. The mechanics were G.L. "Monk" Jordan and Bob Hurst.

There was a dispute involving Howdy Wilcox II. His diabetic condition was misdiagnosed as epilepsy by medics and he was ruled not fit to drive. Drivers formed a protest, but track owner Eddie Rickenbacker would not back down. Mauri Rose eventually replaced Wilcox. He started last and drove to fourth by the forty-eighth lap, when mechanical problems ended his day.

Bill Cummings won the pole at 118.5 mph and led the first 32 laps before Fred Frame and Babe Stapp took over, trading the lead between them through lap 129. Louis Meyer took the lead and led from lap 130 to the finish in his Tydol Special, averaging a record 104.2 mph in his eight-cylinder rear-drive Miller to become the second two-time winner.

Wilbur Shaw, in Leon Duray's Mallory Special, finished second almost six minutes behind Meyer, and Lou Moore finished in third place.

The five-car Studebaker Team finished seventh with Tony Gulotta, and ninth through twelfth with Zeke Meyer, Luther Johnson, Cliff Bergere, and L.L. Corum.

The first four finishers had Miller engines while most of the other finishers utilized stock engines. Prior to the race most of the experts did not foresee the racing engines being successful with only six gallons of oil total.

Louis Meyer would go on to win the 1933 AAA National Championship.

Louis Meyer sports a bow tie in the Miller he and riding mechanic Lawson Harris took to the finish line for first place in 1933.

RACE RESULTS FOR THE 1933 INDIANAPOLIS 500

Finish	Start	Car Num.	Driver	Car Name/Entrant*	Make/Model	Status	Laps	Led	Winnings
1	6	36	Louis Meyer (W)	Tydol	Miller/Miller	104.162	200	71	$18,000
2	23	17	Wilbur Shaw	Mallory	Stevens/Miller	101.795	200	0	$9,100
3	4	37	Lou Moore	Foreman Axle	Duesenberg/Miller	101.599	200	0	$4,100
4	15	21	Chet Gardner	Sampson Radio	Stevens/Miller	101.182	200	0	$2,400
5	10	8	H.W. Stubblefield	Abels & Fink Auto	Rigling/Buick	100.762	200	0	$3,250
6	36	38	Dave Evans	Art Rose	Rigling/Studebaker	100.425	200	0	$1,450
7	12	34	Tony Gulotta	Studebaker	Rigling/Studebaker	99.071	200	0	$1,300
8	17	4	Russ Snowberger	Russell "8"	Snowberger/Studebaker	99.011	200	0	$1,200
9	16	9	Zeke Meyer	Studebaker	Rigling/Studebaker	98.122	200	0	$1,150
10	20	46	Luther Johnson	Studebaker	Rigling/Studebaker	97.287	200	0	$1,100
11	9	6	Cliff Bergere	Studebaker	Rigling/Studebaker	96.536	200	0	$500
12	18	47	L.L. Corum (W)	Studebaker	Rigling/Studebaker	96.454	200	0	$475
13	40	49	Willard Prentiss (R)	Jack C. Carr	Rigling/Duesenberg	93.595	200	0	$450
14	27	14	Raul Riganti	Golden Seal	Chrysler/Chrysler	93.244	200	0	$425
15	28	29	Gene Haustein	Martz	Hudson/Hudson	Running	197	0	$380
16	14	26	Deacon Litz	Bowes Seal Fast	Miller/Miller	Running	197	0	$370
17	31	18	Joe Russo	Wonder Bread	Duesenberg/Duesenberg	Running	192	0	$340
18	39	51	Doc MacKenzie	Ray Brady	Duesenberg/Studebaker	Rear axle	192	0	$330
19	25	27	Kelly Petillo	Sacks Bros.	Smith/Miller	Spun	168	0	$320
20	32	28	Chet Miller	Marr	Hudson/Hudson	Rod	163	0	$305
21	24	19	Al Miller	Marr	Hudson/Hudson	Rod	161	0	$295
22	19	68	Bennett Hill	Goldberg Brothers	Cooper/Cooper	Rod	158	0	$285
23	29	45	Babe Stapp	Boyle Products	Miller/Miller	Out of fuel	156	60	$1,380
24	26	32	Wesley Crawford	Boyle Valve	Stevens/Miller	Accident	147	0	$275
25	1	5	Bill Cummings	Boyle Products	Miller/Miller	Radiator	136	32	$1,065
26	7	15	Lester Spangler (R)	Miller	Miller/Miller	Accident	132	0	$260
27	35	65	Freddie Winnai	Kemp	Duesenberg/Duesenberg	Mechanical	125	0	$255
28	30	57	Malcolm Fox	Universal Service Garage	Studebaker/Studebaker	Accident	121	0	$250
29	3	12	Fred Frame (W)	Miller-Hartz	Wetteroth/Miller	Valve	85	37	$645
30	22	64	Mark Billman (R)	Kemp-Mannix	Duesenberg/Duesenberg	Accident	79	0	$240
31	34	53	Johnny Sawyer (R)	Lencki-Madis	Miller/Miller	Clutch	77	0	$235
32	11	2	Peter Kreis	Frame-Miller	Summers/Miller	Universal joint	63	0	$230
33	5	16	Ernie Triplett	Floating Power	Weil/Miller	Piston	61	0	$225
34	13	25	Shorty Cantlon	Sullivan & O'Brien	Stevens/Miller	Rod	50	0	$220
35	42	3	Mauri Rose (R)	Gilmore	Stevens/Miller	Timing gear	48	0	$215
36	2	58	Frank Brisko	F.W.D.	Miller/Miller	Oil	47	0	$210
37	8	10	Ira Hall	Denny Duesenberg	Stevens/Duesenberg	Accident	37	0	$206
38	41	23	Ralph Hepburn	Highway Truck Parts	Cooper/Cooper	Rod	33	0	$205
39	37	59	Ray Campbell	G&D	Hudson/Hudson	Magneto	24	0	$204
40	33	24	Paul Bost	Frame-Miller Duesenberg	Duesenberg/Miller	Oil	13	0	$203
41	38	61	Rick Decker	Miller	Miller/Miller	Manifold	13	0	$202
42	21	22	Louis Schneider (W)	Edelweiss	Stevens/Miller	Stalled	0	0	$200

* - complete car name/entrant data not available for all entries
(R) - Indicated Rookie
(W) - Indicates Past Winner

1934

Fuel was restricted to forty-five gallons per car for the entire race in an attempt to slow the cars for safety reasons.

A return to thirty-three starters was determined for safety reasons. There were seven rookies and one former winner in the field (Louis Meyer).

Kelly Petillo won the pole at 119.3 mph and led the first six laps. Frank Brisko then led 69 laps. Mauri Rose and Bill Cummings traded the lead for the second half of the race, with Cummings leading from lap 175 to the finish.

The attrition rate was extremely high with one-third of the field out of the race by the 30th lap and only sixteen cars running at the halfway point.

Cummings edged Rose, in a Leon Duray Special, by twenty-seven seconds at the finish, the closest race to date. Cummings averaged a new record of 104.9 mph in Chicago labor organizer Mike Boyle's front-wheel-drive Miller. He averaged 13.9 miles per gallon of fuel.

In the victory enclosure, the winner suggested that he be called "Conservative William" rather than "Wild Bill!" Cummings was from Indianapolis and was raised less than four miles from the track.

Second place was Mauri Rose and third was Lou Moore in a Miller.

Mauri Rose's car owner, Leon Duray, filed a protest that Cummings passed cars under yellow flag conditions. AAA officials denied the protest.

The race was relatively safe with several accidents but no serious injuries. Unfortunately, Peter Kreis, one of the best-liked drivers, and his mechanic Bob Hahn were killed in a practice accident.

Bill Cummings would go on to win the 1934 AAA National Championship.

Champion Spark Plug Company organized the Champion 100-Mile-An-Hour-Club. The club honored those drivers who completed the full distance without relief at an average over 100 mph.

"Wild Bill" Cummings with riding mechanic Earl Unversaw outdueled Mauri Rose to win in Mike Boyle's front-drive Miller.

RACE RESULTS FOR THE 1934 INDIANAPOLIS 500

Finish	Start	Car Num.	Driver	Car Name/Entrant*	Make/Model	Status	Laps	Led	Winnings
1	10	7	Bill Cummings	Boyle Products	Miller/Miller	104.863	200	57	$29,725
2	4	9	Mauri Rose	Leon Duray	Stevens/Miller	104.697	200	68	$14,350
3	20	2	Lou Moore	Foreman Axle	Miller/Miller	102.625	200	0	$6,675
4	19	12	Deacon Litz	Stokely Foods	Miller/Miller	100.749	200	0	$4,250
5	24	16	Joe Russo	Duesenberg	Duesenberg/Duesenberg	99.893	200	0	$3,600
6	8	36	Al Miller	Shafer "8"	Rigling/Buick	98.264	200	0	$2,200
7	18	22	Cliff Bergere	Floating Power	Weil/Miller	97.818	200	0	$1,850
8	9	10	Russ Snowberger	Russell "8"	Snowberger/Studebaker	97.297	200	0	$1,650
9	3	32	Frank Brisko	F.W.D.	Miller/Miller	96.787	200	69	$2,850
10	14	24	Herb Ardinger (R)	Lucenti	Graham/Graham	95.936	200	0	$1,425
11	1	17	Kelly Petillo	Red Lion	Adams/Miller	93.432	200	6	$900
12	29	5	H.W. Stubblefield	Cummins Diesel	Duesenberg/Cummins	88.566	200	0	$880
13	28	49	Charlie Crawford (R)	Detroit Gasket & Mfg.	Ford/Ford V8	Hd gskt (in pit)	110	0	$860
14	11	31	Ralph Hepburn	Art Rose	Miller/Miller	Rod	164	0	$840
15	12	18	George Barringer (R)	Boyle Products	Miller/Miller	Front axle	161	0	$815
16	6	26	Phil Shafer	Shafer "8"	Rigling/Buick	Camshaft	130	0	$790
17	7	8	Tony Gulotta	Schroeder	Cooper/Studebaker	Rod	94	0	$770
18	13	1	Louis Meyer (W)	Ring Free	Stevens/Miller	Oil tank	92	0	$745
19	22	6	Dave Evans	Cummins Diesel	Duesenberg/Cummins	Transmission	81	0	$720
20	15	15	Shorty Cantlon	Sullivan & O'Brien	Stevens/Miller	Crankshaft	76	0	$700
21	5	4	Chet Gardner	Sampson Radio	Stevens/Miller	Rod	72	0	$675
22	17	51	Al Gordon	Abels & Fink	Adams/Miller	Steering	66	0	$650
23	23	35	Rex Mays (R)	Frame Miller-Duesenberg	Duesenberg/Miller	Front axle	53	0	$630
24	25	42	Dusty Fahrnow (R)	Superior Trailer	Cooper/Cooper	Rod	28	0	$600
25	21	41	Johnny Sawyer	Burd Piston Ring	Miller/Lencki	Rods	27	0	$585
26	33	33	Johnny Seymour	Streamline Miller	Adams/Miller	Pinion	22	0	$560
27	27	45	Rick Decker	Carter Carburetor	Miller/Miller	Clutch	17	0	$540
28	2	3	Wilbur Shaw	Lion Head	Stevens/Miller	Lost oil	15	0	$515
29	26	73	Doc MacKenzie	Cresco	Mikan-Carson/Studebaker	Accident	15	0	$490
30	31	29	Gene Haustein	Martz	Hudson/Hudson	Accident	13	0	$470
31	30	63	Harry McQuinn (R)	DeBaets	Rigling/Miller	Rod	13	0	$445
32	16	58	George Bailey (R)	Scott	Snowberger/Studebaker	Accident	12	0	$420
33	32	46	Chet Miller	Bohnalite Ford	Ford/Ford V8	Accident	11	0	$400

* - complete car name/entrant data not available for all entries
(R) - Indicated Rookie
(W) - Indicates Past Winner

1935

Protective helmets were required for the first time.

New warning lights were located at six locations around the track.

Total fuel allotment was reduced to forty-two and a half gallons from forty-five last year.

Eddie Edenburn passed away and Charlie Merz became the new chief steward.

Amelia Earhart, the first woman to fly across the Atlantic Ocean, served as an honorary referee for the race.

Rex Mays won the pole at a speed of 120.7 mph at only twenty-two years old. He became the youngest pole winner ever.

Kelly Petillo qualified on his third and final attempt and started twenty-second. Petillo actually had the fastest qualifying speed, but his run was disallowed for having exceeded fuel allotment by less than a pint.

The field included eight rookies and three former winners.

Rex Mays led most of the first half of the race, 89 of the first 99 laps, then dropped out on lap 123.

Kelly Petillo led the entire second half of the race with the exception of five laps led by Wilbur Shaw when he pitted. Petillo set a new race record at 106.2 mph in his Gilmore Speedway Special.

Rain fell in the late stages of the race, from lap 177 to 190, but not hard enough to bring out the red flag. The last nine laps were run under green, but Wilbur Shaw didn't have the time to catch Petillo and finished just over forty seconds behind.

Petillo's birth name was Cavino Michelli Petillo.

Wilbur Shaw finished second and Bill Cummings, third in his Boyle Products Special.

Petillo's car was the first winning car to be powered by an Offenhauser engine. The Offenhauser engine would soon become the dominant power source, powering every winner from 1947 through 1964.

Ford Motor Company teamed up with Harry Miller to enter ten Ford V8-powered cars. Only four managed to qualify and all were forced out of the race with steering failure.

Several deaths occurred during the month, which resulted in significant safety and track modifications for the following year. Johnny Hannon and Stubby Stubblefield were killed in separate accidents on May 21. Hannon's accident occurred on his first practice lap at speed in his rookie year as his car went over the outside retaining wall. Stubblefield's riding mechanic, Leo Whitaker, was also killed in their accident as the car also went over the outside wall. Rookie Clay Weatherly was fatally injured on his tenth lap in the race, driving the same car owned by Leon Duray that Johnny Hannon was killed in just nine days earlier.

A stronger focus on safety was the result of the fact that since the track opened in 1909 there had been 27 drivers and mechanics and four spectators lose their lives.

Kelly Petillo went on to win the 1935 AAA National Championship.

1935 Winner Kelly Petillo is shown in his "Offy"-powered car with riding mechanic Jimmy Dunham.

RACE RESULTS FOR THE 1935 INDIANAPOLIS 500

Finish	Start	Car Num.	Driver	Car Name/Entrant*	Make/Model	Status	Laps	Led	Winnings
1	22	5	Kelly Petillo	Gilmore Speedway	Wetteroth/Offy	106.240	200	102	$30,600
2	20	14	Wilbur Shaw	Pirrung	Shaw/Offy	105.990	200	5	$13,500
3	5	1	Bill Cummings (W)	Boyle Products	Miller/Miller	104.758	200	0	$6,650
4	3	22	Floyd Roberts (R)	Abels & Fink	Miller/Miller	103.228	200	0	$4,000
5	7	21	Ralph Hepburn	Veedol	Miller/Miller	103.177	200	0	$3,500
6	19	9	Shorty Cantlon	Sullivan & O'Brien	Stevens/Miller	101.140	200	0	$2,200
7	9	18	Chet Gardner	Sampson Radio	Stevens/Miller	101.129	200	0	$1,800
8	13	16	Deacon Litz	Sha-litz	Miller/Miller	100.907	200	0	$1,600
9	15	8	Doc MacKenzie	Pirrung	Rigling/Miller	100.598	200	0	$1,500
10	17	34	Chet Miller	Milac Front Drive	Summers/Miller	100.474	200	0	$1,475
11	8	19	Fred Frame (W)	Miller-Hartz	Wetteroth/Miller	100.436	200	0	$850
12	4	36	Louis Meyer (W)	Ring Free	Stevens/Miller	100.256	200	0	$700
13	16	15	Cliff Bergere	Victor Gasket	Rigling/Buick	Out of fuel	196	0	$600
14	31	62	Harris Insinger (R)	Cresco	Mikan-Carson/Studebaker	Running	185	0	$535
15	21	4	Al Miller	Boyle Products	Rigling/Miller	Engine	178	0	$520
16	26	43	Ted Horn (R)	Ford V-8	Miller-Ford/Ford V8	Steering	145	0	$505
17	1	33	Rex Mays	Gilmore	Adams/Miller	Spring	123	89	$2,490
18	23	7	Lou Moore	Foreman Axle	Miller/Miller	Rod	116	0	$475
19	14	37	George Connor (R)	Marks Miller	Stevens/Miller	Transmission	112	0	$460
20	10	2	Mauri Rose	F.W.D.	Miller/Miller	Studs	103	0	$445
21	6	44	Tony Gulotta	Bowes Seal Fast	Stevens/Miller	Magneto	102	0	$430
22	30	39	Jimmy Snyder (R)	Blue Prelude	Snowberger/Studebaker	Spring	97	0	$415
23	24	41	Frank Brisko	Art Rose	Rigling/Studebaker	Universal joint	79	0	$400
24	27	42	Johnny Seymour	Ford V-8	Miller-Ford/Ford V8	Grease leak	71	0	$385
25	12	17	Babe Stapp	Marks Miller	Adams/Miller	Radiator	70	4	$470
26	29	35	George Bailey	Ford V-8	Miller-Ford/Ford V8	Steering	65	0	$355
27	11	3	Russ Snowberger	Boyle Products	Miller/Miller	Exhaust pipe	59	0	$340
28	32	26	Louis Tomei (R)	Burd Piston Ring	Miller/Lencki	Valve	47	0	$325
29	33	46	Bob Sall (R)	Ford V-8	Miller-Ford/Ford V8	Steering	47	0	$310
30	2	6	Al Gordon	Cocktail Hour Cigarette	Weil/Miller	Accident	17	0	$295
31	28	27	Freddie Winnai	Gyro-Duesenberg	Duesenberg/Miller	Rod	16	0	$280
32	25	45	Clay Weatherly (R)	Bowes Seal Fast	Stevens/Miller	Accident	9	0	$265
33	18	66	Harry McQuinn	DeBaets	Rigling/Miller	Rod	4	0	$250

* - complete car name/entrant data not available for all entries
(R) - Indicated Rookie
(W) - Indicates Past Winner

1936

The steeper-angled banking was removed from the track. A new outer retaining wall was installed in front of the existing one and the inner wall was removed for safety reasons.

The Borg-Warner trophy for the winner was unveiled. The sterling silver trophy stands nearly five feet tall, weighs over 100 pounds and has a likeness of each winner's face, date of victory and average winning speed.

Fuel allotment for the entire race was reduced to thirty-seven and a half gallons. One car had run out of fuel before the end of the race in 1935 after none in 1934. Seven cars would run out of fuel in 1936, with four of them running in the top ten. The fuel shortage victims included: Harry McQuinn, Shorty Cantlon, Rex Mays, Doc Williams, Lou Moore, Floyd Roberts and Frank Brisko.

Rex Mays won the pole for the second year in a row at a speed of 119.6 mph.

Kelly Petillo decided not to defend his title, opting to have Doc MacKenzie drive his car. Petillo did drive relief for MacKenzie.

The field included four rookies and three former winners.

Mays, Babe Stapp and Wilbur Shaw led for the first half. Shaw was effectively eliminated from winning when a seventeen-minute pit stop to repair loose hood rivets dropped him from contention.

Louis Meyer, after a tough month with two cracked cylinder blocks, had to have a third flown in for a last minute qualifying run. His speed of 114.17 mph resulted in a 28th starting position. Meyer's crew then had to work nearly all night the night before the race fixing a valve problem in the engine. Meyer led most of the second half of the race. He led ninety-six laps total. Meyer averaged 109.1 mph in his Ring Free Special for a new speed record and averaged 14.46 miles per gallon. He became the first three-time winner in history.

Ted Horn, who led sixteen laps in the second half, finished second a lap behind in a Hartz Special, and Doc MacKenzie, who was relieved by Kelly Petillo, finished third in the Gilmore Special. A scoring mishap actually had Mauri Rose being flagged third and Petillo fourth in the MacKenzie car, but an audit after the race reversed the positions.

The first five finishers all exceeded last year's record speed.

George Barringer drove the Kennedy Tank Special to an eighth-place finish after starting in the fourteenth position.

Two-time Indy 500 winner Tommy Milton drove the Packard pace car and suggested it be given to the winner. A new tradition was born.

Louis Meyer also unknowingly started another tradition when he refreshed himself by drinking buttermilk in Victory Lane.

The improvement in the track construction helped result in a relatively safe race.

George Barringer and riding mechanic Dick Wilkes drove the Kennedy Tank Special to an eighth-place finish in 1936.

RACE RESULTS FOR THE 1936 INDIANAPOLIS 500

Finish	Start	Car Num.	Driver	Car Name/ Entrant*	Make/Model	Status	Laps	Led	Winnings
1	28	8	Louis Meyer (W)	Ring Free	Stevens/Miller	109.069	200	96	$31,300
2	11	22	Ted Horn	Miller-Hartz	Wetteroth/Miller	108.170	200	16	$13,775
3	4	10	Doc MacKenzie	Gilmore Speedway	Wetteroth/Offy	107.460	200	0	$6,900
4	30	36	Mauri Rose	F.W.D.	Miller/Miller	107.272	200	0	$4,000
5	3	18	Chet Miller	Boyle Products	Summers/Miller	106.919	200	0	$3,653
6	25	41	Ray Pixley (R)	Fink Auto	Miller/Miller	105.253	200	0	$2,328
7	9	3	Wilbur Shaw	Gilmore	Shaw/Offy	104.233	200	51	$3,650
8	14	17	George Barringer	Kennedy Tank	Rigling/Offy	102.630	200	0	$1,650
9	32	53	Zeke Meyer	Boyle Products	Cooper/Studebaker	101.331	200	0	$1,550
10	5	38	George Connor	Marks Miller	Adams/Miller	98.931	200	0	$1,425
11	12	35	Freddie Winnai	Midwest Red Lion	Stevens/Offy	Running	199	0	$850
12	24	9	Ralph Hepburn	Art Rose	Miller/Offy	Running	195	0	$700
13	27	28	Harry McQuinn	Sampson Radio	Stevens/Miller	Out of fuel	196	0	$600
14	10	7	Shorty Cantlon	Hamilton-Harris	Weil/Miller	Out of fuel	194	0	$535
15	1	33	Rex Mays	Gilmore	Adams/Sparks	Out of fuel	192	12	$920
16	23	54	Doc Williams (R)	Superior Trailer	Cooper/Miller	Out of fuel	192	0	$505
17	29	32	Lou Moore	Burd Piston Ring	Miller/Offy	Out of fuel	185	0	$490
18	33	19	Emil Andres (R)	Carew	Whippet/Cragar	Running	184	0	$475
19	15	4	Floyd Roberts	Burd Piston Ring	Stevens/Offy	Out of fuel	183	0	$460
20	20	14	Frank Brisko	Elgin Piston Pin	Miller/Brisko	Out of fuel	180	0	$445
21	17	12	Al Miller	Boyle Products	Smith/Miller	Accident	119	0	$430
22	7	42	Cliff Bergere	Bowes Seal Fast	Stevens/Miller	Engine support	116	0	$415
23	26	15	Deacon Litz	Litz	Miller/Miller	Crankshaft	108	0	$400
24	2	21	Babe Stapp	Pirrung	Shaw/Offy	Crankshaft	89	25	$1,585
25	19	5	Billy Winn	Harry A. Miller	Miller/Miller	Crankshaft	78	0	$370
26	22	52	Frank McGurk (R)	Abels Auto Ford	Adams/Cragar	Crankshaft	51	0	$355
27	8	27	Louis Tomei	Wheeler's	Wetteroth/Miller	Engine support	44	0	$340
28	6	44	Herb Ardinger	Bowes Seal Fast	Stevens/Miller	Transmission	38	0	$325
29	18	6	Chet Gardner	Gardner	Duesenberg/Offy	Clutch	38	0	$310
30	16	43	Jimmy Snyder	Belanger Miller	Stevens/Miller	Oil leak	21	0	$295
31	21	47	Johnny Seymour	Sullivan & O'Brien	Stevens/Miller	Clutch	13	0	$280
32	31	46	Fred Frame (W)	Burd Piston Ring	Miller/Miller	Piston	4	0	$265
33	13	2	Bill Cummings (W)	Boyle Products	Miller/Offy	Clutch	0	0	$250

* - complete car name/entrant data not available for all entries
(R) - Indicated Rookie
(W) - Indicates Past Winner

1937

This was the twenty-fifth running of the race—the Silver Jubilee.

The fuel limit was lifted.

Lee Oldfield practiced but did not qualify the first rear-engine car ever entered.

After failing to qualify, the wealthy Joel Thorne caused a controversy by trying to buy his way into the field. He was stopped by the officials.

Ralph DePalma, legendary Indy 500 driver and 1915 winner, paced the race in a LaSalle.

The first second-generation driver, Billy Devore, started fourteenth and finished seventh. His dad Earl finished second in 1927.

Bill Cummings started from the pole after qualifying at 123.455 mph.

Jimmy Snyder eclipsed the 130 mph barrier for one lap on a qualifying run that was not completed. He later became the fastest qualifier at 125.3 mph, but started nineteenth. Snyder broke Leon Duray's qualifying record set in 1928. He took the lead by the third lap and led to the twenty-seventh lap, when transmission problems eliminated him.

Wilbur Shaw took the lead on lap 27 and pretty much controlled the race except when pitting. He led a total of 131 laps in his first 500 win in his ninth attempt. He nicknamed his "catfish"-influenced streamliner "the Pay Car."

Second-place finisher Ralph Hepburn was overcome by heat and was relieved by Bob Swanson from lap 108 to 163. Swanson led from lap 130 to 163 during his relief stint.

At lap 180, Shaw led by nearly two minutes, or about a lap and a half, but experienced oil pressure problems with his four-cylinder normally aspirated 255 Offy and began to slow. Shaw slowed in the turns as his oil pressure dropped then sped up on the straight-aways.

Prior to 1937, the closest finish was in 1934, when Cummings beat Rose by twenty-seven seconds.

With one lap to go, Shaw led by 14 seconds, but he beat Hepburn's Hamilton Harris Cigar sponsored Stevens/Offy to the line by only 2.16 seconds. This was the closest finish in 500 history until 1982. Even with the slowdown Shaw averaged 113.6 mph for a new speed record and eclipsed the record set in 1936 by 4 mph.

The first four finishers all broke the previous race record set by Louis Meyer in 1936.

John "Jigger" Johnson was the riding mechanic for winner Louis Schneider in 1931 and Wilbur Shaw in 1937.

Of the thirty-three starters, only fourteen were running at the finish.

Wilbur Shaw went on to win the 1937 AAA National Championship.

Wilbur Shaw and riding mechanic "Jigger" Johnson drove Shaw's "Pay Car" to the victory in 1937.

RACE RESULTS FOR THE 1937 INDIANAPOLIS 500

Finish	Start	Car Num.	Driver	Car Name/Entrant*	Make/Model	Status	Laps	Led	Winnings
1	2	6	Wilbur Shaw	Shaw-Gilmore	Shaw/Offy	113.580	200	131	$35,075
2	6	8	Ralph Hepburn	Hamilton-Harris	Stevens/Offy	113.565	200	9	$15,937
3	32	3	Ted Horn	Miller-Hartz	Wetteroth/Miller	113.434	200	0	$7,087
4	5	2	Louis Meyer (W)	Boyle	Miller/Miller	110.730	200	0	$4,275
5	16	45	Cliff Bergere	Midwest Red Lion	Stevens/Offy	108.935	200	0	$3,725
6	1	16	Bill Cummings (W)	Boyle	Miller/Offy	107.124	200	0	$3,187
7	14	28	Billy DeVore (R)	Miller	Stevens/Miller	106.995	200	0	$1,962
8	7	38	Tony Gulotta	Burd Piston Ring	Rigling/Offy	105.015	200	0	$1,787
9	12	17	George Connor	Marks Miller	Adams/Miller	103.830	200	0	$1,862
10	18	53	Louis Tomei	Sobonite Plastics	Rigling/Studebaker	101.825	200	0	$1,487
11	9	31	Chet Gardner	Burd Piston Ring	Duesenberg/Offy	Running	199	0	$912
12	10	23	Ronney Householder (R)	Topping	Viglioni/Miller	Running	194	0	$737
13	17	62	Floyd Roberts	Thorne	Miller/Miller	Running	194	0	$600
14	11	35	Deacon Litz	Motorola Auto Radio	Miller/Miller	Out of oil	191	0	$535
15	24	32	Floyd Davis (R)	Thorne	Snowberger/Miller	Accident	190	0	$520
16	25	34	Shorty Cantlon	Bowes Seal Fast	Weil/Miller	Running	182	0	$505
17	26	42	Al Miller	Thorne	Snowberger/Miller	Carburetor	170	0	$490
18	8	1	Mauri Rose	Burd Piston Ring	Miller/Offy	Oil line	127	0	$475
19	29	41	Ken Fowler (R)	Lucky Teeter	Wetteroth/McDowell	Car pushed	116	0	$460
20	20	25	Kelly Petillo (W)	Petillo	Wetteroth/Offy	Out of oil	109	0	$1,445
21	28	43	George Bailey	Duray-Sims	Stevens/Miller	Clutch	107	0	$430
22	3	54	Herb Ardinger	Chicago Raw Hide Oil Seal	Welch/Offy	Rod	106	2	$915
23	15	24	Frank Brisko	Elgin Piston Pin	Stevens/Brisko	No oil pressure	105	0	$400
24	33	44	Frank Wearne (R)	Duray	Stevens/Miller	Carburetor	99	0	$385
25	27	26	Tony Willman (R)	F.W.D.	Miller/Miller	Rod	95	0	$370
26	4	10	Billy Winn	Harry A. Miller	Miller/Miller	Oil line	85	0	$605
27	30	12	Russ Snowberger	R.S.	Snowberger/Packard	Clutch	66	0	$340
28	21	33	Bob Swanson (R)	Fink Auto	Adams/Sparks	Carburetor	52	34	$825
29	22	47	Harry McQuinn	Sullivan & O'Brien	Stevens/Miller	Piston	47	0	$560
30	13	7	Chet Miller	Boyle	Summers/Miller	Ignition	36	0	$295
31	31	15	Babe Stapp	Topping	Maserati/Maserati	Clutch	36	0	$280
32	19	5	Jimmy Snyder	Sparks	Adams/Sparks	Transmission	27	24	$3,165
33	23	14	Rex Mays	Bowes Seal Fast	Alfa Romeo/Alfa Romeo	Overheating	24	0	$500

* - complete car name/entrant data not available for all entries
(R) - Indicated Rookie
(W) - Indicates Past Winner

1938

Riding mechanics were no longer required, though the entry form included terminology making riding mechanics optional through 1963.

Specifications for the European Grand Prix races were adopted. They called for a maximum of 183 cubic-inches on engines with a supercharger and 274 cubic-inches without a supercharger. All types and any amount of fuel were allowed, which enabled the use of alcohol for super-charged engines.

Floyd Roberts, from Van Nuys, California, won the pole at a new record of 125.7 mph and then went on to win the race for now-retired driver Lou Moore. This was the first of five wins for Moore, and Roberts became the fourth pole winner to win the race.

Ronney Householder actually became the fastest qualifier at 125.8 mph on the second day of qualifications, but was forced to start tenth.

The field included four rookies and four former winners.

Jimmy Snyder and Floyd Roberts made it pretty much a two-car race, each leading ninety-two laps.

Snyder experienced supercharger problems after 151 laps and was eliminated. Roberts led from lap 145 to the finish in his Burd Piston Ring Special powered by a four-cylinder Miller 270.

Spectator Everett Spence was fatally injured by a thrown wheel from the car of Emil Andres.

Roberts finished three laps ahead of second place Wilbur Shaw and averaged 117.2 mph, which was a record that would stand for ten years. Roberts made only one pit stop during the race. A late pit stop by Chet Miller resulted in dropping from second place to a third place finish.

The first three finishers all eclipsed the race record set in 1937 by Wilbur Shaw.

The Victory Area was now called "The Bull Pen."

Floyd Roberts went on to win the AAA National Driving Championship for the 1938 season.

Eddie Rickenbacker had taken over Eastern Airlines in 1938.

The 1938 winner Floyd Roberts, with owner Lou Moore, completes the "500" with only one pit stop.

RACE RESULTS FOR THE 1938 INDIANAPOLIS 500

Finish	Start	Car Num.	Driver	Car Name/Entrant*	Make/Model	Status	Laps	Led	Winnings
1	1	23	Floyd Roberts	Burd Piston Ring	Wetteroth/Miller	117.200	200	92	$32,075
2	7	1	Wilbur Shaw (W)	Shaw	Shaw/Offy	115.580	200	0	$14,425
3	5	3	Chet Miller	I.B.E.W.	Summers/Offy	114.946	200	0	$7,350
4	6	2	Ted Horn	Miller-Hartz	Wetteroth/Miller	112.203	200	0	$4,600
5	18	38	Chet Gardner	Burd Piston Ring	Rigling/Offy	110.311	200	0	$4,100
6	14	54	Herb Ardinger	Offenhauser	Miller-Ford/Offy	Running	199	0	$2,625
7	25	45	Harry McQuinn	Marchese	Marchese/Miller	Running	197	0	$2,175
8	30	58	Billy DeVore	P.R.&W.	Stevens/Offy	Running	185	0	$1,925
9	13	22	Joel Thorne (R)	Thorne Engineering	Shaw/Offy	Running	185	0	$1,775
10	17	29	Frank Wearne	Indiana Fur	Adams/Offy	Running	181	0	$1,650
11	33	43	Duke Nalon (R)	Kohlert-Miller	Fengler/Miller	Running	178	0	$1,025
12	29	12	George Bailey	Leon Duray Barbasol	Weil/Duray	Clutch	166	0	$825
13	9	27	Mauri Rose	I.B.E.W.	Maserati/Maserati	Supercharger	165	0	$650
14	10	16	Ronney Householder	Thorne-Sparks	Adams/Sparks	Supercharger	154	0	$695
15	15	6	Jimmy Snyder	Sparks-Thorne	Adams/Sparks	Supercharger	150	92	$3,390
16	12	5	Louis Meyer (W)	Bowes Seal Fast	Stevens/Winfield	Oil Pump	149	0	$635
17	4	17	Tony Gulotta	Hamilton-Harris	Stevens/Offy	Rod	130	0	$680
18	22	55	Al Miller	Domont's Pepsi-Cola	Miller/Miller	Clutch	125	0	$625
19	19	15	George Connor	Marks Miller	Adams/Miller	Engine	119	0	$620
20	32	9	Cliff Bergere	Kraft's Real Rye	Stevens/Miller	Piston	111	0	$615
21	31	33	Henry Banks (R)	Detroit Sporting World	Miller/Voelker	Rod bearing	109	0	$610
22	21	35	Kelly Petillo (W)	Petillo	Wetteroth/Offy	Camshaft	100	0	$955
23	24	21	Louis Tomei	P.O.B. Perfect Seal	Miller/Miller	Rod	88	0	$625
24	16	7	Bill Cummings (W)	I.B.E.W.	Miller/Miller	Radiator	72	0	$620
25	2	14	Russ Snowberger	D-X	Snowberger/Miller	Rod	56	0	$640
26	8	34	Babe Stapp	McCoy Auto Service	Weil/Miller	Valve	54	0	$585
27	26	10	Tony Willman	Belanger	Stevens/Miller	Valve	47	0	$580
28	3	8	Rex Mays	Alfa-Romeo	A.R.-Weil/Alfa-Romeo	Supercharger	45	16	$1,125
29	28	42	Emil Andres	Elgin Piston Pin	Adams/Brisko	Accident	45	0	$620
30	27	37	Ira Hall	Greenfield Super Service	Nowiak/Studebaker	Accident	44	0	$565
31	11	26	Frank Brisko	Shur-Stop Mech. Brake Equal.	Stevens/Brisko	Oil line	39	0	$585
32	23	36	Al Putnam (R)	Troy Tydol	Stevens/Miller	Crankshaft	15	0	$555
33	20	47	Shorty Cantlon	Kamm's	Stevens/Miller	Supercharger	13	0	$550

* - complete car name/entrant data not available for all entries
(R) - Indicated Rookie
(W) - Indicates Past Winner

1939

Qualification attempts were changed from ten laps back to four laps, the procedure that was last used in 1932.

The field included one rookie and four former winners.

Jimmy Snyder won the pole at 130.138 mph in one of the Thorne Engineering cars and set a new record. This speed record would hold up until 1946. He led the opening thirty-six laps before pitting.

George Bailey qualified on the outside of row two in the first rear-engine car to ever make the race. He would last forty-seven laps.

The second half of the race was mainly a battle between Louis Meyer and Wilbur Shaw.

Louis Meyer led from lap 135 to lap 182 when he blew a right front tire and spun in turn one. He was able to continue, but Shaw took the lead at that time.

Meyer chased Shaw and came within ten feet of Shaw's Maserati before spinning and crashing on lap 198. He was thrown from his car, fortunately was not injured seriously, though he pretty much decided on the spot to retire from racing.

Shaw's Mike Boyle-owned maroon-colored 8CTF Maserati was the first foreign-built car to win since Howdy Wilcox's Peugeot in 1919. He averaged 115 mph and became a two-time winner.

Jimmy Snyder finished second and Cliff Bergere, third.

Just past halfway, defending champion Floyd Roberts, who was driving his winning car from the previous year, was fatally injured in a fiery three-car accident in the second turn. Roberts sustained a broken neck. He became the first 500 winner to perish in the 500 mile race. He was thirty-nine years old. The serious accident caused a thirty-two minute caution and resulted in Shaw not breaking the race record.

Laps led were as follows: Shaw, 51, Snyder, 65, and Meyer, 79. This group led a total of 195 laps.

Estimated attendance was 145,000.

Wilbur Shaw would go on to win the 1939 AAA National Championship.

George Bailey drives the first rear-engine car to compete in the 500—starting sixth and finishing twenty-sixth.

RACE RESULTS FOR THE 1939 INDIANAPOLIS 500

Finish	Start	Car Num.	Driver	Car Name/Entrant*	Make/Model	Status	Laps	Led	Winnings
1	3	2	Wilbur Shaw (W)	Boyle	Maserati/Maserati	115.035	200	51	$27,375
2	1	10	Jimmy Snyder	Thorne Engineering	Adams/Sparks	114.245	200	65	$16,100
3	10	54	Cliff Bergere	Offenhauser	Miller-Ford/Offy	113.698	200	0	$7,400
4	4	4	Ted Horn	Boyle	Miller/Miller	111.879	200	4	$4,750
5	16	31	Babe Stapp	Alfa Romeo	A.R.-Weil/ Alfa Romeo	111.230	200	0	$4,225
6	15	41	George Barringer	Bill White	Weil/Offy	111.025	200	0	$2,800
7	20	8	Joel Thorne	Thorne Engineering	Adams/Sparks	110.416	200	0	$2,150
8	8	16	Mauri Rose	Wheeler's	Shaw/Offy	109.544	200	0	$2,150
9	17	14	Frank Wearne	Burd Piston Ring	Wetteroth/Offy	107.806	200	0	$1,800
10	33	26	Billy DeVore	Leon Duray-Barbasol	Weil/Duray	104.267	200	0	$1,600
11	27	62	Tony Gulotta	Burd Piston Ring	Stevens/Offy	103.938	200	0	$1,000
12	2	45	Louis Meyer (W)	Bowes Seal Fast	Stevens/Winfield	Accident	197	79	$3,200
13	12	18	George Connor	Marks	Adams/Offy	Stalled	195	0	$650
14	26	51	Tony Willman	Burd Piston Ring	Lencki/Lencki	Fuel pump	188	0	$620
15	30	58	Louis Tomei	Alfa-Romeo	Alfa Romeo/Alfa Romeo	Running	186	0	$590
16	19	15	Rex Mays	Thorne Engineering	Adams/Sparks	Rings	145	1	$685
17	9	9	Herb Ardinger	Miller-Hartz	Wetteroth/Miller	Clutch	141	0	$680
18	24	35	Kelly Petillo (W)	Kay Jewelers	Wetteroth/Offy	Pistons	141	0	$600
19	14	49	Mel Hansen (R)	Joel Thorne, Inc.	Shaw/Offy	Accident	113	0	$595
20	32	38	Harry McQuinn	Elgin Piston Pin	Blume/Brisko	Ignition	110	0	$590
21	5	3	Chet Miller	Boyle	Summers/Miller	Accident	109	0	$635
22	13	25	Ralph Hepburn	Hamilton-Harris	Stevens/Offy	Accident	107	0	$605
23	23	1	Floyd Roberts (W)	Burd Piston Ring	Wetteroth/Offy	Accident	106	0	$650
24	18	37	Ira Hall	Greenfield Super Service	Nowiak/Studebaker	Head gasket	89	0	$570
25	25	21	Russ Snowberger	D-X	Snowberger/Miller	Radiator	50	0	$590
26	6	17	George Bailey	Miller	Miller/Miller	Valve	47	0	$610
27	29	56	Floyd Davis	W.B.W.	Miller/Offy	Shock absorber	43	0	$555
28	28	42	Al Miller	Kennedy Tank	Adams/Offy	Accelerator	41	0	$575
29	11	29	Frank Brisko	National Seal	Stevens/Brisko	Air pump	38	0	$570
30	21	44	Emil Andres	Chicago Flash	Stevens/Offy	Spark plugs	22	0	$540
31	22	32	Bob Swanson	S.M.I.	Stevens/Sampson	Rear axle	19	0	$510
32	7	47	Shorty Cantlon	Automotive Service	Stevens/Offy	Bearing	15	0	$605
33	31	53	Deacon Litz	Maserati	Maserati/Maserati	Valve	7	0	$525

* - complete car name/entrant data not available for all entries
(R) - Indicated Rookie
(W) - Indicates Past Winner

1940

Rex Mays won the pole at 127.85 mph, with Wilbur Shaw second at 127.065 mph.

The field included six rookies and two former winners.

Wilbur Shaw became the first driver to win consecutive 500s, driving the same eight-cylinder dual supercharged Maserati for Mike Boyle that was "wrenched" by Cotton Henning. He averaged 114.3 mph.

Shaw now had finished first, second, first and first in four consecutive years, and second in 1933 and 1935.

Second place went to Rex Mays in his Bowes Seal Fast Special and third to Mauri Rose. This was, and continues to be, the only year that the front row starters also finished in the top three positions

Rain fell for the last 125 miles (fifty laps) and the race was run under yellow flag conditions at a speed of approximately 100 mph. Prior to the caution for rain, Shaw led Mays by nearly a lap.

There were nineteen cars running at the finish.

Three-time national champion Eylard Amandus "Ted" Horn was one lap down at the time of the rain and the race was immediately halted when Shaw took the checkered flag. The fact that Horn completed 199 laps caused him to only complete 1,799 of a possible 1,800 laps in the races from 1936 to 1948.

Horn would later drive Shaw's winning Maserati in the 1946-1948 "500s" with finishes of third, third, and fourth. Lee Wallard led the 1949 "500" for 19 laps in the famous car. Bill Vukovich passed his rookie test in the car in 1950.

Wilbur Shaw becomes the first to win two in a row.

RACE RESULTS FOR THE 1940 INDIANAPOLIS 500

Finish	Start	Car Num.	Driver	Car Name/Entrant*	Make/Model	Status	Laps	Led	Winnings
1	2	1	Wilbur Shaw (W)	Boyle	Maserati/Maserati	114.277	200	136	$30,725
2	1	33	Rex Mays	Bowes Seal Fast	Stevens/Winfield	113.742	200	59	$15,950
3	3	7	Mauri Rose	Elgin Piston Pin	Wetteroth/Offy	113.572	200	5	$6,688
4	4	3	Ted Horn	Boyle	Miller/Miller	Running	199	0	$4,575
5	10	8	Joel Thorne	Thorne Donnelly	Adams/Sparks	Running	197	0	$3,850
6	20	32	Bob Swanson	Sampson	Stevens/Sampson	Running	196	0	$2,463
7	7	9	Frank Wearne	Boyle	Stevens/Offy	Running	195	0	$2,038
8	5	31	Mel Hansen	Hartz	Wetteroth/Miller	Running	194	0	$1,813
9	8	16	Frank Brisko	Elgin Piston Pin	Stevens/Brisko	Running	193	0	$1,863
10	31	49	Rene LeBegue (R)	Lucy O'Reilly Schell	Maserati/Maserati	Running	192	0	$1,488
11	15	41	Harry McQuinn	Hollywood Pay Day	A.R.-Weil/Alfa Romeo	Running	192	0	$938
12	22	25	Emil Andres	Belanger-Folz	Stevens/Offy	Running	192	0	$788
13	14	28	Sam Hanks (R)	Duray	Weil/Duray	Running	192	0	$650
14	16	6	George Barringer	Hollywood Pay Day	Weil/Offy	Running	191	0	$620
15	26	42	Joie Chitwood (R)	Kennedy Tank	Adams/Offy	Running	190	0	$615
16	18	26	Louis Tomei	Falstaff	Miller/Offy	Exhaust	190	0	$610
17	27	34	Chet Miller	Alfa Romeo	Alfa Romeo/Alfa Romeo	Running	189	0	$605
18	32	14	Billy DeVore	Bill Holabird	Shaw/Offy	Running	181	0	$600
19	28	44	Al Putnam	Refinoil Motor Oil	Adams/Offy	Running	179	0	$595
20	33	61	Floyd Davis	Lencki	Lencki/Lencki	Running	157	0	$590
21	13	35	Kelly Petillo (W)	Indiana Fur	Wetteroth/Offy	Bearing	128	0	$660
22	25	21	Duke Nalon	Marks	Silnes/Offy	Rod	120	0	$580
23	23	17	George Robson (R)	Keller	Miller-Ford/Offy	Shock absorber	67	0	$575
24	12	24	Babe Stapp	Surber	Stevens/Offy	Oil line	64	0	$595
25	19	36	Doc Williams	Quillen Bros. Refrigerator	Cooper/Miller	Oil line	61	0	$590
26	17	10	George Connor	Lencki	Lencki/Lencki	Rod	52	0	$610
27	6	5	Cliff Bergere	Noc-Out Hose Clamp	Wetteroth/Offy	Oil line	51	0	$605
28	29	38	Paul Russo (R)	Elgin Piston Pin	Blume/Brisko	Oil leak	48	0	$550
29	21	54	Ralph Hepburn	Bowes Seal Fast	Miller-Ford/Offy	Steering	47	0	$595
30	30	58	Al Miller	Alfa Romeo	Alfa Romeo/Alfa Romeo	Clutch	41	0	$540
31	11	19	Russ Snowberger	Snowberger	Snowberger/Miller	Water pump	38	0	$535
32	9	27	Tommy Hinnershitz (R)	Marks	Adams/Offy	Accident	32	0	$530
33	24	29	Raul Riganti	Maserati	Maserati/Maserati	Accident	24	0	$500

* - complete car name/entrant data not available for all entries
(R) - Indicated Rookie
(W) - Indicates Past Winner

1941

The new chief steward was Ted Doescher, who took over for Charlie Merz.

Mauri Rose won the pole in the Elgin Piston Pin Maserati at 128.7 mph.

The field included two rookies and two former winners.

The front row of Rose, Mays and Shaw in 1941 featured the same drivers on the front row in 1940 (but not in the same order).

A garage fire at 6:45 am on the morning of the race destroyed George Barringer's car. Sam Hanks had a serious accident the day before the race and was unable to start. Hanks was awarded thirty-third, and Barringer thirty-second, as there were only thirty-one actual starters for the race. The start was delayed by two hours because of the fire.

The very unique Chrysler Newport paced the race. The Newport featured: two separate seating compartments, full enclosed rear wheel wells, hidden headlights and a gold paint job.

Mays led the first 38 laps. Shaw then led nearly all of the laps up to the 152nd lap, when a wheel collapsed and he crashed. He was leading Cliff Bergere by more than a lap at the time of his accident. Shaw suffered a compression fracture to his back. Shaw claimed that his team had marked a tire with chalk "use last" because of the wheel not being properly balanced. He contended that the water from fighting the garage fire had washed the chalk message from the tire, and as a result that wheel may have been the culprit for his accident.

On lap 72, car owner Lou Moore had Floyd Davis pit and replaced him with his teammate Mauri Rose. Rose had led early in the race, but dropped out with carburetor issues at sixty laps. Davis complied with Moore's order with reluctance. The personal relations between all three individuals would never be the same.

At the time Rose took over the car, Davis was running eleventh and was two and a half minutes behind the leader Shaw. After the pit stop and driver change, Rose was running in thirteenth position. Rose steadily moved up through the field and took the lead on lap 162, leading to the checker.

Floyd Davis and Mauri Rose averaged 115.1 mph in the Noc-Out Hose Clamp Special and were declared co-winners. Rose had driven the car to a third place finish the previous year. Floyd Davis became the second driver to become a co-winner and never lead a lap.

Rex Mays finished second with Ted Horn in third place. Mays went on to win his second consecutive AAA National Championship in 1941.

Cliff Bergere became the first driver to complete the full distance without a pit stop while driving a gasoline-fueled car. Bergere's sickness from fumes and exhaustion most likely factored in him dropping from first place to a fifth place finish in the final fifty laps.

Estimated attendance was 160,000.

Floyd Davis and Mauri Rose (inset) became 1941 co-winners in the Lou Moore-owned car.

RACE RESULTS FOR THE 1941 INDIANAPOLIS 500

Finish	Start	Car Num.	Driver	Car Name/Entrant*	Make/Model	Status	Laps	Led	Winnings
1	17	16	Floyd Davis / Mauri Rose	Noc-Out Hose Clamp	Wetteroth/Offy	115.117	200	39	$29,200
2	2	1	Rex Mays	Bowes Seal Fast	Stevens/Winfield	114.459	200	38	$14,850
3	28	4	Ted Horn	T.E.C.	Adams/Sparks	113.864	200	0	$6,863
4	10	54	Ralph Hepburn	Bowes Seal Fast	Miller-Ford/Novi	113.631	200	0	$4,575
5	7	34	Cliff Bergere	Noc-Out Hose Clamp	Wetteroth/Offy	113.528	200	10	$4,375
6	9	41	Chet Miller	Boyle	Miller/Miller	111.921	200	0	$2,438
7	4	15	Harry McQuinn	Ziffrin	A.R.-Weil/Alfa Romeo	111.795	200	0	$2,063
8	6	7	Frank Wearne	Bill Holabird	Shaw/Offy	110.818	200	0	$1,788
9	18	45	Paul Russo	Leader Card	Marchese/Miller	105.628	200	0	$1,738
10	20	27	Tommy Hinnershitz	Marks	Adams/Offy	105.152	200	0	$1,538
11	24	53	Louis Tomei	H-3	Miller-Ford/Offy	104.437	200	0	$938
12	31	55	Al Putnam	Schoof	Wetteroth/Offy	101.391	200	0	$763
13	26	26	Overton Phillips (R)	Phillips	Bugatti/Miller	Running	187	0	$625
14	27	25	Joie Chitwood	Blue Crown Spark Plug	Lencki/Lencki	Running	177	0	$620
15	30	17	Duke Nalon	Elgin Piston Pin	Maserati/Maserati	Running	173	0	$640
16	13	14	George Connor	Boyle	Stevens/Offy	Transmission	167	0	$660
17	12	47	Everett Saylor (R)	Mark Bowles	Weil/Offy	Accident	155	0	$605
18	3	2	Wilbur Shaw (W)	Boyle	Maserati/Maserati	Accident	151	107	$5,875
19	8	23	Billy DeVore	Hollywood PayDay Candy	Stevens/Offy	Rod	121	0	$595
20	25	62	Tony Willman	Lyons	Stevens/Offy	Rod	117	0	$615
21	11	42	Russ Snowberger	Hussey's Sportsman Club	Snowberger/Offy	Water pump	107	0	$585
22	29	32	Deacon Litz	Sampson 16	Stevens/Sampson	Oil	89	0	$555
23	22	8	Frank Brisko	Zollner Piston	Stevens/Brisko	Valve	70	0	$600
24	5	36	Doc Williams	Indiana Fur	Cooper/Offy	Radiator	68	0	$620
25	16	10	George Robson	Gilmore Red Lion	Weil/Duray	Oil leak	66	0	$565
26	1	3	Mauri Rose	Elgin Piston Pin	Maserati/Maserati	Spark plugs	60	6	$1,035
27	19	22	Kelly Petillo (W)	Air Liner Sandwich Shop	Wetteroth/Offy	Rod	48	0	$605
28	14	12	Al Miller	Miller	Miller/Miller	Transmission	22	0	$575
29	21	9	Mel Hansen	Fageol	Miller-Ford/Offy	Rod	11	0	$595
30	15	19	Emil Andres	Kennedy Tank	Lencki/Lencki	Accident	4	0	$540
31	23	5	Joel Thorne	Thorne Engineering	Adams/Sparks	Accident	4	0	$535
32	DNS	35	George Barringer	Miller	Miller/Miller	Garage fire	DNS	0	$530
33	DNS	28	Sam Hanks	Tom Joyce 7-Up	Kurtis/Offy	Practice acc.	DNS	0	$525

* - complete car name/entrant data not available for all entries
(R) - Indicated Rookie
(W) - Indicates Past Winner

1942

No race scheduled—United States in World War II.

On July 15, 1942, motor racing of all types was halted by a Federal Mandate as a result of World War II.

1943

No race scheduled—United States in World War II.

1944

No race scheduled—United States in World War II.

In November of 1944, Wilbur Shaw drove a 500-mile test for Firestone on the dilapidated track and facility.

1945

No race scheduled—United States in World War II.

Eddie Rickenbacker was seriously considering selling the Speedway to a land developer who wanted to build homes on the property.

Wilbur Shaw came to the rescue and united Anton Hulman, Jr. and Eddie Rickenbacker.

On November 14, 1945, Anton Hulman, Jr., purchased the Indianapolis Motor Speedway from Eddie Rickenbacker for approximately $700,000. Hulman graduated from Yale with an engineering degree. He was an extremely successful businessman residing in Terre Haute, Indiana. Hulman named Wilbur Shaw president and general manager of the Indianapolis Motor Speedway. A tremendous clean-up and refurbishment would be a huge challenge, but Hulman held a race just over six months from purchase.

Clean-up of the track and facility, shown here before Hulman purchased the Speedway, was a tremendous challenge.

1946

There was a surprising number of fifty-seven cars entered for the return of the "500."

The lap prize fund was sold out for the first time since 1927 and for just the third time ever.

Practice actually started on May 1, but the gates did not open to the public until May 15 because clean-up work was still being performed on the "born again" Speedway.

The pole winner was Cliff Bergere, at 126.5 mph in the 1938-winning car of Floyd Roberts. Starting second was Paul Russo in the bulbous Fageol's Twin Coach Special, which actually had an Offenhauser midget engine in front of the driver and one behind him operated by the same pedal.

Ralph Hepburn, at fifty years old, drove the V8 supercharged Novi and was the fastest qualifier, breaking the track record by nearly 4 mph. He set a one-lap record at 134.449 mph and a record average of 133.944, but started nineteenth.

A massive crowd turned out for the return of the 500. A huge traffic jam resulted in a significant proportion of the crowd missing the 11:00 am race start.

Thirty-three cars started the race.

The pre-race tradition of singing "Back Home Again in Indiana" began with the Metropolitan Opera star James Melton.

Mauri Rose started ninth, but led the first lap. Rose crashed into the parked crashed car of Russo on the forty-first lap while trying to avoid another car.

Hepburn in the Novi started nineteenth and was in the lead by lap twelve.

Hepburn was in the lead by more than a minute when a lengthy pit stop on lap fifty-six dropped him back to thirteenth place.

Steady George Robson, driving the Thorne Engineering Special, led 138 laps total and led most of the race after Hepburn's long pit stop. Robson averaged 114.8 mph in his eight-year-old car. This was Robson's first finish in his fourth "500" attempt and his first win in a major automobile race.

Robson's car was only the second six-cylinder engine to win. Harroun's Marmon Wasp being the first in 1911. A six-cylinder engine would not win again until 2012.

Jimmy Jackson, an Indianapolis Tech High School graduate, defied superstition and finished second forty-four seconds back in his green-painted car. Ted Horn finished third in the Boyle Maserati. Had it not been for a nearly seven-minute stop on the ninth lap, Ted Horn might have won.

Only nine cars were running at the finish.

In September of 1946 George Robson and George Barringer lost their lives in a racing accident at the Lakewood Park track in Atlanta. Robson was driving Floyd Roberts' winning car from the 1938 "500."

New track owner Anton "Tony" Hulman Jr. admires the Borg Warner trophy.

RACE RESULTS FOR THE 1946 INDIANAPOLIS 500

Finish	Start	Car Num.	Driver	Car Name/Entrant*	Make/Model	Status	Laps	Led	Winnings
1	15	16	George Robson	Thorne Engineering	Adams/Sparks	114.820	200	138	$42,350
2	5	61	Jimmy Jackson (R)	Jackson	Miller/Offy	114.498	200	5	$13,838
3	7	29	Ted Horn	Boyle Maserati	Maserati/Maserati	109.759	200	0	$7,988
4	11	18	Emil Andres	Elgin Piston Pin	Maserati/Maserati	108.902	200	0	$5,425
5	12	24	Joie Chitwood	Noc-Out Hose Clamp	Wetteroth/Offy	108.399	200	0	$4,375
6	6	33	Lewis Durant (R)	Marion Engineering	Alfa Romeo/Alfa Romeo	105.073	200	0	$3,238
7	28	52	Luigi Villoresi (R)	Maserati	Maserati/Maserati	100.783	200	0	$2,375
8	29	7	Frank Wearne	Wolfe Motors Co., Tulsa	Shaw/Offy	Running	197	0	$2,438
9	25	39	Bill Sheffler (R)	Jack Maurer	Bromme/Offy	Running	139	0	$2,114
10	31	17	Billy DeVore	Schoof	Wetteroth/Offy	Throttle	167	0	$1,888
11	27	4	Mel Hansen	Ross Page	Kurtis/Duray	Crankshaft	143	0	$1,700
12	10	25	Russ Snowberger	Jim Hussey's Sportsman's Club	Maserati/Maserati	Differential	134	0	$1,675
13	18	14	Harry McQuinn	Mobilgas	Adams/Sparks	Out of oil	124	0	$1,600
14	19	2	Ralph Hepburn	Novi Governor	Kurtis/Novi	Stalled	121	44	$7,025
15	13	12	Al Putnam	L.G.S. Spring Clutch	Stevens/Offy	Magneto	120	0	$1,250
16	1	3	Cliff Bergere	Noc-Out Clamp	Wetteroth/Offy	Out of oil	82	2	$1,625
17	8	45	Duke Dinsmore (R)	Johnston	Adams/Offy	Rod	82	0	$1,075
18	17	5	Chet Miller	Miller	Cooper/Offy	Oil line	64	0	$1,000
19	16	63	Jimmy Wilburn (R)	Mobiloil	A.R.-Weil/Alfa Romeo	Block	52	0	$1,000
20	26	42	Tony Bettenhausen (R)	Bristow-McManus	Wetteroth/Miller	Rod	47	0	$925
21	33	59	Danny Kladis (R)	Grancor V8	Miller-Ford/Ford V8	Towed-Disq.	46	0	$875
22	32	54	Duke Nalon	Maserati	Maserati/Maserati	Universal joint	45	0	$825
23	9	8	Mauri Rose	Blue Crown Spark Plug	Lencki/Lencki	Accident	40	8	$1,675
24	30	38	George Connor	Walsh	Kurtis/Offy	Piston	38	0	$800
25	23	48	Hal Robson (R)	Phillips Miller	Bugatti/Miller	Rod	37	0	$775
26	22	15	Louis Tomei	Boxar Tool	Stevens/Brisko	Oil line	34	0	$750
27	21	31	Henry Banks	Automobile Shippers	Snowberger/Offy	Pinion shaft	32	0	$725
28	20	64	Shorty Cantlon	H-3	Miller-Ford/Offy	Clutch	28	0	$725
29	24	26	George Barringer	Tucker Torpedo	Miller/Miller	Gears	27	0	$675
30	14	1	Rex Mays	Bowes Seal Fast	Stevens/Winfield	Manifold	26	3	$1,025
31	3	32	Sam Hanks	Spike Jones	Stevens/Sampson	Oil line	18	0	$675
32	4	47	Hal Cole (R)	Don Lee	Alfa Romeo/Alfa Romeo	Fuel leak	16	0	$600
33	2	10	Paul Russo	Fageol Twin Coach	Fageol/Twin Offys	Accident	16	0	$650

* - complete car name/entrant data not available for all entries
(R) - Indicated Rookie
(W) - Indicates Past Winner

1947

After 1946 it was no longer mandatory for the driver to climb out of the car during a pit stop.

In 1947, a participant's strike over prize money by the members of American Society of Professional Automobile Racing (ASPAR) was eventually settled with The Indianapolis News sports editor William Fox acting as a mediator. Ten ASPAR drivers eventually made the field.

There were thirty starters after several qualifying extensions were allowed.

Ted Horn won the pole at 126.6 mph and was joined on the front row by Cliff Bergere and Mauri Rose. Bill Holland was actually the fastest qualifier at 128.8 mph, but he started eighth.

Cliff Bergere led the first twenty-three laps, then pitted because of tire wear. The rest of the race was led by the front-wheel-drive Blue Crown cars.

Bill Holland led 143 laps and Mauri Rose led thirty-four laps in their Blue Crown Spark Plug Specials.

Holland led from lap 86 to 192. Holland was in his first 500 start at thirty-nine years old. Holland had made two pit stops to Rose's one, but still led by about a half minute when owner Lou Moore gave an "EZY" sign to both his drivers with about 20 laps to go. Holland slowed down, thinking he was more than a lap ahead of Rose, while Rose continued to charge.

Rose passed Holland on the 193rd lap, as Holland acknowledged with a wave what he thought was Rose unlapping himself. Rose went on to win by thirty-two seconds, averaging 116.3 mph.

Holland was extremely upset after the race and called it "a lousy deal".

Holland's car was originally supposed to be driven by Tony Bettenhausen, but as a result of Bettenhausen's involvement with the ASPAR dispute, Lou Moore made a deal with Bill Holland to drive his car.

Shorty Cantlon crashed on lap forty and was fatally injured trying to avoid a skidding Bill Holland in the first turn.

Duke Nalon drove a V12-powered Mercedes to an 18th starting position and finished 16th when a piston problem finished his day on lap 119.

Forty-five year-old Cy Marshall returned to Indy for an eighth place finish after a seventeen year absence. Roland Free also started his second "500" seventeen years after his first race.

Rookie Les Anderson, from Portland, Oregon, drove the Kennedy Tank Special to an eleventh-place finish after starting in the seventh position.

1947 eleventh-place finisher Les Anderson in the Kennedy Tank Special. Bill Kennedy Jr. (author's dad) in white t-shirt and sunglasses nearest driver and "Big John" Berry in suit and hat (author's great-uncle).

RACE RESULTS FOR THE 1947 INDIANAPOLIS 500

Finish	Start	Car Num.	Driver	Car Name/Entrant*	Make/Model	Status	Laps	Led	Winnings
1	3	27	Mauri Rose	Blue Crown Spark Plug	Deidt/Offy	116.338	200	34	$35,125
2	8	16	Bill Holland (R)	Blue Crown Spark Plug	Deidt/Offy	116.097	200	143	$31,300
3	1	1	Ted Horn	Bennett Brothers	Maserati/Maserati	114.997	200	0	$10,115
4	4	54	Herb Ardinger	Novi Governor Mobil	Kurtis/Novi	113.404	200	0	$6,825
5	10	7	Jimmy Jackson	Jim Hussey	Miller/Offy	112.834	200	0	$5,675
6	20	9	Rex Mays	Bowes Seal Fast	Kurtis/Winfield	111.056	200	0	$4,000
7	14	33	Walt Brown (R)	Permafuse	Alfa Romeo/Alfa Romeo	101.744	200	0	$3,700
8	28	34	Cy Marshall	Tattersfield	A.R.-Weil/Alfa Romeo	Running	197	0	$2,850
9	23	41	Fred Agabashian (R)	Ross Page	Kurtis/Duray	Running	191	0	$2,905
10	27	10	Duke Dinsmore	Schoof	Wetteroth/Offy	Running	167	0	$2,310
11	7	58	Les Anderson (R)	Kennedy Tank	Maserati/Offy	Running	131	0	$2,480
12	17	59	Pete Romcevich (R)	Camco Motors Ford	Miller-Ford/Ford V8	Oil line	167	0	$2,360
13	30	3	Emil Andres	Preston Tucker Partners	Lencki/Lencki	Oil line	149	0	$1,740
14	15	31	Frank Wearne	Superior Industries	Miller/Offy	Spun out	128	0	$2,020
15	9	47	Ken Fowler	Don Lee Alfa Romeo	Alfa Romeo/Alfa Romeo	Axle	119	0	$2,050
16	18	46	Duke Nalon	Don Lee Mercedes	Mercedes/Mercedes	Piston	119	0	$1,945
17	12	28	Roland Free	Bristow-McManus	Wetteroth/Miller	Rod	86	0	$1,450
18	25	29	Tony Bettenhausen	Belanger	Stevens/Offy	Gear train	79	0	$1,130
19	6	25	Russ Snowberger	Federal Engineering	Maserati/Maserati	Oil pump	73	0	$1,500
20	16	52	Hal Robson	Palmer	Adams/Offy	Universal joint	67	0	$1,595
21	2	18	Cliff Bergere	Novi Governor Mobil	Kurtis/Novi	Piston	63	23	$3,815
22	22	8	Joie Chitwood	Peters	Wetteroth/Offy	Gears	50	0	$1,135
23	5	24	Shorty Cantlon	Automobile Shippers	Snowberger/Miller	Accident	40	0	$1,505
24	26	43	Henry Banks	Federal Engineering	Miller-Ford/Offy	Lost oil	36	0	$1,250
25	19	66	Al Miller	Preston Tucker	Miller/Miller	Magneto	33	0	$1,370
26	13	14	George Connor	Walsh	Kurtis/Offy	Fuel leak	32	0	$1,465
27	29	38	Mel Hansen	Flavell-Duffy	Adams/Sparks	Pushed-DQ	31	0	$860
28	21	15	Paul Russo	Wolfe Motors, Tulsa	Shaw/Offy	Accident	25	0	$1,080
29	24	44	Charlie Van Acker (R)	Preston Tucker Partners	Stevens/Lencki	Accident	24	0	$800
30	11	53	Milt Fankhauser (R)	Jack Maurer	Stevens/Offy	Stalled	15	0	$1,070

* - complete car name/entrant data not available for all entries
(R) - Indicated Rookie
(W) - Indicates Past Winner

1948

Cliff Bergere, after a couple of spins in the supercharged V8 Novi, felt it was unsafe and left the team. Ralph Hepburn, at fifty-two years old, became the driver. Hepburn was later fatally injured in a practice run on the second day of qualifications. Duke Nalon then became the driver and was dubbed "The Man Who Tamed the Novi."

Rex Mays won the pole for the fourth time at a speed of 130.6 mph, but Nalon's qualification speed was actually higher (131.6 mph), though he started eleventh.

Upon the suggestion of Grace Smith Hulman, Tony Hulman's mother, the tradition of releasing brightly colored balloons just before the start of the race is believed to have started in 1948.

The Chevrolet Fleetmaster Six-Series was driven by three-time "500" winner and Speedway President Wilbur Shaw. This was the first time America's number one selling car company in every year since the 1920's had paced the race.

The race was a battle between Mays, Horn, Nalon and Rose.

Nalon's front-drive Kurtis/Novi had a 112-gallon fuel tank. His team planned on one stop. On lap 101 Nalon pitted, but as a result of aeration in the fuel, his tank was not filled. This resulted in another stop on lap 186 where he stalled his engine, resulting in a best ever third-place finish for a Novi. Ted Horn finished fourth after leading 74 laps. A long pit stop took Horn out of contention for the win.

Rose led for 81 laps total, including all laps from 143 to the finish. His teammate Bill Holland finished second for the second year in a row in the front-wheel-drive Blue Crown Spark Plug Special. Rose averaged a new record of 119.8 mph and pitted just one time in this clear-cut win.

Pat Clancy's six-wheel car, driven by Billy Devore, started twentieth and finished twelfth and was running at the finish.

While attempting to qualify, a rookie named Andy Granatelli crashed and broke a wrist and did not make the race.

A thirty-seven-year-old rookie named Lee Wallard established a new pattern to drive the track, virtually the current "groove." He finished in seventh place.

The Indianapolis Motor Speedway Medical Center was built in 1948.

Ted Horn was fatally injured at Du Quoin, Illinois, in October 1948. He had won three straight AAA championships.

Billy Devore drives the Pat Clancy Special, the only six-wheel car ever, to a twelfth-place finish.

RACE RESULTS FOR THE 1948 INDIANAPOLIS 500

Finish	Start	Car Num.	Driver	Car Name/Entrant*	Make/Model	Status	Laps	Led	Winnings
1	3	3	Mauri Rose (W)	Blue Crown Spark Plug	Deidt/Offy	119.814	200	81	$42,800
2	2	2	Bill Holland	Blue Crown Spark Plug	Deidt/Offy	119.147	200	0	$19,100
3	11	54	Duke Nalon	Novi Grooved Piston	Kurtis/Novi	118.034	200	9	$15,675
4	5	1	Ted Horn	Bennett Brothers	Maserati/Maserati	117.844	200	74	$16,175
5	21	35	Mack Hellings (R)	Don Lee	KK2000/Offy	113.361	200	0	$7,675
6	14	63	Hal Cole	City of Tacoma	KK2000/Offy	111.587	200	0	$5,425
7	28	91	Lee Wallard (R)	Iddings	Meyer/Offy	109.177	200	0	$5,040
8	27	33	Johnny Mauro (R)	Phil Kraft Alfa Romeo	Alfa Romeo/Alfa Romeo	Running	198	0	$4,115
9	23	7	Tommy Hinnershitz	Kurtis-Kraft	Kurtis/Offy	Running	198	0	$4,270
10	4	61	Jimmy Jackson	Howard Keck	Deidt/Offy	Left spindle	193	0	$4,120
11	12	4	Charlie Van Acker	City of South Bend	Stevens/Offy	Running	192	0	$3,120
12	20	19	Billy DeVore	Pat Clancy (6 Wheels)	Kurtis/Offy	Running	190	0	$2,930
13	8	98	Johnny Mantz (R)	Agajanian	KK2000/Offy	Running	185	0	$2,230
14	22	6	Tony Bettenhausen	Belanger Motors	Stevens/Offy	Clutch	167	0	$2,560
15	18	64	Hal Robson	Palmer Construction	Adams/Offy	Valve	164	0	$1,990
16	7	36	Bill Cantrell (R)	Fageol Twin Coach	Stevens/Fageol	Steering	161	0	$1,870
17	10	55	Joie Chitwood	Nyquist	Shaw/Offy	Fuel leak	138	0	$2,375
18	24	53	Bill Sheffler	Jack Maurer	Bromme/Offy	Spark plugs	132	0	$1,830
19	1	5	Rex Mays	Bowes Seal Fast	Kurtis/Winfield	Fuel leak	129	36	$5,775
20	19	31	Chet Miller	Don Lee Mercedes	Mercedes/Mercedes	Oil trouble	108	0	$2,120
21	13	52	Jack McGrath (R)	Sheffler Offy	Bromme/Offy	Stalled	70	0	$1,865
22	29	16	Duane Carter (R)	Belanger Motors	Wetteroth/Offy	Accident	59	0	$1,960
23	32	26	Fred Agabashian	Ross Page	Kurtis/Duray	Oil line	58	0	$1,580
24	9	34	Les Anderson	Kennedy Tank	Kurtis/Offy	Gears	58	0	$1,550
25	33	17	Mel Hansen	Schafer Gear Works	Adams/Sparks	Disqualified	42	0	$1,420
26	15	76	Sam Hanks	Flavell	Adams/Sparks	Clutch	34	0	$1,490
27	30	51	Spider Webb (R)	Fowle Brothers	Bromme/Offy	Oil line	27	0	$1,685
28	17	9	George Connor	Bennett Brothers	Stevens/Miller	Drive shaft	24	0	$1,330
29	6	74	Doc Williams	Clarke Motors	Cooper/Offy	Ignition	19	0	$1,300
30	31	86	Mike Salay (R)	Terman Marine Supply	Wetteroth/Offy	Stalled	13	0	$1,470
31	16	8	Emil Andres	Tuffy's Offy	KK2000/Offy	Steering	11	0	$1,340
32	25	25	Paul Russo	Federal Engineering	Maserati/Maserati	Oil leak	7	0	$1,310
33	26	65	Harry McQuinn	Frank Lynch Motors	Maserati/Maserati	Supercharger	1	0	$1,180

* - complete car name/entrant data not available for all entries
(R) - Indicated Rookie
(W) - Indicates Past Winner

1949

An illustrious group of rookie racers from California showed up: Troy Ruttman, Jim Rathmann, Johnnie Parsons and Manny Ayulo.

A relatively unknown racing fan started an Indianapolis 500 tradition in 1949. Larry Bisceglia would become the first fan in line for the gates to open. He would continue the tradition through 1986 and became a Speedway celebrity.

Rex Mays joined Duke Nalon on the Novi team. Mays finished second twice and won the pole four times during his sterling career, leading in nine of the twelve races in which he competed.

Nalon won the pole at 132.0 mph, with Mays second (129.6 mph), both driving Kurtis/Novis. The Novis were heavy favorites to win their first 500. The confident drivers reputedly made an agreement to split the first and second place winnings.

Nalon led the first twenty-three laps before a rear axle broke in the third turn, resulting in a fiery crash which hospitalized him.

Mays took the lead in the other Novi, but engine trouble sidelined him after forty-eight laps.

Lee Wallard took the lead for a short time until gear problems sidelined him after fifty-five laps. Bill Holland took the lead and led the rest of the way in his Blue Crown Spark Plug Special. Holland averaged a race record 121.3 mph and led 146 laps.

Second place went to Johnnie Parsons, with George Connor in a rear-wheel-drive Blue Crown Special in third place.

Mauri Rose was running second but dropped out on lap 191 with magneto problems and finished thirteenth. This would be the last race Rose drove for Lou Moore.

Holland's win made it three consecutive victories for car owner Lou Moore. In the past eight races, Lou Moore's cars had finished first five times, second twice, third twice and fifth and ninth once each.

Jimmy Jackson and Johnny Mantz completed the race without a pit stop. Jackson finished sixth and Mantz seventh respectively.

On race day, WFBM TV Channel 6 became the first television station to broadcast locally; it carried the entire race "live" to central Indiana. Earl Townsend Jr. was the primary announcer for the broadcast. After two years the local broadcasts were discontinued as a result of track attendance dropping by approximately 20%.

The great Rex Mays was fatally injured in an accident at the Del Mar, California track in November of 1949. Attempting to avoid a crashed car, Mays' car flipped throwing him from the cockpit. A trailing car struck him.

Rex Houston Mays, Jr. was a two-time AAA champion. He won the pole starting position for the Indianapolis 500 four times (1935, 1936, 1940, 1948). He finished in second place in 1940 and 1941.

Duke Nalon crashes the Novi as eventual winner Bill Holland passes through the flame trail.

RACE RESULTS FOR THE 1949 INDIANAPOLIS 500

Finish	Start	Car Num.	Driver	Car Name/Entrant*	Make/Model	Status	Laps	Led	Winnings
1	4	7	Bill Holland	Blue Crown Spark Plug	Deidt/Offy	121.327	200	146	$51,575
2	12	12	Johnnie Parsons (R)	Kurtis-Kraft	Kurtis/Offy	119.785	200	0	$18,250
3	6	22	George Connor	Blue Crown Spark Plug	Lesovsky/Offy	119.595	200	0	$11,675
4	13	2	Myron Fohr (R)	Marchese	Marchese/Offy	118.791	200	0	$8,575
5	16	77	Joie Chitwood	Wolfe	KK2000/Offy	118.757	200	0	$6,950
6	7	61	Jimmy Jackson	Howard Keck	Deidt/Offy	117.870	200	0	$5,625
7	9	98	Johnny Mantz	Agajanian	KK2000/Offy	117.142	200	0	$4,690
8	19	19	Paul Russo	Tuffy's Offy	Silnes/Offy	111.862	200	0	$4,940
9	32	9	Emil Andres	Tuffy's Offy	Silnes/Offy	Running	197	0	$4,420
10	24	71	Norm Houser (R)	Troy Oil Co.	Langley/Offy	Running	181	0	$4,075
11	21	68	Jim Rathmann (R)	Pioneer Auto Repair	Wetteroth/Offy	Running	175	0	$3,195
12	18	64	Troy Ruttman (R)	Carter	Wetteroth/Offy	Running	151	0	$3,150
13	10	3	Mauri Rose (W)	Blue Crown Spark Plug	Deidt/Offy	Magneto strap	192	0	$2,605
14	5	17	Duane Carter	Belanger Motors	Stevens/Offy	Steering	182	0	$2,610
15	15	29	Duke Dinsmore	Norm Olson	Olson/Offy	Radius rod	174	0	$2,565
16	14	8	Mack Hellings	Don Lee	KK2000/Offy	Valves	172	0	$2,570
17	22	4	Bill Sheffler	Sheffler	Bromme/Offy	Rod	160	0	$2,175
18	28	32	Johnny McDowell (R)	Iddings	Meyer/Offy	Magneto	142	0	$2,005
19	11	14	Hal Cole	Gancor	KK2000/Offy	Rod bearing	117	0	$1,975
20	25	38	George Fonder (R)	Ray Brady	Adams/Sparks	Valve	116	0	$1,945
21	30	74	Bill Cantrell	Kennedy Tank	Kurtis/Offy	Drive shaft	95	0	$2,315
22	17	57	Jackie Holmes (R)	Pat Clancy (6 Wheels)	Kurtis/Offy	Drive shaft	65	0	$2,410
23	20	6	Lee Wallard	IRC Maserati	Maserati/Maserati	Gears	55	19	$4,405
24	29	69	Bayliss Levrett (R)	Wynn's Oil	KK2000/Offy	Drain plug	52	0	$2,375
25	2	5	Rex Mays	Novi Mobil	Kurtis/Novi	Engine	48	12	$3,470
26	3	33	Jack McGrath	City of Tacoma	KK2000/Offy	Oil pump	39	0	$2,115
27	31	15	Fred Agabashian	IRC Maserati	Maserati/Maserati	Overheating	38	0	$2,035
28	33	52	Manuel Ayulo (R)	Sheffler	Bromme/Offy	Rod	24	0	$1,805
29	1	54	Duke Nalon	Novi Mobil	Kurtis/Novi	Accident	23	23	$5,650
30	23	18	Sam Hanks	Love Machine & Tool	KK2000/Offy	Oil leak	20	0	$1,645
31	27	10	Charlie Van Acker	Redmer	Stevens/Offy	Accident	10	0	$1,615
32	8	26	George Lynch (R)	Automobile Shippers	Rassey/Offy	Accident	1	0	$1,585
33	26	37	Spider Webb	Grancor	Bromme/Offy	DNS-Transmission	0	0	$1,555

* - complete car name/entrant data not available for all entries
(R) - Indicated Rookie
(W) - Indicates Past Winner

1950

Lou Moore brought a four-car team, with Bill Holland and George Connor in the same cars they drove in 1949. Lee Wallard drove a rear-wheel-drive dirt track car and Tony Bettenhausen was in the former Mauri Rose car.

Nalon was back driving a Novi and Chet Miller was his teammate.

Novi owner Lew Welch threatened not to enter unless the prize money was increased. He eventually did enter two cars, but failed to qualify either one.

Rookie Walt Faulkner took the pole right at six p.m. on Pole Day from mentor Fred Agabashian, who started second. Faulkner set a one-lap record of 136.0 mph and a four-lap average of 134.3 mph, which broke the late Ralph Hepburn's four-year-old record. Johnnie Parsons qualified in the fifth starting position in the Wynn's Friction Proofing car.

Twenty drivers passed rookie tests in 1950.

In 1949, rookies had put streamers on their goggles so other drivers would know they were rookies. In 1950, three strips of colored tape were located on the back of a rookie's car until the rookie test was passed.

Bill Vukovich, a rookie from Fresno, California, passed his rookie test in Shaw's winning Maserati of 1939 and 1940. He failed to qualify for the race.

In 1950, the "500" was included in the brand new World Driving Championship. The "500" results would award points toward the World Driving Championship through 1960.

The race ended at 345 miles (138 laps) because of rain.

With rain falling, Seth Klein, at the order of Chief Steward Tommy Milton, displayed the checkered flag and the red flag to Johnnie Parsons to signal completion of the race at 138 laps. This was only the second time the race had not gone the distance.

Bill Holland finished second and Mauri Rose, third.

Holland had now finished second, second, first and second in his first four "500s."

Parsons had finished second in 1949 and gone on to win the AAA National Championship.

Johnnie Parsons' crew supposedly spotted a small crack in the engine block on race morning. Parsons' apparent plan was to go out and lead as many laps as the engine held together for the lap prize money. His strategy was successful, as he led 115 of the 138 laps and was in the lead by more than a lap when the race was called. Parsons averaged a record of 124 mph.

It is fact that Mike Nazaruk drove the Parsons' winning car in the 1951 "500" and finished second with the same "cracked block" engine. The supposed "crack" was likely porosity in the metal.

This was the first win for the innovative car builder Frank Kurtis. His cars incorporated lightweight tubular frames, independent front suspension and torsion bars instead of springs.

In 1950 the movie To Please a Lady was filmed at the Speedway with Clark Gable and Barbara Stanwyck.

Johnnie Parsons drove his Kurtis/Offy to the win in 1950.

RACE RESULTS FOR THE 1950 INDIANAPOLIS 500

Finish	Start	Car Num.	Driver	Car Name/Entrant*	Make/Model	Status	Laps	Led	Winnings
1	5	1	Johnnie Parsons	Wynn's Friction Proofing	Kurtis/Offy	124.022	138	115	$57,459
2	10	3	Bill Holland (W)	Blue Crown Spark Plug	Deidt/Offy	Running	137	8	$21,899
3	3	31	Mauri Rose (W)	Howard Keck	Deidt/Offy	Running	137	15	$15,269
4	12	54	Cecil Green (R)	John Zink	KK3000/Offy	Running	137	0	$10,964
5	9	17	Joie Chitwood	Wolfe	KK2000/Offy	Running	136	0	$8,789
6	23	8	Lee Wallard	Blue Crown Spark Plug	Moore/Offy	Running	136	0	$6,864
7	1	98	Walt Faulkner (R)	Grant Piston Ring	KK2000/Offy	Running	135	0	$7,664
8	4	5	George Connor	Blue Crown Spark Plug	Lesovsky/Offy	Running	135	0	$5,039
9	19	7	Paul Russo	Russo-Nichels	Nichels/Offy	Running	135	0	$4,989
10	11	59	Pat Flaherty (R)	Granatelli-Sabourin	KK3000/Offy	Running	135	0	$4,639
11	16	2	Myron Fohr	Bardahl	Marchese/Offy	Running	133	0	$3,734
12	13	18	Duane Carter	Belanger Motors	Stevens/Offy	Running	133	0	$3,464
13	26	15	Mack Hellings	Tuffy's Offy	Silnes/Offy	Running	132	0	$2,979
14	6	49	Jack McGrath	Hinkle	KK3000/Offy	Accident	131	0	$2,799
15	24	55	Troy Ruttman	Bowes Seal Fast	Lesovsky/Offy	Running	130	0	$2,979
16	31	75	Gene Hartley (R)	Troy Oil	Langley/Offy	Running	128	0	$2,509
17	27	22	Jimmy Davies (R)	Pat Clancy	Ewing/Offy	Running	128	0	$2,339
18	33	62	Johnny McDowell	Pete Wales	KK2000/Offy	Running	128	0	$2,769
19	20	4	Walt Brown	Tuffy's Offy	Silnes/Offy	Running	127	0	$2,339
20	14	21	Spider Webb	Fadely-Anderson	Maserati/Offy	Running	126	0	$2,509
21	15	81	Jerry Hoyt (R)	Morris	KK2000/Offy	Running	125	0	$2,379
22	29	27	Walt Ader (R)	Sampson	Rae/Offy	Running	123	0	$2,149
23	30	77	Jackie Holmes	Norm Olson	Olson/Offy	Accident	123	0	$2,119
24	28	76	Jim Rathmann	Pioneer Auto Repair	Wetteroth/Offy	Running	122	0	$2,089
25	21	12	Henry Banks	I.R.C.	Maserati/Offy	Oil line	112	0	$2,059
26	22	67	Bill Schindler (R)	Automobile Shippers	Rassey/Offy	Universal joint	111	0	$2,604
27	17	24	Bayliss Levrett	Palmer	Adams/Offy	Oil pressure	108	0	$2,424
28	2	28	Fred Agabashian	Wynn's Friction Proofing	KK3000/Offy	Oil line	64	0	$2,444
29	32	61	Jimmy Jackson	Cummins Diesel	Kurtis/Cummins	Supercharger	52	0	$1,939
30	25	23	Sam Hanks	Merz Engineering	KK2000/Offy	Oil pressure	42	0	$2,134
31	8	14	Tony Bettenhausen	Blue Crown Spark Plug	Deidt/Offy	Wheel	30	0	$1,879
32	18	45	Dick Rathmann (R)	City of Glendale	Watson/Offy	Stalled	25	0	$2,149
33	7	69	Duke Dinsmore	Brown Motor Co.	KK2000/Offy	Oil leak	10	0	$1,844

* - complete car name/entrant data not available for all entries
(R) - Indicated Rookie
(W) - Indicates Past Winner

1951

Duke Nalon won the pole in a Kurtis/Novi at 136.5 mph and Lee Wallard started second (135.0 mph), but the fastest qualifier was Walt Faulkner (136.9 mph), in an Agajanian dirt car, for the second year in a row. Faulkner set a track record, but would start fourteenth.

Wallard led 159 laps total in his lightweight dirt track-type car but had his share of problems during the race: right rear shock absorber mount broke; exhaust pipe broke; and lost brakes with 12 laps to go. The tremendous effort required to overcome these obstacles resulted in Wallard losing fifteen pounds and receiving treatment at the infield hospital after the race.

Wallard still won by one minute and forty-seven seconds over Mike Nazaruk and averaged a new race record of 126.2 mph. He led from lap eighty-one to the finish. Wallard became the first winner to finish the race in less than four hours and was able to complete the race with only one pit stop.

Wallard sat up on the headrest as he came down the pits victorious in a memorable Indianapolis Motor Speedway moment.

Attrition was very high and there were only eight cars running at the finish, with only two of the twenty-five eliminated because of accidents.

Bill Holland's remarkable finishing streak came to an end as he was not in the line-up in 1951 or 1952 because of disputes with the American Automobile Association.

Veteran Tony Bettenhausen turned down the eventual winning Belanger Motors dirt car, preferring to drive the 1947 and 1948 front-drive winning car. His decision opened the seat to Lee Wallard. Bettenhausen spun out late in the race while running fifth and finished in ninth place.

Lee Wallard received near fatal burns in a sprint car race in Reading, Pennsylvania a few days after the "500" and required twenty-seven skin grafts. Wallard returned to the Speedway in 1954, but was unable to qualify.

Mauri Rose retired in January of 1952 at forty-five years old after starting in fifteen "500s" and winning three times. Rose finished in fourteenth place in his final race after his wheel collapsed and his Deidt/Offy flipped while running in third place.

Lee Wallard—the "Cinderella Man"—wins the "500" at forty years of age.

RACE RESULTS FOR THE 1951 INDIANAPOLIS 500

Finish	Start	Car Num.	Driver	Car Name/Entrant*	Make/Model	Status	Laps	Led	Winnings
1	2	99	Lee Wallard	Belanger Motors	Kurtis/Offy	126.244	200	159	$63,612
2	7	83	Mike Nazaruk (R)	Jim Robbins	Kurtis/Offy	125.302	200	0	$21,362
3	3	9	Jack McGrath	Hinkle	KK3000/Offy	124.745	200	11	$14,962
4	31	57	Andy Linden (R)	Leitenberger	Silnes-Sherman/Offy	123.812	200	0	$10,012
5	29	52	Bobby Ball (R)	Blakely Oil	Schroeder/Offy	123.709	200	0	$8,612
6	17	1	Henry Banks	Blue Crown Spark Plug	Moore/Offy	123.304	200	0	$6,962
7	24	68	Carl Forberg (R)	Automobile Shippers	KK3000/Offy	Running	193	0	$5,862
8	4	27	Duane Carter	Mobilgas	Deidt/Offy	Running	180	0	$5,162
9	9	5	Tony Bettenhausen	Mobiloil	Deidt/Offy	Spun	178	0	$4,662
10	1	18	Duke Nalon	Novi Purelube	Kurtis/Novi	Stalled	151	0	$5,062
11	22	69	Gene Force (R)	Brown Motor Co.	KK2000/Offy	Vibration	142	0	$3,182
12	12	25	Sam Hanks	Schmidt	KK3000/Offy	Rod	135	0	$3,412
13	16	10	Bill Schindler	Chapman	KK2000/Offy	Rod	129	0	$3,142
14	5	16	Mauri Rose (W)	Pennzoil	Deidt/Offy	Accident	126	0	$3,022
15	14	2	Walt Faulkner	Agajanian Grant Piston Ring	Kuzma/Offy	Crankshaft	123	0	$4,552
16	27	76	Jimmy Davies	Parks	Silnes-Pawl/Offy	Drive gears	110	25	$5,482
17	11	59	Fred Agabashian	Granatelli-Bardahl	KK3000/Offy	Clutch	109	0	$2,862
18	15	73	Carl Scarborough (R)	McNamara	KK2000/Offy	Axle	100	0	$2,642
19	33	71	Bill Mackey (R)	Karl Hall	Stevens/Offy	Clutch shaft	97	0	$2,212
20	19	8	Chuck Stevenson (R)	Bardahl	Marchese/Offy	Caught fire	93	0	$2,182
21	8	3	Johnnie Parsons (W)	Wynn's Friction Proofing	KK3000/Offy	Magneto	87	0	$2,252
22	10	4	Cecil Green	John Zink	KK3000/Offy	Piston	80	5	$2,622
23	6	98	Troy Ruttman	Agajanian Featherweight	KK2000/Offy	Crankshaft	78	0	$2,092
24	32	6	Duke Dinsmore	Brown Motors Co.	Schroeder/Offy	Overheating	73	0	$2,162
25	28	32	Chet Miller	Novi Purelube	Kurtis/Novi	Ignition	56	0	$2,532
26	13	44	Walt Brown	Federal Engineering	KK3000/Offy	Magneto	55	0	$2,302
27	25	48	Rodger Ward (R)	Deck Manufacturing Co.	Bromme/Offy	Oil line	34	0	$2,472
28	18	23	Cliff Griffith (R)	Morris	KK2000/Offy	Rear axle	30	0	$2,042
29	20	81	Bill Vukovich (R)	Central Excavating	Trevis/Offy	Oil tank	29	0	$1,912
30	21	22	George Connor	Blue Crown Spark Plug	Lesovsky/Offy	Drive shaft	29	0	$1,882
31	23	19	Mack Hellings	Tuffanelli-Derrico	Deidt/Offy	Piston	18	0	$1,852
32	26	12	Johnny McDowell	W & J	Maserati/Offy	Fuel tank	15	0	$2,222
33	30	26	Joe James (R)	Bob Estes Lincoln-Mercury	Watson/Offy	Drive shaft	8	0	$2,092

* - complete car name/entrant data not available for all entries
(R) - Indicated Rookie
(W) - Indicates Past Winner

1952

The four-day qualifying format on two weekends was introduced for the 1952 500.

Freddie Agabashian won the pole at a record speed of 138.0 mph in the Cummins Engine Kurtis-Kraft car powered by a 401-cubic-inch six-cylinder turbocharged truck diesel engine. Frank Kurtis designed the car with an extremely low center of gravity. By placing the Cummins diesel engine on its side, Agabashian's seat rode just four inches above the race track. The car weighed approximately 2400 pounds versus the 1800-1900 pounds for other cars.

Bill Vukovich (138.2 mph) and Chet Miller (139.0 mph) eventually qualified faster, but started eighth and twenty-seventh.

Qualifying was extended to Monday as a result of two unfilled starting positions because of rain on the final Sunday.

The eventual 1952 and 1953 World Driving Champion, Alberto Ascari, qualified nineteenth and finished thirty-first after a wheel broke on his Ferrari. This was the Ferrari team's only attempt at the "500."

Owner/driver Johnny Mauro had purchased a Ferrari, but was unable to qualify his Kennedy Tank Special Ferrari.

The Novis of Chet Miller and Duke Nalon were eliminated early because of supercharger problems, while Agabashian's run ended before the halfway point with turbocharger problems.

Bill Vukovich and Troy Ruttman made it a two-car race. Vukovich led 150 laps, while Ruttman led 44 laps. Ruttman overcame a pit fire on his first stop that could have easily taken him out of the race. He sustained serious burns on his right arm but was able to continue.

Vukovich led by around thirty seconds for a good part of the second half of the race in his Kurtis-Kraft roadster owned by Howard Keck.

Vukovich began having steering problems, and at 190 laps, Ruttman had cut the lead to twenty-two seconds.

On lap 192, with a nineteen second lead, Vukovich's steering arm broke and he was eliminated. Ruttman went on to win in his Eddie Kuzma-built dirt-track car with a record average speed of 128.9 mph.

Ruttman became the youngest winner at twenty-two years and eighty-six days old in his fourth "500." Ruttman was driving for J.C. Agajanian. He reportedly weighed just under 250 pounds at the time of his Indianapolis win.

Jim Rathmann finished second, driving for the Granatelli brothers, but trailed the winner by more than four minutes.

Nineteen-fifty-two was the first race in history in which no relief drivers were used.

Art Cross finished fifth and received the inaugural Stark & Wetzel Rookie of the Year Award.

Bill Vukovich was referred to as the "Mad Russian," but was actually of Yugoslavian parentage.

The Indianapolis Motor Speedway Radio Network was started in 1952 with Sid Collins as the lead broadcaster.

Troy Ruttman was seriously injured in August of 1952 in a sprint car accident in Cedar Rapids, Iowa. A severely injured right arm led to an eighteen-month rehabilitation before returning to Indy cars.

Troy Ruttman with owner J.C. Agajanian, in Stetson and bolo tie, Chief mechanic Clay Smith and crew.

RACE RESULTS FOR THE 1952 INDIANAPOLIS 500

Finish	Start	Car Num.	Driver	Car Name/Entrant*	Make/Model	Status	Laps	Led	Winnings
1	7	98	Troy Ruttman	Agajanian	Kuzma/Offy	128.922	200	44	$61,743
2	10	59	Jim Rathmann	Grancor-Wynn's Oil	KK3000/Offy	126.723	200	0	$24,368
3	5	18	Sam Hanks	Bardahl	KK3000/Offy	125.580	200	0	$14,768
4	6	1	Duane Carter	Belanger Motors	Lesovsky/Offy	125.259	200	0	$11,818
5	20	33	Art Cross (R)	Bowes Seal Fast	KK4000/Offy	124.292	200	0	$9,718
6	21	77	Jimmy Bryan (R)	Schmidt	KK3000/Offy	123.914	200	0	$7,468
7	23	37	Jimmy Reece (R)	John Zink	KK4000/Offy	123.312	200	0	$6,368
8	14	54	George Connor	Federal Engineering	KK3000/Offy	122.595	200	0	$6,118
9	9	22	Cliff Griffith	Tom Sarafoff	KK2000/Offy	122.402	200	0	$5,768
10	31	5	Johnnie Parsons (W)	Jim Robbins	Kurtis/Offy	121.789	200	0	$5,518
11	3	4	Jack McGrath	Hinkle	KK3000/Offy	121.428	200	6	$4,263
12	26	29	Jim Rigsby (R)	Bob Estes	Watson/Offy	120.587	200	0	$3,193
13	16	14	Joe James	Bardahl	KK4000/Offy	120.108	200	0	$2,923
14	15	7	Bill Schindler	Chapman	Stevens/Offy	119.280	200	0	$2,903
15	13	65	George Fonder	Leitenberger	Silnes-Sherman/Offy	Running	197	0	$2,683
16	24	81	Eddie Johnson (R)	Central Excavating	Trevis/Offy	Running	193	0	$2,663
17	8	26	Bill Vukovich	Fuel Injection	KK500A/Offy	Steering	191	150	$18,693
18	11	16	Chuck Stevenson	Springfield Welding/Clay Smith	KK4000/Offy	Running	187	0	$2,623
19	12	2	Henry Banks	Blue Crown Spark Plug	Lesovsky/Offy	Running	184	0	$2,693
20	28	8	Manuel Ayulo	Coast Grain Co.	Lesovsky/Offy	Running	184	0	$2,763
21	33	31	Johnny McDowell	McDowell	Kurtis/Offy	Running	182	0	$2,333
22	29	48	Spider Webb	Granatelli Racing Enterprises	Bromme/Offy	Oil line	162	0	$2,603
23	22	34	Rodger Ward	Federal Engineering	KK4000/Offy	Oil leak	130	0	$2,273
24	30	27	Tony Bettenhausen	Blue Crown Spark Plug	Deidt/Offy	Stalled	93	0	$2,443
25	4	36	Duke Nalon	Novi Pure Oil	Kurtis/Novi	Supercharger	84	0	$2,413
26	32	73	Bob Sweikert (R)	McNamara	KK2000/Offy	Differential	77	0	$2,183
27	1	28	Fred Agabashian	Cummins Diesel	Kurtis/Cummins	Supercharger	71	0	$2,653
28	18	67	Gene Hartley	Mel-Rae	KK4000/Offy	Wheels	65	0	$2,123
29	25	93	Bob Scott (R)	Morris	KK2000/Offy	Drive shaft	49	0	$2,093
30	27	21	Chet Miller	Novi Pure Oil	Kurtis/Novi	Supercharger	41	0	$3,663
31	19	12	Alberto Ascari (R)	Ferrari	Ferrari/Ferrari	Spun out	40	0	$1,983
32	17	55	Bobby Ball	Ansted Rotary	Stevens/Offy	Gear case	34	0	$2,003
33	2	9	Andy Linden	Miracle Power	KK4000/Offy	Sump pump	20	0	$2,273

* - complete car name/entrant data not available for all entries
(R) - Indicated Rookie
(W) - Indicates Past Winner

1953

Novi driver Chet Miller, "the Dean of the Speedway", was fatally injured on the day before the first qualification day in an accident similar to Ralph Hepburn's in 1948. Miller had raced in sixteen "500s," the same number as Cliff Bergere, which was the record for the time. He was fifty years old.

Bill Vukovich won the pole in Howard Keck's Fuel Injection Special with a speed of 138.4 mph, while completing his qualifying run in a driving rainstorm.

Nineteen forty-nine winner Bill Holland finally returned to the Speedway and qualified late, starting twenty-eighth but actually with the second fastest time. He finished fifteenth.

This was the hottest "500" in years, with temperatures in the mid-nineties and track temperatures up to 130 degrees.

Vukovich dominated the race, leading 195 laps, only losing the lead during his first pit stop. He led from lap 54 to the checker. Vukovich averaged 127.7 mph.

Vukovich and second-place finisher Art Cross did not use relief, but many drivers did. Vukovich led Cross by three minutes and thirty seconds at the checker.

Gene Hartley crashed his car, then was driving relief and crashed a second car.

The lap prize was increased to $150 per lap led, up from the $100 awarded since 1920.

Carl Scarborough collapsed from heat exhaustion during a pit stop on lap seventy and later died. Bob Scott finished the race in twelfth position in Scarborough's McNamara Kurtis-Kraft dirt-track car.

Nineteen fifty-three was the first year the race was broadcast in its entirety on the recently formed Indianapolis Motor Speedway Radio Network.

Jimmy Daywalt, of Wabash, Indiana, finished sixth in the Sumar Special and won Rookie of the Year.

The wear and tear shows as winner Bill Vukovich walks back to his garage on a very hot race day.

RACE RESULTS FOR THE 1953 INDIANAPOLIS 500

Finish	Start	Car Num.	Driver	Car Name/Entrant*	Make/Model	Status	Laps	Led	Winnings
1	1	14	Bill Vukovich	Fuel Injection	KK500A/Offy	127.740	200	195	$89,497
2	12	16	Art Cross	Springfield Welding/Clay Smith	KK4000/Offy	126.827	200	0	$27,297
3	9	3	Sam Hanks	Bardahl	KK4000/Offy	126.465	200	3	$16,422
4	2	59	Fred Agabashian	Grancor-Elgin Piston Pin	KK500B/Offy	126.219	200	1	$12,947
5	3	5	Jack McGrath	Hinkle	KK4000/Offy	124.556	200	0	$10,622
6	21	48	Jimmy Daywalt (R)	Sumar	KK3000/Offy	124.379	200	0	$8,197
7	25	2	Jim Rathmann	Travelon Trailer	KK500B/Offy	124.072	200	1	$6,847
8	20	12	Ernie McCoy (R)	Chapman	Stevens/Offy	123.404	200	0	$5,947
9	6	98	Tony Bettenhausen	Agajanian	Kuzma/Offy	Accident	196	0	$5,647
10	32	53	Jimmy Davies	Pat Clancy	KK500B/Offy	Running	193	0	$5,547
11	26	9	Duke Nalon	Novi Governor	Kurtis/Novi	Spun out	191	0	$3,317
12	19	73	Carl Scarborough	McNamara	KK2000/Offy	Running	190	0	$3,147
13	4	88	Manuel Ayulo	Schmidt	Kuzma/Offy	Rod	184	0	$3,177
14	31	8	Jimmy Bryan	Blakely Oil	Schroeder/Offy	Running	183	0	$3,057
15	28	49	Bill Holland (W)	Crawford	KK500B/Offy	Cam gear	177	0	$3,237
16	10	92	Rodger Ward	M.A. Walker Electric	Kurtis/Offy	Stalled	177	0	$2,917
17	14	23	Walt Faulkner	Automobile Shippers	KK500A/Offy	Running	176	0	$2,497
18	22	22	Marshall Teague (R)	Hart Fullerton	KK4000/Offy	Oil Leak	169	0	$2,377
19	18	62	Spider Webb	Lubri-Loy	KK3000/Offy	Oil Leak	166	0	$2,347
20	29	51	Bob Sweikert	Dean Van Lines	Kuzma/Offy	Radius rod	151	0	$2,717
21	23	83	Mike Nazaruk	Kalamazoo	Turner/Offy	Stalled	146	0	$2,287
22	24	77	Pat Flaherty	Schmidt	KK3000/Offy	Accident	115	0	$2,257
23	7	55	Jerry Hoyt	John Zink	KK4000/Offy	Overheating	107	0	$2,227
24	27	4	Duane Carter	Miracle Power	Lesovsky/Offy	Ignition	94	0	$2,197
25	17	7	Paul Russo	Federal Engineering	KK3000/Offy	Magneto	89	0	$2,167
26	8	21	Johnnie Parsons (W)	Belond Equa-Flow	KK500B/Offy	Crankshaft	86	0	$2,637
27	15	38	Don Freeland (R)	Bob Estes	Watson/Offy	Accident	76	0	$2,107
28	13	41	Gene Hartley	Federal Engineering	KK4000/Offy	Accident	53	0	$2,077
29	16	97	Chuck Stevenson	Agajanian	Kuzma/Offy	Fuel Leak	42	0	$2,047
30	30	99	Cal Niday (R)	Miracle Power	Kurtis/Offy	Magneto	30	0	$2,317
31	11	29	Bob Scott	Belond Equa-Flow	Bromme/Offy	Oil Leak	14	0	$2,187
32	33	56	Johnny Thomson (R)	Dr. Sabourin	Del Roy-Allen/Offy	Ignition	6	0	$1,907
33	5	32	Andy Linden	Cop-Sil-Loy	Stevens/Offy	Accident	3	0	$2,127

*- complete car name/entrant data not available for all entries
(R) - Indicated Rookie
(W) - Indicates Past Winner

1954

Jack McGrath eclipsed the 140 mph barrier and won the pole with a fast lap record of 141.287 mph and a record average of 141.0 mph.

The second fastest qualifier and thirteenth-place starter was Cal Niday, a professional barber who at seventeen years old lost a leg in a motorcycle accident.

Two-time pole sitter Duke Nalon, in the only Novi at the track, failed to make the race. He qualified due to a misunderstanding with a speed that eventually did not hold up.

Bill Vukovich struggled in qualifying and actually made the race on the third day of qualifications, starting nineteenth.

The entire field was powered by Offenhausers, marking the first time every car was powered by the same type of engine.

The Dodge Royal 500 paced the race, giving Dodge it's first pacer in its forty-year history.

Jack McGrath led the first forty-four laps, but had to stop for tires because his fast pace caused excessive tire wear.

An extremely hot and humid race day resulted in twenty-eight driver changes involving fifteen cars.

The second half of the race was a battle between Vukovich and Jimmy Bryan. Bryan, driving a dirt car, ended up making three stops to Vukovich's two. After Bryan's last stop on lap 149, Vukovich led to the finish, averaging a record 130.8 mph in his second consecutive win. He became only the third driver to win back-to-back races.

Vukovich led ninety laps, McGrath, forty-seven, and Bryan, forty-six.

Flagman Seth Klein had retired and Bill Vandewater had taken over the flagging duties.

Vukovich and Bryan were nearly side by side at the finish, with Vukovich a lap ahead, prompting Vandewater to wave both the checkered and white flags simultaneously.

Bryan, who battled a rough ride for the last forty laps due to a broken shock absorber, led third-place Jack McGrath by seven seconds at the checker.

After being out of an Indy car for nearly two years, Troy Ruttman qualified for the eleventh starting position and finished an impressive fourth.

Art Cross' car had a total of five drivers that day, finishing eleventh. Cross started twenty-seventh and actually took the lead on lap fifty-six, but began the relief driver sequence when he personally overheated on lap seventy-nine.

Rookie of the Year went to ninth-place finisher Larry Crockett.

The first car out of the race was Bill Homeier after seventy-four laps due to a pit accident, a record for the most laps completed by a last-place-finishing car.

The Howard Keck Fuel Injection Special winning car for Vukovich in 1953 and 1954 was retired.

On October 30, 1954, Wilbur Shaw, president and general manager of the Indianapolis Motor Speedway, was fatally injured in a plane accident near Decatur, Indiana. Anton (Tony) Hulman Jr. did not replace Shaw, but stepped into his role personally, as well as handling his other duties in the family-owned companies.

A happy "Mad Russian" after winning in consecutive years, Bill Vukovich celebrates in the "bull pen."

RACE RESULTS FOR THE 1954 INDIANAPOLIS 500

Finish	Start	Car Num.	Driver	Car Name/Entrant*	Make/Model	Status	Laps	Led	Winnings
1	19	14	Bill Vukovich (W)	Fuel Injection	KK500A/Offy	130.840	200	90	$74,935
2	3	9	Jimmy Bryan	Dean Van Lines	Kuzma/Offy	130.178	200	46	$35,885
3	1	2	Jack McGrath	Hinkle	KK500C/Offy	130.086	200	47	$27,410
4	11	34	Troy Ruttman (W)	Automobile Shippers	KK500A/Offy	129.218	200	0	$12,710
5	14	73	Mike Nazaruk	McNamara	KK500C/Offy	128.923	200	0	$10,935
6	24	77	Fred Agabashian	Merz Engineering	KK500C/Offy	128.711	200	0	$8,035
7	6	7	Don Freeland	Bob Estes	Phillips/Offy	128.474	200	0	$6,885
8	32	5	Paul Russo	Ansted Rotary	KK500A/Offy	128.037	200	0	$6,260
9	25	28	Larry Crockett (R)	Federal Engineering	KK3000/Offy	126.899	200	0	$6,985
10	13	24	Cal Niday	Jim Robbins	Stevens/Offy	126.895	200	0	$6,310
11	27	45	Art Cross	Bardahl	KK4000/Offy	126.232	200	8	$5,255
12	5	98	Chuck Stevenson	Agajanian	Kuzma/Offy	Running	199	0	$3,710
13	22	88	Manuel Ayulo	Schmidt	KK500C/Offy	Running	197	0	$3,465
14	9	17	Bob Sweikert	Lutes	KK4000/Offy	Running	197	0	$3,345
15	8	16	Duane Carter	Automobile Shippers	KK4000/Offy	Running	196	0	$3,225
16	20	32	Ernie McCoy	Crawford	KK500B/Offy	Running	194	0	$3,105
17	7	25	Jimmy Reece	Malloy	Pankratz/Offy	Running	194	0	$2,985
18	31	27	Ed Elisian (R)	Chapman	Stevens/Offy	Running	193	0	$2,865
19	33	71	Frank Armi (R)	Martin Brothers	Silnes/Offy	Running	193	0	$2,835
20	10	1	Sam Hanks	Bardahl	KK4000/Offy	Spun out	191	1	$2,955
21	12	35	Pat O'Connor (R)	Hopkins	KK500C/Offy	Spun out	181	0	$3,275
22	16	12	Rodger Ward	Dr. Sabourin	Allen/Offy	Stalled	172	0	$2,945
23	17	31	Gene Hartley	John Zink	KK4000/Offy	Clutch	168	0	$2,815
24	4	43	Johnny Thomson	Chapman	Nichels/Offy	Stalled	165	0	$2,885
25	23	74	Andy Linden	Brown Motor Co.	Schroeder/Offy	Torsion bar	165	0	$3,655
26	30	99	Jerry Hoyt	Belanger Motors	Kurtis/Offy	Engine	130	0	$2,625
27	2	19	Jimmy Daywalt	Sumar	KK500C/Offy	Accident	111	8	$4,445
28	28	38	Jim Rathmann	Bardahl	KK500C/Offy	Accident	110	0	$2,765
29	21	10	Tony Bettenhausen	Mel Wiggers	KK500C/Offy	Bearing	105	0	$2,535
30	29	65	Spider Webb	Advance Muffler	Bromme/Offy	Fuel pump	104	0	$2,605
31	26	33	Len Duncan (R)	Brady	Schroeder/Offy	Brake cylinder	101	0	$2,875
32	15	15	Johnnie Parsons (W)	Belond Equa-Flow Exhaust	KK500B/Offy	Engine died	79	0	$2,745
33	18	51	Bill Homeier (R)	Jones & Maley	KK500C/Offy	Pit Accident	74	0	$2,415

* - complete car name/entrant data not available for all entries
(R) - Indicated Rookie
(W) - Indicates Past Winner

1955

Bill Vukovich drove for Lindsey Hopkins as Howard Keck, his winning owner the previous two years, was out of racing.

Hopkins owned cars at Indy each year from 1951 to 1982.

Jimmy Daywalt's streamlined Sumar Special arrived at the track in early May more resembling a sports car. As the month progressed, streamlining, such as fenders and enclosed cockpit, was removed to gain speed and handling. Daywalt would eventually start seventeenth and finish ninth.

The first day of qualifying was very windy. The teams made an informal agreement not to go out, assuming the next day would become pole day.

Jerry Hoyt and his team were supposedly unaware of the "agreement" and went out very late in the day and qualified at 140.0 mph to win the pole. Tony Bettenhausen qualified as time nearly expired but was slower than Hoyt.

Manny Ayulo crashed in practice on the second day of qualifications and died.

Jack McGrath was the fastest qualifier at 142.6 mph, but started in the third position.

After qualifications were complete, there were ten drivers with speeds faster than Jerry Hoyt, the pole sitter.

Bob Sweikert actually tore down his own engine after qualifying in the fourteenth position and reassembled it for the race when A.J. Watson, his chief mechanic, was called home for a family emergency.

Jack McGrath took the early lead. Vukovich and McGrath traded the lead through the first twenty-six laps before Vukovich took control.

On lap fifty-seven Rodger Ward, driving Ruttman's 1952-winning car, crashed coming out of the second turn because of a broken axle. Several cars became involved in the accident with Vukovich, who was leading by seventeen seconds, hitting the Sumar Special of Johnny Boyd. Vukovich cartwheeled over the retaining fence. He died instantly of a head injury.

Vukovich's remarkable career at Indy included a four year span (1952-1955) where he led more than 70% of the laps he competed and was in strong contention of winning four consecutive Indianapolis 500's.

After the Vukovich accident, the race turned into a three-driver duel between Bob Sweikert, Don Freeland and Art Cross.

Mechanical problems hampered both Freeland and Cross, as Sweikert led from lap 160 to the finish and averaged 128.2 mph.

Sweikert led for a total of eighty-six laps in the "tropical rose" colored John Zink Special. He was greeted by Dinah Shore during the victory celebration. The car was given the nickname of the "Pink Zink".

Tony Bettenhausen, "The Tinley Park Express", finished second with Jimmy Davies finishing third.

The 1955 Rookie of the Year was Al Herman who finished seventh.

After Sweikert's Indy 500 victory, he went on to win the AAA National and Mid-West Sprint Car championships. He became the only driver to do so.

The tragic 1955 season took the lives of Larry Crockett, Mike Nazaruk, Vuky, Ayulo, Jack McGrath, Jerry Hoyt and Alberto Ascari. Two weeks after the Indianapolis 500, eighty-three spectators were killed at LeMans when a car went into a grandstand.

AAA decided to discontinue sanctioning motorsports; The United States Auto Club (USAC) was formed as a result and became the new sanctioning body.

Bob Sweikert celebrates his 1955 "500" win with Dinah Shore and Tony Hulman.

RACE RESULTS FOR THE 1955 INDIANAPOLIS 500

Finish	Start	Car Num.	Driver	Car Name/Entrant*	Make/Model	Status	Laps	Led	Winnings
1	14	6	Bob Sweikert	John Zink	KK500D/Offy	128.209	200	86	$76,139
2	2	10	Tony Bettenhausen	Chapman	KK500C/Offy	126.733	200	0	$30,089
3	10	15	Jimmy Davies	Bardahl	KK500B/Offy	126.299	200	0	$16,989
4	33	44	Johnny Thomson	Schmidt	Kuzma/Offy	126.241	200	0	$12,889
5	7	77	Walt Faulkner	Merz Engineerng	KK500C/Offy	125.377	200	0	$10,764
6	8	19	Andy Linden	Massaglia	KK4000/Offy	125.022	200	0	$8,514
7	16	71	Al Herman (R)	Martin Brothers	Silnes/Offy	124.794	200	0	$7,564
8	19	29	Pat O'Connor	Ansted Rotary	KK500D/Offy	124.644	200	0	$6,414
9	17	48	Jimmy Daywalt	Sumar	Kurtis/Offy	124.401	200	0	$6,414
10	12	89	Pat Flaherty	Dunn Engineering	KK500B/Offy	124.086	200	0	$6,114
11	18	98	Duane Carter	Agajanian	Kuzma/Offy	Running	197	0	$3,884
12	25	41	Chuck Weyant (R)	Federal Engineering	KK3000/Offy	Running	196	0	$3,614
13	32	83	Eddie Johnson	McNamara	Trevis/Offy	Running	196	0	$3,344
14	20	33	Jim Rathmann	Belond Miracle Power	Epperly/Offy	Running	191	0	$3,324
15	21	12	Don Freeland	Bob Estes	Phillips/Offy	Transmission	178	3	$4,054
16	9	22	Cal Niday	D-A Lubricant	KK500B/Offy	Accident	170	0	$3,484
17	24	99	Art Cross	Belanger Motors	KK500D/Offy	Rod	168	24	$6,664
18	31	81	Shorty Templeman (R)	Central Excavating	Trevis/Offy	Transmission	142	0	$2,744
19	6	8	Sam Hanks	Jones & Maley	KK500C/Offy	Transmission	134	0	$2,914
20	28	31	Keith Andrews (R)	McDaniel	Schroeder/Offy	Drop. In pit	120	0	$2,684
21	27	16	Johnnie Parsons (W)	Trio Brass Foundry	KK500D/Offy	Magneto	119	0	$2,654
22	13	37	Eddie Russo (R)	Dr. Sabourin	Allen/Offy	Ignition	112	0	$2,724
23	23	49	Ray Crawford (R)	Crawford	KK500B/Offy	Valve	111	0	$2,894
24	11	1	Jimmy Bryan	Dean Van Lines	Kuzma/Offy	Fuel pump	90	31	$7,514
25	5	4	Bill Vukovich (W)	Hopkins	KK500C/Offy	Accident	56	50	$10,884
26	3	3	Jack McGrath	Hinkle	KK500C/Offy	Magneto	54	6	$6,354
27	22	42	Al Keller (R)	Sam Traylor	KK2000/Offy	Accident	54	0	$2,874
28	30	27	Rodger Ward	Aristo Blue	Kuzma/Offy	Accident	53	0	$2,444
29	26	39	Johnny Boyd (R)	Sumar	KK500C/Offy	Accident	53	0	$2,414
30	29	68	Ed Elisian	Westwood Gauge & Tool	KK4000/Offy	Stopped	53	0	$2,734
31	1	23	Jerry Hoyt	Jim Robbins	Stevens/Offy	Oil leak	40	0	$2,854
32	4	14	Fred Agabashian	Federal Engineering	KK500D/Offy	Spun	39	0	$2,724
33	15	5	Jimmy Reece	Malloy	Pankratz/Offy	Rod	10	0	$2,294

* - complete car name/entrant data not available for all entries
(R) - Indicated Rookie
(W) - Indicates Past Winner

1956

The entire track was repaved with asphalt with the exception of the front stretch which remained brick.

The new Speedway office and museum building opened at Sixteenth and Georgetown in the spring of 1956. Initially there were six cars on display in the museum and Karl Kizer was the curator.

Lou Welch gave up on the ten-year-old front-wheel-drive Novis and had Frank Kurtis build two rear-wheel-drives with tail fins.

George Francis Flaherty, Jr. (Pat), replaced Bob Sweikert on the John Zink team and won the pole at a new record of 145.6 mph.

Rain washed out all but fifty-seven minutes of the second weekend of qualifications, which resulted in numerous fine cars missing the show, including one driven by Giuseppe "Nino" Farina, former World Driving Champion.

The "Cagle Miracle" came about when heavy rains for several days during race week required track officials to pump several hundred thousand gallons of water from the tunnels beneath the track in order for the race to be run. Track superintendent Clarence Cagle supervised the successful project.

Paul Russo, in the new rear-drive Novi, took command of the race early but a tire exploded and he crashed in the first turn on the twenty-second lap.

Flaherty was never headed from lap 76 on. He led three times for a total of 127 laps, averaging 128.5 mph. The win gave owner John Zink consecutive victories with A.J. Watson as his chief mechanic.

Flaherty's car had magnesium panels that cut the weight of the car to 1700 pounds.

Flaherty would "dirt track" his car through the turns with the left front tire several inches off the surface.

Just after Flaherty took the checker, his throttle linkage broke, prompting Watson to comment "we only build these things to last 200 laps".

Flaherty was the last driver to win wearing a T-shirt.

The fourteenth, fifteenth, and sixteenth place finishing cars were dirt track cars and were the last of this type to compete in the race.

Sam Hanks would finish second, twenty seconds behind, with Don Freeland third. Bob Veith finished seventh and won Rookie of the Year.

Bob Sweikert, the 1955 Indy 500 champion, was fatally injured in a sprint car race at Salem Speedway on June 17, 1956.

George Francis "Pat" Flaherty Jr. celebrates in Victory Lane. He is the last driver to win not wearing a fire-retardant uniform.

RACE RESULTS FOR THE 1956 INDIANAPOLIS 500

Finish	Start	Car Num.	Driver	Car Name/Entrant*	Make/Model	Status	Laps	Led	Winnings
1	1	8	Pat Flaherty	John Zink	Watson/Offy	128.490	200	127	$93,819
2	13	4	Sam Hanks	Jones & Maley	KK500C/Offy	128.303	200	0	$32,919
3	26	16	Don Freeland	Bob Estes	Phillips/Offy	127.668	200	4	$20,419
4	6	98	Johnnie Parsons (W)	Agajanian	Kuzma/Offy	126.631	200	16	$15,769
5	4	73	Dick Rathmann	McNamara	KK500C/Offy	126.133	200	0	$10,744
6	10	1	Bob Sweikert (W)	D-A Lubricant	Kuzma/Offy	125.489	200	0	$7,594
7	23	14	Bob Veith (R)	Federal Engineering	KK500E/Offy	125.048	200	0	$7,494
8	15	19	Rodger Ward	Filter Queen	KK500C/Offy	124.990	200	0	$6,294
9	21	26	Jimmy Reece	Massaglia Hotels	Lesovsky/Offy	124.938	200	0	$6,044
10	30	27	Cliff Griffith	Jim Robbins	Stevens/Offy	Running	199	0	$6,194
11	22	82	Gene Hartley	Central Excavating	KK500C/Offy	Running	196	0	$3,714
12	7	42	Fred Agabashian	Federal Engineering	KK500C/Offy	Running	196	0	$3,644
13	25	57	Bob Christie (R)	Helse	KK500D/Offy	Running	196	0	$3,374
14	28	55	Al Keller	Sam Traylor	KK4000/Offy	Running	195	0	$3,254
15	32	81	Eddie Johnson	Central Excavating	Kuzma/Offy	Running	195	0	$3,434
16	29	41	Billy Garrett (R)	Greenman-Casale	Kuzma/Offy	Running	194	0	$3,014
17	33	64	Duke Dinsmore	Shannon's	KK500A/Offy	Running	191	0	$3,094
18	3	7	Pat O'Connor	Ansted Rotary	KK500D/Offy	Running	187	39	$8,924
19	19	2	Jimmy Bryan	Dean Van Lines	Kuzma/Offy	Running	185	0	$3,144
20	2	24	Jim Rathmann	Hopkins	KK500C/Offy	Rings	175	3	$3,564
21	31	34	Johnnie Tolan (R)	Trio Brass Foundry	KK500D/Offy	Mechanical	173	0	$3,084
22	5	99	Tony Bettenhausen	Belanger Motors	KK500D/Offy	Accident	160	0	$2,754
23	14	10	Ed Elisian	Hoyt Machine	KK500C/Offy	Brakes	160	0	$2,624
24	16	48	Jimmy Daywalt	Sumar	KK500C/Offy	Accident	134	0	$2,594
25	24	54	Jack Turner (R)	Travelon Trailer	KK500B/Offy	Mechanical	131	0	$2,564
26	20	89	Keith Andrews	Dunn Engineering	KK500B/Offy	Transmission	94	0	$2,804
27	9	5	Andy Linden	Chapman	KK500C/Offy	Oil leak	90	0	$2,534
28	27	12	Al Herman	Bardahl	KK500B/Offy	Accident	74	0	$2,474
29	17	49	Ray Crawford	Crawford	KK500B/Offy	Accident	49	0	$2,444
30	12	15	Johnny Boyd	Bowes Seal Fast	KK500G/Offy	Oil leak	35	0	$2,414
31	11	53	Troy Ruttman (W)	John Zink	KK500D/Offy	Spun out	22	0	$2,384
32	18	88	Johnny Thomson	Schmidt	Kuzma/Offy	Spun out	22	0	$2,854
33	8	29	Paul Russo	Novi Vespa	Kurtis/Novi	Accident	21	11	$3,974

* - complete car name/entrant data not available for all entries
(R) - Indicated Rookie
(W) - Indicates Past Winner

1957

A new modern eight story master control tower replaced the pagoda which had been built in 1926.

A new pit area separate from the track now extended north of the start/finish line.

The 500 Festival Committee was formed to coordinate race-celebrating events.

Pat Flaherty had been seriously injured with a severe arm injury in August of 1956 at Springfield, Illinois, which prevented him from defending his championship and kept him out of action for nearly two years.

Pat O'Connor won the pole in the Sumar Special at 143.9 mph, but Paul Russo was the fastest qualifier in a Novi at a 144.8 mph average. He started tenth. Rookie Eddie Sachs qualified second.

Sam Hanks qualified George Salih's "lay-down" Offy in thirteenth position. The car was built in Salih's home garage in Whittier, California. The innovative Salih set the engine only eighteen degrees from horizontal allowing a much lower center of gravity, which resulted in better handling in the corners. Salih was the winning chief mechanic for Lee Wallard in 1951. He attempted to find a buyer for the "lay-down", but was unsuccessful and was forced to campaign the car himself.

Dick Rathmann qualified for the seventeenth starting position in the field in the Sumar Special for his third "500". An altercation in downtown Indianapolis left Rathmann unfit to race, and Johnnie Parsons drove the car to a sixteenth-place finish.

At the start, the cars left the new pits in single file. The parade lap, an additional pre-race lap, was added.

Two cars were eliminated on the parade lap when Elmer George hit Eddie Russo in the rear while trying to get in position for the start.

Early in the race, it was a battle between Hanks' Belond Exhaust Special and Russo's Novi, and later a battle developed between Hanks and Jim Rathmann.

Hanks led from lap 135 to the finish in his Belond Exhaust Special. Jim Rathmann was second in the Chiropractic Special twenty-one seconds behind. Jimmy Bryan finished third and Paul Russo fourth. Hanks averaged a new record of 135.6 mph and won in his thirteenth attempt at Indy.

The top ten finishers all broke the record for average speed for 500 miles.

Don Edmunds won Rookie of the Year with a nineteenth place finish. Eddie Sachs was the next rookie in twenty-third place.

Hanks' victory was one of the most popular in history. The forty-two year old Hanks retired in Victory Lane. He became the first winner since Ray Harroun to retire in Victory Lane. The winner's share of the purse was a record $103,844, the first time the first-place prize had eclipsed $100,000.

The Race of Two Worlds, also known as the 500 Miglia di Monza, was run on June 23, 1957. The race pitted Europe's finest Grand Prix cars and drivers versus the top Indianapolis teams. Jimmy Bryan won the Monza championship. He also went on to win the 1957 AAA National Championship.

Sam Hanks drives George Salih's "sidewinder" to first place in 1957.

RACE RESULTS FOR THE 1957 INDIANAPOLIS 500

Finish	Start	Car Num.	Driver	Car Name/Entrant*	Make/Model	Status	Laps	Led	Winnings
1	13	9	Sam Hanks	Belond Exhaust	Salih/Offy	135.601	200	136	$103,844
2	32	26	Jim Rathmann	Chiropractic	Epperly/Offy	135.382	200	24	$38,494
3	15	1	Jimmy Bryan	Dean Van Lines	Kuzma/Offy	134.246	200	0	$21,794
4	10	54	Paul Russo	Novi Auto Air Conditioner	Kurtis/Novi	133.818	200	24	$19,369
5	12	73	Andy Linden	McNamara/Veedol	KK500G/Offy	133.645	200	0	$11,094
6	5	6	Johnny Boyd	Bowes Seal Fast	KK500G/Offy	132.846	200	0	$8,194
7	28	48	Marshall Teague	Sumar	KK500C/Offy	132.745	200	0	$6,819
8	1	12	Pat O'Connor	Sumar	KK500G/Offy	132.281	200	7	$8,619
9	16	7	Bob Veith	Bob Estes	Phillips/Offy	131.855	200	0	$5,969
10	14	22	Gene Hartley	Massaglia Hotels	Lesovsky/Offy	131.345	200	0	$5,844
11	19	19	Jack Turner	Bardahl	KK500G/Offy	130.906	200	0	$3,639
12	11	10	Johnny Thomson	D-A Lubricant	Kuzma/Offy	Running	199	5	$5,069
13	33	95	Bob Christie	Jones & Maley	KK500C/Offy	Running	197	0	$3,299
14	25	82	Chuck Weyant	Central Excavating	KK500C/Offy	Running	196	0	$3,429
15	22	27	Tony Bettenhausen	Novi Auto Air Conditioner	Kurtis/Novi	Running	195	0	$4,059
16	17	18	Johnnie Parsons (W)	Sumar	KK500G/Offy	Running	195	0	$2,989
17	21	3	Don Freeland	Ansted Rotary	KK500D/Offy	Running	192	0	$2,869
18	6	5	Jimmy Reece	Hoyt Machine	KK500C/Offy	Throttle	182	0	$2,749
19	27	92	Don Edmunds (R)	McKay	KK500G/Offy	Spun out	170	0	$3,169
20	31	28	Johnnie Tolan	Greenman-Casale	Kuzma/Offy	Clutch	138	0	$2,639
21	30	89	Al Herman	Dunn Engineering	Dunn/Offy	Accident	111	0	$2,659
22	4	14	Fred Agabashian	Bowes Seal Fast	KK500G/Offy	Fuel leak	107	0	$2,879
23	2	88	Eddie Sachs (R)	Schmidt	Kuzma/Offy	Fuel pump	105	0	$3,299
24	18	77	Mike Magill (R)	Dayton Steel Foundry	KK500G/Offy	Accident	101	0	$2,519
25	20	43	Eddie Johnson	Chapman	KK500G/Offy	Wheel bearing	93	0	$2,489
26	23	31	Bill Cheesbourg (R)	Schildmeier Seal Line	KK500G/Offy	Fuel leak	81	0	$3,209
27	8	16	Al Keller	Bardahl	KK500G/Offy	Accident	75	0	$2,429
28	29	57	Jimmy Daywalt	Helse	KK500C/Offy	Accident	53	0	$2,449
29	7	83	Ed Elisian	McNamara	KK500C/Offy	Timing gear	51	0	$2,369
30	24	8	Rodger Ward	Wolcott Fuel Injection	Lesovsky/Offy	Supercharger	27	0	$2,889
31	3	52	Troy Ruttman (W)	John Zink	Watson/Offy	Piston	13	4	$3,459
32	26	55	Eddie Russo	Sclavi & Amos	KK500C/Offy	Accident	0	0	$2,404
33	9	23	Elmer George (R)	Travelon Trailer	KK500B/Offy	Accident	0	0	$2,249

* - complete car name/entrant data not available for all entries
(R) - Indicated Rookie
(W) - Indicates Past Winner

1958

The new chief steward was Harlan Fengler, who took over for Harry McQuinn. Fengler actually raced in the 1923 500, finishing sixteenth as a rookie in his only start. Fengler was the riding mechanic for Harry Hartz in 1922, finishing second.

The much anticipated appearance of five-time world champion Juan Manuel Fangio never fully developed as he exited prior to making a qualification attempt.

There was a month-long speed battle between Dick Rathmann in Lee Elkins's car and Ed Elisian in John Zink's car.

Rathmann took the pole at a new record of just under 146.0 mph, with Elisian second.

Retired defending champion Sam Hanks drove the Pontiac Bonneville pace car. This was the first time a Pontiac paced the race.

After a parade lap foul up, which resulted in the start being waved off for the first time in history, Elisian passed Rathmann on the first lap going into turn three, then lost control, causing a huge chain reaction accident. Rathmann and a total of fifteen cars were involved in the accident, with eight being eliminated. Pat O'Connor was fatally injured when his car ran over the car of Jimmy Reece. His car landed upside down before rolling onto its wheels. Jerry Unser went over the wall, but only suffered a dislocated shoulder. He had used Paul Goldsmith's car as a launching ramp.

The race became a battle between Jimmy Bryan, Tony Bettenhausen, George Amick and Johnny Boyd.

Bryan led a total of 139 laps, leading from lap 126 to the finish. He finished twenty-seven seconds ahead of Rookie of the Year George Amick. It was the second year in a row that George Salih's car was victorious. Bryan averaged 133.8 mph.

Twenty-three-year-old rookie A.J. Foyt spun out on lap 149 and finished sixteenth in the Dean Van Lines car. Jimmy Bryan had exited Al Dean's car to drive George Salih's car.

Jimmy Reece, in a car damaged in the first lap accident, finished sixth but actually had the shortest actual running time. He lost precious minutes in the early laps while damage to his car was repaired.

Jerry Unser goes over the wall in the disastrous start to the 1958 "500."

RACE RESULTS FOR THE 1958 INDIANAPOLIS 500

Finish	Start	Car Num.	Driver	Car Name/Entrant*	Make/Model	Status	Laps	Led	Winnings
1	7	1	Jimmy Bryan	Belond A.P.	Salih/Offy	133.791	200	139	$105,574
2	25	99	George Amick (R)	Demler	Epperly/Offy	133.517	200	18	$38,874
3	8	9	Johnny Boyd	Bowes Seal Fast	KK500G/Offy	133.099	200	18	$24,999
4	9	33	Tony Bettenhausen	Jones & Maley	Epperly/Offy	132.855	200	24	$17,199
5	20	2	Jim Rathmann	Leader Card 500 Roadster	Epperly/Offy	132.847	200	0	$11,399
6	3	16	Jimmy Reece	John Zink	Watson/Offy	132.443	200	0	$8,699
7	13	26	Don Freeland	Bob Estes	Phillips/Offy	132.403	200	0	$6,999
8	19	44	Jud Larson (R)	John Zink	Watson/Offy	130.550	200	0	$7,049
9	26	61	Eddie Johnson	Bryant Heating & Cooling	KK500G/Offy	130.156	200	0	$5,999
10	33	54	Bill Cheesbourg	Novi Auto Air Conditioner	Kurtis/Novi	129.149	200	0	$6,399
11	21	52	Al Keller	Bardahl	KK500G-2/Offy	128.498	200	0	$3,919
12	6	45	Johnnie Parsons (W)	Gerhardt	KK500G/Offy	128.254	200	0	$3,599
13	30	19	Johnnie Tolan	Greenman-Casale	Kuzma/Offy	128.150	200	0	$3,329
14	17	65	Bob Christie	Federal Engineering	KK500E/Offy	Spun out	189	0	$4,209
15	32	59	Dempsey Wilson (R)	Sorenson	Kuzma/Offy	Refueling fire	151	0	$4,089
16	12	29	A.J. Foyt (R)	Dean Van Lines	Kuzma/Offy	Spun out	148	0	$2,969
17	31	77	Mike Magill	Dayton Steel Foundry	KK500G/Offy	Running	136	0	$2,849
18	14	15	Paul Russo	Novi Auto Air Conditioner	Kurtis/Novi	Throttle	122	0	$2,779
19	23	83	Shorty Templeman	McNamara	KK500C/Offy	Brakes	116	0	$2,699
20	11	8	Rodger Ward	Wolcott Fuel Injection	Lesovsky/Offy	Magneto	93	0	$2,719
21	15	43	Billy Garrett	Chapman	KK500G/Offy	Gears	80	0	$2,639
22	18	88	Eddie Sachs	Schmidt	Kuzma/Offy	Transmission	68	1	$3,759
23	22	7	Johnny Thomson	D-A Lubricant	Kurtis/Offy	Steering	52	0	$2,754
24	29	89	Chuck Weyant	Dunn Engineering	Dunn/Offy	Accident	38	0	$2,549
25	10	25	Jack Turner	Massaglia Hotels	Lesovsky/Offy	Fuel pump	21	0	$2,569
26	4	14	Bob Veith	Bowes Seal Fast	KK500G/Offy	Accident	1	0	$2,789
27	1	97	Dick Rathmann	McNamara	Watson/Offy	Accident	0	0	$6,259
28	2	5	Ed Elisian	John Zink	Watson/Offy	Accident	0	0	$3,179
29	5	4	Pat O'Connor	Sumar	KK500G/Offy	Accident	0	0	$2,574
30	16	31	Paul Goldsmith (R)	City of Daytona Beach	KK500G/Offy	Accident	0	0	$2,369
31	24	92	Jerry Unser (R)	McKay	KK500G/Offy	Accident	0	0	$2,339
32	27	68	Len Sutton (R)	Jim Robbins	KK500G/Offy	Accident	0	0	$2,309
33	28	57	Art Bisch (R)	Helse	Kuzma/Offy	Accident	0	0	$2,279

* - complete car name/entrant data not available for all entries
(R) - Indicated Rookie
(W) - Indicates Past Winner

1959

Jerry Unser was practicing on May 2 when he crashed in the fourth turn and was burnt on his arms. Complications ensued and he passed away on May 17.

After this accident, fire-treated uniforms became mandatory on May 14, 1959.

Roll bars also became mandatory at Indy in 1959.

Rookie Bob Cortner was fatally injured in practice on an extremely windy May day.

Johnny Thomson won the pole at 145.9 mph, with Eddie Sachs and Jim Rathmann joining him on the front row.

Defending champion Jimmy Bryan completed one lap and finished thirty-third in the winning car from the previous two "500s."

The first eighty-four laps was a contest between Ward, Thomson, Jim Rathmann and Pat Flaherty.

This was Flaherty's first 500 since his win in 1956, as he had sustained a serious arm injury and had been out of action for two years. He was running fourth late in the race but spun with 38 laps to go on the main straightaway and hit the pit wall.

Ward led from lap eighty-five to the checker and led second-place Jim Rathmann, in the Simoniz Special, by twenty-three seconds at the finish. Ward averaged a new record of 135.9 mph. This was the third time Rathmann finished in the runner-up position.

The cars of Ward and Rathmann incorporated air jacks to expedite tire changes on pit stops.

Ward drove for Bob Wilke of Leader Card with A.J. Watson as his chief mechanic.

The 500 Festival selected a queen for the first time, but the queen did not participate in the victory lane ceremonies until 1960.

Nineteen fifty-nine was Ward's ninth 500, with a best prior finish of eighth in 1956. Ward was thirty-eight years old when he won his first 500.

From 1959 to 1964, with the Leader Card cars wrenched by A.J. Watson, Ward's finishes were first, second, third, first, fourth and second. The "Flying W's" referred to Rodger Ward, A.J. Watson and car owner Bob Wilke.

Bobby Grim, from Coal City, Indiana, won Rookie of the Year with a twenty-sixth-place finish and a fifth-place starting position. Grim was injured in an odd circumstance when he exited the race. His car was slowing due to a failing magneto. He threw his arm in the air to warn the cars behind that he was slowing. The force of the air dislocated his shoulder.

Ward led 130 laps, while Thomson led 40.

In Victory Lane, Ward was surrounded by his wife, his dog Skippy and actress Erin O'Brien. This was the last year Borg-Warner brought in a Hollywood actress for the race.

The first electronic scoring pylon was installed in 1959 on the front straight-away. It was later replaced in 1994 then again in 2014.

The Daytona 500 was run for the first time in 1959.

Rodger Ward would go on to win the 1959 USAC National Championship.

Rodger Ward and Johnny Thomson duel in turn one.

RACE RESULTS FOR THE 1959 INDIANAPOLIS 500

Finish	Start	Car Num.	Driver	Car Name/Entrant*	Make/Model	Status	Laps	Led	Winnings
1	6	5	Rodger Ward	Leader Card 500 Roadster	Watson/Offy	135.857	200	130	$106,850
2	3	16	Jim Rathmann	Simoniz	Watson/Offy	135.619	200	19	$39,800
3	1	3	Johnny Thomson	Racing Associates	Lesovsky/Offy	135.340	200	40	$32,375
4	15	1	Tony Bettenhausen	Hoover Motor Express	Epperly/Offy	134.768	200	0	$15,475
5	16	99	Paul Goldsmith	Demler	Epperly/Offy	134.573	200	0	$11,975
6	11	33	Johnny Boyd	Bowes Seal Fast	Epperly/Offy	133.867	200	0	$8,475
7	12	37	Duane Carter	Smokey's Reverse Torque	Kurtis/Offy	133.342	200	0	$7,275
8	8	19	Eddie Johnson	Bryant Heating & Cooling	KK500G/Offy	133.336	200	0	$6,625
9	27	45	Paul Russo	Bardahl	KK500G/Offy	133.331	200	0	$6,325
10	17	10	A.J. Foyt	Dean Van Lines	Kuzma/Offy	133.297	200	0	$6,575
11	9	88	Gene Hartley	Drewry's	Kuzma/Offy	132.434	200	0	$4,795
12	7	74	Bob Veith	John Zink Heater	Moore/Offy	132.169	200	0	$4,675
13	23	89	Al Herman	Dunn Engineering	Dunn/Offy	131.872	200	0	$4,455
14	13	66	Jimmy Daywalt	Federal Engineering	KK500E/Offy	131.861	200	0	$5,335
15	21	71	Chuck Arnold (R)	Hall-Mar	Curtis/Offy	130.918	200	0	$4,165
16	33	58	Jim McWithey (R)	Ray Brady	KK500C/Offy	129.024	200	0	$4,045
17	2	44	Eddie Sachs	Schmidt	Kuzma/Offy	Running	182	0	$4,675
18	28	57	Al Keller	Helse	Kuzma/Offy	Pistons	163	0	$3,980
19	18	64	Pat Flaherty (W)	John Zink Heater	Watson/Offy	Accident	162	11	$5,725
20	4	73	Dick Rathmann	McNamara Chiropractic	Watson/Offy	Fire in pit	150	0	$4,045
21	30	53	Bill Cheesbourg	Greenman-Casale	Kuzma/Offy	Magneto	147	0	$3,765
22	25	15	Don Freeland	Jim Robbins	KK500G/Offy	Magneto	136	0	$4,485
23	32	49	Ray Crawford	Meguiar's Mirror Glaze	Elder/Offy	Accident	115	0	$3,655
24	10	9	Don Branson (R)	Bob Estes	Phillips/Offy	Torsion bar	112	0	$3,625
25	24	65	Bob Christie	Federal Engineering	KK500D/Offy	Rod	109	0	$4,595
26	5	48	Bobby Grim (R)	Sumar	KK500G/Offy	Magneto	85	0	$4,190
27	14	24	Jack Turner	Travelon Trailer	Christensen/Offy	Fuel tank	47	0	$4,335
28	29	47	Chuck Weyant	McKay	KK500J/Offy	Accident	45	0	$3,505
29	19	7	Jud Larson	Bowes Seal Fast	KK500J/Offy	Accident	45	0	$3,650
30	31	77	Mike Magill	Dayton Steel Foundry	KK500G/Offy	Accident	45	0	$3,445
31	26	87	Red Amick (R)	Wheeler-Foutch	KK500C/Offy	Accident	45	0	$3,915
32	22	8	Len Sutton	Wolcott Memorial	Lesovsky/Offy	Accident	34	0	$3,385
33	20	6	Jimmy Bryan (W)	Belond A.P. Muffler	Salih/Offy	Cam housing	1	0	$3,405

* - complete car name/entrant data not available for all entries
(R) - Indicated Rookie
(W) - Indicates Past Winner

1960

Eddie Sachs won the pole with a new record of 146.6 mph, with Jim Rathmann and Rodger Ward joining him on the front row.

On the last day of qualifications, rookie Jim Hurtubise broke the one-lap and four-lap records with almost a 150 mph lap to average 149.1 mph. He beat Sachs by 2 ½ mph in his Watson-designed purple Travelon Trailer Special but started twenty-third. After the record breaking run, Hurtubise stated "just wait until next year when my buddy Parnelli gets here."

Every car in the field was powered by an Offenhauser engine and shod with Firestone tires.

There was a record total of twenty-nine lead changes between five drivers, with fourteen of them between Jim Rathmann and Rodger Ward in the second half of the race.

Ward, Sachs, Troy Ruttman, Jim Rathmann and Johnny Thomson traded the lead for the first half of the race.

The second half was a two-car battle between Ward and Jim Rathmann.

On Ward's first stop, he stalled his car and was in the pits for more than one minute. As a result, he charged hard and put stress on his tires. He was thirty seconds down after the stop, but charged to the front on lap 123.

As Rathmann and Ward battled in the second half of the race, third-place Johnny Thomson started making up ground. This forced Ward and Rathmann to pick up the pace.

Ward led with four laps to go, but the white cord began to show on his right front tire, causing him to slow.

Rathmann passed Ward and led laps 197 to the finish, with Ward twelve seconds back at the checker. Rathmann averaged a new record of 138.8 mph in the Ken Paul Special (named for co-owners Kenny Rich and Paul Lacy). After three second-place finishes (1952, 1957, 1959), Rathmann's win was highly celebrated.

Rathmann led 100 laps, while Ward led 58.

Paul Goldsmith finished third in the Demler Special. His third place finish is the highest by a NASCAR driver.

Jim Hurtubise ("Herk") got up to as high as fifth place and was running eighth when an oil leak put him out with 15 laps left. He won Rookie of the Year.

A homemade spectator scaffold collapsed in the infield during the parade lap and Fred H. Linder and William C. Craig were killed and forty others were injured. Homemade scaffolding was no longer allowed after this tragedy.

Three-time national champion (1954, 1956 and 1957) and 1958 "500" winner Jimmy Bryan was fatally injured at Langhorne, Pennsylvania, in June of 1960 at the age of thirty-four.

Jim Rathmann and Rodger Ward in their classic duel, which results in fourteen lead changes between themselves.

RACE RESULTS FOR THE 1960 INDIANAPOLIS 500

Finish	Start	Car Num.	Driver	Car Name/Entrant*	Make/Model	Status	Laps	Led	Winnings
1	2	4	Jim Rathmann	Ken-Paul	Watson/Offy	138.767	200	100	$110,000
2	3	1	Rodger Ward (W)	Leader Card 500 Roadster	Watson/Offy	138.631	200	58	$48,025
3	26	99	Paul Goldsmith	Demler	Epperly/Offy	136.792	200	0	$24,350
4	8	7	Don Branson	Bob Estes	Phillips/Offy	136.785	200	0	$15,475
5	17	3	Johnny Thomson	Adams Quarter Horse Farm	Lesovsky/Offy	136.750	200	10	$15,100
6	7	22	Eddie Johnson	Jim Robbins	Trevis/Offy	136.137	200	0	$9,200
7	12	98	Lloyd Ruby (R)	Agajanian	Watson/Offy	135.983	200	0	$7,900
8	25	44	Bob Veith	Schmidt	Meskowski/Offy	135.452	200	0	$7,850
9	28	18	Bud Tingelstad (R)	Jim Robbins	Trevis/Offy	133.717	200	0	$6,900
10	14	38	Bob Christie	Federal Engineering	KK500D/Offy	133.416	200	0	$6,700
11	22	27	Red Amick	King O'Lawn	Salih/Offy	131.946	200	0	$5,520
12	27	17	Duane Carter	Thompson Industries	Kuzma/Offy	131.882	200	0	$5,450
13	31	39	Bill Homeier	Ridgewood Builders	Kuzma/Offy	131.367	200	0	$4,980
14	24	48	Gene Hartley	Sumar	KK500G/Offy	Running	196	0	$5,710
15	9	65	Chuck Stevenson	Leader Card 500 Roadster	Watson/Offy	Running	196	0	$4,740
16	21	14	Bobby Grim	Bill Forbes	Meskowski/Offy	Running	194	0	$4,920
17	19	26	Shorty Templeman	Federal Engineering	KK500E/Offy	Running	191	0	$5,100
18	23	56	Jim Hurtubise (R)	Travelon Trailer	Christensen/Offy	Rod	185	0	$8,880
19	10	10	Jimmy Bryan (W)	Metal-Cal	Salih/Offy	Fuel Pump	152	0	$4,400
20	6	28	Troy Ruttman (W)	John Zink Heater	Watson/Offy	Gear	134	11	$6,220
21	1	6	Eddie Sachs	Dean Van Lines	Ewing/Offy	Magneto	132	21	$9,390
22	11	73	Don Freeland	Ross-Babcock Traveler	Kurtis/Offy	Magneto	129	0	$4,310
23	18	2	Tony Bettenhausen	Dowgard	Watson/Offy	Rod	125	0	$5,080
24	15	32	Wayne Weiler (R)	Ansted Rotary	Kuzma/Offy	Accident	103	0	$4,200
25	16	5	A.J. Foyt	Bowes Seal Fast	Kurtis/Offy	Clutch	90	0	$4,220
26	29	46	Eddie Russo	Go-Kart	KK500G/Offy	Accident	84	0	$4,140
27	13	8	Johnny Boyd	Bowes Seal Fast	Epperly/Offy	Piston	77	0	$4,160
28	20	37	Gene Force	McKay	KK500J/Offy	Brakes	74	0	$4,480
29	32	16	Jim McWithey	Hoover Motor Express	Epperly/Offy	Brakes	60	0	$4,100
30	5	9	Len Sutton	S-R Racing Enterprises	Watson/Offy	Piston ring	47	0	$4,320
31	4	97	Dick Rathmann	Jim Robbins	Watson/Offy	Brake Line	42	0	$4,440
32	30	76	Al Herman	Joe Hunt Magneto	Ewing/Offy	Clutch	34	0	$4,010
33	33	23	Dempsey Wilson	Bryant Heating & Cooling	KK500G/Offy	Magneto	11	0	$4,380

* - complete car name/entrant data not available for all entries
(R) - Indicated Rookie
(W) - Indicates Past Winner

1961

The Golden Anniversary 500

A second deck of seating was added to the grandstand on the front straightaway for the 1961 "500".

Thirty-two front-engine cars and one rear-engine car made up the field.

Two-time Formula One Champion (1959, 1960) Jack Brabham started thirteenth and finished ninth in the rear-engine British Racing green Cooper Climax. The start of the rear-engine revolution had begun! The traditionalists referred to them as "funny cars".

There had been rear-engine cars in the late 1930s and 1940s, but none had been entered since 1951.

The Granatelli brothers purchased Lew Welch's Novis but were unable to make the show.

The day before pole day, Tony Bettenhausen was fatally injured while test driving Paul Russo's car when a steering bolt failed. He had been at the top of the speed charts nearly all month in his own car.

Eddie Sachs won the pole for the second year in a row at 147.5 mph. Don Branson and Jim Hurtubise joined Sachs on the front row. The field was so evenly matched that there was just over 3 mph from Sachs's speed to Bobby Grim's slowest speed of 144.0.

The pre-race festivities included Ray Harroun, Earl Cooper and Eddie Rickenbacker driving their cars from the early era in celebration of the Golden Anniversary 500.

A beautiful gold-colored Ford Thunderbird paced the race piloted by Sam Hanks. This was the fourth consecutive year Hanks drove the pace car.

Hurtubise led the first thirty-five laps. The first half of the race was a battle between Jim Rathmann, rookie Parnelli Jones, Sachs, A.J. Foyt and Troy Ruttman.

On lap fifty-two, a five-car accident on the front straight resulted in "Cactus" Jack Turner flipping several times. All of the drivers were able to walk from the accident scene. Turner was an accomplished driver, winning the AAA National Midget championship twice. He was running in second position, after leader pit stops, when the accident occurred.

The second half of the race was almost totally a Sachs vs. Foyt battle.

It appeared that Foyt had the advantage, but on what was supposed to be his last stop on lap 160, a fueling malfunction didn't allow a full tank. In the lead with 15 laps left, Foyt was forced to pit again in his Bowes Seal Fast Special.

It appeared Sachs would win, then, unexpectedly, with three laps left, he pitted to replace a worn right rear tire.

Foyt passed Sachs on lap 198 and won by eight seconds while averaging a new record of 139.1 mph. Rodger Ward finished third. Ward's most recent "500" finishes were first, second and third.

Lloyd Ruby, driving the car originally assigned to Tony Bettenhausen, finished eighth.

Parnelli Jones eventually finished twelfth after leading twenty-seven laps total. He lost a cylinder and a long pit stop cost him a much better finish. He also was hit in the face by a piece of metal and continued driving despite blood seeping into his goggles.

Foyt led for seventy-one laps and Sachs led for sixty-six. Foyt became the first driver to win the Indy 500 and repeat as national champion in the same year.

Rufus Parnell "Parnelli" Jones and seventh-place finisher Bobby Marshman were Rookie of the Year winners. Marshman started 33rd and charged through the field.

Jack Brabham finished in ninth place, his Cooper becoming the first rear-engine car to ever finish.

George Bignotti, the legendary chief mechanic, won his first 500 with Foyt in the Bowes Seal Fast car.

The bricks on the front straight were covered with asphalt in October of 1961, now leaving only a yard of bricks at the start/finish line, utilizing a total of 588 bricks.

Rear-engine is here to stay—Jack Brabham in the Cooper-Climax leads the front-engine roadsters of Shorty Templeman and Parnelli Jones.

RACE RESULTS FOR THE 1961 INDIANAPOLIS 500

Finish	Start	Car Num.	Driver	Car Name/Entrant*	Make/Model	Status	Laps	Led	Winnings
1	7	1	A.J. Foyt	Bowes Seal Fast	Trevis/Offy	139.130	200	71	$117,975
2	1	12	Eddie Sachs	Dean Van Lines	Ewing/Offy	139.041	200	44	$53,400
3	4	2	Rodger Ward (W)	Del Webb's Sun City	Watson/Offy	138.539	200	7	$26,500
4	18	7	Shorty Templeman	Bill Forbes Racing Team	Meskowski/Offy	136.873	200	0	$16,025
5	26	19	Al Keller	Konstant Hot	Phillips/Offy	136.034	200	0	$13,725
6	28	18	Chuck Stevenson	Metal-Cal	Epperly/Offy	135.742	200	0	$9,875
7	33	31	Bobby Marshman (R)	Hoover Motor Express	Epperly/Offy	135.534	200	0	$9,550
8	25	5	Lloyd Ruby	Autolite Dealer's Assn.	Epperly/Offy	134.860	200	0	$8,750
9	13	17	Jack Brabham (R)	Kimberly Cooper-Climax	Cooper/Climax	134.116	200	0	$7,250
10	32	34	Norm Hall (R)	Federal Engineering	KK500E/Offy	134.104	200	0	$8,250
11	15	28	Gene Hartley	John Chalik	Trevis/Offy	Running	198	0	$5,820
12	5	98	Parnelli Jones (R)	Agajanian Willard Battery	Watson/Offy	Running	192	27	$10,350
13	6	97	Dick Rathmann	Jim Robbins	Watson/Offy	Fuel pump	164	0	$5,580
14	17	10	Paul Goldsmith	Racing Associates	Lesovsky/Offy	Oil leak	160	0	$5,210
15	12	15	Wayne Weiler	Hopkins Coral Harbour	Watson/Offy	Wheel	147	0	$5,040
16	31	35	Dempsey Wilson	Lysle Greenman	Kuzma/Offy	Fuel pump	145	0	$4,920
17	16	32	Bob Christie	North Electric	Kurtis/Offy	Piston	132	0	$4,850
18	10	33	Eddie Johnson	Jim Robbins	Kuzma/Offy	Accident	127	0	$4,730
19	8	8	Len Sutton	Bryant Heating & Cooling	Watson/Offy	Transmission	110	0	$4,650
20	22	52	Troy Ruttman (W)	John Zink Trackburner	Watson/Offy	Clutch	105	10	$6,970
21	20	41	Johnny Boyd	Leader Card 500 Roadster	Watson/Offy	Clutch	105	0	$4,650
22	3	99	Jim Hurtubise	Demler	Epperly/Offy	Piston	102	35	$10,410
23	19	86	Ebb Rose (R)	Meyer Speedway	Porter/Offy	Oil line	93	0	$4,530
24	30	26	Cliff Griffith	McCullough Engineering	Elder/Offy	Piston	55	0	$4,750
25	21	45	Jack Turner	Bardahl	Kurtis/Offy	Accident	52	0	$5,720
26	14	73	A.J. Shepherd (R)	Travelon Trailer	Christensen/Offy	Accident	51	0	$4,440
27	29	22	Roger McCluskey (R)	Racing Associates	Moore/Offy	Accident	51	0	$4,710
28	9	14	Bill Cheesbourg	Dean Van Lines	Kuzma/Offy	Accident	50	0	$4,430
29	27	83	Don Davis (R)	Dart-Kart by Rupp	Trevis/Offy	Accident	49	0	$4,950
30	11	4	Jim Rathmann (W)	Simoniz	Watson/Offy	Magneto	48	6	$5,270
31	23	55	Jimmy Daywalt	Schultz Fueling Equipment	KK500G/Offy	Brakes	27	0	$4,890
32	24	16	Bobby Grim	Thompson Industries	Watson/Offy	Fuel injection	26	0	$4,660
33	2	3	Don Branson	Hoover Motor Express	Epperly/Offy	Valves	2	0	$5,080

* - complete car name/entrant data not available for all entries
(R) - Indicated Rookie
(W) - Indicates Past Winner

1962

Pat Vidan became the starter, succeeding Bill Vandewater, who passed away.

Parnelli Jones won the pole, officially eclipsing 150 mph for the first time, with all four laps over 150 mph.

Jones took off at the start and ran away, leading by more than a lap at the halfway point. He led as late as the 125th lap, after leading all but five laps up to that point

Jones attempted to swerve to avoid A.J. Foyt, who had lost a wheel on lap seventy, and realized he had no brakes. His exhaust pipe had burned a hole in the brake line.

Jones fought the brakeless car the second half of the race, with his two remaining pit stops presenting serious problems, and he eventually finished seventh. Spare wheels were set-up in his pit as restraints to help stop the car.

Rodger Ward led all but nine laps from the 126th lap to the checker and averaged a new record of 140.3 mph for his second win.

Ward led his teammate Len Sutton by eleven seconds at the checker for the Leader Card Team, owned by Bob Wilke.

Eddie Sachs started twenty-seventh and finished third.

Jim McElreath finished sixth and won Rookie of the Year.

Jones led 120 laps, and Ward led 66.

Rookie Daniel Sexton Gurney was originally assigned to John Zink's rear-engine turbine-powered car, but eventually switched to Mickey Thompson's rear-engine car. He started eighth and finished twentieth in the only rear-engine car in the field. Gurney's only oval track experience had been at Daytona in 1962. His father was once a singer in the Metropolitan Opera.

For the second consecutive year Jack Turner was involved in an accident on the front stretch and flipped his car. Turner was not as fortunate this year as he sustained a fractured pelvis and broken toe.

Rodger Ward won his second USAC National Championship in 1962.

Rodger Ward drives his A.J. Watson-built roadster to the win in 1962.

RACE RESULTS FOR THE 1962 INDIANAPOLIS 500

Finish	Start	Car Num.	Driver	Car Name/Entrant*	Make/Model	Status	Laps	Led	Winnings
1	2	3	Rodger Ward (W)	Leader Card 500 Roadster	Watson/Offy	140.293	200	66	$125,015
2	4	7	Len Sutton	Leader Card 500 Roadster	Watson/Offy	140.167	200	9	$44,566
3	27	2	Eddie Sachs	Dean-Autolite	Ewing/Offy	140.075	200	0	$26,591
4	12	27	Don Davis	J.H. Rose Truck Line	Lesovsky/Offy	139.768	200	0	$16,716
5	3	54	Bobby Marshman	Bryant Heating & Cooling	Epperly/Offy	138.790	200	0	$14,316
6	7	15	Jim McElreath (R)	Schulz Fueling Equipment	KK500G/Offy	138.653	200	0	$10,366
7	1	98	Parnelli Jones	Agajanian Willard Battery	Watson/Offy	138.534	200	120	$32,966
8	24	12	Lloyd Ruby	Thompson Industries	Watson/Offy	138.182	200	0	$8,541
9	23	44	Jim Rathmann (W)	Simoniz Vista	Watson/Offy	136.913	200	0	$8,041
10	28	38	Johnny Boyd	Metal-Cal	Epperly/Offy	136.600	200	0	$8,841
11	6	4	Shorty Templeman	Bill Forbes Racing Team	Watson/Offy	135.844	200	0	$6,461
12	11	14	Don Branson	Mid-Continent Securities	Epperly/Offy	135.836	200	0	$6,041
13	29	91	Jim Hurtubise	Jim Robbins	Watson/Offy	135.655	200	0	$6,621
14	32	86	Ebb Rose	J.H. Rose Truck Line	Porter/Offy	134.001	200	0	$6,001
15	10	5	Bud Tingelstad	Konstant Hot	Phillips/Offy	133.170	200	0	$5,631
16	9	17	Roger McCluskey	Bell Lines Trucking	Watson/Offy	Spun out	168	3	$5,911
17	17	21	Elmer George	Sarkes Tarzian	Lesovsky/Offy	Engine	146	0	$5,341
18	30	26	Troy Ruttman (W)	Jim Robbins	Kuzma/Offy	Piston	140	0	$5,871
19	15	18	Bobby Grim	Morcroft	Trevis/Offy	Oil Leak	96	0	$5,191
20	8	34	Dan Gurney (R)	Thompson Harvey Aluminum	Thompson/Buick	Rear end	92	0	$5,161
21	16	19	Chuck Hulse (R)	Federal Engineering	KK500E/Offy	Fuel pump	91	0	$5,531
22	33	79	Jimmy Daywalt	City of Albany, NY	Kurtis/Offy	Transmission	74	0	$5,351
23	5	1	A.J. Foyt (W)	Bowes Seal Fast	Trevis/Offy	Lost wheel	69	2	$5,721
24	13	9	Dick Rathmann	Chapman	Watson/Offy	Magneto	51	0	$5,091
25	18	32	Eddie Johnson	Polyaire Foam	Trevis/Offy	Magneto	38	0	$6,261
26	26	53	Paul Goldsmith	American Rubber & Plastics	Epperly/Offy	Magneto	26	0	$5,031
27	20	88	Gene Hartley	Drewry's	Watson/Offy	Steering	23	0	$6,201
28	14	62	Paul Russo	Denver-Chicago Trucking	Watson/Offy	Piston	20	0	$4,921
29	25	45	Jack Turner	Bardahl	Kurtis/Offy	Accident	17	0	$5,141
30	31	29	Bob Christie	North Electric	Kurtis/Offy	Accident	17	0	$5,311
31	22	83	Allen Crowe (R)	S-R Racing Enterprises	Watson/Offy	Accident	17	0	$5,431
32	21	67	Chuck Rodee (R)	Travelon Trailer	Christensen/Offy	Accident	17	0	$5,601
33	19	96	Bob Veith	Meguiar's Mirror Glaze	Elder/Offy	Piston	12	0	$5,871

* - complete car name/entrant data not available for all entries
(R) - Indicated Rookie
(W) - Indicates Past Winner

1963

The Speedway Motel was built on the outside of the second turn in 1963 with 96 rooms and a Golf Clubhouse.

Seat belts became mandatory for the first time.

Mickey Thompson returned with two cars nicknamed "skateboards" because of their low profile. World Champion Graham Hill was to drive one of the cars. Hill later stepped out of the car after crashing.

Eddie Sachs in the beautiful yellow and red roadster, sponsored by Bryant Heating & Cooling, was the first on the track on May 1st.

Parnelli Jones broke the track record in qualifying with a 151.2 mph average to win the pole. Jones went on to win the race in "Calhoun," a car he was driving for the third consecutive year.

Jim Hurtubise started second in the Hotel Tropicana Novi, the first start for a Novi since 1958.

Fifty-year-old Duane Carter qualified one of the "skateboard" cars of Mickey Thompson, while Al Miller ("Mr. Clean") qualified another.

Three Novis were in the field for the first time ever, with Bobby Unser and Art Malone joining Hurtubise. The overzealous rookie Unser crashed his powerful Novi on the second lap and finished thirty-third.

Four of the thirty-three cars were rear-engine cars.

Len Sutton, second-place finisher in 1962, failed to qualify.

Jack Turner flipped down the main straight for the third year in a row, this time in practice on the second day of qualifying. Coming out of turn four, Turner's car barrel-rolled thirteen times. Turner sustained a crushed vertebra and spent nearly three months in the hospital, prompting his retirement from racing.

Sam Hanks paced the race for the sixth and final time in a unique metallic-turquoise Chrysler "300".

Parnelli Jones and Jim Hurtubise battled for the first several laps until Jones pulled away and led until his first stop on lap sixty-four.

Rookie Jim Clark, driving a Lotus with a stock-block Ford V8 engine, pretty much led until his only pit stop (forty-two seconds) then Jones retook the lead on lap ninety-six and led to the checker. Jones averaged a new record 143.1 mph, while making three pit stops.

Jones led for 167 laps, while Clark led 28 laps.

Jones led by forty-eight seconds, with 50 laps to go.

An oil leak from Jones' car nearly resulted in him receiving the black flag, which would have cost him victory.

Jones' owner J.C. Agajanian pleaded with chief steward Harlan Fengler, claiming the crack in the oil tank was above the oil level.

Having spun in turn one on the previous lap, Eddie Sachs,—the "Clown Prince of Auto Racing"- lost a wheel in turn three on lap 181. Sachs retrieved the wheel and rolled it back to the pit area, while waving to the crowd to a tremendous ovation.

Roger McCluskey also spun late in the race and claimed that oil from Jones' car was the culprit. Neither Sachs nor McCluskey elected to attend the Victory Banquet.

The controversy over the oil leak was raging during the race and after. Eddie Sachs confronted Parnelli the day after the race and ended up on the ground at the Speedway Motel.

Jim Clark finished second, thirty-four seconds behind, and was Rookie of the Year. His teammate, Dan Gurney, finished seventh in his Lotus. Foyt finished third in his 1961-winning car.

This was car owner J.C. Agajanian's second win (Ruttman in 1952 being his first).

Rufus Parnell Jones, "Parnelli," celebrates in Victory Lane with owner J.C. Agajanian.

RACE RESULTS FOR THE 1963 INDIANAPOLIS 500

Finish	Start	Car Num.	Driver	Car Name/Entrant*	Make/Model	Status	Laps	Led	Winnings
1	1	98	Parnelli Jones	Agajanian Willard Battery	Watson/Offy	143.137	200	167	$148,513
2	5	92	Jim Clark (R)	Lotus powered by Ford	Lotus/Ford	142.752	200	28	$56,238
3	8	2	A.J. Foyt (W)	Sheraton-Thompson	Trevis/Offy	142.210	200	0	$32,614
4	4	1	Rodger Ward (W)	Kaiser Aluminum	Watson/Offy	141.090	200	0	$21,288
5	3	4	Don Branson	Leader Card 500 Roadster	Watson/Offy	140.866	200	0	$18,588
6	6	8	Jim McElreath	Bill Forbes Racing Team	Watson/Offy	140.862	200	0	$14,888
7	12	93	Dan Gurney	Lotus powered by Ford	Lotus/Ford	140.071	200	0	$18,063
8	11	10	Chuck Hulse	Dean Van Lines	Ewing/Offy	140.064	200	0	$12,163
9	31	84	Al Miller (Krulac) (R)	Thompson Harvey Aluminum	Thompson/Chevrolet	139.524	200	0	$12,513
10	17	22	Dick Rathmann	Chapman	Watson/Offy	138.845	200	0	$10,463
11	30	29	Dempsey Wilson	Vita Fresh Orange Juice	Kuzma/Offy	138.574	200	0	$8,300
12	33	17	Troy Ruttman (W)	Robbins Autocrat Seat Belt	Kuzma/Offy	138.244	200	0	$8,450
13	18	65	Bob Christie	Travelon Trailer	Christensen/Offy	136.104	200	0	$7,900
14	32	32	Ebb Rose	Sheraton-Thompson	Watson/Offy	132.347	200	0	$7,550
15	14	14	Roger McCluskey	Konstant Hot	Watson/Offy	Spun out	198	4	$7,100
16	7	5	Bobby Marshman	Econo-Car Rental	Epperly/Offy	Rear end	196	0	$6,300
17	10	9	Eddie Sachs	Bryant Heating & Cooling	Watson/Offy	Accident	181	0	$7,100
18	9	99	Paul Goldsmith	Demler	Watson/Offy	Crankshaft	149	0	$7,350
19	19	52	Lloyd Ruby	John Zink Trackburner	Watson/Offy	Accident	126	0	$6,350
20	21	88	Eddie Johnson	Drewry's	Watson/Offy	Accident	112	0	$6,300
21	22	45	Chuck Stevenson	Bardahl	Watson/Offy	Cylinder	110	0	$5,700
22	2	56	Jim Hurtubise	Hotel Tropicana, Las Vegas	Kurtis/Novi	Oil leak	102	1	$7,400
23	15	83	Duane Carter	Thompson Harvey Aluminum	Thompson/Chevrolet	Rod	100	0	$5,700
24	29	16	Jim Rathmann (W)	Hopkins Coral Harbour	Watson/Offy	Fuel system	99	0	$5,650
25	20	26	Bobby Grim	Morcroft	Trevis/Offy	Oil tank leak	79	0	$5,900
26	24	86	Bob Veith	Sheraton-Thompson	Porter/Offy	Valve	74	0	$5,600
27	13	35	Allen Crowe	Gabriel Shocker	Trevis/Offy	Accident	47	0	$5,700
28	25	54	Bud Tingelstad	Hoover, Inc.	Epperly/Offy	Accident	46	0	$5,500
29	26	37	Johnny Rutherford (R)	US Equipment Co.	Watson/Offy	Transmission	43	0	$5,400
30	28	21	Elmer George	Sarkes Tarzian	Lesovsky/Offy	Handling	21	0	$5,350
31	23	75	Art Malone (R)	STP	Kurtis/Novi	Clutch	18	0	$5,150
32	27	23	Johnny Boyd	Bowes Seal Fast	Epperly/Offy	Oil	12	0	$5,300
33	16	6	Bobby Unser (R)	Hotel Tropicana, Las Vegas	Kurtis/Novi	Accident	2	0	$6,250

* - complete car name/entrant data not available for all entries
(R) - Indicated Rookie
(W) - Indicates Past Winner

1964

A twenty-one year old young man named Donald Davidson from England showed up for the first time in Indy with a savant-like type mind and recall of Indianapolis 500 history that awed everyone with whom he came in contact. He would become an institution at the great racetrack!

The Indianapolis 500 was shown on closed-circuit in black-and-white at more than 100 movie theatres and convention centers across the country for the first time.

Parnelli Jones opted for his front-engine "Calhoun" over his rear-engine car. This was the fifth year at Indianapolis for the car.

A.J. Foyt made the same decision, choosing a front-engine over a rear-engine.

Smokey Yunick entered his unique Offy-powered "sidecar." Bobby Johns was unable to qualify it.

The Granatellis entered Jim McElreath, Bobby Unser and Art Malone in Novis. STP (Scientifically Treated Petroleum) was the sponsor for the Granatelli's Novis.

Cliff Griffith attempted unsuccessfully to qualify a dirt car. Dirt cars last started the race in 1956, and this was the last time one made a qualifying attempt.

The field was composed of: 18 traditional front-engine roadsters with Offenhauser power, seven rear-engine Fords, five were rear-engine Offy powered and three were front-engine Novis.

Jim Clark, Bobby Marshman and Rodger Ward, all in rear-engine cars, made up the front row. Clark (158.8 mph) eclipsed Parnelli Jones' record from the previous year by almost 8 mph. This was the first time a rear-engine car would start from the pole in "500" history. This was the fastest field in history with the average of 152.50 mph being faster than the track record set the previous year.

The newly-introduced Ford Mustang paced the race with Benson Ford at the wheel.

Clark took the early lead, but as he was coming to the line for lap two, Dave MacDonald lost control in turn four and hit the inside wall, then ricocheted back across the track and was t-boned by Eddie Sachs' Shrike, resulting in one of the worst fiery accidents in history.

Sachs died instantly, while MacDonald died a couple of hours later. This remains the only accident in Indy 500 history to claim the lives of two drivers.

Seven cars were eliminated.

Public address announcer Tom Carnegie informed the stunned crowd that Eddie Sachs had been fatally injured. Sid Collins, the radio voice of the Indy 500, delivered a very memorable impromptu eulogy of his friend and fan favorite.

The race was stopped for nearly two hours, this being the first time the race was stopped because of an accident.

After the restart, Clark led briefly before Marshman took the lead. He was attempting to lap the field in his Pure Oil #51 Lotus/Ford when on lap thirty-nine, while attempting to pass Johnny White, he went too low on the apron and bottomed out, ripping out an oil plug and ending his day.

Clark took the lead, but on lap forty-seven his Dunlop tires began chunking, resulting in suspension failure that ended his race.

On lap fifty-five, Parnelli Jones pitted while leading and a pit fire took him out of the race.

A battle between Ward and Foyt never materialized as Ward was forced to pit five times versus two stops for Foyt. Ward's fuel mixture lever was turned in the wrong direction by mistake, causing poor fuel mileage and likely took him out of contention for the win.

Foyt led 146 laps in his Sheraton-Thompson Watson roadster and set a new record by averaging 147.4 mph in winning his second "500."

Ward was second, one minute and twenty-four seconds behind; Ruby was third and fourth was Johnny White, who won Rookie of the Year.

Ward's rear-engine was the only rear-engined car in the top ten. Ward had now finished in the top four for six consecutive years.

This was the first year that the total purse exceeded $500,000.

A week after the "500," Jim Hurtubise was severely burned at Milwaukee in an accident. Hurtubise's hands were so terribly burnt that he elected to have surgeons mold his hands so that he could grip a steering wheel and continue racing.

Foyt won the USAC National Championship by winning ten of the thirteen races.

Bobby Marshman was fatally injured in a fiery crash while testing at Phoenix in November.

The 1964 winner A.J. Foyt drives the last front-engine car to win.

RACE RESULTS FOR THE 1964 INDIANAPOLIS 500

Finish	Start	Car Num.	Driver	Car Name/Entrant*	Make/Model	Status	Laps	Led	Winnings
1	5	1	A.J. Foyt (W)	Sheraton-Thompson	Watson/Offy	147.350	200	146	$153,650
2	3	2	Rodger Ward (W)	Kaiser Aluminum	Watson/Ford	146.339	200	0	$56,925
3	7	18	Lloyd Ruby	Bill Forbes Racing Team	Watson/Offy	144.320	200	0	$35,650
4	21	99	Johnny White (R)	Demler	Watson/Offy	143.206	200	0	$21,200
5	13	88	Johnny Boyd	Vita Fresh Orange Juice	Kuzma/Offy	142.345	200	0	$17,625
6	19	15	Bud Tingelstad	Federal Engineering	Trevis/Offy	Running	198	0	$15,425
7	12	23	Dick Rathmann	Chapman	Watson/Offy	Running	197	0	$13,500
8	27	4	Bob Harkey (R)	Wally Weir Mobilgas	Watson/Offy	Running	197	0	$12,200
9	32	68	Bob Wente (R)	Morcroft-Taylor	Trevis/Offy	Running	197	0	$11,350
10	20	16	Bobby Grim	Konstant-Hot	Kurtis/Offy	Running	196	0	$10,000
11	30	3	Art Malone	Studebaker-STP	Kurtis/Novi	Running	194	0	$9,200
12	9	5	Don Branson	Wynn's Friction Proofing	Watson/Offy	Transmission	187	0	$7,600
13	10	53	Walt Hansgen (R)	MG Liquid Suspension	Huffaker/Offy	Running	176	0	$7,150
14	11	56	Jim Hurtubise	Tombstone Life	Watson/Offy	Lost oil	141	0	$6,650
15	8	66	Len Sutton	Bryant Heating & Cooling	Vollstedt/Offy	Magneto	140	0	$6,450
16	33	62	Bill Cheesbourg	Arizona Apache Airlines	Epperly/Offy	Gear box	131	0	$6,400
17	6	12	Dan Gurney	Lotus powered by Ford	Lotus/Ford	Withdrawn-tires	110	0	$6,450
18	18	14	Troy Ruttman (W)	Dayton Steel Wheel	Watson/Offy	Spun out	99	0	$6,500
19	23	54	Bob Veith	MG Liquid Suspension	Huffaker/Offy	Piston	88	0	$6,550
20	25	52	Jack Brabham	Zink-Urschel Trackburner	Brabham/Offy	Fuel tank	77	0	$6,000
21	26	28	Jim McElreath	Studebaker-STP	Kurtis/Novi	Filter system	77	0	$5,850
22	28	77	Bob Mathouser (R)	Dayton Disc Brake	Walther/Offy	Spun out	77	0	$5,450
23	4	98	Parnelli Jones (W)	Agajanian Bowes Seal Fast	Watson/Offy	Pit fire	55	7	$8,200
24	1	6	Jim Clark	Lotus powered by Ford	Lotus/Ford	Suspension	47	14	$12,400
25	2	51	Bobby Marshman	Pure Oil Firebird	Lotus/Ford	Transmission	39	33	$12,000
26	24	84	Eddie Johnson	Thompson-Sears Allstate	Thompson/Ford	Fuel Pump	6	0	$5,900
27	15	86	Johnny Rutherford	Bardahl	Watson/Offy	Accident	2	0	$5,200
28	29	95	Chuck Stevenson	Diet Rite Cola	Watson/Offy	Accident	2	0	$5,200
29	14	83	Dave MacDonald (R)	Thompson-Sears Allstate	Thompson/Ford	Accident	1	0	$5,100
30	17	25	Eddie Sachs	American Red Ball	Halibrand/Ford	Accident	1	0	$6,300
31	16	64	Ronnie Duman (R)	Clean Wear Service Co.	Trevis/Offy	Accident	1	0	$5,000
32	22	9	Bobby Unser	Studebaker-STP	Ferguson/Novi	Accident	1	0	$6,750
33	31	26	Norm Hall	Hurst Floor Shift	Watson/Offy	Accident	1	0	$5,750

* - complete car name/entrant data not available for all entries
(R) - Indicated Rookie
(W) - Indicates Past Winner

1965

ABC's "Wide World of Sports" began airing an edited version of the Indianapolis 500 in color on a one-week delay.

In 1965, it became mandatory to make at least two pit stops during the race, strongly encouraging the use of methanol over gasoline. A maximum of seventy-five gallons of fuel could be stored on-board.

Rubberized fuel cells to contain fuel in the car's tank also became mandatory and pressurized refueling had been banned after the 1964 race.

The season opened at Phoenix, with Don Branson giving the front-engine car its last victory in USAC competition.

Qualifications adopted a new procedure, that being a draw for qualifying order.

The front row was A.J. Foyt, with a new record of 161.2 mph, with Jim Clark and Dan Gurney both in Lotus Fords. This was Foyt's first pole start. He stirred the crowd by commenting: "I just wanted to bring the record back to the United States".

Jim Clark was the first driver to officially break the 160 mph barrier in qualifications.

The tire war was on between Firestone and Goodyear.

Twenty-seven of thirty-three cars were rear-engined. Seventeen cars were shod with Firestone and sixteen with Goodyear.

Jim Hurtubise was able to return to Indy after recovering from severe burns from the year before sustained at the Milwaukee race.

Eleven rookies, including Mario Andretti, Al Unser and Gordon Johncock made a stellar first year group.

Rodger Ward failed to qualify after finishes of first, second, third, first, fourth, and second in the previous six "500s."

Jim Clark's Lotus Ford team hired NASCAR's Wood Brothers Team to handle pit stops.

The Plymouth Sports Fury paced the race. This was the first and only pace car appearance by Plymouth.

Clark led pretty much from start to finish and at the finish was almost two laps ahead of second-place Parnelli Jones. At the halfway point, he had led Jones by more than a lap. He averaged a new record of 150.7 mph. Jones drove Clark's pole-winning Lotus/Ford from 1964.

Clark's win resulted in:

the first rear-engine car to win;

just the second car colored green to win (Gaston Chevrolet—1920);

first to average over 150 mph for the race;

first foreign driver to win since Dario Resta in 1916.

Mario Andretti finished third, won Rookie of the Year and nearly caught Jones before the checker. Johncock finished fifth in a roadster. Al Unser finished ninth in a Foyt back-up. Andretti would go on to win the USAC National Championship.

Formula One driver, Masten Gregory, qualified for the race for the first time after two previous unsuccessful attempts. He qualified 31st and passed fourteen cars on the first lap. The Kansas-born Gregory stormed in the top five before retiring with engine problems after 59 laps.

In contrast to the tragic race of 1964, the 1965 race was one of the safest in history with only one wall contact and no injuries.

Hurtubise and Bobby Unser experienced mechanical problems and were eliminated in the last Novis to ever start an Indy 500.

Clark led 190 laps, and Foyt led 10.

*Jim Clark, A.J. Foyt and Parnelli Jones duel it out.
Clark dominates by leading 190 laps.*

RACE RESULTS FOR THE 1965 INDIANAPOLIS 500

Finish	Start	Car Num.	Driver	Car Name/Entrant*	Make/Model	Status	Laps	Led	Winnings
1	2	82	Jim Clark	Lotus powered by Ford	Lotus/Ford	150.686	200	190	$166,621
2	5	98	Parnelli Jones (W)	Agajanian Hurst	Kuzma-Lotus/Ford	149.200	200	0	$64,661
3	4	12	Mario Andretti (R)	Dean Van Lines	Brawner/Ford	149.121	200	0	$42,551
4	7	74	Al Miller (Krulac)	Jerry Alderman Ford	Lotus/Ford	146.581	200	0	$26,641
5	14	76	Gordon Johncock (R)	Weinberger Homes	Watson/Offy	146.417	200	0	$21,981
6	15	81	Mickey Rupp (R)	G.C. Murphy	Gerhardt/Offy	Running	198	0	$18,971
7	22	83	Bobby Johns (R)	Lotus powered by Ford	Lotus/Ford	Running	197	0	$16,886
8	18	4	Don Branson	Wynn's	Watson/Ford	Running	197	0	$16,376
9	32	45	Al Unser (R)	Sheraton-Thompson	Lola/Ford	Running	196	0	$14,416
10	28	23	Eddie Johnson	Chapman	Watson/Offy	Running	195	0	$14,656
11	9	7	Lloyd Ruby	Dupont Golden 7	Halibrand/Ford	Blown engine	184	0	$11,846
12	12	16	Len Sutton	Bryant Heating & Cooling	Vollstedt/Ford	Running	177	0	$11,586
13	29	14	Johnny Boyd	George R. Bryant & Staff	BRP/Ford	Rear gears	140	0	$11,976
14	21	53	Walt Hansgen	MG-Liquid Suspension	Huffaker/Offy	Overheating	117	0	$10,566
15	1	1	A.J. Foyt (W)	Sheraton-Thompson	Lotus/Ford	Gearbox	115	10	$20,517
16	24	5	Bud Tingelstad	American Red Ball	Lola/Ford	Accident	115	0	$9,596
17	6	66	Billy Foster (R)	Jim Robbins	Vollstedt/Offy	Water line	85	0	$9,936
18	19	18	Arnie Knepper (R)	Konstant Hot	Kurtis/Offy	Cylinder	80	0	$10,326
19	8	9	Bobby Unser	STP Gas Treatment	Ferguson/Novi	Oil fitting	69	0	$9,216
20	13	52	Jim McElreath	Zink-Urschel Trackburner	Brabham/Offy	Gear chain	66	0	$8,656
21	16	94	George Snider (R)	Gerhardt	Gerhardt/Offy	Rear end	64	0	$8,696
22	25	65	Ronnie Duman	Travelon Trailer/ H&H Bookbinding	Gerhardt/Offy	Rear end	62	0	$8,786
23	31	41	Masten Gregory (R)	George R. Bryant & Staff	BRP/Ford	Oil Pressure	59	0	$9,076
24	10	54	Bob Veith	MG-Liquid Suspension	Huffaker/Offy	Piston	58	0	$8,266
25	26	88	Chuck Stevenson	Vita Fresh Orange Juice	Kuzma/Offy	Piston	50	0	$8,306
26	3	17	Dan Gurney	Yamaha	Lotus/Ford	Timing gears	42	0	$9,596
27	17	48	Jerry Grant (R)	Bardahl/MG Liquid Susp.	Huffaker/Offy	Magneto	30	0	$7,786
28	30	19	Chuck Rodee	Wally Weir's Mobilgas	Halibrand/Offy	Rear end	28	0	$8,726
29	27	29	Joe Leonard (R)	All American Racers	Halibrand/Ford	Oil leak	27	0	$7,816
30	23	25	Roger McCluskey	All American Racers	Halibrand/Ford	Clutch	18	0	$8,106
31	11	24	Johnny Rutherford	Racing Associates	Halibrand/Ford	Rear end	15	0	$7,596
32	33	47	Bill Cheesbourg	WIFE Good Guy	Gerhardt/Offy	Magneto	14	0	$7,836
33	20	59	Jim Hurtubise	STP-Tombstone Life	Kurtis/Novi	Transmission	1	0	$8,626

* - complete car name/entrant data not available for all entries
(R) - Indicated Rookie
(W) - Indicates Past Winner

1966

Norman Graham Hill substituted for Walt Hansgen, who had lost his life in spring testing at Le Mans. Hill had won the World Driving Championship in 1962 and would win the title again in 1968.

George Bignotti led the John Mecom-owned team with Jackie Stewart, Rodger Ward and Graham Hill as the drivers.

Team Lotus was now sponsored by STP with Jim Clark and Al Unser as their drivers.

The Agajanian team had two new Shrikes for Parnelli Jones and Dick Atkins.

GCR Racers entered a car for NASCAR rookie Lee Roy Yarbrough. GCR stood for Gus Grissom, Gordon Cooper and Jim Rathmann. Lee Roy did not make the race.

Bill Cheesbourg was entered in a unique car powered by two Porsche engines. One engine powered the rear wheels, while the other the front wheels. Cheesbourg could only muster about 149 mph, which fell short of what he needed to make the field by 10 mph.

Art Malone was fined by USAC officials for not wearing shoes following an accident during practice. Malone was having difficulty fitting into his Halibrand-Offy.

The front row was Mario Andretti, Jim Clark and George Snider. Andretti set a new record at 165.9 mph to win the pole in his Brawner/Hawk.

Graham Hill started fifteenth in his rookie race in a Lola/Ford.

Mel Kenyon was returning from serious injuries from a fiery crash at Langhorne the previous summer that had cost him the fingers on his left hand.

Chuck Rodee was driving the car Rodger Ward failed to qualify in 1965. Rodee crashed as he was warming up for a qualifying attempt and backed into the first turn wall hard. He was fatally injured when his aorta ruptured.

A.J. Foyt crashed in practice on the first day of qualifying. He qualified for eighteenth starting position on the second day.

Bobby Grim's front-engine Watson roadster was the only of its type in the field.

At the green flag, a front-stretch accident involved thirteen cars and eliminated eleven cars, including A.J. Foyt's. Billy Foster hit the outside wall while trying to dodge Gordon Johncock's lagging car. Foster had a five-speed gear box, while Johncock's car had a two-speed gear box.

The race was stopped by an accident for only the second time in history and was restarted 100 minutes later. Fortunately the only injury sustained was a cut hand to A.J. Foyt as he climbed the fence to safety.

Andretti led early but mechanical problems took him out by lap twenty-seven. Clark led from lap seventeen until spinning in the fourth turn without contact on lap sixty-four.

Clark spun again, this time on lap eighty-six and once again in turn four without contact. He was able to continue after both spins and didn't pit because he didn't flat spot the tires.

At the halfway mark there were only thirteen cars still running.

Lloyd Ruby and Clark swapped the lead until lap 150, when Jackie Stewart took over.

An oil leak ended Ruby's chances of winning near the three-quarter mark.

Steady-driving Jackie Stewart took the lead on lap 150 and led until lap 190 when oil pressure problems ended his day. This was Stewart's first race on an oval. Stewart would eventually win three World Driving Championships and 27 Grand Prix races.

Graham Hill led the last ten laps for the win. He averaged 144.3 mph.

As the race finished a dispute ensued because Clark and his team felt they had won. A scoring error was later noticed. It had given Clark one of his teammate's (Al Unser) laps. No protest was made. Hill won by forty-one seconds.

Jimmy McElreath finished third with Gordon Johncock fourth. Johncock actually had the least amount of time on the track for 500 miles, but was involved in the first lap accident and lost valuable time in the pits for repairs.

A record low of seven cars were running at the finish.

Rodger Ward retired at the victory banquet, stating it was no longer fun. He had pulled his car in the pits with handling problems.

Jackie Stewart won Rookie of the Year, even though another rookie actually won the race.

Ruby led sixty-eight laps, Clark, sixty-six laps, and Stewart, forty laps. Hill led only the last ten laps.

Hill became the first rookie winner since George Souders in 1927.

Johnny Rutherford missed the 1966 race because of two broken arms sustained in a sprint car accident at Eldora.

Graham Hill celebrates his win as a confused Jim Clark attempts to pull into Victory Lane.

RACE RESULTS FOR THE 1966 INDIANAPOLIS 500

Finish	Start	Car Num.	Driver	Car Name/Entrant*	Make/Model	Status	Laps	Led	Winnings
1	15	24	Graham Hill (R)	American Red Ball	Lola/Ford	144.317	200	10	$156,297
2	2	19	Jim Clark (W)	STP Gas Treatment	Lotus/Ford	143.843	200	66	$76,992
3	7	3	Jim McElreath	Zink-Urschel-Slick	Brabham/Ford	143.742	200	0	$42,586
4	6	72	Gordon Johncock	Weinberger Homes	Gerhardt/Ford	143.084	200	0	$26,381
5	17	94	Mel Kenyon (R)	Gerhardt	Gerhardt/Offy	Running	198	0	$21,987
6	11	43	Jackie Stewart (R)	Bowes Seal Fast	Lola/Ford	Oil pressure	190	40	$25,767
7	29	54	Eddie Johnson	Valvoline II	Huffaker/Offy	Stalled	175	0	$17,615
8	28	11	Bobby Unser	Vita Fresh Orange Juice	Huffaker/Offy	Running	171	0	$16,562
9	20	6	Joe Leonard	Yamaha Eagle	Eagle/Ford	Stalled	170	0	$15,822
10	10	88	Jerry Grant	Bardahl-Pacesetter Homes	Eagle/Ford	Running	167	0	$15,055
11	5	14	Lloyd Ruby	Bardahl Eagle	Eagle/Ford	Cam	166	68	$24,926
12	23	18	Al Unser	STP Oil Treatment	Lotus/Ford	Accident	161	0	$14,965
13	21	8	Roger McCluskey	G.C. Murphy	Eagle/Ford	Oil leak	129	0	$13,123
14	4	98	Parnelli Jones (W)	Agajanian's Rev 500	Shrike/Offy	Wheel bearing	87	0	$13,462
15	13	26	Rodger Ward (W)	Bryant Heating & Cooling	Lola/Offy	Handling	74	0	$11,857
16	25	77	Carl Williams (R)	Dayton Steel Wheel	Gerhardt/Ford	Valve, oil	38	0	$12,171
17	22	56	Jim Hurtubise	Gerhardt	Gerhardt/Offy	Oil	29	0	$11,604
18	1	1	Mario Andretti	Dean Van Lines	Brawner/Ford	Valve	27	16	$25,121
19	3	82	George Snider	Sheraton-Thompson	Coyote/Ford	Accident	22	0	$12,075
20	8	12	Chuck Hulse	Wynn's	Watson/Ford	Accident	22	0	$10,463
21	27	22	Bud Tingelstad	Federal Engineering	Gerhardt/Offy	Overheating	16	0	$10,470
22	14	28	Johnny Boyd	Prestone	B.R.P./Ford	Accident	5	0	$9,896
23	9	4	Don Branson	Leader Cards Racer	Gerhardt/Ford	Accident	0	0	$9,791
24	12	27	Billy Foster	Jim Robbins	Vollstedt/Ford	Accident	0	0	$9,554
25	16	53	Gary Congdon (R)	Valvoline	Huffaker/Offy	Accident	0	0	$9,386
26	18	2	A.J. Foyt (W)	Sheraton-Thompson	Lotus/Ford	Accident	0	0	$10,887
27	19	31	Dan Gurney	All American Racers	Eagle/Ford	Accident	0	0	$9,806
28	24	66	Cale Yarborough (R)	Jim Robbins	Vollstedt/Ford	Accident	0	0	$9,794
29	26	37	Arnie Knepper	Sam Liosi	Cecil/Ford	Accident	0	0	$9,301
30	30	75	Al Miller (Krulac)	Jerry Alderman Ford	Lotus/Ford	Accident	0	0	$8,876
31	31	39	Bobby Grim	Racing Associates	Watson/Offy	Accident	0	0	$8,720
32	32	34	Larry Dickson (R)	Michner Petroleum	Lola/Ford	Accident	0	0	$9,933
33	33	96	Ronnie Duman	Harrison	Eisert/Ford	Accident	0	0	$9,564

* - complete car name/entrant data not available for all entries
(R) - Indicated Rookie
(W) - Indicates Past Winner

1967

A.J. Foyt's cars were "Foyt Orange," or as Foyt claimed, "poppy red," for the first time.

Don Branson had been fatally injured at Ascot in the fall of 1966 and was replaced on the Leader Card team by Bobby Unser.

The very innovative Granatelli STP #40 turbine car was designed by Ken Wallis. The Pratt-Whitney turbine engine was normally used in helicopters. The annulus intake on the turbine engine was restricted to 23.999 square inches. The car also had four-wheel drive.

The turbine car was nicknamed "Whooshmobile" and "Silent Sam."

The public-address system was used for the first time on practice days.

Mario Andretti won the pole for the second year in a row, at a new record of almost 169 mph. Dan Gurney and Gordon Johncock joined Andretti on the front row. Parnelli Jones qualified sixth in the Granatelli turbine.

Jim Clark qualified sixteenth, Jackie Stewart was twenty-ninth after being bumped in another car, and Graham Hill started thirty-first.

No front-engine cars made the race for the first time in history.

Three-time "500" winner Mauri Rose drove the newly-introduced Chevrolet Camaro to pace the field.

Mario Andretti took the lead at the green flag, but Parnelli Jones passed him on the inside coming out of turn two on the first lap. Andretti signaled his disgust to Jones as he was overtaken. Jones led until rain stopped the race for the day on lap nineteen. This was the first time in history the race was run over a two-day period.

Andretti had experienced a clutch problem which was repaired overnight. He was six laps down when the race was restarted the following day.

After the restart, Jones led virtually all day, leading a total of 171 laps, but he retired on lap 197 with a broken transmission resulting from a malfunction of a $6 ball bearing. Foyt trailed by three quarters of a lap at the time. Jones claimed that if he had just "taken it a little easier" exiting the pits, we would have won.

Foyt took the lead and avoided a last-lap front stretch crash involving five cars to win his third 500. Al Unser finished second and Parnelli salvaged sixth. Foyt led twenty-seven laps and set a new race record with a 151.2 mph average.

Foyt became the fourth three-time winner in history.

Denis Hulme won Rookie of the Year with a fourth-place finish. The New Zealand-born Hulme would go on to win the 1967 Formula One World Championship for the Brabham team.

Until near the end of the race, the only problem encountered by Jones was when he and Lee Roy Yarbrough made slight contact on lap fifty-two. Both cars spun but were able to continue.

The turbo car ran on kerosene.

Who predicted before the race that the turbine would have gearbox failure? A.J. Foyt.

Just two weeks later, A.J. Foyt teamed with Dan Gurney and won the Le Mans 24-Hours Race.

Foyt would go on to win the 1967 USAC National Championship.

The revolutionary STP Granatelli Turbine with Parnelli Jones was in the lead, but dropped out late to finish sixth.

RACE RESULTS FOR THE 1967 INDIANAPOLIS 500

Finish	Start	Car Num.	Driver	Car Name/Entrant*	Make/Model	Status	Laps	Led	Winnings
1	4	14	A.J. Foyt (W)	Sheraton-Thompson	Coyote/Ford	151.207	200	27	$171,527
2	9	5	Al Unser	Retzloff Chemical	Lola/Ford	Running	198	0	$67,127
3	5	4	Joe Leonard	Sheraton-Thompson	Coyote/Ford	Running	197	0	$43,177
4	24	69	Denis Hulme (R)	City of Daytona Beach	Eagle/Ford	Running	197	0	$28,177
5	11	2	Jim McElreath	John Zink Trackburner	Moore/Ford	Running	197	0	$22,957
6	6	40	Parnelli Jones (W)	STP Oil Treatment	Granatelli/ Pratt & Whitney	Bearing	196	171	$55,767
7	27	8	Chuck Hulse	Hopkins	Lola/Offy	Accident	195	0	$18,397
8	13	16	Art Pollard (R)	Thermo-King Auto Air Conditioning	Gerhardt/Offy	Running	195	0	$16,928
9	8	6	Bobby Unser	Rislone	Eagle/Ford	Running	193	0	$15,773
10	23	41	Carl Williams	George R. Bryant	B.R.P./Ford	Accident	189	0	$16,173
11	28	46	Bob Veith	Thermo-King Auto Air Conditioning	Gerhardt/Offy	Running	189	0	$14,461
12	3	3	Gordon Johncock	Gilmore Broadcasting	Gerhardt/Ford	Accident	188	0	$15,518
13	12	39	Bobby Grim	Racing Associates	Gerhardt/Offy	Accident	187	0	$13,244
14	25	10	Bud Tingelstad	Federal Engineering	Gerhardt/Ford	Spun out	182	0	$13,376
15	21	22	Larry Dickson	Vita Fresh Orange Juice	Lotus/Ford	Spun out	180	0	$12,565
16	14	15	Mel Kenyon	Thermo-King Auto Air Conditioning	Gerhardt/Offy	Spun out	177	0	$12,273
17	20	21	Cale Yarborough	Bryant Heating & Cooling	Vollstedt/Ford	Accident	176	0	$11,900
18	29	24	Jackie Stewart	Bowes Seal Fast	Lola/Ford	Engine	168	0	$12,796
19	22	12	Roger McCluskey	G.C. Murphy	Eagle/Ford	Engine	165	0	$12,961
20	30	42	Jerry Grant	All American Racers	Eagle/Ford	Radiator	162	0	$11,845
21	2	74	Dan Gurney	Wagner Lockheed Brake Fluid	Eagle/Ford	Black flag	160	2	$15,498
22	18	19	Arnie Knepper	M.V.S. Racers	Cecil/Ford	Engine	158	0	$10,570
23	17	98	Ronnie Duman	Agajanian's Rev 500	Shrike/Offy	Fuel trouble	154	0	$10,261
24	32	48	Jochen Rindt (R)	Wagner Lockheed Brake Fluid	Eagle/Ford-Weslake	Mechanical	108	0	$10,571
25	19	45	Johnny Rutherford	Weinberger Homes	Eagle/Ford	Accident	103	0	$10,000
26	10	26	George Snider	Wagner Lockheed Brake Fluid	Mongoose/Ford	Accident	99	0	$9,898
27	26	67	Lee Roy Yarbrough (R)	Jim Robbins Seat Belt	Vollstedt/Ford	Accident	87	0	$10,015
28	33	32	Al Miller (Krulac)	Cleaver-Brooks	Gerhardt/Ford	Oil filter	74	0	$9,951
29	15	53	Wally Dallenbach (R)	Valvoline	Huffaker/Offy	Accident	73	0	$9,406
30	1	1	Mario Andretti	Dean Van Lines	Hawk/Ford	Lost wheel	58	0	$21,049
31	16	31	Jim Clark (W)	STP Oil Treatment	Lotus/Ford	Piston	35	0	$9,373
32	31	81	Graham Hill (W)	STP Oil Treatment	Lotus/Ford	Piston	23	0	$9,935
33	7	25	Lloyd Ruby	American Red Ball	Mongoose/Offy	Valves	3	0	$9,666

* - complete car name/entrant data not available for all entries
(R) - Indicated Rookie
(W) - Indicates Past Winner

1968

"Pelican Joe" Leonard was a three-time American Motorcyclist Association national champion (1954, 1956, and 1957).

For the turbine engines, the annulus intake area was reduced from 23.999 square inches to 15.999 square inches.

The Granatelli wedge turbines were actually Lotus type-56 with four-wheel drive.

In the spring of 1968, two-time World Champion and Indianapolis 500 champion, Jim Clark was fatally injured in an accident at Hockenheim, Germany in a Formula 2 race. Clark won twenty-five Grand Prix races, the record at that time, before passing at just thirty-two years old.

Upon the death of Al Dean, Mario Andretti became a new team owner and drove a brand new Brawner Hawk.

Second-generation drivers Bill Vukovich Jr. and Gary Bettenhausen were entered as rookies.

Jackie Stewart missed the 1968 race because of a fractured wrist sustained in an accident in Spain.

Early in the month (May 7), England's Mike Spence tested teammate Greg Weld's turbine car and crashed in turn one. Spence died a few hours later.

The next week, Joe Leonard crashed the 1967 #40 Parnelli Jones turbine car, upon which it was withdrawn and never raced again. Jones had retired from racing Indy cars at what seemed to be the peak of his career and focused on sports car and off-road racing.

A hot air balloon race was held on a qualifying day in commemoration of the first contest ever held at the Speedway in 1909.

The front row was Leonard in an STP turbine with a new track record (171.6 mph), Hill in a turbine and Bobby Unser in his Leader Card Rislone Special Eagle/Offy.

Graham Hill was the first driver to officially eclipse the 170 mph barrier.

Because of numerous rain delays, at six p.m. on the fourth day of qualifying there were only twenty-five cars qualified. An extra qualifying session until 7:40 p.m. added two cars to the grid. It was continued on Monday and the field was filled. Rain had fallen at some point for twenty-three straight days and was the culprit in the qualification extension.

Jim Hurtubise qualified during the Monday session and started in thirtieth position in the last front-engine car to ever qualify for the race. Bob Hurt was critically injured (paralyzed) in this Monday session.

Joe Leonard took the lead at the start, but Bobby Unser passed for the lead on lap eight and led until pitting on lap fifty-six.

Unser, Lloyd Ruby and Leonard alternated the lead until Unser lost all but top gear (fourth), resulting in extremely slow exits from the pits on his last two stops.

Ruby led from lap 166 to 174, then experienced mechanical problems resulting in a long pit stop.

Leonard took the lead on lap 175 and held it until the restart on lap 192 after Carl Williams's crash. A broken fuel pump drive shaft eliminated Leonard as the green flag waved and Bobby Unser led the last nine laps to victory. Unser set a new race record at 152.9 mph and won by fifty-four seconds over Dan Gurney. Gurney wore the first full-face helmet at the Speedway.

Unser's Rislone Eagle/Offy was the first winner with a turbocharged engine.

Unser led 127 laps total, with Ruby leading 42, and Leonard, 31 laps.

Dan Gurney finished second and Mel Kenyon third. Billy Vukovich Jr. finished seventh and won Rookie of the Year.

On the final yellow, Leonard led with several cars between himself and second place Unser, including his teammate Art Pollard. Pollard attempted to slow down to increase the gap between Leonard and Unser but the officials ordered him to speed up as the crowd voiced their displeasure of Pollard's interference.

Bobby Unser would go on to win the 1968 USAC National Championship.

The movie Winning, with Paul Newman, was filmed at the track in 1968.

1968 Front row: Joe Leonard—Lotus/Turbine, Graham Hill—Lotus/Turbine and Bobby Unser—Eagle/Offy.

RACE RESULTS FOR THE 1968 INDIANAPOLIS 500

Finish	Start	Car Num.	Driver	Car Name/Entrant*	Make/Model	Status	Laps	Led	Winnings
1	3	3	Bobby Unser	Rislone	Eagle/Offy	152.882	200	127	$175,140
2	10	48	Dan Gurney	Olsonite	Eagle/Ford-Weslake	152.187	200	0	$65,095
3	17	15	Mel Kenyon	City of Lebanon	Gerhardt/Offy	149.224	200	0	$44,960
4	20	42	Denis Hulme	Olsonite	Eagle/Ford	149.140	200	0	$26,625
5	5	25	Lloyd Ruby	Gene White Company	Mongoose/Offy	148.529	200	42	$30,365
6	26	59	Ronnie Duman	Cleaver-Brooks	Brabham/Offy	148.232	200	0	$19,205
7	23	98	Bill Vukovich II (R)	Wagner-Lockheed	Shrike/Offy	Running	198	0	$18,520
8	27	90	Mike Mosley (R)	Zecol-Lubaid	Watson/Offy	Running	197	0	$17,490
9	31	94	Sam Sessions (R)	Valvoline	Finley/Offy	Running	197	0	$15,730
10	25	6	Bobby Grim	Gene White Company	Mongoose/Offy	Running	196	0	$15,170
11	24	16	Bob Veith	Thermo-King Auto Air Conditioning	Gerhardt/Offy	Running	196	0	$14,510
12	1	60	Joe Leonard	STP Oil Treatment	Lotus/Pratt & Whitney	Fuel shaft	191	31	$37,520
13	11	20	Art Pollard	STP Oil Treatment	Lotus/Pratt & Whitney	Fuel shaft	188	0	$12,950
14	13	82	Jim McElreath	Jim Greer	Coyote/Ford	Stalled	179	0	$12,910
15	28	84	Carl Williams	Sheraton-Thompson	Coyote/Ford	Accident	163	0	$14,255
16	18	10	Bud Tingelstad	Federal Engineering	Gerhardt/Ford	Oil pressure	158	0	$12,670
17	12	54	Wally Dallenbach	Valvoline	Finley/Offy	Engine failure	146	0	$11,530
18	21	18	Johnny Rutherford	City of Seattle	Eagle/Ford	Collision	125	0	$11,585
19	2	70	Graham Hill (W)	STP Oil Treatment	Lotus/Pratt & Whitney	Accident	110	0	$13,810
20	8	1	A.J. Foyt (W)	Sheraton-Thompson	Coyote/Ford	Rear end	86	0	$11,130
21	19	45	Ronnie Bucknum (R)	Weinberger Homes	Eagle/Ford	Fuel leak	76	0	$10,970
22	14	27	Jim Malloy (R)	Jim Robbins Co.	Vollstedt/Ford	Rear end	64	0	$10,130
23	15	78	Jerry Grant	Bardahl Eagle	Eagle/Ford	Oil leak	50	0	$9,760
24	22	11	Gary Bettenhausen (R)	Thermo-King Auto Air Conditioning	Gerhardt/Offy	Damage	43	0	$9,860
25	32	21	Arnie Knepper	Bryant Heating & Cooling	Vollstedt/Ford	Hit wheel	42	0	$9,760
26	6	24	Al Unser	Retzloff Chemical	Lola/Ford	Accident	40	0	$10,120
27	9	4	Gordon Johncock	Gilmore Broadcasting	Gerhardt/Offy	Rear end	37	0	$9,480
28	33	64	Larry Dickson	Overseas National Airways	Hawk II/Ford	Piston	24	0	$9,160
29	7	8	Roger McCluskey	G.C. Murphy	Eagle/Offy	Oil filter	16	0	$9,460
30	30	56	Jim Hurtubise	Pepsi-Frito Lay	Mallard/Offy	Piston	9	0	$9,330
31	29	29	George Snider	Vel's Parnelli Jones	Mongoose/Ford	Oil leak	9	0	$9,470
32	16	35	Jochen Rindt	Repco-Brabham	Brabham/Repco-Brabham	Piston	5	0	$9,830
33	4	2	Mario Andretti	Overseas National Airways	Hawk III/Ford	Piston	2	0	$9,960

* - complete car name/entrant data not available for all entries
(R) - Indicated Rookie
(W) - Indicates Past Winner

1969

This was the first year at Indy for Penske Racing, led by thirty-two year old Roger Penske.

Vel's Parnelli Jones Racing purchased Al Retzloff's team and hired Al Unser and chief mechanic George Bignotti.

Rain nearly washed out pole day, but during the afternoon rookie Jigger Sirois made an attempt and waved off a time that very well might have put him on the pole. It rained immediately after.

Al Unser fell from a motorcycle during the rain delay and broke his ankle, eliminating his chances of participating in the race. Bud Tinglestad replaced Unser in the Vel's Parnelli Jones Lola/Offy.

Rain prevented any cars from qualifying on the first weekend.

A.J. Foyt and Mario Andretti continued their speed duel for the second week, until Andretti crashed hard in turn four in his Granatelli-entered four-wheel-drive STP Lotus on Wednesday, forcing him to go to his rear-drive Brawner Hawk back-up.

The front row was Foyt on the pole at 170.6 mph, Andretti and Bobby Unser.

Because of burns on Mario's face from his accident, his twin brother Aldo subbed for him in the "front row" picture.

A.J. Foyt led most of the first seventy-eight laps, but turbocharger problems on lap seventy-nine resulted in a twenty-two-minute pit stop.

Lloyd Ruby and Andretti traded the lead until Ruby pitted while leading on lap 105 and started rolling before the fuel hose was released. It tore the nozzle opening out of the tank, eliminating Ruby from the race.

Andretti led the remaining ninety-four laps and averaged a record 156.867 mph, but was fighting an engine overheating problem throughout.

Dan Gurney was runner-up for the second year in a row, Bobby Unser third and Mel Kenyon fourth for his third top-five finish in four years. Gurney was more than two laps behind Andretti.

Mark Donohue, driving for Roger Penske, finished seventh after a lengthy stop to replace a magneto, which took him out of a better finish. Donohue won Rookie of the Year. He was a graduate of Brown University with a degree in mechanical engineering.

Andretti led 116 laps, and Foyt 66 laps.

Winning entrant Andy Granatelli kissed Mario in Victory Lane after finally getting his first Indy 500 win. He had been trying since 1946.

Mario Andretti would go on to win the 1969 USAC National Championship.

Car owner Andy Granatelli kisses Mario Andretti in celebratory jubilation as twin brother Aldo Andretti watches.

RACE RESULTS FOR THE 1969 INDIANAPOLIS 500

Finish	Start	Car Num.	Driver	Car Name/Entrant*	Make/Model	Status	Laps	Led	Winnings
1	2	2	Mario Andretti	STP Oil Treatment	Hawk III/Ford	156.867	200	116	$206,727
2	10	48	Dan Gurney	Olsonite	Eagle/Weslake-Ford	155.337	200	0	$67,732
3	3	1	Bobby Unser (W)	Bardahl	Lola/Offy	154.090	200	0	$45,647
4	24	9	Mel Kenyon	Krohne Grain Transport	Gerhardt/Offy	152.177	200	0	$30,612
5	33	92	Peter Revson (R)	Repco-Brabham	Brabham/Repco	Running	197	0	$25,722
6	11	44	Joe Leonard	City of Daytona Beach	Eagle/Ford	Running	193	0	$21,602
7	4	66	Mark Donohue (R)	Sunoco-Simoniz	Lola/Offy	Running	190	0	$21,512
8	1	6	A.J. Foyt (W)	Sheraton-Thompson	Coyote/Ford	Running	181	66	$50,252
9	31	21	Larry Dickson	Bryant Heating & Cooling	Vollstedt/Ford	Running	180	0	$17,426
10	32	97	Bobby Johns	Wagner-Lockheed	Shrike/Offy	Running	171	0	$19,841
11	13	10	Jim Malloy	Jim Robbins Co.	Vollstedt/Offy	Running	165	0	$17,358
12	23	11	Sam Sessions	Valvoline	Finley/Offy	Running	163	0	$15,846
13	22	90	Mike Mosley	Zecol-Lubaid	Eagle/Offy	Piston	162	0	$14,755
14	6	82	Roger McCluskey	G.C. Murphy	Coyote/Ford	Split header	157	0	$15,493
15	18	15	Bud Tingelstad	Vel's Parnelli Jones	Lola/Offy	Engine	155	0	$13,894
16	15	84	George Snider	Sheraton-Thompson	Coyote/Ford	Running	152	0	$14,016
17	14	59	Sonny Ates (R)	Krohne Grain Transport	Brabham/Offy	Magneto	146	0	$13,609
18	25	42	Denis Hulme	Olsonite Eagle	Eagle/Ford	Clutch	145	0	$12,823
19	5	12	Gordon Johncock	Gilmore Broadcasting	Gerhardt/Offy	Piston	137	0	$13,585
20	20	4	Lloyd Ruby	Wynn's Spitfire	Mongoose/Offy	Fuel hose	105	11	$13,864
21	19	22	Wally Dallenbach	Sprite	Eagle/Offy	Clutch	82	7	$12,991
22	21	29	Arnie Knepper	M.V.S.	Cecil/Ford	Accident	82	0	$12,189
23	8	67	Lee Roy Yarbrough	Jim Robbins Co.	Vollstedt/Ford	Split header	65	0	$12,258
24	29	95	Jack Brabham	Repco-Brabham	Brabham/Repco	Ignition	58	0	$11,725
25	30	57	Carl Williams	STP Gas Treatment	Gerhardt/Offy	Clutch	50	0	$11,809
26	9	8	Gary Bettenhausen	Thermo-King Auto Air Conditioner	Gerhardt/Offy	Piston	35	0	$11,541
27	27	62	George Follmer (R)	Retzloff Chemical	Gilbert/Ford	Engine failure	26	0	$11,994
28	7	38	Jim McElreath	Jack Adams Airplanes	Hawk II/Offy	Engine fire	24	0	$11,768
29	17	36	Johnny Rutherford	Patrick Petroleum	Eagle/Offy	Oil tank	24	0	$10,963
30	16	45	Ronnie Bucknum	Weinberger Homes	Eagle/Offy	Piston	16	0	$10,929
31	12	40	Art Pollard	STP Oil Treatment	Lotus/Offy	Drive line	7	0	$10,816
32	26	98	Bill Vukovich II	Wagner Lockheed	Mongoose/Offy	Rod	1	0	$11,974
33	28	16	Bruce Walkup (R)	Thermo-King Auto Air Conditioner	Gerhardt/Offy	Transmission	0	0	$11,353

* - complete car name/entrant data not available for all entries
(R) - Indicated Rookie
(W) - Indicates Past Winner

1970

Al Unser drove a new PJ Colt-Ford for Vel's Parnelli Jones Racing, sponsored by Johnny Lightning. His teammate was Joe Leonard.

Defending national champion Mario Andretti was driving a new McNamara/Ford for STP.

Team McLaren made its Indy debut with Chris Amon and Denis Hulme. Carl Williams and Peter Revson eventually ended up driving the McLaren cars in the race.

In practice, the McLaren of Denis Hulme caught fire. He sustained serious hand burns and was unable to compete. Peter Revson took over his McLaren.

Three-time Formula One champion Jack Brabham returned to Indy in his final season of racing.

Mark Donohue, with Penske Racing, looked formidable the entire month.

Al Unser took the pole at 170.2 mph. Johnny Rutherford missed the pole in his Patrick Petroleum four-year old Eagle by three thousandths of a second and A.J. Foyt started third.

Jigger Sirois did not make the field in the last turbine-powered car to run at Indy.

Bruce Walkup qualified an Agajanian car that was the only car in history to race with a full roll cage.

Two-time 500 winner Rodger Ward drove the Oldsmobile 4-4-2 pace car.

The race started a little late due to morning rain. Jim Malloy, starting ninth, spun and hit the fourth turn wall coming to the green to start the race. A half-shaft failure caused the wreck, which resulted in a red flag before the start, causing a thirty-minute delay. Somehow everyone in the eight rows behind Malloy avoided the accident.

Al Unser led from lap one for a total of 190 laps, only relinquishing the lead on pit stops. He led the last 95 laps and averaged 155.7 mph in a dominating performance. He lapped all but four cars.

Johnny Rutherford was the only driver to pass Al Unser on the track. Rutherford nipped Unser to turn one at the start, but Unser regained the lead on the back stretch.

Lloyd Ruby appeared to be the only formidable opposition. He charged from twenty-fifth starting position to the lead on the fiftieth lap, but his seventh blown engine of the month ended his chances. Ruby's car was memorable as it was painted like the American Flag.

Mark Donohue finished in second place, thirty-two seconds behind, while Dan Gurney finished third in his last 500 before retirement.

Donnie Allison, driving for Foyt, finished fourth and won Rookie of the Year. Allison was part of the "Alabama Gang" in NASCAR.

Foyt experienced gear box problems late in the race, after running second behind Unser for most of the race. As he completed his 195th lap, Foyt did a hairpin turn at the pit exit and proceeded up the pit in the wrong direction. He finished tenth.

The total purse exceeded $1,000,000 for the first time in history.

Al and Bobby Unser became the first siblings to win the race.

Nineteen-seventy was the last year in which Victory Lane was located at the south end of the pits.

This was chief mechanic George Bignotti's fourth Indy win. Parnelli Jones became the first "500" winner to later win as a car owner.

Al led 1,527 laps during the season and Bobby Unser was next, leading only 130 laps.

Al Unser dominated the inaugural Ontario 500, but on lap 186, with a one lap lead, was eliminated with mechanical problems. Jim McElreath was the winner.

Al Unser won his first USAC National Championship.

Al Unser wins his first in the beautiful Johnny Lightning Special.

RACE RESULTS FOR THE 1970 INDIANAPOLIS 500

Finish	Start	Car Num.	Driver	Car Name/Entrant*	Make/Model	Status	Laps	Led	Winnings
1	1	2	Al Unser	Johnny Lightning 500	P.J. Colt/Ford	155.749	200	190	$271,698
2	5	66	Mark Donohue	Sunoco	Lola/Ford	155.317	200	5	$86,427
3	11	48	Dan Gurney	Olsonite Eagle	Eagle/Offy	153.201	200	0	$58,977
4	23	83	Donnie Allison (R)	Greer	Eagle/Ford	152.777	200	0	$36,002
5	33	14	Jim McElreath	Sheraton-Thompson	Coyote/Ford	152.182	200	0	$32,577
6	8	1	Mario Andretti (W)	STP Oil Treatment	McNamara/Ford	Running	199	0	$28,202
7	29	89	Jerry Grant	Nelson Iron Works	Eagle/Offy	Running	198	0	$26,977
8	15	38	Rick Muther (R)	The Tony Express	Hawk II/Offy	Running	197	0	$25,302
9	19	75	Carl Williams	McLaren	McLaren/Offy	Running	197	0	$22,352
10	3	7	A.J. Foyt (W)	Sheraton-Thompson	Coyote/Ford	Running	195	2	$24,902
11	7	3	Bobby Unser (W)	Wagner-Lockheed	Eagle/Ford	Running	192	0	$20,552
12	32	67	Sam Sessions	Jim Robbins Co.	Vollstedt/Ford	Running	190	0	$19,752
13	26	32	Jack Brabham	Gilmore Broadcasting-Brabham	Brabham/Offy	Piston	175	1	$20,227
14	31	44	Dick Simon (R)	Bryant Heating & Cooling	Vollstedt/Ford	Running	168	0	$18,427
15	27	19	Ronnie Bucknum	M.V.S.	Morris/Ford	Accident	162	0	$18,602
16	22	23	Mel Kenyon	Sprite	Coyote/Offy	Accident	160	0	$17,552
17	24	22	Wally Dallenbach	Sprite	Eagle/Offy	Coil	143	0	$17,077
18	2	18	Johnny Rutherford	Patrick Petroleum	Eagle/Offy	Header	135	0	$18,327
19	13	27	Lee Roy Yarbrough	Jim Robbins Co.	Vollstedt/Ford	Turbo gear	107	0	$16,302
20	10	84	George Snider	Greer	Coyote/Ford	Suspension	105	0	$16,002
21	12	9	Mike Mosley	G.C. Murphy	Eagle/Offy	Radiator	96	0	$15,627
22	16	73	Peter Revson	McLaren	McLaren/Offy	Magneto	87	0	$16,627
23	30	58	Bill Vukovich II	Sugaripe Prune	Brabham/Offy	Clutch	78	0	$15,252
24	18	15	Joe Leonard	Johnny Lightning 500	P.J. Colt/Ford	Ignition switch	73	0	$15,452
25	4	11	Roger McCluskey	Quickick	Scorpion/Ford	Suspension	62	0	$15,727
26	20	16	Gary Bettenhausen	Thermo-King Auto Air Conditioner	Gerhardt/Offy	Valve	55	0	$14,677
27	25	25	Lloyd Ruby	Daniels Cablevision	Mongoose/Offy	Drive gear	54	2	$17,252
28	17	5	Gordon Johncock	Gilmore Broadcasting	Gerhardt/Ford	Piston	45	0	$14,902
29	14	97	Bruce Walkup	Wynn's Spit-Fire	Mongoose/Offy	Timing gear	44	0	$13,927
30	6	10	Art Pollard	Art Pollard Car Wash Systems	Kingfish/Offy	Piston	28	0	$14,427
31	21	20	George Follmer	STP Oil Treatment	Hawk III/Ford	Oil gasket	18	0	$14,002
32	28	93	Greg Weld (R)	Art Pollard Car Wash Systems	Gerhardt/Offy	Piston	12	0	$14,102
33	9	31	Jim Malloy	Stearns Mfg. Transi-Trend	Gerhardt/Offy	Accident	0	0	$13,677

* - complete car name/entrant data not available for all entries
(R) - Indicated Rookie
(W) - Indicates Past Winner

1971

George Bignotti built new PJ Colts for Al Unser and Joe Leonard.

Team McLaren had new cars for Denis Hulme and Peter Revson. Penske had a new McLaren M16 for Mark Donohue.

Although bolt-on rear wings were still not permitted, the new McLarens had wings designed into the engine cover, which were considered "an integral part of the body."

This year brought a change in qualification procedure. Any car that had drawn a number and was properly presented in line would be entitled to make an attempt as a "first day" qualifier. The previous year, Lloyd Ruby drew a high number and rain caused him to be a second day qualifier.

The front row was Revson with a new track record (178.7 mph), Donohue and Bobby Unser. Donohue had topped the speed charts virtually every day, but a missed chassis set-up put him in the second starting position. Defending Indy 500 and national champion Al Unser started fifth.

Bobby Unser hit a bird while attempting to qualify. He had just ran a lap over 176 mph. He pitted and talked to officials, who allowed him to go back out, and qualified at 175.816.

George Snider qualified twenty-first with three identical laps at 52.45 seconds and one lap at 52.44 seconds. At the time, this was the most consistent run in history.

John Mahler qualified as the fastest rookie, but team owner Dick Simon, who had been bumped, replaced Mahler with himself and started thirty-third.

Just as the race started, pace car driver Eldon Palmer, a local car dealer, lost control of the bright orange Dodge Challenger pace car near the pit exit and swerved into a photographers' stand. Passengers included Speedway owner Tony Hulman, ABC's Chris Schenkel and astronaut John Glenn. Dr. Vicente Alvarez, from Argentina, was critically injured and twenty people were injured.

Donohue jumped to the lead at the start and his first lap was four mph faster than the previous record.

On lap 11, Steve Krisiloff blew an engine and hit the turn three wall. Mel Kenyon spun in the oil and also hit the wall. As Kenyon was exiting his car, Gordon Johncock spun in the oil and hit Kenyon's car. Kenyon was barely able to duck back into the cockpit. He avoided injury, but actually had tire marks on his helmet.

Donohue dominated the early part of the race until gearbox problems eliminated him as he led lap sixty-six. On his previous lap, he set the fastest lap of the race.

Rick Muther and David Hobbs had an accident on the main stretch as Muther's car momentarily skidded on two wheels.

Al Unser and teammate Joe Leonard battled back and forth for several laps, but Unser took over and led almost the entire second half of the race. He averaged a record 157.7 mph in his second Indy 500 win.

Mike Mosley crashed in the fourth turn on lap 167 and sustained a broken leg and elbow. Veteran Gary Bettenhausen actually stopped at the crash scene to assist the injured Mosley then returned to the race and finished in tenth position.

Al Unser became only the fourth driver to win back to back "500s." His second win came on his thirty-second birthday.

For the first time the victory celebration was in front of the master control tower.

Unser was the first "500" winner to use a one-way helmet radio with his team.

Peter Revson finished second and A.J. Foyt third.

Denny Zimmerman finished eighth and won Rookie of the Year in a five-year-old car owned by Frank Fiore. Fiore was a machinist for United Airlines in San Francisco and his total expenses for the month were just over $18,000. The eighth place finish was worth $27,658.

Al Unser led 103 laps, and Donohue led 52.

Al Unser repeats victory in his Johnny Lightning Special.

RACE RESULTS FOR THE 1971 INDIANAPOLIS 500

Finish	Start	Car Num.	Driver	Car Name/Entrant*	Make/Model	Status	Laps	Led	Winnings
1	5	1	Al Unser (W)	Johnny Lightning	P.J. Colt/Ford	157.735	200	103	$238,454
2	1	86	Peter Revson	McLaren	McLaren/Offy	157.419	200	0	$103,198
3	6	9	A.J. Foyt (W)	ITT Thompson	Coyote/Ford	156.069	200	0	$64,753
4	10	42	Jim Malloy	Olsonite Eagle	Eagle/Offy	154.577	200	0	$38,669
5	11	32	Bill Vukovich II	Sugaripe Prune	Brabham/Offy	154.563	200	0	$32,447
6	20	84	Donnie Allison	Purolator	Coyote/Ford	Running	199	0	$30,093
7	17	58	Bud Tingelstad	Sugaripe Prune	Brabham/Offy	Running	198	0	$28,206
8	28	43	Denny Zimmerman (R)	Fiore Racing	Vollstedt/Offy	Running	189	0	$27,658
9	22	6	Roger McCluskey	Sprite	Kuzma/Ford	Running	188	0	$22,980
10	13	16	Gary Bettenhausen	Thermo-King	Gerhardt/Offy	Running	178	0	$24,419
11	7	12	Lloyd Ruby	Utah Stars	Mongoose/Ford	Gears	174	3	$21,866
12	3	2	Bobby Unser (W)	Olsonite Eagle	Eagle/Offy	Accident	164	21	$24,842
13	19	4	Mike Mosley	G.C. Murphy	Eagle Watson/Ford	Accident	159	0	$20,345
14	33	44	Dick Simon	TraveLodge Sleeper	Vollstedt/Ford	Running	151	0	$18,870
15	29	41	George Follmer	Grant King Racers	Kingfish/Offy	Piston	147	0	$18,281
16	14	21	Cale Yarborough	Gene White Firestone	Mongoose/Ford	Cam cover	140	0	$17,370
17	4	85	Denis Hulme	McLaren	McLaren/Offy	Valve	137	0	$17,887
18	24	18	Johnny Rutherford	Patrick Petroleum	Eagle/Offy	Running	128	0	$16,682
19	8	15	Joe Leonard	Samsonite	P.J. Colt/Ford	Turbocharger	123	21	$19,906
20	16	68	David Hobbs (R)	Penske Products	Lola/Ford	Accident	107	0	$16,009
21	18	38	Rick Muther	Arkansas Aviation	Hawk II/Offy	Accident	85	0	$16,190
22	32	99	Bob Harkey	Joe Hunt Magneto	Gerhardt/Offy	Gears	77	0	$15,399
23	15	95	Bentley Warren (R)	Classic Wax	Eagle/Offy	Gears	76	0	$14,486
24	23	22	Wally Dallenbach	Sprite	Kuzma/Offy	Valve	69	0	$14,602
25	2	66	Mark Donohue	Sunoco	McLaren/Offy	Gears	66	52	$26,697
26	31	64	Art Pollard	Gilmore Broadcasting	Scorpion/Ford	Valve	45	0	$14,770
27	25	98	Sam Sessions	Wynn's Kwik-Kool	Lola/Ford	Valve	43	0	$13,721
28	26	45	Larry Dickson	Grant King Racers	Kingfish/Offy	Engine failure	33	0	$13,600
29	12	7	Gordon Johncock	Norris Industries	McLaren/Offy	Accident	11	0	$13,458
30	9	5	Mario Andretti (W)	STP Oil Treatment	McNamara/Ford	Accident	11	0	$13,245
31	27	20	Steve Krisiloff (R)	STP Gas Treatment	McNamara/Ford	Oil-Spun out	10	0	$13,260
32	30	23	Mel Kenyon	Sprite	Kuzma/Ford	Accident	10	0	$14,153
33	21	80	George Snider	G.C. Murphy	Eagle/Offy	Stalled	6	0	$13,974

* - complete car name/entrant data not available for all entries
(R) - Indicated Rookie
(W) - Indicates Past Winner

1972

Vel's Parnelli Jones Racing formed the "Super Team" of Al Unser, Joe Leonard and Mario Andretti. Viceroy sponsored Unser and Andretti, while Samsonite sponsored Leonard.

Maurice Phillippe designed the cars for the Super Team that initially incorporated dihedral wings sprouting from the side bodywork. They were soon permanently removed.

The "Manta," or Antares, was entered by Michner Racing and Lindsey Hopkins. This car was commonly known as one of the ugliest cars in history. It had the appearance of an upside down boat. The Antares was the first Indianapolis car designed on a computer. It was also the first Indy car that was fully instrumental with on-board telemetry and used aluminum honeycombed composite materials. The very unique car's design incorporated early ground effects. Veteran driver Roger McCluskey was the pilot. He struggled in practice and qualifications, eventually starting 20th. McCluskey soldiered in the race and climbed as high as fifth before burning a valve on lap 92, finishing 24th.

The Pacer Light System was installed at the track in an attempt to maintain spreads between cars during caution periods.

Rain plagued the first weekend of qualifying. On Sunday in practice, Jim Malloy was seriously injured when he hit the turn three wall nearly head on. He died four days later after he was taken off life support.

Later on Sunday Bobby Unser shattered Peter Revson's one-year-old record by more than 17 mph and took the pole (195.9 mph). This was the biggest margin increase in the history of the track and was primarily the result of bolt-on rear wings being allowed. Unser's Eagle was designed by Roman Slobodynskj.

Because of rain during the first weekend, five drivers actually could still be "first day" qualifiers on the following Saturday. Two of the five ended up on row one, Peter Revson and Mark Donohue.

Art Pollard crashed his qualified car on Tuesday during the second week of practice and broke his leg. Wally Dallenbach substituted for him, starting thirty-third and finishing fifteenth.

Jim Hurtubise made the field for the first time in four years driving a rear-engine Coyote. On the final day of qualifying, "Herk" put his Mallard in the qualifying line and supposedly threatened to withdraw his rear-engine car. When the gun went off at six p.m., Herk opened the engine compartment of the Miller-sponsored Mallard to show that he had converted it into a beer cooler full of his sponsor's product.

The 1972 race was the last time in which American drivers made up the entire "500" field.

On race morning, the scheduled singer of "Back Home Again in Indiana" didn't show up, so Tony Hulman asked Jim Nabors, who was attending the race as a celebrity, to sing the traditional song. A tradition was born, with Nabors performing 35 times with his last race in 2014.

Jim Rathmann drove the Hurst/Olds pace car. This was the first time in pace car history that an automotive supplier was included in the pace car name.

A.J. Foyt was unable to start his car after the command of, "Gentlemen, start your engines." He finally got started but fell a lap down immediately.

Bobby Unser took a commanding lead at the start and led the first thirty laps, but a broken distributor rotor ended his day on lap thirty-one.

For the next 145 laps Gary Bettenhausen dominated, leading 138 of them, but ignition failure ended his hopes of winning.

Jerry Grant took the lead, but was forced to pit for an unscheduled fifth pit stop to replace a deflating front tire on lap 188. Grant pitted in his teammate Bobby Unser's pit and was serviced by Unser's crew.

Eventually this situation resulted in a penalty and his last 12 laps were disallowed. He "finished" second on the track, but was officially dropped to twelfth. The difference in prize money was $72,000.

Mark Donohue took the lead and led the last 13 laps, giving Roger Penske his first of many wins to come at Indy. Penske brought a new level of organization and a philosophy of "winning is where preparation and hard work intersect."

Donohue averaged 162.962 mph, a new record that would stand until 1984. Al Unser finished second officially, with Joe Leonard placing third.

Mike Mosley crashed while leading on lap 98 in the fourth turn for the second straight year and suffered burns.

Mike Hiss finished seventh and won Rookie of the Year, though Sam Posey finished fifth in this, his rookie year.

Mark Donohue wins and gives Roger Penske his first Indy 500 victory.

RACE RESULTS FOR THE 1972 INDIANAPOLIS 500

Finish	Start	Car Num.	Driver	Car Name/Entrant*	Make/Model	Status	Laps	Led	Winnings
1	3	66	Mark Donohue	Sunoco McLaren	McLaren/Offy	162.962	200	13	$218,763
2	19	4	Al Unser (W)	Viceroy	Parnelli/Offy	160.192	200	0	$95,258
3	6	1	Joe Leonard	Samsonite	Parnelli/Offy	159.327	200	0	$58,793
4	24	52	Sam Sessions	Gene White Firestone	Lola/Ford	158.411	200	0	$39,583
5	7	34	Sam Posey (R)	Norris Eagle	Eagle/Offy	Running	198	0	$37,411
6	11	5	Lloyd Ruby	Wynn's	Atlanta/Foyt	Running	196	0	$29,557
7	25	60	Mike Hiss (R)	STP Pylon Windshield Wiper Blade	Eagle/Offy	Running	196	0	$30,814
8	5	9	Mario Andretti (W)	Viceroy	Parnelli/Offy	Out of fuel	194	0	$24,822
9	31	11	Jimmy Caruthers (R)	US Armed Forces/Steed	Scorpion/Foyt	Running	194	0	$23,094
10	32	21	Cale Yarborough	Bill Daniels GOP	Atlanta/Foyt	Running	193	0	$22,133
11	21	84	George Snider	ITT-Thompson	Coyote/Foyt	Running	190	0	$23,080
12	15	48	Jerry Grant	Mystery Eagle	Eagle/Offy	Penalty	188	16	$24,156
13	23	44	Dick Simon	TraveLodge Sleeper	Lola/Foyt	Out of fuel	186	0	$19,759
14	4	7	Gary Bettenhausen	Sunoco McLaren	McLaren/Offy	Ignition	182	138	$41,284
15	33	40	Wally Dallenbach	STP Oil Treatment	Lola/Foyt	Running	182	0	$19,645
16	14	89	John Martin (R)	Unsponsored	Brabham/Offy	Fuel leak	161	0	$18,084
17	30	37	Lee Kunzman (R)	Caves Buick Company	Gerhardt/Offy	Lost tire	131	0	$17,901
18	12	23	Mel Kenyon	Gilmore Racing	Coyote/Ford	Fuel injection	126	0	$17,146
19	28	17	Denny Zimmerman	Bryant Heating & Cooling	McLaren/Offy	Ignition rotor	116	0	$17,320
20	26	24	Gordon Johncock	Gulf McLaren	McLaren/Offy	Exhaust valve	113	0	$17,823
21	10	15	Steve Krisiloff	Ayr-Way/Lloyd's	Kingfish/Offy	Ignition rotor	102	0	$15,954
22	29	31	John Mahler (R)	Harbor Fuel Oil	McLaren/Offy	Piston	99	0	$16,013
23	13	56	Jim Hurtubise	Miller High Life	Coyote/Foyt	Penalty	94	0	$15,350
24	20	14	Roger McCluskey	American Marine Underwriters	Antares/Offy	Valve	92	0	$15,016
25	17	2	A.J. Foyt (W)	ITT-Thompson	Coyote/Foyt	Turbocharger	60	0	$15,611
26	16	98	Mike Mosley	Vivitar	Eagle/Offy	Accident	56	3	$15,984
27	8	18	Johnny Rutherford	Patrick Petroleum	Brabham/Offy	Rod	55	0	$14,535
28	18	3	Bill Vukovich II	Sugaripe Prune	Eagle/Offy	Rear end	54	0	$14,364
29	22	95	Carl Williams	City of Terre Haute	Eagle/Offy	Oil cooler	52	0	$14,022
30	1	6	Bobby Unser (W)	Olsonite Eagle	Eagle/Offy	Ignition rotor	31	30	$30,830
31	2	12	Peter Revson	Gulf McLaren	McLaren/Offy	Gearbox	23	0	$15,924
32	9	42	Swede Savage (R)	Michner Industries	Eagle/Offy	Rod	5	0	$13,767
33	27	33	Salt Walther (R)	Dayton Disc Brakes	P.J. Colt/Foyt	Magneto	0	0	$14,538

* - complete car name/entrant data not available for all entries
(R) - Indicated Rookie
(W) - Indicates Past Winner

1973

Master Chief Mechanic George Bignotti moved from the Vel's Parnelli Team to Pat Patrick's STP Team.

The Speedway had a new main entrance. Instead of at the corner of Sixteenth and Georgetown, it was now further east on 16th Street, with a four-lane tunnel under the south short chute between turns one and two.

Swede Savage posted the fastest speed of the month, 197.802 mph, prior to qualifications during a rainy first half of the month.

On the morning of the first day of qualifications, crowd favorite Art Pollard crashed in turn one. He died about an hour later.

Johnny Rutherford took the pole in his McLaren at a record 198.4 mph. Bobby Unser and Mark Donohue joined him in row one.

The winner from 1914, René Thomas, delighted the race day crowd as he was driven around on several pre-race laps. The eighty-nine-year-old former winner waved his checkered cap from the riding mechanic's seat of his winning Delage.

The fancy Cadillac Eldorado, at almost 5000 pounds, paced the field with Jim Rathmann at the wheel.

As the race started under threatening skies, Salt Walther's car veered to the right, hit the outer wall and tore some fencing. The front end of the car was torn off and his legs were exposed. The car spun upside down through the air, spraying some fuel on the crowd near the track and injuring 13 spectators.

Ten cars total were involved in the chain reaction accident.

Walther was seriously injured with burns to his hand and face but unbelievably, he had no fractures.

Rain fell during the cleanup and continued, causing the race to be postponed until the next day (Tuesday).

On Tuesday, thirty-two cars (Walther the only one missing) were prepared to start but rain started on the pace lap, causing further postponement until Wednesday.

On Wednesday, rain caused delay of the start until 2:10 p.m.

Bobby Unser took off at the start and led the first thirty-nine laps until pitting. Gordon Johncock, Swede Savage and Al Unser exchanged the lead.

On lap fifty-eight, just after pitting, Swede Savage crashed viciously into the inside wall in turn four. Savage's car held a full load of approximately seventy-five gallons of fuel and exploded like a bomb and was enveloped in flames. Savage sustained broken legs, broken arm, internal injuries and numerous burns. He would die from his injuries about a month later. The race was stopped for an hour for the cleanup. In the confusion of the serious accident, mechanic Armando Teran was struck and fatally injured by a cleanup truck going the wrong direction in the pits.

When the race re-started, Al Unser led for fifteen laps before an engine problem sidelined him.

Gordon Johncock took the lead in his STP Eagle/Offy on lap 73 and led until rain ended this tragic race on lap 133. Johncock averaged 159 mph. Johncock's victory was bittersweet to say the least as Swede Savage was his teammate and Armando Teran was a pit crew member of teammate Graham McRae.

Bill Vukovich finished second in the Sugaripe Prune car and was the only other driver on the lead lap. Roger McCluskey finished third in Lindsey Hopkins' McLaren.

This was George Bignotti's sixth Indy 500 win.

Graham McRae finished sixteenth and won Rookie of the Year.

Several rule changes resulted from this tragic month of May: reduction of the size of the rear wing; on-board fuel only allowed on the left side of the car; and reduction of fuel allowed on board from seventy-five gallons to forty gallons.

The year 1973 marked the last year a qualifier signaled a qualification attempt by raising his arm from the cockpit. In the future, the driver's crew would signal a qualification attempt.

The first corporate suites were constructed in 1973 on the outside of turn 2.

A multi-car accident during the initial start of the "500" seriously injured David "Salt" Walther.

RACE RESULTS FOR THE 1973 INDIANAPOLIS 500

Finish	Start	Car Num.	Driver	Car Name/Entrant*	Make/Model	Status	Laps	Led	Winnings
1	11	20	Gordon Johncock	STP Double Oil Filter	Eagle/Offy	159.036	133	64	$236,023
2	16	2	Bill Vukovich II	Sugaripe Prune	Eagle/Offy	157.262	133	0	$97,513
3	14	3	Roger McCluskey	Lindsey Hopkins Buick	McLaren/Offy	Running	131	0	$60,753
4	19	19	Mel Kenyon	Atlanta Falcons	Eagle/Foyt	Running	131	0	$34,488
5	5	5	Gary Bettenhausen	Sunoco DX	McLaren/Offy	Running	130	0	$37,966
6	7	24	Steve Krisiloff	Elliott-Norton Spirit	Kingfish/Offy	Running	129	0	$30,862
7	25	16	Lee Kunzman	Ayr-Way/Lloyd's	Eagle/Offy	Running	127	0	$26,350
8	24	89	John Martin	Unsponsored	McLaren/Offy	Running	124	0	$25,377
9	1	7	Johnny Rutherford	Gulf McLaren	McLaren/Offy	Running	124	0	$29,904
10	21	98	Mike Mosley	Lodestar	Eagle/Offy	Rod bolt	120	0	$23,675
11	22	73	David Hobbs	Carling Black Label	Eagle/Offy	Running	107	0	$20,935
12	30	84	George Snider	Gilmore Racing Team	Coyote/Foyt	Gearbox	101	0	$21,511
13	2	8	Bobby Unser (W)	Olsonite	Eagle/Offy	Blown engine	100	39	$30,264
14	27	44	Dick Simon	TraveLodge	Eagle/Foyt	Piston	100	0	$19,489
15	3	66	Mark Donohue (W)	Sunoco DX	Eagle/Offy	Piston	92	0	$19,950
16	13	60	Graham McRae (R)	STP Gas Treatment	Eagle/Offy	Header	91	0	$19,039
17	26	6	Mike Hiss	Thermo-King	Eagle/Offy	Drive train	91	0	$18,156
18	29	1	Joe Leonard	Samsonite	Parnelli/Offy	Hub bearing	91	0	$17,301
19	18	48	Jerry Grant	Olsonite	Eagle/Offy	Blown engine	77	0	$16,675
20	8	4	Al Unser (W)	Viceroy	Parnelli/Offy	Piston	75	18	$20,628
21	9	21	Jimmy Caruthers	Cobre	Eagle/Offy	Suspension	73	0	$16,009
22	4	40	Swede Savage	STP Oil Treatment	Eagle/Offy	Accident	57	12	$19,368
23	33	35	Jim McElreath	Norris Eagle	Eagle/Offy	Blown engine	54	0	$15,655
24	20	62	Wally Dallenbach	Olsonite	Eagle/Offy	Broken rod	48	0	$14,971
25	23	14	A.J. Foyt (W)	Gilmore Racing Team	Coyote/Foyt	Rod Bolt	37	0	$14,716
26	28	30	Jerry Karl (R)	Oriente Express	Eagle/Chevrolet	Running	22	0	$17,689
27	15	18	Lloyd Ruby	Commander Motor Homes	Eagle/Offy	Piston	21	0	$14,290
28	32	9	Sam Sessions	M.V.S.	Eagle/Foyt	Out of oil	17	0	$14,719
29	31	28	Bob Harkey	Bryant Heating & Cooling	Kenyon-Eagle/Foyt	Seized engine	12	0	$14,777
30	6	11	Mario Andretti (W)	Viceroy	Parnelli/Offy	Piston	4	0	$14,564
31	10	15	Peter Revson	Gulf McLaren	McLaren/Offy	Accident	3	0	$13,779
32	12	12	Bobby Allison (R)	Sunoco DX	McLaren/Offy	Rod	1	0	$13,722
33	17	77	Salt Walther	Dayton-Walther	McLaren/Offy	Accident	0	0	$13,963

* - complete car name/entrant data not available for all entries
(R) - Indicated Rookie
(W) - Indicates Past Winner

1974

The "tire war" was about to end as Firestone made the decision to pull out of major auto racing at the end of the 1974 season. After 1974, every Indy car would be on Goodyears for the next twenty years.

The chassis war was between McLarens and Eagles, or cars that were very similar to these.

The entrance to the pits was moved to the head of the front stretch. This allowed easier access and greater spacing for the cars.

Jan Opperman replaced an injured Joe Leonard on the Vel's Parnelli Jones team. Leonard's leg injury, sustained at the Ontario 500 in March, ultimately ended his racing career.

Mark Donohue had retired at the end of 1973. Peter Revson was to replace him, but was fatally injured testing for the South African Grand Prix. Mike Hiss was hired by Penske.

Tom Binford replaced Harlan Fengler as Chief Steward. Fengler had been the Chief Steward since 1958.

As a result of the accidents in 1973, the outer wall was raised from 36 inches to 54 inches high.

The flagman was moved from a small platform on the inside of the track to an elevated platform on the outside.

In an attempt to slow down the cars, turbo-charged engines now employed a pop-off valve to limit boost.

A scaled-down schedule was adopted because of the energy crisis caused by the OPEC oil embargo. This meant two days of qualifications rather than four. Each qualifying day was split in half to equate to four sessions of qualifying.

The front row was A.J. Foyt on the pole (his speed, 191.6 mph, would have placed him seventeenth the year before), Wally Dallenbach and Mike Hiss.

Johnny Rutherford blew his engine in the pre-qualifying practice session, which caused him to be a "second day" qualifier. Despite being the second fastest qualifier in the field, Rutherford was relegated to start twenty-fifth.

For the first time the race was run on Sunday, as it has been ever since.

A second parade lap was added to the pre-start for the first time.

Dallenbach jumped to an early lead. He set records on the first two laps, but engine problems eliminated him on lap three. Rutherford moved from twenty-fifth to third in the first eleven laps.

Foyt led most of the race until lap sixty-five, when a long pit stop resulted in Rutherford leading the "500" for the first time in his career.

From lap 65 it was basically a two-man race between Foyt and Rutherford until Foyt was black flagged with an oil leak on lap 140. Foyt pitted, then rejoined the race only to be black flagged again. His race ended on lap 142.

Rutherford, in his Gulf McLaren, led virtually the rest of the race. Bobby Unser finished second in his Olsonite Eagle, 22 seconds behind Rutherford and was the only car on the lead lap. J.R. ended up leading 120 laps with Foyt leading 70. Rutherford averaged 158.6 mph.

Pancho Carter finished seventh and won Rookie of the Year. This was his first Indy car ride and his first time driving a rear-engine car.

Lloyd Ruby finished ninth wearing an open-face helmet with goggles, the last time an open face helmet would be used in the "500." Ruby was running fourth but ran out of his fuel allotment on lap 187 and fell in the standings to ninth.

Johnny Rutherford wins his first "500" in a McLaren/Offy.

RACE RESULTS FOR THE 1974 INDIANAPOLIS 500

Finish	Start	Car Num.	Driver	Car Name/Entrant*	Make/Model	Status	Laps	Led	Winnings
1	25	3	Johnny Rutherford	McLaren	McLaren/Offy	158.589	200	122	$245,032
2	7	48	Bobby Unser (W)	Olsonite Eagle	Eagle/Offy	158.278	200	6	$99,504
3	16	4	Bill Vukovich II	Sugaripe Prune	Eagle/Offy	Running	199	0	$63,811
4	4	20	Gordon Johncock (W)	STP Double Oil Filter	Eagle/Offy	Running	198	0	$37,079
5	9	73	David Hobbs	Carling Black Label	McLaren/Offy	Running	196	0	$32,074
6	30	45	Jim McElreath	Thermo-King	Eagle/Offy	Running	194	0	$27,970
7	21	11	Pancho Carter (R)	Cobre Firestone	Eagle/Offy	Running	191	0	$27,758
8	31	79	Bob Harkey	Peru Circus	Kenyon/Foyt	Running	189	0	$23,985
9	18	9	Lloyd Ruby	Unlimited Racing	Eagle/Offy	Out of fuel	187	0	$23,182
10	17	55	Jerry Grant	Cobre Firestone	Eagle/Offy	Running	175	0	$22,016
11	22	89	John Martin	Sea Snack Shrimp Cocktail	McLaren/Offy	Running	169	0	$21,393
12	23	27	Tom Bigelow (R)	Bryant Heating & Cooling	Vollstedt/Offy	Running	166	0	$20,769
13	20	18	Bill Simpson (R)	American Kids Racer	Eagle/Offy	Piston	163	0	$19,922
14	3	68	Mike Hiss	Norton Spirit	McLaren/Offy	Running	158	0	$21,697
15	1	14	A.J. Foyt (W)	Gilmore Racing Team	Coyote/Foyt	Oil fitting	142	70	$38,674
16	27	1	Roger McCluskey	English Leather	Riley/Offy	Rear end	141	0	$19,097
17	14	77	Salt Walther	Dayton-Walther	McLaren/Offy	Piston	141	0	$18,197
18	26	15	Al Unser (W)	Viceroy	Eagle/Offy	Valve	131	0	$17,492
19	19	42	Jerry Karl	Ayr-Way/Lloyd's	Eagle/Offy	Accident	115	0	$17,333
20	8	24	Tom Sneva (R)	Raymond Companies	Kingfish/Offy	Drive gear	94	0	$19,136
21	32	51	Jan Opperman (R)	Viceroy Parnelli	Parnelli/Offy	Spun out	85	0	$15,617
22	15	60	Steve Krisiloff	STP Gas Treatment	Eagle/Offy	Clutch	72	0	$16,026
23	12	21	Jimmy Caruthers	Cobre Firestone	Eagle/Offy	Gearbox	64	0	$16,063
24	33	59	Larry Cannon (R)	American Financial Corp.	Eagle/Offy	Differential	49	0	$15,429
25	28	56	Jim Hurtubise	Miller High Life	Eagle/Offy	Blown engine	31	0	$15,324
26	29	94	Johnny Parsons (R)	Vatis	Finley/Offy	Turbocharger	18	0	$14,497
27	24	61	Rick Muther	Eisenhour/Brayton	Coyote/Foyt	Piston	11	0	$14,748
28	13	82	George Snider	Gilmore Racing Team	Atlanta/Foyt	Valve	7	0	$14,027
29	6	98	Mike Mosley	Lodestar	Eagle/Offy	Blown engine	6	0	$16,435
30	2	40	Wally Dallenbach	STP Oil Treatment	Eagle/Offy	Piston	3	2	$16,222
31	5	5	Mario Andretti (W)	Viceroy	Eagle/Offy	Valve	2	0	$15,587
32	11	8	Gary Bettenhausen	Score	McLaren/Offy	Valve	2	0	$14,230
33	10	44	Dick Simon	TraveLodge	Eagle/Foyt	Valve	1	0	$14,551

* - complete car name/entrant data not available for all entries
(R) - Indicated Rookie
(W) - Indicates Past Winner

1975

Gary Bettenhausen lost his ride with Penske after suffering a severe injury to his left arm in a dirt-car race in Syracuse, New York, in 1974.

A.J. Foyt and Gordon Johncock had a speed duel during the first week of practice.

The front row was Foyt on the pole at 194 mph (his fourth pole), Gordon Johncock and Bobby Unser.

Jimmy Caruthers had been diagnosed and treated for cancer the previous year but was able to come back and qualify tenth best.

James Garner, actor, racing enthusiast and amateur racer, drove a Buick Century to pace the start of the race.

Johncock took the lead at the start. Johncock and Foyt led most of the first fifty-eight laps. Wally Dallenbach, who started twenty-first, passed Foyt on lap fifty-eight for the lead.

Dallenbach led 97 of the next 103 laps, but a burned piston eliminated him while leading on lap 162, giving him a ninth place finish.

Rutherford led for a couple of laps until Bobby Unser took the lead. Unser was in the lead when a rain deluge stopped the race on lap 174. It was the fourth time in history the race failed to go the distance because of rain. Unser averaged 149.2 mph in his Dan Gurney All American Racers Jorgensen Eagle for his second "500" win. This would be Dan Gurney's only win as a car-owner.

Johnny Rutherford finished in second place in his Gatorade McLaren, and Foyt, who had run out of fuel and coasted in on lap 124, in third place.

The rain eliminated a potentially spectacular finish as each of the top three finishers felt they had the car to win. Rutherford was catching the leader Unser, while third-place Foyt was making-up ground on both.

On lap 125, after just pitting, Tom Sneva was running fifth for Penske in his second year at Indy. Sneva touched wheels with Eldon Rasmussen and flipped and crashed hard into the turn two fencing. Unbelievably, he was not seriously injured. Largely, as a result of mandatory aircraft-type break-away fuel systems, Sneva survived the horrendous crash at the base of the turn two suites. Post-accident investigation showed his fuel tank still had 37 ½ gallons on-board.

Bill Puterbaugh, driving the McNamara Motor Express, that company's first sponsorship since the late 1950s, finished seventh and won Rookie of the Year in his seventh attempt to race at Indy.

Indy 500 champion Mark Donohue, aka "Captain Nice", passed away on August 19, 1975 from a cerebral hemorrhage sustained in a pre-race practice session at the Austrian Grand Prix at Osterreichring.

Graham Hill, 1966 Indy 500 champion and two-time Formula One World Champion, was killed in a plane crash in London on November 29, 1975.

Bobby Unser wins the rain-shortened 1975 race.

RACE RESULTS FOR THE 1975 INDIANAPOLIS 500

Finish	Start	Car Num.	Driver	Car Name/Entrant*	Make/Model	Status	Laps	Led	Winnings
1	3	48	Bobby Unser (W)	Jorgensen Eagle	Eagle/Offy	149.213	174	11	$214,032
2	7	2	Johnny Rutherford (W)	Gatorade	McLaren/Offy	148.308	174	5	$97,886
3	1	14	A.J. Foyt (W)	Gilmore Racing Team	Coyote/Foyt	147.684	174	53	$74,677
4	18	11	Pancho Carter	Cobre Tire	Eagle/Offy	Running	169	0	$33,424
5	22	15	Roger McCluskey	Silver Floss	Riley/Offy	Running	167	0	$31,002
6	8	6	Bill Vukovich II	Cobre Tire	Eagle/Offy	Running	166	0	$28,473
7	15	83	Bill Puterbaugh (R)	McNamara-D.I.A.	Eagle/Offy	Running	165	0	$28,786
8	24	97	George Snider	Leader Card Lodestar	Eagle/Offy	Running	165	0	$24,688
9	21	40	Wally Dallenbach	Sinmast Wildcat	Wildcat/SGD	Piston	162	96	$42,712
10	23	33	Bob Harkey	Dayton-Walther	McLaren/Offy	Running	162	0	$22,899
11	29	98	Steve Krisiloff	Leader Card Lodestar	Eagle/Offy	Running	162	0	$22,796
12	26	19	Sheldon Kinser (R)	Spirit of Indiana	Kingfish/Offy	Running	161	0	$20,772
13	20	30	Jerry Karl	Jose Johnson	Eagle/Chevrolet	Running	161	0	$19,975
14	10	78	Jimmy Caruthers	Alex Foods	Eagle/Offy	Running	161	0	$19,350
15	19	45	Gary Bettenhausen	Thermo-King	Eagle/Offy	Accident	158	0	$19,811
16	11	4	Al Unser (W)	Viceroy	Eagle/Offy	Rod	157	0	$18,300
17	25	36	Sam Sessions	Commander Motor Homes	Eagle/Offy	Engine	155	0	$18,117
18	33	17	Tom Bigelow	Bryant Heating & Cooling	Vollstedt/Offy	Magneto	151	0	$18,162
19	12	93	Johnny Parsons	Ayr-Way WNAP Buzzard	Eagle/Offy	Transmission	140	0	$16,936
20	14	73	Jerry Grant	Spirit of Orange County	Eagle/Offy	Piston	137	0	$16,539
21	30	44	Dick Simon	Bruce Cogle Ford	Eagle/Foyt	Running	133	0	$17,070
22	4	68	Tom Sneva	Norton Spirit	McLaren/Offy	Accident	125	0	$17,829
23	17	24	Bentley Warren	THE BOTTOMHALF	Kingfish/Offy	Running	120	0	$15,516
24	32	58	Eldon Rasmussen (R)	Anacomp-Wild Rose	Ras-Car/Foyt	Valve	119	0	$16,432
25	13	16	Bobby Allison	CAM2 Motor Oil	McLaren/Offy	Gearbox	112	1	$14,827
26	5	12	Mike Mosley	Sugaripe Prune	Eagle/Offy	Engine	94	0	$16,550
27	16	89	John Martin	Unsponsored	McLaren/Offy	Radiator	61	0	$14,551
28	27	21	Mario Andretti (W)	Viceroy	Eagle/Offy	Accident	49	0	$15,880
29	31	94	Mike Hiss	Ayr-Way WNAP Buzzard	Finley/Offy	Accident	39	0	$14,538
30	28	63	Larry McCoy (R)	Shurfine Foods	Ras-Car/Offy	Piston	24	0	$14,925
31	2	20	Gordon Johncock (W)	Sinmast Wildcat	Wildcat/SGD	Ignition	11	8	$18,120
32	6	7	Lloyd Ruby	Allied Polymer	McLaren/Offy	Piston	7	0	$15,583
33	9	77	Salt Walther	Dayton-Walther	McLaren/Offy	Ignition	2	0	$14,954

* - complete car name/entrant data not available for all entries
(R) - Indicated Rookie
(W) - Indicates Past Winner

1976

The new IMS Hall of Fame Museum was opened between turns one and two inside the track.

Arlene Hiss (wife of 1972 Rookie of the Year Mike Hiss) became the first woman to compete in an Indy car race by finishing a distant fourteenth in the season opener at Phoenix. She did not enter the "500."

Thirty-eight-year-old Janet Guthrie, a former aerospace engineer, with Rolla Vollstedt as owner and Phil Hedback as sponsor, was the first woman to be entered at Indy. She had competed at Trenton in early May by starting fourteenth and finishing fifteenth.

The turbocharger boost level was dropped from eighty inches to sixty-five.

Johnny Rutherford won the pole (188.957 mph), his second in four 500s. Gordon Johncock and Tom Sneva filled out the front row.

Mario Andretti missed the first weekend of qualifying because he was competing in the Belgian Grand Prix. He eventually qualified the fastest (189.404 mph) in the field in his McLaren/Offy but had to start nineteenth.

Guthrie was unable to get her car up to speed and the team actually withdrew her car on the third day of qualifications after several blown engines.

A.J. Foyt let Guthrie run some laps in his backup car on the final day of qualifications and she was able to get the car up to competitive speed fairly quickly, but Foyt decided to run only his own car in the race.

Al Loquasto made the field, after trying for eight years, starting twenty-fourth and finishing twenty-fifth in the Frostie Root Beer McLaren/Offy.

Country singer and Daytona 500 competitor Marty Robbins drove the Buick Century pace car to start the 60th Indianapolis 500.

At the start, Rutherford took the lead, but Foyt passed him on the fourth lap and led until his first stop on lap fourteen.

Rutherford led a total of three times for forty-eight laps, while Foyt led two times for twenty-nine laps and Johncock led a stint of eighteen laps.

Rutherford led from lap 80 until rain hit on lap 102, and the race was stopped.

The track was dried and drivers were in their machines ready to restart when rain appeared again and race was made official with 102 laps completed or 255 miles.

Rain had stopped the "500" only twice in the previous 57 years, while now it happened for the third time in four years.

Rutherford became the first winner to walk into the victory circle in the shortest race in history. He averaged 148.7 mph.

Rutherford had now finished first, second and first in the last three "500s."

Foyt finished second, Johncock third and Dallenbach fourth. Each felt they very well may have had something for Rutherford if the second half of the race had taken place. Six former winners and a future winner were all running in the top ten when the race was called.

During the red flag, Foyt repaired a broken sway bar and was ready to do battle with Rutherford.

There were twenty-seven cars still running when the race was called.

Australian Vern Schuppan finished eighteenth and won Rookie of the Year.

Johnny Rutherford is the 1976 winner in his McLaren.

RACE RESULTS FOR THE 1976 INDIANAPOLIS 500

Finish	Start	Car Num.	Driver	Car Name/Entrant*	Make/Model	Status	Laps	Led	Winnings
1	1	2	Johnny Rutherford (W)	Hy-Gain	McLaren/Offy	148.725	102	48	$255,321
2	5	14	A.J. Foyt (W)	Gilmore Racing Team	Coyote/Foyt	148.355	102	29	$103,097
3	2	20	Gordon Johncock (W)	Sinmast	Wildcat/DGS	146.238	102	18	$67,676
4	7	40	Wally Dallenbach	Sinmast	Wildcat/DGS	Running	101	3	$38,050
5	6	48	Pancho Carter	Jorgensen	Eagle/Offy	Running	101	3	$33,778
6	3	68	Tom Sneva	Norton Spirit	McLaren/Offy	Running	101	1	$30,960
7	4	21	Al Unser (W)	American Racing	Parnelli/Cosworth	Running	101	0	$27,442
8	19	6	Mario Andretti (W)	CAM2 Motor Oil	McLaren/Offy	Running	101	0	$28,331
9	22	77	Salt Walther	Dayton-Walther	McLaren/Offy	Running	100	0	$23,728
10	12	3	Bobby Unser (W)	Cobre Tire	Eagle/Offy	Running	100	0	$23,992
11	30	51	Lloyd Ruby	Fairco Drugs	Eagle/Offy	Running	100	0	$23,039
12	14	93	Johnny Parsons	Ayr-Way/WIRE	Eagle/Offy	Running	98	0	$21,215
13	27	23	George Snider	Hubler Chevrolet	Eagle/Offy	Running	98	0	$20,718
14	32	24	Tom Bigelow	Leader Card Racers	Eagle/Offy	Running	98	0	$20,193
15	11	12	Mike Mosley	Sugaripe Prune	Eagle/Offy	Running	98	0	$20,954
16	33	8	Jan Opperman	Routh Meat Packing	Eagle/Offy	Running	97	0	$18,943
17	10	69	Larry Cannon	American Financial Corp.	Eagle/Offy	Running	97	0	$18,060
18	17	9	Vern Schuppan (R)	Jorgensen	Eagle/Offy	Running	97	0	$18,605
19	29	97	Sheldon Kinser	THE BOTTOMHALF	Dragon/Offy	Running	97	0	$17,179
20	28	96	Bob Harkey	Dave McIntire Chevy/Ford Centers	Kingfish/Offy	Running	97	0	$16,782
21	15	98	John Martin	Genesse Beer	Dragon/Offy	Running	96	0	$17,213
22	18	83	Bill Puterbaugh	McNamara Motor Express	Eagle/Offy	Running	96	0	$16,072
23	21	28	Billy Scott (R)	Spirit of Public Enterprise	Eagle/Offy	Running	96	0	$17,859
24	23	92	Steve Krisiloff	1st National City Travelers Checks	Eagle/Offy	Running	95	0	$15,775
25	24	86	Al Loquasto (R)	Frostie Root Beer	McLaren/Offy	Running	95	0	$15,420
26	26	63	Larry McCoy	Shurfine Foods	Ras-Car/Offy	Running	91	0	$14,993
27	20	73	Jerry Grant	California/Oklahoma	Eagle/AMC	Running	91	0	$15,594
28	8	45	Gary Bettenhausen	Thermo-King	Eagle/Offy	Turbocharger	52	0	$15,623
29	31	33	David Hobbs	Dayton-Walther	McLaren/Offy	Water leak	10	0	$15,281
30	13	7	Roger McCluskey	Hopkins	Lightning/Offy	Accident	8	0	$15,468
31	9	5	Bill Vukovich II	Alex Foods	Eagle/Offy	Rod	2	0	$15,283
32	16	17	Dick Simon	Bryant Heating & Cooling	Vollstedt/Offy	Rod	1	0	$15,926
33	25	19	Spike Gehlhausen (R)	Spirit of Indiana	McLaren/Offy	Oil pressure	0	0	$14,197

* - complete car name/entrant data not available for all entries
(R) - Indicated Rookie
(W) - Indicates Past Winner

1977

After the 1976 race, virtually the entire track was paved with asphalt for the first time in history, save for a three-foot strip of bricks and mortar at the start/finish line.

Gordon Johncock turned the first unofficial 200-mph lap during spring testing.

Longtime Speedway safety director Joe Quinn had passed away in the winter, and Sid Collins, the voice of the "500," died at fifty-four years old on May 2 after suffering with ALS.

For the first time a father/son combo was attempting to qualify at Indy, Jim and James McElreath. James failed to qualify.

Belgium's Teddy Pilette became the first third-generation driver to run at Indianapolis. His grandfather, Theodore Pilette, finished fifth in the 1913 "500." Pilette failed to qualify in 1977.

J.C. Agajanian and Grant King entered Gary Bettenhausen, their car sponsored by famous stuntman Evel Knievel.

Turbocharger boost was increased from sixty-five to eighty inches.

On Wednesday, May 11, Mario Andretti turned the first unofficial 200-mph lap of the month.

On the fourth day of practice Janet Guthrie crashed in turn four.

In qualifying Tom "The Gas Man" Sneva broke the 200-mph barrier on his first two laps in his Norton Spirit McLaren/Cosworth.

The front row was Sneva, setting a record of 198.9 mph, Bobby Unser and Al Unser.

On the final day of qualifying, Janet Guthrie became the first woman to qualify at Indy at 188.403 mph, which actually made her the eighteenth fastest in the field. She was the fastest of the entire second weekend. Guthrie started twenty-sixth and finished twenty-ninth, completing twenty-seven laps in her Rolla Vollstadt owned Bryant Heating & Cooling Lightning/Offy.

A young man from Bakersfield, California named Rick Ravon Mears made his debut at Indianapolis but failed to qualify in his three-year old Eagle. He would be back at Indy in a big way in the future!

To start the race, Tony Hulman's command was: "In company with the first lady ever to qualify at Indianapolis, gentlemen, start your engines!"

At the start, Al Unser took the lead and led the first seventeen laps.

On lap thirty-four, Lloyd Ruby crashed hard in turn two and was eliminated. Ruby had climbed from a starting position of nineteenth to seventh place in just thirty laps. This would be the perennial hard luck driver's last Indy 500.

The race became a two-man contest between Johncock and A.J. Foyt, with the two leading all but eight laps after Al Unser led the opening seventeen laps.

From lap 97, Gordon Johncock led 84 of the next 87 laps before a crankshaft failure caused his elimination. He was leading Foyt by 16 seconds on lap 184.

A.J. Foyt led the remaining laps and became the first four-time "500" winner in history. He averaged 161.3 mph in his Bob Riley designed Coyote/Foyt. This was the last time that the winning chassis and engine were built in the United States.

Tom Sneva finished second and Al Unser third. Jerry Sneva finished tenth and won Rookie of the Year.

The four-time winner became the only driver in history to win in both a front-engine and a rear-engine car.

Foyt invited Tony Hulman to ride with him on his victory lap in the Oldsmobile Delta 88 pace car, a very memorable moment in Speedway history.

Larry "Boom Boom" Cannon relieved John Mahler, becoming the last "pure" relief driver to take over for another driver during a pit stop.

Johncock led 129 laps total, with Foyt leading 46 laps.

Clarence Cagle retired in July as superintendent of the track since 1948.

Anton Hulman Jr. passed away on October 27, 1977, at seventy-six years old.

Anthony Joseph Foyt, Jr. becomes the first to win four "500s."

RACE RESULTS FOR THE 1977 INDIANAPOLIS 500

Finish	Start	Car Num.	Driver	Car Name/Entrant*	Make/Model	Status	Laps	Led	Winnings
1	4	14	A.J. Foyt (W)	Gilmore Racing Team	Coyote/Foyt	161.331	200	46	$259,791
2	1	8	Tom Sneva	Norton Spirit	McLaren/Cosworth	160.918	200	3	$109,947
3	3	21	Al Unser (W)	American Racing	Parnelli/Cosworth	Running	199	17	$67,232
4	10	40	Wally Dallenbach	STP Oil Treatment	Wildcat/DGS	Running	199	0	$41,192
5	11	60	Johnny Parsons	STP Wildcat	Wildcat/DGS	Running	193	0	$33,170
6	22	24	Tom Bigelow	Thermo-King	Watson/Offy	Running	192	0	$30,466
7	24	65	Lee Kunzman	City of Syracuse	Eagle/Offy	Running	191	0	$29,129
8	18	11	Roger McCluskey	1st National City Travelers Checks	Lightning/Offy	Running	191	0	$27,256
9	25	92	Steve Krisiloff	Dave McIntire Chevrolet	Eagle/Offy	Running	191	0	$26,653
10	16	36	Jerry Sneva (R)	21st Amendment	McLaren/Offy	Running	187	0	$26,617
11	5	20	Gordon Johncock (W)	STP Double Oil Filter	Wildcat/DGS	Crankshaft	184	129	$45,014
12	28	16	Bill Puterbaugh	Dayton-Walther	Eagle/Offy	Valve	170	0	$22,890
13	32	58	Eldon Rasmussen	Rent-a-Racer, Inc.	Ras-Car/Foyt	Running	168	0	$21,093
14	31	42	John Mahler	Mergard 20th Century	Eagle/Offy	Running	157	0	$20,668
15	8	48	Pancho Carter	Jorgensen	Eagle/Offy	Engine	156	0	$21,679
16	21	98	Gary Bettenhausen	Agajanian/Evil Knievel	Kingfish/Offy	Clutch	138	0	$19,718
17	23	84	Bill Vukovich II	Gilmore Racing Team	Coyote/Foyt	Wing strut	110	1	$19,885
18	2	6	Bobby Unser (W)	Cobre Tire/Clayton Dyno-Tune	Lightning/Offy	Oil leak	94	2	$22,130
19	9	5	Mike Mosley	Sugaripe Prune	Lightning/Offy	Timing gear	91	0	$19,154
20	7	25	Danny Ongais (R)	Interscope Racing	Parnelli/Cosworth	Header	90	0	$21,257
21	33	72	Bubby Jones (R)	Bruce Cogle Ford	Eagle/Offy	Valve	78	0	$17,388
22	27	29	Cliff Hucul (R)	Team Canada	McLaren/Offy	Gearbox	72	0	$17,747
23	20	73	Jim McElreath	Carrillo Rods	Eagle/AMC	Turbocharger	71	0	$22,434
24	13	18	George Snider	Melvin Simon Greenwood Center	Wildcat/DGS	Valve	65	2	$16,650
25	14	78	Bobby Olivero (R)	Alex Foods	Lightning/Offy	Piston	57	0	$17,245
26	6	9	Mario Andretti (W)	CAM2 Motor Oil	McLaren/Offy	Header	47	0	$17,468
27	19	10	Lloyd Ruby	1st National City Travelers Checks	Lightning/Offy	Accident	34	0	$16,619
28	15	86	Al Loquasto	Frostie Root Beer	McLaren/Offy	Magneto	28	0	$17,448
29	26	27	Janet Guthrie (R)	Bryant Heating & Cooling	Lightning/Offy	Timing gear	27	0	$16,556
30	29	38	Clay Regazzoni (R)	Theodore Racing Hong Kong	McLaren/Offy	Fuel cell	25	0	$15,643
31	30	17	Dick Simon	Bryant Heating & Cooling	Vollstedt/Offy	Overheating	24	0	$16,458
32	12	97	Sheldon Kinser	Genesee Beer	Kingfish/Offy	Piston	14	0	$15,101
33	17	2	Johnny Rutherford (W)	1st National City Travelers Checks	McLaren/Cosworth	Gearbox	12	0	$19,472

* - complete car name/entrant data not available for all entries
(R) - Indicated Rookie
(W) - Indicates Past Winner

1978

Joe Cloutier, Tony Hulman's right hand man for decades, became president of the Indianapolis Motor Speedway.

A plane returning from the spring race at Trenton crashed, fatally injuring eight USAC officials.

From the middle of 1969 until the middle of the 1971 season, Al Unser won twenty out of thirty-eight races, including two Indy 500s, driving for Vel's Parnelli Jones Racing. For the 1978 season, Unser decided to depart the Vel's Parnelli Jones team to join sports car driving legend Jim Hall's new Chaparral Race Team, driving a new Lola Cosworth.

Roger Penske had reigning national champ Tom Sneva, Mario Andretti and rookie Rick Mears in his stable.

Bobby Unser was back with Dan Gurney's All American Racers in a new Eagle after a two-year sabbatical.

Pancho Carter was returning from serious leg injuries sustained at Phoenix in an off-season testing accident. He started twenty-first and finished twenty-fourth, completing ninety-two laps.

Rain washed out the first weekend of qualifications.

Danny Ongais crashed hard in turn three on Tuesday before qualifying. He was driving his backup car, which was to have been driven by Lloyd Ruby, effectively knocking Ruby out of the event.

As a result of the rain postponing the first weekend of qualifications, Mario Andretti now had a schedule conflict with the Belgian Grand Prix. Mike Hiss qualified Andretti's car in the middle of row three, but Andretti would have to start thirty-third. Andretti won the Belgian Grand Prix on his way to winning the 1978 World Championship.

Tom Sneva took the pole with a record speed of 202.156 mph in his Penske/Cosworth. Danny Ongais and rookie Rick Mears completed the front row. It was an all 200+ mph front row.

Janet Guthrie qualified for the fifteenth starting position.

A.J. Foyt had a problem on his original qualification attempt and qualified as a third-day qualifier even though he was the third fastest. He would start twentieth.

Jim Hurtubise, who was still attempting to qualify his front-engine Mallard, was ruled ineligible for a run on the last day of qualifications. He made quite a scene by running out on the track to try to disrupt qualifications. He was tackled by fellow driver John Martin and banned from the track for the rest of the month.

On race morning, Louis Meyer delighted the crowd when he drove pre-race laps in his 1928-winning car in celebration of the fiftieth anniversary of his first win.

Mary Fendrich Hulman commanded, "Lady and gentlemen, start your engines!" This was the first time since 1954 that someone other than Tony Hulman voiced the starting command.

The Chevrolet Corvette, in its 25th model year, paced the field with Jim Rathmann at the wheel.

Danny Ongais took the lead at the start and led sixty-eight of the first seventy-five laps in his Parnelli/Cosworth.

Andretti charged through the field, but an eight-minute stop to replace an electrical coil would take him out of contention.

By mid-race it was a three-driver race between Sneva, Ongais and Al Unser.

Ongais blew his engine on lap 145.

Unser led all but four laps from lap 108. On his last stop on lap 179, he hit a tire with his front wing but did not significantly affect the balance of his car.

He returned to the race with a thirty second lead on Sneva. Unser slowed to preserve his car and Sneva began cutting into his lead.

Unser led Sneva by eight seconds at the checker and Gordon Johncock was third. Unser averaged 161.363 mph and became a three-time winner of the "500."

Sneva finished second for the second year in a row, with Gordon Johncock one lap down in third.

Al Unser led 121 laps, and Ongais led 71 laps.

Janet Guthrie finished a career-high ninth driving with a "secret" cracked wrist incurred while playing tennis a few days before the race.

Rick Mears, who started third but dropped out with engine failure and finished twenty-third, and eleventh-place finisher Larry Rice shared Rookie of the Year honors.

Al Unser won only two more races in 1978 but they were biggies: the Pocono 500 and the Ontario 500. He became the only driver to win the Triple Crown of Auto Racing.

Al Unser wins his third "500" in Jim Hall's Lola/Cosworth.

RACE RESULTS FOR THE 1978 INDIANAPOLIS 500

Finish	Start	Car Num.	Driver	Car Name/Entrant*	Make/Model	Status	Laps	Led	Winnings
1	5	2	Al Unser (W)	1st National City Travelers Checks	Lola/Cosworth	161.363	200	121	$290,364
2	1	1	Tom Sneva	Norton Spirit	Penske/Cosworth	161.244	200	3	$112,704
3	6	20	Gordon Johncock (W)	North American Van Lines	Wildcat/DGS	Running	199	0	$61,769
4	13	40	Steve Krisiloff	Foreman Industries	Wildcat/DGS	Running	198	5	$39,504
5	7	6	Wally Dallenbach	Sugaripe Prune	McLaren/Cosworth	Running	195	0	$35,632
6	19	48	Bobby Unser (W)	ARCO Graphite	Eagle/Cosworth	Running	195	0	$29,478
7	20	14	A.J. Foyt (W)	Gilmore Racing/Citicorp	Coyote/Foyt	Running	191	0	$29,628
8	23	84	George Snider	Gilmore Racing/Citicorp	Coyote/Foyt	Running	191	0	$25,818
9	15	51	Janet Guthrie	Texaco Star	Wildcat/DGS	Running	190	0	$24,115
10	8	16	Johnny Parsons	1st National City Travelers Checks	Lightning/Offy	Running	186	0	$26,129
11	30	35	Larry Rice (R)	Bryant Heating/WIBC	Lightning/Offy	Engine	186	0	$24,276
12	33	7	Mario Andretti (W)	Gould Charge	Penske/Cosworth	Running	185	0	$23,252
13	4	4	Johnny Rutherford (W)	1st National City Travelers Checks	McLaren/Cosworth	Running	180	0	$31,805
14	28	88	Jerry Karl	Machinists Union	McLaren/Offy	Running	176	0	$20,930
15	24	69	Joe Saldana (R)	Mr. Wize Buys Carpet Shop	Eagle/Offy	Running	173	0	$20,691
16	31	98	Gary Bettenhausen	Oberdorfer	Kingfish/Offy	Engine	147	0	$20,130
17	25	78	Mike Mosley	Alex XLNT Foods	Lightning/Offy	Turbocharger	146	0	$20,247
18	2	25	Danny Ongais	Interscope Racing	Parnelli/Cosworth	Blown engine	145	71	$33,242
19	10	17	Dick Simon	La Machine	Vollstedt/Offy	Wheel bearing	138	0	$18,516
20	26	26	Jim McElreath	Circle City Coal	Eagle/Offy	Engine	132	0	$19,119
21	18	43	Tom Bigelow	Armstrong Mould	Wildcat/DGS	Rod	107	0	$18,000
22	9	80	Larry Dickson	Polak/Stay-On Car Glaze	Penske/Cosworth	Oil pressure	104	0	$22,659
23	3	71	Rick Mears (R)	CAM2 Motor Oil	Penske/Cosworth	Engine	103	0	$22,396
24	21	8	Pancho Carter	Budweiser	Lightning/Cosworth	Header	92	0	$20,262
25	11	11	Roger McCluskey	National Engineering Co.	Eagle/AMC	Clutch	82	0	$18,707
26	17	39	John Mahler	Tibon	Eagle/Offy	Timing gear	58	0	$16,330
27	14	22	Tom Bagley (R)	Kent Oil	Watson/Offy	Oil leak	25	0	$16,281
28	22	77	Salt Walther	Dayton-Walther	McLaren/Cosworth	Clutch	24	0	$16,560
29	16	19	Spike Gehlhausen	Hubler Chevrolet/WIRE Radio	Eagle/Offy	Accident	23	0	$15,968
30	29	47	Phil Threshie (R)	Circle City Chevrolet/Tutweiler Cadillac	Lightning/Offy	Oil pressure	22	0	$15,705
31	32	30	Jerry Sneva	Smock Material Handling	McLaren/Offy	Transmission	18	0	$18,120
32	12	24	Sheldon Kinser	Thermo-King	Watson/Offy	Oil pressure	15	0	$15,813
33	27	29	Cliff Hucul	Wendy's Hamburgers	McLaren/Offy	Oil line	4	0	$15,534

* - complete car name/entrant data not available for all entries
(R) - Indicated Rookie
(W) - Indicates Past Winner

1979

Championship Auto Racing Teams (CART) was established by several car owners in an attempt to raise the purses and to race at facilities that better accommodated corporate partners.

CART had its schedule of races, and USAC had its schedule.

USAC attempted to restrict CART from competing at Indianapolis, but a judge issued a temporary injunction allowing them.

Jim Hall's new Chaparral, nicknamed the "Yellow Submarine," was the first car at Indy with "ground effects" incorporated into its design. Al Unser was the driver for Hall again.

Penske had released Tom Sneva at the end of the 1978 season after Sneva had won the season championship and the pole at Indy the previous two years.

Sneva was driving the Sugaripe Prune Special for O'Connell Racing.

Mario Andretti did not enter the 1979 "500" in an attempt to concentrate on defending his 1978 Formula One World Championship.

Jim Hurtubise was back with his beloved front-engine Mallard, despite the previous year's antics.

Turbocharger boost level was reduced to fifty inches.

The first day of qualifications was rained out, but Danny Ongais did crash hard during pre-qualification practice in turn four, sustaining a concussion.

Tom Sneva was attempting to become the first driver ever to win the pole three years in a row, but Rick Mears beat him out (193.736 mph). This was Mears first pole position in Indy car. Sneva started second and Al Unser started on the outside of row one. Each front row starter's car was powered by a Cosworth engine.

Because of a controversy involving attempts by some teams to override the pop-off valves furnished by USAC, eleven non-qualifiers were given one attempt to exceed the bump speed (Roger McCluskey 183.908 mph), and be added to the original thirty-three-car field.

On the morning before the race, eight of the eleven took advantage of the opportunity to practice and have one attempt to qualify.

Bill Vukovich and George Snider were the only two fast enough, so thirty-five cars took the green flag, which was the first time since 1933 that more than thirty-three cars started the race.

Jackie Stewart, three-time World Driving Champion and Indy 500 veteran, drove the Ford Mustang pace car.

The pacer light system, used since 1972, had been retired and the "pack-up" rule was initiated at Indianapolis for the first time, with the pace car going on to the track during caution periods.

Al Unser took off at the green flag in the Yellow Submarine and led 85 out of the first 100 laps, relinquishing the lead only on pit stops. On lap 97, transmission problems cropped up, and Unser was out of the race by lap 104.

Penske driver Bobby Unser led from lap 97 to lap 182 and looked like he was going to win his third "500" when he lost fourth gear and was passed by teammate Rick Mears. Unser would eventually finish in fifth place.

Foyt was chasing Mears when a yellow on lap 191 for Tom Sneva's accident cut the lead from 47 seconds to 17 seconds.

The green appeared on lap 196 and Foyt cut the lead to six seconds. Foyt lost a cylinder on the last lap and crept to the checker flag for a second-place finish to a tremendous ovation. He finished just 2.5 seconds ahead of a third-place and fast-closing Mike Mosley. The top three finishers were the only cars on the lead lap.

Rick Mears gave Roger Penske his second Indy 500 win in only Rick's second start. Mears averaged 158.9 mph in his first "500" win.

The only rookie in the field, Howdy Holmes, finished seventh and won Rookie of the Year.

Bobby Unser led eighty-nine laps, Al Unser led eighty-five laps, and Rick Mears led twenty-five laps.

Rick Mears wins in only his second Indy 500.

RACE RESULTS FOR THE 1979 INDIANAPOLIS 500

Finish	Start	Car Num.	Driver	Car Name/Entrant*	Make/Model	Status	Laps	Led	Winnings
1	1	9	Rick Mears	The Gould Charge	Penske/Cosworth	158.899	200	25	$270,401
2	6	14	A.J. Foyt (W)	Gilmore Racing Team	Parnelli/Cosworth	158.260	200	1	$107,291
3	12	36	Mike Mosley	Theodore Racing	Eagle/Cosworth	158.228	200	0	$65,031
4	27	25	Danny Ongais	Interscope Racing	Penske/Cosworth	Running	199	0	$41,197
5	4	12	Bobby Unser (W)	Norton Spirit	Penske/Cosworth	Running	199	89	$62,319
6	5	3	Gordon Johncock (W)	North American Van Lines	Penske/Cosworth	Running	197	0	$34,815
7	13	46	Howdy Holmes (R)	Armstrong Mould/Jiffy Mix	Wildcat/Cosworth	Running	195	0	$38,503
8	34	22	Bill Vukovich II	Hubler/WNDE/Thermo-King	Watson/Offy	Running	194	0	$31,305
9	15	11	Tom Bagley	Dairy Queen/Kent Oil	Penske/Cosworth	Running	193	0	$26,927
10	31	19	Spike Gehlhausen	Sta-On Car Glaze/WIRE	Wildcat/Cosworth	Running	192	0	$26,366
11	28	7	Steve Krisiloff	Frosty Acres/Winton Sales	Lightning/Offy	Running	192	0	$25,713
12	16	77	Salt Walther	Dayton-Walther	Penske/Cosworth	Running	191	0	$24,739
13	25	72	Roger McCluskey	National Engineering Co.	McLaren/Cosworth	Running	191	0	$26,392
14	30	44	Tom Bigelow	Armstrong Mould	Lola/Cosworth	Running	190	0	$25,817
15	2	1	Tom Sneva	Sugaripe Prune	McLaren/Cosworth	Accident	188	0	$30,578
16	26	69	Joe Saldana	KBHL/Spirit of Nebraska	Eagle/Offy	Running	186	0	$24,467
17	29	97	Phil Threshie	Guiffre Brothers Crane	King/Chevrolet	Running	172	0	$24,634
18	8	4	Johnny Rutherford (W)	Budweiser	McLaren/Cosworth	Running	168	0	$30,729
19	23	31	Larry Rice	S&M Electric	Lightning/Offy	Accident	142	0	$21,053
20	17	10	Pancho Carter	Alex XLNT Foods	Lightning/Offy	Wheel bearing	129	0	$21,656
21	22	34	Vern Schuppan	Wysard Motor Co.	Wildcat/DGS	Transmission	111	0	$20,537
22	3	2	Al Unser (W)	Pennzoil	Chaparral/Cosworth	Transmission	104	85	$39,646
23	33	50	Eldon Rasmussen	Vans by Bivouac/WFMS	Antares/Offy	Header pipe	89	0	$19,433
24	24	80	Larry Dickson	Russ Polak	Penske/Cosworth	Fuel pump	86	0	$19,149
25	32	92	John Mahler	Intercomp/Sports Magazine	Eagle/Offy	Fuel pump	66	0	$18,894
26	20	17	Dick Simon	Sanyo	Vollstedt/Offy	Clutch	57	0	$19,267
27	7	6	Wally Dallenbach	Foreman Industries	Penske/Cosworth	Lost wheel	43	0	$19,768
28	10	24	Sheldon Kinser	Genesee Beer	Watson/Offy	Piston	40	0	$18,297
29	18	29	Cliff Hucul	Hucul Racing	McLaren/Offy	Rod	22	0	$21,605
30	11	89	Lee Kunzman	Vetter Windjammer	Parnelli/Cosworth	Scavenger pump	18	0	$18,042
31	21	73	Jerry Sneva	National Engineering Co.	Spirit/AMC	Piston	16	0	$18,357
32	9	15	Johnny Parsons	Hopkins	Lightning/Offy	Piston	16	0	$18,900
33	35	59	George Snider	KBHL/Spirit of Nebraska	Lightning/Offy	Fuel pump	7	0	$18,921
34	14	45	Janet Guthrie	Texaco Star	Lola/Cosworth	Piston	3	0	$18,121
35	19	23	Jim McElreath	Amax Coal	Penske/Cosworth	Valves	0	0	$18,671

* - complete car name/entrant data not available for all entries
(R) - Indicated Rookie
(W) - Indicates Past Winner

1980

John Cooper was now president of the Speedway, succeeding Joseph Cloutier in October of 1979. Cooper was the first paid employee hired when USAC was formed back in 1955.

Al Unser left Jim Hall's Chaparral team and was replaced with Johnny Rutherford. Team McLaren had pulled out of Indy car racing at the end of 1979.

Rutherford was fast from the start of practice. Rookie Timothy Lee Richmond from Ashland, Ohio surprised everyone with the month's fastest lap of 193.5 mph on the Friday before pole day.

Richmond crashed in the practice session before pole day qualifying, forcing him to qualify on the second weekend instead.

J.R. won his third pole at 192.3 mph, with Mario Andretti and Bobby Unser joining him on row one. Rutherford was more than a mile per hour faster than second starter Andretti.

Spike Gehlhausen and Jerry Sneva surprised the fans by starting fourth and fifth respectively.

Roger Rager qualified tenth with a Chevrolet that had an engine block from an old school bus with 250,000 miles on it.

During the second week of practice, a third Sneva brother—Jan—crashed and decided Indy was not for him.

Tom Sneva qualified fourteenth but crashed his car during the second week of practice. He eventually jumped into the team car originally assigned to Vern Schuppan, starting thirty-third.

Jim McElreath started eleventh and finished twenty-fourth, becoming the oldest driver to race at Indy (fifty-two) at that time.

Janet Guthrie failed to qualify.

Johnnie Parsons, the 1950 winner, drove the Pontiac Turbo-Trans Am pace car after driving his winning Kurtis-Offenhauser in pre-race festivities. This was the first time the pace car driver had a son in the race. Johnny Parsons would start seventh and finish twenty-sixth.

Rutherford took the early lead. By lap twenty, Sneva had moved from thirty-third to fourth.

The lead primarily changed during the first half between Rutherford, Gordon Johncock, Pancho Carter, Bobby Unser, Andretti and Tom Sneva.

The second half was dominated by Rutherford, who led 90 of the final 100 laps in his Chaparral 2K. He beat Sneva to the checker by thirty seconds. J.R. averaged 142.9 mph for his third Indy 500 win. This was J.R.'s third win in seven races. Thirteen caution periods for sixty-five laps greatly reduced the race speed.

The last row starters had outstanding races. Tom Sneva finished second in "Old Hound" and Gary Bettenhausen was third in a four-year-old Wildcat, not bad when considering they started thirty-third and thirty-second. This was Sneva's third second-place finish in four years, tying Harry Hartz, Bill Holland and Jim Rathmann's record of three second-place finishes. Tom Bigelow started thirty-first and finished a very respectable eighth place.

Pancho Carter seemed to have had the second best car, but a black flag for passing the pace car relegated him to a sixth-place finish.

Tim Richmond won the Rookie of the Year award by finishing ninth after running out of fuel on his last lap, then provided a memorable moment when he hitched a ride back to the pits on the sidepod of Rutherford's car on J.R.'s victory lap.

Johnny Rutherford would go on to win both the USAC and CART Championships.

1980 Winner Johnny Rutherford drives passenger Tim Richmond back to the pits on his Yellow Submarine Chaparral.

RACE RESULTS FOR THE 1980 INDIANAPOLIS 500

Finish	Start	Car Num.	Driver	Car Name/Entrant*	Make/Model	Status	Laps	Led	Winnings
1	1	4	Johnny Rutherford (W)	Pennzoil	Chaparral/Cosworth	142.862	200	118	$318,820
2	33	9	Tom Sneva	Bon Jour Action Jeans	McLaren/Cosworth	142.524	200	16	$128,945
3	32	46	Gary Bettenhausen	Armstrong Mould	Wildcat/DGS	142.485	200	0	$86,945
4	17	20	Gordon Johncock (W)	North American Van Lines	Penske/Cosworth	142.482	200	11	$56,495
5	6	1	Rick Mears (W)	The Gould Charge	Penske/Cosworth	Running	199	10	$45,505
6	8	10	Pancho Carter	Alex XLNT Foods	Penske/Cosworth	Running	199	5	$39,175
7	16	25	Danny Ongais	Interscope/Panasonic	Parnelli/Cosworth	Running	199	0	$37,414
8	31	43	Tom Bigelow	Armstrong Mould/Jiffy Mix	Lola/Cosworth	Running	198	0	$44,707
9	19	21	Tim Richmond (R)	UNO/Q95 Starcruiser	Penske/Cosworth	Out of fuel	197	1	$43,447
10	23	44	Greg Leffler (R)	Starcraft R.V.	Lola/Cosworth	Running	197	0	$39,047
11	22	29	Billy Engelhart (R)	Master Lock	McLaren/Cosworth	Running	193	0	$32,303
12	30	2	Bill Vukovich II	Hubler Chevrolet/WFMS	Watson/Offy	Running	192	0	$31,087
13	18	96	Don Whittington (R)	Sun System	Penske/Cosworth	Running	178	0	$30,928
14	12	14	A.J. Foyt (W)	Gilmore Racing Team	Parnelli/Cosworth	Valve	173	0	$29,512
15	21	16	George Snider	Gilmore Racing Team	Parnelli/Cosworth	Engine	169	1	$30,351
16	24	18	Dennis Firestone (R)	Scientific Drilling Controls	Penske/Cosworth	Transmission	137	0	$28,776
17	5	7	Jerry Sneva	Hugger's Beverage Holders	Lola/Cosworth	Accident	130	0	$30,271
18	25	99	Hurley Haywood (R)	Sta-On Car Glaze/ KISS99/Guarantee Auto	Lightning/Chevrolet V6	Fire	126	0	$28,273
19	3	11	Bobby Unser (W)	Norton Spirit	Penske/Cosworth	Turbo	126	26	$37,432
20	2	12	Mario Andretti (W)	Essex	Penske/Cosworth	Engine	71	10	$33,611
21	28	38	Jerry Karl	Tonco Trailer	McLaren/Chevrolet	Clutch	64	0	$26,747
22	29	8	Dick Simon	Vermont American/ Shihouette Spas/ Regal 8 Inns	Vollstedt/Offy	Lost wheel	58	0	$26,411
23	10	66	Roger Rager (R)	Advance Clean Sweep/ Carpenter Bus	Wildcat/Chevrolet	Accident	55	2	$26,503
24	11	23	Jim McElreath	McElreath	Penske/Cosworth	Accident	54	0	$26,323
25	20	70	Gordon Smiley (R)	Valvoline/ Diamond Head Ranch	Phoenix/Cosworth	Turbo	47	0	$26,771
26	7	15	Johnny Parsons	Wynn's	Lightning/Offy	Piston	44	0	$26,597
27	9	5	Al Unser (W)	Longhorn Racing	Longhorn/Cosworth	Cylinder	33	0	$25,151
28	13	40	Tom Bagley	Kent Oil	Wildcat/Cosworth	Pump	29	0	$25,983
29	4	35	Spike Gehlhausen	Winton Sales	Penske/Cosworth	Accident	20	0	$26,143
30	27	94	Bill Whittington (R)	Sun System	Parnelli/Cosworth	Accident	9	0	$24,361
31	15	26	Dick Ferguson (R)	AMS Oil	Penske/Cosworth	Accident	9	0	$26,647
32	26	48	Mike Mosley	Theodore Racing	Eagle/Chevrolet	Gasket	5	0	$24,591
33	14	95	Larry Cannon	Kraco Car Stereo	Wildcat/DGS	Camshaft	2	0	$25,063

* - complete car name/entrant data not available for all entries
(R) - Indicated Rookie
(W) - Indicates Past Winner

1981

In 1976, there was one Cosworth engine-powered car in the race. In 1981, twenty-nine of the thirty-three starters were powered by Cosworth.

Roman Slobodynskj's new black "Batmobile" for Ted Field's Interscope Racing was a cool-looking car with Danny Ongais as the driver. Ted Field is the son of department store magnate Marshall Field.

Mario Andretti was driving for Pat Patrick, while Bill Alsup joined Rick Mears and Bobby Unser at Penske.

A Rookie Orientation Program (ROP) was held in April.

Rain during the first weekend of qualifying and a Formula One commitment for Mario Andretti required recently retired Wally Dallenbach to qualify Andretti's car.

Rookie Josele Garza qualified in sixth position to become the first person from Mexico to make the race.

Rookie Geoff Brabham qualified fifteenth, making him and his dad, Jack, the only non-American father/son combination to race in the "500."

Bobby Unser qualified for the pole at 200.546 mph in his Penske/Cosworth, and Mike Mosley and A.J. Foyt made up the front row.

Tom Sneva, whose March/Cosworth didn't arrive at the track until the second week of practice, was considered a second weekend qualifier.

He actually became the fastest qualifier at 200.7 mph, but started twentieth.

George Snider qualified seventeenth in Foyt's back-up after only three practice laps. Foyt later decided to pull Snider and put Tim Richmond, who had been "bumped," in the car for the race and start thirty-third.

Dallenbach qualified Andretti's car. Andretti would start thirty-second.

Jim Hurtubise did not enter a car for himself, the first time since 1967, but did make an attempt in Norm Hall's Kingfish. Herk could only run 174 mph and did not make the show. This was Hurtubise last attempt at Indy.

Mrs. Mary Fendrich Hulman was ill in the hospital on race day, and as a result, Mari Hulman George gave the command to "Start your engines."

The legendary ten-time Indy 500 starter Dennis "Duke" Nalon drove the Buick Regal pace car.

Bobby Unser jumped in the lead at the start and led until his first stop on lap twenty-two. Johnny Rutherford led briefly until he stopped on lap twenty-four and never returned to the race. The defending champ was out of the race with fuel pump problems.

Mike Mosley had qualified a normally-aspirated Chevrolet/Eagle on the front row and became the first car out of the race.

Tom Sneva moved up from twentieth starting position to take the lead before his first stop. He passed Unser for the lead on lap thirty-three and stayed there until lap fifty-six.

Rick Mears took the lead and then pitted on lap fifty-eight. A major pit fire took him out of the race.

Danny Ongais led briefly before he was seriously injured in a horrendous crash in turn three on lap sixty-four.

Gordon Johncock, Bobby Unser and Andretti battled the last two-thirds of the race.

A yellow light on lap 146, caused by Gordon Smiley's crash, resulted in one of the biggest disputes in "500" history.

The leaders pitted, and when they returned to the track under caution, Bobby Unser passed eleven cars before blending in. Andretti initially passed several cars but dropped back and actually gained only a position or two.

Bobby Unser led fifty of the last fifty-three laps and beat Andretti to the checker by five seconds. Unser averaged 139.2 mph as a result of eleven caution periods for sixty-nine laps. This was Unser's third Indy 500 victory—or was it?

There was a total of twenty-four lead changes between eight drivers during the very competitive race.

Soon after the race it rained hard.

Josele Garza led for thirteen laps before finishing twenty-third in his first race. He won Rookie of the Year.

At eight a.m. the morning after the race, the official results were posted to show Andretti the winner and Bobby Unser penalized to second place.

Mario Andretti participated in the "day after the race" winner's pictures and victory banquet.

Roger Penske protested and the official result was not determined until 138 days later on October 9th, when an arbitration committee for USAC ruled that Bobby Unser had won his third "500" and Mario Andretti had finished second because Unser's move had no effect on the outcome. Unser was fined rather than penalized a position and the victory.

Mario Andretti and Bobby Unser become the focal point of this disputed "500."

RACE RESULTS FOR THE 1981 INDIANAPOLIS 500

Finish	Start	Car Num.	Driver	Car Name/Entrant*	Make/Model	Status	Laps	Led	Winnings
1	1	3	Bobby Unser (W)	Norton Spirit	Penske/Cosworth	139.184	200	89	$299,124
2	32	40	Mario Andretti (W)	STP Oil Treatment	Wildcat/Cosworth	139.029	200	12	$128,974
3	18	33	Vern Schuppan	Red Roof Inns	McLaren/Cosworth	Running	199	0	$87,974
4	12	32	Kevin Cogan (R)	Jerry O'Connell Racing	Phoenix/Cosworth	Running	197	0	$59,024
5	15	50	Geoff Brabham (R)	Psachie/Garza/ESSO	Penske/Cosworth	Running	197	0	$55,684
6	23	81	Sheldon Kinser	Sergio Valente Jeans	Longhorn/Cosworth	Running	195	0	$44,754
7	16	16	Tony Bettenhausen Jr. (R)	Provimi Veal	McLaren/Cosworth	Running	195	0	$44,064
8	17	53	Steve Krisiloff	Psachie/Garza/ESSO	Penske/Cosworth	Running	194	0	$39,986
9	4	20	Gordon Johncock (W)	STP Oil Treatment	Wildcat/Cosworth	Engine	194	52	$62,501
10	28	4	Dennis Firestone	Rhoades Aircraft Sales	Wildcat/Cosworth	Engine	193	0	$36,376
11	7	7	Bill Alsup (R)	AB Dick Pacemaker	Penske/Cosworth	Running	193	0	$35,632
12	25	74	Michael Chandler (R)	National Engineering Co.	Penske/Cosworth	Running	192	0	$34,116
13	3	14	A.J. Foyt (W)	Valvoline-Gilmore	Coyote/Cosworth	Running	191	0	$35,795
14	33	84	Tim Richmond	UNO/WTTV/Guarantee Auto	Parnelli/Cosworth	Running	191	0	$33,612
15	31	38	Jerry Karl	Tonco Trailer	McLaren/Chevrolet	Running	189	0	$35,480
16	29	37	Scott Brayton (R)	Forsythe Industries	Penske/Cosworth	Engine	173	0	$32,176
17	9	88	Al Unser (W)	Valvoline-Longhorn	Longhorn/Cosworth	Running	166	0	$31,600
18	19	31	Larry Dickson	Machinist Union	Penske/Cosworth	Piston	165	0	$30,652
19	13	35	Bob Lazier (R)	Montgomery Ward Auto Club	Penske/Cosworth	Engine	154	0	$33,732
20	14	56	Tom Bigelow	Genesee Beer	Penske/Chevrolet	Engine	152	0	$30,140
21	27	90	Bill Whittington	Kraco Car Stereo	March/Cosworth	Stalled	146	0	$31,243
22	8	60	Gordon Smiley	Intermedics	Wildcat/Cosworth	Accident	141	1	$29,240
23	6	55	Josele Garza (R)	Psachie/Garza/ESSO	Penske/Cosworth	Accident	138	13	$40,282
24	24	79	Pete Halsmer (R)	Hubler Chevrolet/KISS 99/Colonial Bread	Penske/Cosworth	Accident	123	0	$30,702
25	20	2	Tom Sneva	Blue Poly	March/Cosworth	Clutch	96	25	$38,000
26	11	8	Gary Bettenhausen	Hopkins	Lightning/Cosworth	Rod	69	0	$27,976
27	21	25	Danny Ongais	Interscope Racing	Interscope/Cosworth	Accident	64	4	$30,380
28	10	5	Pancho Carter	Alex Foods	Penske/Cosworth	Compression	63	0	$27,712
29	30	51	Tom Klausler (R)	IDS Idea	Schkee/Chevrolet	Gearbox	60	0	$27,972
30	22	6	Rick Mears (W)	The Gould Charge	Penske/Cosworth	Pit fire	58	1	$28,560
31	26	91	Don Whittington	Whittington Brothers	March/Cosworth	Accident	32	0	$28,743
32	5	1	Johnny Rutherford (W)	Pennzoil	Chaparral/Cosworth	Fuel pump	25	3	$29,620
33	2	48	Mike Mosley	Pepsi Challenger	Eagle/Chevrolet	Radiator	16	0	$31,392

* - complete car name/entrant data not available for all entries
(R) - Indicated Rookie
(W) - Indicates Past Winner

1982

There was a record of 109 entries.

Warm-up laps on qualification attempts were reduced from three to two in an attempt to speed up the qualification process.

Shortly before the track opened, John Cooper resigned as IMS president and Joe Cloutier took control again. Cooper would later become the first person to serve as president of the Indianapolis Motor Speedway and Daytona International Speedway.

Defending champion Bobby Unser was back as a driving coach for Josele Garza, not as a driver defending his championship.

Just a few of Bobby Unser's accomplishments in a remarkable career:

    Three Indy 500 wins (1968, 1975, 1981)

    National Champion in 1968 and 1974, with three runner-ups

    Led ten races for a total of 440 laps

    Started from the pole position twice

    Started on the front row nine times

    Competed in nineteen consecutive Indy 500's

The Whittingtons entered cars for brothers Bill, Don and Dale.

Theodore Racing entered a Cosworth/Eagle for Desiré Wilson from South Africa, the second woman in history to attempt to qualify for Indy.

Penske teammates Rick Mears and Kevin Cogan and Patrick's Mario Andretti topped the speed charts daily and almost guaranteed a new track record in qualifications.

During qualifications, on his second warm-up lap, Gordon Smiley lost control of his car in the third turn and hit the wall head on. He died instantly. He was the first fatality at the track since 1973.

The front row consisted of Rick Mears, on the pole for the second time with a record of 207.0 mph, Kevin Cogan and A.J. Foyt.

The year 1982 proved to be a record for brothers in the race: Bill, Don and Dale Whittington; Gary and Tony Bettenhausen; Tom and Jerry Sneva; Rick and Roger Mears; and half-brothers Pancho Carter and Johnny Parsons. A third of the field was made up of brother combinations.

Desiré Wilson failed to make the race. Josele Garza struggled mightily, but qualified for the thirty-third position. During Garza's struggles, Bobby Unser tested the car. These would be the last practice laps run at Indy by three-time winner Unser.

Mike Mosley, driving for Dan Gurney, failed to make the race after repeated engine failures.

The Kraco Team, with Bill Vukovich and Vern Schuppan, also failed to make the race.

Roger Mears was the older brother of Rick Mears. Roger was driving in his second "500." He started in the eighth position.

Jim Rathmann paced the race for his sixth and final time in a Chevrolet Z28. Rathmann's six times pacing the start equaled that of Sam Hanks.

At the start of the race, coming to the green flag, Kevin Cogan's car veered to the right and hit Foyt, then spun across the track and collected Mario Andretti. A broken halfshaft was blamed for the incident. All of the other drivers were able to avoid the accident, with the exception of Dale Whittington, who came charging through the field and hit Roger Mears.

The race was red-flagged before it actually started. During the stoppage, Foyt was able to repair his car so he could start the race when it resumed. The other four drivers were eliminated from the race.

When the race was restarted, Foyt shot into the lead and stayed there for the first twenty-two laps until he pitted. This was the first time Foyt led the opening lap in his illustrious career despite starting on the pole four times.

During the first third of the race, the lead shuffled between Foyt, Gordon Johncock, Don Whittington, Danny Ongais, Rick Mears and Tom Sneva.

The final two-thirds of the race was a battle between Johncock and Mears, with Sneva also leading twelve laps.

Johncock, in his Patrick STP Wildcat, took the lead on lap 160 and expanded it when Mears pitted on lap 183. As Mears pitted, the slower car of Herm Johnson held Mears up getting to his pit. Mears actually made contact with the back of Johnson's car on pit lane. Mears's crew then filled his fuel tank when a partial fill-up would have sufficed, as there were only 17 laps remaining. This caused Mears's stop to be longer than necessary (eighteen seconds), and after Johncock's timed stop (thirteen seconds) on lap 186, Mears was 11 seconds behind with 14 laps to go. That's when Mears went to work!

Johncock was fighting handling problems and Mears was able to cut the deficit to two seconds with three laps left.

Mears made a strong run at Johncock going into turn one on the final lap, but got the door shut. Mears made another run at the checker, but Johncock held him off by sixteen hundredths of a second for his second "500" win. Johncock averaged 162 mph.

Many suggest that Johncock was able to avenge his 1973 Indy win – "The race that nobody wanted to remember", with the 1982 victory – "The race nobody could ever forget".

It was the closest "500" finish in history, eclipsing Wilbur Shaw's 2.16 second victory over Ralph Hepburn in 1937.

Pancho Carter finished third, with Tom Sneva fourth, after blowing his engine on lap 197 and losing one position. Al Unser finished fifth.

Jim Hickman finished seventh and won Rookie of the Year. Chip Ganassi, a recent graduate of Duquesne University, started eleventh and finished fifteenth in his rookie race.

Mears led seventy-seven laps, Johncock fifty-seven, Foyt thirty-two, and Sneva thirty-one.

Bobby Rahal was able to win two races in his rookie season in CART to finish second in the standings behind champion Rick Mears.

The 1982 winner Gordon Johncock holds off Rick Mears by 16/100s of a second.

RACE RESULTS FOR THE 1982 INDIANAPOLIS 500

Finish	Start	Car Num.	Driver	Car Name/Entrant*	Make/Model	Status	Laps	Led	Winnings
1	5	20	Gordon Johncock (W)	STP Oil Treatment	Wildcat/Cosworth	162.029	200	57	$290,609
2	1	1	Rick Mears (W)	The Gould Charge	Penske/Cosworth	162.026	200	77	$215,859
3	10	3	Pancho Carter	Alex Foods	March/Cosworth	Running	199	0	$103,559
4	7	7	Tom Sneva	Texaco Star	March/Cosworth	Engine	197	31	$88,309
5	16	10	Al Unser (W)	Longhorn Racing	Longhorn/Cosworth	Running	197	0	$60,326
6	8	91	Don Whittington	The Simoniz Finish	March/Cosworth	Running	196	2	$57,159
7	24	42	Jim Hickman (R)	Stroh's March	March/Cosworth	Running	189	0	$59,209
8	12	5	Johnny Rutherford (W)	Pennzoil	Chaparral/Cosworth	Engine	187	0	$50,329
9	14	28	Herm Johnson (R)	Menard Cashway Lumber	Eagle/Chevrolet	Running	186	0	$53,454
10	18	30	Howdy Holmes	Domino's Pizza	March/Cosworth	Running	186	0	$48,679
11	17	19	Bobby Rahal (R)	Red Roof Inns	March/Cosworth	Engine	174	0	$47,989
12	30	8	Gary Bettenhausen	Kraco Car Stereo	Lightning/Cosworth	Engine	158	0	$49,679
13	15	52	Hector Rebaque (R)	Carta Blanca	March/Cosworth	Fire	150	0	$55,116
14	13	53	Danny Sullivan (R)	Forsythe-Brown Racing	March/Cosworth	Accident	148	0	$46,889
15	11	12	Chip Ganassi (R)	First Commercial Corp.	Wildcat/Cosworth	Engine	147	0	$45,819
16	6	94	Bill Whittington	Whittington/Warner W. Hogdon	March/Cosworth	Engine	121	0	$43,779
17	22	68	Michael Chandler	Freeman Gurney Eagle	Eagle/Chevrolet	Gearbox	104	0	$48,269
18	31	27	Tom Bigelow	H.B.K. Racing	Eagle/Chevrolet	Engine	96	0	$44,289
19	3	14	A.J. Foyt (W)	Valvoline/Gilmore	March/Cosworth	Transmission	95	32	$71,239
20	25	34	Johnny Parsons	Silhouette Spas/WIFE/Tombstone Pizza	March/Cosworth	Spin	92	0	$42,919
21	26	35	George Snider	Cobre Tire/Intermedics	March/Cosworth	Engine	87	0	$41,529
22	9	25	Danny Ongais	Interscope Racing	Interscope/Cosworth	Accident	62	1	$41,319
23	28	69	Jerry Sneva	Great American Spirit	March/Cosworth	Accident	61	0	$40,839
24	29	39	Chet Fillip (R)	Circle Bar Truck Corral	Eagle/Cosworth	Accident	60	0	$40,539
25	32	66	Pete Halsmer	Colonial Bread/Pay Less	Eagle/Chevrolet	Transmission	38	0	$41,269
26	27	16	Tony Bettenhausen Jr.	Provimi Veal	March/Cosworth	Accident	37	0	$40,429
27	21	75	Dennis Firestone	B.C.V. Racing	Eagle/Chevrolet	Rear End	37	0	$41,319
28	20	21	Geoff Brabham	Pentax Super	March/Cosworth	Engine	12	0	$42,139
29	33	55	Josele Garza	Schlitz Gusto	March/Cosworth	Engine	1	0	$40,489
30	2	4	Kevin Cogan	Norton Spirit	Penske/Cosworth	Accident	0	0	$44,769
31	4	40	Mario Andretti (W)	STP Oil Treatment	Wildcat/Cosworth	Accident	0	0	$44,279
32	19	31	Roger Mears (R)	Machinist's Union	Penske/Cosworth	Accident	0	0	$41,719
33	23	95	Dale Whittington (R)	Whittington/Warner W. Hogdon	March/Cosworth	Accident	0	0	$40,356

* - complete car name/entrant data not available for all entries
(R) - Indicated Rookie
(W) - Indicates Past Winner

1983

Dan Gurney did not enter a team in 1983, nor did Jim Hall.

As a result of Gordon Smiley's accident and death and the fatality with Jim Hickman at Milwaukee the prior year, changes were made to slow speeds. Turbocharger boost was reduced to forty-five inches, but then raised to forty-seven after significant complaints from participants.

Rain on the first weekend of qualifications postponed the race for the pole.

Before qualifying, John Paul Jr. and Johnny Rutherford crashed and both suffered broken ankles and eliminated their chance of driving in the race. This was the first 500 start Rutherford had missed since 1966.

Teo Fabi, driving for Forsythe, surprised everyone by taking the pole with a record run of 207.4 mph in his Skoal Bandit March/Cosworth. He was the first rookie to win the pole since Walt Faulkner in 1950.

Mike Mosley and Rick Mears joined Fabi on the front row.

Al Unser Sr. (starting position seventh) and twenty-one-year-old rookie Al Unser Jr. (starting position fifth) became the first father/son combination to race against each other in the "500."

Thirty-two of the thirty-three qualifiers were powered by Cosworth.

At the start Fabi took off and led the first twenty-three laps until pitting. This was the first time a rookie led the first lap since Paul Bost in 1931.

The first half of the race was contested by Al Unser, second-year driver Bobby Rahal, Rick Mears and Tom Sneva.

Fabi pitted for the second time on lap forty-seven, but when the nozzle of the refueling hose was removed, an o-ring popped out of its seat inside the fuel port. The malfunction eliminated Fabi from the race.

Rahal's strong run ended on lap 110 with radiator problems.

Unser in his Hertz Penske Cosworth battled Sneva, in his Bignotti-Cotter Texaco Star March/Cosworth, for the second half of the race.

After the final round of pit stops on lap 173, Unser led with Sneva in second and twenty-one-year-old rookie Al Unser Jr. followed them though five laps down and in tenth place.

On a green restart on lap 177, Unser Jr. passed his dad and Sneva. Unser Jr. was given a two-lap penalty for jumping the start, but coming to the restart on lap 178, he allowed his dad to pass and positioned himself between his dad and Sneva.

For the next several laps, Unser Sr. tried to break away while Unser Jr. held up Sneva.

On lap 191, Sneva was able to pass both Unsers and go on to win his first "500" after finishing second in 1977, 1978 and 1980. Sneva averaged 162.1 mph.

Three-time winner Al Unser Sr. finished second for the third time, tying Harry Hartz, Bill Holland, Jim Rathmann and Tom Sneva for most second-place finishes.

Tom Sneva's win was the first for a March chassis and it was master mechanic George Bignotti's seventh and final win.

Teo Fabi, who finished twenty-sixth, won Rookie of the Year on the strength of his pole run and leading the first twenty-three laps of the race.

Al Unser Jr. finished as the top rookie with a tenth-place finish, but his blocking of Sneva may have hurt him in the balloting for the rookie award.

Late in the race Al Unser Jr. runs interference for his father on Tom Sneva, to no avail.

RACE RESULTS FOR THE 1983 INDIANAPOLIS 500

Finish	Start	Car Num.	Driver	Car Name/Entrant*	Make/Model	Status	Laps	Led	Winnings
1	4	5	Tom Sneva	Texaco Star	March/Cosworth	162.117	200	98	$385,886
2	7	7	Al Unser (W)	Hertz Penske	Penske/Cosworth	161.954	200	61	$179,086
3	3	2	Rick Mears (W)	Pennzoil Penske	Penske/Cosworth	161.799	200	2	$135,086
4	26	12	Geoff Brabham	UNO/British Sterling	Penske/Cosworth	Running	199	0	$108,286
5	22	16	Kevin Cogan	Caesar's Palace/Master Mechanic	March/Cosworth	Running	198	0	$73,856
6	12	30	Howdy Holmes	Domino's Pizza	March/Cosworth	Running	198	0	$71,696
7	14	21	Pancho Carter	Alex Foods Pinata	March/Cosworth	Running	197	0	$77,491
8	16	60	Chip Ganassi	Sea Ray Boats	Wildcat/Cosworth	Running	195	0	$60,580
9	29	37	Scott Brayton	SME Cement	March/Cosworth	Running	195	0	$57,085
10	5	19	Al Unser Jr. (R)	Coors Light Silver Bullet	Eagle/Cosworth	Out of fuel	192	0	$59,110
11	19	56	Steve Chassey (R)	Genesee Beer Wagon/Sizzler/WLHN	Eagle/Chevrolet	Running	192	0	$60,982
12	25	72	Chris Kneifel (R)	Primus/C.F.I	Primus/Cosworth	Running	191	0	$53,690
13	2	18	Mike Mosley	Kraco Car Stereo	March/Cosworth	Accident	169	1	$61,484
14	10	20	Gordon Johncock (W)	STP Oil Treatment	Wildcat/Cosworth	Gearbox	163	0	$53,442
15	20	22	Dick Simon	Vermont American	March/Cosworth	Running	161	0	$56,758
16	30	29	Michael Chandler	Agajanian/Mike Curb	Rattlesnake/Cosworth	Gearbox	153	0	$50,610
17	9	10	Tony Bettenhausen Jr.	Provimi Veal	March/Cosworth	Half shaft	152	0	$49,998
18	15	94	Bill Whittington	Whittington Brothers	March/Cosworth	Gearbox	144	0	$49,922
19	28	34	Derek Daly (R)	Wysard Motor Co.	March/Cosworth	Engine	126	0	$48,882
20	6	4	Bobby Rahal	Red Roof Inns	March/Cosworth	Radiator	110	15	$55,378
21	21	25	Danny Ongais	Interscope Racing	March/Cosworth	Handling	101	0	$48,588
22	23	66	Johnny Parsons	Colonial Bread/Arciero	Penske/Cosworth	Accident	80	0	$47,478
23	11	3	Mario Andretti (W)	Budweiser/Electrolux	Lola/Cosworth	Accident	79	0	$47,082
24	33	90	Dennis Firestone	Simpson Sports	March/Cosworth	Oil leak	77	0	$49,222
25	18	55	Josele Garza	Machinists Union/Silhouette	Penske/Cosworth	Oil leak	64	0	$59,898
26	1	33	Teo Fabi (R)	Skoal Bandit	March/Cosworth	Fuel gasket	47	23	$84,960
27	27	91	Don Whittington	The Simoniz Finish	March/Cosworth	Ignition	44	0	$45,858
28	8	9	Roger Mears	Machinists Union	Penske/Cosworth	Accident	43	0	$45,642
29	31	43	Steve Krisiloff	Armstrong Mould	Lola/Cosworth	U-joint	42	0	$45,462
30	17	35	Patrick Bedard (R)	Escort Radar Warning	March/Cosworth	Accident	25	0	$45,818
31	24	14	A.J. Foyt (W)	Valvoline-Gilmore	March/Cosworth	Shift linkage	24	0	$44,888
32	13	1	George Snider	Calumet Farms	March/Cosworth	Ignition	22	0	$45,138
33	32	38	Chet Fillip	Circle Bar Truck Corral	Eagle/Cosworth	Black flagged	11	0	$50,102

* - complete car name/entrant data not available for all entries
(R) - Indicated Rookie
(W) - Indicates Past Winner

1984

New Hulman Terrace suites were built on the outside of the main straight in time for the 1984 race.

There were 117 entries in 1984, a record which still holds.

Dan Gurney was back in 1984 with a pair of Eagle-Pontiacs for Mike Chandler.

Formula One team Ligier was entered for the first time, with Kevin Cogan as driver, but ultimately didn't make the race.

Two-time Formula One champion Emerson Fittipaldi came out of a three-year retirement to resume his driving career as a thirty-seven year old rookie at Indy, He drove a shocking pink car.

Mike Chandler crashed hard in turn three on the Friday before Pole Day. He sustained a serious head injury that would end his driving career.

Tom Sneva set a new track record in his Texaco Star March/Cosworth and won the pole for the third time in seven years (210.0 mph). He became the first driver to officially break the 210 mph barrier. His teammate, Howdy Holmes, started second, with Rick Mears third.

Canadian Jacques Villeneuve, younger brother of Formula One great Gilles Villeneuve, qualified on the first day of qualifications, but crashed during the second week of practice and sustained a head injury. The team decided to withdraw the car, rather than assign another driver and start last.

First alternate Chris Kneifel became the thirty-third starter. This was the first time the first alternate started the race since 1929.

Mario and Michael Andretti became the second father/son duo to compete in the same "500." Michael started fourth in this, his rookie race, and Mario sixth.

The Pontiac Fiero became the only mid-engine car to ever pace the "500." It also became the shortest car to pace the race at just 93.4 inches.

Mears, Sneva and Mario Andretti shared the lead for most of the first 100 laps, but from lap 110 Mears led all but two laps to win his second "500." Rick Mears averaged a record 163.6 mph in his Pennzoil March/Cosworth, breaking Mark Donohue's race record of 162.962 mph set in 1972.

Mears had now finished in the top three for three consecutive races, and had won twice in seven starts.

On lap fifty-eight, Patrick Bedard, a columnist for Car & Driver magazine, had a serious accident at the north end of the track. He flipped and his car broke in half. Bedard suffered only a broken jaw and bruises but never raced at Indy again.

Sneva's strong run ended on lap 168 when a CV joint failed. He was in second place behind Mears at the time.

Roberto Guerrero finished second, two laps down, despite a spin with no contact and two stalls in the pits.

Al Unser Sr. finished third, sports car ace Al Holbert fourth and Michael Andretti fifth.

Roberto Guerrero and Michael Andretti shared Rookie of the Year.

Rick Mears sustained very serious leg and foot injuries that summer at the Sanair Speedway in Quebec, Canada. His injuries included breaking every bone in his right foot (27). He was able to recover enough to keep driving.

The Lola car showed its superiority with eight straight wins during the summer by Danny Sullivan and Mario Andretti.

Mario won his fourth Indy car title in 1984.

Rick Mears wins in 1984, here with four-time Indy 500 winning car owner Roger Penske.

RACE RESULTS FOR THE 1984 INDIANAPOLIS 500

Finish	Start	Car Num.	Driver	Car Name/Entrant*	Make/Model	Status	Laps	Led	Winnings
1	3	6	Rick Mears (W)	Pennzoil Z-7	March/Cosworth	163.612	200	119	$434,061
2	7	9	Roberto Guerrero (R)	Master Mechanic Tools	March/Cosworth	Running	198	0	$171,666
3	10	2	Al Unser (W)	Miller High Life	March/Cosworth	Running	198	0	$117,416
4	16	21	Al Holbert (R)	CRC Chemical	March/Cosworth	Running	198	0	$106,261
5	4	99	Michael Andretti (R)	Electrolux/Kraco	March/Cosworth	Running	198	0	$119,231
6	12	14	A.J. Foyt (W)	Gilmore/Foyt	March/Cosworth	Running	197	0	$79,276
7	18	5	Bobby Rahal	7-Eleven/Red Roof Inns	March/Cosworth	Running	197	0	$74,996
8	9	28	Herm Johnson	3M/Menard Cashway	March/Cosworth	Running	194	0	$73,560
9	11	25	Danny Ongais	Interscope Racing	March/Cosworth	Running	193	3	$68,085
10	24	55	Josele Garza	Schaefer/Machinist's Union	March/Cosworth	Running	193	0	$66,910
11	31	4	George Snider	Calumet Farms	March/Cosworth	Running	193	0	$69,357
12	32	50	Dennis Firestone	Hoosier Transportation	March/Cosworth	Running	186	0	$62,765
13	2	41	Howdy Holmes	Jiffy Mixes	March/Cosworth	Running	185	0	$85,209
14	13	77	Tom Gloy (R)	Simoniz Finish	March/Cosworth	Engine	179	0	$62,467
15	33	73	Chris Kneifel	Spa*erobics/Living Well	Primus/Cosworth	Transmission	175	0	$61,683
16	1	1	Tom Sneva (W)	Texaco Star	March/Cosworth	CV joint	168	31	$112,935
17	6	3	Mario Andretti (W)	Budweiser Lola	Lola/Cosworth	Nose cone	153	29	$72,323
18	26	37	Scott Brayton	Buick Dealers of America	March/Buick	Transmission	150	0	$64,397
19	21	10	Pancho Carter	American Dream	March/Cosworth	Engine	141	0	$59,057
20	27	98	Kevin Cogan	Dubonnet/Curb Racing	Eagle/Pontiac	Wheel	137	0	$65,853
21	15	7	Al Unser Jr.	Coors Light Silver Bullet	March/Cosworth	Water pump	131	4	$67,985
22	30	84	Johnny Rutherford (W)	Gilmore/Greer/Foyt	March/Cosworth	Engine	116	0	$56,453
23	20	22	Dick Simon	Break Free	March/Cosworth	In pits	112	0	$64,057
24	14	33	Teo Fabi	Skoal Bandit	March/Cosworth	Fuel system	104	14	$71,197
25	5	20	Gordon Johncock (W)	STP Oil Treatment	March/Cosworth	Accident	103	0	$61,373
26	17	16	Tony Bettenhausen Jr.	Provimi Veal	March/Cosworth	Piston	86	0	$55,585
27	29	61	Derek Daly	Provimi Veal	March/Cosworth	Handling	76	0	$55,333
28	22	40	Chip Ganassi	Old Milwaukee	March/Cosworth	Engine	61	0	$54,617
29	28	30	Danny Sullivan	Domino's Pizza	Lola/Cosworth	Broken wheel	57	0	$57,937
30	19	35	Patrick Bedard	Escort Radar Warning	March/Buick	Accident	55	0	$56,793
31	25	57	Spike Gehlhausen	Little Kings	March/Cosworth	Spun out	45	0	$54,185
32	23	47	Emerson Fittipaldi (R)	W.I.T. Promotions	March/Cosworth	Oil pressure	37	0	$53,800
33	8	18	Geoff Brabham	Kraco Car Stereo	March/Cosworth	Fuel line	1	0	$54,077

* - complete car name/entrant data not available for all entries
(R) - Indicated Rookie
(W) - indicates Past Winner

1985

During the first week of practice, two-time Indy 500 champ Gordon Johncock decided to hang it up. Don Whittington replaced Johncock in Pat Patrick's car.

Herm Johnson, who had been near the top of the speed charts, crashed hard in practice in turn one and suffered chest and arm injuries, knocking him out of the race.

Pancho Carter set a new four-lap record in his Valvoline March/Buick and won the pole at 212.6 mph. Scott Brayton, also in a Buick, was second and Bobby Rahal, in a March Cosworth, was third. These were the only two Buick engines in the race.

Derek Daly, having come back from serious foot and leg injuries, made the field in thirty-first position. Three-time winner Johnny Rutherford started thirtieth.

The year 1985 was the first field in history made up of all new cars.

At the start, Rahal took the early lead. The Buicks did not fare well; Carter was out of the race after six laps and finished last, while Brayton lasted thirty-one laps.

Carter became the first pole-sitter to finish last since Cliff Woodbury in 1929.

Mario Andretti took the lead on lap 16 and led 75 of the first 100 laps.

Andretti developed a push and Danny Sullivan began reeling him in. On lap 120, Sullivan attempted an inside pass in turn one. After he had made the pass he did almost a 420-degree spin without contact and was able to continue. Unbelievably, Sullivan did not even flat-spot his tires in the spin.

Andretti made an inside move (the opposite of what he had done two years before when he hit a spinning Johnny Parsons) to avoid the spinning Sullivan.

Sullivan pitted and rejoined the race in second position, continuing his pursuit of Andretti. At virtually the same spot on lap 140, Sullivan successfully passed Mario and led the final sixty laps to win his first 500 by 2.5 seconds.

The "spin and win" move by Sullivan would become one of the most spectacular moments in Indy 500 history. Sullivan averaged 153.0 mph in his Miller High Life March/Cosworth.

Sullivan's win gave Roger Penske his fifth victory and fourth in the past seven years.

Mario Andretti finished second, Roberto Guerrero third, and Al Unser Sr. fourth. Andretti led 107 laps, and Sullivan led 67.

Arie Luyendyk finished seventh and won Rookie of the Year.

Nineteen-eighty five was Dan Gurney's last race as an entrant and constructor. He entered in 1986 but didn't qualify.

March chassis won ten of fifteen races in 1985.

Al Unser Sr. won the season championship over his son and namesake by one point.

The 1985 winner Danny Sullivan spins as he attempts to overtake Mario Andretti.

RACE RESULTS FOR THE 1985 INDIANAPOLIS 500

Finish	Start	Car Num.	Driver	Car Name/Entrant*	Make/Model	Status	Laps	Led	Winnings
1	8	5	Danny Sullivan	Miller American	March/Cosworth	152.982	200	67	$517,663
2	4	3	Mario Andretti (W)	Beatrice Foods	Lola/Cosworth	152.950	200	107	$290,363
3	16	9	Roberto Guerrero	Master Mechanics/True Value	March/Cosworth	152.832	200	0	$157,113
4	7	11	Al Unser (W)	Hertz	March/Cosworth	Running	199	0	$102,533
5	26	76	Johnny Parsons	Canadian Tire	March/Cosworth	Running	198	0	$98,863
6	30	21	Johnny Rutherford (W)	Vermont American	March/Cosworth	Running	198	0	$119,583
7	20	61	Arie Luyendyk (R)	Dutch Treat/Provimi Veal	Lola/Cosworth	Running	198	0	$99,233
8	15	99	Michael Andretti	Electrolux/Kraco	March/Cosworth	Running	196	0	$76,813
9	22	98	Ed Pimm (R)	Skoal Bandit	Eagle/Cosworth	Running	195	0	$79,463
10	19	33	Howdy Holmes	Jiffy Mixes	Lola/Cosworth	Running	194	0	$88,088
11	32	18	Kevin Cogan	Kraco/Wolff Sun Systems	March/Cosworth	Running	191	0	$73,663
12	31	29	Derek Daly	Kapsreiter Bier	Lola/Cosworth	Running	189	0	$77,963
13	5	40	Emerson Fittipaldi	7-Eleven	March/Cosworth	Fuel line	188	11	$78,163
14	12	12	Bill Whittington	Arciero Wines	March/Cosworth	Accident	183	0	$69,333
15	24	43	John Paul Jr. (R)	STS/Indianapolis Heliport	March/Cosworth	Accident	164	0	$68,563
16	27	34	Jim Crawford (R)	Wysard/Canadian Tire	Lola/Cosworth	Electrical	142	0	$72,383
17	17	25	Danny Ongais	Interscope Racing	March/Cosworth	Engine	141	0	$64,913
18	23	23	Raul Boesel (R)	Break Free	March/Cosworth	Radiator	134	0	$83,633
19	9	7	Geoff Brabham	Coors Light Silver Bullet	March/Cosworth	Engine	130	0	$66,871
20	13	2	Tom Sneva (W)	Skoal Bandit	Eagle/Cosworth	Accident	123	0	$63,163
21	10	1	Rick Mears (W)	Pennzoil Z-7	March/Cosworth	Linkage	122	0	$67,333
22	25	84	Chip Ganassi	Calumet Farms	March/Cosworth	Fuel line	121	0	$57,833
23	33	60	Rich Vogler (R)	Byrd's Kentucky Fried Chicken	March/Cosworth	Accident	119	0	$71,183
24	6	20	Don Whittington	STP Oil Treatment	March/Cosworth	Engine	97	0	$60,683
25	11	30	Al Unser Jr.	Domino's Pizza	Lola/Cosworth	Engine	91	0	$60,133
26	14	22	Dick Simon	Break Free	March/Cosworth	Oil pressure	86	0	$64,833
27	3	10	Bobby Rahal	Budweiser	March/Cosworth	Waste gate	84	14	$83,463
28	21	14	A.J. Foyt (W)	Copenhagen-Gilmore	March/Cosworth	Front wing	62	0	$53,863
29	29	97	Tony Bettenhausen Jr.	Skoal Bandit	Lola/Cosworth	Wheel bearing	31	0	$63,613
30	2	37	Scott Brayton	Hardee's 37	March/Buick	Cylinder wall	19	1	$86,863
31	18	55	Josele Garza	Schaefer/Machinists	March/Cosworth	Engine	15	0	$59,083
32	28	44	George Snider	A.J. Foyt Chevrolet	March/Chevrolet	Engine	13	0	$53,263
33	1	6	Pancho Carter	Valvoline Buick	March/Buick	Oil pump	6	0	$121,533

* - complete car name/entrant data not available for all entries
(R) - Indicated Rookie
(W) - Indicates Past Winner

1986

By the 1986 race, the old white and green wooden garages were gone, replaced with concrete structures to house the cars.

Herm Johnson was seriously injured for the second year in a row when part of his bodywork flew off his car and he hit the turn one wall. He sustained foot and ankle injuries, plus a back fracture.

Qualifying records were smashed by Rick Mears' pole run at 216.828 mph in his Pennzoil March/Cosworth. Danny Sullivan and Michael Andretti joined him on row one.

Phil Krueger made the race in a year-old March for Leader Card, starting twenty-fourth. Krueger was not only the driver, he basically was his own chief mechanic as well—a throwback to years gone by.

During the second week of practice, Jim Crawford found top speed. Mario Andretti had a suspension failure and crashed his qualified car. He ended up driving his backup car, starting in the back of the field.

On carb day, an accident coming out of the fourth turn approaching the pit entrance eliminated Dennis Firestone from the race because he didn't have a backup car. Also involved in the accident were Roberto Moreno and the parked cars of George Snider and Josele Garza.

As a result, first alternate Dick Simon would start thirty-third. It was the second time in three years that a first alternate started the race.

As a result of sporadic rain on race day, the race could not be run. It rained again on Monday, so the race was postponed until the following Saturday for the first and only time in history. The main reason for postponing the start until Saturday was that the race was being broadcast live on television to a worldwide audience by ABC Sports for the first time.

Retired United States Air Force Brigadier General Chuck Yeager drove a bright yellow Chevrolet Corvette to pace the 70th Indianapolis 500.

On the pace lap, Tom Sneva's car snapped sideways exiting turn two and hit the inside wall. The race was red-flagged before it even started.

Once the race started, Michael Andretti took the lead and led the first forty-two laps.

The first half of the race also saw Bobby Rahal, Kevin Cogan, Al Unser Jr. and Rick Mears share the lead.

The second half featured a battle between Rahal and Mears, with Cogan running a strong third. On lap 188, Cogan passed both Mears and Rahal for the lead and began pulling away.

Second-year driver Arie Luyendyk caused a yellow on lap 195 when he brushed the fourth turn wall and came to a stop at the pit entrance.

Coming to the restart at the completion of lap 198, Rahal passed Cogan on the inside by the time they got to turn one and went on to win his first "500." Rahal's last lap speed (209.152 mph) was the fastest lap in the race. During the last several laps, Rahal was extremely concerned that he might run out of fuel.

Rahal beat Cogan to the line by just under 1.5 seconds and Mears by just under 1.9 seconds for the closest 1-2-3 finish in history. Rahal averaged a record 170.7 mph in his Budweiser March/Cosworth.

Randy Lanier, who had been sent home for lack of experience in 1985, finished tenth and won Rookie of the Year.

Indy 500 Festival Queen Wendy Barth greeted Rahal in the victory circle that employed a new scissor lift platform for elevation. Barth's mother was the "500" queen in 1961.

Mears led seventy-six laps and Rahal led fifty-eight.

Eleven days after Rahal's win, his car owner and mentor, Jim Trueman, would die of cancer at fifty-one years of age.

Rahal won six times in 1986 and won the season championship.

Bobby Rahal and car owner Jim Trueman celebrate.

RACE RESULTS FOR THE 1986 INDIANAPOLIS 500

Finish	Start	Car Num.	Driver	Car Name/Entrant*	Make/Model	Status	Laps	Led	Winnings
1	4	3	Bobby Rahal	Budweiser	March/Cosworth	170.722	200	58	$581,063
2	6	7	Kevin Cogan	7-Eleven	March/Cosworth	170.698	200	13	$253,363
3	1	4	Rick Mears (W)	Pennzoil Z-7	March/Cosworth	170.691	200	76	$332,263
4	8	5	Roberto Guerrero	True Value	March/Cosworth	170.551	200	1	$139,513
5	9	30	Al Unser Jr.	Domino's Pizza	Lola/Cosworth	Running	199	6	$113,463
6	3	18	Michael Andretti	Kraco/STP/Lean Machine	March/Cosworth	Running	199	45	$171,763
7	11	20	Emerson Fittipaldi	Marlboro	March/Cosworth	Running	199	1	$104,563
8	12	21	Johnny Rutherford (W)	Vermont American	March/Cosworth	Running	198	0	$97,513
9	2	1	Danny Sullivan (W)	Miller American	March/Cosworth	Running	197	0	$134,088
10	13	12	Randy Lanier (R)	Arciero Racing	March/Cosworth	Running	195	0	$103,438
11	29	24	Gary Bettenhausen	Vita Fresh Orange Juice/Timex	March/Cosworth	Running	193	0	$108,913
12	20	8	Geoff Brabham	Valvoline Spirit	Lola/Cosworth	Running	193	0	$94,613
13	22	22	Raul Boesel	Duracell Copper Top	Lola/Cosworth	Running	192	0	$90,063
14	33	23	Dick Simon	Duracell Copper Top	Lola/Cosworth	Running	189	0	$93,463
15	19	61	Arie Luyendyk	MCI/Race For Life	Lola/Cosworth	Accident	188	0	$86,013
16	14	15	Pancho Carter	Coors Light	Lola/Cosworth	Wheel bearing	179	0	$84,713
17	10	66	Ed Pimm	Skoal/Pace Electronics	March/Cosworth	Ignition	168	0	$83,863
18	17	55	Josele Garza	Schaefer/Machinists	March/Cosworth	Running	167	0	$88,363
19	32	9	Roberto Moreno (R)	Valvoline Spirit II	Lola/Cosworth	Engine	158	0	$82,301
20	15	81	Jacques Villeneuve (U) (R)	Living Well/Labatts	March/Cosworth	Main bearing	154	0	$81,613
21	25	59	Chip Ganassi	Bryant Heating & Cooling	March/Cosworth	Blown engine	151	0	$81,163
22	5	11	Al Unser (W)	Hertz	Penske/Ilmor	Vibration	149	0	$81,563
23	16	25	Danny Ongais	GM Goodwrench	March/Buick	Ignition	136	0	$79,713
24	21	14	A.J. Foyt (W)	Copenhagen/Gilmore	March/Cosworth	Spun in pits	135	0	$97,713
25	27	6	Rich Vogler	Byrd's Ky Fr Ckn/Vermont American	March/Cosworth	Accident	132	0	$90,563
26	31	84	George Snider	Copenhagen/Gilmore	March/Cosworth	Ignition	110	0	$80,163
27	28	95	Johnny Parsons	Pizza Hut/Machinists	March/Cosworth	CV joint	100	0	$78,013
28	18	16	Tony Bettenhausen Jr.	Bettenhausen & Associates	March/Cosworth	Valve	77	0	$77,713
29	26	31	Jim Crawford	American Sunroofs Inc.	March/Buick	Head gasket	70	0	$95,263
30	23	71	Scott Brayton	Hardee's/Living Well/WTTV	March/Buick	Engine	69	0	$78,263
31	24	42	Phil Krueger (R)	Squirt/Moran Electric	March/Cosworth	Engine	67	0	$82,413
32	30	2	Mario Andretti (W)	Newman-Haas Racing	Lola/Cosworth	Ignition	19	0	$77,013
33	7	33	Tom Sneva (W)	Skoal Bandit	March/Cosworth	Accident	0	0	$76,963

* - complete car name/entrant data not available for all entries
(R) - Indicated Rookie
(W) - Indicates Past Winner

1987

Penske Racing had Rick Mears, Danny Sullivan and Danny Ongais, whose Panavision sponsorship helped him secure the ride. As a result, Al Unser Sr. was released as the odd man out.

Unser showed up for the first weekend of practice looking for a ride, but returned to Albuquerque after not being able to secure a good one.

Early in the month, Pancho Carter spun between turns three and four. He got uplifted for almost 100 feet and landed upside down. Carter was unhurt.

During the month, there were an abnormal number of accidents (twenty-five). After years of testing, Goodyear used its radial tires and problems resulted for many teams.

On the Friday before the first weekend of qualifications, Danny Ongais crashed hard in turn four and sustained a head injury that sidelined him for the month.

Al Unser Sr. took over for the injured Ongais and qualified a 1986 March Cosworth that started the month in a hotel lobby in Reading, Pennsylvania, as a show car. He qualified for the twentieth starting position.

Mario Andretti was fast all month, winning his third pole (215.4 mph) at more than two mph faster than second-place starter Bobby Rahal (213.3 mph). Rick Mears started third and qualified a March after parking his new Penske because it lacked speed.

Jim Crawford crashed hard in turn one on his qualification attempt and sustained severe leg and ankle injuries. Gordon Johncock came out of retirement to take over Crawford's ride. He qualified for the eighteenth starting position.

Carburetion day was eventful, with A.J. Foyt and Emerson Fittipaldi crashing in separate incidents. Foyt's car was repaired, but Fittipaldi was forced to drive his backup car and start last in the field.

The legendary Carroll Shelby drove the Chrysler LeBaron pace car.

Mario Andretti took the early lead, but Josele Garza spun in turn one of the first lap. Al Unser Sr. and Garza made very slight contact with both cars able to continue.

Mario dominated the race in his Hanna Auto Wash Lola/Chevrolet, leading 170 of the first 177 laps until an electrical problem ended his chances for victory. He led by over a lap on second-place Roberto Guerrero and had more than a two-lap lead on third-place Al Unser Sr.

Guerrero's run had not been without problems. On lap 131, Tony Bettenhausen lost a wheel and Guerrero punted it in the stands between turns three and four. A spectator by the name of Lyle Kurtenbach was struck and fatally injured. He was the first spectator fatally injured in a race-related accident since 1938.

On lap 182, Guerrero made his last pit stop while leading Al Unser Sr. by more than a lap. Attempting to return to the race after service, Guerrero stalled his car. As a result of the contact with Bettenhausen's wheel, the fluid reserve container for his clutch had sustained damage, causing fluid to leak out. Guerrero was finally able to rejoin the race after a nearly seventy second stop, but he fell a lap behind Al Unser Sr.

Guerrero was able to unlap himself before a yellow on lap 192 allowed him to come around at the back of the pack with only six cars between himself and Unser.

The green came out at the completion of lap 196 and Unser had clear sailing, winning by 4.5 seconds over Guerrero to become the second four-time Indy 500 winner. Unser averaged 162.2 mph in his Cummins Sponsored March/Cosworth.

Unser became the oldest "500" winner in history at 47 years old and 360 days old. He also became the winner with the largest span of years between his first win and last (1970-1987).

Italian Fabrizio Barbazza finished third in his only Indy 500 and won Rookie of the Year.

Mario Andretti led 170 laps, and Al Unser Sr. led 18 to surpass Ralph DePalma's sixty-six-year-old record as the all-time lap leader with 613.

Unlikely winner, Al Unser, Sr., becomes the second four-time winner of the Indianapolis 500.

RACE RESULTS FOR THE 1987 INDIANAPOLIS 500

Finish	Start	Car Num.	Driver	Car Name/Entrant*	Make/Model	Status	Laps	Led	Winnings
1	20	25	Al Unser (W)	Cummins/Holset Turbo	March/Cosworth	162.175	200	18	$526,763
2	5	4	Roberto Guerrero	True Value/STP	March/Cosworth	162.109	200	8	$305,013
3	17	12	Fabrizio Barbazza (R)	Arciero Winery	March/Cosworth	Running	198	0	$204,663
4	22	30	Al Unser Jr.	Domino's Pizza	March/Cosworth	Running	196	0	$142,963
5	15	56	Gary Bettenhausen	Genesee Beer Wagon	March/Cosworth	Running	195	0	$132,213
6	6	22	Dick Simon	Soundesign	Lola/Cosworth	Running	193	0	$131,813
7	26	41	Stan Fox (R)	Kerker Exhaust/Skoal Classic	March/Cosworth	Running	192	0	$111,263
8	12	11	Jeff MacPherson (R)	McHoward Leasing	March/Brab./Hon. (Judd)	Running	182	0	$117,313
9	1	5	Mario Andretti (W)	Hanna Auto Wash	Lola/Chevrolet Indy	Ignition	180	170	$368,063
10	27	16	Tony Bettenhausen Jr.	Nationwise/Payless	March/Cosworth	Running	171	0	$105,838
11	8	21	Johnny Rutherford (W)	Vermont American	March/Cosworth	Running	171	0	$104,313
12	13	91	Scott Brayton	Amway/Autostyle	March/Cosworth	Engine	167	0	$103,063
13	16	3	Danny Sullivan (W)	Miller American	March/Chevrolet Indy	Engine	160	4	$120,713
14	21	33	Tom Sneva (W)	Skoal Bandit	March/Buick	Accident	143	0	$103,313
15	19	77	Derek Daly	Scheid Tire/Superior Training/Metrolink	March/Buick	Engine	133	0	$100,763
16	33	20	Emerson Fittipaldi	Marlboro	March/Chevrolet Indy	Engine	131	0	$98,263
17	25	55	Josele Garza	Bryant Heating & Cooling/Schaefer	March/Cosworth	Running	129	0	$103,350
18	7	71	Arie Luyendyk	Living Well/Provimi Veal/WTTV	March/Cosworth	Suspension	125	0	$97,113
19	4	14	A.J. Foyt (W)	Copenhagen/Gilmore	Lola/Cosworth	Oil seal	117	0	$102,963
20	11	81	Rich Vogler	Byrd's Kentucky Fried Chicken/Living Well	March/Buick	Rocker arm	109	0	$98,263
21	30	98	Ed Pimm	Skoal Classic	March/Cosworth	Turbocharger	109	0	$95,513
22	18	2	Gordon Johncock (W)	STP Oil Treatment	March/Buick	Valve	76	0	$94,913
23	3	8	Rick Mears (W)	Pennzoil Z-7	March/Chevrolet Indy	Coil wire	75	0	$112,463
24	14	15	Geoff Brabham	Team Valvoline	March/Brab./Hon. (Judd)	Oil pressure	71	0	$92,963
25	32	87	Steve Chassey	United Oil/Life of Indiana	March/Cosworth	Engine	68	0	$97,913
26	2	1	Bobby Rahal (W)	Budweiser	Lola/Cosworth	Ignition	57	0	$123,013
27	29	29	Pancho Carter	Hardee's	March/Cosworth	Valve	45	0	$93,263
28	28	44	Davy Jones (R)	Skoal Classic/Gilmore/UNO	March/Cosworth	Engine	34	0	$115,463
29	9	18	Michael Andretti	Kraco/STP	March/Cosworth	Pit fire	28	0	$91,113
30	10	23	Ludwig Heimrath, Jr. (R)	MacKenzie Financial/Tim Horton Doughnuts	Lola/Cosworth	Spun out	25	0	$111,513
31	24	7	Kevin Cogan	Marlboro	March/Chevrolet Indy	Oil pump	21	0	$90,763
32	23	24	Randy Lewis (R)	Toshiba/Altos/Oracle	March/Cosworth	Gearbox	8	0	$90,763
33	31	84	George Snider	Calumet/Copenhagen	March/Chevrolet	Engine fire	0	0	$92,713

* - complete car name/entrant data not available for all entries
(R) - Indicated Rookie
(W) - Indicates Past Winner

1988

Team Penske had the new Penske PC-17 car designed by Nigel Bennett and it was a rocket!

Billy Vukovich III was a rookie attempting to be the first third-generation "500" starter (grandfather, father and son). He accomplished this.

The Honda name was gone and the engine was now called the Judd.

Roberto Guerrero had returned after sustaining a serious head injury while testing at Indianapolis the previous fall.

For the first time in history, a Porsche engine competed in the "500," with Teo Fabi starting seventeenth and finishing twenty-eighth.

Jim Crawford was back from injuries the previous year to drive, but was walking with a cane.

Mario Andretti and Rick Mears practiced at over 220 mph, the first time 220 was unofficially eclipsed.

Rick Mears won his fourth pole position, tying A.J. Foyt and Rex Mays. His top lap was 220.453 mph and he averaged 219.2 mph for a new record. Mears became the first driver to officially break the 220 mph barrier.

Penske teammates Danny Sullivan and Al Unser Sr. filled out the all Penske front row, the first time one team occupied the entire first row.

Rookies Billy Vukovich III and John Andretti qualified for their first "500s" in the twenty-third and twenty-seventh starting positions.

As the race started, Sullivan took the lead, but Scott Brayton spun coming out of turn two and collected Roberto Guerrero, while Tony Bettenhausen checked up and hit the wall.

Danny Sullivan dominated the first half of the race, leading 91 of the first 94 laps. He was leading Mears by almost a lap when his right front wing began to flutter. On lap 101, Sullivan's car drifted into the wall between turns one and two.

A caution period from lap 109-111 was the result of Al Unser Sr. hitting a rabbit on the track.

Mears took command of the race upon Sullivan's departure and led 89 of the last 100 laps and from lap 123 to the finish for his third "500" win. Mears' win gave Penske it's fourth win in five years.

A yellow came out on lap 198 for bodywork from Michael Andretti's car on the track. As a result the race finished under caution.

Emerson Fittipaldi finished second and Al Unser Sr. third. Fittipaldi was the only driver on the lead lap with Mears. Mears averaged 144.9 mph in his Pennzoil Penske/Chevrolet. Fourteen cautions for 68 laps slowed the pace.

Jim Crawford had a great ride, finishing sixth after initially having been posted in third.

Vukovich III finished fourteenth to win Rookie of the Year.

The total purse exceeded $5 million for the first time in history.

For the first time, Borg Warner presented a "Baby Borg" to the winning driver. The Baby Borg is a fourteen-inch replica of the big trophy valued at about $25,000.

Penske teammates Mears, Sullivan and Unser Sr. led 192 of the 200 laps, with Jim Crawford leading the other eight.

Danny Sullivan won the season championship in 1988.

Rick Mears wins the 1988 "500" in his Pennzoil Penske.

RACE RESULTS FOR THE 1988 INDIANAPOLIS 500

Finish	Start	Car Num.	Driver	Car Name/Entrant*	Make/Model	Status	Laps	Led	Winnings
1	1	5	Rick Mears (W)	Pennzoil Z-7	Penske/Chevrolet Indy	144.809	200	89	$809,853
2	8	20	Emerson Fittipaldi	Marlboro	March/Chevrolet Indy	144.726	200	0	$337,603
3	3	1	Al Unser (W)	Hertz	Penske/Chevrolet Indy	Running	199	12	$228,903
4	10	18	Michael Andretti	Kraco	March/Cosworth	Running	199	0	$192,953
5	19	4	Bobby Rahal (W)	Budweiser	Lola/Judd	Running	199	0	$151,553
6	18	15	Jim Crawford	Mac Tools/King/Protofab	Lola/Buick	Running	198	8	$170,503
7	20	30	Raul Boesel	Domino's Pizza	Lola/Cosworth	Running	198	0	$148,403
8	15	97	Phil Krueger	CNC Systems/Taylor Dist.	March/Cosworth	Running	196	0	$131,053
9	16	22	Dick Simon	Uniden/Soundesign	Lola/Cosworth	Running	196	0	$127,428
10	6	7	Arie Luyendyk	Provimi Veal	Lola/Cosworth	Running	196	0	$123,028
11	13	11	Kevin Cogan	Schaefer/Playboy Fashions	March/Cosworth	Running	195	0	$141,278
12	33	21	Howdy Holmes	Jiffy Mixes	March/Cosworth	Running	192	0	$123,728
13	5	3	Al Unser Jr.	Team Valvoline/Strohs	March/Chevrolet Indy	Running	180	0	$117,753
14	23	56	Bill Vukovich III (R)	Genesee Beer/EZ Wider	March/Cosworth	Running	179	0	$125,603
15	11	24	Randy Lewis	Toshiba/Oracle/Altos	Lola/Cosworth	Running	175	0	$115,478
16	28	48	Rocky Moran (R)	Skoal/Trench Shoring	March/Cosworth	Engine	159	0	$107,228
17	32	29	Rich Vogler	Byrd's/Pepsi/Bryant	March/Cosworth	Accident	159	0	$106,053
18	21	92	Dominic Dobson (R)	Moore Industries/Columbia Helecopters	Lola/Cosworth	Coolant	145	0	$107,753
19	25	23	Tero Palmroth (R)	Bronson/Neste/Editor	Lola/Cosworth	Engine	144	0	$103,728
20	4	6	Mario Andretti (W)	Amoco/Kmart	Lola/Chevrolet Indy	Electrical	118	0	$130,828
21	27	98	John Andretti (R)	Skoal Bandit	Lola/Cosworth	Engine	114	0	$106,703
22	30	17	Johnny Rutherford (W)	Mac Tools/King/Protofab	Lola/Buick	Accident	107	0	$102,303
23	2	9	Danny Sullivan (W)	Miller High Life	Penske/Chevrolet Indy	Accident	101	91	$214,378
24	26	35	Steve Chassey	Kasale Recycling	March/Cosworth	Accident	73	0	$99,128
25	31	71	Ludwig Heimrath, Jr.	MacKenzie Funds	Lola/Cosworth	Accident	59	0	$100,253
26	22	14	A.J. Foyt (W)	Copenhagen-Gilmore	Lola/Cosworth	Accident	54	0	$98,853
27	14	81	Tom Sneva (W)	Pizza Hut/WRTV	Lola/Judd	Accident	32	0	$97,328
28	17	8	Teo Fabi	Quaker State/Porsche	March/Porsche Indy	Wheel off	30	0	$101,878
29	9	10	Derek Daly	Raynor Garage Doors	Lola/Cosworth	Gearbox	18	0	$97,503
30	29	84	Stan Fox	Copenhagen/Calumet Farms	March/Chevrolet	Engine	2	0	$113,703
31	7	91	Scott Brayton	Amway Spirit/Lifecycle	Lola/Buick	Accident	0	0	$96,078
32	12	2	Roberto Guerrero	STP/Dianetics	Lola/Cosworth	Accident	0	0	$100,828
33	24	16	Tony Bettenhausen Jr.	Hardee's/Sony	Lola/Cosworth	Accident	0	0	$95,753

* - complete car name/entrant data not available for all entries
(R) - Indicated Rookie
(W) - Indicates Past Winner

1989

The track was totally repaved for the 1989 race, with bricks and mortar still exposed at the start/finish line.

The Prest-O-Lite stack just south of the track was torn down. Since 1913, drivers had used the direction of the smoke from the stack as a windsock.

Michael Andretti joined Newman-Haas, and he and Mario made a father/son team.

The track opened on May 6, but was closed early because of extreme cold and a brief snow flurry. Two-tenths of an inch was recorded, the first snow in May in twenty-nine years.

On the first Monday of practice, Rick Mears posted the first unofficial laps over 225 mph (225.5 mph and 225.7 mph).

During the first week of practice, Danny Sullivan lost a section of cowling from his car and crashed. He sustained a broken wrist.

Rain washed away the first day of qualifications.

On Sunday, Rick Mears became the first driver to win the pole five times, setting the track record at almost a 224 mph average.

Al Unser Sr. for Penske and Emerson Fittipaldi for Patrick, joined Mears on the front row—all driving Penskes.

Danny Sullivan made the field the second weekend of qualification and started twenty-sixth, wearing a cast on his wrist.

The average speed of the field was six mph higher than the year before, the fastest in history.

Three-time Indy 500 champion Bobby Unser drove the Pontiac Trans Am to start the 73rd Indianapolis 500.

At the start, two-time World Champion Emerson Fittipaldi jumped into the lead and led the first thirty-four laps.

Kevin Cogan had a serious accident on lap three coming out of turn four, and the tub ended up in the pit entrance. Miraculously, he was not injured.

Fittipaldi gave up the lead on his first pit stop for two laps and then led the next fifty-one laps straight.

Several of the top drivers started dropping out and basically left Fittipaldi and Michael Andretti to battle it out.

Andretti was leading on lap 163 when his engine blew, ending his day.

Fittipaldi took the lead with Al Unser Jr. in second. A yellow on lap 181 resulted in Fittipaldi pitting, while Unser remained on the track to gain track position. The Galles team gambled on sufficient fuel to finish as Unser last pitted on lap 165.

On lap 195, Unser surprised Fittipaldi and made the pass for the lead.

With less than two laps left, Unser got bogged down slightly by lapped traffic in turn two. Fittipaldi got a run and attempted an inside pass going into turn three. Fittipaldi had the inside line and drifted slightly up into Unser, touching wheels. Unser spun and crashed, while Fittipaldi got out of shape but was able to recover the car.

The race finished under yellow, with Fittipaldi winning his first 500. Al Unser, Jr. still finished second, because Raul Boesel, in third place was six laps behind. Fittipaldi averaged 167.6 mph in his Marlboro Penske/Chevrolet.

As Fittipaldi passed the Unser crash scene, "Little Al" gave his tough competitor a double thumbs-up signal in a memorable Speedway moment.

Unser's second-place finish was the highest ever by a driver who was not running at the end of a race that went the distance.

When the last caution occurred, Raul Boesel's engine was sick and fourth-place finisher Mario Andretti was also experiencing a sick engine. A.J. Foyt finished fifth.

Fittipaldi was the first winner to receive over one million dollars.

Fittipaldi led 158 laps, Michael Andretti, 35, and Al Unser Jr., 5 laps.

Bernard Jourdain finished ninth after qualifying with the slowest speed in the field. He and tenth-place finisher Scott Pruett shared Rookie of the Year honors.

Emerson Fittipaldi becomes the first "500" winner to collect over $1,000,000 winnings.

RACE RESULTS FOR THE 1989 INDIANAPOLIS 500

Finish	Start	Car Num.	Driver	Car Name/Entrant*	Make/Model	Status	Laps	Led	Winnings
1	3	20	Emerson Fittipaldi	Marlboro	Penske/Chevrolet Indy	167.581	200	158	$1,001,604
2	8	2	Al Unser Jr.	Valvoline	Lola/Chevrolet Indy	Accident	198	5	$390,453
3	9	30	Raul Boesel	Domino's Pizza	Lola/Judd	Running	194	1	$306,603
4	5	5	Mario Andretti (W)	Kmart/Havoline	Lola/Chevrolet Indy	Running	193	1	$193,853
5	10	14	A.J. Foyt (W)	Copenhagen/Gilmore	Lola/Cosworth DFX	Running	193	0	$177,403
6	6	22	Scott Brayton	Amway/Speedway/Uniden	Lola/Buick	Running	193	0	$190,903
7	31	50	Davy Jones	Euromotorsport/UNO	Lola/Cosworth DFX	Running	192	0	$151,328
8	33	29	Rich Vogler	Byrd's/Bryant/Saturday Evening Post	March/Cosworth DFX	Running	192	0	$153,203
9	20	69	Bernard Jourdain (R)	Corona-Monarch	Lola/Cosworth DFX	Running	191	0	$150,153
10	17	3	Scott Pruett (R)	Budweiser	Lola/Judd	Running	190	0	$141,053
11	25	65	John Jones (R)	Labatt's	Lola/Cosworth DFX	Running	189	0	$134,103
12	30	81	Bill Vukovich III	Hemelgarn/Consani/Sierra	Lola/Judd	Running	186	0	$147,203
13	18	71	Ludwig Heimrath, Jr.	MacKenzie Funds	Lola/Judd	Running	185	0	$123,803
14	28	33	Rocky Moran	Skoal Classic	March/Cosworth DFX	Running	181	0	$122,503
15	24	10	Derek Daly	Raynor Garage Doors	Lola/Judd	Running	167	0	$125,103
16	16	56	Tero Palmroth	Neste/Rotator/Nanso	Lola/Cosworth DFX	Spindle	165	0	$122,803
17	21	6	Michael Andretti	Kmart/Havoline	Lola/Chevrolet Indy	Engine	163	35	$164,353
18	29	86	Dominic Dobson	Texaco Havoline Star	Lola/Cosworth DFX	Drive train	161	0	$113,003
19	4	15	Jim Crawford	Mac Tools/Planters	Lola/Buick	Drive train	135	0	$119,403
20	19	12	Didier Theys (R)	Arciero MacPherson	Penske/Cosworth DFX	Engine	131	0	$111,503
21	15	9	Arie Luyendyk	Provimi/Dutch Boy	Lola/Cosworth DFS	Engine	123	0	$110,203
22	32	24	Pancho Carter	Hardee's	Lola/Cosworth DFX	Electrical	121	0	$108,503
23	1	4	Rick Mears (W)	Pennzoil Z-7	Penske/Chevrolet Indy	Engine	113	0	$267,903
24	2	25	Al Unser (W)	Marlboro	Penske/Chevrolet Indy	Clutch	68	0	$132,903
25	12	70	John Andretti	Tuneup Masters/Granatelli/STP	Lola/Buick	Engine	61	0	$104,503
26	7	18	Bobby Rahal (W)	Kraco	Lola/Cosworth DFS	Valve	58	0	$103,703
27	22	7	Tom Sneva (W)	STP/Granatelli	Lola/Buick	Pit fire	55	0	$106,003
28	26	1	Danny Sullivan (W)	Miller High Life	Penske/Chevrolet Indy	Clutch	41	0	$125,903
29	11	28	Randy Lewis	Toshiba-Oracle	Lola/Cosworth DFX	Wheel bearing	24	0	$101,903
30	13	8	Teo Fabi	Quaker State/Porsche	March/Porsche	Ignition	23	0	$113,753
31	23	91	Gordon Johncock (W)	STP/Pizza Hut/WRTV	Lola/Buick	Engine	19	0	$103,703
32	27	11	Kevin Cogan	Schaefer/Playboy Fashions	March/Cosworth DFX	Accident	2	0	$102,503
33	14	99	Gary Bettenhausen	ATEC Environmental	Lola/Buick	Bent valve	0	0	$101,903

* - complete car name/entrant data not available for all entries
(R) - Indicated Rookie
(W) - Indicates Past Winner

1990

Joe Cloutier had passed away in December of 1989 at 81 years of age.

In January 1990, Tony George, grandson of Anton Hulman Jr., was named president of the Indianapolis Motor Speedway at the age of 30.

There were new "Tower Suites" built and located at the north end of the pits on the outside of the track for corporate hospitality.

The era of transponders with transmitters attached to every car for timing and scoring arrived at the Speedway.

Rick Mears, Emerson Fittipaldi and Al Unser Jr. had a speed battle prior to qualifications. Unser topped the speed chart at 228.5 mph.

Jim Crawford crashed on the Friday before pole day in the first turn and air got under the car, lifting it high into the air before landing it in the infield.

The first day of qualifications was rained out. Rain on Sunday didn't allow qualifications to start until 4:30 p.m. As a result, several potential pole qualifiers would have to wait until the second weekend to get their shot at the pole.

Fittipaldi took the temporary pole with a new track record of 225.3 mph. Mears and eventually Arie Luyendyk joined first-time pole-sitter Fittipaldi on the front row.

Three-time winner Johnny Rutherford failed to make the race, as did Mario Andretti's youngest son, Jeff.

There were numerous accidents during the month, mostly in older cars using the required underwing "diffuser."

The new Dodge Viper with Carroll Shelby behind the wheel paced the 74th Indianapolis 500. Shelby never raced in the "500," but was one of the most accomplished road racers in the 1950's.

As the race started, Fittipaldi jumped into the lead and stayed there for the first ninety-two laps, breaking Frank Lockhart's record of leading the opening eighty-one laps in 1927.

Fittipaldi was the primary leader until several sets of his tires blistered, causing more pit stops. The race became a two-driver duel between Bobby Rahal and Arie Luyendyk, whom some considered somewhat of a dark horse.

Rahal led from lap 136 to 167, but after his last pit stop, his tires didn't work as well as the previous set. Luyendyk passed Rahal on lap 168 and led to the checker, winning by eleven seconds over Rahal. This was Luyendyk's first Indy Car series win. He became the first driver from the Netherlands to win the Indy 500.

Luyendyk set a race record with an average of 185.981 mph in his Domino's Pizza Lola/Chevrolet, completing the race in two hours and forty-one minutes. The speed would remain the race speed record for the next twenty-seven years. Only four fairly brief cautions assisted Luyendyk in setting the record.

Luyendyk's win gave the Lola chassis it's first win since Al Unser Sr.'s 1978 victory.

There were only three leaders in the race. Third-place finisher Fittipaldi led 128 laps, second-place Rahal led 35 laps, and winner Luyendyk led 37 laps.

Former Formula One driver Eddie Cheever Jr. finished eighth and won Rookie of the Year. Cheever competed in 132 Formula One races before his IndyCar career. This ranks number one for Formula One starts for an American driver.

Arie Luyendyk sets a new race record in his first "500" win.

RACE RESULTS FOR THE 1990 INDIANAPOLIS 500

Finish	Start	Car Num.	Driver	Car Name/Entrant*	Make/Model	Status	Laps	Led	Winnings
1	3	30	Arie Luyendyk	Domino's Pizza	Lola/Chevrolet Indy	185.981	200	37	$1,090,940
2	4	18	Bobby Rahal (W)	STP/Kraco	Lola/Chevrolet Indy	185.772	200	35	$488,566
3	1	1	Emerson Fittipaldi (W)	Marlboro	Penske/Chevrolet Indy	185.183	200	128	$592,874
4	7	5	Al Unser Jr.	Team Valvoline	Lola/Chevrolet Indy	Running	199	0	$227,691
5	2	2	Rick Mears (W)	Pennzoil Z-7	Penske/Chevrolet Indy	Running	198	0	$201,610
6	8	14	A.J. Foyt (W)	Copenhagen	Lola/Chevrolet Indy	Running	194	0	$184,804
7	26	22	Scott Brayton	Amway/Speedway	Lola/Cosworth DFS	Running	194	0	$201,448
8	14	25	Eddie Cheever Jr. (R)	Target Stores	Penske/Chevrolet Indy	Running	193	0	$172,786
9	15	11	Kevin Cogan	Tuneup Masters	Penske/Buick	Running	191	0	$150,472
10	21	28	Scott Goodyear (R)	Mackenzie/O'Donnell	Lola/Judd	Running	191	0	$146,970
11	20	70	Didier Theys	Tuneup Masters	Penske/Buick	Running	190	0	$142,384
12	16	23	Tero Palmroth	Hoechst/Celanese/Neste	Lola/Cosworth DFS	Running	188	0	$138,756
13	30	40	Al Unser (W)	Miller High Life	March/Alfa Romeo	Running	186	0	$136,387
14	12	12	Randy Lewis	AMP/Oracle	Penske/Buick	Running	186	0	$134,275
15	29	15	Jim Crawford	Glidden Paints	Lola/Buick	Running	183	0	$130,022
16	32	93	John Paul Jr.	ATEC Environmental	Lola/Buick	Radiator	176	0	$150,276
17	24	39	Dean Hall (R)	Insight	Lola/Cosworth DFS	Suspension	165	0	$134,306
18	23	4	Teo Fabi	Foster's/Quaker State	March/Porsche	Transmission	162	0	$156,060
19	19	21	Geoff Brabham	Mac Tools Distributors	Lola/Judd	Running	161	0	$131,688
20	5	3	Michael Andretti	Kmart/Havoline	Lola/Chevrolet Indy	Vibration	146	0	$130,942
21	10	41	John Andretti	Foster's/Quaker State	March/Porsche	Accident	136	0	$118,320
22	11	86	Dominic Dobson	Texaco Havoline Star	Lola/Cosworth DFS	Engine	129	0	$116,823
23	28	20	Roberto Guerrero	Miller Genuine Draft	March/Alfa Romeo	Suspension	118	0	$115,129
24	31	81	Bill Vukovich III	Hemelgarn	Lola/Buick	Engine	102	0	$119,503
25	33	56	Rocky Moran	Glidden Paints	Lola/Buick	Engine	88	0	$124,580
26	13	16	Tony Bettenhausen Jr.	AMAX	Lola/Buick	Engine	76	0	$112,083
27	6	6	Mario Andretti (W)	Kmart/Havoline	Lola/Chevrolet Indy	Engine	60	0	$111,209
28	17	19	Raul Boesel	Budweiser	Lola/Judd	Engine	60	0	$110,461
29	22	29	Pancho Carter	Hardee's/Machinists	Lola/Cosworth DFS	Accident	59	0	$110,837
30	25	9	Tom Sneva (W)	RCA	Penske/Buick	CV joint	48	0	$110,338
31	18	51	Gary Bettenhausen	Glidden Paints	Lola/Buick	Wheel bearing	39	0	$109,464
32	9	7	Danny Sullivan (W)	Marlboro	Penske/Chevrolet Indy	Accident	19	0	$109,778
33	27	97	Stan Fox	Miyano/CNC Systems	Lola/Buick	Gearbox	10	0	$108,021

* - complete car name/entrant data not available for all entries
(R) - Indicated Rookie
(W) - Indicates Past Winner

1991

The 1991 Indianapolis 500 was the 75th running of the great race—The Diamond Jubilee.

The previous September, A.J. Foyt had sustained very serious leg and foot injuries in an accident at Elkhart Lake, Wisconsin, but by May he was fit to drive.

On the Friday before the first weekend of qualifications, Rick Mears experienced a wheel failure and crashed for the first time in his fourteen years at the Speedway.

Mears returned to the track in his backup car the same afternoon and recorded the second-fastest speed of the month at 226.557 mph.

The same day, Mark Dismore also crashed coming out of turn four and was seriously injured, with multiple fractures of the neck, wrist, feet and legs.

Mears won the pole the next day (224.1 mph), with Foyt and Mario Andretti joining him on the front row. This was Mears's sixth pole—a record. It was also the eleventh time in fourteen starts that Rick Mears qualified on the front row.

Four Andrettis made the race: father Mario, sons Michael and Jeff and cousin John. Mario became the first driver to compete against two of his sons.

On the second day of qualification, Gary Bettenhausen, in a Lola/Buick, became the fastest qualifier at 224.468 mph, but would have to start thirteenth. It occurred on the thirtieth anniversary of his father's death at the Speedway.

Hiro Matsushita qualified twenty-fourth and became the first Asian driver to qualify for Indy.

On the final day of qualifications, Willy T. Ribbs qualified Derrick Walker's car, becoming the first African-American starter in the "500." After qualifying Ribbs received sponsorship from McDonald's. This was the first time McDonald's had ever sponsored a race car. Bill Cosby was also a sponsor of the car.

Two former winners were absent from the field: Al Unser, who did not turn a wheel all month, and Tom Sneva, who struggled and was bumped.

Gulf War hero General H. Norman Schwartzkopf was the parade's grand marshal and Vice President Dan Quayle attended the race.

Morning rain on race day delayed the start of the race by nearly an hour.

The Dodge Viper paced the race.

Rick Mears took off at the start, but Gary Bettenhausen momentarily got loose in turn one and rookie Buddy Lazier spun and crashed trying to avoid him, ending his day.

Ribbs's day ended on lap five with a blown engine.

Mario Andretti took the lead from Mears on lap twelve and led through lap thirty-three. Rick Mears experienced a bad push in the early part of the race and nearly got lapped by Michael Andretti on lap seventy.

Up until almost the 140th lap, the lead was swapped primarily between Michael Andretti and Emerson Fittipaldi, with Mears keeping the leaders in sight.

Mears took the lead on lap 139 and the race became a three-way battle between Mears, teammate Fittipaldi and Michael Andretti.

Fittipaldi's day ended on lap 171 with gearbox problems.

Mears and Andretti continued to exchange the lead.

After a yellow for Danny Sullivan's smoking car, Andretti got a run on Mears upon completing lap 186 and made a rare bold outside pass in turn one. At the same spot on the very next lap, Mears made "The Pass" on the outside of Andretti. Mears then began pulling away before Mario Andretti's stalled car brought out the yellow on lap 191.

On the restart on lap 195, Mears again pulled away and took the checker three seconds in front of Michael Andretti. Mears ran the last five laps at better than a 220 mph average. He became the third driver to become a four-time winner. Mears averaged 176.5 mph in his Marlboro Penske/Chevrolet. It was the third time he had won from the pole. He matched Bobby Unser's record by having won the Indy 500 in three different decades.

Jeff Andretti finished fifteenth after being sidelined on lap 150 with engine problems, but still won Rookie of the Year. He joined father Mario and brother Michael as winners of the coveted award.

Michael Andretti led ninety-seven laps, Fittipaldi, forty-six, and Mears, thirty.

Several weeks later it was learned that Rick Mears had actually broken a bone in his foot in his "Fast Friday" accident. He experienced quite a bit of pain pushing on the throttle, but was able to overcome it. He drove a portion of the race with his left foot pushing on the top of his right foot to keep the throttle open.

Rick Mears and Michael Andretti put on an epic battle toward the end of the 1991 "500."

RACE RESULTS FOR THE 1991 INDIANAPOLIS 500

Finish	Start	Car Num.	Driver	Car Name/Entrant*	Make/Model	Status	Laps	Led	Winnings
1	1	3	Rick Mears (W)	Marlboro	Penske/Chevrolet Indy A	176.457	200	30	$1,219,704
2	5	10	Michael Andretti	Kmart/Havoline	Lola/Chevrolet Indy A	176.402	200	97	$607,753
3	14	1	Arie Luyendyk (W)	RCA/UNO Granatelli	Lola/Chevrolet Indy A	Running	199	0	$317,053
4	6	2	Al Unser Jr.	Valvoline	Lola/Chevrolet Indy A	Running	198	4	$223,916
5	7	4	John Andretti	Pennzoil Z-7	Lola/Chevrolet Indy A	Running	197	0	$205,153
6	33	92	Gordon Johncock (W)	Jack's Tool Rental/Bryant	Lola/Cosworth DFS	Running	188	0	$275,690
7	3	6	Mario Andretti (W)	Kmart/Havoline	Lola/Chevrolet Indy A	Engine	187	22	$203,478
8	17	91	Stan Fox	Byrd's Cafeteria/Bryant	Lola/Buick	Running	185	0	$201,090
9	20	16	Tony Bettenhausen Jr.	AMAX Coal	Penske/Chevrolet Indy A	Running	180	0	$170,016
10	9	20	Danny Sullivan (W)	Miller Genuine Draft/Patrick	Lola/Alfa Romeo	Engine	173	0	$194,403
11	15	5	Emerson Fittipaldi (W)	Marlboro	Penske/Chevrolet Indy A	Gearbox	171	46	$183,728
12	27	19	Scott Pruett	Budweiser/Truesports	Truesports/Judd	Engine	166	0	$159,191
13	30	66	Dominic Dobson	Coors/Kroger/Burns	Lola/Judd	Running	164	0	$159,190
14	31	39	Randy Lewis	AMP/Orbit/Jenn-Air/Epson	Lola/Cosworth DFS	Running	159	0	$150,490
15	11	86	Jeff Andretti (R)	Texaco Havoline Star	Lola/Cosworth DFS	Engine	150	0	$167,490
16	24	7	Hiro Matsushita (R)	Panasonic	Lola/Buick	Running	149	0	$145,891
17	19	22	Scott Brayton	Amway/Hoechst Celanese	Lola/Chevrolet Indy A	Engine	146	0	$172,191
18	21	48	Bernard Jourdain	Monarch/Foyt/Deutz	Lola/Buick	Gearbox	141	0	$140,190
19	4	18	Bobby Rahal (W)	STP/Kraco	Lola/Chevrolet Indy A	Engine	130	1	$153,741
20	22	21	Geoff Brabham	Mac Tools	Truesports/Judd	Electrical	109	0	$136,491
21	32	12	Pancho Carter	Arciero/Alfa LAVAL	Lola/Buick	Engine	94	0	$139,703
22	13	51	Gary Bettenhausen	Glidden Paints	Lola/Buick	Radiator	89	0	$177,890
23	26	23	Tero Palmroth	Neste/Rotator	Lola/Cosworth DFS	Engine	77	0	$131,990
24	18	50	Mike Groff (R)	Fendi-Hawaiian Tropic	Lola/Cosworth DFS	Water leak	68	0	$133,290
25	25	93	John Paul Jr.	ATEC Environmental	Lola/Buick	Oil leak	53	0	$130,690
26	8	26	Jim Crawford	Quaker State	Lola/Buick	Engine	40	0	$133,690
27	12	15	Scott Goodyear	Mackenzie Financial	Lola/Judd	Engine	38	0	$127,791
28	2	14	A.J. Foyt (W)	Foyt/Gilmore/Copenhagen	Lola/Chevrolet Indy A	Suspension	25	0	$153,591
29	16	9	Kevin Cogan	Glidden Paints	Lola/Buick	Accident	24	0	$127,391
30	28	40	Roberto Guerrero	Sharp's/Patrick	Lola/Alfa Romeo	Accident	23	0	$125,203
31	10	8	Eddie Cheever Jr.	Target/Scotch Video	Lola/Chevrolet Indy A	Electrical	17	0	$125,591
32	29	17	Willy T. Ribbs (R)	McDonalds/Cosby	Lola/Buick	Engine	5	0	$147,791
33	23	71	Buddy Lazier (R)	Vail Beaver Creek	Lola/Buick	Accident	1	0	$162,690

* - complete car name/entrant data not available for all entries
(R) - Indicated Rookie
(W) - Indicates Past Winner

1992

During April tests, Roberto Guerrero and Jim Crawford both topped 230 mph in Lola-Buicks.

On Wednesday of the first week of practice, Rick Mears crashed for the second consecutive year after going fourteen years without a mishap. Leaking fluid from his car caused him to spin and hit the wall hard, and then his car turned upside down. Mears sustained a fractured foot and sprained wrist, but he was able to practice the next day.

Three-time F-1 champion Nelson Piquet crashed hard nearly head-on in turn four on Thursday and sustained serious leg and foot injuries. He was replaced on the Menard team by Al Unser Sr.

On Friday the first fatality in ten years occurred when rookie Philippine driver Jovy Marcelo crashed between turns one and two.

Rain on pole day morning caused a late start to qualifying. Roberto Guerrero's record run averaged 232.482 mph. Guerrero became the first driver to officially eclipse the 230 mph barrier. Several drivers would get a pole attempt on Sunday because they were not able to get through the entire qualifying line on Saturday. Guerrero remained on the pole, with Eddie Cheever and Mario Andretti also on the front row.

A.J. Foyt started twenty-third as a result of blowing his engine on his first qualification attempt. This made the thirty-fifth consecutive year Foyt had qualified for the race.

Al Unser Sr. was back after not running a lap the prior year. Johnny Rutherford missed the race for the fourth consecutive year. This would be J.R.'s last attempt at Indy. He had last qualified and raced in 1988.

Lyn St. James became the second woman to qualify at Indy. She started in twenty-seventh position.

Scott Goodyear was bumped but took over his backup car (because of a sponsor stipulation), which had been qualified by Mike Groff. He was forced to start thirty-third.

Ten former winners competed in the "500," which also included two World Driving champions (Mario Andretti and Emerson Fittipaldi).

For the second straight year, four Andrettis would race in the "500."

Race day was very cool, with temperatures in the low 50s and strong wind causing "cold tire" accidents all day.

Pole sitter Roberto Guerrero spun his Quaker State Lola/Buick on the back stretch, hit the inside wall on the parade lap, and was eliminated.

Eddie Cheever brought the field to the green, but Mario and Michael Andretti immediately passed him on each side going into turn one.

Numerous restarts after yellows resulted in accidents because of cold tires. Those involved included Tom Sneva, Philippe Gache, Jim Crawford, Rick Mears, Emerson Fittipaldi and Mario Andretti. Eventually fourteen drivers would be eliminated in accidents.

On lap 115, Jeff Andretti had a serious accident in turn two, suffering serious foot and leg injuries.

Michael Andretti dominated most of the race, pretty much only losing the lead when he pitted.

On lap 189, after leading 160 laps, Michael Andretti was enjoying a big lead when he came to a stop because of a broken fuel pump. The Andretti "jinx" again! This Indy 500 left Michael heartbroken and Mario and Jeff hospitalized with foot and leg injuries.

Andretti's stalled car on the track caused a yellow. The track went green on lap 193 with Scott Goodyear on leader Unser Jr.'s tail.

Al Unser Jr. held Goodyear off as a Goodyear surge at the finish line fell just short. Unser averaged 134.5 mph because of thirteen cautions for 85 laps.

The margin of victory was the closest in history, .043 seconds.

Prior to the race, Unser felt his chance of victory was marginal in view of his new Galmer Chassis. After the race the extremely emotional winner said, "You just don't know what it means to win here at Indianapolis." The 1992 Indy 500 victory came in Al Jr's. tenth attempt.

Al Unser Sr. finished third in a Buick V-6. This was the best finish in history for that power-plant.

Lyn St. James finished eleventh and won Rookie of the Year.

Michael Andretti led 160 laps, and Unser Jr. led 25 laps.

The Speedway golf course was revamped by master golf designer Pete Dye with four holes inside the track and fourteen on the outside.

Al Unser Jr. outduels Scott Goodyear in 1992 in the closest finish in history.

RACE RESULTS FOR THE 1992 INDIANAPOLIS 500

Finish	Start	Car Num.	Driver	Car Name/Entrant*	Make/Model	Status	Laps	Led	Winnings
1	12	3	Al Unser Jr.	Valvoline	Galmer/Chevrolet Indy A	134.477	200	25	$1,244,184
2	33	15	Scott Goodyear	Mackenzie Financial	Lola/Chevrolet Indy A	134.476	200	0	$609,333
3	22	27	Al Unser (W)	Menard-Conseco	Lola/Buick	134.375	200	4	$368,533
4	2	9	Eddie Cheever Jr.	Target-Scotch Video	Lola/Ford Cosworth XB	134.374	200	9	$271,103
5	8	18	Danny Sullivan (W)	Molson/Kraco/STP	Galmer/Chevrolet Indy A	Running	199	0	$211,803
6	10	12	Bobby Rahal (W)	Miller Genuine Draft	Lola/Chevrolet Indy A	Running	199	0	$237,703
7	25	11	Raul Boesel	Panasonic	Lola/Chevrolet Indy A	Running	198	0	$191,503
8	14	8	John Andretti	Pennzoil	Lola/Chevrolet Indy A	Running	195	0	$186,203
9	23	14	A.J. Foyt (W)	Copenhagen	Lola/Chevrolet Indy A	Running	195	0	$189,883
10	18	93	John Paul Jr.	D.B. Mann Development	Lola/Buick	Running	194	0	$171,403
11	27	90	Lyn St. James (R)	Agency Rent-A-Car / JC Penney	Lola/Chevrolet Indy A	Running	193	0	$187,953
12	29	68	Dominic Dobson	Burns/Tobacco Free America	Lola/Chevrolet Indy A	Running	193	0	$179,983
13	6	1	Michael Andretti	Kmart/Texaco Havoline	Lola/Ford Cosworth XB	Fuel pressure	189	160	$295,383
14	24	21	Buddy Lazier	Leader Cards	Lola/Buick	Engine	139	0	$164,283
15	4	6	Arie Luyendyk (W)	Target/Scotch Video	Lola/Ford Cosworth XB	Accident	135	1	$166,953
16	32	31	Ted Prappas (R)	PIG/Say No To Drugs	Lola/Chevrolet Indy A	Gear box	135	0	$163,253
17	5	51	Gary Bettenhausen	Glidden Paints	Lola/Buick	Accident	112	0	$150,803
18	20	48	Jeff Andretti	Gillette/Carlo	Lola/Chevrolet Indy A	Accident	109	0	$153,703
19	26	39	Brian Bonner (R)	Applebee's	Lola/Buick	Accident	97	0	$156,953
20	19	7	Paul Tracy (R)	Mobil 1	Penske/Chevrolet Indy A	Engine	96	0	$160,053
21	28	47	Jimmy Vasser (R)	Kodalux	Lola/Chevrolet Indy A	Accident	94	0	$170,853
22	7	22	Scott Brayton	Amway/Northwest Airlines	Lola/Buick	Engine	93	0	$173,683
23	3	2	Mario Andretti (W)	Kmart/Texaco Havoline	Lola/Ford Cosworth XB	Accident	78	1	$156,633
24	11	5	Emerson Fittipaldi (W)	Marlboro	Penske/Chevrolet Indy B	Accident	75	0	$138,703
25	21	26	Jim Crawford	Quaker State	Lola/Buick	Accident	74	0	$167,503
26	9	4	Rick Mears (W)	Marlboro	Penske/Chevrolet Indy B	Accident	74	0	$136,403
27	13	91	Stan Fox	Jonathan Byrd's Cafeteria	Lola/Buick	Accident	63	0	$136,683
28	16	44	Philippe Gache (R)	Rhone-Poulenc Rorer	Lola/Chevrolet Indy A	Accident	61	0	$136,128
29	31	92	Gordon Johncock (W)	STP/Jacks Tool Rental	Lola/Buick	Engine	60	0	$136,003
30	17	10	Scott Pruett	Budweiser	Truesports/Chevrolet Indy A	Engine	52	0	$143,503
31	30	59	Tom Sneva (W)	Glidden Paints	Lola/Buick	Accident	10	0	$139,778
32	15	19	Eric Bachelart (R)	Royal Oak Charcoal	Lola/Buick	Engine	4	0	$144,228
33	1	36	Roberto Guerrero	Quaker State	Lola/Buick	Accident	0	0	$286,378

* - complete car name/entrant data not available for all entries
(R) - Indicated Rookie
(W) - Indicates Past Winner

1993

Formula One's reigning champion, thirty-nine year-old Nigel Mansell, moved to Indy car while Indy car's fastest driver, Michael Andretti, moved to F-1. Mansell was a former aerospace engineer who had won thirty-one Formula One races in his career. Mansell had never raced an oval when he arrived at Indy, as he had crashed in practice at the season opener at Phoenix.

Three-time Formula One champion Nelson Piquet returned as a rookie after sustaining serious injuries in a practice accident in May of 1992. Piquet spun early in the month, qualified and started thirteenth and finished thirty-second.

Dale Coyne Racing entered a car for Eric Bachelart, with sponsorship from the Marmon Group. The car had a yellow and black paint scheme similar to the Marmon Wasp driven by winner Ray Harroun in the first "500."

Rick Mears was not entered; he surprised the racing world with his retirement announcement in December of 1992.

A few of Mears accomplishments in his storied career are:

>four Indy 500 wins
>
>a record six Indy 500 pole starts
>
>eleven front row starts in fifteen races
>
>twenty-nine IndyCar wins

four CART championships (1979, 1981, 1982, 1991)

The apron had been replaced with rumble strips in an attempt to slow the cars down. The result was speeds were generally down about 10 mph.

Crash recorders were mandatory for the first time to provide information for safety improvements.

A.J. Foyt stunned the crowd on the morning of pole day when he tearfully retired after Robby Gordon had a minor accident with his team car in practice.

A.J. Foyt's career—1958 to 1992:

> ran in thirty-five consecutive "500s"
>
> four firsts, two seconds, three thirds, and eight other top tens
>
> four pole starts; five other front row starts
>
> led 555 laps—fourth highest
>
> led in thirteen races, top in history
>
> only driver in history to win "500's" in a front-engine and a rear-engine car
>
> seven IndyCar Season Titles
>
> twenty-four-hour LeMans winner (1967)
>
> Daytona 500 winner (1972)
>
> winning Indy 500 car owner (1999).

Arie Luyendyk took the pole at 224 mph for Ganassi Racing, with Mario Andretti and Raul Boesel joining him on the front row.

Bobby Rahal, defending Indy car champion and 1986 "500" winner, failed to qualify for the first time in his career dating back to 1982. He became the first series champion to fail to make the race since the 1930's.

Boesel took the early lead for the first seventeen laps.

Several drivers swapped the lead up to lap 70, when Mansell took it. (Gregoire, Cogan, Unser Sr., Mario Andretti, Luyendyk, John Andretti, Gordon and Goodyear.)

The second half of the race was between Luyendyk, Mansell and Fittipaldi.

Mansell was leading on the restart on lap 185 when he was passed by both Fittipaldi and Luyendyk.

On lap 193, Mansell brushed the wall exiting turn two and the yellow flashed, but he was able to continue.

The green appeared on lap 196 and Fittipaldi was able to beat Luyendyk to the checker by 2.8 seconds, becoming a two-time winner. Mansell finished third and won Rookie of the Year. Mansell became the first rookie to finish the full 500 miles since Donnie Allison in 1970.

Fittipaldi, the two-time Formula One World Champion, averaged 157.2 mph in his Marlboro Penske/Chevrolet.

An abnormally high number of twenty-four of the thirty-three cars were running at the finish.

John Andretti drove for A.J. Foyt and finished tenth.

Al Unser Sr. finished twelfth and was able to lead 15 laps to increase his total led laps to a record of 644. It would be his last "500."

Fittipaldi elected to drink orange juice in victory lane before the traditional milk.

A record of twelve different drivers led the race.

Mario Andretti led seventy-two laps, Mansell, thirty-four, Boesel, eighteen, Unser Jr., seventeen, and Fittipaldi, sixteen laps.

Nigel Mansell would go on to win the 1993 PPG IndyCar World Series Championship.

Emerson Fittipaldi drinks the traditional milk after refreshing himself with orange juice first.

RACE RESULTS FOR THE 1993 INDIANAPOLIS 500

Finish	Start	Car Num.	Driver	Car Name/Entrant*	Make/Model	Status	Laps	Led	Winnings
1	9	4	Emerson Fittipaldi (W)	Marlboro	Penske/Chevrolet Indy C	157.207	200	16	$1,155,304
2	1	10	Arie Luyendyk (W)	Target/Scotch Video	Lola/Ford Cosworth XB	157.168	200	14	$681,303
3	8	5	Nigel Mansell (R)	Kmart/Texaco Havoline	Lola/Ford Cosworth XB	157.149	200	34	$391,203
4	3	9	Raul Boesel	Duracell/Mobil 1/Sadia	Lola/Ford Cosworth XB	157.142	200	18	$317,903
5	2	6	Mario Andretti (W)	Kmart/Texaco Havoline	Lola/Ford Cosworth XB	157.133	200	72	$313,953
6	11	22	Scott Brayton	Amway/Byrd's Cafeteria	Lola/Ford Cosworth XB	157.117	200	0	$248,253
7	4	2	Scott Goodyear	Mackenzie Financial	Lola/Ford Cosworth XB	157.099	200	5	$234,953
8	5	3	Al Unser Jr. (W)	Valvoline	Lola/Chevrolet Indy C	157.070	200	17	$243,253
9	17	8	Teo Fabi	Pennzoil	Lola/Chevrolet Indy C	156.968	200	0	$206,703
10	24	84	John Andretti	Copenhagen/Marmon Group	Lola/Ford Cosworth XB	156.964	200	2	$228,303
11	6	16	Stefan Johansson (R)	AMAX Energy & Metals	Penske/Chevrolet Indy C	Running	199	0	$186,020
12	23	80	Al Unser (W)	Budweiser King	Lola/Chevrolet Indy C	Running	199	15	$194,870
13	19	18	Jimmy Vasser	Kodalux/STP	Lola/Ford Cosworth XB	Running	198	0	$188,003
14	14	11	Kevin Cogan	Conseco	Lola/Chevrolet Indy C	Running	198	4	$180,603
15	28	50	Davy Jones	Agip/Andrea Moda/Marcelo	Lola/Chevrolet Indy A	Running	197	0	$166,003
16	33	59	Eddie Cheever Jr.	Glidden/Menard/Quorum	Lola/Buick	Running	197	0	$184,403
17	18	51	Gary Bettenhausen	Glidden Paints	Lola/Menard	Running	197	0	$155,053
18	26	15	Hiro Matsushita	Panasonic	Lola/Ford Cosworth XB	Running	197	0	$157,503
19	15	36	Stephan Gregoire (R)	Formula Project/Maalox	Lola/Buick	Running	195	1	$189,603
20	22	76	Tony Bettenhausen Jr.	AMAX Energy & Metals	Penske/Chevrolet Indy C	Running	195	0	$151,069
21	30	75	Willy T. Ribbs	Cosby/Service Merchandise	Lola/Ford Cosworth XB	Running	194	0	$146,653
22	32	92	Didier Theys	Kinko's/Delta Faucet	Lola/Buick	Running	193	0	$176,053
23	27	66	Dominic Dobson	Coors Light/Indy Parks	Galmer/Chevrolet Indy A	Running	193	0	$146,203
24	31	60	Jim Crawford	Budweiser King	Lola/Chevrolet Indy C	Running	192	0	$148,270
25	21	90	Lyn St. James	JCPenney/Nike/Amer. Woman	Lola/Ford Cosworth XB	Stalled	176	0	$146,403
26	29	27	Geoff Brabham	Glidden/Menard	Lola/Menard	Engine	174	0	$139,203
27	25	41	Robby Gordon (R)	Copenhagen/Foyt	Lola/Ford Cosworth XB	Gearbox	165	2	$155,453
28	10	40	Roberto Guerrero	Budweiser King	Lola/Chevrolet Indy C	Accident	125	0	$137,303
29	16	21	Jeff Andretti	Interstate Batt/Gillette/Taesa	Lola/Buick	Accident	124	0	$154,370
30	7	12	Paul Tracy	Marlboro	Penske/Chevrolet Indy C	Accident	94	0	$136,003
31	20	91	Stan Fox	Delta Faucet-Jacks Tool Rental	Lola/Buick	Engine	64	0	$136,703
32	13	77	Nelson Piquet (R)	ARISCO/STP	Lola/Menard	Engine	38	0	$137,219
33	12	7	Danny Sullivan (W)	Molson	Lola/Chevrolet Indy C	Accident	29	0	$137,203

* - complete car name/entrant data not available for all entries
(R) - Indicated Rookie
(W) - Indicates Past Winner

1994

A new administration building at the corner of West 16th Street and Georgetown Road had been built for Indianapolis Motor Speedway headquarters.

Al Unser Jr. left the Galles team after six years and joined Team Penske with Emerson Fittipaldi and Paul Tracy.

Two former winners announced their retirements during practice. Al Unser Sr. had been entered to drive the Arizona Motor Sport car, but decided it was time to quit. Johnny Rutherford had not driven at Indy for two years when he took a ceremonial lap in one of Foyt's cars.

A few of Al Unser's accomplishments in his stellar career are:

    four Indy 500 wins (1970, 1971, 1978, 1987)

    record holder for laps led at 644

    led laps in eleven of his twenty-seven Indy 500 starts

    oldest Indy 500 winner at 47 years and 360 days

    record of eleven top-three finishes

    won eight 500 mile races (two Pocono, two Ontario and four Indy 500's)

    thirty-nine IndyCar wins

    three IndyCar championships

A few of Johnny Rutherford's accomplishments in his storied career are:

three Indy 500 wins (1974, 1976, 1980)

twenty-four Indy 500 starts

twenty-seven IndyCar wins

CART National Champion in 1980

Rain delayed the start of qualifying, so several drivers made pole attempts on Sunday, although twenty-one made the field on Saturday.

Al Unser Jr.'s speed of 228.011 mph stood up for the pole, with Raul Boesel and Emerson Fittipaldi also on the front row.

Lyn St. James surprised the crowd with a sixth-place starting spot.

Paul Tracy, in his Penske, experienced mechanical problems in his bid for the pole and started twenty-fifth.

Bobby Rahal struggled again in 1994, this time with the Honda/Lola combination, and ended up leasing Penske cars for himself and teammate Mike Groff. He had missed the field in 1993. Rahal would start twenty-eighth.

Gary Bettenhausen missed the show in his brother Tony's car. The year 1994 was his last effort at Indy after twenty-one starts.

The Penske/Mercedes, using a 209 cubic-inch turbocharged pushrod engine generating 900 horsepower, was a heavy favorite to win. The development project was a top secret of Mercedes-Benz, Ilmor Engineering and Team Penske. This dominant engine was never raced again.

Rufus Parnell "Parnelli" Jones, the 1963 "500" champion, paced the 78th Indianapolis 500 in a Ford Mustang Cobra.

Unser Jr. took the early lead for the first twenty-three laps before Fittipaldi took over and led the next thirty-eight laps.

On lap ninety-two, a caution on the track resulted in Dennis Vitolo vaulting over the wheel of John Andretti and landing on Nigel Mansell's car on the warm-up lane in turn three. That would be the last time Mansell would compete in the "500."

The second half of the race was pretty much a Fittipaldi/Unser show. Fittipaldi was able to break away from his teammate and actually put him a lap down.

Emmo pitted on lap 164 and would likely need a later "splash and go" to make it to the finish. Unser pitted on lap 168 and felt he likely had sufficient fuel to finish.

Unser unlapped himself, but on lap 185, Fittipaldi, with nearly a lap lead, pushed too hard coming out of turn four and hit the wall, ending his day for a seventeenth-place finish. Team Penske was just ready to call Fittipaldi to the pits for fuel when he crashed.

Al Unser Jr. was able to lead the last fifteen laps to win his second 500, the ninth overall win for the Unser family and tenth win for Penske Racing. Unser averaged 160.9 mph on his father's birthday. Unser had no radio communication with his team all day.

Jacques Villeneuve finished second just nine seconds back to win Rookie of the Year. Bobby Rahal was able to charge through the field and finish third in his Penske/Ilmor.

Fittipaldi led 145 laps, Unser, 48, and Villeneuve, 7. Penske cars led a total of 193 laps.

Emmo had made the winning pass on lap 185 in the 1993 race. In 1994 he crashed while leading on lap 185.

John Andretti finished tenth, then flew to Charlotte to compete in the NASCAR World 600, the first driver to do the "double header."

Al Unser Jr. would go on to win his second CART championship in 1994.

Three Indy 500 legends retired in 1994: Mario Andretti, Johnny Rutherford and Al Unser Sr. The trio accumulated eight Indy 500 wins.

A few of Mario Andretti's accomplishments are:

> won the 1969 Indy 500
>
> won the pole for the Indy 500 three times (1966, 1967, 1987)
>
> won the IndyCar championship four times (1965, 1966, 1969, 1984)

won the World Driving Championship in 1978

won twelve Grand Prix races

won the Daytona 500 in 1967

only driver in history to win the Indianapolis 500, a Formula One race and NASCAR Sprint Cub Series race.

Al Unser Jr., 1994 winner, with the Team Penske crew.

RACE RESULTS FOR THE 1994 INDIANAPOLIS 500

Finish	Start	Car Num.	Driver	Car Name/Entrant*	Make/Model	Status	Laps	Led	Winnings
1	1	31	Al Unser Jr. (W)	Marlboro Penske	Penske/Mercedes Benz	160.872	200	48	$1,373,813
2	4	12	Jacques Villeneuve (R)	Player's Ltd.	Reynard/Ford Cosworth XB	160.749	200	7	$622,713
3	28	4	Bobby Rahal (W)	Miller Genuine Draft	Penske/Ilmor D	Running	199	0	$411,163
4	16	18	Jimmy Vasser	Conseco/STP	Reynard/Ford Cosworth XB	Running	199	0	$295,163
5	19	9	Robby Gordon	Valvoline/Cummins	Lola/Ford Cosworth XB	Running	199	0	$227,563
6	5	8	Michael Andretti	Target/Scotch Video	Reynard/Ford Cosworth XB	Running	198	0	$245,563
7	24	11	Teo Fabi	Pennzoil	Reynard/Ilmor D	Running	198	0	$216,563
8	11	27	Eddie Cheever Jr.	Quaker State	Lola/Menard	Running	197	0	$238,563
9	22	14	Bryan Herta (R)	AJ Foyt/Copenhagen	Lola/Ford Cosworth XB	Running	197	0	$212,213
10	10	33	John Andretti	Byrd's Cafeteria/Bryant	Lola/Ford Cosworth XB	Running	196	0	$191,750
11	29	88	Mauricio Gugelmin (R)	Hollywood	Reynard/Ford Cosworth XB	Running	196	0	$182,063
12	21	19	Brian Till (R)	The Mi-Jack Car	Lola/Ford Cosworth XB	Running	194	0	$180,763
13	13	91	Stan Fox	Delta Faucet-Jacks Tools	Reynard/Ford Cosworth XB	Accident	193	0	$186,313
14	18	22	Hiro Matsushita	Panasonic/Duskin	Lola/Ford Cosworth XB	Running	193	0	$177,013
15	27	16	Stefan Johansson	Alumax Aluminum	Penske/Ilmor D	Running	192	0	$164,113
16	17	71	Scott Sharp (R)	PacWest	Lola/Ford Cosworth XB	Running	186	0	$161,663
17	3	2	Emerson Fittipaldi (W)	Marlboro Penske	Penske/Mercedes Benz	Accident	184	145	$298,163
18	8	28	Arie Luyendyk (W)	Indy Regency Racing	Lola/Ilmor D	Engine	179	0	$161,412
19	6	90	Lyn St. James	Spirit of American Woman/JC Penney	Lola/Ford Cosworth XB	Running	170	0	$161,212
20	23	59	Scott Brayton	Glidden Paints	Lola/Menard	Engine	116	0	$177,112
21	2	5	Raul Boesel	Duracell Charger	Lola/Ford Cosworth XB	Water Pump	100	0	$173,112
22	7	1	Nigel Mansell	Kmart/Texaco/Havoline	Lola/Ford Cosworth XB	Accident	92	0	$153,312
23	25	3	Paul Tracy	Marlboro Penske	Penske/Mercedes Benz	Turbo	92	0	$151,612
24	14	99	Hideshi Matsuda (R)	Beck Motorsports	Lola/Ford Cosworth XB	Accident	90	0	$150,362
25	30	45	John Paul Jr.	Pro Formance Team Losi	Lola/Ilmor D	Accident	89	0	$168,812
26	15	79	Dennis Vitolo (R)	Hooligans/Carlo	Lola/Ford Cosworth XB	Accident	89	0	$143,862
27	32	25	Marco Greco (R)	International Sports, Ltd.	Lola/Ford Cosworth XB	Electrical	53	0	$171,762
28	26	7	Adrian Fernandez (R)	Tecate/Quaker State	Reynard/Ilmor D	Suspension	30	0	$146,612
29	12	17	Dominic Dobson	Columbia Helecopters	Lola/Ford Cosworth XB	Accident	29	0	$139,912
30	33	40	Scott Goodyear	Budweiser	Lola/Ford Cosworth XB	Mechanical	29	0	$159,312
31	31	10	Mike Groff	Motorola	Penske/Ilmor D	Accident	28	0	$138,812
32	9	6	Mario Andretti (W)	Kmart/Texaco/Havoline	Lola/Ford Cosworth XB	Fuel System	23	0	$138,512
33	20	21	Roberto Guerrero	Interstate Batteries	Lola/Buick	Accident	20	0	$143,912

* - complete car name/entrant data not available for all entries
(R) - Indicated Rookie
(W) - Indicates Past Winner

1995

Firestone was back at Indy for the first time since 1974. Arie Luyendyk set a speed of 233.281 mph on opening day.

Menard teammates Arie Luyendyk and Scott Brayton set fast times prior to qualifications in their Lola/Menard V-6.

Tony George made an announcement regarding the formation of the IRL—Indy Racing League—for 1996.

Rain on pole day allowed only a few qualification attempts.

The front row ended up with Scott Brayton on the pole at 231.6 mph, with Arie Luyendyk and Scott Goodyear.

The Penskes of Emerson Fittipaldi and Al Unser Jr. did not have the speed to qualify on the first weekend.

Team Penske had decided not to test with the Goodyear tires, Goodyear having developed its Speedway tire based on the Lola and Reynard cars.

Fittipaldi qualified on the final day of qualifications, but was bumped with fifteen minutes left.

Neither of Penske's drivers made the field, an astounding situation no one had envisioned. This marked the first year Roger Penske missed having a car in the "500" since his 1969 debut.

At the start, Scott Goodyear took the lead, but an accident occurred in turn one on the first lap, with Stan Fox crashing hard and collecting Eddie Cheever. Fox sustained a serious head injury that ended his racing career.

Goodyear and Michael Andretti swapped the lead for most of the first seventy-seven laps, when Andretti brushed the wall trying to avoid Mauricio Gugelmin, ending his day.

Gugelmin was able to lead 50 of the laps from 82 to 138 before slowing down and eventually finishing sixth.

Moving through the field, after receiving a two-lap penalty on lap 36 for passing the pace car due to a misunderstanding regarding what he thought was a wave-around, was Jacques Villeneuve. He was able to take the lead on lap 156 aided by some excellent pit strategy and fine driving.

The contenders were Jimmy Vasser, Goodyear, Scott Pruett and Villeneuve.

Vasser crashed on lap 171 and Pruett crashed on lap 185. Goodyear was leading Villeneuve on the final restart when Goodyear pulled away from the pack, coming to the green with 10 laps remaining and passed the Chevrolet Corvette pace car in view of a stunned crowd. Goodyear was black-flagged but remained on the track though he was not scored after lap 195. He officially finished fourteenth. Goodyear claimed that the green light was on when he accelerated. Video evidence later proved that Goodyear passed the pace car while the yellow light was on.

Villeneuve took the checker 2.4 seconds ahead of Rookie of the Year Christian Fittipaldi. The win gave Villeneuve a second and a first-place finish in his first two starts. Villeneuve averaged 153.6 mph in his V-8 Team Green Ford Cosworth/Reynard for the 500 miles. He became the first Canadian to win the "500."

Gugelmin led fifty-nine laps, Michael Andretti, forty-five, Goodyear, forty-two, Vasser, twenty, and Villeneuve, fifteen.

Villeneuve would go on to win the CART championship for the 1995 season.

The winner for 1995, Jacques Villeneuve scored a second place and first place finish in his first two starts at Indy.

RACE RESULTS FOR THE 1995 INDIANAPOLIS 500

Finish	Start	Car Num.	Driver	Car Name/Entrant*	Make/Model	Status	Laps	Led	Winnings
1	5	27	Jacques Villeneuve	Player's LTD/Team Green	Reynard/Ford Cosworth XB	153.616	200	15	$1,312,019
2	27	15	Christian Fittipaldi (R)	Marlboro Chapeco	Reynard/Ford Cosworth XB	153.583	200	0	$594,668
3	21	9	Bobby Rahal (W)	Miller Genuine Draft	Lola/Mercedes Benz	153.577	200	1	$373,267
4	24	7	Eliseo Salazar (R)	Cristal/Mobil 1/Copec	Lola/Ford Cosworth XB	153.553	200	0	$302,417
5	7	5	Robby Gordon	Valvoline/Cummins	Reynard/Ford Cosworth XB	153.420	200	1	$247,917
6	6	18	Mauricio Gugelmin	Hollywood/PacWest	Reynard/Ford Cosworth XB	153.392	200	59	$284,667
7	2	40	Arie Luyendyk (W)	Glidden/Quaker State	Lola/Menard V6	153.067	200	7	$247,417
8	15	33	Teo Fabi	ABB/Indeck	Reynard/Ford Cosworth XB	Running	199	0	$206,853
9	18	17	Danny Sullivan (W)	VISA Bank of America/PacWest	Reynard/Ford Cosworth XB	Running	199	0	$193,453
10	10	25	Hiro Matsushita	Panasonic Duskin YKK	Reynard/Ford Cosworth XB	Running	199	0	$196,053
11	17	34	Alessandro Zampedri (R)	The Mi-Jack Car	Lola/Ford Cosworth XB	Running	198	0	$199,153
12	13	21	Roberto Guerrero	Upper Deck/General Components	Reynard/Mercedes Benz	Running	198	0	$181,203
13	33	4	Bryan Herta	Target/Scotch Video	Reynard/Ford Cosworth XB	Running	198	0	$175,903
14	3	24	Scott Goodyear	LCI/Motorola/CNN	Reynard/Honda Indy	Penalty	195	42	$246,403
15	20	54	Hideshi Matsuda	Beck Motorsports/Taisan/Zunne Group	Lola/Ford Cosworth XB	Running	194	0	$200,503
16	31	16	Stefan Johansson	Team Alumax	Reynard/Ford Cosworth XB	Running	192	0	$182,703
17	1	60	Scott Brayton	Quaker State/Glidden	Lola/Menard V6	Running	190	0	$306,503
18	12	31	Andre Ribiero (R)	LCI International	Reynard/Honda Indy	Running	187	0	$176,753
19	8	20	Scott Pruett	Firestone Patrick Racing	Lola/Ford Cosworth XB	Accident	184	8	$164,953
20	22	11	Raul Boesel	The Duracell Charger	Lola/Mercedes Benz	Oil line	184	2	$169,053
21	25	10	Adrian Fernandez	Tecate Beer/Quaker State/Galles	Lola/Mercedes Benz	Engine	176	0	$183,903
22	9	12	Jimmy Vasser	Target/STP	Reynard/Ford Cosworth XB	Accident	170	20	$162,003
23	32	77	Davy Jones	Jonathan Byrd's Cafeteria/Bryant H. & C.	Lola/Ford Cosworth XB	Accident	161	0	$182,303
24	16	3	Paul Tracy	Kmart/Budweiser/Newman/Haas Racing	Lola/Ford Cosworth XB	Electrical	136	0	$149,703
25	4	6	Michael Andretti	Kmart/Texaco Havoline/Newman/Haas	Lola/Ford Cosworth XB	Suspension	77	45	$192,053
26	30	41	Scott Sharp	AJ Foyt/Copenhagen Racing	Lola/Ford Cosworth XB	Accident	74	0	$158,003
27	23	80	Buddy Lazier	Glidden/Quaker State	Lola/Menard V6	Fuel system	45	0	$145,903
28	26	19	Eric Bachelart	The AGFA Car	Lola/Ford Cosworth XB	Mechanical	6	0	$155,003
29	19	8	Gil de Ferran (R)	Pennzoil Special/Hall Racing	Reynard/Mercedes Benz	Accident	1	0	$149,453
30	11	91	Stan Fox	Delta Faucet/Bowling/Hemelgarn	Reynard/Ford Cosworth XB	Accident	0	0	$143,603
31	14	14	Eddie Cheever Jr.	AJ Foyt/Copenhagen Racing	Lola/Ford Cosworth XB	Accident	0	0	$144,103
32	28	90	Lyn St. James	Whitlock Auto Supply	Lola/Ford Cosworth XB	Accident	0	0	$157,803
33	29	22	Carlos Guerrero (R)	Herdez-Viva Mexico!	Lola/Ford Cosworth XB	Accident	0	0	$172,853

* - complete car name/entrant data not available for all entries
(R) - Indicated Rookie
(W) - Indicates Past Winner

1996

The rumble strips that had been added to the track in 1993 were removed, which helped in achieving record speeds.

The year 1996 was the first year of the Indy Racing League (IRL). Virtually all of the CART teams elected not to enter Indy.

As a result, there were seventeen rookies in the 1996 "500," the most since the 1930 race when there were nineteen.

Year-old cars were used as the IRL was putting together a new car and engine package.

Menard had cars for four drivers: Scott Brayton, Tony Stewart, Eddie Cheever and Mark Dismore.

Scandia, formerly Dick Simon Racing, entered cars for seven drivers: Alessandro Zampedri, Eliseo Salazar, Michel Jourdain Jr., Fermin Velez, Joe Gosek, Michele Alboreto and Racin Gardner. All seven would qualify, which became the largest number of cars in history to qualify for one team.

Danny Ongais, after a ten-year absence, was a surprise starter.

Buddy Lazier was involved in an accident while practicing for the Phoenix race in March. He sustained multiple (sixteen) back fractures.

During the first week of practice, Tony Stewart, Eddie Cheever, Scott Brayton and Arie Luyendyk ran 235, 236, and 237 mph laps. On Friday before pole day Luyendyk ran a lap at 239.260 mph, still the fastest unofficial lap in history.

On pole day, toward the end of the day, Brayton withdrew his car and qualified another to win the pole with a new record of 233.718 mph average. Brayton's teammate, Tony Stewart, qualified second and Davy Jones third.

Luyendyk had qualified at 233.390, but his car was determined to be underweight and the run was disallowed. He was forced to qualify on Sunday. He set track records of 236.986 mph average, and 237.498 mph for a one-lap record but would have to start twentieth.

This was the last year for turbo-charged engines, almost guaranteeing slower speeds in the future.

On the Friday before the second weekend of qualifications, Scott Brayton was fatally injured with a basal skull fracture in a second-turn, one-car practice accident in his backup. A right rear blown tire was likely the cause of the tragic accident.

John Menard elected to put Danny Ongais in the Brayton car and start at the back of the field. As a result, Tony Stewart would start from the pole, with Davy Jones and Eliseo Salazar joining him on row one.

Rain on race morning caused a fifteen-minute delay to the start.

Tony Stewart started from the pole in his Lola/Menard V-6 and led the first thirty-one laps before pitting.

Roberto Guerrero, Buddy Lazier and Stewart swapped the lead up to lap seventy.

Stewart's day ended on lap eighty-two with a sour engine.

Davy Jones, Buddy Lazier and Roberto Guerrero then swapped the lead up to lap 170. Lazier fought extreme back pain throughout the race in a courageous effort.

Alessandro Zampedri led from lap 170 to lap 189. Davy Jones passed for the lead on lap 190.

Buddy Lazier passed Jones on lap 192 for the lead. This was the first time in history that three different drivers led the race in the final 12 laps.

A yellow on lap 196 bunched the cars. The green appeared on lap 198 and Lazier led Jones to the checker by .7 of a second. Lazier averaged 148.0 mph for the win in his Hemelgarn Delta Faucet Reynard/Ford Cosworth. This was his first IndyCar win.

As the checkered flag was given, Guerrero lost control and slammed into Zampedri's car, which lifted into the catch fence. Eliseo Salazar actually drove under the flying Zampedri car. Zampedri sustained serious leg and foot injuries.

Rookie Richie Hearn finished third, while Zampedri was still able to finish fourth. Ongais ended up finishing seventh after surviving an early race spin.

Eddie Cheever set the fastest lap in race competition history with a 236.103 mph lap despite being several laps down at the time.

Tony Stewart won Rookie of the Year with a twenty-fourth place finish and the first starting position.

Second-generation driver Buddy Lazier is elated with his 1996 win.

RACE RESULTS FOR THE 1996 INDIANAPOLIS 500

Finish	Start	Car Num.	Driver	Car Name/Entrant*	Make/Model	Status	Laps	Led	Winnings
1	5	91	Buddy Lazier	Hemelgarn Racing-Delta Faucet-Montana	Reynard/Ford Cosworth XB	147.956	200	43	$1,367,854
2	2	70	Davy Jones	Delco Electronics High Tech Team Galles	Lola/Mercedes Ilmor	147.948	200	46	$632,503
3	15	4	Richie Hearn (R)	Della Penna Mtspts. Ralph's Food 4 Less Fuji	Reynard/Ford Cosworth XB	147.871	200	0	$375,203
4	7	8	Alessandro Zampedri	Mi-Jack/AGIP/Xcel	Lola/Ford Cosworth XB	Accident	199	20	$270,853
5	6	21	Roberto Guerrero	WavePhore/Pennzoil	Reynard/Ford Cosworth XB	Accident	198	47	$315,503
6	3	7	Eliseo Salazar	Cristal/Copec Mobil	Lola/Ford Cosworth XB	Accident	197	0	$226,653
7	33	32	Danny Ongais	Glidden Menards	Lola/Menard V6	Running	197	0	$228,253
8	30	52	Hideshi Matsuda	Team Taisan/Beck Motorsports	Lola/Ford Cosworth XB	Running	197	0	$233,953
9	23	54	Robbie Buhl (R)	Original Coors/Beck Motorsports	Lola/Ford Cosworth XB	Running	197	0	$195,403
10	21	11	Scott Sharp	Conseco AJ Foyt Racing	Lola/Ford Cosworth XB	Running	194	0	$202,053
11	4	3	Eddie Cheever Jr.	Quaker State Menards	Lola/Menard V6	Running	189	0	$206,103
12	10	14	Davey Hamilton (R)	AJ Foyt Copenhagen Racing	Lola/Ford Cosworth XB	Running	181	0	$184,003
13	8	22	Michel Jourdain Jr. (R)	Herdez Quaker State/Viva Mexico!	Lola/Ford Cosworth XB	Running	177	0	$193,653
14	18	45	Lyn St. James	Spirit of San Antonio	Lola/Ford Cosworth XB	Accident	153	0	$182,603
15	32	44	Scott Harrington (R)	Gold Eagle/Mechanics Laundry/Harrington/LP	Reynard/Ford Cosworth XB	Accident	150	0	$190,753
16	20	5	Arie Luyendyk (W)	Jonathan Byrd's Cafeteria/Bryant H. & C.	Reynard/Ford Cosworth XB	Damage	149	0	$216,503
17	9	12	Buzz Calkins (R)	Bradley Food Marts/Hoosier Lottery	Reynard/Ford Cosworth XB	Brake	148	0	$173,553
18	19	27	Jim Guthrie (R)	Team Blueprint Racing	Lola/Menard V6	Engine	144	0	$168,453
19	14	30	Mark Dismore (R)	Quaker State Menards	Lola/Menard V6	Engine	129	0	$161,253
20	11	60	Mike Groff	Valvoline Cummins Craftsman	Reynard/Ford Cosworth XB	Tire	122	0	$158,503
21	28	34	Fermin Velez (R)	Scandia/Xcel/Royal Purple	Lola/Ford Cosworth XB	Engine fire	107	0	$176,653
22	31	43	Joe Gosek (R)	Scandia/Fanatics Only/Xcel	Lola/Ford Cosworth XB	Radiator	106	0	$169,653
23	26	10	Brad Murphey (R)	Hemelgarn Racing-Delta Faucet	Reynard/Ford Cosworth XB	Suspension	91	0	$177,853
24	1	20	Tony Stewart (R)	Menards/Glidden/Quaker State	Lola/Menard V6	Engine	82	44	$222,053
25	25	90	Racin Gardner (R)	Team Scandia/Slick Gardner Enterprises	Lola/Ford Cosworth XB	Suspension	76	0	$149,853
26	22	41	Marco Greco	AJ Foyt Enterprises	Lola/Ford Cosworth XB	Engine	64	0	$153,303
27	13	9	Stephan Gregoire	Hemelgarn Racing/Delta Faucet	Reynard/Ford Cosworth XB	Coil fire	59	0	$147,103
28	27	16	Johnny Parsons	Team Blueprint Racing	Lola/Menard V6	Radiator	48	0	$161,203
29	29	75	Johnny O'Connell (R)	Mechanics Laundry/Cunningham	Reynard/Ford Cosworth XB	Fuel system	47	0	$145,553
30	12	33	Michele Alboreto (R)	Rio Hotel & Casino/Perry Ellis/Royal Purple	Reynard/Ford Cosworth XB	Gear box	43	0	$144,953
31	17	18	John Paul Jr.	V-Line/Earl's Perf. Prod./Crowne Plaza/Keco	Lola/Menard V6	Ignition	10	0	$144,203
32	24	96	Paul Durant (R)	ABF Motorsports/Sunrise Rentals	Lola/Buick	Engine	9	0	$149,153
33	16	64	Johnny Unser (R)	Ruger-Titanium/Project Indy	Reynard/Ford Cosworth XB	Transmission	0	0	$143,953

* - complete car name/entrant data not available for all entries
(R) - Indicated Rookie
(W) - Indicates Past Winner

1997

The Dallara and the G Force were the chassis options for the teams. The engine options were either a 4.0-liter normally-aspirated Aurora V-8 or an Infiniti.

The new equation reduced speeds significantly by design.

Two drivers, John Paul Jr. and Scott Sharp, were sidelined for the month from accident injuries during the first week of practice.

Arie Luyendyk took the pole at 218.263 mph, almost 19 mph slower than his record of the year before. Tony Stewart and rookie Vincenzo Sospiri joined Luyendyk on the front row.

Fourteen-time World of Outlaws sprint-car king Steve Kinser qualified for the first time, after failing to make the field back in 1981.

A decision was made to include the runs of Lyn St. James and Johnny Unser, who were not "guaranteed" a spot but did have speeds among the fastest thirty-three. As a result, there were thirty-five starters.

Rain on race day eliminated any racing on Sunday.

A communication misunderstanding resulted in Mari Hulman George commanding to "Start Engines" twice in the pre-race ceremonies. The "mishap" began a series of unique happenings.

Three-time Indy 500 champion Johnny Rutherford piloted the Oldsmobile Aurora pace car for the start of the 81st Indianapolis 500.

On Monday, Alessandro Zampedri never made it to the green flag as he limped in the pits. The fifth row of Stephan Gregoire, Alfonso Giaffone and Kenny Brack collided going into turn four prior to the green flag. All the cars were eliminated. Then Sam Schmidt experienced engine problems prior to the green and was eliminated as well.

Tony Stewart took the early lead when the race finally started, but rain stopped the race on lap fifteen. It had to be resumed Tuesday.

After a third command to "Start Engines" the race was restarted with Stewart in the lead until pitting on lap fifty.

Luyendyk took the lead on lap sixty-three. Over the next eighty laps, Arie Luyendyk, Buddy Lazier and Robbie Buhl would swap the lead.

Five-time National Motocross champion and Indy rookie Jeff Ward, driving in only his second IndyCar race, led from lap 142 to 166 when he pitted. He took the lead back on lap 169 to 192, when he pitted again and Scott Goodyear took the top spot. Luyendyk took the lead on lap 194 from Goodyear (his teammate) on a restart.

The caution appeared on lap 199, as a result of Tony Stewart brushing the wall, but the pace car did not come out and pick up the leader. Drivers and crews expected the race would end under caution. To the surprise of nearly everyone, the green and the white flags were displayed to start the final lap. The lights around the course remained yellow for several seconds after the green/white appeared adding to the confusion. Luyendyk beat Goodyear to the checker by .57 seconds, with Rookie of the Year Jeff Ward third. Luyendyk averaged 145.8 mph for his second Indy 500 win.

This was the first time in history that three different drivers had led in the last ten laps.

Fred Treadway was the first owner to finish first and second since Bob Wilke's Leader Card Team of Rodger Ward and Len Sutton in 1962.

Stewart led for sixty-four laps, Luyendyk, sixty-one, and Ward, forty-nine laps.

Arie Luyendyk wins his second "500" in 1997.

RACE RESULTS FOR THE 1997 INDIANAPOLIS 500

Finish	Start	Car Num.	Driver	Car Name/Entrant*	Make/Model	Status	Laps	Led	Winnings
1	1	5	Arie Luyendyk (W)	Wavephore/Sprint PCS/Miller Lite/Provimi	G Force/Oldsmobile Aurora	145.827	200	61	$1,568,150
2	5	6	Scott Goodyear	Nortel/Sprint PCS/Quebecor Printing	G Force/Oldsmobile Aurora	145.820	200	2	$513,300
3	7	52	Jeff Ward (R)	FirstPlus Team Cheever	G Force/Oldsmobile Aurora	145.779	200	49	$414,250
4	10	91	Buddy Lazier (W)	Delta Faucet-Montana-Hemelgarn	Dallara/Oldsmobile Aurora	145.705	200	7	$279,250
5	2	2	Tony Stewart	Glidden/Menards	G Force/Oldsmobile Aurora	145.490	200	64	$345,050
6	8	14	Davey Hamilton	AJ Foyt PowerTeam Racing	G Force/Oldsmobile Aurora	Running	199	0	$214,000
7	22	11	Billy Boat (R)	Conseco A.J. Foyt Racing	Dallara/Oldsmobile Aurora	Running	199	1	$269,700
8	4	3	Robbie Buhl	Quaker State/Menards	G Force/Oldsmobile Aurora	Running	199	16	$235,200
9	21	30	Robbie Groff (R)	Alfa-Laval/Team Losi/McCormack Mtspts.	G Force/Oldsmobile Aurora	Running	197	0	$222,350
10	29	33	Fermin Velez	Old Navy Scandia Royal Purple Alta Xcel	Dallara/Oldsmobile Aurora	Running	195	0	$216,400
11	16	12	Buzz Calkins	Bradley Food Marts	G Force/Oldsmobile Aurora	Half shaft	188	0	$201,000
12	18	10	Mike Groff	Jonathan Byrd's Cafeteria/Visionaire/Bryant	G Force/Oldsmobile Aurora	Running	188	0	$197,300
13	34	90	Lyn St. James	Lifetime TV-Cinergy-Delta Faucet-Hemelgarn	Dallara/Nissan Infiniti Indy	Accident	186	0	$188,000
14	20	44	Steve Kinser (R)	SRS/One Call/Menards/Quaker St./St. Elmo's	Dallara/Oldsmobile Aurora	Accident	185	0	$193,250
15	28	54	Dennis Vitolo	SmithKline Beechman/Kroger/Beck Mtspts.	Dallara/Nissan Infiniti Indy	Running	173	0	$210,000
16	27	22	Marco Greco	Side Play Int'l Sport Scandia Alta Xcel	Dallara/Oldsmobile Aurora	Gear box	166	0	$193,000
17	3	8	Vincenzo Sospiri (R)	Old Navy Scandia Royal Purple Alta Xcel	Dallara/Oldsmobile Aurora	Running	163	0	$196,250
18	35	9	Johnny Unser	Delta Faucet-Montana-Cinergy-Hemelgarn	Dallara/Nissan Infiniti Indy	Oil pressure	158	0	$158,000
19	26	18	Tyce Carlson (R)	Klipsch Tnemec Overhead Door Pyle V-Line	Dallara/Oldsmobile Aurora	Accident	156	0	$173,250
20	17	40	Jack Miller (R)	AMS/Crest Racing/Trane/Spot-On	Dallara/Nissan Infiniti Indy	Accident	131	0	$171,250
21	33	1	Paul Durant	Conseco A.J. Foyt Racing	G Force/Oldsmobile Aurora	Accident	111	0	$178,000
22	24	50	Billy Roe (R)	Sega/Progressive Elect./KECO/U.J.T./Euroint'l	Dallara/Oldsmobile Aurora	Accident	110	0	$150,250
23	11	51	Eddie Cheever Jr.	FirstPlus Team Cheever	G Force/Oldsmobile Aurora	Timing chain	84	0	$176,000
24	9	7	Eliseo Salazar	Copec/Cristal/Scandia	Dallara/Oldsmobile Aurora	Accident	70	0	$164,000
25	30	97	Greg Ray (R)	Tobacco Free Kids	Dallara/Oldsmobile Aurora	Water pump	48	0	$171,250
26	6	27	Jim Guthrie	Blueprint/Jacuzzi/Armour Golf/ERTL	Dallara/Oldsmobile Aurora	Engine	43	0	$164,500
27	19	21	Roberto Guerrero	Pennzoil-Pagan Racing	Dallara/Nissan Infiniti Indy	Steering	25	0	$160,000
28	25	28	Mark Dismore	Kelley Auto./Mech Laundry/Bombardier	Dallara/Oldsmobile Aurora	Accident	24	0	$159,000
29	12	42	Robby Gordon	Coors Light	G Force/Oldsmobile Aurora	Fire	19	0	$139,500
30	32	72	Claude Bourbonnais (R)	Blueprint/Jacuzzi/Armour Golf/ERTL	Dallara/Oldsmobile Aurora	Engine	9	0	$152,250
31	13	77	Stephan Gregoire	Chastain Motorsports-Estridge-Miller Eads	G Force/Oldsmobile Aurora	Accident	0	0	$158,000
32	14	17	Affonso Giaffone (R)	General Motors Brazil Chitwood	Dallara/Oldsmobile Aurora	Accident	0	0	$158,250
33	15	4	Kenny Brack (R)	Monsoon Galles Racing	G Force/Oldsmobile Aurora	Accident	0	0	$202,250
34	23	16	Sam Schmidt (R)	Blueprint/HOPE Prepaid Fuel Card	Dallara/Oldsmobile Aurora	Engine	0	0	$150,250
35	31	34	Alessandro Zampedri	Mi-Jack Scandia Royal Purple	Dallara/Oldsmobile Aurora	Oil leak	0	0	$145,000

* - complete car name/entrant data not available for all entries
(R) - Indicated Rookie
(W) - Indicates Past Winner

1998

Eddie Cheever entered two cars, one for himself and the other for rookie Robby Unser, the youngest of Bobby Unser's sons.

The Riley & Scott chassis joined the Dallara and the G Force as options.

The Aurora engine was being used by almost all the teams.

As a cost-cutting measure, there would only be six days of practice before the race and two for qualifying, plus "carb" day.

Danny Ongais crashed in practice and could not get clearance to qualify.

Robby Unser qualified on the first day and became the sixth member of the family to make the race in his Eddie Cheever-owned car.

Billy Boat, driving for A.J. Foyt, took the pole at 223.503 mph, with Greg Ray and Kenny Brack on the front row.

Former Formula One driver Eddie Cheever qualified in seventeenth position for his ninth Indy 500.

Morning rain on race day delayed the start for about 35 minutes from the 11:00 am scheduled start.

Boat took the lead at the start and led for the first twelve laps before being passed by Greg Ray.

The Menard team of Tony Stewart and Robbie Buhl were out early with engine problems.

Cheever and Arie Luyendyk came through the field after starting seventeenth and twenty-eighth. Cheever took the lead on lap sixty-eight, while Luyendyk took the lead on lap ninety-eight.

At the halfway point it looked like a battle between Kenny Brack, Buddy Lazier, Cheever, Luyendyk and John Paul Jr.

Gearbox problems hindered Luyendyk after leading laps 147-149, taking him out of the race on lap 151. By lap 157, only Cheever, Lazier and rookie Steve Knapp were on the lead lap.

On his final pit stop on lap 177, Cheever's crew got him out ahead of the leading Lazier and he led to the finish. Cheever beat Lazier to the checker by 3.2 seconds, with Knapp finishing third and winning Rookie of the Year.

Cheever averaged 145.2 mph, as twelve cautions for sixty-one laps slowed the pace. Cheever became the first owner/driver to win since A.J. Foyt in 1977. His sponsor was Rachel's Potato Chips. Rachel's had just signed on to sponsor Cheever's car two weeks before the race. The win came in Cheever's ninth attempt and at forty years of age, but was not achieved without overcoming several obstacles in the race. On the first lap in turn one Cheever and J.J. Yeley touched wheels with Yeley spinning and bringing out the first caution of the race. On lap 49, Cheever narrowly missed the spinning car of Sam Schmidt. Then during a pit stop on lap 85, the fuel nozzle stuck in the fuel port and Cheever nearly pulled away with it still engaged.

Kenny Brack finished sixth for A.J. Foyt Racing. Had it not been for running out of fuel just before the mid-point he very well may have been victorious.

There were twenty-three lead changes between ten different drivers in the very competitive race.

Cheever led seventy-six laps, Paul, thirty-nine, Brack, twenty-three, Lazier, twenty, and Ray, eighteen.

Eddie Cheever celebrates his "500" win in victory circle.

RACE RESULTS FOR THE 1998 INDIANAPOLIS 500

Finish	Start	Car Num.	Driver	Car Name/Entrant*	Make/Model	Status	Laps	Led	Winnings
1	17	51	Eddie Cheever Jr.	Rachel's Potato Chips	Dallara/Oldsmobile Aurora	145.155	200	76	$1,433,000
2	11	91	Buddy Lazier (W)	Delta Faucet/Coors Light/Hemelgarn	Dallara/Oldsmobile Aurora	145.118	200	20	$483,200
3	23	55	Steve Knapp (R)	Primadonna Resorts/Miller Milling/ISM	G Force/Oldsmobile Aurora	145.076	200	0	$338,750
4	8	6	Davey Hamilton	Reebok/Nienhouse Motorsports	G Force/Oldsmobile Aurora	Running	199	3	$301,650
5	21	52	Robby Unser (R)	Team Cheever	Dallara/Oldsmobile Aurora	Running	198	0	$209,400
6	3	14	Kenny Brack	AJ Foyt PowerTeam Racing	Dallara/Oldsmobile Aurora	Running	198	23	$310,750
7	16	81	John Paul Jr.	Team Pelfrey	Dallara/Oldsmobile Aurora	Running	197	39	$216,350
8	19	17	Andy Michner (R)	Konica/Syan Racing	Dallara/Oldsmobile Aurora	Running	197	0	$182,050
9	13	44	J.J. Yeley (R)	One Call Comm. Quaker State Menards SRS	Dallara/Oldsmobile Aurora	Running	197	0	$198,550
10	18	12	Buzz Calkins	Int'l Star Registry/Bradley Food Marts	G Force/Oldsmobile Aurora	Running	195	4	$248,500
11	26	7	Jimmy Kite (R)	Royal Purple Synthetic/Synerlec/Scandia	Dallara/Oldsmobile Aurora	Running	195	0	$287,300
12	22	18	Jack Hewitt (R)	Parker Machinery	G Force/Oldsmobile Aurora	Running	195	0	$265,800
13	27	35	Jeff Ward	Team Tabasco/Superflo/Prolong/ISM	G Force/Oldsmobile Aurora	Running	194	0	$242,050
14	14	16	Marco Greco	Int. Sports Ltd. Phoenix Racing	G Force/Oldsmobile Aurora	Engine	183	0	$167,800
15	32	10	Mike Groff	Jonathan Byrd's VisionAire Bryant H. & C.	G Force/Oldsmobile Aurora	Running	183	0	$237,600
16	7	8	Scott Sharp	Delphi Automotive Systems	Dallara/Oldsmobile Aurora	Gearbox	181	0	$234,800
17	31	77	Stephan Gregoire	Blue Star/Tokheim/Estridge/Miller-Eads	G Force/Oldsmobile Aurora	Running	172	0	$225,300
18	2	97	Greg Ray	TMS/TNN/True Value/Dixie Chopper	Dallara/Oldsmobile Aurora	Gearbox	167	18	$175,400
19	30	30	Raul Boesel	Beloit/Fast Rod/Team Losi/TransWorld	G Force/Oldsmobile Aurora	Running	164	0	$221,300
20	28	5	Arie Luyendyk (W)	Sprint PCS/Radio Shack/Qualcomm	G Force/Oldsmobile Aurora	Gearbox	151	4	$242,100
21	15	40	Jack Miller	Crest Racing	Dallara/Nissan Infiniti Indy	Running	128	0	$159,800
22	9	21	Roberto Guerrero	Pagan Racing	Dallara/Oldsmobile Aurora	Running	125	0	$165,300
23	1	11	Billy Boat	Conseco AJ Foyt Racing	Dallara/Oldsmobile Aurora	Drive line	111	12	$364,200
24	10	4	Scott Goodyear	Pennzoil Panther	G Force/Oldsmobile Aurora	Clutch	100	0	$253,300
25	25	9	Johnny Unser	Hemelgarn Racing	Dallara/Oldsmobile Aurora	Engine	98	0	$136,300
26	6	99	Sam Schmidt	Best Western Gold Crown Racing	Dallara/Oldsmobile Aurora	Accident	48	0	$215,300
27	12	28	Mark Dismore	Kelley Automotive	Dallara/Oldsmobile Aurora	Accident	48	0	$209,300
28	29	19	Stan Wattles (R)	Metro Racing Systems/NCLD	Riley & Scott/Oldsmobile Aurora	Accident	48	0	$138,550
29	20	53	Jim Guthrie	Delco Remy/Goodyear/ISM Racing Aurora	G Force/Oldsmobile Aurora	Accident	48	0	$133,300
30	33	33	Billy Roe	Royal Purple/ProLink/Scandia	Dallara/Oldsmobile Aurora	Accident	48	0	$137,300
31	5	3	Robbie Buhl	Johns Manville/Menards	Dallara/Oldsmobile Aurora	Engine	44	0	$222,300
32	24	98	Donnie Beechler (R)	Cahill Auto Racing	G Force/Oldsmobile Aurora	Engine	34	0	$132,300
33	4	1	Tony Stewart	Glidden/Menards	Dallara/Oldsmobile Aurora	Engine	22	1	$220,250

* - complete car name/entrant data not available for all entries
(R) - Indicated Rookie
(W) - Indicates Past Winner

1999

The shortened schedule of 1998 was also used in 1999.

Arie Luyendyk won his third pole position at 225.179 mph, with Greg Ray and Billy Boat joining him on row one.

Jay Leno, host of the Tonight Show and car aficionado, drove the Chevrolet Monte Carlo pace car to start the race.

Luyendyk paced the first 32 laps of the race and swapped the lead mostly with Ray and Brack until lap 117. He had paced 63 of the first 117 laps, but was eliminated when, while leading, he attempted a low pass of the slower Tyce Carlson and spun and hit the wall in turn three.

The race became a battle between Robby Gordon and Kenny Brack. Brack took the lead on lap 125 and led almost every lap until he pitted on lap 171.

Robby Gordon decided not to pit, as he had last stopped on lap 164. His team felt if another caution came out in the next 29 laps, he would have sufficient fuel to finish. Gordon took the lead on lap 171.

When the green came out on lap 173, the order was Gordon, Ward and Brack. Brack passed Ward with 12 laps remaining.

Brack attempted to run Gordon down, and with just over a lap to go Gordon was forced into the pits for a "splash and go."

The Swedish-born Brack led Ward to the checker by 6.5 seconds. Gordon finished a disappointing fourth. Brack averaged 153.2 mph for

A.J. Foyt's first win as an owner since his retirement from driving, and a self-proclaimed "fifth win."

Brack became the only Swedish-born driver to win the Indianapolis 500, prompting a congratulatory call from the king of Sweden. Brack was the IndyCar Series champion in 1998.

Robby McGehee finished fifth and won Rookie of the Year.

Brack led for sixty-six laps, Luyendyk, sixty-three, Ray, thirty-two, and Gordon, twenty-eight laps.

1999 Winner Kenny Brack gives A.J. Foyt his first win as a car owner after his retirement from driving.

RACE RESULTS FOR THE 1999 INDIANAPOLIS 500

Finish	Start	Car Num.	Driver	Car Name/Entrant*	Make/Model	Status	Laps	Led	Winnings
1	8	14	Kenny Brack	A.J. Foyt PowerTeam Racing	Dallara/Oldsmobile Aurora	153.176	200	66	$1,465,190
2	14	21	Jeff Ward	Yahoo/MerchantOnline	Dallara/Oldsmobile Aurora	153.091	200	3	$583,150
3	3	11	Billy Boat	A.J. Foyt Racing	Dallara/Oldsmobile Aurora	152.853	200	0	$435,200
4	4	32	Robby Gordon	Glidden/Menards	Dallara/Oldsmobile Aurora	152.180	200	28	$253,270
5	27	55	Robby McGehee (R)	Energizer Advanced Formula	Dallara/Oldsmobile Aurora	Running	199	0	$247,750
6	32	84	Robbie Buhl	A.J. Foyt Racing	Dallara/Oldsmobile Aurora	Running	199	0	$257,500
7	22	91	Buddy Lazier (W)	Delta Faucet/Coors Light/Tae-Bo/Hemelgarn	Dallara/Oldsmobile Aurora	Running	198	0	$285,100
8	17	81	Robby Unser	PetroMoly/Team Pelfrey	Dallara/Oldsmobile Aurora	Running	197	0	$195,500
9	24	22	Tony Stewart	The Home Depot	Dallara/Oldsmobile Aurora	Running	196	0	$186,670
10	10	54	Hideshi Matsuda	Mini Juke-Beck Motorsports	Dallara/Oldsmobile Aurora	Running	196	0	$186,000
11	11	9	Davey Hamilton	Galles Racing Spinal Conquest	Dallara/Oldsmobile Aurora	Running	196	0	$220,500
12	33	3	Raul Boesel	Brant Racing R&S MKV	Riley & Scott/Olds. Aurora	Running	195	0	$248,600
13	12	42	John Hollansworth Jr. (R)	pcsave.com/Lycos	Dallara/Oldsmobile Aurora	Running	192	0	$265,400
14	15	20	Tyce Carlson	Pennzoil/Damon's/Bluegreen	Dallara/Oldsmobile Aurora	Running	190	0	$247,000
15	21	96	Jeret Schroeder (R)	Purity Farms/Cobb Racing	G Force/Infiniti Indy	Engine	175	0	$176,250
16	5	28	Mark Dismore	MCI WorldCom	Dallara/Oldsmobile Aurora	Accident	168	0	$235,300
17	20	19	Stan Wattles	Metro Racing Systems/NCLD	Dallara/Oldsmobile Aurora	Running	147	0	$158,000
18	16	51	Eddie Cheever Jr. (W)	Team Cheever/Children's Beverage Group	Dallara/Infiniti Indy	Engine	139	4	$246,800
19	26	12	Buzz Calkins	Bradley Food Marts/Sav-O-Mat	G Force/Oldsmobile Aurora	Running	133	0	$228,000
20	23	33	Roberto Moreno	Truscelli Team Racing/Warner Bros.	G Force/Oldsmobile Aurora	Gearbox	122	0	$225,670
21	2	2	Greg Ray	Glidden/Menards	Dallara/Oldsmobile Aurora	Accident pits	120	32	$204,900
22	1	5	Arie Luyendyk (W)	Sprint PCS/Meijer	G Force/Oldsmobile Aurora	Accident	117	63	$382,350
23	29	52	Wim Eyckmans (R)	EGP/Beaulieu of America	Dallara/Oldsmobile Aurora	Timing chain	113	0	$145,250
24	28	30	Jimmy Kite	Alfa Laval/Team Losi/Fastrod	G Force/Oldsmobile Aurora	Engine	111	0	$228,000
25	25	50	Roberto Guerrero	Cobb Racing	G Force/Infiniti Indy	Engine	105	0	$217,000
26	13	35	Steve Knapp	Delco Remy-ThermoTech-Microphonics	G Force/Oldsmobile Aurora	Handling	104	0	$216,000
27	9	4	Scott Goodyear	Pennzoil Panther	G Force/Oldsmobile Aurora	Engine	101	0	$217,500
28	6	8	Scott Sharp	Delphi Automotive Systems	Dallara/Oldsmobile Aurora	Transmission	83	0	$221,500
29	19	98	Donnie Beechler	Cahill Racing/Big Daddy's BBQ	Dallara/Oldsmobile Aurora	Engine	74	0	$143,000
30	7	99	Sam Schmidt	Unistar Auto Insurance	G Force/Oldsmobile Aurora	Accident	62	4	$213,800
31	31	17	Jack Miller	Dean's Milk Chug	Dallara/Oldsmobile Aurora	Clutch	29	0	$146,000
32	30	92	Johnny Unser	Tae-Bo/Hemelgarn/Homier Tool/Delta Faucet	Dallara/Oldsmobile Aurora	Brakes	10	0	$161,000
33	18	6	Eliseo Salazar	FUBU Nienhouse Racing	G Force/Oldsmobile Aurora	Accident	7	0	$141,000

* - complete car name/entrant data not available for all entries
(R) - Indicated Rookie
(W) - Indicates Past Winner

2000

A new ten-story pagoda-like structure took the place of the master control tower.

New suites were built atop the north tower terrace on the inside of the track.

The first top CART team to enter the "500" since the IRL/CART split was the Ganassi Team, which was coming off four straight CART titles. Juan Pablo Montoya and veteran Jimmy Vasser were the Ganassi drivers. Montoya was the reigning CART champion in his rookie season. Chip Ganassi himself raced in five "500s" (1982-1986).

Goodyear Tire & Rubber Co. was not at the Speedway for the first time in thirty-six years.

Al Unser Jr. was back at Indy, driving for Rick Galles.

Greg Ray took the pole at 223.988 mph for Team Menard, with Montoya and Eliseo Salazar on the front row. Ray had started second the previous two years. (He would also qualify second in 2001.)

Sarah Fisher became the third woman to qualify for the "500" with a nineteenth-place starting position at only nineteen years old.

Lyn St. James qualified for the thirty-second starting position. For the first time in history, two women would compete in the same "500."

Andy Hillenburg, a rookie, qualified a car sponsored by Sumar with a similar white and blue paint scheme as the Sumar Specials that raced in the 1950s.

Greg Ray took the early lead and led the first twenty-six laps.

Montoya took the lead and held it for all but seven of the remaining laps.

Ray had one brush with the wall while attempting to keep up with Montoya, and later crashed in pursuit on lap sixty-seven. He finished in thirty-third position. Only Bill Homeier in 1954 raced more laps (seventy-four laps) to finish thirty-third.

Lyn St. James and Sarah Fisher got together and crashed at about the one-third point in the race, resulting in thirty-second and thirty-first-place finishes. This would be St. James's last 500.

Montoya led Buddy Lazier to the checker by seven seconds and averaged 167.6 mph in his Target G Force/Oldsmobile.

Montoya led 167 laps, Ray, 26, Vasser, 5, and Robby McGehee, 2 laps.

Montoya was the first rookie to win since Graham Hill in 1966 and the first Columbian winner in history.

This was Chip Ganassi's first 500 victory as a sole owner, as Pat Patrick and Ganassi had been co-owners of Emerson Fittipaldi's car in 1989.

Rookie winner Juan Pablo Montoya becomes the first rookie winner since Graham Hill in 1966. He is shown with the Target/Ganassi crew.

RACE RESULTS FOR THE 2000 INDIANAPOLIS 500

Finish	Start	Car Num.	Driver	Car Name/Entrant*	Make/Model	Status	Laps	Led	Winnings
1	2	9	Juan Pablo Montoya (R)	Target	G Force/Oldsmobile	167.607	200	167	$1,235,690
2	16	91	Buddy Lazier (W)	Delta Faucet/Coors Light/Tae-Bo/Hemelgarn	Dallara/Oldsmobile	167.495	200	0	$574,600
3	3	11	Eliseo Salazar	Rio A.J. Foyt Racing	G Force/Oldsmobile	167.362	200	0	$474,900
4	6	14	Jeff Ward	Harrah's A.J. Foyt Racing	G Force/Oldsmobile	167.320	200	0	$361,000
5	10	51	Eddie Cheever Jr. (W)	#51 Excite@Home Indy Race Car	Dallara/Nissan Infiniti	167.315	200	0	$364,500
6	4	32	Robby Gordon	Turtle Wax/Burger King/Moen/JM	Dallara/Oldsmobile	167.309	200	0	$216,355
7	7	10	Jimmy Vasser	Target	G Force/Oldsmobile	Running	199	5	$207,505
8	20	7	Stephan Gregoire	Mexmil/Tokheim/Viking Air Tools	G Force/Oldsmobile	Running	199	0	$306,900
9	13	4	Scott Goodyear	Pennzoil Panther	Dallara/Oldsmobile	Running	199	0	$348,800
10	5	8	Scott Sharp	Delphi Automotive Systems/MCI WorldCom	Dallara/Oldsmobile	Running	198	0	$313,000
11	11	28	Mark Dismore	On Star/GM BuyPower/Bryant H. & C.	Dallara/Oldsmobile	Running	198	0	$294,500
12	15	98	Donnie Beechler	Cahill Racing	Dallara/Oldsmobile	Running	198	0	$283,000
13	26	33	Jaques Lazier (R)	Miles of Hope/Truscelli Team Racing	G Force/Oldsmobile	Running	198	0	$290,250
14	29	6	Jeret Schroeder	Kroger/Tri Star Motorsports Inc.	Dallara/Oldsmobile	Running	198	0	$279,000
15	31	41	Billy Boat	Harrah's A.J. Foyt Racing	G Force/Oldsmobile	Running	198	0	$211,000
16	24	55	Raul Boesel	Epson	G Force/Oldsmobile	Running	197	0	$213,000
17	17	50	Jason Leffler (R)	UnitedAuto Group	G Force/Oldsmobile	Running	197	0	$170,905
18	22	12	Buzz Calkins	Bradley Motorsports/Team CAN	Dallara/Oldsmobile	Running	194	0	$169,000
19	27	23	Steve Knapp	Dreyer & Reinbold Racing	G Force/Nissan Infiniti	Running	193	0	$167,000
20	28	16	Davey Hamilton	FreeInternet.com/TeamXtreme	G Force/Oldsmobile	Running	188	0	$166,500
21	12	5	Robby McGehee	Meijer/Energizer Advanced Formula/Mall.com	G Force/Oldsmobile	Running	187	2	$281,400
22	30	22	Johnny Unser	Delco Remy/Microdigicom/Homier Tools	G Force/Oldsmobile	Running	186	0	$161,000
23	8	92	Stan Wattles	Hemelgarn/Metro Racing	Dallara/Oldsmobile	Engine	172	0	$159,000
24	14	18	Sam Hornish Jr. (R)	Hornish Bros. Trucking/APC	Dallara/Oldsmobile	Accident	153	0	$268,250
25	21	88	Airton Daré (R)	TeamXtreme/USACredit.com/FreeInternet.com	G Force/Oldsmobile	Engine	126	0	$262,250
26	9	24	Robbie Buhl	Team Purex Dreyer & Reinbold Racing	G Force/Oldsmobile	Engine	99	0	$258,500
27	23	75	Richie Hearn	Pagan Racing	Dallara/Oldsmobile	Electrical	97	0	$155,000
28	33	48	Andy Hillenburg (R)	SUMAR Special by Irwindale Speedway	Dallara/Oldsmobile	Wheel bearing	91	0	$154,250
29	18	3	Al Unser Jr. (W)	Galles ECR Racing Tickets.com Starz	G Force/Oldsmobile	Overheating	89	0	$256,000
30	25	27	Jimmy Kite	Big Daddy's BBQ/Founders Bank	G Force/Oldsmobile	Engine	74	0	$164,000
31	19	15	Sarah Fisher (R)	Walker Racing Cummins	Dallara/Oldsmobile	Accident	71	0	$165,750
32	32	90	Lyn St. James	Yellow Freight Systems	G Force/Oldsmobile	Accident	69	0	$152,000
33	1	1	Greg Ray	Team Conseco/Quaker State/Menards	Dallara/Oldsmobile	Accident	67	26	$388,700

* - complete car name/entrant data not available for all entries
(R) - Indicated Rookie
(W) - Indicates Past Winner

2001

Defending champion Juan Pablo Montoya was racing Formula One for the Williams Team and not at Indy to defend his title.

Jimmy Vasser and Tony Stewart drove for Ganassi, joining Bruno Junqueira and Nicolas Minassian.

Roger Penske returned to the "500" with Gil de Ferran and Helio Castroneves.

Team Green returned with Michael Andretti.

Arie Luyendyk made a comeback with Treadway Racing after a two-year retirement.

William N. Salin II, President of Salin Bank, joined the 500 Festival Board of Directors for his first year of a six year term.

For the first time in history, a truck would pace the race, the Oldsmobile Bravada. Also for the first time in history a woman would drive the pace vehicle, supermodel Elaine Irwin-Mellencamp.

Scott Sharp won the pole at 226.037 mph in his Delphi Automotive Dallara/Oldsmobile, with Greg Ray and Robby Gordon joining him on the front row.

Scott Sharp took the lead at the start but spun and hit the wall in the first turn of lap one to finish thirty-third.

Gordon and Ray split the lead for the first forty-five laps.

Michael Andretti started twenty-first and took the lead on lap forty-seven.

Rain appeared just past the halfway point and forced a yellow from lap 107 to 118.

Penske's Gil de Ferran led laps 110 to 136. Tony Stewart led the next 12 laps. Stewart was trying to win two races in one day, the Indy 500 and the NASCAR World 600.

Rain returned on lap 148 and the race was stopped on lap 155 before being resumed fifteen minutes later.

The race went green on lap 157 with Castroneves in the lead. He would lead to the checker. Castroneves averaged 141.6 mph in his Marlboro sponsored Dallara/Oldsmobile because of eight cautions for fifty-six laps.

Castroneves beat teammate de Ferran by 1.7 seconds, with Michael Andretti third. After his cool-down lap, Castroneves drove to the start/finish line, exited his car and climbed the fence, to the delight of the crowd.

The Brazilian Castroneves also won the Rookie of the Year award.

Penske Racing's first and second-place finishes were a first for the team. It was also the eleventh win for Team Penske.

Bruno Junqueira, driving for Chip Ganassi, made up a deficit of five laps early in the race and finished in fifth place on the lead lap.

Castroneves joined Ray Harroun, Jules Goux, René Thomas, Frank Lockhart, George Souders, Louis Meyer, Graham Hill, and Juan Pablo Montoya as drivers who won in their first start. It was the first time since 1928 that there were back-to-back rookie winners.

Castroneves led fifty-two laps, Ray, forty, Mark Dismore, twenty-nine, Gil de Ferran, twenty-seven, Gordon, twenty-two, and Michael Andretti, sixteen.

Rookie winner Helio Castroneves climbs the fence in celebration, to the delight of the crowd.

RACE RESULTS FOR THE 2001 INDIANAPOLIS 500

Finish	Start	Car Num.	Driver	Car Name/Entrant*	Make/Model	Status	Laps	Led	Winnings
1	11	68	Helio Castroneves (R)	Marlboro Team Penske	Dallara/Oldsmobile	141.574	200	52	$1,270,475
2	5	66	Gil de Ferran	Marlboro Team Penske	Dallara/Oldsmobile	141.555	200	27	$482,775
3	21	39	Michael Andretti	Motorola/Archipelago	Dallara/Oldsmobile	141.510	200	16	$346,225
4	12	44	Jimmy Vasser	Target Chip Ganassi Racing	G Force/Oldsmobile	141.419	200	0	$233,325
5	20	50	Bruno Junqueira (R)	Target Chip Ganassi Racing	G Force/Oldsmobile	141.271	200	0	$255,825
6	7	33	Tony Stewart	Target Chip Ganassi Racing	G Force/Oldsmobile	141.157	200	13	$218,850
7	28	14	Eliseo Salazar	Harrah's A.J. Foyt Racing	Dallara/Oldsmobile	Running	199	0	$356,300
8	30	88	Airton Daré	1-800-BAR NONE TeamXtreme	G Force/Oldsmobile	Running	199	0	$320,325
9	32	98	Billy Boat	CURB Records	Dallara/Oldsmobile	Running	199	0	$337,325
10	33	21	Felipe Giaffone (R)	Hollywood	G Force/Oldsmobile	Running	199	0	$211,575
11	14	10	Robby McGehee	Cahill Racing Cure Autism Now	Dallara/Oldsmobile	Running	199	0	$290,825
12	24	12	Buzz Calkins	Bradley Food Marts/Sav-O-Mat	Dallara/Oldsmobile	Running	198	0	$286,025
13	6	5	Arie Luyendyk (W)	Meijer	G Force/Oldsmobile	Running	198	1	$182,275
14	13	4	Sam Hornish Jr.	Pennzoil Panther	Dallara/Oldsmobile	Running	196	0	$308,825
15	9	24	Robbie Buhl	Team Purex Dreyer & Reinbold Racing	G Force/Infiniti	Running	196	0	$300,325
16	4	28	Mark Dismore	Delphi Auto. Systems/Bryant H. & C.	Dallara/Oldsmobile	Running	195	29	$287,375
17	2	2	Greg Ray	Johns Manville/Menards	Dallara/Oldsmobile	Running	192	40	$335,325
18	10	91	Buddy Lazier (W)	Tae-Bo/Coors Light/Delta Faucet	Dallara/Oldsmobile	Running	192	0	$262,325
19	31	16	Cory Witherill (R)	Radio Shack	G Force/Oldsmobile	Running	187	0	$159,575
20	23	9	Jeret Schroeder	Purity Products	G Force/Oldsmobile	Running	187	0	$256,325
21	3	41	Robby Gordon	Team Conseco/Foyt/RCR Childress Racing	Dallara/Oldsmobile	Running	184	22	$173,225
22	17	77	Jaques Lazier	Classmates.com/Jonathan Byrd's Cafeteria	G Force/Oldsmobile	Running	183	0	$161,325
23	26	99	Davey Hamilton	Sam Schmidt Motorsports Racing	Dallara/Oldsmobile	Engine	182	0	$280,325
24	8	35	Jeff Ward	Aerosmith/Heritage Motorsports/Menards	G Force/Oldsmobile	Running	168	0	$248,325
25	27	84	Donnie Beechler	Harrah's A.J. Foyt Racing	Dallara/Oldsmobile	Running	160	0	$172,325
26	25	51	Eddie Cheever Jr. (W)	#51 Excite@Home Indy Race Car	Dallara/Infiniti	Electrical	108	0	$247,325
27	18	6	Jon Herb (R)	Tri Star Motorsports Inc.	Dallara/Oldsmobile	Accident	104	0	$245,575
28	29	36	Stephan Gregoire	Heritage Motorsports/Delco Remy/Menards	G Force/Oldsmobile	Oil leak	86	0	$154,325
29	22	49	Nicolas Minassian (R)	Target Chip Ganassi Racing	G Force/Oldsmobile	Gearbox	74	0	$149,575
30	19	3	Al Unser Jr. (W)	Galles Racing Starz Super-Pak Budweiser	G Force/Oldsmobile	Accident	16	0	$255,825
31	15	15	Sarah Fisher	Walker Racing Kroger	Dallara/Oldsmobile	Accident	7	0	$247,325
32	16	52	Scott Goodyear	#52 Thermos Grill2Go Cheever Indy Racing	Dallara/Infiniti	Accident	7	0	$143,325
33	1	8	Scott Sharp	Delphi Automotive Systems	Dallara/Oldsmobile	Accident	0	0	$427,325

* - complete car name/entrant data not available for all entries
(R) - Indicated Rookie
(W) - Indicates Past Winner

2002

Penske Racing had decided to be a full-time competitor in the IRL rather than CART.

The SAFER barrier (Steel and Foam Energy Reduction), spearheaded by Tony George, was installed on high impact areas of the Speedway's walls.

On opening day Robbie McGehee took the dubious honor of being the first to hit the highly effective SAFER barrier.

Bruno Junqueira, driving for Ganassi, was a surprise pole winner at 231.342 mph. Robbie Buhl and Raul Boesel joined him on row one.

Helio Castroneves qualified thirteenth and Gil de Ferran fourteenth for Penske Racing. Paul Tracy qualified twenty-ninth on the final day of qualifications.

Rookie George Mack qualified for the 32nd starting position, becoming the second African American to compete in the Indy 500. Mack was one of the world's top KART drivers.

Junqueira took the lead at the start and led the first thirty-two laps.

After the first 32 laps, rookie Tomas Scheckter led the majority of the race to lap 172 (actually, all but 55 laps).

On lap 173, Scheckter, leading by ten seconds, was eliminated when he went high coming out of turn four and hit the wall.

Felipe Giaffone took the lead briefly, but pitted on lap 177. Helio Castroneves took the lead for the first time, but was very tight on fuel to make it to the checker.

Paul Tracy had moved up through the field all day and was now in second place.

Tracy hounded Castroneves and finally made his move in turn three with just over a lap to go. Just before Tracy passed Castroneves, the cars of Laurent Redon and Buddy Lazier tangled in turn two and the caution came on.

Tracy actually took the checkered flag first, but shortly after, it was determined that Castroneves was still in the lead when the yellow came on. Castroneves averaged 166.5 mph for his second consecutive win.

In the post-race interview Tracy handled himself in a very professional manner in view of the difficult situation.

Scheckter and fourth-place finisher Alex Barron shared the Rookie of the Year award.

Castroneves became the first driver in history to win the 500 in each of his first two attempts. He was undefeated at Indy!

He also became only the fifth driver to win back to back: Shaw, Rose, Vukovich, Al Unser Sr. and Castroneves.

Paul Tracy and team owner Barry Green disputed the Castroneves win, but Tony George ended the controversy by deciding some six weeks later that the race day decision would stand.

Scheckter led eighty-five laps, Junqueira, thirty-two, Castroneves, twenty-four, and Tony Kanaan, twenty-three laps.

The SAFER (steel and foam energy reduction) barrier being installed.

RACE RESULTS FOR THE 2002 INDIANAPOLIS 500

Finish	Start	Car Num.	Driver	Car Name/Entrant*	Make/Model	Status	Laps	Led	Winnings
1	13	3	Helio Castroneves (W)	Marlboro Team Penske	Dallara/Chevrolet	166.499	200	24	$1,606,215
2	29	26	Paul Tracy	Team Green 7-Eleven	Dallara/Chevrolet	166.484	200	0	$489,315
3	4	21	Felipe Giaffone	Hollywood Mo Nunn Racing	G Force/Chevrolet	166.482	200	12	$480,315
4	26	44	Alex Barron (R)	Rayovac Blair Racing	Dallara/Chevrolet	166.477	200	7	$412,115
5	6	51	Eddie Cheever Jr. (W)	Red Bull Cheever Racing	Dallara/Infiniti	166.461	200	0	$348,515
6	22	20	Richie Hearn	Grill 2 Go Sam Schmidt Motorsports	Dallara/Chevrolet	166.450	200	0	$330,815
7	25	39	Michael Andretti	Motorola/Archipelago	Dallara/Chevrolet	166.444	200	0	$218,715
8	11	31	Robby Gordon	Menards/Childress/Cingular	Dallara/Chevrolet	166.405	200	0	$204,000
9	15	9	Jeff Ward	Target Chip Ganassi Racing	G Force/Chevrolet	166.383	200	0	$308,815
10	14	6	Gil de Ferran	Marlboro Team Penske	Dallara/Chevrolet	166.061	200	13	$293,165
11	21	22	Kenny Brack (W)	Target Chip Ganassi Racing	G Force/Chevrolet	165.995	200	0	$188,315
12	12	7	Al Unser Jr. (W)	Corteco/Bryant	Dallara/Chevrolet	Running	199	1	$288,765
13	30	14	Airton Daré	Harrah's A.J. Foyt Racing	Dallara/Chevrolet	Running	199	0	$281,815
14	24	55	Arie Luyendyk (W)	Meijer	G Force/Chevrolet	Running	199	0	$338,815
15	20	91	Buddy Lazier (W)	Coors Light/Life Fitness/Tae-Bo/Delta Faucet	Dallara/Chevrolet	Accident	198	0	$277,615
16	2	24	Robbie Buhl	Team Purex/Aventis/Dreyer & Reinbold Racing	G Force/Infiniti	Running	198	0	$288,315
17	32	30	George Mack (R)	310 Racing	G Force/Chevrolet	Running	198	0	$283,565
18	23	98	Billy Boat	CURB Records	Dallara/Chevrolet	Running	198	0	$286,315
19	28	27	Dario Franchitti (R)	Team Green 7-Eleven	Dallara/Chevrolet	Running	197	0	$153,565
20	27	12	Shigeaki Hattori (R)	Epson	Dallara/Infiniti	Running	197	0	$161,565
21	3	2	Raul Boesel	Menards/Johns Manville	Dallara/Chevrolet	Running	197	0	$268,315
22	16	34	Laurent Redon (R)	Mi-Jack	Dallara/Infiniti	Accident	197	0	$256,565
23	18	53	Max Papis (R)	Red Bull Cheever Racing	Dallara/Infiniti	Running	196	0	$153,565
24	9	23	Sarah Fisher	Team Allegra/Dreyer & Reinbold Racing	G Force/Infiniti	Running	196	0	$163,315
25	7	4	Sam Hornish Jr.	Pennzoil Panther	Dallara/Chevrolet	Running	186	0	$253,815
26	10	52	Tomas Scheckter (R)	Red Bull Cheever Racing	Dallara/Infiniti	Accident	172	85	$294,815
27	8	8	Scott Sharp	Delphi	Dallara/Chevrolet	Accident	137	3	$255,665
28	5	17	Tony Kanaan (R)	Hollywood Mo Nunn Racing	G Force/Chevrolet	Accident	89	23	$167,665
29	17	5	Rick Treadway (R)	Sprint/Kyocera Wireless/Airlink Enterprises	G Force/Chevrolet	Accident	88	0	$147,565
30	19	19	Jimmy Vasser	Miller Lite/Rahal Letterman Racing	Dallara/Chevrolet	Gearbox	87	0	$151,315
31	1	33	Bruno Junqueira	Target Chip Ganassi Racing	G Force/Chevrolet	Gearbox	87	32	$282,715
32	33	99	Mark Dismore	Grill 2 Go Sam Schmidt Motorsports	Dallara/Chevrolet	Handling	58	0	$145,315
33	31	11	Greg Ray	AJ Foyt Racing/Harrah's	Dallara/Chevrolet	Accident	28	0	$245,315

* - complete car name/entrant data not available for all entries
(R) - Indicated Rookie
(W) - Indicates Past Winner

2003

Team Green, Target Chip Ganassi, Rahal-Letterman, Mo Nunn and Fernandez/Suzuki, had joined the IRL.

Honda and Toyota became engine options, along with the Chevrolet V-8.

Mario Andretti, the 1969 Indianapolis 500 champion, walked away from a spectacular testing accident on April 23rd. Andretti, at 63 years old, had volunteered to drive a testing session for the injured Tony Kanaan for Andretti Green Racing. After hitting a chunk of debris, his Dallara/Honda became airborne and went into several reverse somersaults before landing right-side up. Andretti had been retired since 1994.

Helio Castroneves was attempting to be the first driver in history to win the Indianapolis 500 three consecutive years. His first two races at Indy had resulted in victories.

Gil de Ferran had been injured in an accident at Phoenix in the spring. He sustained a broken vertebrae and concussion and missed the next race in Japan. de Ferran was medically cleared to drive just days before opening of practice.

Helio Castroneves won the pole at 231.725 mph, with Tony Kanaan and Robby Gordon on the front row.

Michael Andretti announced this would be his last race. Andretti was now the majority owner of Andretti Green Racing, and planned on focusing on team management. He qualified thirteenth.

A.J. Foyt IV qualified twenty-third and would become the youngest driver to ever compete in the race. He turned nineteen years old on race day.

Castroneves took the lead at the start and led the first sixteen laps. Scott Dixon, Michael Andretti and Tomas Scheckter led almost all of the laps to the halfway point. Andretti dropped out on lap 94 with a throttle linkage problem.

The second half was a battle between Castroneves and Scheckter, with Gil de Ferran climbing steadily from his tenth starting position.

Scheckter led from lap 101 to 128. Castroneves led from lap 129 to 165. Castroneves pitted on lap 165 and the lead was swapped by Tony Kanaan, Scheckter and Tora Tokagi. In the meantime, de Ferran had passed his teammate Castroneves, who was attempting to win his third straight "500."

On lap 170, de Ferran took the lead.

On lap 187, Dan Wheldon crashed seriously between turns three and four, but was uninjured as his car turned upside down.

The race went green on lap 194 and de Ferran, in his Toyota-powered Panoz G Force, held off Castroneves by .2990 seconds. This represented the first Indy 500 win for Toyota. Gil de Ferran averaged 156.3 mph. Kanaan finished third, Scheckter fourth and Tora Takagi fifth, winning Rookie of the Year and becoming the highest-finishing Japanese driver in history.

Roger Penske tied Lou Moore for being the winning car owner in three straight "500s" (Moore won in 1947, 1948, and 1949). This was Penske's thirteenth win at the "500."

Gil de Ferran climbed the fence in celebration and was joined by teammate Castroneves. A very emotional de Ferran was overjoyed in Victory Circle.

Scheckter led sixty-three laps, Castroneves, fifty-eight, de Ferran, thirty-one, and Andretti, twenty-eight.

On a cool October morning, Tony Renna lost his life in a tire testing accident in turn three in his newly acquired Ganassi ride.

Helio Castroneves joins his teammate and "500" winner Gil de Ferran climbing the fence in celebration.

RACE RESULTS FOR THE 2003 INDIANAPOLIS 500

Finish	Start	Car Num.	Driver	Car Name/Entrant*	Make/Model	Status	Laps	Led	Winnings
1	10	6	Gil de Ferran	Marlboro Team Penske	Panoz G Force/Toyota	156.291	200	31	$1,353,265
2	1	3	Helio Castroneves (W)	Marlboro Team Penske	Dallara/Toyota	156.287	200	58	$739,665
3	2	11	Tony Kanaan	Team 7-Eleven	Dallara/Honda	156.274	200	2	$486,465
4	12	10	Tomas Scheckter	Target Chip Ganassi Racing	Panoz G Force/Toyota	156.268	200	63	$448,415
5	7	12	Tora Takagi (R)	Pioneer Mo Nunn Racing	Panoz G Force/Toyota	156.264	200	2	$363,515
6	25	20	Alex Barron	Meijer Mo Nunn Racing	Panoz G Force/Toyota	156.209	200	0	$297,265
7	8	32	Tony Renna (R)	Cure Autism Now/HomeMed	Dallara/Toyota	156.189	200	0	$206,315
8	14	13	Greg Ray	TrimSpa	Panoz G Force/Honda	156.134	200	0	$299,065
9	17	31	Al Unser Jr. (W)	Corteco	Dallara/Toyota	156.055	200	0	$296,565
10	11	55	Roger Yasukawa (R)	Panasonic ARTA	Dallara/Honda	155.320	199	0	$288,815
11	19	52	Buddy Rice (R)	Red Bull Cheever Racing	Dallara/Chevrolet	Running	199	0	$323,315
12	26	22	Vitor Meira (R)	Metabolife/Johns Manville/Menards	Dallara/Chevrolet	Running	199	0	$192,315
13	32	18	Jimmy Kite	Denny Hecker's Auto Connection	Dallara/Chevrolet	Running	197	0	$273,565
14	15	54	Shinji Nakano (R)	Beard Papa's	Dallara/Honda	Running	196	0	$269,315
15	18	4	Sam Hornish Jr.	Pennzoil Panther	Dallara/Chevrolet	Engine	195	0	$271,065
16	6	15	Kenny Brack (W)	Rahal/Letterman/Miller Lite/Pioneer	Dallara/Honda	Running	195	0	$271,065
17	4	9	Scott Dixon (R)	Target Chip Ganassi Racing	Panoz G Force/Toyota	Accident	191	15	$304,315
18	23	14	A.J. Foyt IV (R)	Conseco/A.J. Foyt Racing	Dallara/Toyota	Running	189	0	$264,315
19	5	26	Dan Wheldon (R)	Klein Tools/Jim Beam	Dallara/Honda	Accident	186	0	$161,815
20	9	8	Scott Sharp	Delphi	Dallara/Toyota	Accident	181	0	$257,815
21	21	91	Buddy Lazier (W)	Victory Brand/Delta Faucet/Life Fitness	Dallara/Chevrolet	Engine	171	0	$276,065
22	3	27	Robby Gordon	Archipelago/Motorola	Dallara/Honda	Gearbox	169	0	$256,250
23	22	24	Robbie Buhl	Purex/Aventis/Dreyer & Reinbold	Dallara/Chevrolet	Engine	147	0	$252,065
24	33	41	Airton Daré	Conseco A.J. Foyt Racing	Panoz G Force/Toyota	Accident	125	0	$166,065
25	31	44	Robby McGehee	Pedigo Chevrolet Panther Racing	Dallara/Chevrolet	Steering	125	0	$151,565
26	27	19	Jimmy Vasser	Argent Rahal/Letterman Racing	Dallara/Honda	Gearbox	102	1	$161,265
27	13	7	Michael Andretti	Team 7-Eleven	Dallara/Honda	Throttle linkage	94	28	$259,415
28	28	99	Richie Hearn	Contour Hardening/Curb Agajanian/SSM	Panoz G Force/Toyota	Accident	61	0	$142,565
29	20	2	Jaques Lazier	Menards/Johns Manville	Dallara/Chevrolet	Accident	61	0	$240,315
30	30	5	Shigeaki Hattori	Epson/A.J. Foyt Racing	Dallara/Toyota	Fuel System	19	0	$240,065
31	24	23	Sarah Fisher	AOL/GMAC/Raybestos/DRR	Dallara/Chevrolet	Engine/accident	14	0	$244,065
32	29	98	Billy Boat	Pedigo Chevrolet Panther Racing	Dallara/Chevrolet	Engine	7	0	$139,065
33	16	21	Felipe Giaffone	Hollywood Mo Nunn Racing	Panoz G Force/Toyota	Electrical	6	0	$242,815

* - complete car name/entrant data not available for all entries
(R) - Indicated Rookie
(W) - Indicates Past Winner

2004

Buddy Rice was a replacement for Kenny Brack for Rahal-Letterman Racing, as Brack had been seriously injured at Texas the previous fall.

Penske Racing had a new driver, two-time IRL champion Sam Hornish Jr., as Gil de Ferran had retired. Hornish rewarded the team by being the first new Penske driver to win his debut race (Homestead).

Engine sizes had been dropped from 3.5 liters to 3.0, which resulted in speeds dropping significantly.

Buddy Rice won the pole at 222.024 mph. Dan Wheldon and Dario Franchitti, both of Andretti Green Racing, joined Rice on the front row.

P.J. Jones, son of 1963 winner Parnelli Jones, qualified thirty-first in a car with the same number and paint scheme as his father's 1963 winning car.

Race day brought overcast skies and rain predictions. The start of the race was delayed for two hours.

Morgan Freeman, Academy award-winning actor, drove the Chevrolet Corvette C5 for the start of the 88th Indianapolis 500.

Buddy Rice took the lead at the start, leading the first twelve laps before an early pit stop.

Rice led twenty-eight of the first fifty laps, while Wheldon led seventeen.

The red flag came out on lap twenty-seven for more than two hours because of rain.

Rice took the lead on lap fifty-nine, leading until pitting on lap ninety-eight.

The lead swapped between Wheldon, Tony Kanaan, Franchitti and Bruno Junqueira before Rice took it on lap 152.

Rice pitted on lap 167 and lost the lead to Bryan Herta, then Adrian Fernandez, but regained it on lap 172 after the leaders pitted for fuel despite threatening weather.

On lap 174, rain caused a yellow light. Rain continued and the red and checkered flags were waved simultaneously on lap 180, with Buddy Rice the winner. Rice averaged 138.5 mph with eight cautions for 56 laps.

Rice's win gave Rahal-Letterman and Honda their first Indy 500 victory.

The month of May was near-perfect for Buddy Rice by winning the pole, the pit stop competition, leading the most laps and winning his first IndyCar race in only his second Indianapolis 500. This was the first time since 1991 with Rick Mears that the race winner also won the pole and the pit stop competition.

The victory celebration was moved inside for the first time in history because of extremely bad weather. An F-2 class tornado missed the Speedway by approximately six miles. Significant damage resulted in south central Indianapolis.

Tony Kanaan finished second, Wheldon, third, and Franchitti, fourth, giving Andretti Green Racing second, third and fourth-place finishes. Honda power finished in the top seven positions.

Kosuke Matsuura finished eleventh to win Rookie of the Year.

Rice led ninety-one laps, Kanaan, twenty-eight, and Wheldon, twenty-six.

Tony Kanaan would go on to win the series championship, while completing every lap of every race in his Dallara/Honda combination.

Buddy Rice celebrates in the "green room" as a result of severe weather.

RACE RESULTS FOR THE 2004 INDIANAPOLIS 500

Finish	Start	Car Num.	Driver	Car Name/Entrant*	Make/Model	Status	Laps	Led	Winnings
1	1	15	Buddy Rice	Rahal-Letterman Argent/Pioneer	Panoz G Force/Honda	138.518	180	91	$1,761,740
2	5	11	Tony Kanaan	Team 7-Eleven	Dallara/Honda	138.516	180	28	$659,240
3	2	26	Dan Wheldon	Klein Tools/Jim Beam	Dallara/Honda	138.491	180	26	$533,040
4	23	7	Bryan Herta	XM Satellite Radio	Dallara/Honda	138.489	180	3	$366,440
5	4	36	Bruno Junqueira	PacifiCare/Secure Horizons	Panoz G Force/Honda	138.474	180	16	$296,240
6	7	17	Vitor Meira	Rahal-Letterman Team Centrix	Panoz G Force/Honda	138.463	180	0	$301,240
7	6	5	Adrian Fernandez	Quaker State Telmex Tecate	Panoz G Force/Honda	138.459	180	3	$294,740
8	13	1	Scott Dixon	Target Chip Ganassi Racing	Panoz G Force/Toyota	138.431	180	0	$283,740
9	8	3	Helio Castroneves (W)	Marlboro Team Penske	Dallara/Toyota	138.414	180	0	$311,990
10	12	16	Roger Yasukawa	Rahal-Letterman Racing Sammy	Panoz G Force/Honda	138.401	180	0	$261,740
11	9	55	Kosuke Matsuura (R)	Panasonic ARTA	Panoz G Force/Honda	138.386	180	0	$294,740
12	24	51	Alex Barron	Red Bull Cheever Racing	Dallara/Chevrolet	138.325	180	3	$269,240
13	20	8	Scott Sharp	Delphi	Dallara/Toyota	138.309	180	0	$253,990
14	3	27	Dario Franchitti	Arca/Ex	Dallara/Honda	138.297	180	1	$255,740
15	25	24	Felipe Giaffone	Team Purex/Dreyer & Reinbold	Dallara/Chevrolet	Running	179	0	$249,490
16	29	21	Jeff Simmons (R)	Pioneer Mo Nunn Racing	Dallara/Toyota	Running	179	0	$224,990
17	17	20	Al Unser Jr. (W)	Patrick Racing	Dallara/Chevrolet	Running	179	0	$220,740
18	10	4	Tomas Scheckter	Pennzoil Panther	Dallara/Chevrolet	Running	179	0	$234,240
19	26	12	Tora Takagi	Pioneer Mo Nunn Racing	Dallara/Toyota	Running	179	0	$230,740
20	30	33	Richie Hearn	Lucas Oil Products/Sam Schmidt	Panoz G Force/Toyota	Running	178	0	$207,740
21	19	39	Sarah Fisher	Bryant Heating & Cooling/Cure Autism Now	Dallara/Toyota	Running	177	0	$208,740
22	33	18	Robby McGehee	Burger King Angus Steak Burger PDM	Dallara/Chevrolet	Running	177	0	$202,740
23	28	91	Buddy Lazier (W)	LifeFitness DRR/Hemelgarn Racing	Dallara/Chevrolet	Fuel system	164	0	$212,240
24	32	25	Marty Roth (R)	Roth Racing	Dallara/Toyota	Accident	128	0	$203,990
25	15	10	Darren Manning (R)	Target Chip Ganassi Racing	Panoz G Force/Toyota	Accident	104	0	$227,490
26	11	6	Sam Hornish Jr.	Marlboro Team Penske	Dallara/Toyota	Accident	104	9	$223,240
27	27	13	Greg Ray	Access Motorsports	Panoz G Force/Honda	Accident	98	0	$239,735
28	31	98	PJ Jones (R)	CURB Records	Dallara/Chevrolet	Accident	92	0	$195,490
29	18	70	Robby Gordon	Meijer/Coca-Cola Robby Gordon	Dallara/Chevrolet	Mechanical	88	0	$192,420
30	14	2	Mark Taylor (R)	Menards/Johns Manville Racing	Dallara/Chevrolet	Accident	62	0	$211,990
31	16	52	Ed Carpenter (R)	Red Bull Cheever Racing	Dallara/Chevrolet	Accident	62	0	$212,485
32	22	41	Larry Foyt (R)	A.J. Foyt Racing	Panoz G Force/Toyota	Accident	54	0	$192,485
33	21	14	A.J. Foyt IV	Conseco/A.J. Foyt Racing	Dallara/Toyota	Handling	26	0	$215,735

* - complete car name/entrant data not available for all entries
(R) - Indicated Rookie
(W) - Indicates Past Winner

2005

Twenty-three-year-old Danica Patrick from Roscoe, Illinois, was entered by Rahal-Letterman Racing.

Patrick sat on the pole and finished fourth at Montegi, Japan, earlier in the year.

Going into qualifications, Patrick had the fast lap of the month at 229.880 mph.

A practice crash in turn two by defending champion Buddy Rice resulted in two broken vertebrae, which eliminated him from competition. Kenny Brack replaced Rice in the Rahal-Letterman car. Brack had overcome serious injury from a 2003 accident at Texas. Rice had replaced the injured Brack for the 2004 500 and won.

A turn two practice accident by Paul Dana broke his neck and put him out of action for the season.

A new qualifying format was unveiled, providing four days of qualifying, with 11 spots to be filled on each of the first three days, the final day being a "bump day."

Tony Kanaan won the pole at 227.566 mph for Andretti Green Racing, with Sam Hornish and Scott Sharp also on row one.

Danica Patrick qualified her Panoz/Honda for the fourth starting position after bobbling in the first turn of her first lap. This was the highest starting position for a woman in history, eclipsing Lyn St. James sixth starting position in 1994. Her second, third and fourth laps were the fastest qualifying laps of 2005.

Kenny Brack actually had the fastest four-lap qualifying speed at 227.698 mph, but was considered a "second day" qualifier so he started twenty-third.

Four-star United States Army General and American statesman Colin Powell drove the Chevrolet Corvette pace car for the noon start of the 89th Indianapolis 500.

Indiana Pacer star Reggie Miller was the honorary flag man for the start.

In the first fifty laps, Hornish, Kanaan and Franchitti traded the lead. On lap fifty-six, Danica Patrick made history by becoming the first woman to ever lead the "500."

Patrick later stalled her car in the pits and lost precious time.

Up to approximately the 150-lap mark Hornish, Kanaan and Franchitti continued to trade the lead.

Hornish was eliminated in a one-car accident in turn one on lap 146.

Patrick was involved in an accident on a restart on lap 155, when she and Tomas Enge hit wheels. She survived, but a chain reaction accident took out Enge, Scheckter and Jeff Bucknum.

Dan Wheldon had started sixteenth, but had moved up consistently to take the lead for the first time on lap 150.

Wheldon pitted for the last time on lap 171. Rahal-Letterman decided to leave Patrick out, banking on further cautions in the hope of conserving fuel. Patrick led from lap 172 to 185.

Wheldon passed Patrick on lap 186, but a caution on lap 187 was caused by Kosuke Matsuura hitting the turn three wall.

On the restart on lap 190, Patrick amazed the crowd by out-dragging Wheldon to the first turn, where she took the lead as the crowd went wild. Patrick led until Wheldon made the winning pass on lap 194. She was forced to back off slightly and nurse her fuel to finish the 500 miles.

Wheldon led to the checker, while Vitor Meira and Bryan Herta were able to overtake Patrick in the final laps.

On lap 199, Sebastian Bourdais was attempting to overtake Patrick when he hit the wall and brought out the yellow. The race ended under yellow with Wheldon, Meira, Herta, Patrick and Buddy Lazier making the top five. Wheldon averaged 157.6 mph.

This was Michael Andretti's first Indy 500 victory as a car owner, after fourteen Indy 500's as a driver without a win.

Danica Patrick won Rookie of the Year, setting off "Danicamania". Patrick's fourth place finish bested Janet Guthrie's ninth place in 1978 for the best finish by a woman.

Hornish led seventy-seven laps, Kanaan, fifty-four, Wheldon, thirty, Patrick, nineteen, and Franchitti, fifteen. There was a total of twenty-seven lead changes between seven drivers.

Dan Wheldon would go on to win the 2005 IRL IndyCar Series Championship for Andretti Green Racing.

Legendary track announcer Tom Carnegie interviews rookie Danica Patrick.

RACE RESULTS FOR THE 2005 INDIANAPOLIS 500

Finish	Start	Car Num.	Driver	Car Name/Entrant*	Make/Model	Status	Laps	Led	Winnings
1	16	26	Dan Wheldon	Klein Tools/Jim Beam	Dallara/Honda	157.603	200	30	$1,537,805
2	7	17	Vitor Meira	Rahal Letterman Menards Johns Manville	Panoz/Honda	157.602	200	3	$656,955
3	18	7	Bryan Herta	XM Satellite Radio	Dallara/Honda	157.601	200	0	$457,505
4	4	16	Danica Patrick (R)	Rahal Letterman Racing Argent Pioneer	Panoz/Honda	157.541	200	19	$378,855
5	9	95	Buddy Lazier (W)	Panther/Jonathan Byrd's/ ESPN 950 AM	Dallara/Chevrolet	157.537	200	0	$288,805
6	6	27	Dario Franchitti	ArcaEx	Dallara/Honda	157.532	200	15	$309,055
7	3	8	Scott Sharp	Delphi	Panoz/Honda	157.526	200	0	$295,305
8	1	11	Tony Kanaan	Team 7-Eleven	Dallara/Honda	157.516	200	54	$467,105
9	5	3	Helio Castroneves (W)	Marlboro Team Penske	Dallara/Toyota	157.496	200	0	$277,805
10	24	33	Ryan Briscoe (R)	Target Chip Ganassi Racing	Panoz/Toyota	Running	199	0	$273,555
11	26	20	Ed Carpenter	Vision Racing	Dallara/Toyota	Running	199	0	$258,305
12	15	37	Sebastien Bourdais (R)	Newman Haas Racing Team Centrix	Panoz/Honda	Accident	198	0	$234,555
13	22	51	Alex Barron	Red Bull Cheever Racing	Dallara/Toyota	Running	197	0	$254,805
14	14	5	Adrian Fernandez	Investment Properties of America	Panoz/Honda	Running	197	0	$226,305
15	33	48	Felipe Giaffone	A.J. Foyt Racing	Panoz/Toyota	Running	194	0	$247,305
16	27	21	Jaques Lazier	Playa Del Racing	Panoz/Toyota	Running	189	0	$219,305
17	8	55	Kosuke Matsuura	Panasonic ARTA	Panoz/Honda	Accident	186	0	$236,305
18	17	24	Roger Yasukawa	Dreyer & Reinbold Racing	Dallara/Honda	Mechanical	167	0	$233,305
19	10	2	Tomas Enge (R)	ROCKSTAR Panther Racing	Dallara/Chevrolet	Accident	155	0	$232,055
20	11	4	Tomas Scheckter	Pennzoil Panther	Dallara/Chevrolet	Accident	154	0	$257,305
21	25	83	Patrick Carpentier (R)	Red Bull Cheever Racing	Dallara/Toyota	Mechanical	153	0	$231,055
22	21	44	Jeff Bucknum (R)	Investment Properties of America	Dallara/Honda	Accident	150	0	$222,555
23	2	6	Sam Hornish Jr.	Marlboro Team Penske	Dallara/Toyota	Accident	146	77	$391,455
24	13	9	Scott Dixon	Target Chip Ganassi Racing	Panoz/Toyota	Accident	113	0	$225,805
25	20	70	Richie Hearn	Meijer/Coca-Cola Racing Special	Panoz/Chevrolet	Accident	112	0	$202,305
26	23	15	Kenny Brack (W)	Rahal Letterman Racing Argent Pioneer	Panoz/Honda	Mechanical	92	0	$275,805
27	31	22	Jeff Ward	Vision Racing	Dallara/Toyota	Handling	92	0	$194,805
28	28	14	A.J. Foyt IV	A.J. Foyt Racing	Dallara/Toyota	Handling	84	0	$218,805
29	19	10	Darren Manning	Target Chip Ganassi Racing	Panoz/Toyota	Mechanical	82	0	$212,805
30	12	36	Bruno Junqueira	Newman Haas Racing Team Centrix	Panoz/Honda	Accident	76	2	$192,205
31	29	25	Marty Roth	Roth Racing/PDM Racing	Dallara/Chevrolet	Handling	47	0	$195,305
32	32	91	Jimmy Kite	Ethanol Hemelgarn Racing	Dallara/Toyota	Handling	47	0	$210,305
33	30	41	Larry Foyt	ABC Supply Co.	Dallara/Toyota	Accident	14	0	$189,305

* - complete car name/entrant data not available for all entries
(R) - Indicated Rookie
(W) - Indicates Past Winner

2006

The ninetieth running of the Indianapolis 500 proved to be one of the most spectacular races in history.

Michael Andretti and Al Unser Jr. came out of retirement to return to the 500. Andretti had last raced in 2003 and Unser last competed in 2004.

Marco Andretti made his rookie debut at only 19 years old, and Arie Luyendyk Jr. also was a rookie.

Paul Dana had been fatally injured in an accident at the season opener at Homestead. Jeff Simmons replaced Dana in the Rahal-Letterman Ethanol sponsored car.

On opening day, three generations of Andrettis opened the track—Marco, Michael and Mario. Michael and Marco drove their current cars, while Mario drove his 1967 pole-winning Brawner Hawk.

Andretti Green Racing entered five cars for Michael Andretti, Marco Andretti, Dario Franchitti, Tony Kanaan and Bryan Herta.

Sam Hornish Jr. for Penske Racing and Dan Wheldon, who was now driving for Ganassi, led the speed charts working toward pole day.

The entire first weekend of qualifications was rained out.

Al Unser Jr., Michael Andretti and Larry Foyt all qualified, which made 2006 the first year since 1992 to have an Andretti, Foyt and Unser in the field.

Sam Hornish Jr. won the pole for Penske Racing at 228.985 mph, with Helio Castroneves and Dan Wheldon joining him on the front row.

Danica Patrick struggled all month with her Panoz Chassis, but qualified well at 224.564 mph and started twelfth.

The record number of former winners in the race was ten in 1992. In 2006, there were six.

The 2006 field had the most number of sons of former drivers in history with nine: Al Unser Jr., Michael Andretti, Marco Andretti, P.J. Jones, Arie Luyendyk Jr., Larry Foyt, Jeff Bucknum, Buddy Lazier, and Jaques Lazier.

Michael Andretti became the only driver in "500" history to race against his father, brother, son, and cousin during his career.

Lance Armstrong, seven-time winner of the Tour de France, drove the Chevrolet Corvette Z-06 pace car for the 1:00 pm start of the 90th Indianapolis 500. Boxing great Sugar Ray Leonard was the honorary starter. Leonard won titles in five weight divisions in his illustrious career.

At the start, Castroneves took the lead. Wheldon passed for the lead on lap 10 and led 141 of the next 171 laps.

Scott Dixon ran in the second position for much of the race, with Hornish running third. On the 151st lap, Hornish pitted and pulled away with the fueling equipment still attached. He received a drive-through penalty under green flag conditions.

As the result of a timely yellow for the Jeff Simmons accident, Hornish was able to stay on the lead lap.

After serving his penalty, Hornish still trailed leader Wheldon by twenty-nine seconds with thirty-four laps remaining. The decision by Roger Penske to pit out of sequence and switch to a fuel conserve mode allowed Hornish to complete the race without another stop. His main competitors were unable to do this.

Dixon's chances of winning were eliminated when he was penalized for blocking Kanaan to protect his teammate, Wheldon, who was leading.

With twenty-five laps remaining, the order was Wheldon, Kanaan, and Marco Andretti.

On lap 183, Kanaan passed Wheldon for the lead. The order was Kanaan, Marco, Franchitti and Michael Andretti for an Andretti Green one-two-three-four.

Kanaan led until the yellow appeared when Felipe Giaffone made wall contact in turn two on lap 191. Prior to the caution, Sam Hornish trailed the leader by more than thirty seconds.

After final pit stops, Michael Andretti took the lead on lap 194 with Marco second and Dixon, Hornish and Wheldon following. Hornish was in fourth place, but was actually ninth in line on the track.

Marco passed his father on lap 198, as did Sam Hornish. At the white flag, Marco led Hornish by .9 second.

Hornish made a final drive just 450 feet before the checker and passed Marco Andretti. It was the second-closest finish in history, with a difference of .0635 second (second only to the Unser Jr./Goodyear finish of 1992). Hornish averaged 157.1 mph, while giving Team Penske its fourteenth Indy 500 victory.

This was the first time in history the lead had changed on the final lap. There were five different leaders within the last 18 laps.

Michael Andretti finished third and Dan Wheldon, fourth.

Marco Andretti was a hands-down Rookie of the Year winner. He became the fourth Andretti to win the award, joining grandfather Mario, father Michael and uncle Jeff.

Wheldon led 148 laps, Hornish, 19, and Kanaan, 12.

Tom Carnegie ended his sixty-one-year-career on the public address system. His contributions to the race were immeasurable.

Sam Hornish, Jr. would go on to win the 2006 IRL IndyCar Series Championship.

Sam Hornish, 2006 winner, nips Marco Andretti at the Yard of Bricks.

RACE RESULTS FOR THE 2006 INDIANAPOLIS 500

Finish	Start	Car Num.	Driver	Car Name/Entrant*	Make/Model	Status	Laps	Led	Winnings
1	1	6	Sam Hornish Jr.	Marlboro Team Penske	Dallara/Honda	157.085	200	19	$1,744,855
2	9	26	Marco Andretti (R)	NYSE Group	Dallara/Honda	157.084	200	2	$688,505
3	13	1	Michael Andretti	Jim Beam/Vonage	Dallara/Honda	157.071	200	4	$455,105
4	3	10	Dan Wheldon (W)	Target Chip Ganassi Racing	Dallara/Honda	157.068	200	148	$571,405
5	5	11	Tony Kanaan	Team 7-Eleven	Dallara/Honda	157.063	200	12	$340,405
6	4	9	Scott Dixon	Target Chip Ganassi Racing	Dallara/Honda	157.043	200	6	$361,005
7	17	27	Dario Franchitti	Klein Tools/Canadian Club	Dallara/Honda	157.008	200	0	$307,905
8	10	16	Danica Patrick	Rahal Letterman Racing Team Argent	Panoz/Honda	157.007	200	0	$285,805
9	8	8	Scott Sharp	Delphi	Dallara/Honda	156.933	200	0	$283,805
10	6	4	Vitor Meira	Harrah's Panther	Dallara/Honda	156.839	200	0	$267,705
11	12	20	Ed Carpenter	Vision Racing	Dallara/Honda	Running	199	0	$264,805
12	25	5	Buddy Lazier (W)	Dreyer & Reinbold Racing	Dallara/Honda	Running	199	0	$274,805
13	19	51	Eddie Cheever Jr. (W)	Cheever Racing	Dallara/Honda	Running	198	0	$255,805
14	18	52	Max Papis	Cheever Racing	Dallara/Honda	Running	197	0	$229,305
15	7	55	Kosuke Matsuura	Panasonic ARTA	Dallara/Honda	Running	196	0	$247,805
16	28	12	Roger Yasukawa	Playa Del Racing	Panoz/Honda	Running	194	0	$228,805
17	24	21	Jaques Lazier	Playa Del Racing	Panoz/Honda	Running	193	0	$219,305
18	29	88	Airton Daré	OCTANE Motors/Sanitec/SSM	Panoz/Honda	Running	193	0	$216,805
19	32	98	PJ Jones	CURB Records	Panoz/Honda	Running	189	0	$214,305
20	16	7	Bryan Herta	XM Satellite Radio	Dallara/Honda	Running	188	0	$234,805
21	21	14	Felipe Giaffone	ABC Supply Co./A.J. Foyt Racing	Dallara/Honda	Accident	177	0	$227,305
22	15	90	Townsend Bell (R)	Rock & Republic	Dallara/Honda	Suspension	161	0	$204,555
23	26	17	Jeff Simmons	Rahal Letterman Racing Team Ethanol	Panoz/Honda	Accident	152	0	$222,305
24	27	31	Al Unser Jr. (W)	A1 Team USA Geico Dreyer & Reinbold	Dallara/Honda	Accident	145	0	$200,305
25	2	3	Helio Castroneves (W)	Marlboro Team Penske	Dallara/Honda	Accident	109	9	$290,355
26	14	15	Buddy Rice (W)	Rahal Letterman Racing Team Argent	Panoz/Honda	Accident	108	0	$224,805
27	11	2	Tomas Scheckter	Vision Racing	Dallara/Honda	Accident	65	0	$215,305
28	31	61	Arie Luyendyk Jr. (R)	CheapCaribbean.com/Blue Star Jets	Panoz/Honda	Handling	54	0	$196,055
29	30	97	Stephan Gregoire	Effen Vodka Team Leader Special	Panoz/Honda	Handling	49	0	$193,305
30	23	41	Larry Foyt	AJ Foyt Racing	Dallara/Honda	Handling	43	0	$192,305
31	33	18	Thiago Medeiros (R)	PDM Racing	Panoz/Honda	Electrical	24	0	$227,555
32	22	92	Jeff Bucknum	Life Fitness	Dallara/Honda	Accident	1	0	$193,805
33	20	91	P.J. Chesson (R)	Carmelo Hemelgarn Racing	Dallara/Honda	Accident	1	0	$211,555

* - complete car name/entrant data not available for all entries
(R) - Indicated Rookie
(W) - Indicates Past Winner

2007

The year 2007 represented A.J. Foyt's fiftieth year of participation at Indy.

For the first time, ethanol fuel was utilized by all the cars. Methanol fuel had been used for the past forty-two years.

Scott Dixon turned the fastest lap in practice prior to the first weekend of qualification with a lap of 227.167 mph.

The "new" qualifying format (11-11-11—Bump Day) adopted in 2005 finally came to fruition, as rain on pole day the previous two years resulted in an adjusted format.

Dario Franchitti held the provisional pole until just a few minutes before closing. Helio Castroneves and Penske Racing withdrew their car and made a second attempt. This time the average was 225.817 mph, eclipsing Franchitti. Just as time was expiring, Tony Kanaan withdrew his first attempt and made another qualifying run. Kanaan looked like he would overtake Castroneves until his last lap.

The front row consisted of Castroneves on the pole for the second time, with Kanaan and Franchitti filling it out.

Jim Nabors missed singing "Back Home Again in Indiana" because of illness. The fans were invited to sing the traditional song in his place.

Patrick Dempsey, actor and racer himself, drove a Chevrolet Corvette to start the 91st Indy 500. Peyton Manning of the Indianapolis Colts was the official starter.

Pole-sitter Helio Castroneves had difficulty starting and finally joined the field in turn four of the first parade lap.

Castroneves took the lead at the start, but Kanaan passed him and led the first lap.

Kanaan, Castroneves, Marco Andretti and Scott Dixon traded the lead during the first seventy laps.

Sam Hornish, Dario Franchitti and Michael Andretti each took the lead before the halfway point.

Near the halfway point, officials warned the teams that rain was nearing the Speedway.

The race was red-flagged because of heavy rain on lap 113, with Kanaan leading, Marco, second and Danica Patrick, third. Would Tony Kanaan get his first 500 win in view of the race having passed the halfway point?

After nearly three hours, the rain stopped and the track was dried. Just after six p.m., the race was restarted.

Kanaan pulled away and led most of the laps up to the pit stops near the three-quarter mark.

After pit stops, Kanaan led, with Hornish in second. On lap 151, Marty Roth crashed, bringing out the yellow.

The skies were very threatening! Some pitted, some stayed out. Franchitti and Dixon elected to stay out to gain track position with a fuel conservation strategy.

The track went green on lap 156, with Franchitti leading and Dixon in second, but then Kanaan and Jaques Lazier crashed in turn four.

The green came out on lap 162, but on the backstretch, Dan Wheldon, Ed Carpenter, Buddy Rice and Marco Andretti tangled, with Andretti's car flipping.

The yellow came on, and before the crash could be cleaned up, a heavy rain fell, ending the race after 166 laps.

Dario Franchitti was declared the winner, making Andretti Green the winning team for the second time in three years. Dixon, Castroneves and Hornish followed the winner. Franchitti averaged 151.774 mph.

Kanaan led eighty-three laps and Franchitti, thirty-four. There were a total of 23 lead changes among 11 different drivers.

Phil Giebler, one of only two rookies (Milka Duno the other) won Rookie of the Year, finishing twenty-ninth.

This race would be the last Indy 500 for two greats—Al Unser Jr. and Michael Andretti.

Al Unser's career included two Indy 500 victories (1992, 1994), two CART IndyCar World Series titles (1990, 1994), two International Race of Champions titles (1986, 1988). Unser won a total of thirty-four IndyCar races.

Michael Andretti competed in sixteen Indy 500's, while leading 431 laps, a record for non-winners. He won the 1991 CART IndyCar World Series championship. He won a total of forty-two IndyCar races.

Dario Franchitti would go on to win the 2007 IRL IndyCar Series Championship.

Dario Franchitti wins in 2007, pictured with wife Ashley Judd.

RACE RESULTS FOR THE 2007 INDIANAPOLIS 500

Finish	Start	Car Num.	Driver	Car Name/Entrant*	Make/Model	Status	Laps	Led	Winnings
1	3	27	Dario Franchitti	Canadian Club	Dallara/Honda	151.774	166	34	$1,645,233
2	4	9	Scott Dixon	Target Chip Ganassi Racing	Dallara/Honda	151.769	166	11	$719,067
3	1	3	Helio Castroneves (W)	Team Penske	Dallara/Honda	151.746	166	19	$646,303
4	5	6	Sam Hornish Jr. (W)	Team Penske	Dallara/Honda	151.703	166	2	$360,389
5	7	12	Ryan Briscoe	Symantec Luczo Dragon Racing	Dallara/Honda	151.649	166	0	$302,305
6	12	8	Scott Sharp	Patron Sharp Rahal Letterman	Dallara/Honda	151.630	166	0	$368,305
7	10	2	Tomas Scheckter	Vision Racing	Dallara/Honda	151.599	166	0	$304,105
8	8	7	Danica Patrick	Motorola	Dallara/Honda	151.537	166	0	$298,005
9	20	02	Davey Hamilton	HP Vision Racing	Dallara/Honda	151.502	166	0	$268,905
10	19	4	Vitor Meira	Delphi Panther	Dallara/Honda	151.471	166	0	$280,305
11	13	17	Jeff Simmons	Rahal Letterman Racing Team Ethanol	Dallara/Honda	151.445	166	1	$278,347
12	2	11	Tony Kanaan	Team 7-Eleven	Dallara/Honda	151.235	166	83	$414,319
13	11	39	Michael Andretti	Motorola/Jim Beam	Dallara/Honda	150.489	166	1	$238,247
14	18	22	A.J. Foyt IV	Vision Racing	Dallara/Honda	Running	165	0	$252,305
15	26	98	Alex Barron	Lenovo/CURB Records	Dallara/Honda	Running	165	0	$249,305
16	17	55	Kosuke Matsuura	Panasonic Panther	Dallara/Honda	Running	165	0	$245,305
17	14	20	Ed Carpenter	Hitachi Power Tools Vision Racing	Dallara/Honda	Accident	164	0	$246,305
18	21	5	Sarah Fisher	Dreyer & Reinbold Racing	Dallara/Honda	Running	164	0	$238,305
19	22	99	Buddy Lazier (W)	Sam Schmidt Motorsports	Dallara/Honda	Running	164	0	$216,805
20	15	14	Darren Manning	ABC Supply Co./AJ Foyt Racing	Dallara/Honda	Running	164	0	$232,305
21	23	24	Roger Yasukawa	Wellman Corbier/DRR	Dallara/Honda	Running	164	0	$234,305
22	6	10	Dan Wheldon (W)	Target Chip Ganassi Racing	Dallara/Honda	Accident	163	0	$231,805
23	32	91	Richie Hearn	Hemelgarn/Racing Professionals	Dallara/Honda	Running	163	0	$224,305
24	9	26	Marco Andretti	NYSE Group	Dallara/Honda	Accident	162	13	$229,351
25	16	15	Buddy Rice (W)	A1TeamUSA/DRR	Dallara/Honda	Accident	162	0	$222,805
26	25	50	Al Unser Jr. (W)	AJ Foyt Racing	Dallara/Honda	Running	161	0	$205,805
27	28	21	Jaques Lazier	Indiana Ice / Venture Logistics	Panoz/Honda	Accident	155	2	$207,389
28	30	25	Marty Roth	Roth Racing	Dallara/Honda	Accident	148	0	$216,305
29	33	31	Phil Giebler (R)	Ethos Fuel Reformulator	Panoz/Honda	Accident	106	0	$230,305
30	24	33	John Andretti	Camping World Panther	Dallara/Honda	Accident	95	0	$204,305
31	29	23	Milka Duno (R)	CITGO Racing	Dallara/Honda	Accident	65	0	$213,555
32	27	19	Jon Herb	Racing Professionals	Dallara/Honda	Accident	51	0	$193,305
33	31	77	Roberto Moreno	Chastain Motorsports Z-Line Designs Miller Eads	Panoz/Honda	Accident	36	0	$224,805

* - complete car name/entrant data not available for all entries
(R) - Indicated Rookie
(W) - Indicates Past Winner

2008

During the off season, the long-anticipated unification was signed between the Indy Racing League and the Champ Car World Series.

Also during the off-season Helio Castroneves gave IndyCar racing tremendous positive publicity by winning the wildly popular "Dancing with the Stars" television program. His dancing partner, Julianne Hough, would sing the national anthem on race day.

Going into pole day, Scott Dixon had run the fastest lap of the month at 226.968 mph on "Fast Friday."

During pole day practice, Marco Andretti recorded a speed of 228.318 mph for the month's fastest.

Scott Dixon won the pole at 226.366 mph for Target Chip Ganassi Racing. Dan Wheldon had withdrawn his speed in the final hour and had requalified in second position. Ryan Briscoe filled out the front row.

For the third time in four years, the 11-11-11 — bump day format had to be adjusted due to a rainout on the second day of qualifications.

With just a few minutes left on the final day of qualifying, 1996 champion Buddy Lazier bumped his way into the field.

Nineteen year old Graham Rahal, qualified for the thirteenth starting position. He would start his first Indy 500 twenty-two years after his father's victory in 1986.

Retired two-time winner Emerson Fittipaldi drove the Chevrolet Corvette Z-06 pace car for the start of the 92nd Indy 500. Olympian ice skater Kristi Yamaguchi was the honorary starter.

Scott Dixon took the early lead and teammate Dan Wheldon passed him for the lead on lap three.

Wheldon led to lap thirty-six, when Dixon passed him. Wheldon and Dixon continued to trade the lead.

Tony Kanaan took the lead on lap ninety-four, which set a record because he had led a lap in seven consecutive races. He broke Rick Mears's record of six consecutive (1979-1984). Unfortunately, Kanaan's bad luck continued, and on lap 105, teammate Marco Andretti tangled with him in turn three and Kanaan hit the wall.

Marco Andretti took the lead on lap 122, with Dixon running second and Wheldon beginning to slip back because of handling problems.

On the lap 159 restart, Vitor Meira stormed into the lead with a spectacular zig-zag pass from third place, overtaking Dixon and Andretti.

During a yellow flag on lap 171, as the leaders made their last pit stops, Danica Patrick and Ryan Briscoe tangled on pit lane while exiting. Both were eliminated. Patrick got out of her car and marched toward Briscoe's pit, but was intercepted by security.

The track went green on lap 176, with Dixon leading Meira and Marco Andretti. Dixon led to the finish, edging Meira by 1.75 seconds, with Andretti finishing third. Dixon averaged 143.6 mph as a result of eight cautions for 60 laps. Meira finished in second position for the second time in four years.

Dixon led 115 laps, Wheldon, 30, Marco Andretti, 15 and Tony Kanaan, 12. There were eighteen lead changes between nine drivers.

Dixon became the nineteenth pole winner to win the race and was the first winner from New Zealand. It also marked the third time that Chip Ganassi was the winning car owner. Ganassi's drivers (Dixon and Wheldon) led almost three-quarters of the race.

Ryan Hunter-Reay won Rookie of the Year with a sixth-place finish.

Scott Dixon would go on to win the 2008 IndyCar Series Championship.

Scott Dixon wins his first "500" in his sixth attempt.

RACE RESULTS FOR THE 2008 INDIANAPOLIS 500

Finish	Start	Car Num.	Driver	Car Name/Entrant*	Make/Model	Status	Laps	Led	Winnings
1	1	9	Scott Dixon	Target Chip Ganassi Racing	Dallara/Honda	143.567	200	115	$2,988,065
2	8	4	Vitor Meira	Delphi National Guard	Dallara/Honda	143.547	200	12	$1,273,215
3	7	26	Marco Andretti	Team Indiana Jones presented by Blockbuster	Dallara/Honda	143.541	200	15	$782,065
4	4	3	Helio Castroneves (W)	Team Penske	Dallara/Honda	143.496	200	0	$482,815
5	10	20	Ed Carpenter	Menards/ Vision Racing	Dallara/Honda	143.492	200	3	$399,665
6	20	17	Ryan Hunter-Reay (R)	Rahal Letterman Racing Team Ethanol	Dallara/Honda	143.487	200	0	$328,065
7	9	27	Hideki Mutoh (R)	Formula Dream	Dallara/Honda	143.477	200	0	$307,115
8	17	15	Buddy Rice (W)	Dreyer & Reinbold Racing	Dallara/Honda	143.466	200	8	$311,415
9	14	14	Darren Manning	ABC Supply Co./AJ Foyt Racing	Dallara/Honda	143.462	200	0	$301,815
10	12	99	Townsend Bell	Dreyer & Reinbold William Rast Racing	Dallara/Honda	143.459	200	0	$275,315
11	25	5	Oriol Servia (R)	Angie's List Special	Dallara/Honda	143.310	200	0	$302,065
12	2	10	Dan Wheldon (W)	Target Chip Ganassi Racing	Dallara/Honda	143.215	200	30	$366,815
13	23	8	Will Power (R)	Aussie Vineyard-Team Australia	Dallara/Honda	143.206	200	0	$300,565
14	18	22	Davey Hamilton	Hewlett-Packard/KR Vision Racing	Dallara/Honda	143.202	200	0	$270,315
15	29	36	Enrique Bernoldi (R)	Sangari Conquest Racing	Dallara/Honda	143.201	200	0	$300,565
16	21	24	John Andretti	Roth Racing	Dallara/Honda	Running	199	0	$300,315
17	32	91	Buddy Lazier (W)	Hemelgarn Johnson	Dallara/Honda	Running	195	0	$327,015
18	28	19	Mario Moraes (R)	Sonny's Bar-B-Q	Dallara/Honda	Running	194	3	$303,415
19	27	23	Milka Duno	CITGO / Dreyer & Reinbold Racing	Dallara/Honda	Running	185	0	$300,315
20	15	18	Bruno Junqueira	Z-Line Designs	Dallara/Honda	Running	184	2	$301,215
21	31	2	A.J. Foyt IV	Lilly Diabetes/Vision Racing	Dallara/Honda	Running	180	0	$311,815
22	5	7	Danica Patrick	Motorola	Dallara/Honda	Contact	171	0	$301,915
23	3	6	Ryan Briscoe	Team Penske	Dallara/Honda	Contact	171	0	$312,315
24	11	12	Tomas Scheckter	Symantec Luczo Dragon Racing	Dallara/Honda	Mechanical	156	0	$270,315
25	19	16	Alex Lloyd (R)	Rahal Letterman with Chip Ganassi	Dallara/Honda	Contact	151	0	$272,065
26	26	33	E.J. Viso (R)	PDVSA HVM Racing	Dallara/Honda	Mechanical	139	0	$301,565
27	16	02	Justin Wilson (R)	McDonald's Racing Team	Dallara/Honda	Contact	132	0	$302,065
28	24	41	Jeff Simmons	ABC Supply/Foyt Racing	Dallara/Honda	Contact	112	0	$270,000
29	6	11	Tony Kanaan	Team 7-Eleven	Dallara/Honda	Contact	105	12	$331,215
30	22	67	Sarah Fisher	Sarah Fisher Racing	Dallara/Honda	Contact	103	0	$277,215
31	30	34	Jaime Camara (R)	Sangari	Dallara/Honda	Contact	79	0	$300,565
32	33	25	Marty Roth	Roth Racing	Dallara/Honda	Contact	59	0	$300,315
33	13	06	Graham Rahal (R)	Hole in the Wall Camps	Dallara/Honda	Contact	36	0	$312,065

* - complete car name/entrant data not available for all entries
(R) - Indicated Rookie
(W) - Indicates Past Winner

2009

The Speedway Motel, which had been opened in 1963, was closed and torn down. Die-hard race fans were disappointed, but safety issues weighed heavily in the decision to close the facility.

The year 2009 ushered in a three-year Centennial Celebration for the Speedway.

The month of May opened with a three-day Balloon Festival in recognition of the first event ever staged at the Speedway in June of 1909.

Ryan Briscoe had the fastest speed in practice prior to pole day at 225.981 mph.

Dan Wheldon crashed in practice on Saturday prior to qualifying.

Helio Castroneves took the pole at 224.864 mph, with Ryan Briscoe and Dario Franchitti making up the front row. This was Helio's third pole win.

John Andretti bumped his way into the field with just a few minutes left on bump day driving for seven-time NASCAR champion Richard Petty.

Alex Tagliani was bumped from the field when Ryan Hunter-Reay finished his qualification run after the six p.m. gun signaled the end of qualifications.

Tagliani ended up taking over the car qualified by his teammate, Bruno Junqueira, and would start thirty-third.

At the start, the green was not waved as it was judged that Castroneves had jumped the start. The second attempt resulted in the green flag.

During the first half of the race, Scott Dixon, Castroneves and Franchitti swapped the lead.

On lap 98, Tony Kanaan was running third when a driveshaft failure caused him to crash on the backstretch and into turn three.

Scott Dixon led from lap 91 to 141, with Dario Franchitti in close pursuit.

Vitor Meira survived a serious-looking pit fire on lap 134 and was able to rejoin the race.

On the restart on lap 142, Castroneves passed Dixon in turn one.

On lap 173, Vitor Meira and Raphael Matos collided in turn one. Meira was injured with two broken vertebrae. Meira's car flipped on its side and rode the wall for several hundred feet, backwards.

Castroneves led the final 59 laps to win over Dan Wheldon, Danica Patrick, Townsend Bell and Will Power. Castroneves averaged 150.3 mph as a result of eight cautions for sixty-one laps. This was Penske's fifteenth Indy 500 win.

Castroneves was extremely emotional on this, his third Indy 500 victory. Just two months before he had been acquitted of federal charges for tax evasion and conspiracy. A conviction may very well have ended his driving career.

Patrick's third-place finish broke her own record of fourth in 2005 for the best finish by a female driver.

Dixon led seventy-three laps, Castroneves, sixty-six, and Franchitti, fifty. Ryan Briscoe led the other eleven laps. There were only six lead changes among the four drivers.

A record nineteen cars finished on the lead lap.

Alex Tagliani won Rookie of the Year with an eleventh-place finish.

Castroneves received a record purse of $3,048,005.

Shortly after the running of the 93rd Indy 500, Joie Chitwood III left to become President of Daytona International Speedway. He was replaced by Jeffrey G. Belskus as President of the Indianapolis Motor Speedway.

The 2009 winner Helio Castroneves and team "kiss the bricks" in celebration.

RACE RESULTS FOR THE 2009 INDIANAPOLIS 500

Finish	Start	Car Num.	Driver	Car Name/Entrant*	Make/Model	Status	Laps	Led	Winnings
1	1	3	Helio Castroneves (W)	Team Penske	Dallara/Honda	150.318	200	66	$3,048,005
2	18	4	Dan Wheldon (W)	National Guard Panther Racing	Dallara/Honda	150.293	200	0	$1,258,805
3	10	7	Danica Patrick	Boost Mobile/Motorola	Dallara/Honda	150.288	200	0	$763,305
4	24	8	Townsend Bell	Herbalife-KV Racing Technology	Dallara/Honda	150.284	200	0	$445,305
5	9	12	Will Power	Team Verizon Wireless	Dallara/Honda	150.272	200	0	$345,305
6	5	9	Scott Dixon (W)	Target Chip Ganassi Racing	Dallara/Honda	150.264	200	73	$374,155
7	3	10	Dario Franchitti (W)	Target Chip Ganassi Racing	Dallara/Honda	150.256	200	50	$386,305
8	17	20	Ed Carpenter	Menards/Vision Racing	Dallara/Honda	150.249	200	0	$302,805
9	13	15	Paul Tracy	GEICO/KV Racing Technology	Dallara/Honda	150.236	200	0	$271,805
10	16	27	Hideki Mutoh	Formula Dream	Dallara/Honda	150.226	200	0	$301,805
11	33	36	Alex Tagliani (R)	All Sport Conquest Racing	Dallara/Honda	150.186	200	0	$295,305
12	26	19	Tomas Scheckter	MONA-VIE	Dallara/Honda	150.180	200	0	$280,305
13	11	99	Alex Lloyd	HER CGR/SSM Racing	Dallara/Honda	150.177	200	0	$270,305
14	20	16	Scott Sharp	Tequila Patrón Panther Racing	Dallara/Honda	150.174	200	0	$270,305
15	2	6	Ryan Briscoe	Team Penske	Dallara/Honda	150.159	200	11	$349,755
16	19	41	A.J. Foyt IV	ABC Supply/Foyt-Greer Racing	Dallara/Honda	150.123	200	0	$271,805
17	21	67	Sarah Fisher	Dollar General/Sarah Fisher Racing	Dallara/Honda	150.117	200	0	$270,305
18	27	24	Mike Conway (R)	Dreyer & Reinbold Racing	Dallara/Honda	150.113	200	0	$300,555
19	28	43	John Andretti	Window World	Dallara/Honda	150.091	200	0	$276,805
20	30	23	Milka Duno	CITGO/Dreyer & Reinbold Racing	Dallara/Honda	Running	199	0	$301,805
21	14	14	Vitor Meira	ABC Supply Co. AJ Foyt Racing	Dallara/Honda	Contact	173	0	$300,305
22	12	2	Raphael Matos (R)	US Air Force Luczo Dragon	Dallara/Honda	Contact	173	0	$308,305
23	15	18	Justin Wilson	Z-Line Designs	Dallara/Honda	Contact	160	0	$300,305
24	29	13	E.J. Viso	PDVSA HVM Racing	Dallara/Honda	Mechanical	139	0	$300,305
25	31	00	Nelson Philippe (R)	i drive green HVM Racing	Dallara/Honda	Contact	130	0	$270,555
26	25	17	Oriol Servia	The Rahal Letterman DAFCA Special	Dallara/Honda	Mechanical	98	0	$271,805
27	6	11	Tony Kanaan	Team 7-Eleven	Dallara/Honda	Contact	97	0	$303,305
28	23	06	Robert Doornbos (R)	Newman/Haas/Lanigan Racing	Dallara/Honda	Contact	85	0	$305,555
29	22	44	Davey Hamilton	Hewlett Packard	Dallara/Honda	Contact	79	0	$271,805
30	8	26	Marco Andretti	Team Venom Energy	Dallara/Honda	Handling	56	0	$315,305
31	4	02	Graham Rahal	McDonald's Racing Team	Dallara/Honda	Contact	55	0	$305,805
32	32	21	Ryan Hunter-Reay	IZOD/WilliamRast/Vision Racing	Dallara/Honda	Contact	19	0	$353,305
33	7	5	Mario Moraes	Azul Tequila-Votorantim-KV Racing	Dallara/Honda	Contact	0	0	$301,805

* - complete car name/entrant data not available for all entries
(R) - Indicated Rookie
(W) - Indicates Past Winner

2010

Qualifying was cut back to just two days, with twenty-four cars to qualify on the first day and nine on the second.

A new qualifying "shootout" format was implemented, with the "fast nine" requalifying for the pole with up to two attempts per car at 4:30 pm on pole day.

Five women attempted to qualify, with four making the race: Danica Patrick, Ana Beatriz, Simona DeSilvestro and Sarah Fisher.

Helio Castroneves won both the first session of qualifying and the "shootout" to start from the pole with a speed of 227.970 mph. This was his fourth pole start, including back to back poles in 2009 and 2010.

Tony Kanaan had difficulty qualifying, as he had two accidents before finally making the field in the thirty-second starting position. After qualifying, Andretti Autosport decided to replace Kanaan's qualified back-up car with the primary car. This resulted in Kanaan being moved to the 33rd starting position.

Paul Tracy was the most notable driver not to make the race.

The Chevrolet Camaro SS pace car was driven by ABC's Robin Roberts, and a two-seater driven by Michael Andretti with actor Mark Wahlberg as passenger paced the race.

Jack Nicholson was the honorary starter. He enthusiastically remained in the flag stand for the first couple of caution periods.

Dario Franchitti took the lead at the start, but a spin and crash by Davey Hamilton, who was pinched by Tomas Scheckter in turn two of the first lap, caused a caution.

Franchitti led until lap thirty-one, when Will Power passed him.

On Power's pit stop on lap thirty-six, he pulled away before the fuel hose was properly disengaged and was penalized with a "drive-through," which dropped him to twenty-fifth position.

From lap 38, Franchitti led 105 of the next 124 laps, while Kanaan was continually moving up through the field.

Near the three-quarter mark, Castroneves stalled in the pits, dropping him from third to sixteenth.

Ryan Briscoe crashed in turn four on lap 148. The running order was Franchitti, Kanaan and Andretti.

A caution on lap 161 for a Sebastian Saavadra spin caused most drivers to make their last stop, but several stayed out (Conway, Wilson, Castroneves and Rahal), hoping for more cautions to assist them in making it to the finish.

Franchitti nursed his car to the finish, as he was able to go the final 36 laps without a pit stop.

Dario regained the lead on lap 192 when the others were forced to pit for fuel.

Dario Franchitti averaged 161.6 mph in winning his second "500."

Franchitti pretty much dominated the race, leading 155 laps, Conway, 15, and Justin Wilson, 11.

Mike Conway was involved in a serious accident on the final lap. Ryan Hunter-Reay ran out of fuel and slowed quickly, with Conway running over the back of his car and being launched into the catch fence. Conway was airlifted to the hospital with multiple back and neck fractures.

Dan Wheldon finished second for Panther Racing for the second year in a row, with Marco Andretti third and Alex Lloyd, fourth. This was the third consecutive year the Panther Racing car finished second.

Simona de Silvestro finished fourteenth and won Rookie of the Year despite fellow rookie Mario Romancini finishing thirteenth.

Dario Franchitti would go on to win the 2010 IndyCar Championship for Target Chip Ganassi Racing. Chip Ganassi's race teams won the Indy 500 with Franchitti and both the Daytona 500 and Brickyard 400 with Jamie McMurray.

The 2010 winner Dario Franchitti receives the checkered flag.

RACE RESULTS FOR THE 2010 INDIANAPOLIS 500

Finish	Start	Car Num.	Driver	Car Name/Entrant*	Make/Model	Status	Laps	Led	Winnings
1	3	10	Dario Franchitti (W)	Target Chip Ganassi Racing	Dallara/Honda	161.623	200	155	$2,752,055
2	18	4	Dan Wheldon (W)	National Guard Panther Racing	Dallara/Honda	161.621	200	0	$1,010,805
3	16	26	Marco Andretti	Team Venom Energy	Dallara/Honda	161.319	200	1	$631,505
4	26	19	Alex Lloyd	Boy Scouts of America	Dallara/Honda	161.319	200	0	$425,305
5	6	9	Scott Dixon (W)	Target Chip Ganassi Racing	Dallara/Honda	161.312	200	0	$377,805
6	23	7	Danica Patrick	Team GoDaddy.com	Dallara/Honda	161.308	200	0	$307,305
7	11	22	Justin Wilson	Team Z-Line Designs/DRR	Dallara/Honda	161.247	200	11	$312,255
8	2	12	Will Power	Verizon Team Penske	Dallara/Honda	161.185	200	5	$385,805
9	1	3	Helio Castroneves (W)	Team Penske	Dallara/Honda	161.146	200	3	$545,655
10	5	77	Alex Tagliani	Bowers & Wilkins/Honda Edmonton Indy	Dallara/Honda	161.128	200	0	$302,805
11	33	11	Tony Kanaan	Team 7-Eleven	Dallara/Honda	160.763	200	0	$328,555
12	7	30	Graham Rahal	The Quick Trim/RLR Special	Dallara/Honda	160.758	200	0	$251,805
13	27	34	Mario Romancini (R)	Conquest Racing	Dallara/Honda	160.733	200	0	$305,555
14	22	78	Simona de Silvestro (R)	Team Stargate Worlds/HVM	Dallara/Honda	160.733	200	0	$327,055
15	20	23	Tomas Scheckter	MonaVie/DRR	Dallara/Honda	Running	199	5	$262,555
16	10	99	Townsend Bell	Herbalife Ganassi/Schmidt Team	Dallara/Honda	Running	199	0	$251,805
17	8	20	Ed Carpenter	Panther/Vision/Fuzzy's Vodka	Dallara/Honda	Running	199	0	$250,305
18	17	37	Ryan Hunter-Reay	Team IZOD	Dallara/Honda	Contact	198	0	$302,305
19	15	24	Mike Conway	Dad's Root Beer/DRR	Dallara/Honda	Contact	198	15	$307,055
20	31	5	Takuma Sato (R)	Lotus-KV Racing Technology	Dallara/Honda	Running	198	0	$302,055
21	21	25	Ana Beatriz (R)	Ipiranga/DRR	Dallara/Honda	Contact	196	0	$250,305
22	24	36	Bertrand Baguette (R)	Conquest Racing RACB	Dallara/Honda	Running	183	0	$300,555
23	32	29	Sebastian Saavedra (R)	William Rast/Bryan Herta Autosport	Dallara/Honda	Contact	159	0	$255,555
24	4	6	Ryan Briscoe	Team Penske	Dallara/Honda	Contact	147	5	$307,305
25	19	8	E.J. Viso	PDVSA-Jet Aviation-KV Racing Technology	Dallara/Honda	Contact	139	0	$301,805
26	29	67	Sarah Fisher	Dollar General/Sarah Fisher Racing	Dallara/Honda	Contact	125	0	$250,305
27	30	14	Vitor Meira	ABC Supply Co. A.J. Foyt Racing	Dallara/Honda	Contact	105	0	$300,305
28	9	06	Hideki Mutoh	Formula Dream/Panasonic	Dallara/Honda	Handling	76	0	$315,305
29	12	2	Raphael Matos	HP de Ferran Dragon Racing	Dallara/Honda	Contact	72	0	$300,305
30	28	43	John Andretti	Team Window World	Dallara/Honda	Contact	62	0	$251,805
31	13	32	Mario Moraes	GEICO-Curb Records/KV Racing Technology	Dallara/Honda	Contact	17	0	$301,805
32	25	33	Bruno Junqueira	Bowers & Wilkins/TorcUP	Dallara/Honda	Contact	7	0	$261,805
33	14	21	Davey Hamilton	HP de Ferran Dragon Racing	Dallara/Honda	Contact	0	0	$255,305

* - complete car name/entrant data not available for all entries
(R) - Indicated Rookie
(W) - Indicates Past Winner

2011

The race was the third and final of a three-year-long Centennial Celebration of the 100th anniversary of the opening of the track (1909) through the first 500 mile race (1911).

The race was billed as "The Most Important Race in History."

Many of the former winners and past race participants attended the 100th anniversary celebration of the first race.

The start of the race was moved back to noon, instead of one p.m., which had been the regular start time between 2006 and 2010.

Donald Trump was originally named as the pace car driver, but was eventually replaced with four-time winner A.J. Foyt.

The final entry list included seventy-nine cars for forty-one entries.

On "Fast Friday", Helio Castroneves topped Alex Tagliani's month's top speed with a 228.611 mph lap.

The qualifying format remained with a first segment, followed by a late-in-the-day "Fast Nine Shootout."

Alex Tagliani took the provisional pole in the first segment with an average of 226.954 mph. He then backed it up with the final run of the day, taking the pole at 227.472 mph for Sam Schmidt Motorsports. Scott Dixon and Oriol Servia joined "Tags" on the front row.

The Ganassi Team miscalculated fuel and Dario Franchitti and Scott Dixon both ran out before the checkered flag in the "shootout."

The Andretti Autosport Team struggled mightily in qualifying. Danica Patrick finally made the field with just over an hour left, and Marco Andretti bumped his teammate, Ryan Hunter-Reay, in the final minute.

The controversial decision by IndyCar of using a two-car abreast start on restarts was implemented for the "500." Many of the drivers were extremely concerned for safety reasons.

Four-time Indy 500 champion A.J. Foyt Jr. drove the Chevrolet Camaro SS pace car to start the 95th Indy 500.

Scott Dixon jumped the start to take the early race lead.

The first half of the race primarily saw Dixon, Tagliani and Dario Franchitti exchanging the lead.

The second half of the race saw eight leaders.

A caution occurred on lap 158, when Ryan Briscoe and Townsend Bell tangled.

As the race was preparing to go green on lap 164, several drivers elected to pit and top off their fuel, including Dario Franchitti and J.R. Hildebrand.

Graham Rahal took the lead from Oriol Servia on lap 166. This was the first time he had ever led the "500."

Scott Dixon took the lead from Rahal on lap 172 and held it until he pitted on lap 179. Danica Patrick took the lead and hoped for a caution that might allow her enough fuel to finish without pitting.

Patrick led for 10 laps, but her pace slowed and she was passed for the lead by second-year driver Bertrand Baguette. Baguette then gave up the lead on lap 197, when he too was forced to pit for fuel.

J.R. Hildebrand took the lead, and it appeared that a rookie would win the "500" for the first time since 2001.

On the final turn of the last lap, Hildebrand attempted to avoid the slowing car of Charlie Kimball, who was decelerating quickly due to running out of fuel, and got out of the groove and clipped the wall exiting turn four.

As Hildebrand rode the wall down the front stretch with his accelerator still mashed, Dan Wheldon was able to pass him, winning by just over two seconds.

Dan Wheldon became a two-time "500" winner and the only driver to lead only the last lap of the race. Wheldon averaged 170.265 mph.

Hildebrand finished second and won Rookie of the Year, with Graham Rahal third, Tony Kanaan fourth and Scott Dixon fifth.

This was the fourth consecutive year a Panther Racing driver finished in the second position.

Scott Dixon led seventy-three laps, Franchitti, fifty-one laps, Alex Tagliani, twenty laps, Oriol Servia, eighteen laps, J.R. Hildebrand, seven laps, Graham Rahal, six laps, Ed Carpenter, three laps and Dan Wheldon, one lap.

There were twenty-three lead changes among ten different drivers.

The winning car's ownership team consisted of: Bryan Herta, Steve Newey, Cary Agajanian, Mike Curb and Sam Schmidt.

This was the last Indy 500 for the normally aspirated Honda V-8 engines with the Dallara IR-05 Chassis.

Two-time Indianapolis 500 winner Dan Wheldon tragically lost his life in the season's final race at Las Vegas.

Dan Wheldon wins his second "500" as J.R. Hildebrand crashes on the final turn of the last lap.

RACE RESULTS FOR THE 2011 INDIANAPOLIS 500

Finish	Start	Car Num.	Driver	Car Name/Entrant*	Make/Model	Status	Laps	Led	Winnings
1	6	98	Dan Wheldon (W)	William Rast - Curb/Big Machine	Dallara/Honda	Running	200	1	$2,567,255
2	12	4	JR Hildebrand (R)	National Guard Panther Racing	Dallara/Honda	Running	200	7	$1,064,895
3	29	38	Graham Rahal	Service Central	Dallara/Honda	Running	200	6	$666,945
4	22	82	Tony Kanaan	GEICO - KV Racing Technology - Lotus	Dallara/Honda	Running	200	0	$438,745
5	2	9	Scott Dixon (W)	Target Chip Ganassi Racing	Dallara/Honda	Running	200	73	$519,345
6	3	2	Oriol Servia	CDW/Telemundo	Dallara/Honda	Running	200	18	$364,845
7	14	30	Bertrand Baguette	The RACB/Aspria RLL Special	Dallara/Honda	Running	200	11	$256,255
8	21	07	Tomas Scheckter	Team REDLINE Xtreme - Circle K	Dallara/Honda	Running	200	0	$253,805
9	27	26	Marco Andretti	Team Venom	Dallara/Honda	Running	200	0	$311,245
10	25	7	Danica Patrick	Team GoDaddy	Dallara/Honda	Running	200	10	$321,745
11	8	67	Ed Carpenter	Dollar General/Sarah Fisher Racing	Dallara/Honda	Running	200	3	$251,655
12	9	10	Dario Franchitti (W)	Target Chip Ganassi Racing	Dallara/Honda	Running	200	51	$369,695
13	28	83	Charlie Kimball (R)	Levemir and Novolog FlexPen	Dallara/Honda	Running	199	0	$251,555
14	5	12	Will Power	Verizon Team Penske	Dallara/Honda	Running	199	0	$318,745
15	11	14	Vitor Meira	ABC Supply Co./A.J. Foyt Racing	Dallara/Honda	Running	199	0	$306,745
16	19	22	Justin Wilson	Z-Line Designs/ Dreyer & Reinbold Racing	Dallara/Honda	Running	199	0	$309,995
17	16	3	Helio Castroneves (W)	Shell V-Power/ Pennzoil Ultra Team Penske	Dallara/Honda	Running	199	0	$320,245
18	7	44	Buddy Rice (W)	Fuzzy's Vodka/Panther Racing	Dallara/Honda	Running	198	0	$252,805
19	30	19	Alex Lloyd	Boy Scouts of America	Dallara/Honda	Running	198	0	$254,805
20	31	36	Pippa Mann (R)	Conquest Racing	Dallara/Honda	Running	198	0	$251,555
21	32	24	Ana Beatriz	Team Ipiranga/ Dreyer & Reinbold Racing	Dallara/Honda	Running	197	0	$306,745
22	17	43	John Andretti	Team Window World	Dallara/Honda	Running	197	0	$251,305
23	33	41	Ryan Hunter-Reay	ABC Supply/DHL/Sun Drop	Dallara/Honda	Running	197	0	$252,805
24	15	11	Davey Hamilton	HP/Dreyer & Reinbold Racing	Dallara/Honda	Running	193	0	$251,305
25	24	23	Paul Tracy	WIX Filters/Dreyer & Reinbold Racing	Dallara/Honda	Running	175	0	$252,805
26	4	99	Townsend Bell	Herbalife Schmidt Pelfrey Racing	Dallara/Honda	Contact	157	0	$252,805
27	26	6	Ryan Briscoe	IZOD Team Penske	Dallara/Honda	Contact	157	0	$356,745
28	1	77	Alex Tagliani	Bowers & Wilkins/ Sam Schmidt Motorsports	Dallara/Honda	Contact	147	20	$492,245
29	13	06	James Hinchcliffe (R)	Sprott Newman Haas Racing	Dallara/Honda	Contact	99	0	$256,305
30	20	88	Jay Howard (R)	Service Central Schmidt RLL Racing	Dallara/Honda	Contact	60	0	$251,555
31	23	78	Simona de Silvestro	Nuclear Clean Air Energy	Dallara/Honda	Handling	44	0	$311,745
32	18	59	E.J. Viso	PDVSA - KV Racing Technology - Lotus	Dallara/Honda	Contact	27	0	$306,745
33	10	5	Takuma Sato	Monavie-KV Racing Technology - Lotus	Dallara/Honda	Contact	20	0	$310,245

* - complete car name/entrant data not available for all entries
(R) - Indicated Rookie
(W) - Indicates Past Winner

Indy 500 Recaps The Short Chute Edition | 381

2012

The 96th Indianapolis 500 resulted in another thrilling finish.

For the first time since 1947, the defending champion was unable to defend his title due to a fatality. Two-time Indy 500 Champion and fan favorite Dan Wheldon had lost his life in a multi-car accident at the final race of the 2011 season in Las Vegas.

Retired Formula One driver, Rubens Barrichello, came out of retirement to make an attempt at Indy. Barrichello won the 2001 U.S. Grand Prix at Indy.

For the first time since 1996 all entries were turbocharged engines. The engine suppliers—Honda, Chevrolet and Lotus—provided 2.2 liter turbocharged power plants. The new Dallara chassis was the result of the ICONIC development project. The late Dan Wheldon did the bulk of the testing on the newly-designed car prior to his fatal accident. As a tribute to Wheldon the chassis was named the Dallara DW12.

On opening day, Josef Newgarden, a rookie driving for Sarah Fisher Hartman Racing, topped the speed chart at 220.250 mph.

Marco Andretti, in a Chevrolet-powered car, was at or near the top of the speed chart each practice day and set the month's top speed on Fast Friday at 227.540 mph.

On Pole Day, Helio Castroneves, in a Chevrolet-powered car, posted a practice lap speed of 227.744 eclipsing Andretti's fast lap of the previous day.

First segment qualifying resulted in the following drivers advancing to the "Fast Nine" qualifying session: James Hinchcliffe, Will Power, Ryan Hunter-Reay, Helio Castroneves, Ryan Briscoe, Tony Kanaan, Marco Andretti, Josef Newgarden and E.J. Viso. Each of these were powered by Chevrolet, with the only exception being Newgarden in a Honda.

In the Fast Nine Session, Ryan Briscoe set an early time to shoot for at 226.484 mph. James Hinchcliffe came closest to overtaking Briscoe, but fell short by .003 mph. The difference in speed represents the closest margin in Indy 500 pole qualifying history.

The front row consisted of Ryan Briscoe with Team Penske, James Hinchcliffe and Ryan Hunter-Reay.

Generally throughout the month the Chevrolet-powered cars had a distinct speed advantage versus Honda.

Bump day proved to be rather uneventful as there were no bump attempts after the field was full.

Unbeknownst to most everyone; Honda had developed a generation two engine they let no one use until Carb Day. Carb Day results had Dario Franchitti and Scott Dixon at the top of the speed chart. They had qualified 16th and 15th respectively.

The Pit Stop Competition was won by the Scott Dixon Ganassi Team. This was the first win in this competition for Chip Ganassi Racing.

May 27, 2012—Race day brought extremely high temperatures. A top temperature of 91 degrees fell one degree short of the 1937 record.

Jim Nabors was unable to sing the traditional "Back Home Again in Indiana" live because of illness, but a video version was the substitute.

Indiana Governor Mitch Daniels was the honorary starter for the 96th Indianapolis 500.

Ryan Briscoe led as the field took the green flag but was drafted by James Hinchcliffe who led the first lap. These two drivers traded the lead six times in the first twenty laps.

The Lotus entries of former Formula One driver Jean Alesi and Simona de Silvestro were black-flagged early for not being able to maintain race pace.

An accident on lap fourteen involving Bryan Clauson brought out the caution. As the majority of cars pitted, Dario Franchitti was hit from behind by E.J. Viso and spun into his pit box. Franchitti's crew replaced his nose piece and he rejoined the race in last place on the track.

Marco Andretti, driving for his father, took the lead from Ryan Briscoe on lap twenty and led fifty-nine of the next seventy laps. Early in the race it became fairly obvious that the Honda engine had similar speed to the Chevrolet, but also had a fuel economy advantage, as they were able to stretch their race stints several more laps.

At the halfway point, the leader board was Dixon, Dario Franchitti, Hunter-Reay, Graham Rahal, Justin Wilson and Takuma Sato. There had been seventeen lead changes by the mid-point of the race.

Takuma Sato became the leader of the Indianapolis 500 for the first time when Dixon pitted on lap 119. Sato led thirty-one laps total just past the three-quarter mark.

The Ganassi teammates, Dario Franchitti and Scott Dixon, led all but seven laps from lap 153.

On lap 178, Franchitti passed Dixon to break the all-time record of 29 lead passes in the 1960 race.

Both Ed Carpenter and Marco Andretti were in contention for the win late in the race but had incidents that foiled their chance of victory.

After the one-car accident which eliminated Andretti, Tony Kanaan led the pack to the restart on lap 194. Kanaan was passed by Franchitti, Dixon and Sato just after they received the green. Dixon overtook Franchitti on the next lap and led until being passed by both Dario and Takuma at the start of lap 199.

As Franchitti took the white flag, Takuma Sato drove deep into turn one and attempted an inside pass. Sato lost control of his car and crashed hard into the turn one wall. Franchitti was able to avoid the accident and took the checkered flag under caution for his third

Indy 500 victory. Sato would finish in the seventeenth position. He joined the very exclusive company of drivers winning at least three Indianapolis 500s: Louis Meyer, Wilbur Shaw, Mauri Rose, A.J. Foyt, Al Unser Sr., Johnny Rutherford, Bobby Unser, Rick Mears and Helio Castroneves.

During the victory celebration, Franchitti dedicated the victory to his close friend and two-time "500" champion Dan Wheldon. Franchitti also asked Susie Wheldon to accompany him and wife, Ashley Judd, on the victory lap in the pace car.

Wheldon's former teammates Franchitti, Dixon and Kanaan honored their fallen friend with a three-wide salute on the front straightaway at the completion of the race.

Franchitti's average speed for the race was 167.73 mph. There was a record of thirty-four lead changes. The victory represented Honda power plant's ninth consecutive Indy 500 win.

Lap leaders included Andretti, 59, Dixon, 53, Sato, 31 and Franchitti 23.

Rubens Barrichello won the Rookie of the Year award with an eleventh place finish.

Dario Franchitti barely avoids a spinning Takuma Sato on the last lap.

RACE RESULTS FOR THE 2012 INDIANAPOLIS 500

Finish	Start	Car Num.	Driver	Car Name/Entrant*	Make/Model	Status	Laps	Led	Winnings
1	16	50	Dario Franchitti (W)	Target Chip Ganassi Racing	Dallara/Honda	Running	200	23	$2,474,280
2	15	9	Scott Dixon (W)	Target Chip Ganassi Racing	Dallara/Honda	Running	200	53	$1,102,280
3	8	11	Tony Kanaan	GEICO/Mouser Electronics KV Racing Technology	Dallara/Chevrolet	Running	200	7	$636,580
4	27	22	Oriol Servia	Panther/ Dreyer & Reinbold Racing	Dallara/Chevrolet	Running	200	0	$443,430
5	1	2	Ryan Briscoe	IZOD Team Penske	Dallara/Chevrolet	Running	200	15	$489,930
6	2	27	James Hinchcliffe	Team GoDaddy.com	Dallara/Chevrolet	Running	200	5	$357,680
7	21	18	Justin Wilson	Sonny's BBQ	Dallara/Honda	Running	200	0	$303,430
8	14	83	Charlie Kimball	NovoLog FlexPen	Dallara/Honda	Running	200	3	$277,655
9	20	99	Townsend Bell	BraunAbility-Schmidt-Pelfrey Motorsports	Dallara/Honda	Running	200	0	$251,305
10	6	3	Helio Castroneves (W)	Shell V-Power/ Pennzoil Ultra Team Penske	Dallara/Chevrolet	Running	200	0	$308,930
11	10	8	Rubens Barrichello (R)	BMC/Embrase KV Racing Technology	Dallara/Chevrolet	Running	200	2	$331,080
12	11	98	Alex Tagliani	Team Barracuda-BHA	Dallara/Honda	Running	200	2	$252,205
13	12	38	Graham Rahal	Service Central	Dallara/Honda	Running	200	0	$306,680
14	18	4	JR Hildebrand	National Guard Panther Racing	Dallara/Chevrolet	Running	200	0	$306,680
15	17	19	James Jakes (R)	Boy Scouts of America	Dallara/Honda	Running	200	0	$252,555
16	23	77	Simon Pagenaud (R)	Schmidt Hamilton HP Motorsports	Dallara/Honda	Running	200	0	$303,680
17	19	15	Takuma Sato	Rahal Letterman Lanigan Racing	Dallara/Honda	Contact	199	31	$301,755
18	9	5	E.J. Viso	CITGO/PDVSA KV Racing Technology	Dallara/Chevrolet	Running	199	0	$303,430
19	22	30	Michel Jourdain Jr.	Office Depot/RLL Racing	Dallara/Honda	Running	199	0	$253,305
20	25	7	Sebastien Bourdais	Dragon Racing	Dallara/Chevrolet	Running	199	0	$252,805
21	28	20	Ed Carpenter	Fuzzy's Vodka Ed Carpenter Racing	Dallara/Chevrolet	Running	199	0	$304,930
22	30	6	Katherine Legge (R)	TrueCar Dragon Racing	Dallara/Chevrolet	Running	199	0	$303,680
23	13	25	Ana Beatriz	Team Ipiranga	Dallara/Chevrolet	Running	190	0	$252,805
24	4	26	Marco Andretti	Team RC Cola	Dallara/Chevrolet	Contact	187	59	$368,480
25	7	67	Josef Newgarden (R)	Sarah Fisher Hartman/ Dollar General	Dallara/Honda	Mechanical	161	0	$257,805
26	24	17	Sebastian Saavedra	Team AFS	Dallara/Chevrolet	Electrical	143	0	$256,305
27	3	28	Ryan Hunter-Reay	Team DHL/Sun Drop Citrus Soda	Dallara/Chevrolet	Suspension	123	0	$346,680
28	5	12	Will Power	Verizon Team Penske	Dallara/Chevrolet	Contact	79	0	$310,430
29	29	14	Mike Conway	ABC Supply Co./A.J. Foyt Racing	Dallara/Honda	Contact	78	0	$305,430
30	31	39	Bryan Clauson (R)	Sarah Fisher Hartman/ Curb Agajanian	Dallara/Honda	Mechanical	46	0	$258,055
31	26	41	Wade Cunningham (R)	Ecat/ABC Supply	Dallara/Honda	Electrical	42	0	$251,555
32	32	78	Simona de Silvestro	Nuclear Clean Air Energy Lotus HVM Racing	Dallara/Lotus	Handling	10	0	$303,430
33	33	64	Jean Alesi (R)	Lotus - FP Journe - Fan Force United	Dallara/Lotus	Handling	9	0	$251,555

* - complete car name/entrant data not available for all entries
(R) - Indicated Rookie
(W) - Indicates Past Winner

2013

Many long-time race fans thought that it would be unlikely the 97th Indianapolis 500 could match the excitement of recent races. Amazingly the race matched, if not exceeded, previous races!

Mark Miles had been hired in December of 2012 as Chief Executive Officer of Hulman & Company. His main goal was to elevate the level of success of the Indianapolis 500 and the IndyCar series.

For the first time since 1987, there were two drivers attempting to win their fourth Indy 500—Helio Castroneves and Dario Franchitti.

Practice sessions were dominated by the team of Andretti Autosport. Either Marco Andretti, James Hinchcliffe, E.J. Viso or rookie Carlos Munoz put Andretti Autosport at the top of the speed charts on five of the seven practice days.

The first day of qualifications was dominated by Chevrolet. During the first segment of qualifying the top ten cars were all powered by Chevrolet. Will Power put his Team Penske car on the provisional pole at an average of 228.844 mph.

The Fast Nine Shootout actually started at 6:30 pm rather than the scheduled 4:30 pm because of an afternoon rain delay.

Team owner and driver Ed Carpenter posted an average of 228.762 to knock Marco Andretti off the pole. He became the first owner/driver to win the pole since A.J. Foyt in 1975.

Carlos Munoz and Marco Andretti joined Carpenter on the front row. Andretti Autosport drivers made up four of the top seven qualifiers.

Highlights of the second day of qualifications included:

Buddy Lazier, 1996 champion, qualified for the thirty-second starting position after not competing in the race since 2008.

Katherine Legge successfully qualified the Schmidt Peterson Motorsports Dallara after taking her first practice laps of the month that morning. Legge joined Ana Beatriz, Simona de Silvestro and Pippa Mann in the field.

Rufus Parnell "Parnelli" Jones led a group of front-engine roadsters on the track prior to the public driver's meeting on Saturday of race weekend. Parnelli drove his 1963 winning car—"Calhoun".

Jim Nabors was able to return and sing the traditional "Back Home Again in Indiana", after missing the 2012 race because of illness.

N.F.L. Super Bowl coach Jim Harbaugh drove the Chevrolet Corvette Stingray pace car to start the 97th Indianapolis 500.

Ed Carpenter took the lead at the start. J.R. Hildebrand, who came within a successful final turn of winning the "500" in 2011, lost control and crashed his National Guard Dallara in turn one on lap four.

Tony Kanaan, who started in the twelfth position, passed for the lead in the third turn on lap nine. This marked the ninth race, of the twelve in which he had participated, that Kanaan had led.

Carpenter, Andretti and Kanaan traded the lead for most of the first half of the race. At the race mid-point, Carpenter had led 37 laps with Kanaan at 18 and Andretti 13.

Rookie A.J. Allmendinger started the 98th lap in fourth position then proceeded to pass the three cars directly ahead of him, including the leader Kanaan, by the end of that lap.

At 100 laps the running order was: Allmendinger, Kanaan, Ryan Hunter-Reay, E.J. Viso and Andretti rounding out the top five positions.

Allmendinger led until pitting on lap 113 as a result of a loose seat belt that needed to be tightened.

The next eighty laps was a continuation of lead changing primarily between Kanaan, Andretti, Hunter-Reay and Allmendinger.

A green flag run from lap 61 to lap 193 set a modern era record for most consecutive laps without a caution.

On lap 194 Graham Rahal spun exiting turn two and hit the inside wall causing a caution.

The restart order on lap 197 was: Ryan Hunter-Reay, Tony Kanaan, Carlos Munoz, Marco Andretti and Justin Wilson

As the green waved, Tony Kanaan passed Hunter-Reay entering turn one for the 68th pass for the lead in the race. Munoz was also able to pass Hunter-Reay before Dario Franchitti crashed in the south short chute.

The 97th Indianapolis 500 ended under the caution with the super popular Tony Kanaan claiming his first win in his 12th attempt at Indy. This was the fourth consecutive year the race ended under caution.

Kanaan drove the race with torn ligaments in his thumb from an accident at Long Beach, California in April.

Rookie Carlos Munoz held on to the second place finish, while Hunter-Reay, Andretti, Wilson, Castroneves, Allmendinger, Simon Pagenaud, Charlie Kimball and Ed Carpenter rounded out the top ten finishers.

Chevrolet continued its domination of the month of May with a sweep of the first four finishers. The win was Chevrolet's first since 2002, after nine straight Honda victories.

The 97th Indianapolis 500 was a race of new records:

A new speed record of 187.433 mph average, breaking Arie Luyendyk's 1990 record of 185.981. The race was completed in 2 hours, 40 minutes and 3.4181 seconds.

A new record of 68 lead changes among fourteen drivers, breaking 2012's record of 34 lead changes and the 1993 record of 12 different leaders. Kanaan and Hunter-Reay exchanged the lead four times in the last eleven laps.

Nineteen cars on the lead lap at the finish, tying the record of 2009.

Fewest caution laps of only twenty-one, breaking the modern era record of twenty-six in 1990.

Twenty-six cars running at the finish, tying the record of 1911 when there were forty starters.

Kanaan won the race for the first time in his twelfth attempt. Sam Hanks won the race in 1957 in his twelfth attempt, though he had qualified thirteen times, but was injured prior to the 1941 race and was unable to compete.

The top lap leaders were: Carpenter—37, Kanaan—34, Andretti—31, Hunter-Reay—26 and Allmendinger—23.

Carlos Munoz won Rookie of the Year after starting in the second position and finishing second while leading twelve laps during the race.

Tony Kanaan's face became the 100th face on the famed Borg-Warner Trophy. Kanaan's win was as popular a victory as any in Speedway history. His full name is Antoine Rizkallah Kanaan Filho.

After the 97th running of the Indianapolis 500 there were several personnel changes at the Indianapolis Motor Speedway:

Doug Boles was named President of IMS

Jeff Belskus was named President and CFO of Hulman & Company

Derrick Walker was named President of IndyCar

Three-time Indianapolis 500 champion Dario Franchitti was seriously injured in the season's final race in Houston. Franchitti sustained a broken back, broken ankle and a concussion. Following his doctors advice, Franchitti announced his retirement from driving in November.

Mike King, the anchor of the IMS Radio Network broadcast of the race, decided to retire after being the "Voice of the 500" for the past fifteen years. Paul Page was named to replace King. Page had replaced Sid Collins in 1977 and was the "Voice of the 500" through the 1987 race.

Tony Kanaan makes the winning pass on Ryan Hunter-Reay.

RACE RESULTS FOR THE 2013 INDIANAPOLIS 500

Finish	Start	Car Num.	Driver	Car Name/Entrant*	Make/Model	Status	Laps	Led	Winnings
1	12	11	Tony Kanaan	Hydroxycut KV Racing Technology-SH Racing	Dallara/Chevrolet	Running	200	34	$2,353,355
2	2	26	Carlos Munoz (R)	Unistraw	Dallara/Chevrolet	Running	200	12	$964,205
3	7	1	Ryan Hunter-Reay	DHL	Dallara/Chevrolet	Running	200	26	$583,005
4	3	25	Marco Andretti	RC Cola	Dallara/Chevrolet	Running	200	31	$469,755
5	14	19	Justin Wilson	Dale Coyne Racing	Dallara/Honda	Running	200	0	$337,805
6	8	3	Helio Castro-neves (W)	Shell V-Power/Pennzoil Ultra Team Penske	Dallara/Chevrolet	Running	200	1	$313,755
7	5	2	AJ Allmendinger (R)	IZOD Team Penske	Dallara/Chevrolet	Running	200	23	$261,155
8	21	77	Simon Pagenaud	Schmidt Hamilton HP Motorsports	Dallara/Honda	Running	200	0	$262,805
9	19	83	Charlie Kimball	NovoLog FlexPen	Dallara/Honda	Running	200	0	$269,305
10	1	20	Ed Carpenter	Fuzzy's Vodka Ed Carpenter Racing	Dallara/Chevrolet	Running	200	37	$405,955
11	13	22	Oriol Servia	Panther DRR	Dallara/Chevrolet	Running	200	0	$271,305
12	23	8	Ryan Briscoe	NTT DATA	Dallara/Honda	Running	200	0	$230,555
13	18	14	Takuma Sato	ABC Supply Co./A.J. Foyt Racing	Dallara/Honda	Running	200	0	$264,805
14	16	9	Scott Dixon (W)	Target Chip Ganassi Racing	Dallara/Honda	Running	200	1	$268,005
15	29	18	Ana Beatriz	Ipiranga	Dallara/Honda	Running	200	0	$262,805
16	28	55	Tristan Vautier (R)	Lucas Oil/Schmidt Peterson Motorsports	Dallara/Honda	Running	200	0	$227,305
17	24	78	Simona de Silvestro	Nuclear Entergy Areva KVRT	Dallara/Chevrolet	Running	200	0	$262,805
18	4	5	E.J. Viso	Team Venezuela PDVSA Citgo	Dallara/Chevrolet	Running	200	5	$276,555
19	6	12	Will Power	Verizon Team Penske	Dallara/Chevrolet	Running	200	16	$273,255
20	20	16	James Jakes	Acorn Stairlifts	Dallara/Honda	Running	199	5	$227,555
21	9	27	James Hinchcliffe	GoDaddy	Dallara/Chevrolet	Running	199	7	$267,955
22	31	41	Conor Daly (R)	ABC Supply Co./A.J. Foyt Racing	Dallara/Honda	Running	198	0	$227,305
23	17	10	Dario Franchitti (W)	Target Chip Ganassi Racing	Dallara/Honda	Contact	197	0	$277,805
24	11	98	Alex Tagliani	Barracuda Racing	Dallara/Honda	Running	196	1	$263,255
25	26	15	Graham Rahal	Midas/Big O Tires	Dallara/Honda	Contact	193	0	$262,805
26	33	81	Katherine Legge	Angie's List Schmidt Peterson Pelfrey	Dallara/Honda	Running	193	0	$225,305
27	22	60	Townsend Bell	Sunoco "Turbo" Panther Racing	Dallara/Chevrolet	Running	192	1	$237,255
28	25	21	Josef Newgarden	Sarah Fisher Hartman/Century 21	Dallara/Honda	Running	191	0	$264,305
29	15	7	Sebastien Bourdais	Dragon Racing	Dallara/Chevrolet	Contact	178	0	$262,805
30	30	63	Pippa Mann	Cyclops Gear.com	Dallara/Honda	Contact	46	0	$225,305
31	32	91	Buddy Lazier (W)	Spirit of Oklahoma	Dallara/Chevrolet	Mechanical	44	0	$230,305
32	27	6	Sebastian Saavedra	Dragon Racing	Dallara/Chevrolet	Contact	34	0	$225,305
33	10	4	JR Hildebrand	National Guard Panther Racing	Dallara/Chevrolet	Contact	3	0	$264,305

* - complete car name/entrant data not available for all entries
(R) - Indicated Rookie
(W) - Indicates Past Winner

2014

The month of May, leading up to the 98th running of the Indianapolis 500 started with the inaugural running of the Grand Prix of Indianapolis on the IMS road course on May 10. Simon Pagenaud was the winner.

Two former winners, Jacques Villeneuve (1995) and Juan Pablo Montoya (2000) returned for the first time since their victories. This resulted in the three champions (Villeneuve, Montoya and Kanaan – 2013) attempting to win "back-to-back" 500's.

NASCAR star Kurt Busch teamed with Andretti Autosport in an attempt to complete "The Double" in one day – The Indianapolis 500 and the Charlotte 600.

Three-time Indy 500 Champion, Dario Franchitti, announced his retirement from racing in November of 2013 after sustaining a broken back, ankle and severe concussion in the season final race in Houston.

A new qualifying format was adopted with the qualifications held over two days, with the pole position not determined until the second day.

Engine specifications required twin-turbos.

Paul Page returned as "Voice of the 500" for the radio broadcast after Mike King retired. King had served in that role from 1999 through 2013.

Practice for the 98th running of the Indianapolis 500 began on Sunday, May 11. James Hinchcliffe was sidelined by a concussion he received during the Grand Prix of Indianapolis.

Team Penske topped opening day of practice on the speed chart with Will Power at 223.057 mph, Juan Pablo Montoya at 222.502 mph and Helio Castroneves at 222.373 mph.

Practice day speed leaders leading up to "Fast Friday" were: Power at 223.057 mph, Hunter-Reay at 225.025 mph, E.J. Viso (subbing for James Hinchcliffe) at 224.488 mph, Simon Pagenaud at 226.122 mph and Helio Castroneves at 227.166 mph.

Fast Friday was somewhat anti-climactic, as there were only 19 minutes of practice time due to rain. Cars were allowed an additional 10 kPa for Fast Friday practice and qualifications. Ed Carpenter posted the top speed of the month at 230.522 mph during the abbreviated practice session.

The top nine qualifiers at the end of the Saturday session became eligible for the Fast Nine Shoot-out scheduled for 2:00 pm on Sunday.

Saturday qualifiers who posted times from 10th fastest to 33rd would requalify on Sunday and their speeds would determine their starting position.

The Fast Nine Shoot-out resulted in Ed Carpenter winning his second consecutive Indy 500 pole position with a speed of 231.067 mph. James Hinchcliffe, with Andretti Autosport at 230.839 mph, and Will Power, for Team Penske at 230.697 mph, joined Carpenter on the front row.

The Monday following the qualification weekend became a post-qualifying practice session for the first time. The session allowed the teams to work on race day set-ups. Early in the session, Kurt Busch lost control of his car in turn two and crashed hard. Fortunately Busch was not injured.

Carb Day practice was dominated by the Target Chip Ganassi Racing Team. Teammates Tony Kanaan and Scott Dixon were at the top of the speed chart at almost 228 mph. Dixon's team then went on to win the 37th Pit Stop Challenge.

Race day brought beautiful blue skies and no chance of rain. Jim Nabors sang Back Home Again in Indiana for the final time. Nabors has added to the pre-race festivities with his rendition for nearly every year since

1972. At almost 84-years-old and residing in Hawaii, Nabors decided that it was time to pass the torch.

Mari Hulman George and her close friend, Jim Nabors, together gave the drivers the command to "Start your engines".

Three-time Indy 500 champion, Dario Franchitti drove the Chevrolet Camaro pace car. The honorary starter was Mark Cuban, an Indiana University graduate, owner of the NBA Dallas Mavericks and a renowned entrepreneur.

James Hinchcliffe took the early lead, as Ryan Briscoe nearly spun in turn two on the first lap.

The race was caution-free for the first 149 laps, setting a record. Only two cars had dropped out at the half-way point.

Tony Kanaan, the defending champion, ran out of fuel prior to his second stop and slowly coasted to the pits. After refueling the car, the starter broke while the team attempted to restart the engine. He finally returned to the race after falling eighteen laps behind.

Pole-sitter Ed Carpenter overtook Hinchcliffe on lap 10 and led through lap 28.

The first half of the race saw Helio Castroneves lead 26 laps, Will Power, 22, Carpenter, 21 and Hinchcliffe, 14.

At the half-way point, James Hinchcliffe led with a new record average speed of an astounding 211.871 mph.

The next quarter of the race saw continued lead changes, primarily between Ryan Hunter-Reay, who started nineteenth, Castroneves, Juan Pablo Montoya and Marco Andretti.

Charlie Kimball spun and crashed on lap 149, coming out of turn two, bringing out the first caution period in the race. The leaders pitted and the green flag waved on lap 158 with Carpenter in the lead, followed by Hunter-Reay, Andretti, Scott Dixon and Castroneves.

Dixon crashed in turn four on lap 168, breaking a consecutive laps-completed streak of 1733, dating back to the 2006 race.

The green flag waved on lap 175 with Hunter-Reay leading Carpenter, Townsend Bell, Hinchcliffe and Castroneves. As the group was entering turn one, Hinchcliffe dove low and made it three-wide with Carpenter and Bell. Hinchcliffe and Carpenter hit wheels and crashed hard. Carpenter was visibly upset with Hinchcliffe for forcing the three-wide scenario in turn one.

The green flag returned on lap 180 with Ryan Hunter-Reay in the lead. The lead changed between Andretti, Castroneves and back to Hunter-Reay before Townsend Bell crashed exiting turn two on lap 191.

In an unprecedented decision, race officials made a popular call for a red flag to stop the race so that the accident could be cleaned up and the SAFER Barrier repaired. The race stoppage lasted for nearly eleven minutes. Eight of the previous 12 Indy 500's had finished under caution as a result of an accident or rain.

Upon the restart, the drivers took two warm-up laps. The green flag waved with six laps remaining. The order was Hunter-Reay in the lead, with Castroneves and Andretti in close pursuit.

Helio Castroneves made an inside pass going into turn one with five laps remaining. On the next lap Hunter-Reay made a bold inside pass of Castroneves going into turn three, with two wheels well below the white line. Castroneves retaliated with an outside pass going into turn one with two laps remaining. Ryan Hunter-Reay then made the winning pass with a slingshot outside pass just prior to receiving the white flag. Castroneves made a last-ditch attempt with a dive to the checkered flag but fell 0.0600 seconds short. This represented the second-closest finish in Indy 500 history, topping all races except 1992.

The average speed of the race of 186.563 mph was also the second fastest in history. Following Hunter-Reay and Castroneves (in the top ten) were: Andretti, Carlos Munoz, Montoya, Kurt Busch, Sebastian Bourdais, Will Power, rookie Sage Karam and J.R. Hildebrand.

The top lap leaders were: Hunter-Reay, 56 laps, Castroneves, 38, Carpenter, 26, Power, 22, Andretti, 20, Montoya, 16 and Hinchcliffe, 14.

The Rookie of the Year award was presented to Kurt Busch at the Victory Banquet. Busch's attempt at completing the full 1100 miles in one day in "The Double" fell short when his engine blew late in the NASCAR Coca-Cola 600.

Andretti Autosport experienced a very successful Indy 500 with Hunter-Reay placing first, Marco Andretti third, Carlos Munoz fourth, and Kurt Busch finishing sixth. This was Michael Andretti's third Indy 500 win as a car owner.

Ryan Hunter-Reay became the first American-born driver to win the Indy 500 since Sam Hornish in 2006, and only the third since 1998. His winnings were $2,491,194.

Will Power went on to win the 2014 IndyCar Series Championship after having finished second in 2010, 2011 and 2012.

Ryan Hunter-Reay makes the winning pass on Helio Castroneves just prior to the white flag.

RACE RESULTS FOR THE 2014 INDIANAPOLIS 500

Finish	Start	Car Num.	Driver	Car Name/Entrant*	Make/Model	Status	Laps	Led	Winnings
1	19	28	Ryan Hunter-Reay	DHL	Dallara/Honda	Running	200	56	$2,491,194
2	4	3	Helio Castroneves (W)	Pennzoil Ultra Platinum Team Penske	Dallara/Chevrolet	Running	200	38	$785,194
3	6	25	Marco Andretti	Snapple	Dallara/Honda	Running	200	20	$585,194
4	7	34	Carlos Munoz	Cinsay AndrettiTV.com HVM	Dallara/Honda	Running	200	0	$449,194
5	10	2	Juan Pablo Montoya (W)	Verizon Team Penske	Dallara/Chevrolet	Running	200	16	$441,944
6	12	26	Kurt Busch (R)	Suretone	Dallara/Honda	Running	200	0	$423,889
7	17	11	Sebastien Bourdais	Hydroxycut/Mistic KVSH Racing	Dallara/Chevrolet	Running	200	0	$384,194
8	3	12	Will Power	Verizon Team Penske	Dallara/Chevrolet	Running	200	22	$442,194
9	31	22	Sage Karam (R)	Comfort Revolution/Brantley Gilbert	Dallara/Chevrolet	Running	200	0	$270,305
10	9	21	JR Hildebrand	Preferred Freezer / Ed Carpenter Racing	Dallara/Chevrolet	Running	200	0	$366,194
11	18	16	Oriol Servia	Rahal Letterman Lanigan Racing	Dallara/Honda	Running	200	0	$247,305
12	5	77	Simon Pagenaud	Schmidt Peterson Hamilton Motorsports	Dallara/Honda	Running	200	0	$374,444
13	24	68	Alex Tagliani	SFHR/RW Motorsports	Dallara/Honda	Running	200	3	$368,694
14	27	5	Jacques Villeneuve (W)	Schmidt Peterson Motorsports	Dallara/Honda	Running	200	0	$354,194
15	32	17	Sebastian Saavedra	KV AFS Racing	Dallara/Chevrolet	Running	200	0	$349,194
16	28	33	James Davison (R)	KVRT/Always Evolving Racing	Dallara/Chevrolet	Running	200	0	$341,194
17	21	18	Carlos Huertas (R)	Dale Coyne Racing	Dallara/Honda	Running	200	0	$339,694
18	30	8	Ryan Briscoe	NTT Data Chip Ganassi Racing	Dallara/Chevrolet	Running	200	0	$344,444
19	23	14	Takuma Sato	ABC Supply A.J. Foyt Racing	Dallara/Honda	Running	200	0	$342,444
20	13	98	Jack Hawksworth (R)	Integrity Energee Drink	Dallara/Honda	Running	200	0	$346,194
21	15	7	Mikhail Aleshin (R)	SMP Racing	Dallara/Honda	Running	198	1	$340,194
22	14	19	Justin Wilson	Dale Coyne Racing	Dallara/Honda	Running	198	0	$339,194
23	29	41	Martin Plowman (R)	ABC Supply/AJ Foyt Racing	Dallara/Honda	Running	196	0	$225,805
24	22	63	Pippa Mann	Dale Coyne Racing	Dallara/Honda	Running	193	0	$226,805
25	25	6	Townsend Bell	Robert Graham KV Racing Technology	Dallara/Chevrolet	Contact	190	0	$226,805
26	16	10	Tony Kanaan (W)	Target Chip Ganassi Racing	Dallara/Chevrolet	Running	177	1	$343,194
27	1	20	Ed Carpenter	Fuzzy's Vodka/Ed Carpenter Racing	Dallara/Chevrolet	Contact	175	26	$463,694
28	2	27	James Hinchcliffe	United Fiber & Data	Dallara/Honda	Contact	175	14	$376,194
29	11	9	Scott Dixon (W)	Target Chip Ganassi Racing	Dallara/Chevrolet	Contact	167	3	$390,694
30	8	67	Josef Newgarden	Hartman Oil/Sarah Fisher Hartman Racing	Dallara/Honda	Contact	156	0	$344,194
31	26	83	Charlie Kimball	Novo Nordisk Ganassi Racing	Dallara/Chevrolet	Contact	149	0	$341,194
32	33	91	Buddy Lazier	Wynn Institute for Vision Research	Dallara/Chevrolet	Mechanical	87	0	$225,305
33	20	15	Graham Rahal	National Guard	Dallara/Honda	Electrical	44	0	$341,194

* - complete car name/entrant data not available for all entries
(R) - Indicated Rookie
(W) - Indicates Past Winner

2015

The 99th Indianapolis 500 lived up to the extremely high expectations built over the past several races. Another super exciting Indianapolis 500!

Track time on Sunday May 3rd included a rookie orientation, refresher test time and an open session. Many teams took advantage of the opportunity to test the new oval aero kits, designed, engineered and manufactured by engine suppliers Honda and Chevrolet.

Month of May racing started on May 9th with the second annual Grand Prix of Indianapolis on the Indianapolis Motor Speedway's 2.605-mile road course.

IndyCar Series champion, Will Power, dominated the Grand Prix, leading 65 of the 82 laps. Graham Rahal finished a close second, driving for Rahal Letterman Lanigan Racing.

"Official" practice for the 99th Indianapolis 500 began on Monday, May 11. Sage Karam posted the fast time at 225.802 mph with Scott Dixon and Tony Kanaan next, all driving for Chip Ganassi Racing.

On Wednesday of the first week of practice an accident involving three-time Indy 500 champion Helio Castroneves foreshadowed topsy-turvy things to come. After entering turn one his car did a half-spin and hit the short chute wall. While sliding backward the car lifted and did nearly a complete flip before coming to a rest upright in turn two. Castroneves walked away uninjured and returned to the track in his back-up car before track closing. Carlos Munoz posted the fast lap of the month at 230.121 mph.

Josef Newgarden experienced a major crash in turn one on Thursday which seemed somewhat similar to the Castroneves accident the day before. Newgarden did a three-quarter spin in turn one and hit the wall in the short chute. The rear of his car lifted and flipped and landed upside-down at the entrance to turn two. Newgarden was not injured in the big crash. Simon Pagenaud was on top of the speed chart for Team Penske at 228.793 mph.

Additional boost generating approximately 50 extra horsepower was given for "Fast Friday" and qualifications. Simon Pagenaud was fastest on Friday at 230.698.

Helio Castroneves turned the fastest lap since 1996 on Saturday's early practice session at 233.474 mph. Qualifications started with just three drivers attempting runs before rain ended the session. Officials decided to void the completed qualification attempts and time trials would occur on Sunday.

Practice on Sunday morning prior to qualifications brought more problems! Early in the practice session, two-time pole sitter Ed Carpenter lost control of his car in turn two. The car did a half spin and hit the wall at the exit of the turn. The car slid backwards along the wall, lifted, flipped and landed upside-down. Carpenter was not injured, but the fact that this accident represented the third Chevrolet-powered car to get airborne in less than a week caused serious safety concerns.

Meetings ensued with officials and owners resulting in qualification procedures being modified. Each car would have just one attempt to qualify in "race trim" with no additional boost. The Fast Nine Shootout was also eliminated, but there would be a final row shootout with the four slowest cars vying for the last three starting positions.

Scott Dixon was an early qualifier at an average speed of 226.760 mph, and his speed held up as the fastest of the day. This was the second time in his career that Dixon won the pole. Joining Dixon on the front row were Team Penske drivers Will Power and Simon Pagenaud. Juan Pablo Montoya, the third Penske driver, qualified a rather disappointing fifteenth. There were no incidents during the qualifying session.

The 1996 Indy 500 champion, Buddy Lazier, was the sole participant who failed to make the starting field. He had very limited practice time in his Lazier Partners Chevrolet Dallara.

For the second consecutive year a post-qualifying practice session was scheduled for race week Monday. Early in the session a serious accident involving James Hinchcliff occurred. Entering turn three his car experienced a right front suspension failure. The car veered into the outside wall with great force, slid through the north chute on its side before landing upright. Hinchcliff had to be extricated from his car and lost a tremendous amount of blood as a result of suspension parts piercing his thigh. Quick reaction by the Holmatro IndyCar safety personnel likely saved his life. Major surgery was performed on Hinchcliff at Methodist Hospital.

The track was closed for repairs and further investigation of the serious accident. The track reopened from 4:00 pm to 6:00 pm for IndyCar practice. Sage Karam set fast time of the day at 227.831 mph.

Ryan Briscoe was named as the replacement for the injured Hinchcliff. A special one-hour practice session was allowed for Briscoe on Thursday of race week.

Carb Day was held on Friday May 22, 2015. News sprung that Carlos Huertas was not medically cleared to drive because of an inner ear issue. Tristan Vautier, who had actually qualified a car for James Davison, was named to replace Huertas. There were no incidents during the one hour Carb session. Will Power topped the speed chart at 229.020 mph.

Englishman Jack Harvey won the Indy Lights Freedom 100 for Schmidt Peterson Motorsports. The team carried the first four positions at the finish.

The TAG Heuer Annual Pit Stop Challenge was won by the Helio Castroneves team for the sixth time. This was Team Penske's fifteenth win in the contest.

Four-time Indy 500 champion, Al Unser Sr., was honored on Legends Day.

Race Day brought blue skies and warm temperatures. The a cappella group Straight No Chaser continued the pre-race tradition carried for so many years by Jim Nabors by performing "Back Home Again in Indiana."

Conor Daly experienced a fire underneath his car on the parade lap and became the infamous "first out."

Pole sitter Scott Dixon brought the field to the green flag. The first accident of the race occurred in the first turn on the first lap. Takuma Sato and Sage Karam attempted to occupy the same track space and Karam hit the outside wall. Ryan Briscoe spun trying to avoid the mishap. The cars of Briscoe and Sato were able to be repaired and continued in the race.

The strange start of the race continued. As the field was preparing for the restart on lap 7, Simona de Silvestro rear-ended Juan Pablo Montoya breaking the right-rear wheel guard off his car. Both cars were repaired under a continued caution. Montoya rejoined the field in 30th position.

The green flag finally appeared on lap 13. Dixon, Tony Kanaan and Simon Pagenaud swapped the lead until the first round of green flag pit stops.

Ganassi teammates swapped the lead until lap 64 when Bryan Clauson crashed in turn four. Simon Pagenaud was able to take the lead during the yellow flag pit stops.

Pagenaud, Kanaan and Dixon continued to battle for the lead to the halfway point. On lap 95, Juan Pablo Montoya overshot his pit which cost him precious seconds. The first half of the race had definitely not gone as expected for Montoya.

The third caution of the race occurred on lap 113, as Ed Carpenter and Oriol Servia came together in turn one. This was the second year in a row that Carpenter's race ended against the first turn wall.

An unheard of situation occurred during the caution, as all three of Dale Coyne's cars were involved in a chain reaction pit accident eliminating James Davison, Pippa Mann and Tristan Vautier.

As the race went green on lap 122, Will Power joined the fray fighting for the lead with Kanaan, Dixon and Pagenaud.

Just past the three-quarter mark, 2013 Indy 500 champion, Tony Kanaan lost control in turn three and crashed. He had pitted just prior to the crash and made a significant downforce adjustment.

The race went green on lap 160 with Juan Pablo Montoya joining the lead group. The fifth caution of the day occurred on lap 167 for debris on the track.

The leaders made their final pit stops with Andretti Autosport drivers Carlos Munoz and Justin Wilson electing not to pit. As the race went green on lap 173, Munoz and Wilson briefly led the lead pack before being passed. As Simon Pagenaud was passing Justin Wilson he clipped his rear-end and damaged his front wing. This contact resulted in Pagenaud dropping back through the field.

On lap 176, Jack Hawksworth hit Sebastián Saavedra from behind and Stefano Coletti was collected in the aftermath.

The race went green on lap 184 with Will Power leading. The final shootout would produce five lead changes in the last fourteen laps. Dixon and Power exchanged the lead several times then Montoya went to the front. Power overtook Montoya on lap 193 and led through lap 196. Entering turn one on lap 197 Montoya completed the winning outside pass. Montoya took the checker after leading only nine laps the entire day. Montoya held off Penske teammate Will Power by .1046 of a second. This was the fourth closest finish in history.

The victory was Roger Penske's sixteenth Indy 500 win. Montoya's second Indy 500 win occurred fifteen years after his first, and in only his third start.

Charlie Kimball finished third for his career best "500" result. Scott Dixon finished fourth after having led a race high 84 laps. A late race overheating problem may have cost him a second Indy 500 win. The remainder of the top ten was: Rahal, Andretti, Castroneves, Hildebrand, Newgarden and Pagenaud.

The super competitive race saw a total of 37 lead changes with Dixon leading 84, Pagenaud 35, Kanaan 30, Power 23, Kimball 10 and Montoya 9.

Tragedy struck the IndyCar Series during the Pocono 500 on August 23, 2015. Justin Wilson was hit in the head by flying debris from an accident involving another car. Wilson suffered a traumatic brain injury and passed away the following day. Wilson was at the top of the list of popular drivers in the paddock.

After leading the IndyCar points battle for nearly the entire season, Juan Pablo Montoya lost a championship tiebreak to Scott Dixon in the final race of the season in California at Sonoma Raceway. This championship represented Scott Dixon's fourth series title.

Juan Pablo Montoya makes the winning pass overtaking Will Power on lap 197.

RACE RESULTS FOR THE 2015 INDIANAPOLIS 500

Finish	Start	Car Num.	Driver	Car Name/Entrant*	Make/Model	Status	Laps	Led	Winnings
1	15	2	Juan Pablo Montoya	Verizon Team Penske Chevrolet	Dallara/Chevrolet	Running	200	9	$2,449,055
2	2	1	Will Power	Verizon Team Penske Chevrolet	Dallara/Chevrolet	Running	200	23	$792,555
3	14	83	Charlie Kimball	Novo Nordisk Chip Ganassi Racing Chevrolet	Dallara/Chevrolet	Running	200	10	$564,055
4	1	9	Scott Dixon	Target Chip Ganassi Racing Chevrolet	Dallara/Chevrolet	Running	200	84	$615,805
5	17	15	Graham Rahal	Steak 'n Shake Honda	Dallara/Honda	Running	200	0	$439,555
6	8	27	Marco Andretti	Snapple Honda	Dallara/Honda	Running	200	0	$412,055
7	5	3	Helio Castroneves	Shell V-Power Nitro+ Team Penske Chevrolet	Dallara/Chevrolet	Running	200	2	$482,555
8	10	6	JR Hildebrand	Preferred Freezer CFH Racing Chevrolet	Dallara/Chevrolet	Running	200	0	$246,805
9	9	21	Josef Newgarden	Century 21 CFH Racing Chevrolet	Dallara/Chevrolet	Running	200	0	$382,055
10	3	22	Simon Pagenaud	Avaya Team Penske Chevrolet	Dallara/Chevrolet	Running	200	35	$307,805
11	7	11	Sebastien Bourdais	Hydroxycut-HAUS Vaporizer KVSH Chevrolet	Dallara/Chevrolet	Running	200	0	$378,555
12	31	5	Ryan Briscoe	Arrow/Lucas Oil Schmidt Peterson Honda	Dallara/Honda	Running	200	0	$368,805
13	24	14	Takuma Sato	ABC Supply A.J. Foyt Racing Honda	Dallara/Honda	Running	200	0	$364,055
14	23	24	Townsend Bell	The Robert Graham Special Chevrolet	Dallara/Chevrolet	Running	200	0	$218,555
15	16	28	Ryan Hunter-Reay	DHL Honda	Dallara/Honda	Running	200	0	$355,555
16	26	96	Gabby Chaves	Bowers & Wilkins/Curb Honda	Dallara/Honda	Running	200	0	$399,055
17	20	48	Alex Tagliani	Alfe Heat Treating Special Honda	Dallara/Honda	Running	200	2	$203,305
18	19	7	James Jakes	Schmidt Peterson Motorsports Honda	Dallara/Honda	Running	200	0	$347,555
19	18	29	Simona de Silvestro	TE Connectivity Honda	Dallara/Honda	Running	200	0	$200,305
20	11	26	Carlos Munoz	AndrettiTV Cinsay Honda	Dallara/Honda	Running	200	3	$345,555
21	6	25	Justin Wilson	Andretti Autosport Honda	Dallara/Honda	Running	199	2	$211,305
22	25	63	Pippa Mann	Dale Coyne Racing Honda	Dallara/Honda	Running	197	0	$206,805
23	27	17	Sebastian Saavedra	AFS Chip Ganassi Racing Chevrolet	Dallara/Chevrolet	Contact	175	0	$200,305
24	28	41	Jack Hawksworth	ABC Supply A.J. Foyt Racing Honda	Dallara/Honda	Contact	175	0	$205,055
25	29	4	Stefano Coletti	KV Racing Technology Chevrolet	Dallara/Chevrolet	Contact	175	0	$344,555
26	4	10	Tony Kanaan	NTT Data Chip Ganassi Racing Chevrolet	Dallara/Chevrolet	Contact	151	30	$375,555
27	33	19	James Davison	Dale Coyne Racing Honda	Dallara/Honda	Mechanical	116	0	$344,055
28	32	18	Tristan Vautier	Dale Coyne Racing Honda	Dallara/Honda	Mechanical	116	0	$344,055
29	13	32	Oriol Servia	Rahal Letterman Lanigan Racing Honda	Dallara/Honda	Contact	112	0	$201,805
30	12	20	Ed Carpenter	Fuzzy's Vodka CFH Racing Chevrolet	Dallara/Chevrolet	Contact	112	0	$344,055
31	30	88	Bryan Clauson	Jonathan Byrd's/Cancer Centers of America Chevrolet	Dallara/Chevrolet	Contact	61	0	$200.305
32	21	8	Sage Karam	Comfort Revolution/Big Machine Records Chevrolet	Dallara/Chevrolet	Contact	0	0	$344,055
33	22	43	Conor Daly	Fueled by Bacon Special Honda	Dallara/Honda	Mechanical	0	0	$201,805

2016

The month of May for the 100th running of the Indianapolis 500 opened on May 14, 2016 with the Angie's List Grand Prix on the 2.439-mile road course. Simon Pagenaud dominated by leading 57 of the 82 laps, including the final 21 to the checker.

For the first time in race history, the Indianapolis 500 had a "presenting sponsor". It was called the "100th Indianapolis 500 presented by Penn Grade Motor Oil". Penn Grade Motor Oil is a brand of D-A Lubricant Company. D-A Lubricant sponsored cars in the Indianapolis 500 in the late 1950's.

Simon Pagenaud arrived at Indy red hot, with second place finishes in the first two races of the year, then two consecutive wins prior to the Indy Grand Prix.

Dome skids were required on all cars in an attempt to keep the cars on the ground during a crash. The domed skids were attached to the undertrays of the car body. After the dilemma of cars lifting in accidents during the month of May 2015, the phenomenon did not occur in 2016.

Indy 500 practice started on Monday, May 16, 2016 with Andretti Autosport taking the top three speed positions. Marco Andretti, at 228.978 mph, topped teammates Carlos Munoz and Ryan Hunter-Reay.

Tuesday was a rain-out. Wednesday brought the first accident of the month when rookie Spencer Pigot lost control of his Rahal Letterman Lannigan Racing Dallara/Honda in turn one. Andretti Autosport topped the speed chart again with Ryan Hunter-Reay at 228.202 mph. Josef Newgarden, with Ed Carpenter Racing, led the "no tow" laps at 224.541.

On Thursday, all 33 car entries practiced. Gabby Chavez, driving for Dale Coyne Racing, surprised the larger teams with the fast time of the day at 227.961 mph. Will Power recorded the fastest "no tow" lap at 225.381 mph.

For both Fast Friday and qualifications, the teams were allowed an extra 10kPa of turbocharger boost - from 130 to 140. Early in the Friday practice session, Marco Andretti became the first driver of the month to eclipse the 230 mph barrier. By the end of the session, fourteen drivers exceeded 230 mph with Will Power of Penske Racing at the top of the speed chart at 232.672 mph. Townsend Bell, with Andretti Autosport, set the fastest "no tow" lap at 231.672 mph.

Saturday's pre-qualification morning practice was delayed by rain. Actual practice did not start until 12:30 pm. Early in the session, rookie Max Chilton spun in turn two and crashed. Officials announced that qualifications would be extended to 7:00 pm from the customary 6:00 pm close because of loss of track time due to rain and "weepers".

The top nine qualifiers on Saturday would participate in the Top Nine Shootout on Sunday for the pole position. Qualifiers in positions 10 through 33 would be set in the starting field, but actual starting spots would be determined by Sunday's qualifying speeds.

The Fast Nine qualifiers by speed included James Hinchcliffe, Ryan Hunter-Reay, Will Power, Helio Castroneves, Townsend Bell, Josef Newgarden, Mikhail Aleshin, Carlos Munoz and Simon Pagenaud. Rookie Alexander Rossi, Marco Andretti and defending champion Juan Pablo Montoya just missed.

Pole day qualifications brought warmer temperatures and lower speeds. Early in the qualifying session, Alex Tagliani lost control of his A.J. Foyt car coming out of turn four and hit the outside wall. He would be relegated to start thirty-third. Oriol Servia, driving for Schmidt Peterson Motorsports, would be the fastest of the non-Fast Nine at 229.060 mph.

Josef Newgarden, driving for Ed Carpenter Racing, took the provisional pole early in the session at a speed of 230.700 mph. The speed held up until James Hinchcliffe, in the final run of the day, eclipsed Newgarden for the pole position at 230.770 mph. A very enthusiastic and supportive crowd cheered Hinchcliffe's achievement one year after his near fatal accident at the track.

An extremely busy post-qualifying Monday practice session saw all thirty-three drivers work on race day set-ups. A month high of 2886 laps were completed during the action-packed session. Josef Newgarden was at the top of the speed chart at 227.414 mph.

On May 25th, Speedway officials announced that the race was a total sellout with all grandstand seats and general admission tickets sold. The 100th running of the Indianapolis 500 would be the first official sellout in history. It was also announced that the race would be broadcast live locally for the first time since 1950.

Carb Day Friday was the final practice session prior to the race. Pippa Mann crashed coming out of turn four for her second incident of the month. Tony Kanaan, driving for Chip Ganassi Racing, set the fast time at 226.280 mph.

Race day brought partly cloudy skies and temperatures in the low 80's. Pre-race festivities included celebrating many of the former winning drivers and noteworthy cars in history. Sam Hornish, the 2006 Indy 500 winner, drove the Kennedy Tank Special car that competed in the 1948 and 1949 Indy 500.

Mari Hulman George was joined by numerous members of her family to give the command to start engines.

Sixteen-time winning car owner, Roger Penske, drove the Chevrolet Camaro pace car to start the race.

The jam-packed record crowd was in a frenzy as the green flag fell with pole sitter James Hinchcliffe taking the lead until being passed on the backstretch by Ryan Hunter-Reay. Hunter-Reay led the first lap and battled in the lead group with Hinchcliffe and Josef Newgarden for the first quarter of the race.

The yellow flag flew for the first time on lap 47 because of debris. During pit stops, Will Power forced Tony Kanaan against the inside pit wall. Power was penalized and sent to the rear of the field.

Upon the restart, Hunter-Reay and Hinchcliffe continued their battle for the lead. Defending Indy 500 champion, Juan Pablo Montoya, crashed in turn two on lap 64. In four "500" starts for Montoya, this was his first DNF. He finished in 33rd position.

During the yellow flag, another pit incident occurred as Simon Pagenaud exited his stall and made contact with Mikhail Aleshin. Pagenaud was penalized and sent to the back of the field.

Will Power elected to stay on the track and took the lead. Light rain caused a very short delay in restarting the race. The green flag flew on lap 74 and Power was quickly passed by Hinchcliffe and Hunter-Reay.

Near the halfway point, Sage Karam attempted an outside pass of Townsend Bell entering turn one and crashed.

Just past the halfway point, the leaderboard showed Helio Castroneves, followed by Hunter-Reay, Bell and Tony Kanaan. On lap 114, a rear suspension failure on Mikhail Aleshin's car caused him to crash in turn one. Conor Daly spun to avoid Aleshin and was finished for the day. Aleshin returned to the race after repairs, but was many laps down.

During the yellow flag period, another pit accident occurred. While exiting the pit, Townsend Bell made contact with Helio Castroneves. Bell then spun into Hunter-Reay, causing both to fall off the lead lap. Castroneves's car was not affected significantly.

During this yellow flag period, Alex Tagliani and Alexander Rossi elected not to pit, which put them out of sequence with most of the field.

The green flag fell on lap 121 and Tagliani and Rossi battled for the lead until nearly lap 140 when pitting was required. Castroneves took the lead until his pit stop. Just as he was nearing his pit box, the yellow light came on because of Buddy Lazier losing a tire in turn two. Yellow flag pit stops cycled Castroneves to the lead with Tony Kanaan in second place.

The green flag waved on lap 158 and almost immediately a battle between Castroneves, Kanaan, Newgarden and Hinchcliffe was waged. On lap 161, J.R. Hildebrand made contact with Castroneves's left rear bumper pad. Repairs were needed, but a yellow when Takuma Sato hit the wall coming out of turn four, minimized, to a degree, Castroneves's loss. During the yellow, most drivers pitted, though it seemed that another stop would be required to get to the finish.

Green flag racing resumed on lap 167 with Kanaan, Newgarden and Munoz rounding out the top three. As the finish neared, most teams realized that a "splash and go" would be necessary to complete the race.

Kanaan pitted first, then Newgarden and Munoz pitted with five laps remaining. Rookie Alexander Rossi assumed the lead while trying to nurse his fuel to the finish. Rossi had overcome two poor pit stops that placed him toward the back of the field. He had started 12th and near the mid-point was running 10th. On his stop after the Karam accident, his crew had difficulty engaging the fuel hose. As a result he restarted 26th. At this point the team decided to pit again while the track was being cleaned and effectively put Rossi out of sequence with the bulk of the field for the rest of the race.

As the white flag was waved, Rossi led Andretti Autosport teammate, Carlos Munoz, by just over twenty seconds. In a concerted effort to save fuel, Rossi ran the final lap at less than 180 mph (179.784). He took the checkered flags 4.5 seconds ahead of Munoz, whose final lap was at almost 219 mph. Rossi was able to stretch his fuel load thirty-six laps to the checker, while the average fuel window for Honda was about thirty-two laps.

Following Rossi and Munoz were: Newgarden, Kanaan, Charlie Kimball, Hildebrand, Hinchliffe, Dixon, Sebastien Bourdais and Will Power.

Rossi became the first rookie winner since Castroneves in 2001 and only the tenth rookie winner in history. He averaged 166.634 mph and won $2.54 million of the $13,273,253 purse. He also won the Rookie of the Year award.

Rossi's win gave Michael Andretti his fourth win as a car owner. It also gave Bryan Herta his second as an owner.

Lap leaders were: Hunter-Reay 52, Hinchcliffe 27, Castroneves 24, Kanaan 19, Newgarden 14 and Rossi 14. The race saw thirteen different leaders.

Three-time Indy 500 starter Bryan Clauson died on August 7, 2016 from injuries sustained in the Belleville Nationals midget race. He was competing in his 116th race of the year.

Simon Pagenaud continued his early-season domination after the Indy 500. He won five races and seven pole positions on his way to winning the Verizon IndyCar Series championship. Pagenaud's season championship represented the fourteenth for Team Penske.

Rookie Alexander Rossi becomes the first American-born winner since Sam Hornish in 2006.

RACE RESULTS - INDIANAPOLIS 500 - 2016

Finish	Start	Car Num.	Driver	Car Name/Entrant	Make/Model	Status	Laps	Led	Winnings
1	11	98	Alexander Rossi	NAPA Auto Parts / Curb Honda	Dallara/Honda	166.634	200	14	$2,548,743
2	5	26	Carlos Munoz	United Fiber & Data Honda	Dallara/Honda	166.565	200	10	$788,743
3	2	21	Josef Newgarden	Preferred Freezer Chevrolet	Dallara/Chevrolet	166.588	200	14	$574,243
4	18	10	Tony Kanaan	NTT Data Chip Ganassi Racing Chevrolet	Dallara/Chevrolet	166.473	200	19	$445,743
5	16	42	Charlie Kimball	Tresiba Chevrolet	Dallara/Chevrolet	166.742	200	0	$423,243
6	15	6	JR Hildebrand	Preferred Freezer Fuzzy's Vodka Chevrolet	Dallara/Chevrolet	166.46	200	4	$257,305
7	1	5	James Hinchcliffe	Arrow Schmidt Peterson Motorsports Honda	Dallara/Honda	166.438	200	27	$502,993
8	13	9	Scott Dixon	Target Chip Ganassi Racing Chevrolet	Dallara/Chevrolet	166.401	200	0	$384,493
9	19	11	Sebastien Bourdais	Team Hydroxycut - KVSH Chevrolet	Dallara/Chevrolet	166.31	200	0	$371,743
10	6	12	Will Power	Verizon Team Penske Chevrolet	Dallara/Chevrolet	166.303	200	8	$390,243
11	9	3	Helio Castroneves	Shell V-Power Nitro+ Team Penske Chevrolet	Dallara/Chevrolet	166.294	200	24	$451,243
12	10	77	Oriol Servia	Lucas Oil Special Honda	Dallara/Honda	166.268	200	0	$220,305
13	14	27	Marco Andretti	Snapple Honda	Dallara/Honda	166.25	200	0	$354,243
14	26	15	Graham Rahal	Steak 'n Shake Honda	Dallara/Honda	166.2	200	0	$354,493
15	22	8	Max Chilton	Gallagher Chip Ganassi Racing Chevrolet	Dallara/Chevrolet	166.193	200	0	$346,743
16	31	41	Jack Hawksworth	ABC Supply AJ Foyt Racing Honda	Dallara/Honda	166.14	200	0	$336,243
17	33	35	Alex Tagliani	Alfe Heat Treating Special Honda	Dallara/Honda	166.139	200	11	$215,805
18	25	63	Pippa Mann	Susan G. Komen Honda	Dallara/Honda	165.698	199	0	$205,305
19	8	22	Simon Pagenaud	Menards Team Penske Chevrolet	Dallara/Chevrolet	165.689	199	0	$341,243
20	21	98	Gabby Chaves	Boy Scouts of America Honda	Dallara/Honda	165.592	199	0	$336,243
21	4	29	Townsend Bell	California Pizza Kitchen/Robert Graham Honda	Dallara/Honda	165.592	199	12	$221,305
22	27	61	Matthew Brabham	PIRTEK Team Murray	Dallara/Chevrolet	165.579	199	0	$202,805
23	28	88	Bryan Clauson	Cancer Treatment Centers of America	Dallara/Honda	164.861	198	3	$201,805
24	3	28	Ryan Hunter-Reay	DHL Honda	Dallara/Honda	164.188	198	52	$419,243
25	29	16	Spencer Pigot	RLL / Mi-Jack / Manitowoc	Dallara/Honda	161.997	195	0	$200,805
26	12	14	Takuma Sato	ABC Supply AJ Foyt Racing Honda	Dallara/Honda	Contact	163	0	$338,243
27	7	7	Mikhail Aleshin	SMP Racing Schmidt Peterson Honda	Dallara/Honda	Contact	126	0	$359,243

Finish	Start	Car Num.	Driver	Car Name/Entrant	Make/Model	Status	Laps	Led	Winnings
28	30	25	Stefan Wilson	Driven2SaveLives - KVRT Chevrolet	Dallara/Chevrolet	Electrical	119	0	$200,805
29	24	18	Conor Daly	Shirts for America Honda	Dallara/Honda	Contact	115	0	$336,243
30	32	4	Buddy Lazier	Lazier / Burns Racing Chevrolet	Dallara/Chevrolet	Mechanical	100	0	$200,305
31	20	20	Ed Carpenter	Ed Carpenter Racing Chevrolet	Dallara/Chevrolet	Mechanical	98	0	$200,305
32	23	24	Sage Karam	Gas Monkey Energy Chevrolet	Dallara/Chevrolet	Contact	93	2	$203,305
33	17	2	Juan Pablo Montoya	Verizon Team Penske Chevrolet	Dallara/Chevrolet	Contact	63	0	$339,493

INDIANAPOLIS 500 RACE WINNERS

YEAR	SP	CAR #	DRIVER	CAR NAME/ENTRANT CHASSIS/ENGINE	QUALIFY SPEED	RACE TIME	RACE SPEED
1911	28	32	Ray Harroun	Nordyke & Marmon/Marmon/Marmon	N/A	6:42:08.000	74.602
1912	7	8	Joe Dawson	National Motor Vehicle/National/National	86.130	6:21:06.000	78.719
1913	7	16	Jules Goux	Peugeot/Peugeot/Peugeot	86.030	6:35:05.000	75.933
1914	15	16	Rene Thomas	L. Delage/Delage/Delage	94.540	6:03:45.000	82.474
1915	2	2	Ralph DePalma	Mercedes/E.C. Patterson/Mercedes/Mercedes	98.580	5:33:55.510	89.840
1916	4	17	Dario Resta	Peugeot Auto Racing/Peugeot/Peugeot	94.400	3:34:17.000	84.001a
1919	2	3	Howdy Wilcox	Peugeot/Indpls Spdway Team/Peugeot/Peugeot	100.010	5:40:42.870	88.050
1920	6	4	Gaston Chevrolet	Monroe/William Small/Frontenac/Frontenac	91.550	5:38:32.000	88.618
1921	20	2	Tommy Milton	Frontenac/Louis Chevrolet/Frontenac/Frontenac	93.050	5:34:44.650	89.621
1922	1	35	Jimmy Murphy	Jimmy Murphy/Duesenberg/Miller	100.500	5:17:30.790	94.484
1923	1	1	Tommy Milton	H.C.S. Motor/Miller/Miller	108.170	5:29:50.170	90.954
1924	21	15	L.L. Corum-J. Boyer	Duesenberg/Duesenberg/Duesenberg	93.330	5:05:23.510	98.234
1925	2	12	Peter DePaolo	Duesenberg/Duesenberg/Duesenberg	113.080	4:56:39.460	101.127
1926	20	15	Frank Lockhart	Miller/Peter Kreis/Miller/Miller	95.780	4:10:14.950	95.904b
1927	22	32	George Souders	Duesenberg/William White/Duesenberg/Duesenberg	111.550	5:07:33.080	97.545
1928	13	14	Louis Meyer	Miller/Alden Sampson II/Miller/Miller	111.350	5:01:33.750	99.482
1929	6	2	Ray Keech	Simplex Piston Ring/Yagle/Miller/Miller	114.900	5:07:25.420	97.585
1930	1	4	Billy Arnold	Miller-Hartz/Summers/Miller	113.260	4:58:39.720	100.448
1931	13	23	Louis Schneider	Bowes Seal Fast/Schneider/Stevens/Miller	107.210	5:10:27.930	96.629
1932	27	34	Fred Frame	Miller-Harry Hartz/Wetteroth/Miller	113.850	4:48:03.790	104.144
1933	6	36	Louis Meyer	Tydol/Louis Meyer/Miller/Miller	116.970	4:48:00.750	104.162
1934	10	7	Bill Cummings	Boyle Products/Henning/Miller/Miller	116.110	4:46:05.200	104.863
1935	22	5	Kelly Petillo	Gilmore Speedway/Petillo/Wetteroth/Offy	115.090	4:42:22.710	106.240
1936	28	8	Louis Meyer	Ring Free/Louis Meyer Stevens/Miller	114.170	4:35:03.390	109.069
1937	2	6	Wilbur Shaw	Shaw-Gilmore/Shaw/Offy	122.790	4:24:07.800	113.580
1938	1	23	Floyd Roberts	Burd Piston Ring/Lou Moore/Wetteroth/Miller	125.680	4:15:58.400	117.200
1939	3	2	Wilbur Shaw	Boyle Racing Headquarters/Maserati/Maserati	128.970	4:20:47.390	115.035
1940	2	1	Wilbur Shaw	Boyle Racing Headquarters/Maserati/Maserati	127.060	4:22:31.170	114.277
1941	17	16	F. Davis/M. Rose	Noc-Out Hose Clamp/Moore/Wetteroth/Offy	121.100	4:20:36.240	115.117
1946	15	16	George Robson	Thorne Engineering/ Adams/Sparks	125.540	4:21:16.700	114.820
1947	3	27	Mauri Rose	Blue Crown Spark Plug/Moore/Deidt/Offy	120.040	4:17:52.170	116.338
1948	3	3	Mauri Rose	Blue Crown Spark Plug/Moore/Deidt/Offy	129.120	4:10:23.330	119.814
1949	4	7	Bill Holland	Blue Crown Spark Plug/Moore/Deidt/Offy	128.670	4:07:15.970	121.327
1950	5	1	Johnnie Parsons	Wynn's Friction/Kurtis-Kraft/Kurtis/Offy	132.040	2:46:55.970	124.002c
1951	2	99	Lee Wallard	Murrell Belanger/Kurtis/Offy	135.030	3:57:38.050	126.244
1952	7	98	Troy Ruttman	J.C. Agajanian/Kuzma/Offy	135.360	3:52:41.880	128.922
1953	1	14	Bill Vukovich	Fuel Injection/Howard Keck KK500A/Offy	138.390	3:53:01.690	128.740
1954	19	14	Bill Vukovich	Fuel Injection/Howard Keck KK500A/Offy	138.470	3:49:17.270	130.840
1955	14	6	Bob Sweikert	John Zink KK500C/Offy	139.990	3:53:59.130	128.213
1956	1	8	Pat Flaherty	John Zink/Watson/Offy	145.590	3:53:28.840	128.490
1957	13	9	Sam Hanks	Belond Exhaust/George Salih/Salih/Offy	142.810	3:41:14.250	135.601
1958	7	1	Jimmy Bryan	Belond AP/George Salih/Salih/Offy	144.180	3:44:13.800	133.791
1959	6	5	Rodger Ward	Leader Card 500 Roadster/Watson/Offy	144.030	3:40:49.200	135.857
1960	2	4	Jim Rathmann	Ken-Paul/Watson/Offy	146.370	3:36:11.360	138.767
1961	7	1	A.J. Foyt	Bowes Seal Fast/Bignotti Trevis/Offy	145.900	3:35:37.490	139.130
1962	2	3	Rodger Ward	Leader Card 500 Roadster/Watson/Offy	149.370	3:33:50.330	140.293
1963	1	98	Parnelli Jones	J.C. Agajanian/Willard Battery Watson/Offy	151.150	3:29:35.400	143.137
1964	5	1	A.J. Foyt	Sheraton-Thompson/Ansted Watson/Offy	154.670	3:23:35.830;	147.350
1965	2	82	Jim Clark	Lotus powered by Ford/Lotus/Ford	160.720	3:19:05.340	150.686

YEAR	SP	CAR #	DRIVER	CAR NAME/ENTRANT CHASSIS/ENGINE	QUALIFY SPEED	RACE TIME	RACE SPEED
1966	15	24	Graham Hill	American Red Ball/Mecom Lola/Ford	159.240	3:27:52.530	144.317
1967	4	14	A.J. Foyt	Sheraton-Thompson/Ansted Coyote/Ford	166.280	3:18:24.220	151.207
1968	3	3	Bobby Unser	Rislone/Leader Cards/Eagle/Offy	169.500	3:16:13.760	152.882
1969	2	2	Mario Andretti	STP Oil Treatment/Hawk/Ford	169.850	3:11:14.710	156.867
1970	1	2	Al Unser	Johnny Lightning/Parnelli Jones/P.J. Colt/Ford	170.220	3:12:37.040	155.749
1971	5	1	Al Unser	Johnny Lightning/Parnelli Jones/P.J. Colt/Ford	174.520	3:10:11.560	157.735
1972	3	66	Mark Donohue	Sunoco McLaren/Penske/McLaren/Offy	191.400	3:04:05.540	162.962
1973	11	20	Gordon Johncock	STP Double Oil Filter/Patrick Eagle/Offy	192.550	2:05:26.590	159.036d
1974	25	3	Johnny Rutherford	McLaren Cars/McLaren/Offy	190.440	3:09:10.060	158.589
1975	3	48	Bobby Unser	Jorgensen/All American Racers Eagle/Offy	191.070	2:54:55.080	149.213e
1976	1	2	Johnny Rutherford	Hy-Gain/McLaren/McLaren/Offy	188.950	1:42:52.000	148.725f
1977	4	14	A.J. Foyt	Gilmore Racing/A.J. Foyt	194.560	3:05:57.160	161.331
1978	5	2	Al Unser	First National City/Chaparral	196.470	3:05:54.990	161.363
1979	1	9	Rick Mears	The Gould Charge/Penske/Penske/Cosworth	193.730	3:08:47.970	158.899
1980	1	4	Johnny Rutherford	Pennzoil/Chaparral Racing/Chaparral/Cosworth	192.520	3:29:59.560	142.862
1981	1	3	Bobby Unser	The Norton Spirit/Penske/Penske/Cosworth	200.540	3:35:41.780	139.084
1982	5	20	Gordon Johncock	STP Oil Treatment/Patrick Wildcat/Cosworth	201.880	3:05:09.140	162.029
1983	4	5	Tom Sneva	Texaco Star/Bignotti-Cotter/March/Cosworth	203.680	3:05:03.066	162.117
1984	3	6	Rick Mears	Pennzoil Z-7/Penske/March/Cosworth	207.840	3:03:21.660	163.612
1985	8	5	Danny Sullivan	Miller American/Penske/March/Cosworth	210.290	3:16:06.069	152.982
1986	4	3	Bobby Rahal	Budweiser/Truesports/March/Cosworth	213.550	2:55:43.480	170.722
1987	20	25	Al Unser	Cummins-Holset/Penske/March/Cosworth	207.420	3:04:59.147	162.175
1988	1	5	Rick Mears	Pennzoil Z-7/Penske/Penske/Chevy Indy V8	219.190	3:27:10.204	144.809
1989	3	20	Emerson Fittipaldi	Marlboro/Patrick Racing/Penske/Chevy Indy V8	222.320	2:59:01.049	167.581
1990	3	30	Arie Luyendyk	Domino's Pizza/Shierson - Lola/Chevy Indy V8	223.300	2:41:18.404	185.981i
1991	1	3	Rick Mears	Marlboro Penske Chevy 91/Penske/Chevy Indy V8	224.113	2:50:00.791	176.457
1992	12	3	Al Unser Jr.	Valvoline Galmer '92/Galmer/Chevy Indy V8A	222.989	3:43:05.148	134.477
1993	9	4	Emerson Fittipaldi	Marlboro Penske Chevy '93/Penske/Chevy Indy V8C	220.150	3:10:49.860	157.207
1994	1	31	Al Unser Jr.	Marlboro Penske Mercedes/Penske/Mercedes Benz	228.011	3:06:29.006	160.872
1995	5	27	Jacques Villeneuve	Player's LTD/Team Green Reynard/Ford Cosworth XB	228.397	3:15:17.561	153.616
1996	5	91	Buddy Lazier	Delta Faucet/Montana/Hemelgarn 95 Reynard/Ford Cosworth XB	231.468	3:22:45.753	147.956
1997	1	5	Arie Luyendyk	Wavephore/Sprint PCS/Miller Lite/Provimi/G Force/Aurora	218.263	3:25:43.388	145.827
1998	17	51	Eddie Cheever Jr.	Rachel's Potato Chips/Dallara/Aurora	217.334	3:26:40.524	145.155
1999	8	14	Kenny Brack	A.J. Foyt PowerTeam Racing/Dallara/Aurora	222.659	3:15:51.182	153.176
2000	2	9	Juan Pablo Montoya	Target/G Force Oldsmobile /td>	223.372	2:58:59.431	167.607
2001	11	68	Helio Castroneves	Marlboro Team Penske/Dallara/Oldsmobile	224.142	3:31:54.180	141.574
2002	13	3	Helio Castroneves	Marlboro Team Penske/Dallara/Chevy	229.052	3:00:10.8714	166.499
2003	10	6	Gil de Ferran	Marlboro Team Penske/G Force/Toyota	228.633	3:11:56.9891	156.291
2004	1	15	Buddy Rice	Rahal Letterman Racing/Panoz G Force/Honda	222.024	3:14:55.2395	138.518g
2005	16	26	Dan Wheldon	Andretti Green Racing/Dallara/Honda	224.308	3:10:21.0769	157.603
2006	1	6	Sam Hornish Jr.	Marlboro Team Penske/Dallara/Honda	228.985	3:10:58.7590	157.085
2007	3	27	Dario Franchitti	Andretti Green Racing/Dallara/Honda	225.191	2:44:03.5608	151.774h
2008	1	9	Scott Dixon	Target Chip Ganassi Racing/Dallara/Honda	226.366	3:28:57.6792	143.567
2009	1	3	Helio Castroneves	Team Penske/Dallara/Honda	224.864	3:19:34.6427	150.318
2010	3	9	Dario Franchitti	Target Chip Ganassi Racing/Dallara/Honda	226.990	3:05:37.0131	161.623
2011	6	98	Dan Wheldon	Bryan Herta Autosport with Curb/Agajanian/Dallara/Honda	226.490	2:56:11.7267	170.265
2012	16	50	Dario Franchitti	Target Chip Ganassi Racing/Dallara/Honda	223.582	2:58:51.2532	167.734

YEAR	SP	CAR #	DRIVER	CAR NAME/ENTRANT CHASSIS/ENGINE	QUALIFY SPEED	RACE TIME	RACE SPEED
2013	12	11	Tony Kanaan	KV Racing Technology/Dallara/Chevrolet	226.949	2:40:03.4181	187.433
2014	19	28	Ryan Hunter-Reay	DHL Honda/Dallara/Honda	229.719	2:40:48.2305	186.563
2015	15	2	Juan Pablo Montoya	Verizon Team Penske Chevrolet	224.657	3:05:57.5286	161.341
2016	11	98	Alexander Rossi	Andretti Herta Autosport Dallara/Honda	228.473	3:00:002.0872	166.634

INDIANAPOLIS 500—ALL-TIME LAP LEADERS

RANK	DRIVER	STARTS	RACES LED	LAPS LED	RACE WINS
1	Al Unser	27	11	644	4
2	Ralph DePalma	10	6	612	1
3	Mario Andretti	29	11	556	1
4	A.J. Foyt	35	13	555	4
5	Wilbur Shaw	13	7	508	3
6	Emerson Fittipaldi	11	7	505	2
7	Parnelli Jones	7	5	492	1
8	Bill Vukovich	5	4	485	2
9	Bobby Unser	19	10	440	3
10	Scott Dixon	14	10	434	1
11	Michael Andretti	16	9	431	0
12	Rick Mears	15	9	429	4
13	Billy Arnold	5	3	410	1
14	Gordon Johncock	24	7	339	2
15	Louis Meyer	12	6	332	3
16	Dario Franchitti	10	7	329	3
17	Tony Kanaan	15	12	305	1
18	Jim Clark	5	4	298	1
19	Bill Holland	5	3	297	1
20	Johnny Rutherford	24	5	296	3
21	Helio Castroneves	16	11	296	3
22	Rex Mays	12	9	266	0
23	Rodger Ward	15	4	261	2
24	Mauri Rose	16	7	256	3
25	Dan Wheldon	9	5	235	2
26	Jimmy Murphy	5	3	220	1
27	Tommy Milton	8	2	218	2
28	Jimmy Bryan	9	3	216	1
29	Tom Sneva	18	8	208	1
30	Frank Lockhart	2	2	205	1
31	Juan Pablo Montoya	4	3	192	2
32	Arie Luyendyk	17	8	188	2
33	Jimmy Snyder	5	3	181	0
34	Lee Wallard	4	2	178	1
35	Danny Sullivan	12	3	162	1
36	Howdy Wilcox	11	4	155	1
37	Jim Rathmann	14	6	153	1
	Tomas Scheckter	10	3	153	0
39	Peter DePaolo	7	3	148	1
40	Marco Andretti	10	6	141	0
41	Dario Resta	3	2	140	1
	Sam Hanks	13	3	140	1
43	Jules Goux	5	2	139	1
44	Gary Bettenhausen	21	1	138	0
	George Robson	3	1	138	1
	Pat Flaherty	5	2	138	1
47	Ryan Hunter-Reay	9	3	134	1
48	Johnnie Parsons	10	2	131	1
49	Lloyd Ruby	18	5	126	0
50	Bobby Rahal	13	6	124	1
51	Earl Cooper	7	2	123	0
52	Tony Stewart	5	4	122	0
53	Joe Boyer	6	3	119	1

RANK	DRIVER	STARTS	RACES LED	LAPS LED	RACE WINS
54	Greg Ray	8	4	116	0
55	Rene Thomas	4	2	114	1
56	Al Unser Jr.	19	8	110	2
57	Kelly Petillo	9	2	108	1
	Wally Dallenbach	13	4	108	0
59	Sam Hornish Jr.	8	4	107	1
60	Babe Stapp	12	4	106	0
	Fred Frame	8	3	106	1
62	Buddy Rice	6	2	99	1
63	Ted Horn	10	3	94	0
64	Bill Cummings	9	3	93	1
	Dave Lewis	4	2	93	0
66	Floyd Roberts	5	1	92	1
67	Eddie Cheever Jr.	14	3	89	1
	Kenny Brack	6	2	89	1
69	Ray Harroun	1	1	88	1
70	Bob Sweikert	5	1	86	1
71	David Bruce-Brown	2	1	81	0
72	Danny Ongais	11	4	79	0
73	Arthur Duray	1	1	77	0
74	Will Power	9	5	74	0
75	Gil de Ferran	4	3	71	1
76	Buddy Lazier	18	3	70	1
	Jack McGrath	8	4	70	0
	Mark Donohue	5	3	70	1
79	Frank Brisko	12	1	69	0
	Troy Ruttman	12	4	69	1
	Ed Carpenter	13	4	69	0
82	Leon Duray	8	3	68	0
	Ralph Hepburn	15	3	68	0
84	George Souders	2	2	67	1
85	Eddie Sachs	8	3	66	0
86	Mauricio Gugelmin	2	1	59	0
87	Harry Hartz	6	4	57	0
88	Roberto Guerrero	15	3	56	0
89	Johnny Thomson	8	3	55	0
90	Robby Gordon	10	4	53	0
	James Hinchcliffe	5	4	53	0
92	Bruno Junqueira	6	4	52	0
	Jeff Ward	7	2	52	0
	Joe Leonard	9	2	52	0
95	Deacon Litz	12	1	49	0
	Scott Goodyear	11	3	49	0
97	Davy Jones	5	1	46	0
	Pat O'Connor	5	2	46	0
	Ray Keech	2	1	46	0
100	Gil Anderson	6	2	44	0
101	Jimmy Gleason	4	1	43	0
102	Bob Burman	5	1	41	0
103	Jackie Stewart	2	1	40	0
104	John Paul Jr.	7	1	39	0
	Louis Schneider	6	1	39	1
	Alex Tagliani	8	6	39	0
107	Teo Fabi	8	2	37	0
108	Bob Carey	1	1	36	0-

RANK	DRIVER	STARTS	RACES LED	LAPS LED	RACE WINS
	Jim Hurtubise	10	3	36	0
110	Cliff Bergere	16	3	35	0
	Paul Russo	14	2	35	0
112	Bob Swanson	3	1	34	0
	Nigel Mansell	2	1	34	0
114	Bobby Marshman	4	1	33	0
	Tony Gulotta	13	1	33	0
116	Art Cross	4	2	32	0
	Duke Nalon	10	2	32	0
118	Ryan Briscoe	9	3	31	0
	Takuma Sato	5	1	31	0
120	Danica Patrick	7	2	29	0
	Mark Dismore	7	1	29	0
	Phil Shafer	7	2	29	0
123	Jimmy Vasser	8	3	26	0
124	Jimmy Davies	4	1	25	0
	Carlos Munoz	4	3	25	0
126	Tony Bettenhausen	14	1	24	0
127	AJ Allmendinger	1	1	23	0
	Lou Moore	9	2	23	0
129	Jacques Villeneuve	2	2	22	1
130	Raul Boesel	13	3	21	0
131	Alessandro Zampedri	3	1	20	0
132	George Amick	1	1	18	0
	Johnny Boyd	12	1	18	0
	Oriol Servia	8	1	18	0
135	Kevin Cogan	12	2	17	0
136	Jerry Grant	10	1	16	0
	Johnny Aitken	2	2	16	0
	Robbie Buhl	8	1	16	0
139	Mike Conway	3	1	15	0
	Vitor Meira	9	2	15	0
141	Ernie Triplett	5	1	14	0
	Gaston Chevrolet	2	1	14	1
	Josef Newgarden	5	1	14	0
	Alexander Rossi	1	1	14	1
145	Billy Boat	7	2	13	0
	Josele Garza	7	1	13	0
	Russ Snowberger	15	1	13	0
	Justin Wilson	7	2	13	0
	Charlie Kimball	5	2	13	0
	Townsend Bell	9	2	13	0
151	Felipe Giaffone	6	1	12	0
	Swede Savage	2	1	12	0
153	Bertrand Baguette	2	1	11	0
	JR Hildebrand	5	2	11	0
155	Alex Barron	5	2	10	0
	Graham Hill	3	1	10	1
	Ralph Mulford	10	1	10	0
158	Albert Guyot	5	1	9	0
	Dutch Baumann	1	1	9	0
	Eddie Rickenbacker	4	1	9	0
	Josef Christiaens	2	1	9	0
	Len Sutton	7	1	9	0
	Louis Chevrolet	4	1	9	0
164	Jim Crawford	8	1	8	0

RANK	DRIVER	STARTS	RACES LED	LAPS LED	RACE WINS
	Jimmy Daywalt	8	1	8	0
	Pancho Carter	17	2	8	0
	Scott Pruett	4	1	8	0
168	Don Freeland	8	2	7	0
	Roger McCluskey	18	2	7	0
170	Graham Rahal	6	1	6	0
	Ira Hall	5	1	6	0
172	Cecil Green	2	1	5	0
	EJ Viso	6	1	5	0
	James Jakes	3	1	5	0
	Jimmy Jackson	5	1	5	0
	Spencer Wishart	4	1	5	0
	Steve Krisiloff	11	1	5	0
178	Buzz Calkins	6	1	4	0
	Cliff Durant	6	1	4	0
	Fred Belcher	1	1	4	0
	Mike Mosley	15	2	4	0
	Sam Schmidt	3	1	4	0
183	Adrian Fernandez	4	1	3	0
	Bryan Herta	5	1	3	0
	Davey Hamilton	11	1	3	0
	George Snider	22	2	3	0
	Mario Moraes	3	1	3	0
	Scott Sharp	14	1	3	0
	Bryan Clauson	3	1	3	0
190	Caleb Bragg	3	2	2	0
	Dan Gurney	9	1	2	0
	Don Whittington	5	1	2	0
	Herb Ardinger	6	1	2	0
	Jaques Lazier	6	1	2	0
	Joe Dawson	3	1	2	1
	John Andretti	12	1	2	0
	Paul Bost	3	1	2	0
	Robby McGehee	5	1	2	0
	Robert Evans	1	1	2	0
	Roger Rager	1	1	2	0
	Rubens Barrichello	1	1	2	0
	Teddy Tetzlaff	4	1	2	0
	Tora Takagi	2	1	2	0
	Sage Karam	3	1	2	0
205	Art Klein	5	1	1	0
	Bill Vukovich Jr.	12	1	1	0
	Bobby Allison	2	1	1	0
	Fred Agabashian	11	1	1	0
	Gordon Smiley	2	1	1	0
	Howdy Wilcox II	1	1	1	0
	Jack Brabham	4	1	1	0
	Jean Chassagne	3	1	1	0
	Jeff Simmons	4	1	1	0
	Roscoe Sarles	4	1	1	0
	Scott Brayton	14	1	1	0
	Stephan Gregoire	7	1	1	0
	Tim Richmond	2	1	1	0
	Mikhail Aleshin	2	1	1	0

INDIANAPOLIS 500—POLE POSITION WINNERS

Year	Driver	Entrant	Car/Engine	Speed (mph)
1911	Lewis Strang	J.I. Case T.M. Co.	Case/Wisconsin	First Entered
1912	Gil Anderson*	Ideal Motor Car Co	Stutz/Wisconsin	First Entered
1913	Caleb Bragg*	Mercer Motors Co.	Mercer/Mercer	Drew Pole
1914	Jean Chassagne*	Sunbeam Motor Car Co.	Sunbeam/Sunbeam	Drew Pole
1915	Howard Wilcox	Stutz Motor Car Co.	Stutz/Stutz	98.900
1916	Johnny Aitken	Ind. Speedway Team Co.	Peugeot/Peugeot	96.690
1919	Rene Thomas	Ernest Ballot	Ballot/Ballot	104.780 NR
1920	Ralph DePalma	Ralph DePalma	Ballot/Ballot	99.150
1921	Ralph DePalma	Ralph DePalma	Ballot/Ballot	100.750
1922	Jimmy Murphy	Jimmy Murphy	Duesenberg/Miller	100.500
1923	Tommy Milton	H.C.S. Motor Co.	Miller/Miller	108.170 NR
1924	Jimmy Murphy	Jimmy Murphy	Miller/Miller	108.037
1925	Leon Duray	Harry Hartz	Miller/Miller	113.196 NR
1926	Earl Cooper	Harry A. Miller	Miller/Miller	111.735
1927	Frank Lockhart	Frank S. Lockhart	Miller/Miller	120.100 NR
1928	Leon Duray	Leon Duray	Miller/Miller	122.391 NR
1929	Cliff Woodbury	Cliff R. Woodbury	Miller/Miller	120.599
1930	Billy Arnold	Harry Hartz	Summers/Miller	113.268
1931	Russ Snowberger*	Russell Snowberger	Snowberger/Studebaker	112.769
1932	Lou Moore	M.J.Boyle	Miller/Miller	117.363
1933	Bill Cummings	M.J. Boyle	Miller/Miller	118.530
1934	Kelly Petillo	Joe Marks	Adams/Miller	119.329
1935	Rex Mays	Paul Weirick	Adams/Miller	120.736
1936	Rex Mays	Paul Weirick	Adams/Sparks	119.644
1937	Bill Cummings*	H.C. Henning	Miller/Offy	123.343 NR
1938	Floyd Roberts*	Lou Moore	Wetteroth/Miller	125.681 NR
1939	Jimmy Snyder	Joel Thorne Inc.	Adams/Sparks	130.138 NR
1940	Rex Mays	Bowes Racing Inc.	Stevens/Winfield	127.850
1941	Mauri Rose	Lou Moore	Maserati/Maserati	128.691
1946	Cliff Bergere*	Shirley Bergere	Wetteroth/Offy	126.471
1947	Ted Horn*	H. C. Henning	Maserati/Maserati	126.564
1948	Rex Mays*	Bowes Racing Inc.	Kurtis/Winfield	130.577
1949	Duke Nalon	W.C. Winfield	Kurtis/Novi	132.939
1950	Walt Faulkner	J.C. Agajanian	KK2000/Offy	134.343 NR
1951	Duke Nalon*	Jean Marcenac	Kurtis/Novi	136.498 NR
1952	Fred Agabashian*	Cummins Engine Co.	Kurtis/Cummins	138.010 NR
1953	Bill Vukovich	Howard Keck Co.	KK500A/Offy	138.392
1954	Jack McGrath	Jack B. Hinkle	KK500C/Offy	141.033 NR
1955	Jerry Hoyt*	Jim Robbins	Stevens/Offy	140.045

Year	Driver	Entrant	Car/Engine	Speed (mph)
1956	Pat Flaherty	John Zink Co.	Watson/Offy	145.596 NR
1957	Pat O'Connor*	Chapman S. Root	KK500G/Offy	143.948
1958	Dick Rathmann	Kalamazoo Sports Inc.	Watson/Offy	145.974 NR
1959	Johnny Thomson	Racing Associates	Lesovsky/Offy	145.908
1960	Eddie Sachs*	Dean Van Lines Racing	Ewing/Offy	146.592 NR
1961	Eddie Sachs	Dean Van Lines Racing	Ewing/Offy	147.481
1962	Parnelli Jones	J.C. Agajanian	Watson/Offy	150.370 NR
1963	Parnelli Jones	J.C. Agajanian	Watson/Offy	151.153 NR
1964	Jim Clark	Team Lotus	Lotus/Ford	158.828 NR
1965	A.J. Foyt	Ansted-Thompson Rac.	Lotus/Ford	161.233 NR
1966	Mario Andretti	Dean Racing Enterprises	Brawner/Ford	165.899 NR
1967	Mario Andretti	Dean Racing Enterprises	Hawk/Ford	168.982 NR
1968	Joe Leonard	STP Corporation	Lotus/Pratt & Whitney	171.559 NR
1969	A.J. Foyt	Ansted-Thompson Rac.	Coyote/Ford	170.568
1970	Al Unser	Vel's Parnelli Jones Ford	P.J. Colt/Ford	170.221
1971	Peter Revson	McLaren Cars	McLaren/Offy	178.696 NR
1972	Bobby Unser	Olsonite Division	Eagle/Offy	195.940 NR
1973	Johnny Rutherford	McLaren Cars	McLaren/Offy	198.413 NR
1974	A.J. Foyt	A. J. Foyt Enterprises	Coyote/Foyt	191.632
1975	A.J. Foyt	A. J. Foyt Enterprises	Coyote/Foyt	193.976
1976	Johnny Rutherford*	Team McLaren	McLaren/Offy	188.957
1977	Tom Sneva	Penske Racing	McLaren/Cosworth	198.884 NR
1978	Tom Sneva	Penske Racing	Penske/Cosworth	202.156 NR
1979	Rick Mears	Penske Racing	Penske/Cosworth	193.736
1980	Johnny Rutherford	Chaparral Racing	Chaparral/Cosworth	192.256
1981	Bobby Unser*	Penske Racing	Penske/Cosworth	200.546
1982	Rick Mears	Penske Racing	Penske/Cosworth	207.004 NR
1983	Teo Fabi	Forsythe Racing	March/Cosworth	207.395 NR
1984	Tom Sneva	Mayer Motor Racing	March/Cosworth	210.029 NR
1985	Pancho Carter	Galles Racing	March/Buick	212.583 NR
1986	Rick Mears	Penske Racing	March/Cosworth	216.828 NR
1987	Mario Andretti	Newman-Haas Racing	Lola/Chevy Indy	215.390
1988	Rick Mears	Penske Racing	Penske/Chevy Indy	219.198 NR
1989	Rick Mears	Penske Racing	Penske/Chevy Indy	223.885 NR
1990	Emerson Fittipaldi	Penske Racing	Penske/Chevy Indy	225.301 NR
1991	Rick Mears*	Penske Racing	Penske/Chevy Indy	224.113
1992	Roberto Guerrero	Kenny Bernstein	Lola/Buick	232.482 NR
1993	Arie Luyendyk	Ganassi Racing	Lola/Ford XB	223.967
1994	Al Unser Jr.	Penske Racing	Penske/Mercedes Benz	228.011
1995	Scott Brayton	Team Menard	Lola/Menard	231.604
1996	Scott Brayton*^	Team Menard	Lola/Menard	233.718

Year	Driver	Entrant	Car/Engine	Speed (mph)
1997	Arie Luyendyk	Treadway Racing	G Force/Aurora	218.263
1998	Billy Boat	A.J. Foyt Enterprises	Dallara/Aurora	223.503
1999	Arie Luyendyk	Treadway Racing	G Force/Aurora	225.179
2000	Greg Ray	Team Menard	Dallara/Oldsmobile	223.471
2001	Scott Sharp	Kelley Racing	Dallara/Oldsmobile	226.037
2002	Bruno Junqueira	Ganassi Racing	G Force/Chevy	231.342
2003	Helio Castroneves	Marlboro Team Penske	Dallara/Toyota	231.725
2004	Buddy Rice	Rahal Letterman Racing	Panoz G Force/Honda	222.024
2005	Tony Kanaan*	Andretti Green Racing	Dallara/Honda	227.566
2006	Sam Hornish Jr.	Marlboro Team Penske	Dallara/Honda	228.985
2007	Helio Castroneves	Marlboro Team Penske	Dallara/Honda	225.817
2008	Scott Dixon	Target Chip Ganassi Racing	Dallara/Honda	226.366
2009	Helio Castroneves	Team Penske	Dallara/Honda	224.864
2010	Helio Castroneves	Team Penske	Dallara/Honda	227.970
2011	Alex Tagliani	Sam Schmidt Motorsports	Dallara/Honda	224.472
2012	Ryan Briscoe	Team Penske	Dallara/Honda	226.484
2013	Ed Carpenter	Ed Carpenter Racing	Dallara/Chevrolet	228.762
2014	Ed Carpenter	Ed Carpenter Racing	Dallara/Chevrolet	231.067
2015	Scott Dixon	Target Chip Ganassi Racing	Dallara/Chevrolet	226.760
2016	James Hinchcliffe	Schmidt Peterson Motorsports	Dallara/Honda	230.760

Legend *—Pole winner was not the fastest qualifier; NR—New Record;

- ^—Tony Stewart started the 1996 Indianapolis 500 from the pole position after
- Scott Brayton was fatally injured during practice prior to the race.

MULTIPLE POLE POSITION WINNERS

One driver with six poles:

Rick Mears 1979, 82, 86, 88-89, 91

Three drivers with four poles:

Rex Mays 1935-36, 40, 48, A.J. Foyt 1965, 69, 74-75, Helio Castroneves 2003, 07, 09, 10

Four drivers with three poles:

Johnny Rutherford 1973, 76, 80, Mario Andretti 1966-67, 87, Tom Sneva 1977-78, 84, Arie Luyendyk 1993, 97, 99

Nine drivers with two poles:

Ralph DePalma 1920-21, Eddie Sachs 1960-61, Jimmy Murphy 1922, 24, Parnelli Jones 1962-63, Leon Duray 1925, 28, Bobby Unser 1972, 81, Bill Cummings 1933, 37, Scott Brayton 1995-96, Duke Nalon 1949, 51; Scott Dixon 2008, 2015.

Quick Fact, Records:

Most consecutive pole positions: 2 (10 times)—Ralph DePalma (1920-21), Rex Mays (1935-36), Eddie Sachs (1960-61), Parnelli Jones (1962-63), Mario Andretti (1966-67), A.J. Foyt (1974-75), Tom Sneva (1977-78), Rick Mears (1988-89), Scott Brayton (1995-96), Helio Castroneves (2009-10)

DRIVER RECORDS

Year	Start	Finish	Status	Laps
ADER, Walt (1)				
1950	29	22	Running/rain	123
Died Nov. 25, 1982				
AGABASHIAN, Fred (11)				
1947	23	9	Running	191
1948	32	23	Oil line	58
1949	31	27	Overheating	38
1950	2	28	Oil line	64
1951	11	17	Clutch	109
1952	1	27	Supercharger	71
1953	2	4	Running	200
(Relieved by Paul Russo)				
1954	24	6	Running	200
1955	4	32	Spun	39
1956	7	12	Running	196
1957	4	22	Fuel leak	107
Died Oct. 13, 1989				
AITKEN, Johnny (2)				
1911	4	27	Rod	125
1916	1	15	Valve	69
Died Oct. 15, 1918, influenza				
ALBORETO, Michele (1)				
1996	12	30	Gearbox	43
Died April 25, 2001 in testing crash at Lausitz, Germany				
ALESHIN, Mikhail (2)				
2014	15	21	Running	198
2016	7	27	Contact	126
ALESI, Jean (1)				
2012	33	33	Handling	9
ALLEN, Leslie "Bugs"(1)				
1930	9	9	Running	200

Year	Start	Finish	Status	Laps
(Relieved by Fred Lecklider, Stubby Stubblefield)				

ALLEY, Tom (5)

Year	Start	Finish	Status	Laps
1915	9	8	Running	200
1916	19	11	Running	120
1919	28	5	Running	200
1921	18	11	Rod	133
1922	12	9	Running	200

Died March 26, 1953

ALLISON, Bobby (2)

Year	Start	Finish	Status	Laps
1973	12	32	Rod	1
1975	13	25	Gearbox	112

ALLISON, Donnie (2)

Year	Start	Finish	Status	Laps
1970	23	4	Running	200
1971	20	6	Running	199

ALLMENDINGER, AJ (1)

Year	Start	Finish	Status	Laps
2013	5	7	Running	200

ALSUP, Bill (1)

Year	Start	Finish	Status	Laps
1981	7	11	Running	193

Died August 9, 2016

AMICK, George (1)

Year	Start	Finish	Status	Laps
1958	25	2	Running	200

Died April 4, 1959 in racing accident at Daytona Beach, Fla.

AMICK, Richard "Red" (2)

Year	Start	Finish	Status	Laps
1959	26	31	Accident	45
1960	22	11	Running	200

Died May 16, 1995

ANDERSON (Andersen), Gil (6)

Year	Start	Finish	Status	Laps
1911	10	11	Running	200
1912	1	16	Accident	79
1913	14	12	Camshaft gears	187

(Relieved by Earl Cooper)

Year	Start	Finish	Status	Laps
1914	16	26	Cylinder bolts	42
1915	5	3	Running	200
(Relieved by Johnny Aitken)				
1916	3	13	Oil line	75

Died Sept. 20, 1930

ANDERSON, Les (2)

Year	Start	Finish	Status	Laps
1947	7	11	Running	131
1948	9	24	Gears	58

Died July 10, 1949 in racing accident in Portland, Ore.

ANDRES, Emil (9)

Year	Start	Finish	Status	Laps
1936	33	18	Running	184
(Relieved by Jimmy Snyder)				
1938	28	29	Accident	44
1939	21	30	Spark plugs	22
1940	22	12	Running	192
1941	15	30	Accident	4
1946	11	4	Running	200
1947	30	13	Magneto	149
(Relieved by George Connor)				
1948	16	31	Steering	11
1949	32	9	Running	197
(Relieved by Walt Brown)				

Died July 20, 1999

ANDRETTI, Jeff (3)

Year	Start	Finish	Status	Laps
1991	11	15	Engine	150
1992	20	18	Accident	109
1993	16	29	Accident	124

ANDRETTI, John (12)

Year	Start	Finish	Status	Laps
1988	27	21	Engine	114
1989	12	25	Engine	61
1990	10	21	Accident	136
1991	7	5	Running	197
1992	14	8	Running	195
1993	24	10	Running	200
1994	10	10	Running	196

Year	Start	Finish	Status	Laps
2007	24	30	Accident	95
2008	21	16	Running	199
2009	28	19	Running	200
2010	28	30	Accident	62
2011	17	22	Running	197

ANDRETTI, Marco (11)

Year	Start	Finish	Status	Laps
2006	9	2	Running	200
2007	9	24	Accident	162
2008	7	3	Running	200
2009	8	30	Handling	56
2010	16	3	Running	200
2011	27	9	Running	200
2012	4	24	Contact	187
2013	3	4	Running	200
2014	6	3	Running	200
2015	8	6	Running	200
2016	14	13	Running	200

ANDRETTI, Mario (29)

Year	Start	Finish	Status	Laps
1965	4	3	Running	200
1966	1	18	Valve	27
1967	1	30	Lost wheel	58
1968	4	33	Piston	2
1969	2	1	Running	200
1970	8	6	Running	199
1971	9	30	Accident	11
1972	5	8	Out of fuel	194
1973	6	30	Piston	4
1974	5	31	Valve	2
1975	27	28	Accident	49
1976	19	8	Running/rain	101
1977	6	26	Header	47
1978	33	12	Running	185
1980	2	20	Engine	71
1981	32	2	Running	200
1982	4	31	Accident	0
1983	11	23	Accident	79
1984	6	17	Broken nosecone	153

Year	Start	Finish	Status	Laps
1985	4	2	Running	200
1986	30	32	Ignition	19
1987	1	9	Ignition	180
1988	4	20	Electrical	118
1989	5	4	Running	193
1990	6	27	Engine	60
1991	3	7	Engine	187
1992	3	23	Accident	78
1993	2	5	Running	200
1994	9	32	Fuel system	23

ANDRETTI, Michael (16)

Year	Start	Finish	Status	Laps
1984	4	5	Running	198
1985	15	8	Running	196
1986	3	6	Running	199
1987	9	29	CV joint	28
1988	10	4	Running	199
1989	21	17	Engine	163
1990	5	20	Vibration	146
1991	5	2	Running	200
1992	6	13	Fuel pressure	189
1994	5	6	Running	198
1995	4	25	Suspension	77
2001	21	3	Running	200
2002	25	7	Running	200
2003	13	27	Throttle linkage	94
2006	13	3	Running	200
2007	11	13	Running	166

ANDREWS, Keith (2)

Year	Start	Finish	Status	Laps
1955	28	20	Ignition	120
1956	20	26	Spun	94

Died May 15, 1957 in Indianapolis 500 practice accident

ANSTERBURG, Ernie (1)

Year	Start	Finish	Status	Laps
1924	10	22	Accident	1

Died Oct. 16, 1924 in racing accident at Charlotte, N.C.

ARDINGER, Herb (6)

Year	Start	Finish	Status	Laps
1934	14	10	Running	200
(Relieved by Dan Day)				
1936	6	28	Transmission	38
1937	3	22	Rod	106
(Relieved by Jimmy Snyder)				
1938	14	6	Running	199
(Relieved by Russ Snowberger, Cliff Bergere)				
1939	9	17	Clutch	141
(Relieved by Frank Brisko, Mel Hansen)				
1947	4	4	Running	200
(Relieved by Cliff Bergere)				

Died June 14, 1973

ARMI, Frank (1)

Year	Start	Finish	Status	Laps
1954	33	19	Running	193
(Relieved by George Fonder)				

Died Nov. 28, 1992

ARNOLD, Billy (5)

Year	Start	Finish	Status	Laps
1928	20	7	Running	200
(Relieved by Bill Spence)				
1929	7	8	Running	200
(Relieved by Cliff Woodbury, Fred Roberts)				
1930	1	1	Running	200
1931	18	19	Accident	161
1932	2	31	Accident	59

Died Nov. 10, 1976

ARNOLD, Chuck (1)

Year	Start	Finish	Status	Laps
1959	21	15	Running	200

Died Sept. 4, 1997

ASCARI, Alberto (1)

Year	Start	Finish	Status	Laps
1952	19	31	Spun	40

Died May 26, 1955 in testing accident at Monza, Italy

ASPEN, Al (2)

Year	Start	Finish	Status	Laps
1931	31	14	Running	200
(Relieved by Bill Denver)				
1932	23	34	Rod	31

Year	Start	Finish	Status	Laps
Died 1960				

ATES, Sonny (1)

Year	Start	Finish	Status	Laps
1969	14	17	Magneto	146

Died Oct. 25, 2010

AYULO, Manuel (4)

Year	Start	Finish	Status	Laps
1949	33	28	Rod	24
1952	28	20	Running	184
1953	4	13	Rod	184
1954	22	13	Running	197

Died May 16, 1955 in Indianapolis 500 practice accident

BABCOCK, George C. (1)

Year	Start	Finish	Status	Laps
1915	12	17	Cylinder	117

BABLOT, Paul (1)

Year	Start	Finish	Status	Laps
1919	6	21	Accid. (Chassagne)	63

(Relieved by Jean Chassagne)
Died Dec. 23, 1932

BACHELART, Eric (2)

Year	Start	Finish	Status	Laps
1992	15	32	Engine	4
1995	26	28	Mechanical	6

BAGLEY, Tom (3)

Year	Start	Finish	Status	Laps
1978	14	27	Oil leak	25
1979	15	9	Running	193
1980	13	28	Pump	29

BAGUETTE, Bertrand (2)

Year	Start	Finish	Status	Laps
2010	24	22	Running	183
2011	14	7	Running	200

BAILEY, George (5)

Year	Start	Finish	Status	Laps
1934	16	32	Accident	12
1935	29	26	Steering	65
1937	28	21	Clutch	107
1938	29	12	Clutch	166

Year	Start	Finish	Status	Laps
1939	6	26	Valve	47

Died May 7, 1940 due to burns suffered in Indianapolis 500 practice accident

BAKER, Erwin G. "Cannonball" (1)

Year	Start	Finish	Status	Laps
1922	16	11	Running	200

Died May 10, 1960

BALL, Bobby (2)

Year	Start	Finish	Status	Laps
1951	29	5	Running	200
1952	17	32	Gear case	34

Injured in Jan. 1953 at Gardena, Calif., died Feb. 27, 1954

BANKS, Henry (6)

Year	Start	Finish	Status	Laps
1938	31	21	Rod bearing	109
1946	21	27	Pinion shaft	32
1947	26	24	Oil line	36
1950	21	25	Running/rain	112

(Relieved by Fred Agabashian)

Year	Start	Finish	Status	Laps
1951	17	6	Running	200
1952	12	19	Running	184

Died Dec. 18, 1994

BARBAZZA, Fabrizio (1)

Year	Start	Finish	Status	Laps
1987	17	3	Running	198

BARRICHELLO, Rubens (1)

Year	Start	Finish	Status	Laps
2012	10	11	Running	200

BARRINGER, George (6)

Year	Start	Finish	Status	Laps
1934	12	15	Bent front axle	161

(Relieved by Chet Gardner)

Year	Start	Finish	Status	Laps
1936	14	8	Running	200
1939	15	6	Running	200
1940	16	14	Running	191
1941	32	32	Garage fire	DNS
1946	24	29	Gears	27

Died Sept. 2, 1946 in racing accident at Atlanta

Year	Start	Finish	Status	Laps
BARRON, Alex (5)				
2002	26	4	Running	200
2003	25	6	Running	200
2004	24	12	Running/rain	180
2005	22	13	Running	197
2007	26	15	Running	165
BASLE, Charles (1)				
1911	15	34	Mechanical	46
Died Feb. 4, 1962				
BATTEN, Norman (3)				
1926	16	7	Running/rain	151
1927	10	30	Fire	24
1928	15	5	Running	200
(Relieved by Zeke Meyer)				
Lost aboard SS Vestris, Nov. 12, 1928				
BAUMANN, Charles "Dutch" (1)				
1927	17	20	Pinion shaft	90
Died Aug. 18, 1930 from injuries suffered in racing accident at Kankakee, Ill.				
BEARDSLEY, Ralph (1)				
1911	34	20	Running	Flagged
(Relieved by Frank Goode)				
Died March 18, 1920, boating accident, Norfolk Bay, VA				
BEATRIZ, Ana (4)				
2010	21	21	Accident	196
2011	32	21	Running	197
2012	13	23	Running	190
2013	29	15	Running	200
BEDARD, Patrick (2)				
1983	17	30	Accident	25
1984	19	30	Accident	55
BEECHLER, Donnie (4)				
1998	24	32	Engine	34

Year	Start	Finish	Status	Laps
1999	19	29	Engine	74
2000	15	12	Running	198
2001	27	25	Oil leak	160

BELCHER, Fred (1)

Year	Start	Finish	Status	Laps
1911	13	9	Running	200

(Relieved by John Coffey)
Died Jan. 14, 1957

BELL, Townsend (10)

Year	Start	Finish	Status	Laps
2006	15	22	Suspension	161
2007	12	10	Running	200
2009	24	4	Running	200
2010	10	16	Running	199
2011	4	26	Accident	157
2012	20	9	Running	200
2013	22	27	Running	192
2014	25	25	Contact	190
2015	23	14	Running	200
2016	4	21	Running	199

BELT, C.W. (1)

Year	Start	Finish	Status	Laps
1928	25	27	Valve	32

Died Sept. 15, 1969

BERGERE, Cliff (16)

Year	Start	Finish	Status	Laps
1927	14	9	Running	200

(Relieved by Wesley Crawford)

Year	Start	Finish	Status	Laps
1928	3	28	Supercharger	6
1929	32	9	Running	200

(Relieved by Peter Kreis)

Year	Start	Finish	Status	Laps
1931	14	9	Running	200
1932	10	3	Running	200
1933	9	11	Running	200

(Relieved by Sam Palmer)

Year	Start	Finish	Status	Laps
1934	18	7	Running	200

(Relieved by Tony Gulotta, Billy Winn)

Year	Start	Finish	Status	Laps
1935	16	13	Out of gas	196
1936	7	22	Engine mount	116

Year	Start	Finish	Status	Laps
(Relieved by Tony Gulotta, Herb Ardinger)				
1937	16	5	Running	200
(Relieved by George Barringer)				
1938	32	20	Piston	111
1939	10	3	Running	200
1940	6	27	Oil line	51
1941	7	5	Running	200
1946	1	16	Out of oil	82
(Relieved by Rex Mays)				
1947	2	21	Piston	62

Died June 18, 1980

BERNOLDI, Enrique (1)

Year	Start	Finish	Status	Laps
2008	29	15	Running	200

BETTENHAUSEN, Gary (21)

Year	Start	Finish	Status	Laps
1968	22	24	Accident	43
1969	9	26	Piston	35
1970	20	26	Valve	55
1971	13	10	Running	178
1972	4	14	Ignition	182
1973	5	5	Running/rain	130
1974	11	32	Valve	2
1975	19	15	Accident	158
1976	8	28	Turbocharger	52
1977	21	16	Clutch	138
1978	31	16	Engine	147
1980	32	3	Running	200
1981	11	26	Rod	69
1982	30	12	Engine	158
1986	29	11	Running	193
1987	15	5	Running	195
1989	14	33	Valve	0
1990	18	31	Wheel bearing	39
1991	13	22	Radiator	89
1992	5	17	Accident	112
1993	18	17	Running	197

Died March 16, 2014

Year	Start	Finish	Status	Laps
BETTENHAUSEN, Melvin "Tony" (14)				
1946	26	20	Rod	47
1947	25	18	Timing gear	79
1948	22	14	Clutch	167
1950	8	31	Wheel bearing	30
1951	9	9	Spun	178
1952	30	24	Stalled	93
1953	6	9	Accident (Hartley)	196
(Relieved by Chuck Stevenson, Gene Hartley)				
1954	21	29	Bearing	105
1955	2	2	Running	200
(Relieved by Paul Russo)				
1956	5	22	Accident	160
1957	22	15	Running	195
1958	9	4	Running	200
1959	15	4	Running	200
1960	18	23	Rod	125

Died May 12, 1961 in Indianapolis 500 practice accident

Year	Start	Finish	Status	Laps
BETTENHAUSEN, Tony (11)				
1981	16	7	Running	195
1982	27	26	Accident	37
1983	9	17	Half shaft	152
1984	17	26	Piston	86
1985	29	29	Wheel bearing	31
1986	18	28	Valve spring	77
1987	27	10	Engine	171
1988	24	33	Accident	0
1990	13	26	Engine	76
1991	20	9	Running	180
1993	22	20	Running	195

Died Feb. 14, 2000 in a plane crash at Leesburg, Ky.

Year	Start	Finish	Status	Laps
BIGELOW, Charles (1)				
1911	33	15	Running	Flagged
(Relieved by E.H. Sherwood, Howard Frey)				

Year	Start	Finish	Status	Laps
BIGELOW, Tom (9)				
1974	23	12	Running	166

Year	Start	Finish	Status	Laps
1975	33	18	Magneto	151
1976	32	14	Running/rain	98
1977	22	6	Running	192
1978	18	21	Rod	107
1979	30	14	Running	190
1980	31	8	Running	198
1981	14	20	Engine	152
1982	31	18	Engine	96

BILLMAN, Mark (1)

Year	Start	Finish	Status	Laps
1933	22	30	Accident	79

Died May 30, 1933 in Indianapolis 500 racing accident

BISCH, Art (1)

Year	Start	Finish	Status	Laps
1958	28	33	Accident	0

Died July 4, 1958 in racing accident at Atlanta

BOAT, Billy (7)

Year	Start	Finish	Status	Laps
1997	22	7	Running	199
1998	1	23	Drive line	111
1999	3	3	Running	200
2000	31	15	Running	198
2001	32	9	Running	199
2002	23	18	Running	198
2003	29	32	Engine	7

BOESEL, Raul (13)

Year	Start	Finish	Status	Laps
1985	23	18	Radiator	134
1986	22	13	Running	192
1988	20	7	Running	198
1989	9	3	Running	194
1990	17	28	Engine	60
1992	25	7	Running	198
1993	3	4	Running	200
1994	2	21	Water pump	100
1995	22	20	Oil line	184
1998	30	19	Running	164
1999	33	12	Running	195
2000	24	16	Running	197

Year	Start	Finish	Status	Laps
2002	3	21	Running	197

BOILLOT, Andre (3)

Year	Start	Finish	Status	Laps
1919	32	15	Accident	195
1920	16	23	Engine	16
1921	11	20	Rod bearing	41

Died June 9, 1932 in hillclimb accident near Chateauroux, France

BOILLOT, Georges (1)

Year	Start	Finish	Status	Laps
1914	29	14	Broken frame	141

Died May 20, 1916 in World War I aerial combat

BOLING, John (2)

Year	Start	Finish	Status	Laps
1920	14	11	Running	199

(Relieved by Riley Brett)

Year	Start	Finish	Status	Laps
1931	24	36	Rod	7

Died June 28, 1962

BONNER, Brian (1)

Year	Start	Finish	Status	Laps
1992	26	19	Accident	97

BORDINO, Pietro (1)

Year	Start	Finish	Status	Laps
1925	8	10	Running	200

(Relieved by Antoine Mourre)

Died April 15, 1928 in racing accident at Alessandria, Italy

BORZACHINI, Baconin (1)

Year	Start	Finish	Status	Laps
1930	28	36	Magneto	7

(Relieved by Jimmy Rossi)

Died Sept. 10, 1933 in racing accident at Monza, Italy

BOST, Paul (3)

Year	Start	Finish	Status	Laps
1931	3	31	Crankshaft	35
1932	8	37	Crankshaft	18
1933	33	40	Oil line	13

Died Sept. 4, 1974

BOURBONNAIS, Claude (1)

Year	Start	Finish	Status	Laps
1997	32	30	Engine	9

Year	Start	Finish	Status	Laps
BOURDAIS, Sebastien (6)				
2005	15	12	Accident	198
2012	25	20	Running	199
2013	15	29	Contact	178
2014	17	7	Running	200
2015	7	11	Running	200
2016	19	9	Running	200
BOYD, Johnny (12)				
1955	26	29	Accident	53
1956	12	30	Engine	35
1957	5	6	Running	200
1958	8	3	Running	200
1959	11	6	Running	200
1960	13	27	Piston	77
1961	20	21	Clutch	105
1962	28	10	Running	200
1963	27	32	Oil leak	12
1964	13	5	Running	200
1965	29	13	Gearbox	140
1966	14	22	Accident	5
Died Oct. 26, 2003				
BOYER, Joe (5)				
1919	14	31	Rear axle	30
1920	2	12	Accident (Vail)	192
(Relieved by Ira Vail)				
1921	3	17	Rear axle	74
1923	13	18	Differential	59
1924	4	18	Accident	92
(Relieved by Ernie Ansterburg, L.L. Corum, Thane Houser)				
		1	Running	200
(In relief of L.L. Corum, last 88 laps)				
Died Sept. 2, 1924 of injuries at Altoona, Pa.				
BRABHAM, Geoff (10)				
1981	15	5	Running	197
1982	20	28	Engine	12
1983	26	4	Running	199

Year	Start	Finish	Status	Laps
1984	8	33	Fuel line	1
1985	9	19	Engine	130
1986	20	12	Running	193
1987	14	24	Oil pressure	71
1990	19	19	Running	161
1991	22	20	Electrical	109
1993	29	26	Engine	174

BRABHAM, Jack (4)

Year	Start	Finish	Status	Laps
1961	13	9	Running	200
1964	25	20	Fuel tank	77
1969	29	24	Ignition	58
1970	26	13	Piston	175

Died May 18, 2014

BRABHAM, Matthew (1)

Year	Start	Finish	Status	Laps
2016	27	22	Running	199

BRACK, Kenny (6)

Year	Start	Finish	Status	Laps
1997	15	33	Accident	0
1998	3	6	Running	198
1999	8	1	Running	200
2002	21	11	Running	200
2003	6	16	Running	195
2005	23	26	Mechanical	92

BRAGG, Caleb (3)

Year	Start	Finish	Status	Laps
1911	35	37	Accident	24
1913	1	15	Pump shaft	128

(Relieved by Ralph DePalma)

Year	Start	Finish	Status	Laps
1914	9	19	Camshaft	117

Died Oct. 24, 1943

BRANSON, Don (8)

Year	Start	Finish	Status	Laps
1959	10	24	Torsion bar	112
1960	8	4	Running	200
1961	2	33	Bent valves	2
1962	11	12	Running	200
1963	3	5	Running	200

Indy 500 Recaps The Short Chute Edition | 441

Year	Start	Finish	Status	Laps
1964	9	12	Clutch	187
1965	18	8	Running	197
1966	9	23	Accident	0

Died Nov. 12, 1966 in racing accident at Gardena, Calif.

BRAYTON, Scott (14)

Year	Start	Finish	Status	Laps
1981	29	16	Engine	173
1983	29	9	Running	195
1984	26	18	Transmission	150
1985	2	30	Cylinder wall	19
1986	23	30	Engine	69
1987	13	12	Engine	167
1988	7	31	Accident	0
1989	6	6	Running	193
1990	26	7	Running	194
1991	19	17	Engine	146
1992	7	22	Engine	93
1993	11	6	Running	200
1994	23	20	Engine	116
1995	1	17	Running	190

Died May 17, 1996 in Indianapolis 500 practice accident

BRETT, Riley (1)

Year	Start	Finish	Status	Laps
1921	16	15	Accident	91

(Relieved by Harry Thicksten)
Died Feb. 5, 1982

BRISCOE, Ryan (10)

Year	Start	Finish	Status	Laps
2005	24	10	Running	199
2007	7	5	Running	166
2008	3	23	Accident	171
2009	2	15	Running	200
2010	4	24	Accident	147
2011	26	27	Accident	157
2012	1	5	Running	200
2013	23	12	Running	200
2014	30	18	Running	200
2015	31	12	Running	200

Year	Start	Finish	Status	Laps
BRISKO, Frank (12)				
1929	29	11	Running	180
1931	27	22	Steering arm	138
1932	13	29	Clutch	61
1933	2	36	Oil too hot	47
1934	3	9	Running	200
(Relieved by Rex Mays)				
1935	24	23	Universal joint	79
1936	20	20	Out of gas	180
1937	15	23	Oil pressure	105
1938	11	31	Oil line	39
1939	11	29	Air pump	38
1940	8	9	Running	193
1941	22	23	Valve	70

Died Nov. 26, 1990

Year	Start	Finish	Status	Laps
BROCK, S.F. (1)				
1914	21	30	Camshaft	5

Lost at sea in submarine in 1918, during World War I

Year	Start	Finish	Status	Laps
BROWN, W. W. (1)				
1919	17	32	Rod	14

Died June 14, 1958

Year	Start	Finish	Status	Laps
BROWN, Walt (3)				
1947	14	7	Running	200
1950	20	19	Running/rain	127
1951	13	26	Magneto	55

Died July 29, 1951 in racing accident at Williams Grove, Pa.

Year	Start	Finish	Status	Laps
BRUCE-BROWN, David (2)				
1911	25	3	Running	200
1912	23	22	Valves	24

Died Oct. 1, 1912 in practice accident at Milwaukee

Year	Start	Finish	Status	Laps
BRYAN, Jimmy (9)				
1952	21	6	Running	200
1953	31	14	Running	183
1954	3	2	Running	200

Year	Start	Finish	Status	Laps
1955	11	24	Fuel pump	90
1956	19	19	Running	185
1957	15	3	Running	200
1958	7	1	Running	200
1959	20	33	Clutch/cam gear	1
1960	10	19	Fuel pump	152

Died June 19, 1960 in racing accident at Langhorne, Pa.

BUCKNUM, Jeff (2)

Year	Start	Finish	Status	Laps
2005	21	22	Accident	150
2006	22	32	Accident	1

BUCKNUM, Ronnie (3)

Year	Start	Finish	Status	Laps
1968	19	21	Fuel leak	76
1969	16	30	Piston	16
1970	27	15	Accident	162

Died April 25, 1992

BUHL, Robbie (8)

Year	Start	Finish	Status	Laps
1996	23	9	Running	197
1997	4	8	Running	199
1998	5	31	Engine	44
1999	32	6	Running	199
2000	9	26	Engine	99
2001	9	15	Running	196
2002	2	16	Running	198
2003	22	23	Engine	147

BURMAN, Bob (5)

Year	Start	Finish	Status	Laps
1911	39	19	Running	Flagged
1912	12	12	Accident	157
1913	21	11	Running	Flagged
(Relieved by Hughie Hughes)				
1914	22	24	Rod	47
1915	7	6	Running	200

Died April 8, 1916 in racing accident at Corona, Calif.

BURTON (Berton), Claude (1)

Year	Start	Finish	Status	Laps
1930	16	11	Running	196

Year	Start	Finish	Status	Laps
BUSCH, Kurt (1)				
2014	12	6	Running	200
BUTCHER, Harry (2)				
1930	38	14	Running	128
1931	33	38	Accident	6
Died June 18, 1942				
CACCIA, Joe (1)				
1930	14	25	Accident	43
Died May 26, 1931 in Indianapolis 500 practice accident, along with mechanic Clarence Grove				
CALKINS, Buzz (6)				
1996	9	17	Rear brakes	148
1997	16	11	Half shaft	188
1998	18	10	Running	195
1999	26	19	Running	133
2000	22	18	Running	194
2001	24	12	Running	198
CAMARA, Jaime (1)				
2008	30	31	Accident	79
CAMPBELL, Ray (2)				
1932	34	30	Crankshaft	60
1933	37	39	Oil leak	24
CANNON, Larry "Boom Boom" (3)				
1974	33	24	Differential	49
1976	10	17	Running/rain	97
1980	14	33	Camshaft	2
Died Nov. 6, 1995				
CANTLON, William "Shorty" (11)				
1930	3	2	Running	200
(Relieved by Herman Schurch)				
1931	26	27	Rod	88
1933	13	34	Rod	50

Year	Start	Finish	Status	Laps
1934	15	20	Crankshaft	76
(Relieved by Billy Winn)				
1935	19	6	Running	200
(Relieved by Billy Winn)				
1936	10	14	Out of gas	194
1937	25	16	Running	182
(Relieved by Rex Mays)				
1938	20	33	Supercharger	13
1939	7	32	Main bearing	15
1946	20	28	Clutch	28
1947	5	23	Accident	40

Died May 30, 1947 in Indianapolis 500 racing accident

CANTRELL, Bill (2)

Year	Start	Finish	Status	Laps
1948	7	16	Steering	161
1949	30	21	Drive shaft	95

Died Jan. 22, 1996

CAREY, Bob (1)

Year	Start	Finish	Status	Laps
1932	14	4	Running	200

Died April 16, 1933 in racing accident at Los Angeles

CARLSON, Billy (2)

Year	Start	Finish	Status	Laps
1914	5	9	Running	200
(Relieved by Jack LeCain)				
1915	16	9	Running	200
(Relieved by Hughie Hughes)				

Died July 5, 1915 of injuries suffered in racing accident at Tacoma, Wash.

CARLSON, Tyce (2)

Year	Start	Finish	Status	Laps
1997	26	19	Accident	156
1999	15	14	Running	190

CARPENTER, Ed (12)

Year	Start	Finish	Status	Laps
2004	16	31	Accident	62
2005	26	11	Running	199
2006	12	11	Running	199
2007	14	17	Accident	164
2008	10	5	Running	200

Year	Start	Finish	Status	Laps
2009	17	8	Running	200
2010	8	17	Running	199
2011	8	11	Running	200
2012	28	21	Running	199
2013	1	10	Running	200
2014	1	27	Contact	175
2015	12	30	Contact	112
2016	20	31	Mechanical	98

CARPENTIER, Patrick (1)

Year	Start	Finish	Status	Laps
2005	25	21	Mechanical	153

CARTER, Duane (11)

Year	Start	Finish	Status	Laps
1948	29	22	Accident	59
1949	5	14	Steering-spun	182
1950	13	12	Running/rain	133
1951	4	8	Running	180
1952	6	4	Running	200
1953	27	24	Ignition	94
1954	8	15	Running	196

(Relieved by Jimmy Jackson, Marshall Teague, Tony Bettenhausen)

Year	Start	Finish	Status	Laps
1955	18	11	Running	197
1959	12	7	Running	200
1960	27	12	Running	200
1963	15	23	Rod	100

Died March 7, 1993

CARTER, Duane Jr. "Pancho" (17)

Year	Start	Finish	Status	Laps
1974	21	7	Running	191
1975	18	4	Running/rain	169
1976	6	5	Running/rain	101
1977	8	15	Engine	156
1978	21	24	Header	92
1979	17	20	Wheel bearing	129
1980	8	6	Running	199
1981	10	28	Compression	63
1982	10	3	Running	199
1983	14	7	Running	197
1984	21	19	Engine	141

Year	Start	Finish	Status	Laps
1985	1	33	Oil pump	6
1986	14	16	Wheel bearing	179
1987	29	27	Valve	45
1989	32	22	Electrical	121
1990	22	29	Accident	59
1991	32	21	Engine	94

CARUTHERS, Jimmy (4)

Year	Start	Finish	Status	Laps
1972	31	9	Running	194
1973	9	21	Suspension	73
1974	12	23	Gearbox	64
1975	10	14	Running/rain	161

Died Oct. 26, 1975

CASTRONEVES, Helio (16)

Year	Start	Finish	Status	Laps
2001	11	1	Running	200
2002	13	1	Running	200
2003	1	2	Running	200
2004	8	9	Running/rain	180
2005	5	9	Running	200
2006	2	25	Accident	109
2007	1	3	Running	166
2008	4	4	Running	200
2009	1	1	Running	200
2010	1	9	Running	200
2011	16	17	Running	199
2012	6	10	Running	200
2013	8	6	Running	200
2014	4	2	Running	200
2015	5	7	Running	200
2016	9	11	Running	200

CHANDLER, Billy (2)

Year	Start	Finish	Status	Laps
1914	4	21	Rod	69
1916	15	9	Running	120

(Relieved by Frank Elliott)
Died July 28, 1924

CHANDLER, Michael (3)

Year	Start	Finish	Status	Laps
1981	25	12	Running	192
1982	22	17	Gearbox	104

Year	Start	Finish	Status	Laps
1983	30	16	Gearbox	153

CHASSAGNE, Jean (3)

Year	Start	Finish	Status	Laps
1914	1	29	Accident	20
1920	4	7	Running	200
1921	6	18	Lost hood	65

Died April 13, 1947

CHASSEY, Steve (3)

Year	Start	Finish	Status	Laps
1983	19	11	Running	191
1987	32	25	Engine	68
1988	26	24	Accident	73

CHAVES, Gabby (2)

Year	Start	Finish	Status	Laps
2015	26	16	Running	200
2016	21	20	Running	199

CHEESBOURG, Bill (6)

Year	Start	Finish	Status	Laps
1957	23	26	Fuel leak	81
1958	33	10	Running	200
1959	30	21	Magneto	147
1961	9	28	Accident	50
1964	33	16	Engine	131
1965	33	32	Magneto	14

Died Nov. 6, 1995

CHEEVER, Eddie Jr. (14)

Year	Start	Finish	Status	Laps
1990	14	8	Running	193
1991	10	31	Electrical	17
1992	2	4	Running	200
1993	33	16	Running	197
1994	11	8	Running	197
1995	14	31	Accident	0
1996	4	11	Running	189
1997	11	23	Timing chain	84
1998	17	1	Running	200
1999	16	18	Engine	139
2000	10	5	Running	200
2001	25	26	Electrical	108

Year	Start	Finish	Status	Laps
2002	6	5	Running	200
2006	19	13	Running	199

CHESSON, P.J. (1)

Year	Start	Finish	Status	Laps
2006	20	33	Accident	1

CHEVROLET, Arthur (2)

Year	Start	Finish	Status	Laps
1911	14	36	Mechanical	30
1916	11	18	Magneto	35

Died April 16, 1946

CHEVROLET, Gaston (2)

Year	Start	Finish	Status	Laps
1919	16	10	Running	200

(Relieved by Louis Chevrolet)

Year	Start	Finish	Status	Laps
1920	6	1	Running	200

Died Nov. 25, 1920 in racing accident at Beverly Hills, Calif.

CHEVROLET, Louis (4)

Year	Start	Finish	Status	Laps
1915	23	20	Valve	76
1916	21	12	Rod	82

(Relieved by Joe Boyer)

Year	Start	Finish	Status	Laps
1919	12	7	Running	200

(Relieved by Joe Boyer)

Year	Start	Finish	Status	Laps
1920	3	18	Steering	94

(Relieved by Sal Barbarino, Jerry Wonderlich)

Died June 6, 1941

CHILTON, Max (1)

Year	Start	Finish	Status	Laps
2016	22	15	Running	200

CHIRON, Louis (1)

Year	Start	Finish	Status	Laps
1929	14	7	Running	200

Died June 22, 1979

CHITWOOD, Joie (7)

Year	Start	Finish	Status	Laps
1940	26	15	Running	190
1941	27	14	Running	177
1946	12	5	Running	200

(Relieved by Sam Hanks)

Year	Start	Finish	Status	Laps
1947	22	22	Gears	50
1948	10	17	Fuel leak	138

(Relieved by Paul Russo, Johnny Shackleford)

Year	Start	Finish	Status	Laps
1949	16	5	Running	200
1950	9	5	Running/rain	136

(Relieved by Tony Bettenhausen)

Died Jan. 3, 1988

CHRISTIAENS, Josef (2)

Year	Start	Finish	Status	Laps
1914	7	6	Running	200
1916	14	4	Running	120

Died Feb. 23, 1919 in testing accident in England

CHRISTIE, Bob (8)

Year	Start	Finish	Status	Laps
1956	25	13	Running	196
1957	33	13	Running	197
1958	17	14	Spun	189
1959	24	25	Rod bolt	109
1960	14	10	Running	200
1961	16	17	Piston	132
1962	31	30	Accident	18
1963	18	13	Running	200

Died June 1, 2009

CLARK, George (1)

Year	Start	Finish	Status	Laps
1913	27	10	Running	200

(Relieved by Tom Alley)

CLARK, Jim (5)

Year	Start	Finish	Status	Laps
1963	5	2	Running	200
1964	1	24	Suspension	47
1965	2	1	Running	200
1966	2	2	Running	200
1967	16	31	Piston	35

Died April 7, 1968 in racing accident at Hockenheim, Germany

CLAUSON, Bryan (3)

Year	Start	Finish	Status	Laps
2012	31	30	Mechanical	46
2015	30	31	Contact	61

Year	Start	Finish	Status	Laps
2016	28	23	Running	198

Died August 7, 2016 from racing accident at Lincoln, NE

COBE, Harry (1)

Year	Start	Finish	Status	Laps
1911	22	10	Running	200

Died July 24, 1966

COGAN, Kevin (12)

Year	Start	Finish	Status	Laps
1981	12	4	Running	197
1982	2	30	Accident	0
1983	22	5	Running	198
1984	27	20	Wheel	137
1985	32	11	Running	191
1986	6	2	Running	200
1987	24	31	Oil pump	21
1988	13	11	Running	195
1989	27	32	Accident	2
1990	15	9	Running	191
1991	16	29	Accident	24
1993	14	14	Running	198

COLE, Hal (3)

Year	Start	Finish	Status	Laps
1946	4	32	Fuel leak	16
1948	14	6	Running	200
1949	11	19	Rod bearing	117

Died Nov. 12, 1970

COLETTI, Stefano (1)

Year	Start	Finish	Status	Laps
2015	29	25	Contact	175

COMER, Fred (4)

Year	Start	Finish	Status	Laps
1924	16	7	Running	200

(Relieved by Wade Morton)

Year	Start	Finish	Status	Laps
1925	12	11	Running	200

(Relieved by Ira Vail)

Year	Start	Finish	Status	Laps
1926	13	4	Running/rain	155

(Relieved by Wade Morton)

Year	Start	Finish	Status	Laps
1928	9	9	Running	200

(Relieved by Cliff Woodbury)

Year	Start	Finish	Status	Laps

Died Oct. 12, 1928 in racing accident at Salem, N.H.

CONGDON, Gary (1)

Year	Start	Finish	Status	Laps
1966	16	25	Accident	0

Died Sept. 24, 1967 in racing accident at Terre Haute, Ind.

CONNOR, George (14)

Year	Start	Finish	Status	Laps
1935	14	19	Transmission	112
1936	5	10	Running	200
1937	12	9	Running	200
1938	19	19	Engine	119
1939	12	13	Stalled	195
1940	17	26	Rod	52
1941	13	16	Transmission	167
1946	30	24	Piston	38
1947	13	26	Fuel leak	32
1948	17	28	Drive shaft	24
1949	6	3	Running	200
1950	4	8	Running/rain	135
1951	21	30	Universal joint	29
1952	14	8	Running	200

Died March 28, 2001

CONWAY, Mike (3)

Year	Start	Finish	Status	Laps
2009	27	18	Running	200
2010	15	19	Accident	198
2012	29	29	Contact	78

COOPER, Earl (7)

Year	Start	Finish	Status	Laps
1914	14	18	Broken wheel	118
(Relieved by Bill Rader)				
1915	4	4	Running	200
(Relieved by Johnny Aitken)				
1919	9	12	Running	200
(Relieved by Reeves Dutton)				
1923	12	21	Accident (Alley)	22
(Relieved by Tom Alley)				
1924	6	2	Running	200
1925	4	17	Accident	127

Year	Start	Finish	Status	Laps
1926	1	16	Transmission	74

Died Oct. 23, 1965

COOPER, Joe (1)

Year	Start	Finish	Status	Laps
1915	15	15	Accident	154

Died Aug. 7, 1915 in racing accident at Des Moines, Iowa

CORUM, L.L. "Slim" (6)

Year	Start	Finish	Status	Laps
1922	15	17	Engine	169
1923	7	5	Running	200
1924	21	1	Running	200

(Relieved by Joe Boyer on Lap 111; Boyer finished race)

Year	Start	Finish	Status	Laps
1926	24	20	Shock absorbers	45
1930	17	10	Running	200
1933	18	12	Running	200

Died March 7, 1949

COTEY, Al (1)

Year	Start	Finish	Status	Laps
1927	29	21	Universal joint	87

(Relieved by Eddie Burbach)

COX, C.C. (1)

Year	Start	Finish	Status	Laps
1915	21	24	Timing gears	12

Died July 4, 1915 in racing accident at Sioux City, Iowa

CRAWFORD, Charlie (1)

Year	Start	Finish	Status	Laps
1934	28	13	Head gasket/in pits	110

Died 1958

CRAWFORD, Jim (8)

Year	Start	Finish	Status	Laps
1985	27	16	Electrical	142
1986	26	29	Head gasket	70
1988	18	6	Running	198
1989	4	19	Drive train	135
1990	29	15	Running	183
1991	8	26	Engine	40
1992	21	25	Accident	74
1993	31	24	Running	192

Died Aug. 6, 2002

Year	Start	Finish	Status	Laps
CRAWFORD, Ray (3)				
1955	23	23	Valve	111
1956	17	29	Accident	49
1959	32	23	Accident	115

Died Feb. 1, 1996

Year	Start	Finish	Status	Laps
CRAWFORD (Crafford), Wesley (3)				
1929	24	15	Carburetor	127
(Relieved by Zeke Meyer, Ted Simpson, Dave Evans)				
1932	16	36	Crankshaft	28
1933	26	24	Accident (Winn)	147
(Relieved by Billy Winn)				

Died Jan. 10, 1961

Year	Start	Finish	Status	Laps
CROCKETT, Larry (1)				
1954	25	9	Running	200

Died March 20, 1955 in racing accident at Langhorne, Pa.

Year	Start	Finish	Status	Laps
CROSS, Art (4)				
1952	20	5	Running	200
1953	12	2	Running	200
1954	27	11	Running	200
(Relieved by Johnnie Parsons, Sam Hanks, Andy Linden, Jimmy Davies)				
1955	24	17	Rod	168

Died April 15, 2005

Year	Start	Finish	Status	Laps
CROWE, Allen (2)				
1962	22	31	Accident	17
1963	13	27	Accident	47

Died June 2, 1963 in racing accident at New Bremen, Ohio

Year	Start	Finish	Status	Laps
CUCINOTTA, Letterio (1)				
1930	30	12	Running	185

Year	Start	Finish	Status	Laps
CUMMINGS, Bill (9)				
1930	22	5	Running	200
(Relieved by Freddie Winnai)				
1931	2	28	Oil line	70

Year	Start	Finish	Status	Laps
1932	12	19	Crankshaft	151
(Relieved by Frank Brisko)				
1933	1	25	Radiator	136
(Relieved by Frank Brisko)				
1934	10	1	Running	200
1935	5	3	Running	200
1936	13	33	Clutch	0
1937	1	6	Running	200
(Relieved by Chet Miller)				
1938	16	24	Radiator	72
Died Feb. 8, 1939 in traffic accident				

CUNNINGHAM, Wade (1)

Year	Start	Finish	Status	Laps
2012	26	31	Electrical	42

CURTNER, Jack (1)

Year	Start	Finish	Status	Laps
1922	21	14	Running	165
Died Dec. 18, 1959				

D'ALENE, Wilbur (Ed Aleon) (3)

Year	Start	Finish	Status	Laps
1916	10	2	Running	120
1919	23	17	Axle	120
1922	18	15	Running	160
Died 1966				

DALLENBACH, Wally (13)

Year	Start	Finish	Status	Laps
1967	15	29	Accident	73
1968	12	17	Engine	146
1969	19	21	Clutch	82
1970	24	17	Coil	143
1971	23	24	Valve	69
1972	33	15	Running	182
1973	20	24	Broken rod	48
1974	2	30	Piston	3
1975	21	9	Piston	162
1976	7	4	Running/rain	101
1977	10	4	Running	199
1978	7	5	Running	195
1979	7	27	Lost wheel	43

Year	Start	Finish	Status	Laps
DALY, Conor (3)				
2013	31	22	Running	198
2015	22	33	Mechanical	0
2016	24	18	Contact	116
DALY, Derek (6)				
1983	28	19	Engine	126
1984	29	27	Handling	76
1985	31	12	Running	189
1987	19	15	Engine	133
1988	9	29	Gearbox	18
1989	24	15	Running	167
DARÉ, Airton (5)				
2000	21	25	Engine	126
2001	30	8	Running	199
2002	30	13	Running	199
2003	33	24	Accident	125
2006	29	18	Running	193
DAVIES, Jimmy (4)				
1950	27	17	Running/rain	128
1951	27	16	Rear end gears	110
1953	32	10	Running	193
1955	10	3	Running	200

Died June 11, 1966 of injuries suffered June 3 at Santa Fe Speedway, near Chicago

Year	Start	Finish	Status	Laps
DAVIS, Don (2)				
1961	27	29	Accident	49
1962	12	4	Running	200

Died Aug. 7, 1962 at Dayton, Ohio, of injuries suffered Aug. 5 at New Bremen

Year	Start	Finish	Status	Laps
DAVIS, Floyd (4)				
1937	24	15	Accident	190
1939	29	27	Shock absorber	43
1940	33	20	Running	157

(Relieved by Lou Webb, George Connor)

Year	Start	Finish	Status	Laps
1941	17	1	Running	200

(Relieved by Mauri Rose, Laps 72-200)

Died May 31, 1977

DAVISON, James (2)

2014	28	16	Running	200
2015	33	27	Mechanical	116

DAWSON, Joe (3)

1911	27	5	Running	200

(Relieved by Cyrus Patschke)

1912	7	1	Running	200

(Relieved by Don Herr, Laps 108-144)

1914	17	25	Accident	44

Died June 17, 1946

DAYWALT, Jimmy (8)

1953	21	6	Running	200
1954	2	27	Accident	111
1955	17	9	Running	200
1956	16	24	Accident	134
1957	29	28	Accident	53
1959	13	14	Running	200
1961	23	31	Brake line	27
1962	33	22	Transmission	75

Died April 4, 1966

DE ALZAGA, Martin (1)

1923	4	24	Rod	6

Died Nov. 15, 1982

DE CYSTRIA, Prince Bertrand (1)

1923	22	9	Running	200

Died Feb. 22, 1943

DE FERRAN, Gil (4)

1995	19	29	Accident	1
2001	5	2	Running	200
2002	14	10	Running	200

Year	Start	Finish	Status	Laps
2003	10	1	Running	200

DE SILVESTRO, Simona (5)

Year	Start	Finish	Status	Laps
2010	22	14	Running	200
2011	23	31	Handling	44
2012	32	32	Handling	10
2013	24	17	Running	200
2015	18	19	Running	200

DE VIZCAYA, Pierre (1)

Year	Start	Finish	Status	Laps
1923	6	12	Rod	166

Died July 14, 1933 in a traffic accident in Paris

DECKER, Rick (4)

Year	Start	Finish	Status	Laps
1929	30	23	Fuel line	61

(Relieved by Jimmy Rossi)

Year	Start	Finish	Status	Laps
1930	36	37	Oil tank	8
1933	38	41	Manifold	13
1934	27	27	Clutch	17

Died Feb. 28, 1966

DELANEY, Ernest (1)

Year	Start	Finish	Status	Laps
1911	24	23	Running	Flagged

Died Aug. 29, 1937

DENVER (Orem), Bill (1)

Year	Start	Finish	Status	Laps
1930	35	22	Rod	41

Died May 28, 1933 in Indianapolis 500 qualifying accident, along with mechanic Hugh Hurst

DePALMA, John (1)

Year	Start	Finish	Status	Laps
1915	13	21	Loose flywheel	41

Died Jan 18, 1951

DePALMA, Ralph (10)

Year	Start	Finish	Status	Laps
1911	2	6	Running	200
1912	4	11	Rod	198
1913	12	23	Bearing	15
1915	2	1	Running	200

Year	Start	Finish	Status	Laps
1919	4	6	Running	200
1920	1	5	Running	200
1921	1	12	Rod	112
1922	3	4	Running	200
1923	11	15	Head gasket	69
1925	18	7	Running	200

(Relieved by L.L. Corum)
Died March 31, 1956

DePAOLO, Peter (7)

Year	Start	Finish	Status	Laps
1922	10	20	Accident	110
1924	13	6	Running	200
1925	2	1	Running	200

(Relieved by Norman Batten for Laps 106-127)

1926	27	5	Running/rain	153
1927	2	26	Supercharger	31
1929	5	30	Steering	25
1930	21	33	Accident	19

(Relieved by Fred Roberts)
Died Nov. 26, 1980

DeVIGNE, Jules (1)

Year	Start	Finish	Status	Laps
1916	12	16	Accident (LeCain)	61

(Relieved by Jack LeCain)

DEVORE, Billy (7)

Year	Start	Finish	Status	Laps
1937	14	7	Running	200

(Relieved by Fred Frame)

1938	30	8	Running	185
1939	33	10	Running	200

(Relieved by Henry Banks)

1940	32	18	Running	181

(Relieved by George Connor)

1941	8	19	Rod	121
1946	31	10	Throttle	167
1948	20	12	Running	190

Died Aug. 12, 1985

DEVORE, Earl (3)

Year	Start	Finish	Status	Laps
1925	15	13	Running	198

Year	Start	Finish	Status	Laps
(Relieved by L.L. Corum, Glen Shultz)				
1927	15	2	Running	200
(Relieved by Zeke Meyer)				
1928	24	18	Accident	161
(Relieved by Cy Marshall)				
Lost Nov. 12, 1928 with SS Vestris				

DICKSON, Larry (8)

Year	Start	Finish	Status	Laps
1966	32	32	Accident	0
1967	21	15	Spun	180
1968	33	28	Piston	24
(Relieved by Mario Andretti)				
1969	31	9	Running	180
1971	26	28	Engine	33
1978	9	22	Oil pressure	104
1979	24	24	Fuel pump	86
1981	19	18	Piston	165

DINGLEY, Bert (1)

Year	Start	Finish	Status	Laps
1912	10	13	Rod	116

Died April 7, 1966

DINSMORE, Duke (6)

Year	Start	Finish	Status	Laps
1946	8	17	Rod	82
1947	27	10	Running	167
(Relieved by Billy Devore)				
1949	15	15	Radius rod	174
1950	7	33	Oil leak	10
1951	32	24	Overheating	73
1956	33	17	Running	191

Died Oct. 12, 1985

DISBROW, Louis (4)

Year	Start	Finish	Status	Laps
1911	5	35	Accident	45
1912	24	18	Differ. pin	67
(Relieved by Neil Whalen)				
1913	23	8	Running	200
(Relieved by I.J. Kilpatrick)				
1914	24	16	Rod	128

Year	Start	Finish	Status	Laps
Died July 9, 1939				
DISMORE, Mark (7)				
1996	14	19	Engine	129
1997	25	28	Accident	24
1998	12	27	Accident	48
1999	5	16	Accident	168
2000	11	11	Running	198
2001	4	16	Running	195
2002	33	32	Handling	58
DIXON, Scott (14)				
2003	4	17	Accident	191
2004	13	8	Running/rain	180
2005	13	24	Accident	113
2006	4	6	Running	200
2007	4	2	Running	166
2008	1	1	Running	200
2009	5	6	Running	200
2010	6	5	Running	200
2011	2	5	Running	200
2012	15	2	Running	200
2013	16	14	Running	200
2014	11	29	Contact	167
2015	1	4	Running	200
2016	13	8	Running	200
DOBSON, Dominic (7)				
1988	21	18	Lost coolant	145
1989	29	18	Engine	161
1990	11	22	Engine	129
1991	30	13	Running	164
1992	29	12	Running	193
1993	27	23	Running	193
1994	12	29	Accident	29
DONOHUE, Mark (5)				
1969	4	7	Running	190
1970	5	2	Running	200

Year	Start	Finish	Status	Laps
1971	2	25	Gears	66
1972	3	1	Running	200
1973	3	15	Piston	92

Died Aug. 19, 1975 of injuries in practice for Austrian Grand Prix

DOORNBOS, Robert (1)

Year	Start	Finish	Status	Laps
2009	23	28	Accident	85

DUFF, John (1)

Year	Start	Finish	Status	Laps
1926	28	9	Running/rain	147

Died Jan. 8, 1958

DUMAN, Ronnie (5)

Year	Start	Finish	Status	Laps
1964	16	31	Accident	1
1965	25	22	Rear end gears	62
1966	33	33	Accident	0
1967	17	23	Fuel trouble	154
1968	26	6	Running	200

Died June 9, 1968 in racing accident at Milwaukee

DUNCAN, Len (1)

Year	Start	Finish	Status	Laps
1954	26	31	Brakes	101

(Relieved by George Fonder)
Died Aug. 1, 1998

DUNO, Milka (3)

Year	Start	Finish	Status	Laps
2007	29	31	Accident	65
2008	27	19	Running	185
2009	30	20	Running	199

DURANT, Lewis (1)

Year	Start	Finish	Status	Laps
1946	6	6	Running	200

Died Feb. 13, 1972

DURANT, Paul (2)

Year	Start	Finish	Status	Laps
1996	24	32	Engine	9
1997	33	21	Accident	111

DURANT, R. Clifford "Cliff" (6)

Year	Start	Finish	Status	Laps
1919	20	24	Steering	54
1922	11	12	Running	200
(Relieved by Dave Lewis)				
1923	10	7	Running	200
(Relieved by Eddie Hearne)				
1924	8	13	Out of gas	199
(Relieved by Phil Shafer, Eddie Hearne)				
1926	11	17	Fuel tank leak	61
(Relieved by Eddie Hearne)				
1928	18	16	Supercharger	175
(Relieved by Bob McDonogh)				
Died Oct. 31, 1937				

DURAY, Arthur (1)

Year	Start	Finish	Status	Laps
1914	10	2	Running	200
Died Feb. 11, 1954				

DURAY, Leon (George Stewart) (8)

Year	Start	Finish	Status	Laps
1922	4	22	Axle	94
1923	21	13	Rod	136
(Relieved by Lou Wilson)				
1925	1	6	Running	200
(Relieved by Fred Comer)				
1926	3	23	Broken axle	33
1927	3	27	Fuel tank leak	26
1928	1	19	Overheating	133
(Relieved by Cliff Bergere)				
1929	2	22	Carburetor	65
(Relieved by Ralph Hepburn)				
1931	29	37	Overheating	6
Died May 12, 1956				

EDMUNDS, Don (1)

Year	Start	Finish	Status	Laps
1957	27	19	Spun	170

ELDRIDGE, E.A.D. (1)

Year	Start	Finish	Status	Laps
1926	23	19	Tie rod	46
(Relieved by Herschel McKee)				
Died Oct. 27, 1935				

Year	Start	Finish	Status	Laps
ELISIAN, Ed (5)				
1954	31	18	Running	193
(Relieved by Bob Scott)				
1955	29	30	Stopped	53
1956	14	23	Stalled	160
(Relieved by Eddie Russo)				
1957	7	29	Timing gear	51
1958	2	28	Accident	0

Died Aug. 30, 1959 in racing accident at Milwaukee

Year	Start	Finish	Status	Laps
ELLINGBOE, Jules (6)				
1921	5	19	Steering	49
1922	20	26	Accident	25
1924	7	11	Running	200
1925	7	22	Steering	24
1926	6	22	Supercharger	39
1927	21	29	Accident	25

Died April 26, 1948

Year	Start	Finish	Status	Laps
ELLIOTT, Frank (6)				
1922	8	16	Rear axle	195
(Relieved by Art Klein)				
1923	16	6	Running	200
(Relieved by Dave Lewis)				
1924	12	20	Gas tank	150
1925	10	12	Running	200
(Relieved by Ora Haibe)				
1926	8	6	Running/rain	152
(Relieved by Leon Duray)				
1927	13	10	Running	200
(Relieved by Fred Frame)				

Died 1957

Year	Start	Finish	Status	Laps
ELLIS, Fred (1)				
1911	21	38	Withdrawn	22

Died July 24, 1958

ENDICOTT, Bill (3)

Year	Start	Finish	Status	Laps
1911	37	26	Running	Flagged
(Relieved by John Jenkins)				
1912	15	5	Running	200
(Relieved by Harry Endicott)				
1913	9	27	Drive shaft	1
Died June 7, 1944				

ENDICOTT, Harry (2)

Year	Start	Finish	Status	Laps
1911	3	16	Running	N/A
1913	10	21	Transmission	23
(Relieved by Ed Madden)				
Died Sept. 5, 1913 in racing accident at Jackson, Mich.				

ENGE, Tomas (1)

Year	Start	Finish	Status	Laps
2005	10	19	Accident	155

ENGELHART, Bill (1)

Year	Start	Finish	Status	Laps
1980	22	11	Running	193

EVANS, Dave (6)

Year	Start	Finish	Status	Laps
1927	28	5	Running	200
(Relieved by Steve Nemish)				
1928	23	12	Running	200
1930	33	6	Running	200
1931	17	13	Running	200
1933	36	6	Running	200
1934	22	19	Transmission	81
Died March 31, 1974				

EVANS, Bob (1)

Year	Start	Finish	Status	Laps
1913	4	13	Clutch	158

EYCKMANS, Wim (1)

Year	Start	Finish	Status	Laps
1999	29	23	Timing chain	113

FABI, Teo (8)

Year	Start	Finish	Status	Laps
1983	1	26	Fuel gasket	47
1984	14	24	Fuel system	104
1988	17	28	Accident	30
1989	13	30	Ignition	23

Year	Start	Finish	Status	Laps
1990	23	18	Transmission	162
1993	17	9	Running	200
1994	24	7	Running	198
1995	15	8	Running	199

FAHRNOW, Herbert "Dusty" (1)

Year	Start	Finish	Status	Laps
1934	25	24	Rod	28

Died May 25, 1981

FANKHAUSER, Milt (1)

Year	Start	Finish	Status	Laps
1947	11	30	Stalled	15

Died Feb. 26, 1970

FARMER, Frank (3)

Year	Start	Finish	Status	Laps
1929	26	14	Supercharger	140

(Relieved by Bill Albertson)

Year	Start	Finish	Status	Laps
1930	11	21	Accident	69
1931	22	32	Rod bearing	32

Died Aug. 27, 1932 in racing accident at Woodbridge, N.J.

FAULKNER, Walt (4)

Year	Start	Finish	Status	Laps
1950	1	7	Running/rain	135
1951	14	15	Crankshaft	123
1953	14	17	Running	176

(Relieved by Johnny Mantz)

Year	Start	Finish	Status	Laps
1955	7	5	Running	200

(Relieved by Bill Homeier)

Died April 22, 1956 in racing accident at Vallejo, Calif.

FENGLER, Harlan (1)

Year	Start	Finish	Status	Laps
1923	19	16	Gas tank	69

(Relieved by Lou Wilson)

Died March 26, 1981

FERGUSON, Dick (1)

Year	Start	Finish	Status	Laps
1980	15	31	Accident	9

Died Sept. 26, 2010

FERNANDEZ, Adrian (4)

Year	Start	Finish	Status	Laps
1994	26	28	Suspension	30
1995	25	21	Engine	176
2004	6	7	Running/rain	180
2005	14	14	Running	197

FETTERMAN, I.P. "Red" (1)

Year	Start	Finish	Status	Laps
1922	13	7	Running	200

(Relieved by Phil Shafer)
Died Dec. 5, 1924

FILLIP, Chet (2)

Year	Start	Finish	Status	Laps
1982	29	24	Accident	60
1983	32	33	Black flagged	11

FIRESTONE, Dennis (5)

Year	Start	Finish	Status	Laps
1980	24	16	Transmission	137
1981	28	10	Engine	193
1982	21	27	Rear end	37
1983	33	24	Oil leak	77
1984	32	12	Running	186

FISHER, Sarah (9)

Year	Start	Finish	Status	Laps
2000	19	31	Accident	71
2001	15	31	Accident	7
2002	9	24	Running	196
2003	24	31	Engine/accident	14
2004	19	21	Running/rain	177
2007	21	18	Running	164
2008	22	30	Accident	103
2009	21	17	Running	200
2010	29	26	Accident	125

FITTIPALDI, Christian (1)

Year	Start	Finish	Status	Laps
1995	27	2	Running	200

FITTIPALDI, Emerson (11)

Year	Start	Finish	Status	Laps
1984	23	32	Oil pressure	37
1985	5	13	Fuel line	188
1986	11	7	Running	199

Year	Start	Finish	Status	Laps
1987	33	16	Lost power	131
1988	8	2	Running	200
1989	3	1	Running	200
1990	1	3	Running	200
1991	15	11	Gearbox	171
1992	11	24	Accident	75
1993	9	1	Running	200
1994	3	17	Accident	184

FLAHERTY, Pat (5)

Year	Start	Finish	Status	Laps
1950	11	10	Running/rain	135
1953	24	22	Accident	115
1955	12	10	Running	200
1956	1	1	Running	200
1959	18	19	Accident	162

Died April 9, 2002

FOHR, Myron (2)

Year	Start	Finish	Status	Laps
1949	13	4	Running	200
1950	16	11	Running/rain	133

Died Jan. 14, 1994

FOLLMER, George (3)

Year	Start	Finish	Status	Laps
1969	27	27	Engine	26
1970	21	31	Oil gasket	18
1971	29	15	Piston	147

FONDER, George (2)

Year	Start	Finish	Status	Laps
1949	25	20	Valve	116

(Relieved by Mel Hansen)

Year	Start	Finish	Status	Laps
1952	13	15	Running	197

Died June 14, 1958 in racing accident at Hatfield, Pa.

FONTAINE (Fountaine), Louis (1)

Year	Start	Finish	Status	Laps
1921	7	21	Accident	33

Died March 2, 1960

FORBERG, Carl (1)

Year	Start	Finish	Status	Laps
1951	24	7	Running	193

Died Jan. 17, 2000

Year	Start	Finish	Status	Laps
FORCE, Gene (2)				
1951	22	11	Oil pressure	142
1960	20	28	Brakes	74
Died Aug. 21, 1983				
FORD, Percy (1)				
1921	8	3	Running	200
(Relieved by Andy Burt, Jules Ellingboe)				
Died March 8, 1962				
FOSTER, Billy (2)				
1965	6	17	Water manifold	85
1966	12	24	Accident	0
Died Jan. 20, 1967 in racing accident at Riverside, Calif.				
FOWLER, Kenneth (2)				
1937	29	19	Pushed	116
1947	9	15	Axle	119
Died Jan. 8, 1981				
FOX, Frank (1)				
1911	6	22	Running	Flagged
(Relieved by W.F. Clemens)				
Died April 19, 1931				
FOX, Malcolm (2)				
1932	32	20	Spring	132
1933	30	28	Accident	121
Died Aug. 21, 1968				
FOX, Stan (8)				
1987	26	7	Running	192
1988	29	30	Half shaft	2
1990	27	33	Gearbox	10
1991	17	8	Running	185
1992	13	27	Accident	63
1993	20	31	Engine	64
1994	13	13	Accident	193

Year	Start	Finish	Status	Laps
1995	11	30	Accident	0

Died Dec. 18, 2000 in traffic accident in New Zealand

FOYT, A.J. (35)

Year	Start	Finish	Status	Laps
1958	12	16	Spun	148
1959	17	10	Running	200
1960	16	25	Clutch	90
1961	7	1	Running	200
1962	5	23	Lost wheel	69
1963	8	3	Running	200
1964	5	1	Running	200
1965	1	15	Gearbox	115
1966	18	26	Accident	0
1967	4	1	Running	200
1968	8	20	Rear end	86
1969	1	8	Running	181
1970	3	10	Running	195
1971	6	3	Running	200
1972	17	25	Turbocharger	60
1973	23	25	Rod bolt	37
1974	1	15	Oil fitting	142
1975	1	3	Running/rain	174
1976	5	2	Running/rain	102
1977	4	1	Running	200
1978	20	7	Running	191
1979	6	2	Running	200
1980	12	14	Valve	173
1981	3	13	Running	191
1982	3	19	Transmission	95
1983	24	31	Shift linkage	24
1984	12	6	Running	197
1985	21	28	Front wing	62
1986	21	24	Spun in pits	135
1987	4	19	Oil seal	117
1988	22	26	Accident	54
1989	10	5	Running	193
1990	8	6	Running	194
1991	2	28	Suspension	25
1992	23	9	Running	195

Year	Start	Finish	Status	Laps
FOYT, A.J. IV (6)				
2003	23	18	Running	189
2004	21	33	Handling	26
2005	28	28	Handling	84
2007	18	14	Running	165
2008	31	21	Running	180
2009	19	16	Running	200
FOYT, Larry (3)				
2004	22	32	Accident	54
2005	30	33	Accident	14
2006	23	30	Handling	43
FRAME, Fred (8)				
1927	33	11	Running	199
(Relieved by George Fernic, George Abell)				
1928	14	8	Running	200
(Relieved by Ralph Hepburn, Benny Shoaff)				
1929	22	10	Running	193
(Relieved by Johnny Seymour)				
1931	8	2	Running	200
1932	27	1	Running	200
1933	3	29	Valve	85
1935	8	11	Running	200
(Relieved by Frank Brisko)				
1936	31	32	Piston	4
Died April 25, 1962				
FRANCHI, Aldo (1)				
1916	16	21	Engine	9
Died 1920				
FRANCHITTI, Dario (10)				
2002	28	19	Running	197
2004	3	14	Running/rain	180
2005	6	6	Running	200
2006	17	7	Running	200
2007	3	1	Running	166

Year	Start	Finish	Status	Laps
2009	3	7	Running	200
2010	3	1	Running	200
2011	9	12	Running	200
2012	16	1	Running	200
2013	17	23	Contact	197

FRAYER, Lee (1)

Year	Start	Finish	Status	Laps
1911	26	13	Running	flagged

(Relieved by Eddie Rickenbacher)
Died July 25, 1938

FREE, Roland (2)

Year	Start	Finish	Status	Laps
1930	24	19	Clutch	69
1947	12	17	Spun	86

Died Oct. 11, 1980

FREELAND, Don (8)

Year	Start	Finish	Status	Laps
1953	15	27	Accident	76
1954	6	7	Running	200
1955	21	15	Transmission	178
1956	26	3	Running	200
1957	21	17	Running	192
1958	13	7	Running	200
1959	25	22	Valve spring	136
1960	11	22	Magneto	129

Died Nov. 2, 2007

FRIEDRICH, Ernst (1)

Year	Start	Finish	Status	Laps
1914	18	15	Drive pinion	134

Died Jan. 22, 1954

GACHE, Philippe (1)

Year	Start	Finish	Status	Laps
1992	16	28	Accident	61

GANASSI, Chip (5)

Year	Start	Finish	Status	Laps
1982	11	15	Engine	147
1983	16	8	Running	195
1984	22	28	Engine	61
1985	25	22	Fuel line	121

Year	Start	Finish	Status	Laps
1986	25	21	Engine	151

GARDNER, Chet (7)

Year	Start	Finish	Status	Laps
1930	5	38	Spun	0
1933	15	4	Running	200
1934	5	21	Rod	72
1935	9	7	Running	200
1936	18	29	Clutch	38
1937	9	11	Running	199

(Relieved by Billy Winn)

Year	Start	Finish	Status	Laps
1938	18	5	Running	200

Died Sept. 3, 1938 in racing accident at Flemington, N.J.

GARDNER, Racin (1)

Year	Start	Finish	Status	Laps
1996	25	25	Suspension	76

GARDNER, W.H. "Speed" (3)

Year	Start	Finish	Status	Laps
1929	28	6	Running	200

(Relieved by Chet Gardner)

Year	Start	Finish	Status	Laps
1930	27	35	Main bearing	14
1931	7	25	Frame	107

(Relieved by Wesley Crawford)

Died April 25, 1972

GARRETT, Billy (2)

Year	Start	Finish	Status	Laps
1956	29	16	Running	194
1958	15	21	Cam gear	80

Died Feb. 15, 1999

GARZA, Josele (7)

Year	Start	Finish	Status	Laps
1981	6	23	Accident	138
1982	33	29	Engine	1
1983	18	25	Oil leak	64
1984	24	10	Running	193
1985	18	31	Engine	15
1986	17	18	Running	167
1987	25	17	Running	129

Year	Start	Finish	Status	Laps
GAUDINO, Juan (1)				
1932	36	26	Clutch	71
(Relieved by Joe Bonadeo)				
Died March 23, 1975				
GEHLHAUSEN, Spike (5)				
1976	25	33	Oil pressure	0
1978	16	29	Accident	23
1979	31	10	Running	192
1980	4	29	Accident	20
1984	25	31	Spun	45
GIEBLER, Phil (1)				
2007	33	29	Accident	106
GEORGE, Elmer (3)				
1957	9	33	Accident/DNS	0
1962	17	17	Engine	146
(Relieved by Paul Russo, A.J. Foyt)				
1963	28	30	Handling	21
Died May 30, 1976				
GIAFFONE, Affonso (1)				
1997	14	32	Accident	0
GIAFFONE, Felipe (6)				
2001	33	10	Running	199
2002	4	3	Running	200
2003	16	33	Electrical	6
2004	25	15	Running/rain	179
2005	33	15	Running	194
2006	21	21	Accident	177
GILHOOLY, Ray (1)				
1914	20	27	Accident	41
Died Sep. 18, 1973				
GLEASON, Jimmy (4)				
1928	21	15	Magneto	195

Year	Start	Finish	Status	Laps
(Relieved by Russ Snowberger)				
1929	23	3	Running	200
(Relieved by Thane Houser, Ernie Triplett)				
1930	24	28	Timing gears	22
1931	20	6	Running	200
(Relieved by Wilbur Shaw)				

Died Sept. 12, 1931 in racing accident at Syracuse, N.Y.

GLOY, Tom (1)

Year	Start	Finish	Status	Laps
1984	13	14	Engine	179

GOLDSMITH, Paul (6)

Year	Start	Finish	Status	Laps
1958	16	30	Accident	0
1959	16	5	Running	200
1960	26	3	Running	200
1961	17	14	Connecting rod	160
1962	26	26	Magneto	26
1963	9	18	Crankshaft	149

GOODYEAR, Scott (11)

Year	Start	Finish	Status	Laps
1990	21	10	Running	191
1991	12	27	Engine	38
1992	33	2	Running	200
1993	4	7	Running	200
1994	33	30	Suspension	29
1995	3	14*	Running	195*
1997	5	2	Running	200
1998	10	24	Clutch	100
1999	9	27	Engine	101
2000	13	9	Running	199
2001	16	32	Accident	7

*Last five laps disallowed for ignoring black flag

GORDON, Al (3)

Year	Start	Finish	Status	Laps
1932	37	40	Accident	3
1934	17	22	Accident	66
1935	2	30	Accident	17

Died Jan. 26, 1936 in racing accident at Los Angeles

Year	Start	Finish	Status	Laps
GORDON, Robby (10)				
1993	25	27	Gearbox	165
1994	19	5	Running	199
1995	7	5	Running	200
1997	12	29	Fire	19
1999	4	4	Running	200
2000	4	6	Running	200
2001	3	21	Running	184
2002	11	8	Running	200
2003	3	22	Gearbox	169
2004	18	29	Mechanical	88

(Relieved by Jaques Lazier on Lap 27 due to red flag for rain/Gordon's NASCAR team commitment)

Year	Start	Finish	Status	Laps
GOSEK, Joe (1)				
1996	31	22	Radiator	106

Year	Start	Finish	Status	Laps
GOUX, Jules (5)				
1913	7	1	Running	200
1914	19	4	Running	200
1919	22	3	Running	200
1920	21	15	Engine	148
1922	22	25	Axle	25

Died March 6, 1965

Year	Start	Finish	Status	Laps
GRANT, Harry (4)				
1911	17	33	Bearings	51
1913	6	24	Gas tank	14
1914	26	7	Running	200
1915	10	12	Loose mud apron	184

(Relieved by Carl Limberg)
Died Oct. 8, 1915 from burns suffered Sept. 28 at Sheepshead Bay, N.Y.

Year	Start	Finish	Status	Laps
GRANT, Jerry (10)				
1965	17	27	Magneto	30
1966	10	10	Running	167
1967	30	20	Piston	162
1968	15	23	Oil leak	50
1970	29	7	Running	198

Year	Start	Finish	Status	Laps
1972	15	12*	Running	188*
1973	18	19	Engine	77
1974	17	10	Running	175
1975	14	20	Piston	137
1976	20	27	Running/rain	91

*Last 12 laps disallowed for refueling infraction

Died Aug. 12, 2012

GRECO, Marco (4)

Year	Start	Finish	Status	Laps
1994	32	27	Electrical	53
1996	22	26	Engine	64
1997	27	16	Gearbox	166
1998	14	14	Engine	183

GREEN, Cecil (2)

Year	Start	Finish	Status	Laps
1950	12	4	Running/rain	137
1951	10	22	Rod	80

Died July 29, 1951 in racing accident at Winchester, Ind.

GREGOIRE, Stephan (7)

Year	Start	Finish	Status	Laps
1993	15	19	Running	195
1996	13	27	Coil pack fire	59
1997	13	31	Accident	0
1998	31	17	Running	172
2000	20	8	Running	199
2001	29	28	Oil leak	86
2006	30	29	Handling	49

GREGORY, Masten (1)

Year	Start	Finish	Status	Laps
1965	31	23	Oil pressure	59

Died Nov. 8, 1985

GREINER, Art (1)

Year	Start	Finish	Status	Laps
1911	38	40	Accident	12

Died Dec. 15, 1916

GRIFFITH, Cliff (4)

Year	Start	Finish	Status	Laps
1951	18	28	Rear axle	30
1952	9	9	Running	200

Year	Start	Finish	Status	Laps
1956	30	10	Running	199
1961	30	24	Piston	55

Died Jan. 23, 1996

GRIM, Bobby (9)

Year	Start	Finish	Status	Laps
1959	5	26	Piston	85
1960	21	16	Running	194
1961	24	32	Piston	26
1962	15	19	Oil leak	97
1963	20	25	Oil leak	79
1964	20	10	Running	196
1966	31	31	Accident	0
1967	12	13	Accident	187
1968	25	10	Running	196

Died June 14, 1995

GROFF, Mike (5)

Year	Start	Finish	Status	Laps
1991	18	24	Water leak	68
1994	31	31	Accident	28
1996	11	20	Fire	122
1997	18	12	Running	188
1998	32	15	Running	183

GROFF, Robbie (1)

Year	Start	Finish	Status	Laps
1997	21	9	Running	197

GUERRERO, Carlos (1)

Year	Start	Finish	Status	Laps
1995	29	33	Accident	0

GUERRERO, Roberto (15)

Year	Start	Finish	Status	Laps
1984	7	2	Running	198
1985	16	3	Running	200
1986	8	4	Running	200
1987	5	2	Running	200
1988	12	32	Accident	0
1990	28	23	Suspension	118
1991	28	30	Accident	23
1992	1	33	Accident	0
1993	10	28	Accident	125

Year	Start	Finish	Status	Laps
1994	20	33	Accident	20
1995	13	12	Running	198
1996	6	5	Accident	198
1997	19	27	Steering	25
1998	9	22	Running	125
1999	25	25	Engine	105

GUGELMIN, Mauricio (2)

Year	Start	Finish	Status	Laps
1994	29	11	Running	196
1995	6	6	Running	200

GULOTTA, Tony (13)

Year	Start	Finish	Status	Laps
1926	12	11	Running/rain	142
1927	27	3	Running	200
(Relieved by Peter DePaolo)				
1928	4	10	Running	200
(Relieved by Dutch Baumann)				
1929	11	17	Supercharger	91
1930	20	20	Valve	79
1931	19	18	Accident	167
1932	20	13	Running	184
1933	12	7	Running	200
1934	7	17	Rod	94
1935	6	21	Magneto	102
1937	7	8	Running	200
(Relieved by Rex Mays, Jimmy Snyder)				
1938	4	17	Rod	130
1939	27	11	Running	200
(Relieved by Harry McQuinn)				

Died March 2, 1981

GURNEY, Dan (9)

Year	Start	Finish	Status	Laps
1962	8	20	Rear end	93
1963	12	7	Running	200
1964	6	17	Tire wear	110
1965	3	26	Timing gears	42
1966	19	27	Accident	0
1967	2	21	Piston	160
1968	10	2	Running	200

Year	Start	Finish	Status	Laps
1969	10	2	Running	200
1970	11	3	Running	200

GUTHRIE, Janet (3)

Year	Start	Finish	Status	Laps
1977	26	29	Timing gear	27
1978	15	9	Running	190
1979	14	34	Piston	3

GUTHRIE, Jim (3)

Year	Start	Finish	Status	Laps
1996	19	18	Engine	144
1997	6	26	Engine	43
1998	20	29	Accident	48

GUYOT, Albert (5)

Year	Start	Finish	Status	Laps
1913	2	4	Running	200
1914	11	3	Running	200
1919	3	4	Running	200
1921	14	6	Running	200

(Relieved by Joe Boyer, Eddie Miller)

Year	Start	Finish	Status	Laps
1926	19	28	Piston	9

Died March 24, 1947

HAIBE, Ora (5)

Year	Start	Finish	Status	Laps
1916	13	10	Running	120
1919	26	14	Running	200
1921	13	5	Running	200
1922	14	5	Running	200

(Relieved by Jules Ellingboe)

Year	Start	Finish	Status	Laps
1924	17	15	Running	182

(Relieved by Elmer Dempsey)
Died Dec. 10, 1970

HALL, Dean (1)

Year	Start	Finish	Status	Laps
1990	24	17	Suspension	165

HALL, Howard (1)

Year	Start	Finish	Status	Laps
1911	36	17	Running	Flagged

(Relieved by Rupert Jeffkins)

Year	Start	Finish	Status	Laps
HALL, Ira (5)				
1928	27	21	Accident	115
(Relieved by Jack Petticord)				
1932	5	7	Running	200
(Relieved by Ned Meier)				
1933	8	37	Piston	37
1938	27	30	Accident	44
1939	18	24	Head gasket	89
Died Feb. 6, 1987				
HALL, Norm (2)				
1961	32	10	Running	200
1964	31	33	Accident	1
Died March 11, 1992				
HALSMER, Pete (2)				
1981	24	24	Accident	123
1982	32	25	Transmission	38
HAMILTON, Davey (11)				
1996	10	12	Running	181
1997	8	6	Running	199
1998	8	4	Running	199
1999	11	11	Running	196
2000	28	20	Running	188
2001	26	23	Engine	182
2007	20	9	Running	166
2008	18	14	Running	200
2009	22	29	Accident	79
2010	14	33	Accident	0
2011	15	24	Running	193
HANKS, Sam (13)				
1940	14	13	Running	192
1941	33	33	Accident	DNS
(Qualified 27th, injured, did not start, credited with 33rd)				
1946	3	31	Oil line	18
1948	15	26	Clutch	34
1949	23	30	Oil leak	20

Year	Start	Finish	Status	Laps
1950	25	30	Oil pressure	42
1951	12	12	Rod	135
1952	5	3	Running	200
1953	9	3	Running	200
(Relieved by Duane Carter)				
1954	10	20	Spun (Rathmann)	191
(Relieved by Jimmy Davies, Jim Rathmann)				
1955	6	19	Transmission	134
1956	13	2	Running	200
1957	13	1	Running	200

Died June 27, 1994

HANSEN, Mel (6)

Year	Start	Finish	Status	Laps
1939	14	19	Accident	113
1940	5	8	Running	194
1941	21	29	Rod	11
1946	27	11	Crankshaft	143
1947	29	27	Pushed, disqualified	31
1948	33	25	Ruled off/too slow	42

Died June 5, 1963

HANSGEN, Walt (2)

Year	Start	Finish	Status	Laps
1964	10	13	Running	176
1965	21	14	Overheating	117

Died April 7, 1966 of testing injuries at Le Mans

HARDER, Fred (1)

Year	Start	Finish	Status	Laps
1924	22	17	Running	176

Died March 17, 1956

HARKEY, Bob (6)

Year	Start	Finish	Status	Laps
1964	27	8	Running	197
1971	32	22	Gears	77
1973	31	29	Seized engine	12
1974	31	8	Running	189
1975	23	10	Running/rain	162
(Relieved by Salt Walther)				
1976	28	20	Running/rain	97

Died Jan. 16, 2016

Year	Start	Finish	Status	Laps
HARRINGTON, Scott (1)				
1996	32	15	Accident	150
HARROUN, Ray (1)				
1911	28	1	Running	200
(Relieved by Cyrus Patschke, 35 laps)				
Died Jan. 19, 1968				
HARTLEY, Gene (10)				
1950	31	16	Running/rain	128
1952	18	28	Exhaust pipe	65
1953	13	28	Accident	53
1954	17	23	Engine	168
(Relieved by Marshall Teague)				
1956	22	11	Running	196
1957	14	10	Running	200
1959	9	11	Running	200
1960	24	14	Running	196
1961	15	11	Running	198
1962	20	27	Steering	24
(Relieved by Bill Cheesbourg)				
Died March 13, 1994				
HARTZ, Harry (6)				
1922	2	2	Running	200
1923	2	2	Running	200
1924	2	4	Running	200
1925	3	4	Running	200
1926	2	2	Running/rain	158
1927	4	25	Crankshaft	38
Died Sept. 26, 1974				
HATTORI, Shigeaki (2)				
2002	27	20	Running	196
2003	30	30	Fuel system	19
HAUPT, Willie (4)				
1913	15	9	Running	200

Year	Start	Finish	Status	Laps
(Relieved by Lee Oldfield)				
1914	28	12	Running	200
1915	24	11	Running	200
1920	13	16	Rod	146
(Relieved by Wade Morton)				
Died April 12, 1966				

HAUSTEIN, Gene (3)

Year	Start	Finish	Status	Laps
1931	34	23	Lost wheel	117
1933	28	15	Running	197
1934	31	30	Accident	13
Died June 6, 1984				

HAWKES, W. Douglas (2)

Year	Start	Finish	Status	Laps
1922	19	13	Running	200
1926	17	14	Camshaft	92
(Relieved by E.A.D. Eldridge)				
Died Aug. 2, 1974				

HAWKSWORTH, Jack (3)

Year	Start	Finish	Status	Laps
2014	13	20	Running	200
2015	28	24	Contact	175
2016	31	16	Running	200

HAYWOOD, Hurley (1)

Year	Start	Finish	Status	Laps
1980	25	18	Fire	126

HEARN, Richie (7)

Year	Start	Finish	Status	Laps
1996	15	3	Running	200
2000	23	27	Electrical	97
2002	22	6	Running	200
2003	28	28	Accident	61
2004	30	20	Running/rain	178
2005	20	25	Accident	112
2007	32	23	Running	163

HEARNE, Eddie (9)

Year	Start	Finish	Status	Laps
1911	16	21	Running	Flagged
(Relieved by Ed Parker)				

Year	Start	Finish	Status	Laps
1912	5	20	Burned bearing	54
(Relieved by Neil Whalen)				
1919	8	2	Running	200
1920	9	6	Running	200
1921	4	13	Oil line	111
1922	23	3	Running	200
1923	14	4	Running	200
(Relieved by Earl Cooper)				
1924	14	19	Fuel line	151
(Relieved by Cliff Durant)				
1927	18	7	Running	200
(Relieved by Harry Hartz, Leon Duray, Ira Vail)				
Died Feb. 9, 1955				

HEIMRATH, Ludwig Jr. (3)

Year	Start	Finish	Status	Laps
1987	10	30	Spun-lost wheel	25
1988	31	25	Accident	59
1989	18	13	Running	185

HELLINGS, Mack (4)

Year	Start	Finish	Status	Laps
1948	21	5	Running	200
1949	14	16	Valve	172
1950	26	13	Running/rain	132
1951	23	31	Piston	18
Died in plane crash Nov. 11, 1951 in California				

HENDERSON, George "Pete" (2)

Year	Start	Finish	Status	Laps
1916	9	6	Running	120
(Relieved by Eddie Rickenbacher)				
1920	17	10	Running	200
(Relieved by Tom Alley)				
Died June 19, 1940				

HEPBURN, Ralph (15)

Year	Start	Finish	Status	Laps
1925	6	16	Gas tank	143
1926	15	8	Running/rain	151
(Relieved by Bob McDonogh)				
1927	5	24	Fuel tank leak	39
1928	6	24	Timing gears	48

Year	Start	Finish	Status	Laps
1929	3	31	Transmission	14
1931	10	3	Running	200
(Relieved by Peter Kreis)				
1933	41	38	Rod bearing	33
1934	11	14	Connecting rod	164
(Relieved by Louis Meyer)				
1935	7	5	Running	200
(Relieved by Gene Haustein)				
1936	24	12	Running	195
1937	6	2	Running	200
(Relieved by Bob Swanson)				
1939	13	22	Accident(Swanson) 107	
(Relieved by Bob Swanson)				
1940	21	29	Steering	47
1941	10	4	Running	200
1946	19	14	Stalled	121

Died May 16, 1948 in Indianapolis 500 practice accident

HERB, Jon (2)

Year	Start	Finish	Status	Laps
2001	18	27	Accident	104
2007	27	32	Accident	51

HERMAN, Al (5)

Year	Start	Finish	Status	Laps
1955	16	7	Running	200
1956	27	28	Accident	74
1957	30	21	Accident	111
1959	23	13	Running	200
1960	30	32	Clutch	34

Died June 18, 1960 in racing accident at West Haven, Conn.

HERR, Don (1)

Year	Start	Finish	Status	Laps
1913	5	26	Clutch shaft	7

Died June 21, 1953

HERTA, Bryan (5)

Year	Start	Finish	Status	Laps
1994	22	9	Running	197
1995	33	13	Running	198
2004	23	4	Running/rain	180

Year	Start	Finish	Status	Laps
2005	18	3	Running	200
2006	16	20	Running	188

HEWITT, Jack (1)

Year	Start	Finish	Status	Laps
1998	22	12	Running	195

HICKEY, Denny (1)

Year	Start	Finish	Status	Laps
1919	27	9	Running	200

Died Aug. 10, 1965

HICKMAN, Jim (1)

Year	Start	Finish	Status	Laps
1982	24	7	Running	189

Died Aug. 1, 1982 after crash at Milwaukee Mile

HILDEBRAND, JR (6)

Year	Start	Finish	Status	Laps
2011	12	2	Running	200
2012	18	14	Running	200
2013	10	33	Contact	3
2014	9	10	Running	200
2015	10	8	Running	200
2016	15	6	Running	200

HILL, Bennett "Benny" (8)

Year	Start	Finish	Status	Laps
1920	8	17	Accident (Sarles)	115

(Relieved by Roscoe Sarles)

Year	Start	Finish	Status	Laps
1921	15	8	Running	200

(Relieved by Jerry Wonderlich)

Year	Start	Finish	Status	Laps
1923	18	19	Crankshaft	41
1924	5	5	Running	200
1925	13	18	Rear spring	69

(Relieved by Ray Cariens, Jules Ellingboe,
Jerry Wonderlich)

Year	Start	Finish	Status	Laps
1926	7	12	Running/rain	136

(Relieved by Jules Ellingboe)

Year	Start	Finish	Status	Laps
1927	9	28	Shackle bolt	26
1933	19	22	Rod	158

(Relieved by Frank Brisko)

Died Dec. 9, 1977

Year	Start	Finish	Status	Laps
HILL, George (1)				
1915	22	23	Water pump gear	20
Died March 26, 1967				
HILL, Graham (3)				
1966	15	1	Running	200
1967	31	32	Piston	23
1968	2	19	Accident	110
Died Nov. 29, 1975 in plane crash at London				
HILL, Jimmy (1)				
1927	32	12	Running	197
(Relieved by Don Ostrander)				
HILLENBURG, Andy (1)				
2000	33	28	Wheel bearing	91
HINCHCLIFFE, James (5)				
2011	13	29	Accident	99
2012	2	6	Running	200
2013	9	21	Running	199
2014	2	28	Contact	175
2016	1	7	Running	200
HINNERSHITZ, Tommy (3)				
1940	9	32	Accident	32
1941	20	10	Running	200
(Relieved by George Robson)				
1948	23	9	Running	198
Died Aug. 1, 1999				
HISS, Mike (4)				
1972	25	7	Running	196
1973	26	17	Drive train	91
1974	3	14	Running	158
1975	31	29	Accident	39
HITKE, Kurt (1)				
1919	24	23	Rod bearing	56

Year	Start	Finish	Status	Laps
HOBBS, David (4)				
1971	16	20	Accident	107
1973	22	11	Running/rain	107
1974	9	5	Running	196
1976	31	29	Water leak	10
HOLBERT, Al (1)				
1984	16	4	Running	198

Died Sept. 30, 1988 in plane crash at Columbus, Ohio

Year	Start	Finish	Status	Laps
HOLLAND, Bill (5)				
1947	8	2	Running	200
1948	2	2	Running	200
1949	4	1	Running	200
1950	10	2	Running/rain	137
1953	28	15	Cam gear	177

(Relieved by Jim Rathmann)
Died May 20, 1984

Year	Start	Finish	Status	Laps
HOLLANSWORTH, John Jr. (1)				
1999	12	13	Running	192
HOLMES, Howdy (6)				
1979	13	7	Running	195
1982	18	10	Running	186
1983	12	6	Running	198
1984	2	13	Running	185
1985	19	10	Running	194
1988	33	12	Running	192
HOLMES, Jackie (2)				
1949	17	22	Drive shaft	65
1950	30	23	Spun	123

Died March 1, 1995

Year	Start	Finish	Status	Laps
HOMEIER, Bill (2)				
1954	18	33	Accident	74
1960	31	13	Running	200

Year	Start	Finish	Status	Laps
Died May 2, 2001				

HORAN, Joe (1)

Year	Start	Finish	Status	Laps
1912	18	8	Running	200

(Relieved by George Ainslee)
Died Sept. 16, 1932

HORN, Ted (10)

Year	Start	Finish	Status	Laps
1935	26	16	Steering	145
1936	11	2	Running	200
1937	32	3	Running	200
1938	6	4	Running	200
1939	4	4	Running	200
1940	4	4	Running	199
1941	28	3	Running	200
1946	7	3	Running	200
1947	1	3	Running	200
1948	5	4	Running	200

Died Oct. 10, 1948 in racing accident at DuQuoin, Ill.

HORNISH, Sam Jr. (8)

Year	Start	Finish	Status	Laps
2000	14	24	Accident	153
2001	13	14	Running	196
2002	7	25	Running	186
2003	18	15	Engine	195
2004	11	26	Accident	104
2005	2	23	Accident	146
2006	1	1	Running	200
2007	5	4	Running	166

HOUSEHOLDER, Ronney (2)

Year	Start	Finish	Status	Laps
1937	10	12	Running	194

(Relieved by Al Putnam, Henry Banks, Ken Fowler)

Year	Start	Finish	Status	Laps
1938	10	14	Supercharger	154

(Relieved by Billy Winn)
Died Nov. 11, 1972

HOUSER, Norm (1)

Year	Start	Finish	Status	Laps
1949	24	10	Running	181

Year	Start	Finish	Status	Laps
Died Dec. 3, 1996				
HOUSER, Thane (1)				
1926	21	13	Running/rain	102
Died Nov. 23, 1967				
HOWARD, C. Glenn (1)				
1922	27	18	Engine	163
Died March 29, 1946				
HOWARD, Jay (1)				
2011	20	30	Accident	60
HOWARD, Ray (2)				
1919	21	16	Oil pressure	130
1920	10	13	Camshaft	150
(Relieved by Aldo Franchi)				
HOWIE, George (1)				
1931	30	11	Running	200
(Relieved by L.L. Corum, Herman Schurch)				
Died Nov. 11, 1979				
HOYT, Jerry (4)				
1950	15	21	Running/rain	125
1953	7	23	Overheating	107
(Relieved by Chuck Stevenson, Andy Linden)				
1954	30	26	Engine	130
1955	1	31	Oil leak	40
Died July 10, 1955 in racing accident at Oklahoma City				
HUCUL, Cliff (3)				
1977	27	22	Gearbox	72
1978	27	33	Oil line	4
1979	18	29	Rod	22
HUERTAS, Carlos (1)				
2014	21	17	Running	200

Year	Start	Finish	Status	Laps
HUFF, Joe, (3)				
1930	26	23	Valve	48
(Relieved by Ted Chamberlain, Speed Gardner)				
1931	40	16	Running	180
(Relieved by Speed Gardner)				
1932	15	10	Running	200
(Relieved by Dusty Fahrnow)				
Died Aug. 25, 1971				
HUGHES, Hughie (2)				
1911	32	12	Running	200
1912	17	3	Running	200
Died Dec. 2, 1916 in racing accident at Uniontown, Pa.				
HULME, Denis (4)				
1967	24	4	Running	197
1968	20	4	Running	200
1969	25	18	Clutch	145
1971	4	17	Valve	137
Died Oct. 3, 1992 of heart attack while competing in saloon race in Australia				
HULSE, Chuck (4)				
1962	16	21	Fuel pump	921
1963	11	8	Running	200
1966	8	20	Accident	22
1967	27	7	Accident	195
HUNT, Bill (1)				
1924	19	14	Running	190
Died Dec. 15, 1950				
HUNTER-REAY, Ryan (9)				
2008	20	6	Running	200
2009	32	32	Accident	19
2010	17	18	Accident	198
2011	33	23	Running	197
2012	3	27	Suspension	123
2013	7	3	Running	200
2014	19	1	Running	200

Year	Start	Finish	Status	Laps
2015	16	15	Running	200
2016	3	24	Running	198

HURTUBISE, Jim (10)

Year	Start	Finish	Status	Laps
1960	23	18	Rod	185
1961	3	22	Piston	102
1962	29	13	Running	200
1963	2	22	Oil leak	102
1964	11	14	Oil pressure	141
1965	20	33	Transmission	1
1966	22	17	Oil line	29
1968	30	30	Piston	9
1972	13	23*	Running	94*
1974	28	25	Engine	31

*All laps after lap 94 disallowed for rules infraction

Died Jan. 6, 1989

INSINGER, Harris (1)

Year	Start	Finish	Status	Laps
1935	31	14	Running	185

Died Sept. 8, 1935 in racing accident at Oakland, Calif.

JACKSON, Jimmy (5)

Year	Start	Finish	Status	Laps
1946	5	2	Running	200
1947	10	5	Running	200
1948	4	10	Spindle	193
1949	7	6	Running	200
1950	32	29	Supercharger	52

Died Nov. 25, 1984

JAGERSBERGER, Joe (1)

Year	Start	Finish	Status	Laps
1911	8	31	Accident	87

Died Oct. 5, 1952

JAKES, James (3)

Year	Start	Finish	Status	Laps
2012	17	15	Running	200
2013	20	20	Running	199
2015	19	18	Running	200

Year	Start	Finish	Status	Laps
JAMES, Joe (2)				
1951	30	33	Drive shaft	8
1952	16	13	Running	200

Died Nov. 5, 1952 of injuries suffered Nov. 2 at San Jose, Calif.

Year	Start	Finish	Status	Laps
JENKINS, Johnny (2)				
1912	11	7	Running	200
1913	17	25	Crankshaft	13

Died Nov. 25, 1945

Year	Start	Finish	Status	Laps
JOHANSSON, Stefan (3)				
1993	6	11	Running	199
1994	27	15	Running	192
1995	31	16	Running	192
JOHNCOCK, Gordon (24)				
1965	14	5	Running	200
1966	6	4	Running	200
1967	3	12	Spun	188
1968	9	27	Rear end	37
1969	5	19	Piston	137
1970	17	28	Piston	45
1971	12	29	Accident	11
1972	26	20	Exhaust valve	113
1973	11	1	Running/rain	133
1974	4	4	Running	198
1975	2	31	Ignition	11
1976	2	3	Running/rain	102
1977	5	11	Crankshaft	184
1978	6	3	Running	199
1979	5	6	Running	197
1980	17	4	Running	200
1981	4	9	Engine	194
1982	5	1	Running	200
1983	10	14	Gearbox	163
1984	5	25	Accident	103
1987	18	22	Valve	76
1989	23	31	Engine	19
1991	33	6	Running	188

Year	Start	Finish	Status	Laps
1992	31	29	Engine	60

JOHNS, Bobby (2)

Year	Start	Finish	Status	Laps
1965	22	7	Running	197
1969	32	10	Running	171

Died March 7, 2016

JOHNSON, Art (1)

Year	Start	Finish	Status	Laps
1916	17	8	Running	120

Died 1949

JOHNSON, Eddie (13)

Year	Start	Finish	Status	Laps
1952	24	16	Running	193
1955	32	13	Running	196
1956	32	15	Running	195
1957	20	25	Wheel bearing	93
1958	26	9	Running	200
1959	8	8	Running	200
1960	7	6	Running	200
1961	10	18	Accident	127
1962	18	25	Magneto	39
1963	21	20	Accident	112
1964	24	26	Fuel pump	6
1965	28	10	Running	195
1966	29	7	Stalled	175

Died June 30, 1974 in plane crash at Cleveland

JOHNSON, Herm (2)

Year	Start	Finish	Status	Laps
1982	14	9	Running	186
1984	9	8	Running	194

Died December 10, 2016

JOHNSON, Luther (3)

Year	Start	Finish	Status	Laps
1931	12	20	Accident	156
1932	11	16	Lost wheel	164
1933	20	10	Running	200

(Relieved by Ralph Hepburn, Sam Palmer)

Died April 12, 1978

Year	Start	Finish	Status	Laps
JONES, Ben (1)				
1926	18	18	Accident	54
Died Dec. 23, 1938				
JONES, Bubby (1)				
1977	33	21	Valve	78
JONES, Davy (5)				
1987	28	28	Engine	34
1989	31	7	Running	192
1993	28	15	Running	197
1995	32	23	Accident	161
1996	2	2	Running	200
JONES, Herbert (1)				
1925	17	19	Accident	68
(Relieved by A.E. Moss)				
Died May 27, 1926 in Indianapolis 500 qualifying accident				
JONES, John (1)				
1989	25	11	Running	189
JONES, M.C. (1)				
1925	21	21	Transmission	32
Died May 27, 1932				
JONES, PJ (2)				
2004	31	28	Accident	92
2006	32	19	Running	189
JONES, Parnelli (7)				
1961	5	12	Running	192
1962	1	7	Running	200
1963	1	1	Running	200
1964	4	23	Pit fire	55
1965	5	2	Running	200
1966	4	14	Wheel bearing	87
1967	6	6	Bearing	196

Year	Start	Finish	Status	Laps
JONES, Will (1)				
1911	9	28	Steering	122
Died Jan. 19, 1972				
JOURDAIN, Bernard (2)				
1989	20	9	Running	191
1991	21	18	Gearbox	141
JOURDAIN, Michel Jr. (2)				
1996	8	13	Running	177
2012	22	19	Running	199
JUNQUEIRA, Bruno (6)				
2001	20	5	Running	200
2002	1	31	Engine	87
2004	4	5	Running/rain	180
2005	12	30	Accident	76
2008	15	20	Running	184
2010	25	32	Accident	7
KANAAN, Tony (15)				
2002	5	28	Accident	89
2003	2	3	Running	200
2004	5	2	Running/rain	180
2005	1	8	Running	200
2006	5	5	Running	200
2007	2	12	Running	166
2008	6	29	Accident	105
2009	6	27	Accident	97
2010	33	11	Running	200
2011	22	4	Running	200
2012	8	3	Running	200
2013	12	1	Running	200
2014	16	26	Running	177
2015	4	26	Contact	151
2016	18	4	Runnning	200
KARAM, Sage (3)				
2014	31	9	Running	200

Year	Start	Finish	Status	Laps
2015	21	32	Contact	0
2016	23	32	Contact	93

KARL, Jerry (6)

1973	28	26	Running/rain	22
1974	19	19	Accident	115
1975	20	13	Running/rain	161
1978	28	14	Running	176
1980	28	21	Clutch	64
1981	31	15	Running	189

Died Feb. 16, 2008 from injuries sustained in an automobile accident in Baltimore.

KARNATZ, Albert (1)

1929	31	25	Gas leak	50

Died July 15, 1934 in racing accident at Detroit

KEECH, Ray (2)

1928	10	4	Running	200

(Relieved by Wilbur Shaw)

1929	6	1	Running	200

Died June 15, 1929 in racing accident at Altoona, Pa.

KEENE, Charlie (1)

1914	27	8	Running	200

(Relieved by C. L. Rogers)

KELLER, Al (6)

1955	22	27	Accident	54
1956	28	14	Running	195
1957	8	27	Accident	75
1958	21	11	Running	200
1959	28	18	Piston	163
1961	26	5	Running	200

Died Nov. 19, 1961 in racing accident at Phoenix

KENEALY, Mel (1)

1930	23	15	Valve	114

Died June 29, 1985

Year	Start	Finish	Status	Laps
KENYON, Mel (8)				
1966	17	5	Running	198
1967	14	16	Accident	177
1968	17	3	Running	200
1969	24	4	Running	200
1970	22	16	Acc.(McCluskey)	160
(Relieved by Roger McCluskey)				
1971	30	32	Accident	10
1972	12	18	Fuel injection	126
1973	19	4	Running/rain	131
KIMBALL, Charlie (6)				
2011	28	13	Running	199
2012	14	8	Running	200
2013	19	9	Running	200
2014	26	31	Contact	149
2015	14	3	Running	200
2016	16	5	Running	200
KINSER, Sheldon (6)				
1975	26	12	Running/rain	161
1976	29	19	Running/rain	97
1977	12	32	Piston	14
1978	12	32	Oil pressure	15
1979	10	28	Piston	40
1981	23	6	Running	195
Died Aug. 1, 1988				
KINSER, Steve (1)				
1997	20	14	Accident	185
KIRKPATRICK, Charles (1)				
1919	11	20	Rod	69
KITE, Jimmy (5)				
1998	26	11	Running	195
1999	28	24	Engine	111
2000	25	30	Engine	74
2003	32	13	Running	197

Year	Start	Finish	Status	Laps
2005	32	32	Handling	47

KLADIS, Danny (1)

1946	33	21	Towed in	46

Died April 26, 2009

KLAUSLER, Tom (1)

1981	30	29	Gearbox	60

KLEIN, Art (5)

1914	8	20	Valve	87
1915	8	18	Smoking	111

(Relieved by Billy Chandler)

1919	7	19	Oil line	70
1920	5	21	Accident	40
1922	25	21	Rod	105

Died June 6, 1955

KNAPP, Steve (3)

1998	23	3	Running	200
1999	13	26	Handling	106
2000	27	19	Running	193

KNEIFEL, Chris (2)

1983	25	12	Running	191
1984	33	15	Transmission	175

KNEPPER, Arnie (5)

1965	19	18	Cylinder	80
1966	26	29	Accident	0
1967	18	22	Engine	158
1968	32	25	Hit wheel	42
1969	21	22	Accident	82

Died June 6, 1992 at Belleville, Ill.

KNIGHT, Harry (2)

1911	7	30	Accident	90
1912	9	23	Engine	7

Died July 4, 1913 in racing accident at Columbus, Ohio

Year	Start	Finish	Status	Laps
KNIPPER, Billy (3)				
1911	40	18	Running	Flagged
1913	11	16	Clutch	125
(Relieved by Harry Grant)				
1914	12	13	Running	200
(Relieved by Bob Burman)				
Died September 1968				
KOHLERT, Henry (1)				
1928	28	13	Running	180
(Relieved by Shorty Cantlon, Doc Shattuc)				
Died Dec. 18, 1939				
KREIGER, Johnny (1)				
1932	33	35	Rod	30
Died June 11, 1953				
KREIS, Peter (6)				
1925	9	8	Running	200
(Relieved by Norman Batten)				
1927	12	17	Front axle	123
(Relieved by Bennett Hill, Harry Hartz)				
1928	19	22	Rod bearing	73
1929	17	16	Engine seized	91
1932	17	15	Accident	178
1933	11	32	Universal joint	63

Died May 25, 1934 in Indianapolis 500 practice accident, along with mechanic Bob Hahn

Year	Start	Finish	Status	Laps
KRISILOFF, Steve (11)				
1971	27	31	Oil leak-spun	10
1972	10	21	Ignition rotor	102
1973	7	6	Running/rain	129
1974	15	22	Clutch	72
1975	29	11	Running/rain	162
1976	23	24	Running/rain	95
1977	25	9	Running	191
1978	13	4	Running	198
1979	28	11	Running	192

Year	Start	Finish	Status	Laps
1981	17	8	Running	194
1983	31	29	U-joint	42

KRUEGER, Phil (2)

Year	Start	Finish	Status	Laps
1986	24	31	Engine	67
1988	15	8	Running	196

KUNZMAN, Lee (4)

Year	Start	Finish	Status	Laps
1972	30	17	Lost tire	131
1973	25	7	Running/rain	127
1977	24	7	Running	191
1979	11	30	Scavenger pump	18

LANIER, Randy (1)

Year	Start	Finish	Status	Laps
1986	13	10	Running	195

LARSON, Jud (2)

Year	Start	Finish	Status	Laps
1958	19	8	Running	200
1959	19	29	Accident	45

Died June 11, 1966 in racing accident at Reading, Pa.

LAUTENSCHLAGER, Christian (1)

Year	Start	Finish	Status	Laps
1923	17	23	Accident	14

Died Jan. 3, 1954

LAZIER, Bob (1)

Year	Start	Finish	Status	Laps
1981	13	19	Engine	154

LAZIER, Buddy (19)

Year	Start	Finish	Status	Laps
1991	23	33	Accident	1
1992	24	14	Engine	139
1995	23	27	Fuel system	45
1996	5	1	Running	200
1997	10	4	Running	200
1998	11	2	Running	200
1999	22	7	Running	198
2000	16	2	Running	200
2001	10	18	Running	192
2002	20	15	Accident	198

Year	Start	Finish	Status	Laps
2003	21	21	Engine	171
2004	28	23	Fuel system	164
2005	9	5	Running	200
2006	25	12	Running	199
2007	22	19	Running	164
2008	32	17	Running	195
2013	32	31	Mechanical	44
2014	33	32	Mechanical	87
2016	32	30	Mechanical	100

LAZIER, Jaques (6)

Year	Start	Finish	Status	Laps
2000	26	13	Running	198
2001	17	22	Running	183
2003	20	29	Accident	61
2004		Relief driver. Replaced Robby Gordon on Lap 27 due to red flag for rain/Gordon's NASCAR team commitment; dropped out of race on Lap 88.
2005	27	16	Running	189
2006	24	17	Running	193
2007	28	27	Accident	155

LeBEGUE, Rene (1)

Year	Start	Finish	Status	Laps
1940	31	10	Running	192

(Relieved by Rene Dreyfus)

Died Feb. 24, 1946

LECKLIDER, Fred (2)

Year	Start	Finish	Status	Laps
1926	26	24	Rod	24
1927	30	23	Accident (Kohlert)	49

(Relieved by Henry Kohlert)

Died Jan. 10, 1964

LeCOCQ, Louis (1)

Year	Start	Finish	Status	Laps
1919	25	18	Accident	96

Died May 30, 1919 in Indianapolis 500 racing accident, along with mechanic Robert Bandini

LEFFLER, Greg (1)

Year	Start	Finish	Status	Laps
1980	23	10	Running	197

Year	Start	Finish	Status	Laps
LEFFLER, Jason (1)				
2000	17	17	Running	197
Died June 12, 2013 in a racing accident at Bridgeport, New Jersey				
LEGGE, Kathrine (2)				
2012	30	22	Running	199
2013	33	26	Running	193
LEONARD, Joe (9)				
1965	27	29	Oil leak	27
1966	20	9	Stalled	170
1967	5	3	Running	197
1968	1	12	Fuel shaft	191
1969	11	6	Running	193
1970	18	24	Ignition	73
1971	8	19	Turbocharger	123
1972	6	3	Running	200
1973	29	18	Wheel bearing	91
LEVRETT, Bayliss (2)				
1949	29	24	Drain plug	52
1950	17	27	Oil pressure	108
(Relieved by Bill Cantrell)				
Died March 13, 2002				
LEWIS, Dave (4)				
1916	18	14	Gas tank	71
1925	5	2	Running	200
(Relieved by Bennett Hill)				
1926	4	15	Valve	91
(Relieved by Earl Cooper)				
1927	8	33	Front axle	21
Died May 13, 1928 at Los Angeles				
LEWIS, Randy (5)				
1987	23	32	Gearbox	8
1988	11	15	Running	175
1989	11	29	Wheel bearing	24

Year	Start	Finish	Status	Laps
1990	12	14	Running	186
1991	31	14	Running	159

LIESAW, Billy (2)

Year	Start	Finish	Status	Laps
1912	14	17	Fire	72

(Relieved by Warren Farr)

Year	Start	Finish	Status	Laps
1913	3	14	Loose rods	148

(Relieved by Warren Farr)
Died April 15, 1941

LINDAU, Bill (1)

Year	Start	Finish	Status	Laps
1929	33	19	Valve	70

Died Dec. 18, 1989

LINDEN, Andy (7)

Year	Start	Finish	Status	Laps
1951	31	4	Running	200
1952	2	33	Oil leak	20
1953	5	33	Accident	3
1954	23	25	Torsion bar	165

(Relieved by Bob Scott)

Year	Start	Finish	Status	Laps
1955	8	6	Running	200
1956	9	27	Oil leak	90
1957	12	5	Running	200

Died Feb. 11, 1987

LITZ, A.B. "Deacon" (12)

Year	Start	Finish	Status	Laps
1928	17	14	Running	161

(Relieved by Wesley Crawford)

Year	Start	Finish	Status	Laps
1929	9	24	Rod	56
1930	31	30	Accident	22
1931	4	17	Accid.(Cummings)	177

(Relieved by Bill Cummings)

Year	Start	Finish	Status	Laps
1932	19	18	Rod	152
1933	14	16	Running	197

(Relieved by Louis Schneider)

Year	Start	Finish	Status	Laps
1934	19	4	Running	200

(Relieved by Babe Stapp)

Year	Start	Finish	Status	Laps
1935	13	8	Running	200

(Relieved by Johnny Sawyer, Babe Stapp)

Year	Start	Finish	Status	Laps
1936	26	23	Crankshaft	108
(Relieved by Louis Tomei)				
1937	11	14	Out of oil	191
(Relieved by Harry McQuinn)				
1939	31	33	Valve	7
1941	29	22	Oil trouble	89

Died Jan. 4, 1967

LLOYD, Alex (4)

Year	Start	Finish	Status	Laps
2008	19	25	Accident	151
2009	11	13	Running	200
2010	26	4	Running	200
2011	30	19	Running	198

LOCKHART, Frank (2)

Year	Start	Finish	Status	Laps
1926	20	1	Running/rain	160
1927	1	18	Rod	120

Died April 25, 1928 in racing accident at Daytona Beach, Fla.

LOQUASTO, Al (2)

Year	Start	Finish	Status	Laps
1976	24	25	Running/rain	95
1977	15	28	Magneto	28

Died July 31, 1991 in a plane crash

LUYENDYK, Arie (17)

Year	Start	Finish	Status	Laps
1985	20	7	Running	198
1986	19	15	Accident	188
1987	7	18	Suspension	125
1988	6	10	Running	196
1989	15	21	Engine	123
1990	3	1	Running	200
1991	14	3	Running	199
1992	4	15	Accident	135
1993	1	2	Running	200
1994	8	18	Engine	179
1995	2	7	Running	200
1996	20	16	Damage	149
1997	1	1	Running	200
1998	28	20	Gearbox	151

Year	Start	Finish	Status	Laps
1999	1	22	Accident	117
2001	6	13	Running	198
2002	24	14	Running	199

LUYENDYK, Arie Jr. (1)

Year	Start	Finish	Status	Laps
2006	31	28	Handling	54

LYNCH, George (1)

Year	Start	Finish	Status	Laps
1949	8	32	Accident	1

Died May 5, 1997

LYTLE, Herb (1)

Year	Start	Finish	Status	Laps
1911	31	32	Accident	82

Died 1933

MacDONALD, Dave (1)

Year	Start	Finish	Status	Laps
1964	14	29	Accident	1

Died May 30, 1964 in Indianapolis 500 racing accident

MacKENZIE, George "Doc" (5)

Year	Start	Finish	Status	Laps
1932	39	28	Engine	65
1933	39	18	Rear axle	192
1934	26	29	Accident	15
1935	15	9	Running	200
1936	4	3	Running	200

(Relieved by Kelly Petillo)

Died Aug. 23, 1936 in racing accident at Milwaukee

MACK, George (1)

Year	Start	Finish	Status	Laps
2002	32	17	Running	198

MACKEY, Bill (W.C. Gretsinger Jr.) (1)

Year	Start	Finish	Status	Laps
1951	33	19	Clutch shaft	97

Died July 29, 1951 in racing accident at Winchester, Ind.

MacPHERSON, Jeff (1)

Year	Start	Finish	Status	Laps
1987	12	8	Running	182

Year	Start	Finish	Status	Laps
MAGILL, Mike (3)				
1957	18	24	Accident	101
1958	31	17	Running	136
1959	31	30	Accident	45

Died Aug. 31, 2006

Year	Start	Finish	Status	Laps
MAHLER, John (4)				
1972	29	22	Piston	99
1977	31	14	Running	157
(Relieved by Larry Cannon)				
1978	17	26	Timing gear	58
1979	32	25	Fuel pump	66

Year	Start	Finish	Status	Laps
MAIS, Johnny (1)				
1915	20	22	Left course	23

Died May 26, 1961

Year	Start	Finish	Status	Laps
MALLOY, Jim (4)				
1968	14	22	Rear end	64
1969	13	11	Running	165
1970	9	33	Accident DNS	0
1971	10	4	Running	200

Died May 18, 1972 after Indianapolis 500 practice accident May 14

Year	Start	Finish	Status	Laps
MALONE, Art (2)				
1963	23	31	Clutch	18
1964	30	11	Running	194

Died March 29, 2013

Year	Start	Finish	Status	Laps
MANN, Pippa (5)				
2011	31	20	Running	198
2013	30	30	Contact	46
2014	22	24	Running	193
2015	25	22	Running	197
2016	25	18	Running	199

Year	Start	Finish	Status	Laps
MANNING, Darren (4)				
2004	15	25	Accident	104
2005	19	29	Mechanical	82

Year	Start	Finish	Status	Laps
2007	15	20	Running	164
2008	14	9	Running	200

MANSELL, Nigel (2)

Year	Start	Finish	Status	Laps
1993	8	3	Running	200
1994	7	22	Accident	92

MANTZ, Johnny (2)

Year	Start	Finish	Status	Laps
1948	8	13	Running	185
1949	9	7	Running	200

Died Oct. 25, 1972 in highway accident

MARCHESE, Carl (1)

Year	Start	Finish	Status	Laps
1929	25	4	Running	200

Died June 26, 1984

MARQUETTE, Mel (2)

Year	Start	Finish	Status	Laps
1911	20	25	Running	Flagged
1912	19	19	Broken wheels	63

Died March 17, 1961

MARSHALL, Cy (2)

Year	Start	Finish	Status	Laps
1930	10	26	Accident	29
1947	28	8	Running	197

Died Dec. 20, 1974

MARSHMAN, Bobby (4)

Year	Start	Finish	Status	Laps
1961	33	7	Running	200
1962	3	5	Running	200
1963	7	16	Rear end	196
1964	2	25	Oil plug	39

Died Dec. 4, 1964 after accident in testing at Phoenix

MARTIN, John (5)

Year	Start	Finish	Status	Laps
1972	14	16	Fuel leak	161
1973	24	8	Running/rain	124
1974	22	11	Running	169
1975	16	27	Radiator	61
1976	15	21	Running/rain	96

Year	Start	Finish	Status	Laps
MASON, George (1)				
1914	13	23	Piston	66
Died Sept. 13, 1918 in France, World War I				
MATHOUSER, Bob (1)				
1964	28	22	Brakes	77
Died Nov. 15, 1980				
MATOS, Raphael (2)				
2009	12	22	Accident	173
2010	12	29	Accident	72
MATSON, Joe (1)				
1912	21	14	Crankshaft	107
Died Jan. 4, 1937				
MATSUDA, Hideshi (4)				
1994	14	24	Accident	90
1995	20	15	Running	194
1996	30	8	Running	197
1999	10	10	Running	196
MATSUSHITA, Hiro (4)				
1991	24	16	Running	149
1993	26	18	Running	197
1994	18	14	Running	193
1995	10	10	Running	199
MATSUURA, Kosuke (4)				
2004	9	11	Running/rain	180
2005	8	17	Accident	186
2006	7	15	Running	196
2007	17	16	Running	165
MAURO, Johnny (1)				
1948	27	8	Running	198
(Relieved by Lewis Durant)				
Died Jan. 23, 2003				

Year	Start	Finish	Status	Laps
MAYS, Rex (12)				
1934	23	23	Front axle	53
1935	1	17	Spring shackle	123
1936	1	15	Out of gas	192
1937	23	33	Overheating	24
1938	3	28	Supercharger	45
1939	19	16	Rings	145
1940	1	2	Running	200
1941	2	2	Running	200
1946	14	30	Manifold	26
1947	20	6	Running	200
1948	1	19	Fuel leak	129
1949	2	25	Engine	48

Died Nov. 6, 1949 in racing accident at Del Mar, Calif.

Year	Start	Finish	Status	Laps
McCARVER, Jack (1)				
1926	25	25	Rod	23

Died June 21, 1959

Year	Start	Finish	Status	Laps
McCLUSKEY, Roger (18)				
1961	29	27	Accident	51
1962	9	16	Spun	169
1963	14	15	Spun	198
1965	23	30	Clutch	18
1966	21	13	Oil leak	129
1967	22	19	Engine	165
1968	7	29	Oil filter	16
1969	6	14	Split header	157
1970	4	25	Suspension	62
1971	22	9	Running	188
1972	20	24	Valve	92
1973	14	3	Running/rain	131
1974	27	16	Rear end	141
1975	22	5	Running/rain	167
1976	13	30	Accident	8
1977	18	8	Running	191
1978	11	25	Clutch	82
1979	25	13	Running	191

Year	Start	Finish	Status	Laps
Died Aug. 29, 1993				
McCOY (Musser), Ernie (2)				
1953	20	8	Running	200
1954	20	16	Running	194
Died Feb. 11, 2001				
McCOY, J.J. (1)				
1919	33	30	Oil line	36
McCOY, Larry (2)				
1975	28	30	Piston	24
1976	26	26	Running/rain	91
Died Dec. 9, 1979 at Bristol, Pa.				
McDONALD, J.C. (1)				
1930	13	18	Fuel tank leak	112
(Relieved by Johnny Kreiger)				
McDONOGH, Bob (5)				
1924	18	10	Running	200
1925	20	14	Truss rod	188
(Relieved by Bennett Hill)				
1927	7	6	Running	200
(Relieved by Peter DePaolo)				
1929	19	18	Oil tank	74
(Relieved by Cliff Woodbury)				
1932	24	38	Oil line	17
Died Dec. 10, 1945				
McDOUGALL, Bon (1)				
1926	9	26	Valve	19
Died Dec. 11, 1970				
McDOWELL, Johnny (4)				
1949	28	18	Magneto	142
1950	33	18	Running/rain	128
1951	26	32	Gas tank	15
1952	33	21	Running	182

Year	Start	Finish	Status	Laps

Died June 8, 1952 in racing accident at Milwaukee

McELREATH, Jim (15)

Year	Start	Finish	Status	Laps
1962	7	6	Running	200
1963	6	6	Running	200
1964	26	21	Filter system	77
1965	13	20	Rear end gears	66
1966	7	3	Running	200
1967	11	5	Running	197
1968	13	14	Stalled	179
1969	7	28	Engine fire	24
1970	33	5	Running	200
1973	33	23	Engine	54
1974	30	6	Running	194
1977	20	23	Turbocharger	71
1978	26	20	Engine	132
1979	19	35	Valves	0
1980	11	24	Accident	54

McGEHEE, Robby (5)

Year	Start	Finish	Status	Laps
1999	27	5	Running	199
2000	12	21	Running	187
2001	14	11	Running	199
2003	31	25	Steering	125
2004	33	22	Running/rain	177

McGRATH, Jack (8)

Year	Start	Finish	Status	Laps
1948	13	21	Stalled	70
1949	3	26	Oil pump	39
1950	6	14	Spun in rain	131
1951	3	3	Running	200

(Relieved by Manny Ayulo)

Year	Start	Finish	Status	Laps
1952	3	11	Running	200
1953	3	5	Running	200
1954	1	3	Running	200
1955	3	26	Magneto	54

Died Nov. 6, 1955 in racing accident at Phoenix

Year	Start	Finish	Status	Laps
McGURK, Frank (1)				
1936	22	26	Crankshaft	51
Died Feb. 7, 1982				
McQUINN, Harry (10)				
1934	30	31	Rod	13
1935	18	33	Rod	4
1936	27	13	Out of gas	196
1937	22	29	Piston	47
1938	25	7	Running	197
(Relieved by Tony Willman)				
1939	32	20	Ignition	110
(Relieved by Al Putnam, Frank Brisko, George Robson)				
1940	15	11	Running	192
1941	4	7	Running	200
(Relieved by Kelly Petillo)				
1946	18	13	Out of oil	124
(Relieved by Jimmy Wilburn)				
1948	26	33	Supercharger	1
Died Jan. 1, 1986				
McRAE, Graham (1)				
1973	13	16	Header	91
McWITHEY, Jim (2)				
1959	33	16	Running	200
1960	32	29	Brakes	60
Died Feb. 1, 2009				
MEARS, Rick (15)				
1978	3	23	Engine	103
1979	1	1	Running	200
1980	6	5	Running	199
1981	22	30	Pit fire	58
1982	1	2	Running	200
1983	3	3	Running	200
1984	3	1	Running	200
1985	10	21	Linkage	122
1986	1	3	Running	200

Year	Start	Finish	Status	Laps
1987	3	23	Coil wire	75
1988	1	1	Running	200
1989	1	23	Engine	113
1990	2	5	Running	198
1991	1	1	Running	200
1992	9	26	Accident	74

MEARS, Roger (2)

Year	Start	Finish	Status	Laps
1982	19	32	Accident	0
1983	8	28	Accident	43

MEDEIROS, Thiago (1)

Year	Start	Finish	Status	Laps
2006	33	31	Electrical	24

MEIRA, Vitor (9)

Year	Start	Finish	Status	Laps
2003	26	12	Running	199
2004	7	6	Running/rain	180
2005	7	2	Running	200
2006	6	10	Running	200
2007	19	10	Running	166
2008	8	2	Running	200
2009	14	21	Accident	173
2010	30	27	Accident	105
2011	11	15	Running	199

MELCHER, Al (1)

Year	Start	Finish	Status	Laps
1927	20	15	Supercharger	144

(Relieved by Jack Petticord, Fred Lecklider)
Died Oct. 28, 1944

MERZ, Charlie (4)

Year	Start	Finish	Status	Laps
1911	18	7	Running	200
1912	22	4	Running	200

(Relieved by Billy Knipper)

Year	Start	Finish	Status	Laps
1913	16	3	Running	200

(Relieved by Earl Cooper)

Year	Start	Finish	Status	Laps
1916	8	19	Lubrication	25

Died July 8, 1952

Year	Start	Finish	Status	Laps
MEYER, Louis (12)				
1928	13	1	Running	200
1929	8	2	Running	200
1930	2	4	Running	200
1931	25	34	Oil leak	28
1932	7	33	Crankshaft	50
1933	6	1	Running	200
1934	13	18	Oil tank	92
1935	4	12	Running	200
1936	28	1	Running	200
1937	5	4	Running	200
1938	12	16	Oil pump	149
1939	2	12	Accident	197
Died Oct. 7, 1995				
MEYER, Zeke (4)				
1930	34	16	Rod	115
1932	38	6	Running	200
1933	16	9	Running	200
1936	32	9	Running	200
Died April 27, 1962				
MICHNER, Andy (1)				
1998	19	8	Running	197
MILLER (Krulac), Al (4)				
1963	31	9	Running	200
1965	7	4	Running	200
1966	30	30	Accident	0
1967	33	28	Oil cooler	74
Died July 28, 1978				
MILLER, Al (11)				
1932	18	27	Engine	66
1933	24	21	Rod	161
1934	8	6	Running	200
(Relieved by Zeke Meyer)				
1935	21	15	Magneto	178
1936	17	21	Accident	119

Year	Start	Finish	Status	Laps
1937	26	17	Carburetor	170
(Relieved by Emil Andres, Mauri Rose)				
1938	22	18	Clutch	125
1939	28	28	Accelerator	41
1940	30	30	Clutch	41
1941	14	28	Transmission	22
1947	19	25	Magneto	33

Died Aug. 18, 1967

MILLER, Chet (16)

Year	Start	Finish	Status	Laps
1930	15	13	Running	161
(Relieved by Paul Bost)				
1931	15	10	Running	200
(Relieved by Bryan Saulpaugh)				
1932	29	21	Engine	125
(Relieved by Al Miller)				
1933	32	20	Rod	163
(Relieved by Shorty Cantlon)				
1934	32	33	Accident	11
1935	17	10	Running	200
1936	3	5	Running	200
1937	13	30	Ignition	36
1938	5	3	Running	200
1939	5	21	Accident	109
1940	27	17	Running	189
(Relieved by Henry Banks)				
1941	9	6	Running	200
1946	17	18	Oil line	64
(Relieved by Louis Tomei)				
1948	19	20	Oil trouble	108
(Relieved by Ken Fowler, Louis Tomei)				
1951	28	25	Ignition	56
1952	27	30	Supercharger	41

Died May 15, 1953 in Indianapolis 500 practice accident

MILLER, Eddie (1)

Year	Start	Finish	Status	Laps
1921	9	4	Running	200

(Relieved by Jimmy Murphy)

Died 1965

Year	Start	Finish	Status	Laps
MILLER, Dr. Jack (3)				
1997	17	20	Accident	131
1998	15	21	Running	128
1999	31	31	Clutch	29
MILTON, Tommy (8)				
1919	31	25	Rod	50
1920	11	3	Running	200
1921	20	1	Running	200
1922	24	24	Gas tank	44
1923	1	1	Running	200
(Relieved by Howdy Wilcox for Laps 103-151)				
1924	3	21	Gas tank	110
1925	11	5	Running	200
1927	25	8	Running	200
(Relieved by Leon Duray, C. W. Van Ranst, Ralph Hepburn)				
Died July 11, 1962				
MINASSIAN, Nicolas (1)				
2001	22	29	Gearbox	74
MONTOYA, Juan Pablo (4)				
2000	2	1	Running	200
2014	10	5	Running	200
2015	15	1	Running	200
2016	17	33	Contact	63
MOORE, Lou (9)				
1928	8	2	Running	200
(Relieved by Louis Schneider)				
1929	13	13	Rod	198
(Relieved by Barney Kloepfer)				
1930	12	29	Accident	23
1931	38	26	Differential	103
1932	1	25	Timing gear	79
1933	4	3	Running	200
1934	20	3	Running	200
(Relieved by Wilbur Shaw)				

Year	Start	Finish	Status	Laps
1935	23	18	Rod	116
(Relieved by Tony Gulotta)				
1936	29	17	Out of gas	185
(Relieved by Cliff Bergere)				
Died March 25, 1956				

MORAES, Mario (3)

2008	28	18	Running	194
2009	7	33	Accident	0
2010	13	31	Accident	17

MORAN, Charles Jr. (1)

1930	19	27	Accident	22
Died June 7, 1978				

MORAN, Rocky (3)

1988	28	16	Engine	159
1989	28	14	Running	181
1990	33	25	Engine	88

MORENO, Roberto (3)

1986	32	19	Stalled	158
1999	23	20	Transmission	122
2007	31	33	Accident	36

MORICEAU, Jules (1)

1929	15	29	Accident	30
Died 1977				

MORTON, Wade (3)

1923	24	10	Running	200
(Relieved by Ora Haibe, Jerry Wonderlich and Phil Shafer, who qualified car)				
1925	16	15	Accident (Gleason)	156
(Relieved by Antoine Mourre, Jimmy Gleason)				
1927	26	14	Accident (Winnai)	152
(Relieved by Ralph Holmes, Freddie Winnai)				
Died February 22, 1935, automobile accident, near Auburndale, Fla.				

Year	Start	Finish	Status	Laps
MOSLEY, Mike (15)				
1968	27	8	Running	197
1969	22	13	Piston	162
1970	12	21	Radiator	96
1971	19	13	Accident	159
1972	16	26	Accident	56
1973	21	10	Rod bolt	120
1974	6	29	Engine	6
1975	5	26	Engine	94
1976	11	15	Running/rain	98
1977	9	19	Timing gear	91
1978	25	17	Turbocharger	146
1979	12	3	Running	200
1980	26	32	Gasket	5
1981	2	33	Radiator	16
1983	2	13	Accident	169
Died March 3, 1984 in highway accident				
MOSS, Alfred E. (1)				
1924	20	16	Running	177
Died April 23, 1972				
MOURRE, Antoine (1)				
1924	9	9	Running	200
MULFORD, Ralph (10)				
1911	29	2	Running	200
1912	16	10	Running	200
1913	22	7	Running	200
1914	6	11	Running	200
1915	18	16	Rod	124
(Relieved by Billy Chandler)				
1916	20	3	Running	120
1919	15	29	Driveshaft	37
1920	23	9	Running	200
1921	21	9	Running	177
1922	5	19	Rod	161
Died Oct. 23, 1973				

Year	Start	Finish	Status	Laps
MUNOZ, Carlos (4)				
2013	2	2	Running	200
2014	6	4	Running	200
2015	11	20	Running	200
2016	5	2	Runnning	200
MURPHEY, Brad (1)				
1996	26	23	Suspension	91
MURPHY, Jimmy (5)				
1920	15	4	Running	200
1921	19	14	Accident	107
(Relieved by Eddie Pullen, Eddie Miller)				
1922	1	1	Running	200
1923	9	3	Running	200
1924	1	3	Running	200
Died Sept. 15, 1924 in racing accident at Syracuse, N.Y.				
MUTHER, Rick (3)				
1970	15	8	Running	197
1971	18	21	Accident	85
1974	24	27	Piston	11
Died March 12, 1995				
MUTOH, Hideki (3)				
2008	9	7	Running	200
2009	16	10	Running	200
2010	9	28	Handling	76
NAKANO, Shinji (1)				
2003	15	14	Running	196
NALON, Dennis "Duke" (10)				
1938	33	11	Running	178
1940	25	22	Rod	120
1941	30	15	Running	173
1946	32	22	Universal joint	45
1947	18	16	Piston	119
1948	11	3	Running	200

Year	Start	Finish	Status	Laps
1949	1	29	Accident	23
1951	1	10	Stalled	151
1952	4	25	Supercharger	84
1953	26	11	Spun	191

Died Feb. 26, 2001

NAZARUK, Mike (3)

Year	Start	Finish	Status	Laps
1951	7	2	Running	200
1953	23	21	Stalled	146
1954	14	5	Running	200

Died May 1, 1955 in racing accident at Langhorne, Pa.

NEMESH, Steve (1)

Year	Start	Finish	Status	Laps
1926	22	21	Transmission	41

Died Sep. 18, 1975

NEWGARDEN, Josef (5)

Year	Start	Finish	Status	Laps
2012	7	25	Mechanical	161
2013	25	28	Running	191
2014	8	30	Contact	156
2015	9	9	Running	200
2016	2	3	Runnning	200

NIDAY, Cal (3)

Year	Start	Finish	Status	Laps
1953	30	30	Magneto	30
1954	13	10	Running	200
1955	9	16	Accident	170

Died Feb. 14, 1988 in vintage car racing accident in California

NIKRENT, Joe (1)

Year	Start	Finish	Status	Laps
1913	24	18	Bearing	67

(Relieved by Eddie Hearne)

Died July 25, 1958

O'CONNELL, Johnny (1)

Year	Start	Finish	Status	Laps
1996	29	29	Fuel pickup	47

O'CONNOR, Pat (5)

Year	Start	Finish	Status	Laps
1954	12	21	Spun	181

Year	Start	Finish	Status	Laps
1955	19	8	Running	200
1956	3	18	Running	187
1957	1	8	Running	200
1958	5	29	Accident	0

Died May 30, 1958 in Indianapolis 500 racing accident

O'DONNELL, Eddie (3)

Year	Start	Finish	Status	Laps
1915	11	5	Running	200
1919	5	22	Piston	60
1920	12	14	Oil line	149

Died Nov. 26, 1920 in racing accident at Beverly Hills, Calif.

OLDFIELD, Barney (2)

Year	Start	Finish	Status	Laps
1914	30	5	Running	200
(Relieved by Gil Anderson)				
1916	5	5	Running	120

Died Oct. 4, 1946

OLIVERO, Bobby (1)

Year	Start	Finish	Status	Laps
1977	14	25	Piston	57

ONGAIS, Danny (11)

Year	Start	Finish	Status	Laps
1977	7	20	Header	90
1978	2	18	Engine	145
1979	27	4	Running	199
1980	16	7	Running	199
1981	21	27	Accident	64
1982	9	22	Accident	62
1983	21	21	Handling	101
1984	11	9	Running	193
1985	17	17	Engine	141
1986	16	23	Ignition	136
1996	33	7	Running	197

OPPERMAN, Jan (2)

Year	Start	Finish	Status	Laps
1974	32	21	Spun	85
1976	33	16	Running/rain	97

Died Sept. 4, 1997

Year	Start	Finish	Status	Laps
ORMSBY, Len (1)				
1912	20	24	Rod	5
Died March 13, 1983				
ORR, Tom (1)				
1915	17	13	Axle bearing	168
(Relieved by Billy Carlson)				
Died Dec. 11, 1954				
PAGENAUD, Simon (5)				
2012	23	16	Running	200
2013	21	8	Running	200
2014	5	12	Running	200
2015	3	10	Running	200
2016	8	19	Running	199
PALMROTH, Tero (4)				
1988	25	19	Engine	144
1989	16	16	Spindle	165
1990	16	12	Running	188
1991	26	23	Engine	77
PAPIS, Max (2)				
2002	18	23	Running	196
2006	18	14	Running	197
PARDEE, Phil (1)				
1931	11	30	Accident (Shaw)	60
Relieved by Wilbur Shaw				
Died Dec. 27, 1967				
PARSONS, Johnnie (10)				
1949	12	2	Running	200
1950	5	1	Running/rain	138
1951	8	21	Magneto	87
1952	31	10	Running	200
1953	8	26	Crankshaft	86
1954	15	32	Stalled in pits	79
1955	27	21	Magneto	119

Year	Start	Finish	Status	Laps
1956	6	4	Running	200
1957	17	16	Running	195
1958	6	12	Running	200

Died Sept. 8, 1984

PARSONS, Johnny (12)

Year	Start	Finish	Status	Laps
1974	29	26	Turbocharger	18
1975	12	19	Transmission	140
1976	14	12	Running/rain	98
1977	11	5	Running	193
1978	8	10	Running	187
1979	9	32	Piston	16
1980	7	26	Piston	44
1982	25	20	Spin	92
1983	23	22	Accident	80
1985	26	5	Running	197
1986	28	27	CV joint	100
1996	27	28	Radiator	48

PATRICK, Danica (7)

Year	Start	Finish	Status	Laps
2005	4	4	Running	200
2006	10	8	Running	200
2007	8	8	Running	166
2008	5	22	Accident	171
2009	10	3	Running	200
2010	23	6	Running	200
2011	25	10	Running	200

PAUL, John Jr. (7)

Year	Start	Finish	Status	Laps
1985	24	15	Accident	164
1990	32	16	Radiator	176
1991	25	25	Oil leak	53
1992	18	10	Running	194
1994	30	25	Accident	89
1996	17	31	Ignition	10
1998	16	7	Running	197

PETILLO, Kelly (9)

Year	Start	Finish	Status	Laps
1932	40	12	Running	189

Year	Start	Finish	Status	Laps
1933	25	19	Spun, stalled	168
(Relieved by Sam Hoffman)				
1934	1	11	Running	200
1935	22	1	Running	200
1937	20	20	Out of oil	109
1938	21	22	Camshaft	100
1939	24	18	Pistons	141
1940	13	21	Bearing	128
1941	19	27	Rod	48

Died June 30, 1970

PETTICORD, Jack (1)

Year	Start	Finish	Status	Laps
1927	11	32	Supercharger	22

Died Jan. 2, 1940

PHILIPPE, Nelson (1)

Year	Start	Finish	Status	Laps
2009	31	25	Accident	130

PHILLIPS, Overton (1)

Year	Start	Finish	Status	Laps
1941	26	13	Running	187
(Relieved by Mel Hansen)				

Died April 1, 1999

PIGOT, Spencer (1)

Year	Start	Finish	Status	Laps
2016	29	25	Running	200

PILETTE, Theodore (1)

Year	Start	Finish	Status	Laps
1913	13	5	Running	200

Died May 13, 1921 in testing accident in Belgium

PIMM, Ed (3)

Year	Start	Finish	Status	Laps
1985	22	9	Running	195
1986	10	17	Electrical	168
1987	30	21	Lost boost	109

PIQUET, Nelson (1)

Year	Start	Finish	Status	Laps
1993	13	32	Engine	38

Year	Start	Finish	Status	Laps
PIXLEY, Ray (1)				
1936	25	6	Running	200

Died Aug. 30, 1936 in racing accident at Roby, Ind.

Year	Start	Finish	Status	Laps
PLOWMAN, Martin (1)				
2014	29	23	Running	196

Year	Start	Finish	Status	Laps
POLLARD, Art (5)				
1967	13	8	Running	195
1968	11	13	Fuel shaft	188
1969	12	31	Drive line	7
1970	6	30	Piston	28
1971	31	26	Valve	45

Died May 12, 1973 in Indianapolis practice accident

Year	Start	Finish	Status	Laps
PORPORATO, Jean (2)				
1915	6	14	Piston	164
1920	22	22	Ruled off	23

Year	Start	Finish	Status	Laps
POSEY, Sam (1)				
1972	7	5	Running	198

Year	Start	Finish	Status	Laps
POWER, Will (9)				
2008	23	13	Running	200
2009	9	5	Running	200
2010	2	8	Running	200
2011	5	14	Running	199
2012	5	28	Contact	78
2013	6	19	Running	200
2014	3	8	Running	200
2015	2	2	Running	200
2016	6	10	Running	200

Year	Start	Finish	Status	Laps
PRAPPAS, Ted (1)				
1992	32	16	Gearbox	135

Year	Start	Finish	Status	Laps
PRENTISS, Willard (1)				
1933	40	13	Running	200

(Relieved by Harold Shaw)

Year	Start	Finish	Status	Laps
Died Oct. 6, 1959				

PRUETT, Scott (4)

Year	Start	Finish	Status	Laps
1989	17	10	Running	190
1991	27	12	Transmission	166
1992	17	30	Engine	52
1995	8	19	Accident	184

PUTERBAUGH, Bill (3)

Year	Start	Finish	Status	Laps
1975	15	7	Running/rain	165
1976	18	22	Running/rain	96
1977	28	12	Valve	170

PUTNAM, Al (4)

Year	Start	Finish	Status	Laps
1938	23	32	Crankshaft	15
1940	28	19	Running	179
1941	31	12	Running	200
(Relieved by Lewis Durant)				
1946	13	15	Magneto	120
(Relieved by George Connor)				
Died Sept. 15, 1946 in racing accident at Indiana State Fairgrounds				

QUINN, Francis (1)

Year	Start	Finish	Status	Laps
1931	21	40	Rear axle	3
Died Dec. 13, 1931 in an automobile accident.				

RAGER, Roger (1)

Year	Start	Finish	Status	Laps
1980	10	23	Accident	55

RAHAL, Bobby (13)

Year	Start	Finish	Status	Laps
1982	17	11	Engine	174
1983	6	20	Radiator	110
1984	18	7	Running	197
1985	3	27	Waste gate	84
1986	4	1	Running	200
1987	2	26	Ignition	57
1988	19	5	Running	199
1989	7	26	Valve	58
1990	4	2	Running	200

Year	Start	Finish	Status	Laps
1991	4	19	Engine	130
1992	10	6	Running	199
1994	28	3	Running	199
1995	21	3	Running	200

RAHAL, Graham (9)

Year	Start	Finish	Status	Laps
2008	13	33	Accident	36
2009	4	31	Accident	55
2010	7	12	Running	200
2011	29	3	Running	200
2012	12	13	Running	200
2013	26	25	Contact	193
2014	20	33	Electrical	44
2015	17	5	Running	200
2016	26	14	Running	200

RASMUSSEN, Eldon (3)

Year	Start	Finish	Status	Laps
1975	32	24	Valve	119
1977	32	13	Running	168
1979	33	23	Header pipe	89

RATHMANN, Dick (9)

Year	Start	Finish	Status	Laps
1950	18	32	Stalled	25
1956	4	5	Running	200
1958	1	27	Accident	0
1959	4	20	Fire in pit	150
1960	4	31	Brake line	42
1961	6	13	Fuel pump	164
1962	13	24	Magneto	52
1963	17	10	Running	200
1964	12	7	Running	197

Died Feb. 1, 2000

RATHMANN, Jim (14)

Year	Start	Finish	Status	Laps
1949	21	11	Running	175
1950	28	24	Running/rain	122
1952	10	2	Running	200
1953	25	7	Running	200

(Relieved by Eddie Johnson)

Year	Start	Finish	Status	Laps
1954	28	28	Accid. (Flaherty)	110
(Relieved by Pat Flaherty)				
1955	20	14	Running	191
1956	2	20	Rings	175
1957	32	2	Running	200
1958	20	5	Running	200
1959	3	2	Running	200
1960	2	1	Running	200
1961	11	30	Magneto	48
1962	23	9	Running	200
1963	29	24	Magneto	99

Died Nov. 23, 2011

RAY, Greg (8)

Year	Start	Finish	Status	Laps
1997	30	25	Water pump	48
1998	2	18	Gearbox	167
1999	2	21	Accident	120
2000	1	33	Accident	67
2001	2	17	Running	192
2002	31	33	Accident	28
2003	14	8	Running	200
2004	27	27	Accident	98

REBAQUE, Hector (1)

Year	Start	Finish	Status	Laps
1982	15	13	Fire	150

REDON, Laurent (1)

Year	Start	Finish	Status	Laps
2002	16	22	Accident	196

REECE, Jimmy (6)

Year	Start	Finish	Status	Laps
1952	23	7	Running	200
1954	7	17	Running	194
1955	15	33	Rod	10
1956	21	9	Running	200
1957	6	18	Throttle	182
1958	3	6	Running	200

Died Sept. 28, 1958 in racing accident at Trenton, N.J.

Year	Start	Finish	Status	Laps
REGAZZONI, Clay (1)				
1977	29	30	Fuel cell	25

Died Dec. 15, 2006 in auto accident at Parma, Italy

Year	Start	Finish	Status	Laps
RENNA, Tony (1)				
2003	8	7	Running	200

Died Oct. 22, 2003 in testing accident at IMS

Year	Start	Finish	Status	Laps
RESTA, Dario (3)				
1915	3	2	Running	200
1916	4	1	Running	120
1923	3	14	Differential	87

(Relieved by Ernie Ansterburg, Joe Boyer)
Died Sept. 3, 1924 in racing accident at Brooklands, England

Year	Start	Finish	Status	Laps
REVSON, Peter (5)				
1969	33	5	Running	197
1970	16	22	Magneto	87
1971	1	2	Running	200
1972	2	31	Gearbox	23
1973	10	31	Accident	3

Died March 22, 1974 in testing accident at Johannesburg, South Africa

Year	Start	Finish	Status	Laps
RIBBS, Willy T. (2)				
1991	29	32	Engine failure	5
1993	30	21	Running	194

Year	Start	Finish	Status	Laps
RIBIERO, Andre (1)				
1995	12	18	Running	187

Year	Start	Finish	Status	Laps
RICE, Buddy (6)				
2003	19	11	Running	199
2004	1	1	Running/rain	180
2006	14	25	Accident	108
2007	16	25	Accident	162
2008	17	8	Running	200
2011	7	18	Running	198

Year	Start	Finish	Status	Laps
RICE, Larry (2)				
1978	30	11	Engine	186
1979	23	19	Accident	142
Died May 20, 2009				
RICHMOND, Tim (2)				
1980	19	9	Running	197
1981	33	14	Running	191
(Car qualified by George Snider)				
Died Aug. 13, 1989				
RICKENBACKER (Rickenbacher), Eddie (4)				
1912	13	21	Intake valve	43
1914	23	10	Running	200
1915	19	19	Rod	103
1916	2	20	Steering	9
Died July 23, 1973				
RIGANTI, Raul (3)				
1923	23	22	Gas line	19
1933	27	14	Running	200
(Relieved by Juan Gaudino)				
1940	24	33	Accident	24
Died Oct. 1, 1970				
RIGSBY, Jim (1)				
1952	26	12	Running	200
Died Aug. 31, 1952 in racing accident at Dayton, Ohio				
RINDT, Jochen (2)				
1967	32	24	Valve	108
1968	16	32	Piston	5
Died Sept. 5, 1970 in racing accident at Monza, Italy				
ROBERTS, Floyd (5)				
1935	3	4	Running	200
1936	15	19	Out of gas	183
1937	17	13	Running	194
1938	1	1	Running	200

Year	Start	Finish	Status	Laps
1939	23	23	Accident	106

Died May 30, 1939 in Indianapolis 500 racing accident

ROBSON, George (3)

Year	Start	Finish	Status	Laps
1940	23	23	Shock absorber	67
1941	16	25	Oil leak	66
1946	15	1	Running	200

Died Sept. 2, 1946 in racing accident at Atlanta

ROBSON, Hal (3)

Year	Start	Finish	Status	Laps
1946	23	25	Rod	37
1947	16	20	Universal joint	67
1948	18	15	Valve	164

Died July 2, 1996

RODEE, Chuck (Charles J. Rodeghier) (2)

Year	Start	Finish	Status	Laps
1962	21	32	Accident	18
1965	30	28	Rear end gears	28

Died May 14, 1966 in Indianapolis 500 qualifying accident

ROE, Billy (2)

Year	Start	Finish	Status	Laps
1997	24	22	Accident	110
1998	33	30	Accident	48

ROMANCINI, Mario (1)

Year	Start	Finish	Status	Laps
2010	27	13	Running	200

ROMCEVICH, Pete (1)

Year	Start	Finish	Status	Laps
1947	17	12	Oil line	167

Died June 16, 1952 in racing accident at Detroit

ROONEY, Tom (1)

Year	Start	Finish	Status	Laps
1916	7	17	Accident	48

Died 1939

ROSE, Jesse "Ebb" (3)

Year	Start	Finish	Status	Laps
1961	19	23	Rod	93
1962	32	14	Running	200
1963	32	14	Running	200

Year	Start	Finish	Status	Laps
Died Aug. 27, 2007				
ROSE, Mauri (15)				
1933	42	35	Timing gears	48
1934	4	2	Running	200
1935	10	20	Studs	103
1936	30	4	Running	200
1937	8	18	Oil line	123
1938	9	13	Supercharger	165
1939	8	8	Running	200
1940	3	3	Running	200
1941	1	26	Spark plugs	60
	17	1	Running	200
(In relief of Floyd Davis, last 128 laps)				
1946	9	23	Accident	40
1947	3	1	Running	200
1948	3	1	Running	200
1949	10	13	Magneto strap	192
1950	3	3	Running/rain	137
1951	5	14	Accident	126
Died Jan. 1, 1981				
ROSS, Sam (2)				
1928	16	20	Timing gears	132
1931	37	15	Running	200
Died Sept. 12, 1980				
ROSSI, Alexander (1)				
2016	11	1	Running	200
ROTH, Marty (4)				
2004	32	24	Accident	128
2005	29	31	Handling	47
2007	30	28	Accident	148
2008	33	32	Accident	59
RUBY, Lloyd (18)				
1960	12	7	Running	200
1961	25	8	Running	200

Year	Start	Finish	Status	Laps
1962	24	8	Running	200
1963	19	19	Accident	126
1964	7	3	Running	200
1965	9	11	Engine	184
1966	5	11	Cam stud	166
1967	7	33	Valves	3
1968	5	5	Running	200
1969	20	20	Fuel hose conn.	105
1970	25	27	Drive gear	54
1971	7	11	Gears	174
1972	11	6	Running	196
1973	15	27	Piston	21
1974	18	9	Out of fuel	187
1975	6	32	Piston	7
1976	30	11	Running/rain	100
1977	19	27	Accident	34

Died March 23, 2009

RUPP, Mickey (1)

Year	Start	Finish	Status	Laps
1965	15	6	Running	198

RUSSO, Eddie (3)

Year	Start	Finish	Status	Laps
1955	13	22	Ignition	112
1957	26	32	Accident/DNS	0
1960	29	26	Accident	84

Died Oct. 14, 2012

RUSSO, Joe (4)

Year	Start	Finish	Status	Laps
1931	16	24	Oil leak	109
1932	21	24	Rod	107
1933	31	17	Running	192
1934	24	5	Running	200

Died June 9, 1934 in racing accident at Langhorne, Pa.

RUSSO, Paul (14)

Year	Start	Finish	Status	Laps
1940	29	28	Oil leak	8
1941	18	9	Running	200

(Relieved by Lewis Durant)

Year	Start	Finish	Status	Laps
1946	2	33	Accident	16

Year	Start	Finish	Status	Laps
1947	21	28	Accident	25
1948	25	32	Oil leak	7
1949	19	8	Running	200
1950	19	9	Running/rain	135
1953	17	25	Magneto	89
1954	32	8	Running	200
(Relieved by Jerry Hoyt)				
1956	8	33	Accident	21
1957	10	4	Running	200
1958	14	18	Radiator	122
1959	27	9	Running	200
1962	14	28	Piston	20
Died Feb. 13, 1976				

RUTHERFORD, Johnny (24)

Year	Start	Finish	Status	Laps
1963	26	29	Transmission	43
1964	15	27	Accident	2
1965	11	31	Rear end gears	15
1967	19	25	Accident	103
1968	21	18	Accident	125
1969	17	29	Oil tank	24
1970	2	18	Header	135
1971	24	18	Running	128
1972	8	27	Rod	55
1973	1	9	Running/rain	124
1974	25	1	Running	200
1975	7	2	Running/rain	174
1976	1	1	Running/rain	102
1977	17	33	Gearbox	12
1978	4	13	Running	180
1979	8	18	Running	168
1980	1	1	Running	200
1981	5	32	Fuel pump	25
1982	12	8	Engine	187
1984	30	22	Engine	116
1985	30	6	Running	198
1986	12	8	Running	198
1987	8	11	Running	171
1988	30	22	Accident	107

Year	Start	Finish	Status	Laps
RUTTMAN, Troy (12)				
1949	18	12	Running	151
1950	24	15	Running/rain	130
1951	6	23	Bearing	78
1952	7	1	Running	200
1954	11	4	Running	200
(Relieved by Duane Carter)				
1956	11	31	Spun	22
1957	3	31	Overheating	13
1960	6	20	Rear end gear	134
1961	22	20	Clutch	105
1962	30	18	Piston	141
1963	33	12	Running	200
1964	18	18	Spun	99
Died May 19, 1997				
SAAVEDRA, Sebastian (5)				
2010	32	23	Accident	159
2012	24	26	Electrical	143
2013	27	32	Contact	34
2014	32	15	Running	200
2015	27	23	Contact	175
SACHS, Eddie (8)				
1957	2	23	Piston	105
1958	18	22	Universal joint	68
1959	2	17	Gear tower bolt	182
1960	1	21	Magneto	132
1961	1	2	Running	200
1962	27	3	Running	200
1963	10	17	Accident	181
1964	17	30	Accident	1
Died May 30, 1964 in Indianapolis 500 racing accident				
SAILER, Max (1)				
1923	20	8	Running	200
(Relieved by Karl Sailer)				
Died Feb. 5, 1964				

Year	Start	Finish	Status	Laps

ST. JAMES, Lyn (7)

Year	Start	Finish	Status	Laps
1992	27	11	Running	193
1993	21	25	Gearbox	176
1994	6	19	Running	170
1995	28	32	Accident	0
1996	18	14	Accident	153
1997	34	13	Accident	186
2000	32	32	Accident	69

SALAY (Szalai), Mike (1)

Year	Start	Finish	Status	Laps
1948	31	30	Stalled	13

Died Nov. 14, 1973

SALAZAR, Eliseo (6)

Year	Start	Finish	Status	Laps
1995	24	4	Running	200
1996	3	6	Accident	197
1997	9	24	Accident	70
1999	18	33	Accident	7
2000	3	3	Running	200
2001	28	7	Running	199

SALDANA, Joe (2)

Year	Start	Finish	Status	Laps
1978	24	15	Running	173
1979	26	16	Running	186

SALL, Bob (1)

Year	Start	Finish	Status	Laps
1935	33	29	Steering	47

Died Oct. 14, 1974

SARLES, Roscoe (4)

Year	Start	Finish	Status	Laps
1919	19	33	Rocker arm	8
1920	7	20	Accident	58
1921	2	2	Running	200
1922	6	23	Rod	88

Died Sept. 17, 1922 in racing accident at Kansas City, Mo.

SATO, Takuma (7)

Year	Start	Finish	Status	Laps
2010	31	20	Running	198

Year	Start	Finish	Status	Laps
2011	10	33	Accident	20
2012	19	17	Contact	199
2013	18	13	Running	200
2014	23	19	Running	200
2015	24	13	Running	200
2016	12	26	Contact	163

SAULPAUGH, Bryan (1)

Year	Start	Finish	Status	Laps
1932	3	32	Oil line	55

Died April 22, 1933 in racing accident at Oakland, Calif.

SAVAGE, David "Swede" (2)

Year	Start	Finish	Status	Laps
1972	9	32	Rod	5
1973	4	22	Accident	57

Died July 2, 1973 of injuries suffered in Indianapolis 500 racing accident on May 30, 1973

SAWYER, Johnny (2)

Year	Start	Finish	Status	Laps
1933	34	31	Clutch	77
1934	31	25	Rod	27

Died June 17, 1989

SAYLOR, Everett (1)

Year	Start	Finish	Status	Laps
1941	12	17	Accident	155

Died May 31, 1942 in racing accident at Cape Girardeau, Mo.

SCARBOROUGH, Carl (2)

Year	Start	Finish	Status	Laps
1951	15	18	Axle	100
1953	19	12	Running	190

(Relieved by Bob Scott)

Died May 30, 1953 of heat prostration during Indianapolis 500

SCHECKTER, Tomas (10)

Year	Start	Finish	Status	Laps
2002	10	26	Accident	172
2003	12	4	Running	200
2004	10	18	Running/rain	179
2005	11	20	Accident	154
2006	11	27	Accident	65
2007	10	7	Running	166

Year	Start	Finish	Status	Laps
2008	11	24	Mechanical	156
2009	26	12	Running	200
2010	20	15	Running	199
2011	21	8	Running	200

SCHINDLER, Bill (3)

Year	Start	Finish	Status	Laps
1950	22	26	Universal joint	111
1951	16	13	Rod	129
1952	15	14	Running	200

Died Sept. 20, 1952 in racing accident at Allentown, Pa.

SCHMIDT, Sam (3)

Year	Start	Finish	Status	Laps
1997	23	34	Engine	0
1998	6	26	Accident	48
1999	7	30	Accident	62

SCHNEIDER, Louis (6)

Year	Start	Finish	Status	Laps
1927	23	16	Timing gears	137

(Relieved by L.L. Corum, Dutch Baumann)

Year	Start	Finish	Status	Laps
1928	7	11	Running	200

(Relieved by Lou Wilson)

Year	Start	Finish	Status	Laps
1930	4	3	Running	200
1931	13	1	Running	200
1932	30	23	Frame	125

(Relieved by Bill Cummings)

Year	Start	Finish	Status	Laps
1933	21	42	Stalled	0

Died Sept. 22, 1942

SCHRADER, Gus (1)

Year	Start	Finish	Status	Laps
1932	28	39	Accident	7

Died Oct. 22, 1941 in racing accident at Shreveport, La.

SCHROEDER, Jeret (3)

Year	Start	Finish	Status	Laps
1999	21	15	Engine	175
2000	29	14	Running	198
2001	23	20	Running	187

SCHUPPAN, Vern (3)

Year	Start	Finish	Status	Laps
1976	17	18	Running/rain	97

Year	Start	Finish	Status	Laps
1979	22	21	Transmission	111
1981	18	3	Running	199

SCHURCH, Herman (2)

1929	27	20	Gas tank split	70

(Relieved by Jack Buxton, Bert Karnatz)

1931	39	39	Transmission	5

Died Nov. 10, 1931 of injuries suffered Nov. 7 at Legion Ascot Speedway

SCOTT, Billy (1)

1976	21	23	Running/rain	96

SCOTT, Bob (2)

1952	25	29	Drive shaft	49
1953	11	31	Oil leak	14

Died July 4, 1954 in racing accident at Darlington, S.C.

SERVIA, Oriol (8)

2008	25	11	Running	200
2009	25	26	Mechanical	98
2011	3	6	Running	200
2012	27	4	Running	200
2013	13	11	Running	200
2014	18	11	Running	200
2015	13	29	Contact	112
2016	10	12	Running	200

SESSIONS, Sam (7)

1968	31	9	Running	197
1969	23	12	Running	163
1970	32	12	Running	190
1971	25	27	Valve	43
1972	24	4	Running	200
1973	32	28	Out of oil	17
1975	25	17	Engine	155

Died Dec. 17, 1977 in snowmobile accident

SEYMOUR, Johnny (6)

1928	11	17	Supercharger	170

Year	Start	Finish	Status	Laps
1929	16	21	Rear axle	65
1930	18	32	Accident	21
1934	33	26	Pinion gear	22
1935	27	24	Grease leak	71
(Relieved by George Barringer)				
1936	21	31	Clutch	13

Died Feb. 27, 1958

SHAFER, Phil "Red" (7)

Year	Start	Finish	Status	Laps
1925	22	3	Running	200
(Relieved by Wade Morton)				
1926	5	10	Running/rain	146
(Relieved by Fred Lecklider)				
1929	18	12	Running	150
(Relieved by Cliff Woodbury, Russ Snowberger)				
1930	8	7	Running	200
1931	23	12	Running	200
1932	26	11	Running	197
1934	6	16	Camshaft drive	130
(Relieved by Zeke Meyer)				

Died Jan. 29, 1971

SHANNON, Elmer T. (1)

Year	Start	Finish	Status	Laps
1919	29	13	Running	200
(Relieved by E.E. Rawlings)				

Died Feb. 14, 1961

SHARP, Scott (14)

Year	Start	Finish	Status	Laps
1994	17	16	Running	186
1995	30	26	Accident	74
1996	21	10	Accident	194
1998	7	16	Gearbox	181
1999	6	28	Transmission	83
2000	5	10	Running	198
2001	1	33	Accident	0
2002	8	27	Mechanical	137
2003	9	20	Accident	181
2004	20	13	Running/rain	180
2005	3	7	Running	200

Year	Start	Finish	Status	Laps
2006	8	9	Running	200
2007	12	6	Running	166
2009	20	14	Running	200

SHATTUC, Dr. W.E. "Doc" (3)

Year	Start	Finish	Status	Laps
1925	14	9	Running	200
1926	10	27	Valve	16
1927	16	22	Valve	83

Died 1962

SHAW, Wilbur (13)

Year	Start	Finish	Status	Laps
1927	19	4	Running	200

(Relieved by Louis Meyer)

Year	Start	Finish	Status	Laps
1928	29	25	Timing gears	42
1930	25	24	Wrist pin	54
1932	22	17	Rear axle	157
1933	23	2	Running	200
1934	2	28	Lost oil	15
1935	20	2	Running	200
1936	9	7	Running	200
1937	2	1	Running	200
1938	7	2	Running	200
1939	3	1	Running	200
1940	2	1	Running	200
1941	3	18	Accident	151

Died Oct. 30, 1954 in plane crash near Decatur, Ind.

SHEFFLER, Bill (3)

Year	Start	Finish	Status	Laps
1946	25	9	Running	139
1948	24	18	Spark plugs	132
1949	22	17	Rod	160

Died June 28, 1949 from injuries suffered in racing accident June 19 at Trenton, N.J.

SHEPHERD, A.J. (1)

Year	Start	Finish	Status	Laps
1961	14	26	Accident	51

Died May 8, 2005

SHOAFF, Benny (2)

Year	Start	Finish	Status	Laps
1927	31	13	Rear end gears	198
(Relieved by Babe Stapp)				
1928	26	26	Accident	35
Died April 15, 1960				

SIMMONS, Jeff (4)

2004	29	16	Running/rain	179
2006	26	23	Accident	152
2007	13	11	Running	166
2008	24	28	Accident	112

SIMON, Dick (17)

1970	31	14	Running	168
1971	33	14	Running	151
1972	23	13	Out of fuel	186
1973	27	14	Piston	100
1974	10	33	Valve	1
1975	30	21	Running/rain	133
1976	16	32	Rod	1
1977	30	31	Overheating	24
1978	10	19	Wheel bearing	139
1979	20	26	Clutch	57
1980	29	22	Lost wheel	58
1983	20	15	Running	161
1984	20	23	In pits	112
1985	14	26	Oil pressure	86
1986	33	14	Running	189
1987	6	6	Running	193
1988	16	9	Running	196

SIMPSON, Bill (1)

1974	20	13	Piston	163

SMILEY, Gordon (2)

1980	20	25	Turbocharger	47
1981	8	22	Accident	141

Died May 15, 1982 in Indianapolis 500 qualifying accident

SNEVA, Jerry (5)

Year	Start	Finish	Status	Laps
1977	16	10	Running	187
1978	32	31	Transmission	18
1979	21	31	Piston	16
1980	5	17	Accident	130
1982	28	23	Accident	61

SNEVA, Tom (18)

Year	Start	Finish	Status	Laps
1974	8	20	Drive gear	94
1975	4	22	Accident	125
1976	3	6	Running/rain	101
1977	1	2	Running	200
1978	1	2	Running	200
1979	2	15	Accident	188
1980	33	2	Running	200
1981	20	25	Clutch	96
1982	7	4	Engine	197
1983	4	1	Running	200
1984	1	16	Left CV joint	168
1985	13	20	Accident	123
1986	7	33	Accident - DNS	0
1987	21	14	Accident	143
1988	14	27	Accident	32
1989	22	27	Pit fire	55
1990	25	30	CV joint	48
1992	30	31	Accident	10

SNIDER, George (22)

Year	Start	Finish	Status	Laps
1965	16	21	Rear end gears	64
1966	3	19	Accident	22
1967	10	26	Accident (Ruby)	99

(Relieved by Lloyd Ruby)

Year	Start	Finish	Status	Laps
1968	29	31	Oil leak	9
1969	15	16	Running	152
1970	10	20	Suspension	105
1971	21	33	Stalled	6
1972	21	11	Running	190
1973	30	12	Gearbox	101

(Relieved by A.J Foyt, Lap 58-101)

Year	Start	Finish	Status	Laps
1974	13	28	Valve	7

Year	Start	Finish	Status	Laps
1975	24	8	Running/rain	165
1976	27	13	Running/rain	98
1977	13	24	Valve	65
1978	23	8	Running	191
1979	35	33	Fuel pump	7
1980	21	15	Engine	169
1982	26	21	Engine	87
1983	13	32	Ignition	22
1984	31	11	Running	193
1985	28	32	Engine	13
1986	31	26	Ignition	110
1987	31	33	Fuel leak	0

SNOWBERGER, Russ (15)

Year	Start	Finish	Status	Laps
1928	22	29	Supercharger	4
1929	10	27	Supercharger	45
1930	7	8	Running	200
1931	1	5	Running	200
1932	4	5	Running	200
1933	17	8	Running	200

(Relieved by George Howie, Mauri Rose)

Year	Start	Finish	Status	Laps
1934	9	8	Running	200
1935	11	27	Exhaust pipe	59
1937	30	27	Clutch	66

(Relieved by Johnny Seymour)

Year	Start	Finish	Status	Laps
1938	2	25	Rod	56
1939	25	25	Radiator	50
1940	11	31	Water pump	38
1941	11	21	Water pump	107
1946	10	12	Differential	134

(Relieved by Duke Nalon)

Year	Start	Finish	Status	Laps
1947	6	19	Oil pump	73

Died Sept. 28, 1968

SNYDER, Jimmy (5)

Year	Start	Finish	Status	Laps
1935	30	22	Spring	97
1936	16	30	Oil leak	21
1937	19	32	Transmission	27
1938	15	15	Supercharger	150

Year	Start	Finish	Status	Laps
1939	1	2	Running	200

Died June 29, 1939 in racing accident at Cahokia, Ill.

SOSPIRI, Vincenzo (1)

Year	Start	Finish	Status	Laps
1997	3	17	Running	163

SOUDERS, George (2)

Year	Start	Finish	Status	Laps
1927	22	1	Running	200
1928	12	3	Running	200

Died July 26, 1976

SPANGLER, Lester (1)

Year	Start	Finish	Status	Laps
1933	7	26	Accident	132

Died May 30, 1933 in Indianapolis 500 racing accident, along with mechanic G.L. Jordan

SPENCE, Bill (1)

Year	Start	Finish	Status	Laps
1929	12	32	Accident	9

Died May 30, 1929 in Indianapolis 500 racing accident

STAPP, Elbert "Babe" (12)

Year	Start	Finish	Status	Laps
1927	24	31	Universal joint	24
1928	5	6	Running	200
(Relieved by Ralph Hepburn)				
1929	4	28	Universal joint	40
1930	32	31	Accident	18
1931	6	35	Oil leak/clutch	9
1933	29	23	Out of gas	156
1935	12	25	Radiator	70
1936	2	24	Crankshaft	89
1937	31	31	Clutch	36
1938	8	26	Valve	54
1939	16	5	Running	200
1940	12	24	Oil line	64
(Relieved by Tony Willman)				

Died Sept. 17, 1980

STEVENS, Myron (1)

Year	Start	Finish	Status	Laps
1931	35	4	Running	200

Year	Start	Finish	Status	Laps
(Relieved by Louis Meyer)				
Died July 2, 1988				

STEVENSON, Chuck (9)

Year	Start	Finish	Status	Laps
1951	19	20	Fire	93
1952	11	18	Running	187
1953	16	29	Fuel leak	42
1954	5	12	Running	199
(Relieved by Walt Faulkner)				
1960	9	15	Running	196
1961	28	6	Running	200
1963	22	21	Valve	110
1964	29	28	Accident	2
1965	26	25	Piston	50
Died Aug. 21, 1995				

STEWART, Jackie (2)

Year	Start	Finish	Status	Laps
1966	11	6	Oil pressure	190
1967	29	18	Engine	168

STEWART, Tony (5)

Year	Start	Finish	Status	Laps
1996	1	24	Engine	82
1997	2	5	Running	200
1998	4	33	Engine	22
1999	24	9	Running	196
2001	7	6	Running	200

STRANG, Lewis (1)

Year	Start	Finish	Status	Laps
1911	1	29	Steering	108
(Relieved by Elmer Ray)				

Died July 20, 1911 in passenger car testing accident at Blue River, Wis.

STUBBLEFIELD, Hartwell "Stubby" (4)

Year	Start	Finish	Status	Laps
1931	9	8	Running	200
1932	25	14	Running	178
1933	10	5	Running	200
1934	29	12	Running	200
(Relieved by Dave Evans)				

Died May 21, 1935 in Indianapolis 500 qualifying accident, along with mechanic Leo Whitaker

Year	Start	Finish	Status	Laps
SULLIVAN, Danny (12)				
1982	13	14	Accident	148
1984	28	29	Broken wheel	57
1985	8	1	Running	200
1986	2	9	Running	197
1987	16	13	Engine	160
1988	2	23	Accident	101
1989	26	28	Rear axle	41
1990	9	32	Accident	19
1991	9	10	Turbo	173
1992	8	5	Running	199
1993	12	33	Accident	29
1995	18	9	Running	199
SUTTON, Len (7)				
1958	27	32	Accident	0
1959	22	32	Accident	34
1960	5	30	Piston	47
1961	8	19	Clutch	110
1962	4	2	Running	200
1964	8	15	Magneto	140
1965	12	12	Running	177

Died Dec. 4, 2006

Year	Start	Finish	Status	Laps
SWANSON, Bob (3)				
1937	21	28	Carburetor	52
1939	22	31	Rear axle	19
1940	20	6	Running	196

Died June 13, 1940 from injuries in racing accident at Toledo, Ohio on June 12

Year	Start	Finish	Status	Laps
SWEIKERT, Bob (5)				
1952	32	26	Differential	77
1953	29	20	Radius rod	151
1954	9	14	Running	197
1955	14	1	Running	200
1956	10	6	Running	200

Died June 17, 1956 in racing accident at Salem, Ind.

Year	Start	Finish	Status	Laps
TAGLIANI, Alex (8)				
2009	33	11	Running	200
2010	5	10	Running	200
2011	1	28	Accident	147
2012	11	12	Running	200
2013	11	24	Running	196
2014	24	13	Running	200
2015	20	17	Running	200
2016	33	17	Running	200
TAKAGI, Tora (2)				
2003	7	5	Running	200
2004	26	19	Running/rain	179
TAYLOR, Mark (1)				
2004	14	30	Accident	62
TEAGUE, Marshall (2)				
1953	22	18	Oil	169
1957	28	7	Running	200

Died Feb. 11, 1959 in racing accident at Daytona Beach, Fla.

Year	Start	Finish	Status	Laps
TEMPLEMAN, Clark "Shorty" (5)				
1955	31	18	Stalled	142
1958	23	19	Brakes	116
1960	19	17	Running	191
1961	18	4	Running	200
1962	6	11	Running	200

Died Aug. 24, 1962 of injuries suffered in racing accident Aug. 23 at Marion, Ohio

Year	Start	Finish	Status	Laps
TETZLAFF, Teddy (4)				
1911	30	39	Accident	20
1912	3	2	Running	200
(Relieved by Caleb Bragg)				
1913	8	17	Drive chain	118
1914	2	28	Rocker arm	33

Died Dec. 8, 1929

Year	Start	Finish	Status	Laps
THEYS, Didier (3)				
1989	19	20	Engine	131
1990	20	11	Running	190
1993	32	22	Running	193
THOMAS, Joe (3)				
1920	19	8	Running	200
(Relieved by Art Klein, Harry Thicksten)				
1921	22	22	Accident	24
1922	17	10	Running	200
(Relieved by Wade Morton, Peter DePaolo)				
Died Dec. 28, 1965				
THOMAS, Rene (4)				
1914	15	1	Running	200
1919	1	11	Running	200
1920	18	2	Running	200
1921	17	10	Water hose	144
Died Sept. 23, 1975				
THOMSON, Johnny (8)				
1953	33	32	Ignition	6
1954	4	24	Stalled	165
(Relieved by Andy Linden, Bill Homeier)				
1955	33	4	Running	200
1956	18	32	Spun	22
1957	11	12	Running	199
1958	22	23	Steering	52
1959	1	3	Running	200
1960	17	5	Running	200
Died Sept. 24, 1960 in racing accident at Allentown, Pa.				
THORNE, Joel (4)				
1938	13	9	Running	185
1939	20	7	Running	200
1940	10	5	Running	197
1941	23	31	Accident	4
Died Oct. 17, 1955 in plane crash in Los Angeles				

Year	Start	Finish	Status	Laps
THRESHIE, Phil (2)				
1978	29	30	Oil pressure	22
1979	29	17	Running	172
THURMAN, Arthur (1)				
1919	18	27	Accident	44

Died May 30, 1919 in Indianapolis 500 racing accident

Year	Start	Finish	Status	Laps
TILL, Brian (1)				
1994	21	12	Running	194
TINGELSTAD, Bud (10)				
1960	28	9	Running	200
1962	10	15	Running	200
1963	25	28	Accident	46
1964	19	6	Running	198
1965	24	16	Accident	115
1966	27	21	Overheating	16
1967	25	14	Spun	182
1968	18	16	Oil pressure	158
1969	18	15	Engine	155
1971	17	7	Running	198

Died July 30, 1981

Year	Start	Finish	Status	Laps
TOFT, Omar (1)				
1919	30	28	Rod	44

Died Jan. 12, 1921 in racing accident at Phoenix

Year	Start	Finish	Status	Laps
TOLAN, Johnnie (3)				
1956	31	21	Running	173
1957	31	20	Clutch	138
1958	30	13	Running	200

Died June 2, 1986

Year	Start	Finish	Status	Laps
TOMEI, Louis (8)				
1935	32	28	Valve	47
1936	8	27	Engine support	44
1937	18	10	Running	200
1938	24	23	Rod	88

Year	Start	Finish	Status	Laps
1939	30	15	Running	186
(Relieved by Mel Hansen)				
1940	18	16	Exhaust pipe	190
1941	24	11	Running	200
1946	22	26	Oil line	34

Died May 15, 1955 from injuries suffered in a speed boat accident during filming of a movie.

TOWER, Jack (2)

Year	Start	Finish	Status	Laps
1911	23	24	Running	Flagged
(Relieved by Bob Evans)				
1913	25	19	Accident	51

Died 1950

TRACY, Paul (7)

Year	Start	Finish	Status	Laps
1992	19	20	Engine	96
1993	7	30	Accident	94
1994	25	23	Turbo	92
1995	16	24	Electrical	136
2002	29	2	Running	200
2009	13	9	Running	200
2011	24	25	Running	175

TREADWAY, Rick (1)

Year	Start	Finish	Status	Laps
2002	17	29	Accident	88

TREXLER, Marion (1)

Year	Start	Finish	Status	Laps
1930	29	34	Accident	19

Died Feb. 29, 1968

TRIPLETT, Ernie (5)

Year	Start	Finish	Status	Laps
1929	20	26	Rod	48
1930	6	17	Piston	125
1931	5	7	Running	200
1932	31	22	Clutch	125
1933	5	33	Piston	66

Died March 4, 1934 of injuries at El Centro, Calif.

Year	Start	Finish	Status	Laps
TRUCCO, Vincenzo (1)				
1913	18	20	Loose gas tank	39
TURNER, Jack (6)				
1956	24	25	Engine	131
1957	19	11	Running	200
1958	10	25	Fuel pump	21
1959	14	27	Fuel tank	47
1961	21	25	Accident	52
1962	25	29	Accident	17
Died Sept. 12, 2004				
TURNER, W.H. (1)				
1911	12	8	Running	200
(Relieved by Walter Jones)				
UNSER, Al (27)				
1965	32	9	Running	196
1966	23	12	Accident	161
1967	9	2	Running	198
1968	6	26	Accident	40
1970	1	1	Running	200
1971	5	1	Running	200
1972	19	2	Running	200
1973	8	20	Piston	75
1974	26	18	Valve	131
1975	11	16	Rod	157
1976	4	7	Running/rain	101
1977	3	3	Running	199
1978	5	1	Running	200
1979	3	22	Transmission	104
1980	9	27	Cylinder	33
1981	9	17	Running	166
1982	16	5	Running	197
1983	7	2	Running	200
1984	10	3	Running	198
1985	7	4	Running	199
1986	5	22	Vibration	149
1987	20	1	Running	200

Year	Start	Finish	Status	Laps
1988	3	3	Running	199
1989	2	24	Clutch	68
1990	30	13	Running	186
1992	22	3	Running	200
1993	23	12	Running	199

UNSER, Al Jr. (19)

Year	Start	Finish	Status	Laps
1983	5	10	Out of fuel	192
1984	15	21	Water pump	131
1985	11	25	Engine	91
1986	9	5	Running	199
1987	22	4	Running	196
1988	5	13	Running	180
1989	8	2	Accident	198
1990	7	4	Running	199
1991	6	4	Running	198
1992	12	1	Running	200
1993	5	8	Running	200
1994	1	1	Running	200
2000	18	29	Overheating	89
2001	29	30	Accident	16
2002	12	12	Running	199
2003	17	9	Running	200
2004	17	17	Running/rain	179
2006	27	24	Accident	145
2007	25	26	Running	161

UNSER, Bobby (19)

Year	Start	Finish	Status	Laps
1963	16	33	Accident	2
1964	22	32	Accident	1
1965	8	19	Oil fitting	69
1966	28	8	Running	171
1967	8	9	Running	193
1968	3	1	Running	200
1969	3	3	Running	200
1970	7	11	Running	192
1971	3	12	Accident	164
1972	1	30	Ignition rotor	31
1973	2	13	Engine	100

Year	Start	Finish	Status	Laps
1974	7	2	Running	200
1975	3	1	Running/rain	174
1976	12	10	Running/rain	100
1977	2	18	Oil leak	94
1978	19	6	Running	195
1979	4	5	Running	199
1980	3	19	Turbocharger	126
1981	1	1	Running	200

UNSER, Jerry (1)

Year	Start	Finish	Status	Laps
1958	24	31	Accident	0

Died May 17, 1959 of injuries suffered in Indianapolis 500 practice accident May 2, 1959.

UNSER, Johnny (5)

Year	Start	Finish	Status	Laps
1996	16	33	Transmission	0
1997	35	18	Oil pressure	158
1998	25	25	Engine	98
1999	30	32	Brakes	10
2000	30	22	Running	186

UNSER, Robby (2)

Year	Start	Finish	Status	Laps
1998	21	5	Running	198
1999	17	8	Running	197

VAIL, Ira (5)

Year	Start	Finish	Status	Laps
1919	10	8	Running	200
1921	10	7	Running	200
1922	9	8	Running	200
(Relieved by Dave Koetzla)				
1924	15	8	Running	200
(Relieved by C.W. Van Ranst)				
1925	19	20	Rod	63

Died April 21, 1979

VAN ACKER, Charlie (3)

Year	Start	Finish	Status	Laps
1947	24	29	Accident	24
1948	12	11	Running	192
1949	27	31	Accident	10

Year	Start	Finish	Status	Laps
Died May 31, 1998				
VAN RAALTE, Noel (1)				
1915	14	10	Running	200
Died May 5, 1940				
VAN RANST, C.W. (1)				
1921	23	16	Water hose	87
Died Oct. 11, 1972				
VASSER, Jimmy (8)				
1992	28	21	Accident	94
1993	19	13	Running	198
1994	16	4	Running	199
1995	9	22	Accident	170
2000	7	7	Running	199
2001	12	4	Running	200
2002	19	30	Gearbox	87
2003	27	26	Gearbox	102
VAUTIER, Tristan (2)				
2013	28	16	Running	200
2015	32	28	Mechanical	116
VEITH, Bob (11)				
1956	23	7	Running	200
1957	16	9	Running	200
1958	4	26	Accident	1
1959	7	12	Running	200
1960	25	8	Running	200
1962	19	33	Engine	13
1963	24	26	Valve	74
1964	23	19	Piston	88
1965	10	24	Piston	58
1967	28	11	Running	189
1968	24	11	Running	196
Died March 29, 2006				

Year	Start	Finish	Status	Laps
VELEZ, Fermin (2)				
1996	28	21	Engine	107
1997	29	10	Running	195
Died March 31, 2003				
VILLENEUVE, Jacques (uncle) (1)				
1986	15	20	Main bearing	154
VILLENEUVE, Jacques (nephew) (3)				
1994	4	2	Running	200
1995	5	1	Running	200
2014	27	14	Running	200
VILLORESI, Luigi (1)				
1946	28	7	Running	200
Died Aug. 23, 1997 in Italy				
VISO, E.J. (6)				
2008	26	26	Mechanical	139
2009	29	24	Mechanical	139
2010	19	25	Accident	139
2011	18	32	Accident	27
2012	9	18	Running	200
2013	4	18	Running	200
VITOLO, Dennis (2)				
1994	15	26	Accident	89
1997	28	15	Running	173
VOGLER, Rich (5)				
1985	33	23	Accident	119
1986	27	25	Accident	132
1987	11	20	Rocker arm	109
1988	32	17	Accident	159
1989	33	8	Running	192
Died July 21, 1990 in racing accident at Salem, Ind.				
VUKOVICH, Bill (5)				
1951	20	29	Oil tank	29

Year	Start	Finish	Status	Laps
1952	8	17	Steering	191
1953	1	1	Running	200
1954	19	1	Running	200
1955	5	25	Accident	56

Died May 30, 1955 in Indianapolis 500 racing accident

VUKOVICH, Bill Jr. (12)

Year	Start	Finish	Status	Laps
1968	23	7	Running	198
1969	26	32	Rod	1
1970	30	23	Clutch	78
1971	11	5	Running	200
1972	18	28	Rear end	54
1973	16	2	Running/rain	133
1974	16	3	Running	199
1975	8	6	Running/rain	166
1976	9	31	Rod	2
1977	23	17	Wing strut	110
1979	34	8	Running	194
1980	30	12	Running	192

VUKOVICH, Billy III (3)

Year	Start	Finish	Status	Laps
1988	23	14	Running	179
1989	30	12	Running	186
1990	31	24	Engine	102

Died Nov. 25, 1990 in racing accident at Bakersfield, Calif.

WAGNER, Louis (1)

Year	Start	Finish	Status	Laps
1919	13	26	Broken wheel	44

Died March 13, 1960

WALKUP, Bruce (2)

Year	Start	Finish	Status	Laps
1969	28	33	Transmission	0
1970	14	29	Timing gear	44

WALLARD, Lee (4)

Year	Start	Finish	Status	Laps
1948	28	7	Running	200
1949	20	23	Gears	55
1950	23	6	Running/rain	136

Year	Start	Finish	Status	Laps
1951	2	1	Running	200

Died Nov. 28, 1963

WALTHER, Salt (7)

Year	Start	Finish	Status	Laps
1972	27	33	Magneto	0
1973	17	33	Accident	0
1974	14	17	Piston	141
1975	9	33	Ignition	2

(Relieved Bob Harkey, finished 10th)

Year	Start	Finish	Status	Laps
1976	22	9	Running/rain	100
1978	22	28	Clutch	24
1979	16	12	Running	191

Died December 27, 2012

WARD, Jeff (7)

Year	Start	Finish	Status	Laps
1997	7	3	Running	200
1998	27	13	Running	194
1999	14	2	Running	200
2000	6	4	Running	200
2001	8	24	Running	168
2002	15	9	Running	200
2005	31	27	Handling	92

WARD, Rodger (15)

Year	Start	Finish	Status	Laps
1951	25	27	Oil line	34
1952	22	23	Oil pressure	130
1953	10	16	Stalled	177

(Relieved by Andy Linden, Duke Dinsmore)

Year	Start	Finish	Status	Laps
1954	16	22	Stalled	172

(Relieved by Eddie Johnson)

Year	Start	Finish	Status	Laps
1955	30	28	Accident	53
1956	15	8	Running	200
1957	24	30	Supercharger	27
1958	11	20	Fuel pump	93
1959	6	1	Running	200
1960	3	2	Running	200
1961	4	3	Running	200
1962	2	1	Running	200
1963	4	4	Running	200

Year	Start	Finish	Status	Laps
1964	3	2	Running	200
1966	13	15	Handling	74

Died July 5, 2004

WARREN, Bentley (2)

Year	Start	Finish	Status	Laps
1971	15	23	Gears	76
1975	17	23	Running/rain	120

WATTLES, Stan (3)

Year	Start	Finish	Status	Laps
1998	29	28	Accident	48
1999	20	17	Running	147
2000	8	23	Engine	172

WEARNE, Frank (7)

Year	Start	Finish	Status	Laps
1937	33	24	Carburetor	99
1938	17	10	Running	181
1939	17	9	Running	200
1940	7	7	Running	195
1941	6	8	Running	200
1946	29	8	Running	197
1947	15	14	Spun	128

(Relieved by Louis Tomei)

Died Feb. 21, 1985

WEATHERLY, Clay (1)

Year	Start	Finish	Status	Laps
1935	25	32	Accident	9

Died May 30, 1935 in Indianapolis 500 racing accident

WEBB, Travis "Spider" (6)

Year	Start	Finish	Status	Laps
1948	30	27	Oil line	27
1949	26	33	Transmission	0
1950	14	20	Running/rain	126
1952	29	22	Oil leak	162
1953	18	19	Oil leak	166

(Relieved by Johnny Thomson, Jackie Holmes)

Year	Start	Finish	Status	Laps
1954	29	30	Oil leak	104

(Relieved by Danny Kladis)

Died Jan. 27, 1990

Year	Start	Finish	Status	Laps
WEILER, Wayne (2)				
1960	15	24	Accident	103
1961	12	15	Wheel bearing	147
Died Oct. 13, 2005				
WELD, Greg (1)				
1970	28	32	Piston	12
Died Aug. 4, 2008				
WENTE, Bob (1)				
1964	32	9	Running	197
Died Aug. 12, 2000				
WERNER, Christian (1)				
1923	15	11	Running	200
(Relieved by Max Sailer)				
Died June 17, 1932				
WEYANT, Chuck (4)				
1955	25	12	Running	196
1957	25	14	Running	196
1958	29	24	Accident	38
1959	29	28	Accident	45
WHELDON, Dan (9)				
2003	5	19	Accident	186
2004	2	3	Running/rain	180
2005	16	1	Running	200
2006	3	4	Running	200
2007	6	22	Accident	163
2008	2	12	Running	200
2009	18	2	Running	200
2010	18	2	Running	200
2011	6	1	Running	200
Died Oct. 16, 2011 in IZOD IndyCar Series racing accident at Las Vegas				
WHITE, Johnny (1)				
1964	21	4	Running	200
Died Dec. 24, 1977				

Year	Start	Finish	Status	Laps
WHITTINGTON, Bill (5)				
1980	27	30	Accident	9
1981	27	21	Stalled	146
1982	6	16	Engine	121
1983	15	18	Gearbox	144
1985	12	14	Accident	183
WHITTINGTON, Dale (1)				
1982	23	33	Accident	0
Died June 14, 2003				
WHITTINGTON, Don (5)				
1980	18	13	Running	178
1981	26	31	Accident	32
1982	8	6	Running	196
1983	27	27	Ignition	44
1985	6	24	Engine	97
WILBURN, Jimmy (1)				
1946	16	19	Engine	52
Died Aug. 26, 1984				
WILCOX, Howdy (11)				
1911	19	14	Running	Flagged
1912	8	9	Running	200
(Relieved by Bill Rader)				
1913	20	6	Running	200
(Relieved by Bill Rader)				
1914	3	22	Valve	67
(Relieved by D.W. Helmick)				
1915	1	7	Running	200
1916	6	7	Running	120
(Relieved by Gil Anderson)				
1919	2	1	Running	200
1920	20	19	Engine	65
1921	12	23	Rod	22
1922	26	27	Valve spring	7
1923	8	17	Clutch	60

Year	Start	Finish	Status	Laps

Died Sept. 4, 1923 in racing accident at Altoona, Pa.

WILCOX, Howdy II (1)

Year	Start	Finish	Status	Laps
1932	6	2	Running	200

Died Oct. 14, 1946 while working as flagman at Converse, Ind.

WILLIAMS, Carl (6)

Year	Start	Finish	Status	Laps
1966	25	16	Valve	38
1967	23	10	Accident	189
1968	28	15	Accident	163
1969	30	25	Clutch	50
1970	19	9	Running	197
1972	22	29	Oil cooler	52

Died Feb. 24, 1973 in motorcycle accident

WILLIAMS, Merrill "Doc" (4)

Year	Start	Finish	Status	Laps
1936	23	16	Out of gas	192
1940	19	25	Oil line	61
1941	5	24	Radiator	68
1948	6	29	Clutch	19

Died April 28, 1982

WILLMAN, Tony (4)

Year	Start	Finish	Status	Laps
1937	27	25	Rod	95
1938	26	27	Valve	47
1939	26	14	Fuel pump	188
1941	25	20	Rod	117

Died Oct. 12, 1941 in racing accident at Thompson, Conn.

WILSON, Dempsey (4)

Year	Start	Finish	Status	Laps
1958	32	15	Clutch pedal	151
1960	33	33	Magneto	11
1961	31	16	Fuel pump	145
1963	30	11	Running	200

Died April 23, 1971

WILSON, Justin (8)

Year	Start	Finish	Status	Laps
2008	16	27	Accident	132
2009	15	23	Accident	160

Year	Start	Finish	Status	Laps
2010	11	7	Running	200
2011	19	16	Running	199
2012	21	7	Running	200
2013	14	5	Running	200
2014	14	22	Running	198
2015	6	21	Running	199

Died Aug 24, 2015 from racing accident at Long Pond, PA

WILSON, Stefan (1)

Year	Start	Finish	Status	Laps
2016	30	28	Electrical	119

WINGERTER, George (1)

Year	Start	Finish	Status	Laps
1931	32	33	Fuel tank	29

Died Aug. 20, 1994

WINN, Billy (4)

Year	Start	Finish	Status	Laps
1931	36	21	Running	138
(Relieved by Jimmy Patterson)				
1932	9	9	Running	200
(Relieved by Jimmy Patterson)				
1936	19	25	Crankshaft	78
1937	4	26	Oil line	85

Died Aug. 20, 1938 in racing accident at Springfield, Ill.

WINNAI, Freddy (6)

Year	Start	Finish	Status	Laps
1929	21	5	Running	200
(Relieved by L.L. Corum, Roscoe Ford)				
1931	28	29	Accident	60
1932	35	8	Running	200
1933	35	27	Engine	125
(Relieved by Terry Curley)				
1935	28	31	Rod	16
1936	12	11	Running	199

Died Sept. 4, 1977

WISHART, Spencer (4)

Year	Start	Finish	Status	Laps
1911	11	4	Running	200
(Relieved by Dave Murphy)				
1912	6	15	Water line	82

Year	Start	Finish	Status	Laps
1913	19	2	Running	200
(Relieved by Ralph DePalma)				
1914	25	17	Camshaft	122
Died Aug. 22, 1914 in racing accident at Elgin, Ill.				

WITHERILL, Cory (1)

Year	Start	Finish	Status	Laps
2001	31	19	Running	187

WONDERLICH (Wunderlich), Jerry (2)

Year	Start	Finish	Status	Laps
1922	7	6	Running	200
(Relieved by Jules Ellingboe)				
1924	11	12	Running	200
(Relieved by Wade Morton)				
Died April 13, 1937				

WOODBURY, Cliff (4)

Year	Start	Finish	Status	Laps
1926	14	3	Running/rain	158
1927	6	19	Supercharger	108
1928	2	23	Timing gears	55
1929	1	33	Accident	3
Died Nov. 13, 1984				

YARBOROUGH, Cale (4)

Year	Start	Finish	Status	Laps
1966	24	28	Accident	0
1967	20	17	Accident	176
1971	14	16	Cam cover	140
1972	32	10	Running	193

YARBROUGH, Lee Roy (3)

Year	Start	Finish	Status	Laps
1967	26	27	Accident	87
1969	8	23	Split header	65
1970	13	19	Turbo gear	107
Died Dec. 7, 1984				

YASUKAWA, Roger (5)

Year	Start	Finish	Status	Laps
2003	11	10	Running	199
2004	12	10	Running/rain	180
2005	17	18	Mechanical	167
2006	28	16	Running	194

Year	Start	Finish	Status	Laps
2007	23	21	Running	164

YELEY, J.J. (1)

Year	Start	Finish	Status	Laps
1998	13	9	Running	197

ZAMPEDRI, Alessandro (3)

Year	Start	Finish	Status	Laps
1995	17	11	Running	198
1996	7	4	Accident	199
1997	31	35	Oil leak	0

ZBOROWSKI, Count Louis (1)

Year	Start	Finish	Status	Laps
1923	5	20	Rod	41

Died Oct. 19, 1924 in racing accident at Monza, Italy

ZENGEL, Len (1)

Year	Start	Finish	Status	Laps
1912	2	6	Running	200

(Relieved by Billy Knipper)
Died Sept. 24, 1963

ZIMMERMAN, Denny (2)

Year	Start	Finish	Status	Laps
1971	28	8	Running	189
1972	28	19	Ignition rotor	116

ZUCCARELLI, Paolo "Paul" (1)

Year	Start	Finish	Status	Laps
1913	26	22	Main bearing	18

Died June 19, 1913 in testing accident in France

RESOURCES

Arute, Jack, with Jenna Flyer, Tales from the Indianapolis 500.

Auto Editors of Consumer Guide. Indy 500 Pace Cars.

Bloemker, Al. 500 Miles to Go.

Clymer, Floyd. Indianapolis 500 Mile Race Yearbooks.

Clymer, Floyd. Indianapolis "500" Race History.

Davidson, Donald, and Rick Shaffer. Autocourse Official History of the Indianapolis 500.

Devaney, John and Barbara. The Indianapolis 500.

Engel, Lyle Kenyon. Mario Andretti—The Man Who Can Win Any Kind of Race.

Fox, Jack C. The Illustrated History of the Indianapolis 500.

Garner, Art and Spiegel, Marc B. Indy 500 Memories.

Gates, Bob. California Gold—The Legendary Life of Troy Ruttman.

Granatelli, Andy. They Call Me Mister 500.

Hungess, Carl. Indianapolis 500 Yearbooks.

Indianapolis Motor Speedway. Indianapolis 500 Programs.

Indianapolis 500: The Legacy Series (video collection)

Indianapolis Star. "100 Years, 500 Miles - 2011."

Kennedy, Pat. How Much Do You Really Know About the Indianapolis 500?

Kramer, Ralph. Indianapolis Motor Speedway: 100 Years of Racing.

Olvey, Dr. Stephen. Rapid Response.

Reed, Terry. Indy the Race and Ritual of the Indianapolis 500—Second Edition.

Shaw, Wilbur. Gentlemen, Start Your Engines.

Yates, Brock. Famous Indianapolis Cars and Drivers.

Yates, Brock. The Indianapolis 500.

Pictures courtesy of the Indianapolis Motor Speedway Photo Operations.

INDEX

A

Ader, Walt 126, 426
Agabashian, Fred 115, 118, 122, 124, 126, 129, 133, 137, 141, 145, 149, 153, 421, 422, 426, 433
Agajanian, Cary 383
Agajanian, J.C. 134, 177, 178, 232, 415, 422, 423
Aitken, Johnny 1, 5, 6, 9, 17, 19, 21, 22, 420, 422, 426, 428, 453
Aleshin, Mikhail 398, 410, 411, 412, 413, 421, 426
Alesi, Jean 386, 426
Allen, Leslie "Bugs" 426
Alley, Tom 18, 22, 28, 34, 37, 39, 427, 451, 453, 486
Allison, Bobby 218, 226, 421, 427
Allison, Donnie 206, 207, 210, 306, 427
Allison, James 1, 54, 57
Allmendinger, A.J. 390
Alsup, Bill 249, 252, 427
Alvarez, Dr. Vicente 209
Amick, George 156, 157, 420, 427
Amick, Richard "Red" 160, 164, 427
Amon, Chris 203
Anderson (Andersen), Gil 427
Anderson, Les 115, 116, 118, 428
Andres, Emil 84, 91, 92, 94, 98, 102, 111, 115, 118, 122, 428, 518
Andretti, Aldo 203

Andretti, Jeff 295, 297, 299, 300, 304, 428
Andretti, John 282, 283, 286, 290, 295, 299, 304, 306, 309, 310, 311, 363, 367, 371, 372, 376, 381, 421, 428
Andretti, Marco 356, 358, 359, 360, 363, 364, 365, 367, 368, 369, 371, 376, 378, 381, 382, 384, 386, 387, 389, 392, 397, 398, 400, 406, 409, 410, 413, 418, 429
Andretti, Mario 183, 185, 186, 187, 190, 192, 194, 196, 198, 200, 201, 203, 206, 210, 212, 214, 218, 222, 226, 228, 230, 232, 234, 236, 237, 239, 241, 245, 247, 249, 252, 254, 255, 256, 257, 261, 265, 266, 267, 269, 270, 271, 274, 276, 278, 279, 280, 282, 286, 288, 290, 291, 293, 295, 296, 298, 299, 300, 304, 305, 306, 309, 311, 342, 416, 418, 423, 426, 429, 461
Andretti, Michael 265, 266, 267, 269, 271, 274, 275, 278, 282, 284, 286, 287, 288, 290, 295, 296, 297, 299, 300, 301, 302, 309, 313, 314, 315, 336, 337, 338, 339, 340, 344, 345, 355, 356, 358, 360, 363, 364, 365, 377,

400, 418, 426, 430
Andrews, Keith 145, 149, 430
Ansterburg, Ernie 41, 42, 44, 430, 440, 532
Ardinger, Herb 76, 84, 88, 91, 94, 115, 421, 430, 435
Armi, Frank 141, 431
Armstrong, Lance 358

B

Babcock, George C. 432
Bablot, Paul 28, 432
Bachelart, Eric 299, 302, 313, 432
Bagley, Tom 239, 243, 247, 432
Baguette, Bertrand 376, 381, 383, 420, 432
Bailey, George 76, 80, 88, 91, 92, 94, 95, 432
Baker, Erwin G. "Cannonball" 433
Ball, Bobby 129, 133, 433
Bandini, Robert 26, 504
Banks, Henry 91, 111, 115, 126, 129, 133, 433, 460, 491, 518
Banks, Leo 29
Barbazza, Fabrizio 278, 280, 433
Barrichello, Rubens 384, 386, 388, 421, 433
Barringer, George 76, 84, 85, 94, 98, 99, 102, 111, 112, 433, 436, 543
Barron, Alex 340, 342, 344, 348, 353, 363, 420, 433
Barth, Wendy 276
Basle, Charles 5, 434
Batten, Norman 54, 434, 460, 502
Baumann, Charles "Dutch" 53, 420, 434, 480, 541
Beardsley, Ralph 5, 434
Beatriz, Ana 375, 376, 381, 386, 389, 392, 434
Becker, Maurice 28
Bedard, Patrick 261, 265, 266, 434
Beechler, Donnie 325, 328, 332, 336, 434
Begin, Emil 11

Arnold, Billy 56, 59, 60, 63, 64, 66, 67, 68, 70, 71, 415, 418, 422, 431
Arnold, Chuck 160, 431
Ascari, Alberto 131, 133, 146, 431
Aspen, Al 66, 70, 431
Ates, Sonny 201, 432
Ayulo, Manuel 122, 133, 137, 141, 432

Belcher, Fred 5, 421, 435
Bell, Townsend 358, 367, 371, 373, 376, 381, 382, 386, 392, 398, 399, 406, 409, 410, 411, 412, 413, 421, 435
Belskus, Jeffrey G. (Jeff) 369, 390
Belt, C.W. 56, 435
Benefield, Benny 71
Bennett, Nigel 280
Bergere, Cliff 53, 56, 59, 66, 70, 73, 74, 76, 80, 84, 88, 91, 94, 98, 100, 102, 106, 109, 111, 113, 115, 116, 135, 419, 422, 431, 435, 464, 520
Bernoldi, Enrique 367, 436
Bettenhausen, Gary 196, 198, 201, 206, 210, 211, 214, 215, 218, 222, 224, 226, 230, 232, 234, 239, 247, 248, 252, 257, 274, 278, 286, 290, 293, 295, 296, 299, 304, 307, 418, 436
Bettenhausen, Melvin "Tony" 68, 111, 113, 115, 118, 123, 126, 128, 129, 133, 137, 141, 142, 143, 145, 149, 153, 155, 160, 164, 165, 166, 420, 436, 447, 451
Bettenhausen, Tony 252, 254, 257, 261, 265, 269, 274, 276, 278, 280, 282, 290, 295, 304, 437
Bigelow, Charles 437
Bigelow, Tom 222, 226, 230, 234, 239, 243, 247, 249, 252, 257, 437
Bignotti, George 169, 187, 200, 207, 208, 216, 219, 263
Billman, Mark 71, 73, 438

Binford, Tom 220
Bisceglia, Larry 119
Bisch, Art 156, 438
Boat, Billy 321, 325, 326, 328, 329, 332, 336, 340, 344, 420, 424, 438
Boesel, Raul 269, 274, 282, 286, 288, 290, 299, 304, 305, 307, 309, 313, 325, 328, 332, 340, 341, 420, 438
Boillot, Andre 28, 31, 34, 439
Boillot, Georges 15, 439
Boles, Doug 394
Boling, John 31, 66, 439
Bonner, Brian 299, 439
Bordino, Pietro 47, 439
Borzachini, Baconin 63, 439
Bost, Paul 66, 70, 73, 262, 421, 439, 518
Bourdais, Sebastien 353, 386, 392, 398, 406, 413, 426, 440
Boyd, Johnny 143, 145, 149, 153, 156, 157, 160, 164, 168, 171, 176, 181, 185, 190, 420, 440
Boyer, Joe 28, 29, 30, 31, 34, 40, 41, 42, 44, 45, 60, 418, 440, 450, 454, 481, 532
Boyle, Mike 75, 77, 93, 95
Brabham, Geoff 250, 252, 257, 261, 265, 269, 274, 278, 290, 295, 304, 440
Brabham, Jack 166, 168, 169, 170, 181, 201, 203, 206, 421, 441
Brabham, Matt 413, 441
Brack, Kenny 321, 322, 325, 326, 328, 329, 330, 333, 340, 344, 347, 351, 353, 354, 416, 419, 441

Bragg, Caleb 5, 9, 11, 15, 421, 422, 441, 551
Branson, Don 160, 164, 166, 168, 171, 176, 181, 183, 185, 190, 192, 441
Brayton, Scott 252, 261, 265, 269, 270, 274, 278, 282, 283, 286, 290, 295, 299, 304, 309, 311, 312, 313, 316, 318, 421, 423, 426, 442
Bresnahan, John 32
Brett, Riley 34, 439, 442
Brink, Wilbur 65
Briscoe, Ryan 353, 363, 367, 368, 369, 371, 372, 373, 376, 378, 381, 382, 384, 385, 386, 387, 392, 396, 398, 403, 406, 420, 424, 442
Brisko, Frank 59, 66, 70, 73, 74, 76, 80, 82, 84, 88, 91, 94, 98, 102, 419, 431, 442, 456, 472, 488, 515
Brock, S.F. 15, 443
Brown, Walt 115, 126, 129, 428, 443
Brown, W.W. 28
Bruce-Brown, David 2, 5, 8, 419, 443
Bryan, Jimmy 133, 137, 139, 141, 145, 149, 153, 154, 156, 157, 158, 160, 164, 165, 415, 418, 443
Bucknum, Jeff 353, 354, 356, 358, 444
Bucknum, Ronnie 198, 201, 206, 444
Buhl, Robbie 317, 321, 323, 325, 326, 328, 332, 336, 340, 341, 344, 420, 444
Burman, Bob 5, 8, 11, 15, 18, 419, 444, 502
Burton (Berton), Claude 444
Busch, Kurt 395, 396, 398, 400, 444
Butcher, Harry 63, 66, 445

C

Caccia, Joe 63, 64, 71, 445
Cagle, Clarence 148, 236
Calkins, Buzz 317, 321, 325, 328, 332, 336, 421, 445
Camara, Jaime 367, 445
Campbell, Ray 70, 73, 445
Cannon, Larry "Boom Boom"
236, 445
Cantrell, Bill 118, 122, 446, 505
Carey, Bob 67, 70, 419, 446
Carlson, Billy 12, 15, 18, 446, 525
Carlson, Tyce 321, 328, 330, 446
Carnegie, Tom 179, 355, 360
Carpenter, Ed 348, 353, 358, 363, 365,

367, 371, 376, 381, 383, 386,
387, 389, 390, 392, 393, 396,
397, 398, 402, 406, 407, 409,
410, 414, 419, 424, 446
Carpentier, Patrick 353, 447
Carter, Duane 118, 122, 126, 129, 133,
137, 141, 145, 160, 164, 173,
176, 447, 483, 538
Carter, Duane Jr. "Pancho" 222, 224,
226, 230, 234, 236, 239, 243,
247, 248, 249, 252, 255, 257,
259, 261, 265, 268, 269, 274,
276, 278, 286, 290, 295, 420,
423, 447
Caruthers, Jimmy 214, 218, 222, 224,
226, 448
Castroneves, Helio 336, 337, 340, 341,
342, 344, 345, 346, 348, 353,
356, 358, 361, 363, 364, 365,
367, 371, 372, 373, 376, 379,
381, 384, 386, 388, 389, 392,
395, 397, 398, 399, 400, 401,
403, 406, 410, 412, 413, 416,
418, 424, 426, 448
Chandler, Billy 15, 22, 448, 501, 521
Chandler, Michael 252, 257, 261, 448
Chassagne, Jean 12, 15, 31, 34, 421,
422, 432, 449
Chassey, Steve 261, 278, 282, 449
Chaves, Gabby 406, 413, 449
Cheesbourg, Bill 153, 156, 160, 168,
181, 185, 187, 449, 484
Cheever, Eddie Jr. 288, 290, 295, 296,
297, 299, 304, 309, 311, 313,
314, 316, 317, 321, 322, 323,
324, 325, 328, 332, 336, 340,
358, 416, 419, 449
Chesson, P.J. 358, 450
Chevrolet, Arthur 5, 22, 29, 35,
39, 450
Chevrolet, Gaston 26, 28, 29, 30, 31,
32, 186, 415, 420, 450
Chevrolet, Louis 18, 22, 26, 28, 31, 35,
48, 415, 420, 450
Chilton, Max 408, 413, 450

Chiron, Louis 59, 450
Chitwood III, Joie 373
Chitwood, Joie 98, 102, 111, 115, 118,
122, 126, 373, 450
Christiaens, Josef 15, 22, 420, 451
Christie, Bob 149, 153, 156, 160, 164,
168, 171, 176, 451
Clancy, Pat 118, 119, 122, 126, 137
Clark, George 11, 451
Clark, Jim 175, 176, 177, 178, 181, 183,
184, 185, 187, 190, 192, 194,
196, 415, 418, 423, 451
Clauson, Bryan 386, 387, 404, 406,
413, 426, 451
Cloutier, Joe 236, 254, 288
Cobe, Harry 5, 452
Cogan, Kevin 252, 255, 257, 261, 263,
265, 269, 274, 275, 278, 282,
286, 287, 290, 295, 304, 420, 452
Cole, Hal 111, 118, 122, 452
Coletti, Stefano 406, 407, 452
Collins, Sid 134, 179, 232, 394
Comer, Fred 44, 47, 50, 56, 452, 464
Congdon, Gary 190, 453
Connor, George 80, 84, 88, 91, 94,
98, 102, 111, 115, 118, 120, 122,
123, 126, 129, 133, 428, 453,
457, 460, 529
Conway, Mike 371, 376, 378, 386,
420, 453
Cooper, Earl 15, 17, 18, 28, 39, 40, 42,
44, 45, 47, 48, 50, 166, 418, 422,
427, 453, 486, 505, 516
Cooper, Joe 18, 454
Cooper, John 245, 254
Cortner, Bob 158
Cotey, Al 53, 454
Cox, C.C. 18, 454
Cox, Harry 70
Crawford, Charlie 76, 454
Crawford (Crafford), Wesley 455
Crawford, Jim 269, 271, 274, 277, 281,
282, 284, 286, 288, 290, 295,
297, 299, 300, 304, 420, 454
Crawford, Ray 145, 149, 160, 455

Crockett, Larry 141, 142, 146, 455
Cross, Art 133, 134, 137, 138, 141, 142, 145, 146, 420, 455
Crowe, Allen 171, 176, 455
Cucinotta, Letterio 455
Cummings, Bill 63, 66, 70, 72, 73, 74, 76, 77, 78, 80, 84, 86, 88, 91, 415, 419, 422, 426, 455, 506, 541
Cunningham, Wade 386, 456
Curb, Mike 261, 383
Curtner, Jack 35, 37, 456

D

Dahnke, Bob 23
D'alene, Wilber (Ed Aleon) 456
Dallenbach, Wally 194, 198, 201, 206, 210, 213, 214, 218, 222, 223, 224, 226, 230, 234, 239, 243, 249, 419, 456
Daly, Conor 392, 403, 406, 412, 414, 457
Daly, Derek 261, 265, 269, 270, 278, 282, 286, 457
Dana, Paul 351, 356
Daniels, Mitch 385
Daré, Airton 332, 336, 340, 344, 358, 457
Davies, Jimmy 126, 129, 137, 145, 146, 420, 455, 457, 483
Davis, Don 168, 171, 457
Davis, Floyd 88, 94, 98, 100, 102, 103, 104, 106, 457, 535
Davison, James 398, 403, 406, 407, 458
Dawson, Joe 2, 5, 6, 8, 13, 15, 54, 415, 421, 458
Daywalt, Jimmy 137, 138, 141, 143, 145, 149, 153, 160, 168, 171, 420, 458
De Alzaga, Martin 40, 458
Dean, Al 157, 196
Decker, Rick 59, 63, 73, 76, 459
De Cystria, Prince Bertrand 458
De Ferran, Gil 313, 336, 337, 338, 340, 341, 344, 345, 346, 349, 416, 419, 458
Delaney, Ernest 5, 459
Dempsey, Patrick 364
Denver (Orem), Bill 459
DePalma, John 18, 459
DePalma, Ralph 5, 6, 7, 8, 11, 16, 18, 19, 25, 28, 29, 31, 32, 33, 34, 35, 37, 40, 46, 47, 85, 280, 415, 418, 422, 426, 441, 459, 567
DePaolo, Peter 29, 45, 46, 48, 51, 68, 415, 418, 460, 480, 513, 552
De Silvestro, Simona 376, 378, 381, 386, 389, 392, 404, 406, 459
DeVigne, Jules 22, 460
De Vizcaya, Pierre 459
Devore, Billy 86, 88, 91, 94, 98, 102, 111, 118, 119, 460, 461
Devore, Earl 47, 52, 53, 56, 57, 460
Dickson, Larry 190, 194, 198, 201, 210, 239, 243, 252, 461
Dickson, Sam 2
Diddel, William 57
Dingley, Bert 8, 461
Dinsmore, Duke 111, 115, 122, 126, 129, 149, 461, 561
Disbrow, Louis 5, 8, 11, 15, 461
Dismore, Mark 293, 316, 317, 321, 325, 328, 332, 336, 338, 340, 420, 462
Dixon, Scott 344, 345, 348, 353, 358, 359, 361, 363, 364, 367, 368, 369, 371, 372, 373, 376, 380, 381, 382, 383, 385, 386, 387, 392, 396, 398, 399, 401, 402, 403, 406, 408, 413, 416, 418, 424, 426, 462
Dobson, Dominic 282, 286, 290, 295, 299, 304, 309, 462
Doescher, Ted 99
Donohue, Mark 201, 202, 203, 206, 207, 208, 210, 213, 214, 215, 216, 218, 220, 228, 266, 416, 419, 462

Doornbos, Robert 371, 463
Duff, John 50, 463
Duman, Ronnie 181, 185, 190, 194, 198, 463
Duncan, Len 141, 463
Dunham, Jimmy 81
Duno, Milka 363, 365, 367, 371, 463

Durant, Lewis 111, 463, 511, 529, 536
Durant, Paul 317, 321, 463
Duray, Arthur 12, 15, 419, 464
Duray, Leon (George Stewart) 37, 40, 45, 47, 50, 53, 54, 56, 59, 66, 72, 74, 75, 76, 78, 85, 419, 422, 425
Dye, Pete 301

E

Earhart, Amelia 77
Edenburn, Eddie 77
Edmunds, Don 153, 154, 464
Eldridge, E.A.D. 50, 464, 485
Elisian, Ed 141, 145, 149, 153, 155, 156, 465
Elkins, Lee 155
Ellingboe, Jules 34, 37, 44, 47, 50, 53, 465, 470, 481, 488, 567
Elliott, Frank 37, 40, 44, 47, 50, 53, 448, 465
Ellis, Fred 5, 465
Endicott, Bill 3, 5, 7, 8, 11, 465
Endicott, Harry 5, 11, 466
Engelhart, Bill 466
Enge, Tomas 353, 354, 466
Evans, Bob 11, 466, 554
Evans, Dave 53, 56, 63, 66, 73, 76, 455, 466, 549
Eyckmans, Wim 328, 466

F

Fabi, Teo 259, 261, 263, 265, 280, 282, 286, 290, 304, 309, 313, 419, 423, 466
Fahrnow, Herbert "Dusty" 76, 467, 493
Fangio, Juan Manuel 155
Fankhauser, Milt 115, 467
Farina, Giuseppe "Nino" 147
Farmer, Frank 59, 63, 66, 467
Faulkner, Walt 124, 126, 127, 129, 137, 145, 259, 422, 467, 549
Fengler, Harlan 40, 155, 177, 220, 467
Ferguson, Dick 247, 467
Fernandez, Adrian 309, 313, 348, 350, 353, 421, 467
Fetterman, I.P. "Red" 37, 468
Field, Ted 249
Fillip, Chet 257, 261, 468
Fiore, Frank 211
Firestone, Dennis 247, 252, 257, 261, 265, 272, 468
Fisher, Carl 1, 16, 41, 54
Fisher, Sarah 332, 334, 336, 340, 344, 348, 363, 367, 371, 375, 376, 381, 384, 386, 392, 398, 468
Fittipaldi, Christian 313, 315, 468
Fittipaldi, Emerson 263, 265, 269, 274, 278, 282, 284, 285, 286, 287, 288, 290, 295, 296, 299, 300, 304, 306, 307, 309, 313, 334, 368, 416, 418, 423, 468
Flaherty, George Francis Jr. (Pat) 126, 137, 145, 146, 147, 148, 149, 150, 157, 160, 415, 418, 423, 469, 531
Fohr, Myron 122, 126, 469
Follmer, George 201, 206, 210, 469
Fonder, George 122, 133, 431, 463, 469
Forberg, Carl 129, 469
Force, Gene 129, 164, 470
Ford, Benson 179
Ford, Edsel 67
Ford, Henry 41, 67
Ford, Percy 33, 34, 470
Foster, Billy 185, 188, 190, 470

Fowler, Kenneth 470
Fox, Frank 5, 470
Fox, Malcolm 70, 73, 470
Fox, Stan 278, 282, 290, 295, 299, 304, 309, 313, 314, 470
Fox, William 112
Foyt, A.J. 156, 157, 160, 164, 166, 168, 170, 171, 176, 178, 181, 183, 185, 187, 188, 190, 192, 194, 196, 198, 200, 201, 202, 203, 206, 210, 211, 214, 215, 218, 222, 223, 224, 226, 230, 234, 235, 237, 239, 243, 247, 250, 252, 255, 257, 261, 265, 269, 274, 277, 278, 282, 283, 286, 288, 290, 292, 295, 298, 299, 303, 305, 306, 321, 326, 327, 328, 329, 330, 332, 333, 336, 340, 344, 345, 348, 353, 358, 361, 363, 367, 371, 376, 379, 381, 382, 386, 388, 389, 392, 398, 406, 410, 415, 416, 418, 423, 424, 426, 471, 472, 475
Foyt, A.J. IV 342, 344, 348, 353, 363, 367, 371
Foyt, Larry 348, 353, 356, 358, 472
Frame, Fred 53, 56, 59, 65, 66, 67, 70, 71, 72, 73, 80, 84, 415, 419, 460, 465, 472
Franchi, Aldo 22, 472, 492
Franchitti, Dario 340, 348, 349, 353, 356, 358, 361, 363, 364, 365, 371, 372, 373, 376, 377, 378, 381, 382, 385, 386, 387, 388, 389, 392, 393, 394, 395, 396, 416, 418, 472
Frank, Harry 35
Frayer, Lee 3, 5, 473
Freeland, Don 137, 141, 145, 146, 149, 150, 153, 156, 160, 164, 420, 473
Freeman, Morgan 349
Free, Roland 63, 115, 116, 473
Friedrich, Ernst 15, 473

G

Gable, Clark 127
Gache, Philippe 299, 300, 473
Galles, Rick 333
Ganassi, Chip 257, 259, 261, 265, 269, 274, 333, 334, 336, 338, 340, 342, 344, 348, 353, 358, 363, 367, 368, 369, 371, 376, 378, 381, 385, 386, 392, 396, 398, 401, 406, 411, 413, 416, 424, 473
Gardner, Chet 63, 73, 76, 80, 84, 88, 91, 433, 474
Gardner, Racin 316, 317, 474
Gardner, W.H. "Speed" 59, 63, 66, 474, 493
Garner, James 224
Garrett, Billy 149, 156, 474
Garza, Josele 249, 252, 254, 255, 257, 261, 265, 269, 272, 274, 278, 279, 420, 474
Gaudino, Juan 70, 475, 533
Gehlhausen, Spike 230, 239, 243, 245, 247, 265, 475
George, Elmer 151, 153, 171, 176, 475
George, Tony 288, 311, 341, 342
Giaffone, Affonso 321, 475
Giaffone, Felipe 336, 340, 341, 344, 348, 353, 358, 360, 420, 475
Giebler, Phil 363, 365, 475
Gilhooly, Ray 15, 475
Gleason, Jimmy 55, 56, 58, 59, 63, 66, 419, 475, 520
Glenn, John 209
Gloy, Tom 265, 476
Goldsmith, Paul 156, 157, 160, 164, 165, 168, 171, 176, 476
Goodyear, Scott 290, 295, 298, 299, 301, 304, 309, 312, 313, 314, 315, 321, 323, 325, 328, 332, 336, 419, 476
Gordon, Al 70, 76, 80, 476
Gordon, Robby 304, 309, 313, 321, 328, 330, 332, 336, 337, 340,

344, 345, 348, 419, 477, 504
Gosek, Joe 316, 317, 477
Goux, Jules 9, 10, 11, 12, 15, 26, 28, 31, 37, 338, 415, 418, 477
Granatelli, Andy 15, 119, 203
Grant, Harry 5, 11, 15, 18, 477, 502
Grant, Jerry 185, 190, 194, 198, 206, 214, 215, 218, 222, 226, 230, 420, 477
Greco, Marco 309, 317, 321, 325, 478
Green, Barry 342
Green, Cecil 126, 129, 421, 478
Gregoire, Stephan 304, 317, 321, 322, 325, 332, 336, 358, 421, 478
Gregory, Masten 185, 186, 478
Greiner, Art 2, 5, 478
Griffith, Cliff 129, 133, 149, 168, 178, 478
Grim, Bobby 160, 161, 164, 166, 168, 171, 176, 181, 188, 190, 194, 198, 479
Grissom, Gus 187
Groff, Mike 295, 297, 306, 309, 317, 321, 325, 479

Groff, Robbie 321, 479
Grove, Clarence 64, 445
Guerrero, Carlos 313, 479
Guerrero, Roberto 265, 267, 269, 271, 274, 278, 279, 280, 282, 283, 290, 295, 297, 298, 299, 300, 304, 309, 313, 317, 318, 321, 325, 328, 419, 423, 479
Gugelmin, Mauricio 309, 313, 314, 419, 480
Gulotta, Tony 50, 53, 55, 56, 59, 63, 65, 66, 70, 73, 76, 80, 88, 91, 94, 420, 435, 480, 520
Gurney, Daniel Sexton 170, 171, 174, 176, 181, 182, 185, 190, 191, 192, 194, 196, 197, 198, 200, 201, 203, 206, 223, 235, 254, 258, 262, 267, 421, 480
Guthrie, Janet 228, 233, 234, 237, 239, 241, 243, 248, 355, 481
Guthrie, Jim 317, 321, 325, 481
Guyot, Albert 11, 12, 15, 28, 34, 50, 420, 481

H

Hahn, Bob 77, 502
Haibe, Ora 22, 28, 34, 37, 44, 465, 481, 520
Haines, William 59
Hall, Dean 290, 481
Hall, Howard 5, 481
Hall, Ira 56, 70, 73, 91, 94, 421, 482
Hall, Norm 168, 181, 250, 482
Halsmer, Pete 252, 257, 482
Hamilton, Davey 317, 321, 325, 328, 332, 336, 363, 367, 371, 376, 377, 381, 421, 482
Hanks, Sam 98, 99, 102, 111, 118, 122, 126, 129, 133, 137, 141, 145, 149, 150, 151, 153, 154, 155, 166, 174, 255, 394, 415, 418, 450, 455, 482
Hannon, Johnny 78, 81
Hansen, Mel 94, 98, 102, 111, 115, 118, 431, 469, 483, 527, 554
Hansgen, Walt 181, 185, 187, 483
Harbaugh, Jim 390
Harder, Fred 44, 483
Harkey, Bob 181, 210, 218, 222, 226, 230, 483, 561
Harrington, Scott 317, 484
Harris, Lawson 74
Hartley, Gene 126, 133, 137, 138, 141, 149, 153, 160, 164, 168, 171, 437, 484
Hartz, Harry 35, 37, 39, 40, 44, 47, 48, 49, 50, 53, 60, 64, 68, 155, 249, 263, 415, 419, 422, 484, 486, 502
Harvey, Jack 403
Hattori, Shigeaki 340, 344, 484
Haupt, Willie 11, 15, 18, 31, 484
Haustein, Gene 66, 73, 76, 485, 487
Hawkes, W. Douglas 485

Hawksworth, Jack 398, 406, 407, 413, 485
Haywood, Hurley 247, 485
Hearne, Eddie 5, 8, 26, 28, 31, 34, 35, 37, 39, 40, 44, 53, 464, 485, 523
Hearn, Richie 317, 319, 332, 340, 344, 348, 353, 363, 485
Hedback, Phil 228
Heimrath, Ludwig Jr. 486
Hellings, Mack 118, 122, 126, 129, 486
Henderson, George "Pete" 22, 31, 37, 44, 47, 50, 53, 59, 63, 66, 115, 126, 252, 257, 301, 482, 486, 534
Henning, Cotton 95
Hepburn, Ralph 47, 50, 53, 56, 59, 65, 66, 73, 76, 80, 84, 86, 88, 94, 98, 102, 109, 111, 116, 124, 135, 259, 419, 464, 472, 486, 496, 519, 548
Herb, Jon 336, 363, 487
Herman, Al 145, 146, 149, 153, 160, 164, 487
Herr, Don 6, 11, 458, 487
Herta, Bryan 309, 313, 348, 350, 353, 355, 356, 358, 376, 383, 416, 421, 426, 487
Hewitt, Jack 325, 488
Hickey, Denny 28, 488
Hickman, Jim 257, 259, 488
Hildebrand, JR 381, 386, 392, 398, 406, 413, 420, 488
Hill, Bennett "Benny" 52, 53, 56, 71, 472, 488, 544
Hillenburg, Andy 332, 334, 489
Hill, George 18, 489
Hill, Graham 173, 187, 190, 191, 192, 194, 197, 198, 200, 228, 334, 338, 416, 420, 489
Hill, Jimmy 53, 489
Hinchcliffe, James 381, 384, 385, 386, 389, 392, 395, 396, 397, 398, 410, 411, 413, 420, 424, 489
Hinnershitz, Tommy 98, 102, 118, 489
Hiss, Arlene 228
Hiss, Mike 214, 216, 218, 220, 222, 223, 226, 228, 237, 489
Hitke, Kurt 28, 489
Hobbs, David 210, 211, 218, 222, 230, 490
Holbert, Al 265, 267, 490
Holland, Bill 113, 115, 116, 118, 119, 120, 122, 123, 124, 126, 130, 135, 137, 249, 263, 415, 418, 490
Hollansworth, John Jr. 490
Holmes, Howdy 243, 245, 257, 261, 264, 265, 269, 282, 490
Holmes, Jackie 122, 126, 490, 562
Homeier, Bill 141, 142, 164, 334, 467, 490, 552
Hopkins, Lindsey 143, 212, 218, 219
Horan, Joe 8, 491
Horn, Eylard Amandus "Ted" 68, 80, 82, 84, 88, 91, 94, 98, 99, 102, 105, 111, 112, 113, 115, 117, 118, 119, 249, 299, 419, 422, 455, 491, 493, 528
Hornish, Sam Jr. 491
Houck, Jerry 71
Householder, Ronney 88, 90, 91, 491
Houser, Norm 122, 491
Houser, Thane 41, 50, 440, 476, 492
Howard, C. Glenn 37, 492
Howard, Jay 381, 492
Howard, Ray 28, 31, 492
Howie, George 66, 492, 547
Hoyt, Jerry 126, 137, 141, 143, 145, 146, 422, 492, 537
Hucul, Cliff 234, 239, 243, 492
Huertas, Carlos 398, 403, 492
Huff, Joe 63, 66, 70, 493
Hughes, Hughie 5, 8, 444, 446, 493
Hulman, Anton Jr. "Tony" 36, 106, 110, 116, 139, 144, 208, 212, 232, 233, 235, 236, 287
Hulman George, Mari 250, 322, 396, 411
Hulman, Grace Smith 117
Hulman, Mary Fendrich 240, 250
Hulme, Denis 194, 195, 198, 201, 203, 208, 210, 493

Hulse, Chuck 171, 176, 190, 194, 493
Hunt, Bill 44, 493
Hunter-Reay, Ryan 367, 369, 371, 372, 376, 378, 381, 382, 384, 386, 390, 391, 392, 394, 397, 398, 399, 400, 406, 409, 410, 411, 413, 417, 419, 493

Hurst, Bob 72
Hurt, Bob 198
Hurtubise, Jim 162, 164, 165, 166, 168, 171, 173, 174, 176, 181, 182, 183, 185, 190, 197, 198, 213, 214, 222, 237, 241, 250, 419, 494

I

Insinger, Harris 80, 494

Irwin-Mellencamp, Elaine 337

J

Jackson, Jimmy 111, 112, 115, 118, 122, 126, 421, 447, 494
Jagersberger, Joe 5, 494
Jakes, James 386, 392, 406, 421, 494
James, Joe 129, 133, 495
Jeffkins, Rupert 6, 7, 481
Jenkins, Johnny 8, 11, 495
Johansson, Stefan 304, 309, 313, 495
Johncock, Gordon 183, 185, 188, 190, 191, 192, 194, 198, 201, 206, 210, 211, 214, 217, 218, 219, 222, 224, 226, 228, 230, 232, 234, 235, 239, 241, 243, 247, 248, 252, 253, 257, 258, 259, 261, 265, 267, 277, 278, 286, 295, 299, 416, 418, 495
Johns, Bobby 178, 185, 201, 496
Johnson, Art 22, 496
Johnson, Eddie 133, 145, 149, 153, 156, 160, 164, 168, 171, 176, 181, 185, 190, 496, 530, 561
Johnson, Herm 257, 258, 265, 267, 271, 496
Johnson, John "Jigger" 67, 89, 200, 203

Johnson, Luther 64, 66, 70, 73, 74, 496
Jones, Ben 50, 496
Jones, Bubby 234, 497
Jones, Davy 278, 286, 304, 313, 317, 318, 319, 419, 497
Jones, Herbert 47, 497
Jones, John 286, 497
Jones, M.C. 47, 497
Jones, Milton 71
Jones, Parnelli 166, 168, 169, 170, 171, 173, 174, 176, 178, 181, 182, 185, 186, 187, 190, 192, 194, 196, 198, 200, 201, 203, 207, 212, 220, 236, 349, 415, 416, 418, 423, 426, 497
Jones, P.J. 349, 356
Jones, Will 5, 497
Jordan, G.L. "Monk" 72
Jourdain, Bernard 286, 288, 295, 498
Jourdain, Michel Jr. 498
Judd, Ashley 365, 388
Junqueira, Bruno 336, 337, 338, 340, 341, 348, 350, 353, 367, 372, 376, 419, 424, 498

K

Kanaan, Tony 340, 342, 343, 344, 345, 346, 348, 350, 351, 353, 356, 358, 361, 363, 364, 367, 368, 369, 371, 372, 376, 377, 381, 383, 384, 386, 388, 390, 391, 392, 393, 394, 396, 398, 401, 404, 406, 407, 411, 412, 413, 417, 418, 422, 424, 498
Karam, Sage 398, 400, 401, 403, 406, 411, 414, 498
Karl, Jerry 218, 222, 226, 239, 247, 252, 499

Karnatz, Albert 499
Keck, Howard 118, 122, 126, 131, 135, 142, 143, 415, 422
Keech, Ray 56, 58, 59, 60, 415, 419, 499
Keene, Charlie 15, 499
Keller, Al 145, 149, 153, 156, 160, 168, 499
Kenealy, Mel 499
Kennedy Tank Special 15, 85, 116, 131, 411
Kenyon, Mel 187, 190, 194, 198, 199, 201, 202, 206, 210, 211, 214, 218, 499
Kimball, Charlie 381, 383, 386, 392, 393, 397, 398, 406, 408, 413, 420, 426, 500
King, Grant 210, 232
King, Mike 394, 395
Kinser, Sheldon 226, 230, 234, 239, 243, 252, 500
Kinser, Steve 320, 321, 500
Kirkpatrick, Charles 28, 500
Kite, Jimmy 325, 328, 332, 344, 353, 500
Kizer, Karl 147
Kladis, Danny 111, 501, 562
Klausler, Tom 252, 501
Klein, Art 15, 18, 28, 31, 37, 421, 465, 501, 552
Klein, Seth 124, 139
Knapp, Steve 325, 326, 328, 332, 501
Kneifel, Chris 261, 265, 266, 501
Knepper, Arnie 185, 190, 194, 198, 201, 501
Knievel, Evel 232
Knight, Harry 5, 8, 501
Knipper, Billy 5, 11, 15, 502, 516, 568
Kohlert, Henry 56, 502, 504
Kreiger, Johnny 70, 502, 513
Kreis, Peter 47, 48, 53, 56, 59, 70, 73, 77, 415, 435, 487, 502
Krisiloff, Steve 210, 214, 218, 222, 226, 230, 234, 239, 243, 252, 261, 421, 502
Krueger, Phil 271, 274, 282, 503
Kunzman, Lee 214, 218, 234, 243, 503
Kurtenbach, Lyle 279
Kurtis, Frank 127, 131, 147
Kuzma, Eddie 133

L

Lacy, Paul 165
Laly, Robert 15, 25
Lanier, Randy 274, 276, 503
Larson, Jud 156, 160, 503
Lautenschlager, Christian 40, 503
Lazier, Bob 252, 503
Lazier, Buddy 295, 296, 299, 313, 316, 317, 318, 319, 321, 323, 325, 326, 328, 332, 334, 336, 340, 342, 344, 348, 353, 355, 356, 358, 363, 367, 368, 389, 392, 398, 402, 414, 416, 418, 419, 503
Lazier, Jaques 332, 336, 344, 353, 356, 358, 363, 365, 421, 477, 504
LeBegue, Rene 98, 504
Lecklider, Fred 50, 53, 427, 504, 516, 543
LeCocq, Louis 26, 28, 504
Leffler, Greg 247, 504
Leffler, Jason 332, 505
Legge, Kathrine 386, 388, 392, 505
Leonard, Joe 185, 190, 194, 196, 198, 199, 200, 201, 203, 206, 208, 210, 211, 212, 214, 216, 218, 220, 419, 423, 505
Leonard, Sugar Ray 359
Levrett, Bayliss 122, 126, 505
Lewis, Dave 22, 45, 46, 47, 48, 50, 53, 419, 464, 465, 505
Lewis, Randy 278, 282, 286, 290, 295, 505
Liesaw, Billy 8, 11, 506
Lindau, Bill 59, 506
Linden, Andy 129, 133, 137, 141, 145, 149, 153, 455, 492, 506, 552, 561
Litz, A.B. "Deacon" 56, 57, 59, 63, 66,

70, 73, 76, 80, 84, 88, 94, 102, 419, 506
Lloyd, Alex 367, 371, 376, 378, 381, 507
Lockhart, Frank 48, 50, 51, 53, 54, 291, 338, 415, 418, 422, 507
Loquasto, Al 230, 231, 234, 507
Luyendyk, Arie 269, 271, 274, 275, 278, 282, 286, 290, 291, 292, 295, 299, 304, 305, 309, 311, 312, 313, 316, 317, 319, 321, 323, 325, 326, 328, 329, 336, 337, 340, 356, 358, 393, 416, 418, 423, 424, 426, 507, 508
Luyendyk, Arie Jr. 354, 355, 358, 508
Lynch, George 122, 508
Lytle, Herb 5, 508

M

MacDonald, Dave 179, 181, 508
MacKenzie, George "Doc" 47, 50, 53, 70, 73, 76, 80, 82, 84, 98, 102, 118, 502, 508, 544, 565
Mackey, Bill (W.C. Gretsinger Jr.) 508
Mack, George 340, 341, 508
MacPherson, Jeff 278, 508
Magill, Mike 153, 156, 160, 509
Mahler, John 208, 214, 234, 236, 239, 243, 509
Mais, Johnny 18, 509
Malloy, Jim 198, 201, 203, 206, 210, 212, 509
Malone, Art 173, 176, 178, 181, 187, 509
Manning, Darren 348, 353, 363, 367, 509
Manning, Peyton 364
Mann, Pippa 381, 389, 392, 398, 406, 407, 411, 413, 509
Mansell, Nigel 302, 304, 306, 309, 310, 420, 510
Mantz, Johnny 118, 122, 467, 510
Marcelo, Jovy 297
Marchese, Carl 59, 510
Marquette, Mel 5, 8, 510
Marshall, Cy 61, 63, 115, 116, 461, 510
Marshall, Paul 61
Marshman, Bobby 168, 169, 171, 176, 178, 181, 183, 420, 510
Martin, Harry 6
Martin, John 214, 218, 222, 226, 230, 239, 510
Mason, George 15, 511

Mathouser, Bob 181, 511
Matlock, Spider 64, 67
Matos, Raphael 371, 373, 376, 511
Matson, Joe 8, 511
Matsuda, Hideshi 309, 313, 317, 328, 511
Matsushita, Hiro 293, 295, 304, 309, 313, 511
Matsuura, Kosuke 348, 350, 353, 355, 358, 363, 511
Mauro, Johnny 118, 131, 511
Mays, Rex 76, 77, 78, 80, 82, 84, 88, 91, 94, 95, 96, 98, 102, 105, 111, 115, 116, 118, 120, 122, 123, 283, 418, 422, 426, 436, 443, 446, 480, 512
McCarver, Jack 50, 512
McCluskey, Roger 168, 171, 176, 177, 185, 190, 194, 198, 201, 206, 210, 212, 214, 218, 219, 222, 226, 230, 234, 239, 243, 421, 500, 512
McCoy, J.J. 28, 513
McCoy, Larry 226, 230, 513
McCoy (Musser), Ernie 513
McDonald, J.C. 63, 513
McDonogh, Bob 44, 47, 53, 59, 70, 464, 486, 513
McDowell, Johnny 122, 126, 129, 133, 513
McElreath, James 232
McElreath, Jim 171, 172, 176, 178, 181, 185, 190, 194, 198, 201, 206, 208, 218, 222, 234, 239, 243,

247, 514
McGehee, Robby 328, 331, 332, 334, 336, 344, 348, 421, 514
McGrath, Jack 118, 122, 126, 129, 133, 137, 138, 139, 141, 143, 145, 146, 419, 422, 514
McGurk, Frank 84, 515
McQuinn, Harry 76, 80, 82, 84, 88, 91, 94, 98, 102, 111, 118, 155, 480, 507, 515
McRae, Graham 218, 219, 515
McWithey, Jim 160, 164, 515
Mears, Rick 236, 237, 239, 241, 242, 243, 244, 245, 247, 249, 252, 253, 255, 257, 258, 259, 261, 262, 264, 265, 266, 267, 269, 271, 274, 275, 276, 277, 278, 282, 283, 284, 285, 286, 288, 290, 292, 293, 295, 296, 297, 299, 300, 302, 350, 369, 388, 416, 418, 423, 426, 515
Mears, Roger 255, 256, 257, 261, 516
Mecom, John 187
Medeiros, Thiago 358, 516
Meira, Vitor 344, 348, 353, 355, 358, 363, 367, 369, 371, 373, 376, 381, 420, 516
Melcher, Al 53, 516
Melton, James 109
Menard, John 318
Merz, Charlie 5, 8, 10, 11, 22, 77, 99, 516
Meyer, Louis 54, 55, 56, 57, 58, 59, 61, 63, 66, 70, 72, 73, 74, 76, 80, 82, 84, 85, 88, 89, 91, 93, 94, 240, 338, 388, 415, 418, 487, 517, 544, 548
Meyer, Zeke 63, 70, 73, 74, 84, 434, 455, 461, 517, 543
Michner, Andy 325, 517
Miles, Mark 389
Miller, Al 70, 73, 76, 80, 84, 88, 91, 94, 98, 102, 115, 173, 176, 185, 190, 194, 517, 518
Miller, Chet 62, 63, 66, 70, 73, 76, 80, 84, 88, 91, 92, 94, 98, 102, 111, 118, 124, 129, 131, 133, 135, 456, 518
Miller, Dr. Jack 321, 325, 328, 519
Miller, Eddie 34, 481, 518, 522
Miller, Harry 45, 66, 70, 78
Miller (Krulac), Al 176, 185, 190, 194, 517
Miller, Reggie 354
Milton, Tommy 28, 30, 31, 32, 33, 34, 37, 38, 40, 41, 44, 47, 53, 85, 124, 415, 418, 422, 519
Minassian, Nicolas 336, 337, 519
Montoya, Juan Pablo 332, 333, 334, 336, 338, 395, 397, 398, 402, 404, 405, 406, 407, 408, 410, 411, 414, 416, 417, 418, 519
Moore, Lou 55, 56, 58, 59, 63, 66, 67, 70, 72, 73, 75, 76, 80, 82, 84, 90, 92, 100, 106, 113, 116, 120, 121, 123, 346, 415, 420, 422, 519
Moraes, Mario 367, 371, 376, 421, 520
Moran, Charles Jr. 520
Moran, Rocky 282, 286, 290, 520
Moreno, Roberto 272, 274, 328, 363, 520
Moriceau, Jules 59, 520
Morton, Wade 40, 46, 47, 53, 452, 485, 520, 543, 552, 567
Mosley, Mike 198, 201, 206, 210, 211, 214, 216, 218, 222, 226, 230, 234, 239, 243, 245, 247, 250, 251, 252, 255, 259, 261, 421, 521
Moss, Alfred E. 521
Moss, Stirling 42
Mourre, Antoine 44, 439, 520, 521
Mulford, Ralph 2, 5, 7, 8, 10, 11, 15, 18, 20, 22, 28, 31, 34, 37, 420, 521
Munoz, Carlos 389, 391, 392, 393, 394, 398, 400, 401, 406, 407, 409, 410, 413, 420, 426, 522
Murphey, Brad 317, 522
Murphy, Jimmy 30, 31, 34, 35, 36, 37, 38, 39, 40, 41, 42, 44, 45, 415, 418, 422, 426, 518, 522

N

Muther, Rick 206, 210, 211, 222, 522
Mutoh, Hideki 367, 371, 376, 522

Nabors, Jim 212, 359, 383, 388, 394, 395, 402
Nakano, Shinji 344, 522
Nalon, Dennis "Duke" 91, 98, 102, 111, 115, 116, 118, 120, 122, 123, 126, 127, 129, 131, 133, 137, 139, 149, 250, 420, 422, 426, 461, 522, 547, 561
Nazaruk, Mike 127, 128, 129, 137, 141, 146, 523

Myers, T.E. "Pop" 17, 220, 242

Nemesh, Steve 50, 523
Newby, Arthur 1, 3
Newey, Steve 383
Newgarden, Josef 384, 386, 392, 398, 401, 406, 409, 410, 411, 413, 523
Newman, Paul 199
Nicholson, Jack 377
Niday, Cal 137, 139, 141, 145, 523
Nikrent, Joe 11, 523
Nunn, Mo 340, 342, 344, 348

O

O'Brien, Erin 161
O'Connell, Johnny 317, 523
O'Connor, Pat 141, 145, 149, 151, 153, 156, 157, 419, 423, 523
O'Donnell, Eddie 18, 28, 31, 36, 524
Oldfield, Barney 12, 15, 22, 29, 524
Oldfield, Lee 85, 485
Olivero, Bobby 234, 524

Olsen, Ernie 38
Ongais, Danny 234, 236, 237, 239, 240, 242, 243, 247, 249, 252, 253, 257, 258, 261, 265, 269, 274, 276, 316, 317, 318, 326, 419, 524
Opperman, Jan 220, 222, 230, 524
Ormsby, Len 8, 525
Orr, Tom 18, 525

P

Page, Anita 59
Pagenaud, Simon 386, 392, 393, 395, 398, 401, 402, 404, 406, 407, 408, 409, 410, 411, 413, 426, 525
Page, Paul 394, 395
Palmer, Eldon 209
Palmroth, Tero 282, 286, 290, 295, 525
Papis, Max 340, 358, 525
Pardee, Phil 65, 66, 525
Parsons, Johnnie 119, 120, 122, 124, 126, 127, 129, 133, 137, 141, 145, 149, 151, 153, 156, 248, 415, 418, 455, 525
Parsons, Johnny 222, 226, 230, 234, 239, 243, 247, 248, 255, 257, 261, 269, 270, 274, 317, 526
Patrick, Danica 350, 351, 353, 354, 355, 356, 358, 363, 364, 367, 369, 371, 373, 374, 376, 381, 382, 420, 526
Patrick, Pat 216, 249, 267, 334
Patschke, Cyrus 2, 458, 484
Paul, John Jr. 258, 269, 290, 295, 299, 309, 317, 318, 323, 325, 419, 526
Penske, Roger 200, 202, 215, 216, 236, 245, 254, 267, 271, 314, 337, 346, 359, 408, 411
Petillo, Kelly 70, 73, 74, 76, 78, 80, 81, 82, 88, 91, 94, 98, 102, 415, 419, 422, 508, 515, 526
Petticord, Jack 53, 482, 516, 527
Petty, Richard 372
Philippe, Nelson 371, 527
Phillippe, Maurice 212
Phillips, Overton 102, 527
Pigot, Spencer 407, 413, 528

Pilette, Teddy 232
Pilette, Theodore 11, 232, 527
Pimm, Ed 269, 274, 278, 527
Piquet, Nelson 297, 302, 304, 527
Pixley, Ray 84, 528
Plowman, Martin 398, 528
Pollard, Art 194, 198, 199, 201, 206, 210, 213, 216, 528
Porporato, Jean 18, 31, 528
Posey, Sam 214, 216, 528
Powell, Colin 354
Power, Will 367, 371, 373, 376, 377, 381, 384, 386, 389, 392, 395, 396, 397, 398, 400, 401, 402, 403, 406, 407, 408, 409, 410, 411, 413, 419, 426, 528
Prappas, Ted 299, 528
Prentiss, Willard 73, 528
Pruett, Scott 286, 288, 295, 299, 313, 315, 420, 529
Puterbaugh, Bill 226, 227, 230, 234, 529
Putnam, Al 91, 98, 102, 111, 491, 515, 529

Q

Quayle, Vice President Dan 295
Quinn, Francis 66, 529
Quinn, Joe 232

R

Rager, Roger 245, 247, 421, 529
Rahal, Bobby 257, 259, 261, 262, 265, 269, 270, 274, 275, 276, 277, 278, 282, 286, 290, 291, 295, 299, 305, 307, 309, 311, 313, 416, 418, 529
Rahal, Graham 367, 368, 371, 376, 381, 382, 383, 386, 387, 390, 392, 398, 401, 406, 413, 421, 530
Rasmussen, Eldon 226, 227, 234, 243, 530
Rathmann, Dick 126, 149, 151, 155, 156, 160, 164, 168, 171, 176, 181, 423, 530
Rathmann, Jim 119, 122, 126, 133, 134, 137, 141, 145, 149, 153, 154, 156, 158, 160, 162, 164, 166, 168, 171, 176, 187, 215, 216, 240, 249, 255, 263, 415, 418, 483, 490, 530
Ray, Greg 321, 325, 326, 328, 329, 332, 333, 334, 336, 337, 340, 344, 348, 418, 424, 531
Rebaque, Hector 257, 531
Redon, Laurent 340, 342, 531
Reece, Jimmy 133, 141, 145, 149, 153, 156, 157, 531
Regazzoni, Clay 234, 532
Renna, Tony 344, 346, 532
Resta, Dario 17, 18, 20, 22, 39, 40, 45, 186, 415, 418, 532
Retzloff, Al 200
Revson, Peter 201, 203, 206, 208, 210, 211, 212, 213, 214, 218, 220, 423, 532
Ribbs, Willy T. 293, 295, 304, 532
Ribiero, Andre 313, 532
Rice, Buddy 344, 347, 348, 349, 350, 351, 358, 363, 365, 367, 381, 416, 419, 424, 532
Rice, Larry 239, 241, 243, 533
Rich, Kenny 165
Richmond, Timothy Lee (Tim) 247, 249, 250, 252, 278, 421, 533
Rickenbacker (Rickenbacher), Eddie 3, 6, 8, 12, 15, 18, 19, 22, 45, 54, 71, 90, 106, 166, 420, 533
Riganti, Raul 40, 73, 98, 533
Rigsby, Jim 133, 533
Rindt, Jochen 194, 198, 533
Robbins, Marty 231
Roberts, Floyd 80, 82, 84, 88, 89, 90,

91, 92, 94, 95, 109, 112, 415, 419, 422, 533
Roberts, Robin 377
Robson, George 98, 102, 109, 111, 112, 415, 418, 489, 515, 534
Robson, Hal 111, 115, 118, 534
Rodee, Chuck (Charles J. Rodeghier) 171, 185, 187, 534
Roe, Billy 321, 325, 534
Romancini, Mario 376, 378, 534
Romcevich, Pete 115, 534
Rooney, Tom 22, 534
Rose, Jesse "Ebb" 168, 171, 176, 534
Rose, Mauri 72, 73, 74, 75, 76, 77, 80, 83, 84, 88, 91, 94, 96, 98, 99, 100, 102, 103, 106, 109, 111, 113, 115, 118, 120, 122, 124, 125, 126, 129, 130, 192, 388, 415, 418, 422, 457, 518, 535, 547
Ross, Sam 56, 66, 535
Rossi, Alexander 408, 410, 411, 412, 413, 417, 535
Roth, Marty 348, 353, 363, 364, 367, 535
Ruby, Lloyd 164, 168, 169, 171, 176, 181, 185, 189, 190, 194, 198, 199, 201, 202, 206, 207, 208, 210, 214, 218, 222, 224, 226, 230, 234, 235, 237, 418, 535, 546
Rupp, Mickey 185, 536
Russo, Eddie 145, 151, 153, 164, 465, 536
Russo, Joe 66, 70, 73, 76, 536
Russo, Paul 98, 102, 109, 111, 115, 118, 122, 126, 137, 141, 148, 149, 151, 153, 154, 156, 160, 166, 171, 419, 426, 437, 451, 475, 536
Rutherford, Johnny 176, 181, 185, 192, 194, 198, 201, 203, 206, 210, 214, 216, 218, 222, 223, 224, 226, 227, 228, 230, 232, 234, 239, 243, 245, 247, 249, 250, 252, 257, 259, 265, 269, 270, 274, 278, 282, 291, 298, 307, 311, 322, 388, 416, 418, 423, 426, 537

S

Saavedra, Sebastian 376, 386, 392, 398, 406, 538
Sachs, Eddie 151, 153, 154, 156, 158, 160, 162, 164, 166, 168, 171, 172, 173, 176, 177, 179, 181, 419, 423, 426, 538
SAFER barrier 341, 399
Sailer, Max 40, 538, 563
Salay (Szalai), Mike 539
Salazar, Eliseo 313, 316, 317, 318, 319, 321, 328, 332, 333, 336, 539
Saldana, Joe 239, 243, 539
Salih, George 151, 154, 157, 415
Salin II, William N. 337
Sall, Bob 80, 539
Sarles, Roscoe 28, 30, 31, 33, 34, 37, 421, 488, 539
Sato, Takuma 376, 381, 386, 387, 388, 392, 398, 403, 406, 413, 420, 424, 539
Saulpaugh, Bryan 70, 518, 540
Savage, David "Swede" 214, 216, 217, 218, 219, 420, 540
Sawyer, Johnny 73, 76, 506, 540
Saylor, Everett 102, 540
Scarborough, Carl 129, 137, 138, 540
Scheckter, Tomas 340, 341, 344, 345, 348, 353, 358, 363, 367, 371, 376, 377, 381, 418, 540
Schenkel, Chris 209
Schindler, Bill 126, 129, 133, 541
Schmidt, Sam 321, 322, 325, 328, 329, 336, 340, 348, 363, 379, 381, 383, 421, 424, 541
Schneider, Louis 53, 56, 61, 63, 65, 66, 67, 70, 73, 89, 415, 419, 506, 519, 541
Schrader, Gus 70, 541
Schroeder, Jeret 328, 332, 336, 541
Schuppan, Vern 230, 232, 243, 247,

252, 255, 541
Schurch, Herman 59, 66, 445, 492, 542
Schwartzkopf, General H. Norman 294
Scott, Billy 230, 542
Scott, Bob 133, 137, 138, 465, 506, 540, 542
Servia, Oriol 367, 371, 380, 381, 382, 383, 386, 392, 398, 406, 407, 410, 413, 420, 542
Sessions, Sam 198, 201, 206, 210, 214, 218, 226, 542
Seymour, Johnny 56, 59, 63, 76, 80, 84, 472, 542, 547
Shafer, Phil "Red" 46, 47, 50, 59, 63, 66, 70, 76, 420, 464, 468, 520, 543
Shannon, Elmer T. 543
Sharp, Scott 309, 313, 317, 319, 325, 328, 332, 336, 337, 340, 344, 348, 351, 353, 358, 363, 371, 421, 424, 543
Shattuc, Dr. W.E. "Doc" 47, 50, 53, 502, 544
Shaw, Wilbur 15, 53, 56, 63, 65, 70, 72, 73, 76, 78, 80, 82, 84, 86, 88, 89, 91, 92, 93, 94, 95, 98, 99, 102, 107, 108, 117, 142, 259, 388, 415, 418, 476, 499, 519, 525, 544
Shelby, Carroll 279, 291
Shepherd, A.J. 168, 544
Shoaff, Benny 52, 53, 56, 472, 544
Shore, Dinah 146
Simmons, Jeff 348, 356, 358, 359, 363, 367, 421, 545
Simon, Dick 206, 208, 210, 214, 218, 222, 226, 230, 234, 239, 243, 247, 261, 265, 269, 272, 274, 278, 282, 316, 545
Simpson, Bill 222, 545
Sirois, Jigger 200, 203
Slobodynskj, Roman 212, 249
Smiley, Gordon 247, 252, 253, 255, 259, 421, 545
Smith, Clay 133, 134, 137
Sneva, Jerry 234, 235, 239, 243, 245, 247, 255, 257, 545
Sneva, Tom 222, 226, 227, 228, 230, 234, 235, 236, 237, 239, 241, 242, 243, 245, 247, 248, 250, 252, 253, 257, 258, 259, 261, 262, 263, 265, 269, 274, 275, 278, 282, 286, 290, 293, 299, 300, 416, 418, 423, 426, 546
Snider, George 185, 187, 190, 194, 198, 201, 206, 208, 210, 214, 218, 222, 226, 230, 234, 239, 243, 244, 247, 250, 257, 261, 265, 269, 272, 274, 278, 421, 533, 546
Snowberger, Russ 56, 59, 63, 64, 66, 70, 73, 76, 80, 88, 91, 94, 98, 102, 111, 115, 420, 422, 431, 476, 543, 547
Snyder, Jimmy 80, 84, 86, 88, 90, 91, 92, 94, 418, 422, 428, 431, 480, 547
Sospiri, Vincenzo 319, 321, 548
Souders, George 51, 53, 54, 55, 56, 192, 338, 415, 419, 548
Spangler, Lester 72, 73, 548
Spence, Bill 57, 59, 431, 548
Spence, Everett 91
Spence, Mike 196
Stanwyck, Barbara 127
Stapp, Elbert "Babe" 52, 53, 56, 59, 63, 66, 72, 73, 80, 82, 84, 88, 91, 94, 98, 419, 506, 544, 548
Stark & Wetzel 134
Stevens, Myron 66, 548
Stevenson, Chuck 129, 133, 137, 141, 164, 168, 176, 181, 185, 437, 492, 549
Stewart, Jackie 187, 190, 191, 192, 194, 196, 244, 419, 549
Stewart, Tony 316, 317, 318, 319, 321, 322, 323, 325, 326, 328, 336, 337, 338, 418, 426, 549
St. James, Lyn 298, 299, 301, 304, 307, 309, 313, 317, 321, 322, 332, 334, 354, 538
Straight No Chaser 403

Strang, Lewis 1, 5, 422, 549
Stubblefield, Hartwell "Stubby" 78, 427, 549
Stutz, Harry C. 32
Sullivan, Danny 257, 265, 267, 269, 270, 271, 274, 276, 278, 282, 283, 284, 285, 286, 290, 295, 296, 299, 304, 313, 416, 418, 550
Sutton, Len 156, 160, 164, 168, 171, 172, 173, 181, 185, 323, 420, 550
Swanson, Bob 86, 88, 94, 98, 420, 487, 550
Sweikert, Bob 133, 137, 141, 143, 145, 146, 147, 149, 150, 415, 419, 550

T

Tagliani, Alex 371, 372, 373, 376, 379, 381, 383, 386, 392, 398, 406, 410, 413, 420, 424, 551
Takagi, Tora 344, 346, 348, 421, 551
Taylor, Mark 348, 551
Teague, Marshall 137, 153, 447, 484, 551
Templeman, Clark "Shorty" 145, 156, 164, 167, 168, 171, 551
Teran, Armando 219
Tetzlaff, Teddy 5, 6, 8, 11, 15, 421, 551
Theys, Didier 286, 290, 304, 552
Thomas, Joe 31, 34, 37, 552
Thomas, Rene 15, 28, 31, 34, 415, 419, 422, 552
Thompson, Mickey 172, 173
Thomson, Johnny 137, 141, 145, 149, 153, 156, 158, 160, 162, 164, 419, 423, 552, 562
Thorne, Joel 85, 91, 94, 98, 102, 422, 552
Threshie, Phil 239, 243, 553
Thurman, Arthur 25, 26, 28, 553
Till, Brian 309, 553
Tingelstad, Bud 164, 171, 176, 181, 185, 190, 194, 198, 201, 210, 553
Toft, Omar 28, 553
Tolan, Johnnie 149, 153, 156, 553
Tomei, Louis 80, 84, 88, 91, 94, 98, 102, 111, 507, 518, 553, 562
Tower, Jack 5, 11, 554
Tracy, Paul 299, 304, 307, 309, 313, 340, 341, 342, 371, 377, 381, 554
Treadway, Fred 323
Treadway, Rick 340, 554
Trexler, Marion 63, 554
Triplett, Ernie 59, 63, 66, 70, 73, 420, 476, 554
Trucco, Vincenzo 11, 555
Trueman, Jim 276
Trump, Donald 379
Turner, Jack 149, 153, 156, 160, 167, 168, 171, 172, 173, 555
Turner, W.H. 5, 555

U

Unser, Al 32, 183, 185, 186, 187, 190, 191, 194, 195, 198, 200, 203, 204, 206, 207, 208, 210, 211, 212, 214, 216, 217, 218, 219, 222, 226, 230, 233, 234, 235, 236, 239, 240, 241, 242, 243, 244, 245, 247, 252, 257, 259, 260, 261, 262, 263, 265, 267, 269, 271, 274, 275, 276, 278, 279, 280, 282, 283, 284, 285, 286, 287, 288, 290, 292, 293, 295, 297, 298, 299, 301, 304, 306, 307, 309, 311, 313, 332, 333, 336, 340, 342, 344, 348, 356, 358, 363, 365, 388, 403, 416, 418, 419, 423, 555, 556
Unser, Al Jr. 258, 259, 260, 261, 265, 269, 271, 274, 278, 282, 284, 285, 286, 287, 290, 295, 297, 298, 299, 302, 304, 305, 3306, 307, 308, 309, 310, 329, 332, 336, 340, 344, 348, 354, 355,

356, 358, 361, 363, 416, 419,
423, 556
Unser, Bobby 173, 176, 178, 181, 185,
187, 190, 192, 194, 197, 198,
199, 200, 201, 202, 206, 207,
208, 210, 212, 214, 215, 216,
217, 218, 222, 223, 224, 226,
227, 228, 230, 233, 234, 236,
239, 243, 244, 245, 247, 248,
249, 250, 252, 253, 254, 255,
286, 297, 323, 388, 416, 418,
423, 426, 556
Unser, Jerry 156, 157, 158, 557
Unser, Johnny 317, 321, 322, 325, 328,
332, 557
Unser, Robby 323, 325, 326, 328, 557
Unversaw, Earl 77

V

Vail, Ira 28, 34, 37, 44, 47, 440, 452,
486, 557
Van Acker, Charlie 115, 118, 122, 557
Vandewater, Bill 139, 170
Van Raalte, Noel 18, 558
Vasser, Jimmy 299, 304, 309, 313, 314,
332, 333, 336, 337, 340, 344,
420, 558
Vautier, Tristan 392, 403, 406, 407, 558
Veith, Bob 149, 150, 153, 156, 160,
164, 171, 176, 181, 185, 194,
198, 558
Velez, Fermin 316, 317, 321, 559
Vidan, Pat 170
Villeneuve, Gilles 265
Villeneuve, Jacques (nephew) 307,
311, 312, 313, 393, 398, 416,
420, 559
Villeneuve, Jacques (uncle) 262,
274, 559
Villoresi, Luigi 111, 559
Viso, E.J. 367, 371, 376, 381, 384, 386,
387, 389, 390, 392, 395, 559
Vitolo, Dennis 309, 310, 321, 559
Vogler, Rich 269, 274, 278, 282,
286, 559
Vollstedt, Rolla 228
Vukovich, Bill 99, 124, 129, 131, 133,
134, 135, 137, 138, 139, 141,
142, 143, 145, 196, 198, 201,
206, 210, 214, 218, 219, 222,
226, 230, 234, 243, 244, 247,
255, 282, 286, 290, 415, 418,
421, 422, 559, 560
Vukovich, Bill Jr. 195, 198, 201, 206,
210, 214, 216, 218, 222, 226,
230, 234, 241, 243, 247, 254,
421, 560
Vukovich, Billy III 279, 280, 282, 286,
290, 560

W

Wagner, Louis 28, 560
Wahlberg, Mark 377
Walker, Derrick 293, 394
Walkup, Bruce 201, 203, 206, 560
Wallard, Lee 99, 118, 119, 120, 122,
123, 126, 127, 129, 130, 151,
415, 418, 560
Walther, Salt 214, 216, 218, 222, 226,
230, 239, 243, 483, 561
Ward, Jeff 321, 323, 325, 328, 332, 336,
340, 353, 419, 561
Ward, Rodger 129, 133, 137, 141, 143,
145, 149, 153, 156, 160, 161,
162, 164, 166, 168, 169, 171,
172, 173, 176, 178, 181, 183,
187, 188, 190, 191, 203, 323,
415, 418, 561
Warren, Bentley 210, 226, 562
Watson, A.J. 143, 150, 158, 161, 173
Wattles, Stan 325, 328, 332, 562
Wearne, Frank 88, 91, 94, 98, 102, 111,
115, 562

Weatherly, Clay 80, 81, 562
Webb, Travis "Spider" 64, 67, 118, 122, 126, 133, 137, 141, 562
Weiler, Wayne 164, 168, 563
Welch, Lou 147
Weld, Greg 196, 206, 563
Wente, Bob 181, 563
Werner, Christian 40, 563
Weyant, Chuck 145, 153, 156, 160, 563
Wheeler, Frank 1, 32
Wheldon, Dan 344, 346, 348, 349, 353, 354, 355, 356, 358, 360, 363, 365, 367, 368, 371, 372, 373, 376, 378, 381, 383, 384, 388, 416, 418, 563
Wheldon, Susie 388
Whitaker, Leo 81, 549
White, Johnny 180, 181, 182, 563
Whittington, Bill 247, 252, 257, 261, 269, 564
Whittington, Dale 255, 256, 257, 564
Whittington, Don 247, 252, 257, 258, 261, 267, 269, 421, 564
Wilburn, Jimmy 111, 515, 564
Wilcox, Howdy 5, 8, 11, 15, 16, 18, 22, 25, 26, 27, 28, 31, 34, 37, 38, 40, 41, 60, 69, 70, 72, 93, 415, 418, 421, 519, 564, 565
Wilcox, Howdy II 68, 70, 71, 421, 565
Wilke, Bob 158, 161, 172, 323
Wilkes, Dick 85
Williams, Carl 190, 194, 198, 199, 201, 203, 206, 214, 565
Williams, Merrill "Doc" 81, 84, 98, 102, 118, 565
Willman, Tony 88, 91, 94, 102, 515, 548, 565
Wilson, Dempsey 156, 164, 168, 176, 565
Wilson, Desiré 255
Wilson, Justin 367, 371, 376, 378, 381, 386, 387, 392, 398, 406, 407, 408, 420, 565
Wilson, Stefan 414, 566
Wingerter, George 66, 566
Winnai, Freddy 566
Winn, Billy 66, 70, 84, 88, 435, 445, 446, 455, 474, 491, 566
Wishart, Spencer 5, 8, 10, 11, 15, 421, 566
Witherill, Cory 336, 567
Wonderlich (Wunderlich), Jerry 567
Wood Brothers 185
Woodbury, Cliff 50, 53, 56, 57, 59, 270, 422, 431, 452, 513, 543, 567

Y

Yagle, Maude A. 58
Yamaguchi, Kristi 368
Yarborough, Cale 190, 194, 210, 214, 567
Yarbrough, Lee Roy 187, 194, 195, 201, 206, 567
Yasukawa, Roger 344, 348, 353, 358, 363, 567
Yeager, General Chuck 275
Yeley, J.J. 325, 328, 568
Yunick, Smokey 178

Z

Zampedri, Alessandro 313, 316, 317, 319, 321, 322, 420, 568
Zborowski, Count Louis 40, 568
Zengel, Len 8, 568
Zimmerman, Denny 210, 211, 214, 568
Zink, John 126, 129, 133, 137, 141, 145, 146, 147, 149, 150, 153, 155, 156, 160, 164, 168, 172, 176, 194, 415, 423
Zuccarelli, Paolo "Paul" 11, 568

Author, Pat Kennedy.

ABOUT THE AUTHOR

Pat Kennedy attended his first Indianapolis 500 with his family in 1963 when he was six years old. He has not missed a race since. His interest and passion was immediate and has continued to grow, culminating in his second book and annual updates on the Indianapolis 500.

His grandfather and father sponsored race cars at Indy from 1936 to the early 1950s under the name of their family-owned business: the Kennedy Tank Special. Kennedy Tank and Manufacturing Company has been a supplier of pit fueling tanks for many years at Indy. Pat has continued the family tradition of involvement in the Indianapolis 500.

Pat is the president of a group of family-owned companies, including Kennedy Tank and Manufacturing Company (Indianapolis, Indiana); Southern Tank and Manufacturing Company (Owensboro, Kentucky); and Steel Tank and Fabricating Corporation (Columbia City, Indiana).

In 2010, Pat's first book, How Much Do You Really Know About the Indianapolis 500?, was published. It is the official trivia book of the Indianapolis 500. Currently the Official Indy 500 Trivia book is in its third edition and the Indy 500 Recaps book is in its sixth.

www.autoracingtrivia.com